CREATING WEALTH

ETHICAL
and
ECONOMIC PERSPECTIVES

...

Edited by David Schmidtz
University of Arizona

cognella™
San Diego, CA

First published in the United States of America in 2011 by Cognella, a division of University Readers, Inc.

Trademark Notice: Product or corporate names may be trademarks or registered trademarks, and are used only for identification and explanation without intent to infringe.

15 14 13 12 11   1 2 3 4 5

Printed in the United States of America

ISBN: 978-1-60927-964-6

www.cognella.com 800.200.3908

CONTENTS

Acknowledgments

I wish to thank Kevin Vallier in particular for handling much of the task of editing this collection. I also want to thank all of the people who have helped to invent and to teach the Philosophy Department's course on The Ethics and Economics of Wealth Creation: Jason Brennan, Tom Christiano, Gerald Gaus, Michael Gill, Ben Kearns, Guido Pincione, John Thrasher, John Tomasi, Steve Wall, Matt Zwolinski, and again Kevin Vallier.

I want to thank T.Y. Henderson as well, for teaching me ethics, and for rescuing me from a career carrying mail for Canada Post and diverting me into Philosophy.

100% of the royalties from sales of this book will be donated to an account at the University of Arizona Foundation that will support administrative staff at the University of Arizona.

—David Schmidtz

The Language of Ethics
Introduction

W e have been studying moral philosophy for thousands of years. We have made progress. Only someone who does not know the field's history would say otherwise. On the other hand, the modest, halting, fragile nature of that progress suggests there are few fields of intellectual inquiry whose problems are as intractable as moral philosophy's.

I am a teacher of moral philosophy, so let me say something about what that is like. It is a great privilege to be able to write and teach for a living, but I sometimes teach introductory ethics, and that can be a bit depressing. In introductory economics or biology or calculus, students buckle down, expecting a difficult time, but at least having a sense of how to get started. Introductory ethics is different. Students come in with the vague idea that it will be a sort of encounter group where they tell the professor how they feel about things (and where their strong feelings entitle them to a good grade). Then they find themselves being asked questions that even the professor finds intimidating. Students begin to recoil, insisting it is all arbitrary opinion and that what is true for the grader may not be true for the student. (To a six-year-old, the quadratic equation likewise looks like an arbitrary game whose rules are too complex to be worth learning). The professor assures students that what they say at parties on Friday night is not the last word on moral philosophy, but the very idea that there is that much to learn is something students find disturbing if not downright offensive.

In addition to the intrinsic difficulty of the subject matter, there is a further problem, and here is where the idea of language enters the picture. Moral philosophy has become an academic discipline, and like any such discipline, it has become esoteric. It is a conversation that has been going on for generations and has become a conversation among insiders trained in the discipline. The conversation has been going on for so long and has been sufficiently isolated that it has developed its own dialect, only partly understood by people on the inside and unintelligible to people on the outside. It would be the same if you were to walk into an advanced seminar in physics. You would have no idea what they were talking about.

So, if moral philosophy seems hard, it is not your fault. Neither is it your instructor's fault. Nor is the fault of the authors you will read. It is hard for philosophers to talk even to people who speak the same language, and it is that much harder to talk to those who do not. I work on the fundamental nature of value. I work on the nature of the connection between being rational and being moral. It is hard to bring that sort of research to bear on everyday questions about how to live in such a way that at the end of your life people will be glad you were here. It is a worthy challenge, though, because most of this volume's readers are (or some day will be) people whose jobs really matter and who routinely find themselves in moral dilemmas that really matter. My goal, then, is to describe some of the tools (including some of that jargon) that moral philosophers use to help us understand such dilemmas.

WHAT IS MORAL PHILOSOPHY?

The discipline of philosophy can be divided into fields. Typically it is divided into three. In the simplest terms:

1. Metaphysics is the study of the fundamental nature of reality;
2. Epistemology is the study of knowledge and how we acquire it;
3. Ethics is the study of goodness and rightness—what counts as a good life, a life worth living, and what counts as right action, especially with regard to our obligations to other people.

The study of ethics generally is guided by certain presuppositions. Among the main presuppositions are these.

1. We are more or less rational beings, capable of understanding the world.
2. We can act on the basis of what we understand.
3. Our actions can serve a purpose—we can make a difference.

Ethics itself can be divided into subfields.

1. Normative ethics is the study of rightness and goodness per se.
2. Descriptive ethics is the study of opinions or beliefs about what is right and good. (Descriptive ethics often is considered to be a branch of anthropology rather than

philosophy. However, we insist on separating normative from descriptive ethics in order to emphasize that seeking the truth about ethics is not the same as cataloguing opinions about ethics).

3. Metaethics, studies the meanings and presuppositions of moral theories and moral language. In effect, then, where normative ethics asks what is right and what is good, metaethics steps back to ask what we hope to accomplish by theorizing about it.

Within the subfield of normative ethics, we seek to formulate theories of the good, sometimes called theories of value. We also seek to formulate theories of the right. ("Good" and "right" often are interchangeable in ordinary use, but in philosophy we treat rightness as pertaining to what we should do, whereas goodness pertains to what we should want.)

When we try to apply the results of normative ethics to questions of practical policy and personal conduct such as those discussed in this volume, we move into the realm of applied moral philosophy. Different contexts give rise to slightly different problems, so we seldom teach courses in applied moral philosophy as such. Instead, we teach courses in applied moral philosophy from a more specific perspective, such as engineering ethics, business ethics, and environmental ethics. Each of these perspectives is, of course, relevant to the problems discussed in this volume.

Some people view ethics from a personal perspective, while others view it from an institutional perspective. Thus, in an environmental ethics course, when we ask students what they can do to live a good life that is also an environmentally friendly life, some respond by saying, "We could print our term papers double-sided." Or "We could properly insulate our water heaters." They interpret the question as a personal question about what we as individuals can do here and now, given institutional structure as it is, to reduce personal consumption in ways that are personally as well as environmentally beneficial, even if only in small ways.

Others respond by saying, "We could redefine the role of the US Supreme Court so as to make it responsible for striking down any legislation that has adverse environmental impacts." These people interpret the question not as a question about how to live but as a question about institutional design. Professors sometimes find it disturbing that people would see ethics as primarily about what the government ought to do rather than as primarily about how they ought to live their own lives. Yet, both perspectives are legitimate on their own terms, and each is relevant to problems discussed in this volume.

Suffice it to say that there are two perspectives, which in effect implies that morality is more than one thing. One part of morality ranges over the subject of personal aspiration—which goals we should spend our lives trying to achieve. Another part of morality ranges over the subject of interpersonal constraint—especially which socially or institutionally embedded constraints we ought to respect as we pursue our goals in a social setting. The morality of institutional constraints leads us to ask whether we are meeting our obligations to other people, whether we are obeying the law, and so on.

The morality of personal goals, though, leads us to go beyond what it required of us by the morality of interpersonal constraints. You will find that wealthy businesspeople, late in life, are not content merely with being rich. They spend time looking in the mirror, looking at their lives, and they no longer get much of a thrill from simply counting their money. Neither are they content merely to assure themselves that their way of getting rich was legal. They are asking deeper questions: whether they had a cause, whether they did something that made their lives worth living. They ask whether it was good that they were here on this earth. They ask who will have reason to be glad they were here.

I hope you get rich! If you do, then you too will one day have these questions. These questions will make up this most final of your final exams.

ETHICS IS NOT A JINGLE

Much of the history of moral philosophy revolves around the project of articulating an adequate theory of morality. How do we construct a moral theory? We begin by asking a moral question, which is roughly to say, a question about what makes a particular kind of thing right or good, and that question defines the theory's subject matter. For example, we might ask what makes an act right. (We could have asked more specifically what makes an act permissible, or what makes an act obligatory. Or we could have asked about a different subject altogether, something other than acts. To give a few of the most important examples, we could ask about rules, laws, institutions, or character traits.)

If we ask what makes an action right, one plausible answer is that the right action is the action that does as much good as possible. This is (roughly speaking) the theory known as utilitarianism. The theory is most often associated with John Stuart Mill, and it is one of the simplest theories we have. An alternative theory: What makes an act right is not whether it promotes what is good so much as whether it respects what is good. Associated most often with Immanuel Kant, this theory is known as deontology and says, a bit more precisely, that an action is right if, but only if, it expresses respect for all persons as ends in themselves and therefore treats no person merely as a means to further ends.

Yet another alternative, virtue theory, is so different it might be best to see it not as an alternative answer to the same question but as responding to a different question altogether. Associated most often with Aristotle, virtue theory tells us that what is right is to be a certain kind of person, a person of virtue: courageous, modest, honest, evenhanded, industrious, wise. Moral life is not about doing the right thing so much as it is about taking the best of our potential as persons and making it real. - Aristotle

I wish I could simply tell you which of these theories is right, then specify in simple terms what that correct theory tells you to do. For better or worse, though, moral life is more complicated than that. The three theories just described are the main theories we discuss in introductory classes in moral philosophy, but few philosophy professors believe that any of them comes close to being the complete truth about morality. Each contains a grain of truth, but none can be treated as infallible.

We need to understand, then, that the key to morality will not be found in a jingle, or even in a sophisticated professional code of ethics. Morality is complex. It calls for creativity and judgment in the same way that chess does. You might come to the game of chess hoping to be given a simple algorithm that picks out the winning play no matter what the situation. For human players, though, there is no algorithm. There is no substitute for creativity and good judgment, for the ability to think ahead and expect the unexpected. Even something as simple as a game of chess is full of surprises, yet the complexity involved in playing chess is nothing compared to the complexity involved in being moral.

A MATTER OF PRINCIPLE

Perhaps our first and most important practical task, then, is to understand what we should not be hoping for. What we naturally hope for is to be given a list of rules or a code of professional conduct. When moral philosophers try to do applied ethics, though, it becomes apparent that there is something artificial and unhelpful about trying to interpret morality as a set of rules. Rules function in our reasoning as trump cards. If we have a rule, and if we can really believe with complete confidence that the rule ought to be followed, and if we ascertain that a certain course of action is forbidden by the rule, then that settles it. The rule trumps all further reasoning, so no further reasoning is necessary.

How comforting it would be to have such rules. And of course, sometimes the situation actually is rule-governed. Not always, though. Much of the time, there are reasons in favor of an action, and reasons against, and neither trumps the other.

It may still be possible, though, to decide in a principled way. Principles are not like rules. Where rules function in our reasoning like trump cards, principles function like weights. If the applicable moral rule forbids X, then X is ruled out, so to speak. In contrast, it is possible for a principle to weigh against X without categorically ruling out X.

If you need to figure out what to do, don't look for rules. Look for principles.

Consider an analogy. A home builder might say, in describing his or her philosophy about how to build houses, "You have to minimize ductwork." Question: Is that a rule or a principle? The answer is that, interpreted as a rule, it would be silly. As a rule, it would say, no matter what weighs in favor of more extensive ductwork, minimize ductwork, period. In other words, zero ductwork!

In fact, though, "minimize ductwork" is a good principle rather than a bad rule. As a principle, it tells home builders to be mindful of energy wasted and living space consumed when heated or air-conditioned air is piped to remote parts of the house. Other things equal, get the air to where it has to go by the shortest available route. This principle will seldom outweigh the principle that the ceiling should be a minimum of seven feet above the floor. That is to say, it is not a trump, but it does have weight. A good builder designs houses with that principle in mind, but does not treat the principle as if it were a rule.

When students sign up for introductory courses in ethics, some of the most conscientious of them are expecting to be told the moral rules. It is a shock when we tell them we have been teaching ethics for twenty years, but for the most part, we don't know the moral rules, and we suspect there aren't any. Or more accurately, we suspect there are too few to give comprehensive guidance regarding how we ought to live.

When we are making real-world practical decisions, the considerations we bring to bear are more often principles than rules. So why, when we look to moral philosophy, would we hope to be given rules than principles? What is the attraction of rules? The idea of following a rule is comforting because it has the feel of relieving us of moral responsibility. If we just follow the rules, it seems to guarantee our innocence. Unlike rules, principles offer no such escape. Rules are things we follow. Principles are things we apply. Principles leave us with no doubt as to who is responsible for weighing them, for making choices, and for bearing the consequences of those choices.

The upshot, and it is fundamental to understanding what being a moral agent is like in the real world: If you need to figure out what to do, don't look for rules; look for principles. Needless to say, this too is a principle, not a rule. It has exceptions. There are, after all, rules. They sometimes do trump all other considerations.

COMING TO GRIPS WITH THE SITUATION

A few decades ago, Stanley Milgram ran now-infamous experiments on the phenomenon of obedience to authority. Volunteer subjects were told the experiment was designed to test whether learning is enhanced by the use of pain to motivate subjects to pay maximum attention to the learning task. A volunteer test giver watches as a test taker (actually an actor) is strapped down to a chair and wired to a machine that delivers the pain stimulus in the form of electric shock. The volunteer is asked by the experimenter to administer a multiple-choice word association test, and in the event of an incorrect answer, to hit a switch that sends the electric shock to the test taker. The test giver is also instructed to increase the voltage by fifteen volts after each incorrect answer, beginning at fifteen, and eventually going beyond four hundred and fifty volts to settings marked XXX. After a few (scripted) mistakes the test taker begins to howl with pain, complains of heart pain, then collapses into apparent unconsciousness.

The volunteers for the most part had no idea that it was an act. I have seen films of the experiments. Typically, the volunteer is extremely agitated, begging the experimenter to check the condition of the test taker to make sure he was all right. The volunteer typically and repeatedly begged the experimenter to discontinue the experiment. But when firmly told to continue with the experiment, the volunteer most often did. The volunteer kept asking multiple-choice questions, to which the apparently dead or unconscious test taker did not respond. Having been instructed to treat nonanswers as incorrect answers, the subject kept sending ever more powerful electric shocks to that dead or unconscious body.

Needless to say, there is a moral rule against strapping down innocent people and torturing them to death. It is safe to say none of the volunteer test givers were unaware of this rule. Yet, when told to break this rule, they did, and for no reason other than that they were told to do so. They did not wish to break the rule. Indeed, it was agonizing for them. Many were hysterical. However, they simply lacked whatever psychological resources a person needs to be able to disobey a direct order from someone perceived as an authority figure, even when they knew that what they were being ordered to do was wrong.

If it had been me, I am sure I would not have obeyed. But I am the same as everyone else in that respect. No one thinks they would have obeyed. So, perhaps I should not be so sure of how I would respond. I have been forewarned about the electric shock experiments, so of course I would see through them. But what if I were a Morton Thiokol engineer presenting my boss with reason to believe that seals on the space shuttle's booster rocket were not safe, and what if my boss told me to keep my mouth shut? As it actually happened, the engineers did shut up. The Challenger space shuttle was launched. Seconds later, it exploded. The engineers' worst fears were confirmed.

Now, if I imagine myself in their position, prior to the launch, part of the problem is that if I refuse to back down and succeed in aborting the launch, there will always be an unanswered question. The program would be halted until the seals were redesigned at great expense. The faulty seals would never be tested under full operation. I might be fired without anyone (including me) ever knowing whether I was right or whether I was a troublemaking lunatic. I would be smart enough to see that. Would I also be smart enough, and brave enough, to sound the alarm anyway? In the heat of the moment, would I remain calm enough to be able to call vividly to mind a picture of the kind of person I want to be?[1] In the heat of the moment, would I realize that while life has just raised the price of being that kind of person, it has not changed my reason for resolving to be that kind of person? Would you?

If we are looking for a moral code, the test of a code is not that it presents us with answers to all questions, but that it helps us to decide what questions to ask, when to ask them, and when not to settle for easy answers. Moral philosophy's value is not so much in the infor¬mation it gives us regarding how to pass the test. Moral philosophy can indeed

---

1   A word of caution. Unwary readers could think of this idea as vaguely egoistic, without being careful to sort out what they mean by egoism. Suffice it to say, there is a world of difference between thinking that morality is centrally about getting as much good as you can get and thinking (a part of) morality is centrally about being as good a person as you can be. Only the former is egoistic.

help us prepare for the test. But moral philosophy prepares us not so much by giving us the answers as by training us to recognize when the test has begun.

> *Moral philosophy prepares us not so much by giving us the answers as by training us to recognize when the test has begun.*

One simple principle that often helps: Talk to people. Don't suffer in silence. The point of talking is twofold.

1. Talking helps us to examine our judgment.
2. Talking sometimes gives us the courage us to trust our better judgment when we otherwise might have caved in like a subject in a Milgram experiment. In other words, sometimes, what we need to question is not what we judge to be right so much as whether we're actually doing what we judge to be right.

Talk to the wisest and most honest people you know, to counteract the mind-numbing influence of social pressure.[2] Or, if you'd rather not talk about it—i f you would prefer that the people you most respect not know of your situation or of what you have decided to do—that is a sign that you are in trouble.

I defined deontology as the theory that one ought never to treat persons merely as means but also as ends in themselves, not to be sacrificed to the ends of others. According to Immanuel Kant, another way to express the same idea is to say we ought to do only that which we could will to be a universal law. Whether this really is the same idea is debatable, but in any case this new formulation contains a thought about the secret of being moral that has considerable value in practical terms. The thought is this: Act in such a way that you would be willing to let your action be presented to the whole world as an example of how a person ought to act. If you are doing that, then you are doing the right thing, or at least you are trying to the honest best of your ability.

Studying moral theory can make a person wiser, I believe, but it is not obvious how the process works. Learning is somewhat mysterious. Especially when we are learning something that is more a skill than a list of facts, it can be hard to describe what we have learned or how. For example, we know there is such a thing as learning how to ride a bicycle, yet we cannot teach a person to ride a bicycle simply by explaining how to do it. Being moral is like that. As teachers of moral philosophy, we try to explain how to be moral. But if our students are learning to be moral in our classrooms, it is not because they

---

2   Of course, I do not mean to say talking to people is a panacea. It is only a principle. In the actual case of the failed Morton Thiokol booster rocket, fourteen of the company's engineers opposed the launch, so there was considerable mutual confirmation of each other's best judgment, but even so it evidently did not lead the engineers to go over the heads of their immediate supervisors.

are memorizing information. Ethics is more skill than dogma. If they are learning to be moral, it is because they are getting a feel for what it is like to wrestle with hard choices. At least in their imaginations, they are practicing the art of acting with integrity in cases where integrity is not without cost.

NUMBERS DO NOT ALWAYS COUNT

Adam Smith was one of the greatest moral philosophers who ever lived. He also is credited with inventing economics as an academic discipline. Here is what he says about, in effect, playing God with other people's lives.

> The man of system ... is apt to be very wise in his own conceit; and is often so enamoured with the supposed beauty of his own ideal plan of government, that he cannot suffer the smallest deviation from any part of it. He goes on to establish it completely and in all its parts, without any regard either to the great interests, or to the strong prejudices which may oppose it. He seems to imagine that he can arrange the different members of a great society with as much ease as the hand arranges the different pieces upon a chess-board. He does not consider that the pieces upon the chess-board have no other principle of motion besides that which the hand impresses upon them; but that, in the great chess-board of human society, every single piece has a principle of motion of its own, altogether different from that which the legislature might chose to impress upon it.[3]

Smith's point is as relevant as ever. In moral philosophy, there has been much discussion of the following kind of case: Imagine that five patients lie on operating tables about to die for lack of suitable organ donors. A United Parcel Service delivery person walks into the office. She is a suitable organ donor for all five patients. If you kidnap her and harvest her organs, you will be saving five and killing one. Should you do it? Why or why not?

The answer is not simply a matter of numbers, of one versus five. The issue is more centrally a matter of trust. What gives society its utility for those who live in it? The answer is trust. Hospitals cannot serve their purpose unless people can trust hospitals to treat patients and everyone else as rights bearers. Institutions have utility by creating conditions under which people can trust each other not to operate in a utilitarian way, as if other people were simply pawns to be moved around in such a way as to maximize the overall good.

Moral institutions get the best result not so much by aiming at the best result as by imposing constraints on individual pursuits so as to bring individual pursuits into better

---

3   Adam Smith, *Theory of Moral Sentiments*, Indianapolis: Liberty Fund Press (1976): Part VI ("Of the Character of Virtue").

harmony with each other. Institutions (e.g., hospitals) serve the common good by creating opportunities for mutual benefit, then trusting individuals to take advantage of them. In effect, there are two sides to the sense in which institutional utility is based on trust. First, people have to be able to trust their society to treat them as rights bearers, not as mere pawns. Second, society has to trust people to make use of opportunities that people have as rights bearers within society. Even from a utilitarian perspective, then, numbers do not always count. There are times when simply treating values with respect is the best we can do to promote them.

So, the principle here is: Consider the consequences. However, when applying this principle, we must realize that, even when considering consequences, there are times when the numbers do not count. They paint a misleading picture of what is really at stake.

Here is one more illustration: a case that I used to present in my ethics courses.

TROLLEY: A trolley is rolling down a track on its way to killing five people. If you switch to another track on which there is only one person, you will save five and kill one.

Wherever I lecture, after presenting the TROLLEY case and asking people whether they would switch tracks, about ninety percent would say, "there has to be another way!" On a trip to Kazakhstan, I presented the case to an audience of twenty-one professors from nine post-Soviet republics, and they said the same thing. I responded as I always did. I said, "Please, stay on topic. I'm trying to illustrate a point here! To see the point, you need to decide what to do when there is no other way." When I said this to my class of post-Soviet professors, though, they responded in a way no audience of mine had responded before. They spoke briefly among themselves in Russian, then two of them quietly said (as others nodded, every one of them looking me straight in the eye), "Yes, we understand. We have heard this before. All our lives we were told the few must be sacrificed for the sake of many. We were told there is no other way. What we were told was a lie. There was always another way." They were right. The real world does not stipulate that there is no other way. Justice is about respecting the separateness of persons. We are not to sacrifice one person for the sake of another. If we find ourselves seemingly called upon to sacrifice the few for the sake of the many (or for the sake of profit), justice is about finding another way.

HOW TO SAVE THE WHALES

As mentioned earlier, the moral problems discussed in this volume tend to have institutional as well as personal dimensions. We want to know how to conduct ourselves when we find ourselves in moral dilemmas. We also want to know whether there is anything we could do by way of institutional design to minimize the pressures that lead to dilemmas in the first place. Here is one idea.

We know why consumers are so often thoughtless. We insist on it. We insist on thoughtless consumption when we insist on pricing policies that protect consumers from the true full cost of consumption. Water is a scarce good. When we price it as if it were not, we run out. Electricity is a scarce good. When we price it as if it were not, we run out. If, in the nineteenth century, we had heavily subsidized whale-oil consumption, whales would be extinct today. Would-be producers of alternative energy sources (e.g., petroleum, in the case of whale oil) would not have been able to compete. Imagine selling food by charging each household a flat monthly fee, then simply turning people loose on the supermarkets. We would run out of food. A vast amount of food would be wasted.

From an environmental perspective, we want consumers to economize, to moderate their demand. That will not happen so long as consumers do not pay the true cost of consumption, on a per unit basis. If Paul does not pay for Paul's consumption, then Peter will pay for Paul's overconsumption. We can choose to detach the cost from people as consumers and reattach it to people as taxpayers, but whatever the reasons for doing such a thing, we should not ignore the fact that when we do that, we eliminate the incentive to conserve. To make consumers stop to think before consuming that extra unit, the extra unit needs to have a price.

Likewise, from an economic perspective, we want to "keep an eye on the unseen." Frederic Bastiat warned us long ago (and his warning is as timely as ever) that however many jobs we think we are creating with make-work programs funded by taxes, the inescapable truth remains that the money has to come from somewhere. The unseen cost of transferring those tax dollars from private employers to government programs is that we are taking away money that would have been creating real jobs, if we had only left it alone. When we read that a program creates a new job for every $500,000 that it spends, we can be fairly sure that for every job the program creates, it stopped at least five jobs from being created in the larger economy from which it took those funds.

Ethics is not warm and fuzzy. Business ethics, like environmental ethics, is ethics for a world in which choices have consequences, a world in which mistakes have costs that cannot be wished away. We live in a complex world in which there are many relevant considerations, but as a rule, we should not subsidize consumption. The basic principle is this: If you want to save whales, do not subsidize the consumption of whale oil. Do not give cash prizes to people for doing things you do not want them to do. When you subsidize consumption, you pay people to consume more than they otherwise would. If that is not your objective, eliminate the subsidy. Let prices rise. Let the market do its job of steering consumers and producers toward (for example) alternative energy sources.

SUMMARY

From an environmentalist perspective, one of our primary policy responsibilities in setting public policy is to avoid unmetered consumption. Unmetered consumption is a prescription for irresponsible consumption, thus a prescription for future dilemmas. From a more personal perspective, it is important not to under¬estimate how social pressure affects our moral thinking. This weighs in favor not of deliberating in isolation but in favor of being committed to consulting the most levelheaded people we know.

I explained why being moral is not simply a matter of following the right rules. Nevertheless, there are such things as moral principles (many more than can be enumerated in a useful written code) that carry considerable weight and that fairly reliably lead us in the right direction. One example: Consider the consequences. However, do not treat people as if they were numbers, such that it appears permissible simply to sacrifice low numbers for the sake of high ones. Instead, treat all persons as ends in themselves. Finally, think! Think about what is involved, day to day, in living a life of integrity. Think about what you need to do to be true to yourself, true to the people around you, and true to the highest standards of your profession.

CHAPTER 1

✝

COOPERATION AND DIVISION OF LABOR

Republic

PLATO

A state, I said, arises, as I conceive, out of the needs of mankind; no one is self-sufficing, but all of us have many wants. Can any other origin of a State be imagined?

There can I be no other.

Then, as we have many wants, and many persons are needed to supply them, one takes a helper for one purpose and another for another; and when these partners and helpers are gathered together in one habitation the body of inhabitants is termed a State.

True, he said.

And they exchange with one another, and one gives, and another receives, under the idea that the exchange will be for their good.

Very true.

Then, I said, let us begin and create in idea a State; and yet the true creator is necessity, who is the mother of our invention.

Of course, he replied.

Now the first and greatest of necessities is food, which is the condition of life and existence.

Certainly.

The second is a dwelling, and the third clothing and the like.

True.

And now let us see how our city will be able to supply this great demand: We may suppose that one man is a husbandman, another a builder, some one else a weaver—shall we add to them a shoemaker, or perhaps some other purveyor to our bodily wants?

Quite right.

The barest notion of a State must include four or five men.

Clearly.

And how will they proceed? Will each bring the result of his labours into a common stock?—the individual husbandman, for example, producing for four, and labouring four times as long and as much as he need in the provision of food with which he supplies others as well as himself; or will he have nothing to do with others and not be at the trouble of producing for them, but provide for himself alone a fourth of the food in a fourth of the time, and in the remaining three-fourths of his time be employed in making a house or a coat or a pair of shoes, having no partnership with others, but supplying himself all his own wants?

Adeimantus thought that he should aim at producing food only and not at producing everything.

Probably, I replied, that would be the better way; and when I hear you say this, I am myself reminded that we are not all alike; there are diversities of natures among us which are adapted to different occupations.

Very true.

And will you have a work better done when the workman has many occupations, or when he has only one?

When he has only one.

Further, there can be no doubt that a work is spoilt when not done at the right time?

No doubt.

For business is not disposed to wait until the doer of the business is at leisure; but the doer must follow up what he is doing, and make the business his first object.

He must.

And if so, we must infer that all things are produced more plentifully and easily and of a better quality when one man does one thing which is natural to him and does it at the right time, and leaves other things.

Undoubtedly.

Then more than four citizens will be required; for the husbandman will not make his own plough or mattock, or other implements of agriculture, if they are to be good for anything. Neither will the builder make his tools—and he too needs many; and in like manner the weaver and shoemaker.

True.

Then carpenters, and smiths, and many other artisans, will be sharers in our little State, which is already beginning to grow?

True.

Yet even if we add neatherds, shepherds, and other herdsmen, in order that our husbandmen may have oxen to plough with, and builders as well as husbandmen may have draught cattle, and curriers and weavers fleeces and hides—still our State will not be very large.

That is true; yet neither will it be a very small State which contains all these.

Then, again, there is the situation of the city—to find a place where nothing need be imported is well-nigh impossible.

Impossible.

Then there must be another class of citizens who will bring the required supply from another city?

There must.

But if the trader goes empty-handed, having nothing which they require who would supply his need, he will come back empty-handed.

That is certain.

And therefore what they produce at home must be not only enough for themselves, but such both in quantity and quality as to accommodate those from whom their wants are supplied.

Very true.

Then more husbandmen and more artisans will be required?

They will.

Not to mention the importers and exporters, who are called merchants?

Yes.

Then we shall want merchants?

We shall.

And if merchandise is to be carried over the sea, skillful sailors will also be needed, and in considerable numbers?

Yes, in considerable numbers.

Then, again, within the city, how will they exchange their productions? To secure such an exchange was, as you will remember, one of our principal objects when we formed them into a society and constituted a State.

Clearly they will buy and sell.

Then they will need a market-place, and a money-token for purposes of exchange.

Certainly.

Suppose now that a husbandman, or an artisan, brings some production to market, and he comes at a time when there is no one to exchange with him—is he to leave his calling and sit idle in the market-place?

Not at all; he will find people there who, seeing the want, undertake the office of salesmen. In well-ordered States they are commonly those who are the weakest in bodily strength, and therefore of little use for any other purpose; their duty is to be in the market, and to give money in exchange for goods to those who desire to sell and to take money from those who desire to buy.

This want, then, creates a class of retail-traders in our State. Is not 'retailer' the term which is applied to those who sit in the market-place engaged in buying and selling, while those who wander from one city to another are called merchants?

Yes, he said.

And there is another class of servants, who are intellectually hardly on the level of companionship; still they have plenty of bodily strength for labour, which accordingly they sell, and are called, if I do not mistake, hirelings, hire being the name which is given to the price of their labour.

True.

Then hirelings will help to make up our population?

Yes. And now, Adeimantus, is our State matured and perfected?

I think so.

Where, then, is justice, and where is injustice, and in what part of the State did they spring up?

Probably in the dealings of these citizens with one another. Cannot imagine that they are more likely to be found anywhere else.

I dare say that you are right in your suggestion, I said; we had better think the matter out, and not shrink from the enquiry.

Let us then consider, first of all, what will be their way of life, now that we have thus established them. Will they not produce corn, and wine, and clothes, and shoes, and build houses for themselves? And when they are housed, they will work, in summer, commonly, stripped and barefoot, but in winter substantially clothed and shod. They will feed on barley-meal and flour of wheat, baking and kneading them, making noble cakes and loaves; these they will serve up on a mat of reeds or on clean leaves, themselves reclining the while upon beds strewn with yew or myrtle. And they and their children will feast, drinking of the wine which they have made, wearing garlands on their heads, and hymning the praises of the gods, in happy converse with one another. And they will take care that their families do not exceed their means; having an eye to poverty or war.

But, said Glaucon, interposing, you have not given them a relish to their meal.

True, I replied, I had forgotten; of course they must have a relish-salt, and olives, and cheese, and they will boil roots and herbs such as country people prepare; for a dessert we shall give them figs, and peas, and beans; and they will roast myrtle-berries and acorns at the fire, drinking in moderation. And with such a diet they may be expected to live in peace and health to a good old age, and bequeath a similar life to their children after them.

Yes, Socrates, he said, and if you were providing for a city of pigs, how else would you feed the beasts ?

But what would you have, Glaucon? I replied.

Why, he said, you should give them the ordinary conveniences of life. People who are to be comfortable are accustomed to lie on sofas, and dine off tables, and they should have sauces and sweets in the modern style.

Yes, I said, now I understand: the question which you would have me consider is, not only how a State, but how a luxurious State is created; and possibly there is no harm in this, for in such a State we shall be more likely to see how justice and injustice originate. In my opinion the true and healthy constitution of the State is the one which I have described. But if you wish also to see a State at fever heat, I have no objection. For I suspect that many will not be satisfied with the simpler way of way. They will be for adding sofas, and tables, and other furniture; also dainties, and perfumes, and incense, and courtesans, and cakes, all these not of one sort only, but in every variety; we must go beyond the necessaries of which I was at first speaking, such as houses, and clothes, and shoes: the arts of the painter and the embroiderer will have to be set in motion, and gold and ivory and all sorts of materials must be procured.

True, he said.

Then we must enlarge our borders; for the original healthy State is no longer sufficient. Now will the city have to fill and swell with a multitude of callings which are not required by any natural want; such as the whole tribe of hunters and actors, of whom one large class have to do with forms and colours; another will be the votaries of music—poets and their attendant train of rhapsodists, players, dancers, contractors; also makers of diverse kinds of articles, including women's dresses. And we shall want more servants.

. . .

The Wealth of Nations

Book 1, Chapters 1–4

ADAM SMITH

CHAPTER I
OF THE DIVISION OF LABOUR

The greatest improvement in the productive powers of labour, and the greater part of the skill, dexterity, and judgment with which it is any where directed, or applied, seem to have been the effects of the division of labour.

The effects of the division of labour, in the general business of society, will be more easily understood, by considering in what manner it operates in some particular manufactures. It is commonly supposed to be carried furthest in some very trifling ones; not perhaps that it really is carried further in them than in others of more importance: but in those trifling manufactures which are destined to supply the small wants of but a small number of people, the whole number of workmen must necessarily be small; and those employed in every different branch of the work can often be collected into the same workhouse, and placed at once under the view of the spectator. In those great manufactures, on the contrary, which are destined to supply the great wants of the great body of the people, every different branch of the work employs so great a number of workmen, that it is impossible to collect them all into the same workhouse. We can seldom see more, at one time, than those employed in one single branch. Though in such manufactures, therefore, the work may really be divided into a much greater number of parts, than in those of a more trifling nature, the division is not near so obvious, and has accordingly been much less observed.

To take an example, therefore, from a very trifling manufacture; but one in which the division of labour has been very often taken notice of, the trade of the pin-maker; a workman not educated to this business (which the division of labour has rendered a distinct trade), nor acquainted with the use of the machinery employed in it (to the invention of which the same division of labour has probably given occasion), could scarce, perhaps, with his utmost industry, make one pin in a day, and certainly could not make twenty. But in the way in which this business is now carried on, not only the whole work is a peculiar trade, but it is divided into a number of branches, of which the greater part are likewise peculiar trades. One man draws out the wire, another straights it, a third cuts it, a fourth points it, a fifth grinds it at the top for receiving the head; to make the head requires two or three distinct operations; to put it on, is a peculiar business, to whiten the pins is another; it is even a trade by itself to put them into the paper; and the important business of making a pin is, in this manner, divided into about eighteen distinct operations, which, in some manufactories, are all performed by distinct hands, though in others the same man will sometimes perform two or three of them. I have seen a small manufactory of this kind where ten men only were employed, and where some of them consequently performed two or three distinct operations. But though they were very poor, and therefore but indifferently accommodated with the necessary machinery, they could, when they exerted themselves, make among them about twelve pounds of pins in a day. There are in a pound upwards of four thousand pins of a middling size. Those ten persons, therefore, could make among them upwards of forty-eight thousand pins in a day. Each person, therefore, making a tenth part of forty-eight thousand pins, might be considered as making four thousand eight hundred pins in a day. But if they had all wrought separately and independently, and without any of them having been educated to this peculiar business, they certainly could not each of them have made twenty, perhaps not one pin in a day; that is, certainly, not the two hundred and fortieth, perhaps not the four thousand eight hundredth part of what they are at present capable of performing, in consequence of a proper division and combination of their different operations.

In every other art and manufacture, the effects of the division of labour are similar to what they are in this very trifling one; though, in many of them, the labour can neither be so much subdivided, nor reduced to so great a simplicity of operation. The division of labour, however, so far as it can be introduced, occasions, in every art, a proportionable increase of the productive powers of labour. The separation of different trades and employments from one another, seems to have taken place, in consequence of this advantage. This separation too is generally carried furthest in those countries which enjoy the highest degree of industry and improvement; what is the work of one man in a rude state of society, being generally that of several in an improved one. In every improved society, the farmer is generally nothing but a farmer; the manufacturer, nothing but a manufacturer. The labour too which is necessary to produce any one complete manufacture, is almost always divided among a great number of hands. How many different trades are employed in each branch of the linen and woollen manufactures, from the growers of the flax and the wool, to the bleachers and smoothers of the linen, or to the dyers and dressers of the cloth! The nature of agriculture, indeed, does not admit of so many subdivisions of labour, nor of so complete a separation of one business from another, as manufactures. It is impossible to separate so entirely, the business of the grazier from that of the corn-farmer, as the trade of the carpenter is commonly separated from that of the smith. The spinner is almost always a distinct person from the weaver; but the ploughman, the harrower, the sower of the seed, and the reaper of the corn, are often the same. The occasions for those different sorts of labour returning with the different seasons of the year, it is impossible that one man should be constantly employed in any one of them. This impossibility of making so complete and entire a separation of all the different branches of labour employed in agriculture, is perhaps the reason why the improvement of the productive powers of labour in this art, does not always keep pace with their improvement in manufactures. The most opulent nations, indeed, generally excel all their neighbours in agriculture as well as in manufactures; but they are commonly more distinguished by their superiority in the latter than in the former. Their lands are in general better cultivated, and having more labour and expence bestowed upon them, produce more in proportion to the extent and natural fertility of the ground. But this superiority of produce is seldom much more than in proportion to the superiority of labour and expence. In agriculture, the labour of the rich country is not always much more productive than that of the poor; or, at least, it is never so much more productive, as it commonly is in manufactures. The corn of the rich country, therefore, will not always, in the same degree of goodness, come cheaper to market than that of the poor. The corn of Poland, in the same degree of goodness, is as cheap as that of France, notwithstanding the superior opulence and improvement of the latter country. The corn of France is, in the corn provinces, fully as good, and in most years nearly about the same price with the corn of England, though, in opulence and improvement, France is perhaps inferior to England. The corn-lands of England, however, are better cultivated than those of France, and the corn-lands of France are said to be much better cultivated than those of Poland. But though the poor country, notwithstanding the inferiority of its cultivation, can, in some measure, rival the rich in the cheapness and goodness of its corn, it can pretend to no such competition in its manufactures; at least if those manufactures suit the soil, climate, and situation of the rich country. The silks of France are better and cheaper than those of England, because the silk manufacture, at least under the present high duties upon the importation of raw silk, does not so well suit the climate of England as that of France. But the hard-ware and the coarse woollens of England are beyond all comparison superior to those of France, and much cheaper too in the same degree of goodness. In Poland there are said to be scarce any manufactures of any kind, a few of those coarser household manufactures excepted, without which no country can well subsist.

This great increase of the quantity of work, which, in consequence of the division of labour, the same number of people are capable of performing, is owing to three different circumstances; first, to the increase of dexterity in every particular workman; secondly, to the saving of the time which is commonly lost in passing from one species of work to another; and lastly, to the invention of a great number of machines which facilitate and abridge labour, and enable one man to do the work of many.

First, the improvement of the dexterity of the workman necessarily increases the quantity of the work he can perform; and the division of labour, by reducing every man's business to some one simple operation, and by making this operation the sole employment of his life, necessarily increases very much the dexterity of the workman. A common smith, who, though accustomed to handle the hammer, has never been used to make nails, if upon some particular occasion he is obliged to attempt it, will scarce, I am assured, be able to make above two or three hundred nails in a day, and those too very bad ones. A smith who has been accustomed to make nails, but whose sole or principal business has not been that of a nailer, can seldom with his utmost diligence make more than eight hundred or a thousand nails in a day. I have seen several boys under twenty years of age who had never exercised any other trade but that of making nails, and who, when they exerted themselves, could make, each of them, upwards of two thousand three hundred nails in a day. The making of a nail, however, is by no means one of the simplest operations. The same person blows the bellows, stirs or mends the fire as there is occasion, heats the iron, and forges every part of the nail: In forging the head too he is obliged to change his tools. The different operations into which the making of a pin, or of a metal button, is subdivided, are all of them much more simple, and the dexterity of the person, of whose life it has been the sole business to perform them, is usually much greater. The rapidity with which some of the operations of those manufactures are performed, exceeds what the human hand could, by those who had never seen them, be supposed capable of acquiring.

Secondly, the advantage which is gained by saving the time commonly lost in passing from one sort of work to another, is much greater than we should at first view be apt to imagine it. It is impossible to pass very quickly from one kind of work to another, that is carried on in a different place, and with quite different tools. A country weaver, who cultivates a small farm, must lose a good deal of time in passing from his loom to the field, and from the field to his loom. When the two trades can be carried on in the same workhouse, the loss of time is no doubt much less. It is even in this case, however, very considerable. A man commonly saunters a little in turning his hand from one sort of employment to another. When he first begins the new work he is seldom very keen and hearty; his mind, as they say, does not go to it, and for some time he rather trifles than applies to good purpose. The habit of sauntering and of indolent careless application, which is naturally, or rather necessarily acquired by every country workman who is obliged to change his work and his tools every half hour, and to apply his hand in twenty different ways almost every day of his life; renders him almost always slothful and lazy, and incapable of any vigorous application even on the most pressing occasions. Independent, therefore, of his deficiency in point of dexterity, this cause alone must always reduce considerably the quantity of work which he is capable of performing.

Thirdly, and lastly, every body must be sensible how much labour is facilitated and abridged by the application of proper machinery. It is unnecessary to give any example. I shall only observe, therefore, that the invention of all those machines by which labour is so much facilitated and abridged, seems to have been originally owing to the division of labour. Men are much more likely to discover easier and readier methods of attaining any object, when the whole attention of their minds is directed towards that single object, than when it is dissipated among a great variety of things. But in consequence of the division of labour, the whole of every man's attention comes naturally to be directed towards some one very simple object. It is naturally to be expected, therefore, that some one or other of those who are employed in each particular branch of labour should soon find out easier and readier methods of performing their own particular work, wherever the nature of it admits of such improvement. A great part of the machines made use of in those manufactures in which labour is most subdivided, were originally the inventions of common workmen, who, being each of them employed in some very simple operation, naturally turned their thoughts towards finding out easier and readier methods of performing it. Whoever has been much accustomed to visit such manufactures, must frequently have been shewn very pretty machines, which were the inventions of such workmen, in order to facilitate and quicken their own particular part of the work. In the first fire-engines, a boy was constantly employed to open and shut alternately the communication between the boiler and the cylinder, according as the piston either ascended or descended. One of those boys, who loved to play with his companions, observed that, by tying a string from the handle of the valve which opened this communication to another part of the machine, the valve would open and shut without his assistance, and leave him at liberty to divert himself with his play-fellows. One of the greatest improvements that has been made upon this machine, since it was first invented, was in this manner the discovery of a boy who wanted to save his own labour.

All the improvements in machinery, however, have by no means been the inventions of those who had occasion to use the machines. Many improvements have been made by the ingenuity of the makers of the machines, when to make them became the business of a peculiar trade; and some by that of those who are called philosophers or men of speculation, whose trade it is not to do any thing, but to observe every thing; and who, upon that account, are often capable of combining together the powers of the most distant and dissimilar objects. In the progress of society, philosophy or speculation becomes, like every other employment, the principal or sole trade and occupation of a particular class of citizens. Like every other employment too, it is subdivided into a great number of different branches, each of which affords occupation to a peculiar tribe or class of philosophers; and this subdivision of employment in philosophy, as well as in every other business, improves dexterity, and saves time. Each individual becomes more expert in his own peculiar branch, more work is done upon the whole, and the quantity of science is considerably increased by it.

It is the great multiplication of the productions of all the different arts, in consequence of the division of labour, which occasions, in a well-governed society, that universal opulence which extends itself to the lowest ranks of the people. Every workman has a great quantity of his own work to dispose of beyond what he himself has occasion for; and every other workman being exactly in the same situation, he is enabled to exchange a great quantity of his own goods for a great quantity, or, what comes to the same thing, for the price of a great quantity of theirs. He supplies them abundantly with what they have occasion for, and they accommodate him as amply with what he has occasion for, and a general plenty diffuses itself through all the different ranks of the society.

Observe the accommodation of the most common artificer or day-labourer in a civilized and thriving country, and you will perceive that the number of people of whose industry a part, though but a small part, has been employed in procuring him this accommodation, exceeds all computation. The woollen coat, for example, which covers the day-labourer, as coarse and rough as it may appear, is the produce of the joint labour of a great multitude of workmen. The shepherd, the sorter of the wool, the wool-comber or carder, the dyer, the scribbler, the spinner, the weaver, the fuller, the dresser, with many others, must all join their different arts in order to complete even this homely production. How many merchants and carriers, besides, must have been employed in transporting the materials from some of those workmen to others who often live in a very distant part of the country! How much commerce and navigation in particular, how many ship-builders, sailors, sail-makers, rope-makers, must have been employed in order to bring together the different drugs made use of by the dyer, which often come from the remotest corners of the world! What a variety of labour too is necessary in order to produce the tools of the meanest of those workmen! To say nothing of such complicated machines as the ship of the sailor, the mill of the fuller, or even the loom of the weaver, let us consider only what a variety of labour is requisite in order to form that very simple machine, the shears with which the shepherd clips the wool. The miner, the builder of the furnace for smelting the ore, the feller of the timber, the burner of the charcoal to be made use of in the smelting-house, the brick-maker, the brick-layer, the workmen who attend the furnace, the mill-wright, the forger, the smith, must all of them join their different arts in order to produce them. Were we to examine, in the same manner, all the different parts of his dress and household furniture, the coarse linen shirt which he wears next his skin, the shoes which cover his feet, the bed which he lies on, and all the different parts which compose it, the kitchen-grate at which he prepares his victuals, the coals which he makes use of for that purpose, dug from the bowels of the earth, and brought to him perhaps by a long sea and a long land carriage, all the other utensils of his kitchen, all the furniture of his table, the knives and forks, the earthen or pewter plates upon which he serves up and divides his victuals, the different hands employed in preparing his bread and his beer, the glass window which lets in the heat and the light, and keeps out the wind and the rain, with all the knowledge and art requisite for preparing that beautiful and happy invention, without which these northern parts of the world could scarce have afforded a very comfortable habitation, together with the tools of all the different workmen employed in producing those different conveniencies; if we examine, I say, all these things, and consider what a variety of labour is employed about each of them, we shall be sensible that without the assistance and co-operation of many thousands, the very meanest person in a civilized country could not be provided, even according to, what we very falsely imagine, the easy and simple manner in which he is commonly accommodated. Compared, indeed, with the more extravagant luxury of the great, his accommodation must no doubt appear extremely simple and easy; and yet it may be true, perhaps, that the accommodation of an European prince does not always so much exceed that of an industrious and frugal peasant, as the accommodation of the latter exceeds that of many an African king, the absolute master of the lives and liberties of ten thousand naked savages.

CHAPTER II
OF THE PRINCIPLE WHICH GIVES OCCASION TO THE DIVISION OF LABOUR

This division of labour, from which so many advantages are derived, is not originally the effect of any human wisdom, which foresees and intends that general opulence to which it gives occasion. It is the necessary, though very slow and gradual, consequence of a certain propensity in human nature which has in view no such extensive utility; the propensity to truck, barter, and exchange one thing for another.

Whether this propensity be one of those original principles in human nature, of which no further account can be given; or whether, as seems more probable, it be the necessary consequence of the faculties of reason and speech, it belongs not to our present subject to enquire. It is common to all men, and to be found in no other race of animals, which seem to know neither this nor any other species of contracts. Two greyhounds, in running down the same hare, have sometimes the appearance of acting in some sort of concert. Each turns her towards his companion, or endeavours to intercept her when his companion turns her towards himself. This, however, is not the effect of any contract, but of the accidental concurrence of their passions in the same object at that particular time. Nobody ever saw a dog make a fair and deliberate exchange of one bone for another with another dog. Nobody ever saw one animal by its gestures and natural cries signify to another, this is mine, that yours; I am willing to give this for that. When an animal wants to obtain something either of a man or of another animal, it has no other means of persuasion but to gain the favour of those whose service it requires. A puppy fawns upon its dam, and a spaniel endeavours by a thousand attractions to engage the attention of its master who is at dinner, when it wants to be fed by him. Man sometimes uses the same arts with his brethren, and when he has no other means of engaging them to act according to his inclinations, endeavours by every servile and fawning attention to obtain their good will. He has not time, however, to do this upon every occasion. In civilized society he stands at all times in need of the co-operation and assistance of great multitudes, while his whole life is scarce sufficient to gain the friendship of a few persons. In almost every other race of animals each individual, when it is grown up to maturity, is entirely independent, and in its natural state has occasion for the assistance of no other living creature. But man has almost constant occasion for the help of his brethren, and it is in vain for him to expect it from their benevolence only. He will be more likely to prevail if he can interest their self-love in his favour, and shew them that it is for their own advantage to do for him what he requires of them. Whoever offers to another a bargain of any kind, proposes to do this: Give me that which I want, and you shall have this which you want, is the meaning of every such offer; and it is in this manner that we obtain from one another the far greater part of those good offices which we stand in need of. It is not from the benevolence of the butcher, the brewer, or the baker, that we expect our dinner, but from their regard to their own interest. We address ourselves, not to their humanity but to their self-love, and never talk to them of our own necessities but of their advantages. Nobody but a beggar chuses to depend chiefly upon the benevolence of his fellow-citizens. Even a beggar does not depend upon it entirely. The charity of well-disposed people, indeed, supplies him with the whole fund of his subsistence. But though this principle ultimately provides him with all the necessaries of life which he has occasion for, it neither does nor can provide him with them as he has occasion for them. The greater part of his occasional wants are supplied in the same manner as those of other people, by treaty, by barter, and by purchase. With the money which one man gives him he purchases food. The old cloaths which another bestows upon him he exchanges for other old cloaths which suit him better, or for lodging, or for food, or for money, with which he can buy either food, cloaths, or lodging, as he has occasion.

As it is by treaty, by barter, and by purchase, that we obtain from one another the greater part of those mutual good offices which we stand in need of, so it is this same trucking disposition which originally gives occasion to the division of labour. In a tribe of hunters or shepherds a particular person makes bows and arrows, for example, with more readiness and dexterity than any other. He frequently exchanges them for cattle or for venison with his companions; and he finds at last that he can in this manner get more cattle and venison, than if he himself went to the field to catch them. From a regard to his own interest, therefore, the making of bows and arrows grows to be his chief business, and he becomes a sort of armourer. Another excels in making the frames and covers of their little huts or moveable houses. He is accustomed to be of use in this way to his neighbours, who reward him in the same manner with cattle and with venison, till at last he finds it his interest to dedicate himself entirely to this employment, and to become a sort of house-carpenter. In the same manner a third becomes a smith or a brazier; a fourth a tanner or dresser of hides or skins, the principal part of the clothing of savages. And thus the certainty of being able to exchange all that surplus part of the produce of his own labour, which is over and above his own consumption, for such parts of the produce of other men's labour as he may have occasion for, encourages every man to apply himself to a particular occupation, and to cultivate and bring to perfection whatever talent or genius he may possess for that particular species of business.

The difference of natural talents in different men is, in reality, much less than we are aware of; and the very different genius which appears to distinguish men of different professions, when grown up to maturity, is not upon many occasions so much the cause, as the effect of the division of labour. The difference between the most dissimilar characters, between a philosopher and a common street porter, for example, seems to arise not so much from nature, as from habit, custom, and education. When they came into the world, and for the first six or eight years of their existence, they were, perhaps, very much alike, and neither their parents nor playfellows could perceive any remarkable difference. About that age, or soon after, they come to be employed in very different occupations. The difference of talents comes then to be taken notice of, and widens by degrees, till at last the vanity of the philosopher is willing to acknowledge scarce any resemblance. But without the disposition to truck, barter, and exchange, every man must have procured to himself every necessary and conveniency of life which he wanted. All must have had the same duties to perform, and the same work to do, and there could have been no such difference of employment as could alone give occasion to any great difference of talents.

As it is this disposition which forms that difference of talents, so remarkable among men of different professions, so it is this same disposition which renders that difference useful. Many tribes of animals acknowledged to be all of the same species, derive from nature a much more remarkable distinction of genius, than what, antecedent to custom and education, appears to take place among men. By nature a philosopher is not in genius and disposition half so different from a street porter, as a mastiff is from a greyhound, or a greyhound from a spaniel, or this last from a shepherd's dog. Those different tribes of animals, however, though all of the same species, are of scarce any use to one another. The strength of the mastiff is not in the least supported either by the swiftness of the greyhound, or by the sagacity of the spaniel, or by the docility of the shepherd's dog. The effects of those different geniuses and talents, for want of the power or disposition to barter and exchange, cannot be brought into a common stock, and do not in the least contribute to the better accommodation and conveniency of the species. Each animal is still obliged to support and defend itself, separately and independently, and derives no sort of advantage from that variety of talents with which nature has distinguished its fellows. Among men, on the contrary, the most dissimilar geniuses are of use to one another; the different produces of their respective talents, by the general disposition to truck, barter, and exchange, being brought, as it were, into a common stock, where every man may purchase whatever part of the produce of other men's talents he has occasion for.

CHAPTER III
THAT THE DIVISION OF LABOUR IS LIMITED BY THE EXTENT OF THE MARKET

As it is the power of exchanging that gives occasion to the division of labour, so the extent of this division must always be limited by the extent of that power, or, in other words, by the extent of the market. When the market is very small, no person can have any encouragement to dedicate himself entirely to one employment, for want of the power to exchange all that surplus part of the produce of his own labour, which is over and above his own consumption, for such parts of the produce of other men's labour as he has occasion for.

There are some sorts of industry, even of the lowest kind, which can be carried on no where but in a great town. A porter, for example, can find employment and subsistence in no other place. A village is by much too narrow a sphere for him; even an ordinary market town is scarce large enough to afford him constant occupation. In the lone houses and very small villages which are scattered about in so desert a country as the Highlands of Scotland, every farmer must be butcher, baker and brewer for his own family. In such situations we can scarce expect to find even a smith, a carpenter, or a mason, within less than twenty miles of another of the same trade. The scattered families that live at eight or ten miles distance from the nearest of them, must learn to perform themselves a great number of little pieces of work, for which, in more populous countries, they would call in the assistance of those workmen. Country workmen are almost every where obliged to apply themselves to all the different branches of industry that have so much affinity to one another as to be employed about the same sort of materials. A country carpenter deals in every sort of work that is made of wood: a country smith in every sort of work that is made of iron. The former is not only a carpenter, but a joiner, a cabinet maker, and even a carver in wood, as well as a wheelwright, a ploughwright, a cart and waggon maker. The employments of the latter are still more various. It is impossible there should be such a trade as even that of a nailer in the remote and inland parts of the Highlands of Scotland. Such a workman at the rate of a thousand nails a day, and three hundred working days in the year, will make three hundred thousand nails in the year. But in such a situation it would be impossible to dispose of one thousand, that is, of one day's work in the year.

As by means of water-carriage a more extensive market is opened to every sort of industry than what land-carriage alone can afford it, so it is upon the sea-coast, and along the banks of navigable rivers, that industry of every kind naturally begins to subdivide and improve itself, and it is frequently not till a long time after that those improvements extend themselves to the inland parts of the country. A broad-wheeled waggon, attended by two men, and drawn by eight horses, in about six weeks time carries and brings back between London and Edinburgh near four ton weight of goods. In about the same time a ship navigated by six or eight men, and sailing between the ports of London and Leith, frequently carries and brings back two hundred ton weight of goods. Six or eight men, therefore, by the help of water-carriage, can carry and bring back in the same time the same quantity of goods between London and Edinburgh, as fifty broad-wheeled waggons, attended by a hundred men, and drawn by four hundred horses. Upon two hundred tons of goods, therefore, carried by the cheapest land-carriage from London to Edinburgh, there must be charged the maintenance of a hundred men for three weeks, and both the maintenance, and, what is nearly equal to the maintenance, the wear and tear of four hundred horses as well as of fifty great waggons. Whereas, upon the same quantity of goods carried by water, there is to be charged only the maintenance of six or eight men, and the wear and tear of a ship of two hundred tons burthen, together with the value of the superior risk, or the difference of the insurance between land and water-carriage. Were there no other communication between those two places, therefore, but by land-carriage, as no goods could be transported from the one to the other, except such whose price was very considerable in proportion to their weight, they could carry on but a small part of that commerce which at present subsists between them, and consequently could give but a small part of that encouragement which they at present mutually afford to each other's industry. There could be little or no commerce of any kind between the distant parts of the world. What goods could bear the expense of land-carriage between London and Calcutta? Or if there were any so precious as to be able to support this expence, with what safety could they be transported through the territories of so many barbarous nations? Those two cities, however, at present carry on a very considerable commerce with each other, and by mutually affording a market, give a good deal of encouragement to each other's industry.

Since such, therefore, are the advantages of water-carriage, it is natural that the first improvements of art and industry should be made where this conveniency opens the whole world for a market to the produce of every sort of labour, and that they should always be much later in extending themselves into the inland parts of the country. The inland parts of the country can for a long time have no other market for the greater part of their goods, but the country which lies round about them, and separates them from the sea-coast, and the great navigable rivers. The extent of their market, therefore, must for a long time be in proportion to the riches and populousness of that country, and consequently their improvement must always be posterior to the improvement of that country. In our North American colonies the plantations have constantly followed either the sea-coast or the banks of the navigable rivers, and have scarce any where extended themselves to any considerable distance from both.

The nations that, according to the best authenticated history, appear to have been first civilized, were those that dwelt round the coast of the Mediterranean sea. That sea, by far the greatest inlet that is known in the world, having no tides, nor consequently any waves except such as are caused by the wind only, was, by the smoothness of its surface, as well as by the multitude of its islands, and the proximity of its neighbouring shores, extremely favourable to the infant navigation of the world; when, from their ignorance of the compass, men were afraid to quit the view of the coast, and from the imperfection of the art of ship-building, to abandon themselves to the boisterous waves of the ocean. To pass beyond the pillars of Hercules, that is, to sail out of the Straights of Gibraltar, was, in the ancient world, long considered as a most wonderful and dangerous exploit of navigation. It was late before even the Phenicians and Carthaginians, the most skilful navigators and ship-builders of those old times, attempted it, and they were for a long time the only nations that did attempt it.

Of all the countries on the coast of the Mediterranean sea, Egypt seems to have been the first in which either agriculture or manufactures were cultivated and improved to any considerable degree. Upper Egypt extends itself nowhere above a few miles from the Nile, and in Lower Egypt that great river breaks itself into many different canals, which, with the assistance of a little art, seem to have afforded a communication by water-carriage, not only between all the great towns, but between all the considerable villages, and even to many farm-houses in the country; nearly in the same manner as the Rhine and the Maese do in Holland at present. The extent and easiness of this inland navigation was probably one of the principal causes of the early improvement of Egypt.

...

CHAPTER IV
OF THE ORIGIN AND USE OF MONEY

When the division of labour has been once thoroughly established, it is but a very small part of a man's wants which the produce of his own labour can supply. He supplies the far greater part of them by exchanging that surplus part of the produce of his own labour, which is over and above his own consumption, for such parts of the produce of other men's labour as he has occasion for. Every man thus lives by exchanging, or becomes in some measure a merchant, and the society itself grows to be what is properly a commercial society.

But when the division of labour first began to take place, this power of exchanging must frequently have been very much clogged and embarrassed in its operations. One man, we shall suppose, has more of a certain commodity than he himself has occasion for, while another has less. The former consequently would be glad to dispose of, and the latter to purchase, a part of this superfluity. But if this latter should chance to have nothing that the former stands in need of, no exchange can be made between them. The butcher has more meat in his shop than he himself can consume, and the brewer and the baker would each of them be willing to purchase a part of it. But they have nothing to offer in exchange, except the different productions of their respective trades, and the butcher is already provided with all the bread and beer which he has immediate occasion for. No exchange can, in this case, be made between them. He cannot be their merchant, nor they his customers; and they are all of them thus mutually less serviceable to one another. In order to avoid the inconveniency of such situations, every prudent man in every period of society, after the first establishment of the division of labour, must naturally have endeavoured to manage his affairs in such a manner, as to have at all times by him, besides the peculiar produce of his own industry, a certain quantity of some one commodity or other, such as he imagined few people would be likely to refuse in exchange for the produce of their industry.

Many different commodities, it is probable, were successively both thought of and employed for this purpose. In the rude ages of society, cattle are said to have been the common instrument of commerce; and, though they must have been a most inconvenient one, yet in old times we find things were frequently valued according to the number of cattle which had been given in exchange for them. The armour of Diomede, says Homer, cost only nine oxen; but that of Glaucus cost a hundred oxen. Salt is said to be the common instrument of commerce and exchanges in Abyssinia; a species of shells in some parts of the coast of India; dried cod at Newfoundland; tobacco in Virginia; sugar in some of our West India colonies; hides or dressed leather in some other countries; and there is at this day a village in Scotland where it is not uncommon, I am told, for a workman to carry nails instead of money to the baker's shop or the ale-house.

In all countries, however, men seem at last to have been determined by irresistible reasons to give the preference, for this employment, to metals above every other commodity. Metals can not only be kept with as little loss as any other commodity, scarce any thing being less perishable than they are, but they can likewise, without any loss, be divided into any number of parts, as by fusion those parts can easily be reunited again; a quality which no other equally durable commodities possess, and which more than any other quality renders them fit to be the instruments of commerce and circulation. The man who wanted to buy salt, for example, and had nothing but cattle to give in exchange for it, must have been obliged to buy salt to the value of a whole ox, or a whole sheep, at a time. He could seldom buy less than this, because what he was to give for it could seldom be divided without loss; and if he had a mind to buy more, he must, for the same reasons, have been obliged to buy double or triple the quantity, the value, to wit, of two or three oxen, or of two or three sheep. If, on the contrary, instead of sheep or oxen, he had metals to give in exchange for it, he could easily proportion the quantity of the metal to the precise quantity of the commodity which he had immediate occasion for.

Different metals have been made use of by different nations for this purpose. Iron was the common instrument of commerce among the antient Spartans; copper among the antient Romans; and gold and silver among all rich and commercial nations.

Those metals seem originally to have been made use of for this purpose in rude bars, without any stamp or coinage. Thus we are told by Pliny, upon the authority of Timæus, an antient historian, that, till the time of Servius Tullius, the Romans had no coined money, but made use of unstamped bars of copper, to purchase whatever they had occasion for. These rude bars, therefore, performed at this time the function of money.

The use of metals in this rude state was attended with two very considerable inconveniencies; first with the trouble of weighing; and, secondly, with that of assaying them. In the precious metals, where a small difference in the quantity makes a great difference in the value, even the business of weighing, with proper exactness, requires at least very accurate weights and scales. The weighing of gold in particular is an operation of some nicety. In the coarser metals, indeed, where a small error would be of little consequence, less accuracy would, no doubt, be necessary. Yet we should find it excessively troublesome, if every time a poor man had occasion either to buy or sell a farthing's worth of goods, he was obliged to weigh the farthing. The operation of assaying is still more difficult, still more tedious, and, unless a part of the metal is fairly melted in the crucible, with proper dissolvents, any conclusion that can be drawn from it, is extremely uncertain. Before the institution of coined money, however, unless they went through this tedious and difficult operation, people must always have been liable to the grossest frauds and impositions, and instead of a pound weight of pure silver, or pure copper, might receive in exchange for their goods, an adulterated composition of the coarsest and cheapest materials, which had, however, in their outward appearance, been made to resemble those metals. To prevent such abuses, to facilitate exchanges, and thereby to encourage all sorts of industry and commerce, it has been found necessary, in all countries that have made any considerable advances towards improvement, to affix a public stamp upon certain quantities of such particular metals, as were in those countries commonly made use of to purchase goods. Hence the origin of coined money, and of those public offices called mints; institutions exactly of the same nature with those of the aulnagers and stampmasters of woollen and linen cloth. All of them are equally meant to ascertain, by means of a public stamp, the quantity and uniform goodness of those different commodities when brought to market.

I, Pencil: My Family Tree as told to Leonard E. Read

LEONARD E. READ

I am a lead pencil—the ordinary wooden pencil familiar to all boys and girls and adults who can read and write.[1]

Writing is both my vocation and my avocation; that's all I do.

You may wonder why I should write a genealogy. Well, to begin with, my story is interesting. And, next, I am a mystery—more so than a tree or a sunset or even a flash of lightning. But, sadly, I am taken for granted by those who use me, as if I were a mere incident and without background. This supercilious attitude relegates me to the level of the commonplace. This is a species of the grievous error in which mankind cannot too long persist without peril. For, the wise G. K. Chesterton observed, "We are perishing for want of wonder, not for want of wonders."

I, Pencil, simple though I appear to be, merit your wonder and awe, a claim I shall attempt to prove. In fact, if you can understand me—no, that's too much to ask of anyone—if you can become aware of the miraculousness which I symbolize, you can help save the freedom mankind is so unhappily losing. I have a profound lesson to teach. And I can teach this lesson better than can an automobile or an airplane or a mechanical dishwasher because—well, because I am seemingly so simple.

---

1   My official name is "Mongol 482." My many ingredients are assembled, fabricated, and finished by Eberhard Faber Pencil Company.

Simple? Yet, *not a single person on the face of this earth knows how to make me.* This sounds fantastic, doesn't it? Especially when it is realized that there are about one and one-half billion of my kind produced in the U.S.A. each year.

Pick me up and look me over. What do you see? Not much meets the eye—there's some wood, lacquer, the printed labeling, graphite lead, a bit of metal, and an eraser.

INNUMERABLE ANTECEDENTS

Just as you cannot trace your family tree back very far, so is it impossible for me to name and explain all my antecedents. But I would like to suggest enough of them to impress upon you the richness and complexity of my background.

My family tree begins with what in fact is a tree, a cedar of straight grain that grows in Northern California and Oregon. Now contemplate all the saws and trucks and rope and the countless other gear used in harvesting and carting the cedar logs to the railroad siding. Think of all the persons and the numberless skills that went into their fabrication: the mining of ore, the making of steel and its refinement into saws, axes, motors; the growing of hemp and bringing it through all the stages to heavy and strong rope; the logging camps with their beds and mess halls, the cookery and the raising of all the foods. Why, untold thousands of persons had a hand in every cup of coffee the loggers drink!

The logs are shipped to a mill in San Leandro, California. Can you imagine the individuals who make flat cars and rails and railroad engines and who construct and install the communication systems incidental thereto? These legions are among my antecedents.

Consider the millwork in San Leandro. The cedar logs are cut into small, pencil-length slats less than one-fourth of an inch in thickness. These are kiln dried and then tinted for the same reason women put rouge on their faces. People prefer that I look pretty, not a pallid white. The slats are waxed and kiln dried again. How many skills went into the making of the tint and the kilns, into supplying the heat, the light and power, the belts, motors, and all the other things a mill requires? Sweepers in the mill among my ancestors? Yes, and included are the men who poured the concrete for the dam of a Pacific Gas & Electric Company hydroplant which supplies the mill's power!

Don't overlook the ancestors present and distant who have a hand in transporting sixty carloads of slats across the nation.

Once in the pencil factory—$4,000,000 in machinery and building, all capital accumulated by thrifty and saving parents of mine—each slat is given eight grooves by a complex machine, after which another machine lays leads in every other slat, applies glue, and places another slat atop—a lead sandwich, so to speak. Seven brothers and I are mechanically carved from this "wood-clinched" sandwich.

My "lead" itself—it contains no lead at all—is complex. The graphite is mined in Ceylon. Consider these miners and those who make their many tools and the makers of the paper sacks in which the graphite is shipped and those who make the string that ties the sacks and those who put them aboard ships and those who make the ships. Even the lighthouse keepers along the way assisted in my birth—and the harbor pilots.

The graphite is mixed with clay from Mississippi in which ammonium hydroxide is used in the refining process. Then wetting agents are added such as sulfonated tallow—animal fats chemically reacted with sulfuric acid. After passing through numerous machines, the mixture finally appears as endless extrusions—as from a sausage grinder—cut to size, dried, and baked for several hours at 1,850 degrees Fahrenheit. To increase their strength and smoothness the leads are then treated with a hot mixture which includes candelilla wax from Mexico, paraffin wax, and hydrogenated natural fats.

My cedar receives six coats of lacquer. Do you know all the ingredients of lacquer? Who would think that the growers of castor beans and the refiners of castor oil are a part of it? They are. Why, even the processes by which the lacquer is made a beautiful yellow involve the skills of more persons than one can enumerate!

Observe the labeling. That's a film formed by applying heat to carbon black mixed with resins. How do you make resins and what, pray, is carbon black?

My bit of metal—the ferrule—is brass. Think of all the persons who mine zinc and copper and those who have the skills to make shiny sheet brass from these products of nature. Those black rings on my ferrule are black nickel. What is black nickel and how is it applied? The complete story of why the center of my ferrule has no black nickel on it would take pages to explain.

Then there's my crowning glory, inelegantly referred to in the trade as "the plug," the part man uses to erase the errors he makes with me. An ingredient called "factice" is what does the erasing. It is a rubber-like product made by reacting rape-seed oil from the Dutch East Indies with sulfur chloride. Rubber, contrary to the common notion, is only for binding purposes. Then, too, there are numerous vulcanizing and accelerating agents. The pumice comes from Italy; and the pigment which gives "the plug" its color is cadmium sulfide.

NO ONE KNOWS

Does anyone wish to challenge my earlier assertion that no single person on the face of this earth knows how to make me?

Actually, millions of human beings have had a hand in my creation, no one of whom even knows more than a very few of the others. Now, you may say that I go too far in relating the picker of a coffee berry in far off Brazil and food growers elsewhere to my creation; that this is an extreme position. I shall stand by my claim. There isn't a single person in all these millions, including the president of the pencil company, who contributes more than a tiny, infinitesimal bit of know-how. From the standpoint of know-how the only difference between the miner of graphite in Ceylon and the logger in Oregon is in the *type* of know-how. Neither the miner nor the logger can be dispensed with, any more than can the chemist at the factory or the worker in the oil field—paraffin being a by-product of petroleum.

Here is an astounding fact: Neither the worker in the oil field nor the chemist nor the digger of graphite or clay nor any who mans or makes the ships or trains or trucks nor the one who runs the machine that does the knurling on my bit of metal nor the president of the company performs his singular task because he wants me. Each one wants me less, perhaps, than does a child in the first grade. Indeed, there are some among this vast multitude who never saw a pencil nor would they know how to use one. Their motivation is other than me. Perhaps it is something like this: Each of these millions sees that he can thus exchange his tiny know-how for the goods and services he needs or wants. I may or may not be among these items.

NO MASTER MIND

There is a fact still more astounding: the absence of a master mind, of anyone dictating or forcibly directing these countless actions which bring me into being. No trace of such a person can be found. Instead, we find the Invisible Hand at work. This is the mystery to which I earlier referred.

It has been said that "only God can make a tree." Why do we agree with this? Isn't it because we realize that we ourselves could not make one? Indeed, can we even describe a tree? We cannot, except in superficial terms. We can say, for instance, that a certain molecular configuration manifests itself as a tree. But what mind is there among men that could even record, let alone direct, the constant changes in molecules that transpire in the life span of a tree? Such a feat is utterly unthinkable!

I, Pencil, am a complex combination of miracles: a tree, zinc, copper, graphite, and so on. But to these miracles which manifest themselves in Nature an even more extraordinary miracle has been added: the configuration of creative human energies—millions of tiny know-hows configurating naturally and spontaneously in response to human necessity and desire and *in the absence of any human master-minding!* Since only God can make a tree, I insist that only God could make me. Man can no more direct these millions of know-hows to bring me into being than he can put molecules together to create a tree.

The above is what I meant when writing, "If you can become aware of the miraculousness which I symbolize, you can help save the freedom mankind is so unhappily losing." For, if one is aware that these know-hows will naturally, yes, automatically, arrange themselves into creative and productive patterns in response to human necessity and demand—that is, in the absence of governmental or any other coercive masterminding—then one will possess an absolutely essential ingredient for freedom: *a faith in free people.* Freedom is impossible without this faith.

Once government has had a monopoly of a creative activity such, for instance, as the delivery of the mails, most individuals will believe that the mails could not be efficiently delivered by men acting freely. And here is the reason: Each one acknowledges that he himself doesn't know how to do all the things incident to mail delivery. He also recognizes that no other individual could do it. These assumptions are correct. No individual possesses enough know-how to perform a nation's mail delivery any more than any individual possesses enough know-how to make a pencil. Now, in the absence of faith in free people—in the unawareness that millions of tiny know-hows would naturally and miraculously form and cooperate to satisfy this necessity—the individual cannot help but reach the erroneous conclusion that mail can be delivered only by governmental "master-minding."

TESTIMONY GALORE

If I, Pencil, were the only item that could offer testimony on what men and women can accomplish when free to try, then those with little faith would have a fair case. However, there is testimony galore; it's all about us and on every hand. Mail delivery is exceedingly simple when compared, for instance, to the making of an automobile or a calculating machine or a grain combine or a milling machine or to tens of thousands of other things. Delivery? Why, in this area where men have been left free to try, they deliver the human voice around the world in less than one second; they deliver an event visually and in motion to any person's home when it is happening; they deliver 150 passengers from Seattle to Baltimore in less than four hours; they deliver gas from Texas to one's range or furnace in New York at unbelievably low rates and without subsidy; they deliver each four pounds of oil from the Persian Gulf to our Eastern Seaboard—halfway around the world—for less money than the government charges for delivering a one-ounce letter across the street!

The lesson I have to teach is this: *Leave all creative energies uninhibited.* Merely organize society to act in harmony with this lesson. Let society's legal apparatus remove all obstacles the best it can. Permit these creative know-hows freely to flow. Have faith that free men and women will respond to the Invisible Hand. This faith will be confirmed. I, Pencil, seemingly simple though I am, offer the miracle of my creation as testimony that this is a practical faith, as practical as the sun, the rain, a cedar tree, the good earth.

Leonard E. Read (1898–1983) founded FEE in 1946 and served as its president until his death.

"I, Pencil," his most famous essay, was first published in the December 1958 issue of The Freeman. *Although a few of the manufacturing details and place names have changed over the past forty years, the principles are unchanged.*

Reason and Evolution

> *To relate by whom, and in what connection, the true law of the formation of free states was recognized, and how this discovery, closely akin to those which, under the names of development, evolution, and continuity, have given a new and deeper method to other sciences, solved the ancient problem between stability and change, and determined the authority of tradition on the progress of thought.*
>
> —Lord Acton

CONSTRUCTION AND EVOLUTION

There are two ways of looking at the pattern of human activities which lead to very different conclusions concerning both its explanation and the possibilities of deliberately altering it. Of these, one is based on conceptions which are demonstrably false, yet are so pleasing to human vanity that they have gained great influence and are constantly employed even by people who know that they rest on a fiction, but believe that fiction to be innocuous. The other, although few people will question its basic contentions if they are stated abstractly, leads in some respects to conclusions so unwelcome that few are willing to follow it through to the end.

The first gives us a sense of unlimited power to realize our wishes, while the second leads to the insight that there are limitations to what we can deliberately bring about, and to the recognition that some of our present hopes are delusions. Yet the effect of allowing ourselves to be deluded by the first view has always been that man has actually limited the scope of what he can achieve. For it has always been the recognition of the limits of the possible which has enabled man to make full use of his powers.

The first view holds that human institutions will serve human purposes only if they have been deliberately designed for these purposes, often also that the fact that an institution exists is evidence of its having been created for a purpose, and always that we should so re-design society and its institutions that all our actions will be wholly guided by known purposes. To most people these propositions seem almost self-evident and to constitute an attitude alone worthy of a thinking being. Yet the belief underlying them, that we owe all beneficial institutions to design, and that only such design has made or can make them useful for our purposes, is largely false.

This view is rooted originally in a deeply ingrained propensity of primitive thought to interpret all regularity to be found in phenomena anthropomorphically, as the result of the design of a thinking mind. But just when man was well on the way to emancipating himself from this naïve conception, it was revived by the support of a powerful philosophy with which the aim of freeing the human mind from false prejudices has become closely associated, and which became the dominant conception of the Age of Reason.

The other view, which has slowly and gradually advanced since antiquity but for a time was almost entirely overwhelmed by the more glamorous constructivist view, was that that orderliness of society which greatly increased the effectiveness of individual action was not due solely to institutions and practices which had been invented or designed for that purpose, but was largely due to a process described at first as 'growth' and later as 'evolution', a process in which practices which had first been adopted for other reasons, or even purely accidentally, were preserved because they enabled the group in which they had arisen to prevail over others. Since its first systematic development in the eighteenth century this view had to struggle not only against the anthropomorphism of primitive thinking but even more against the reinforcement these naïve views had received from the new rationalist philosophy. It was indeed the challenge which this philosophy provided that led to the explicit formulation of the evolutionary view.

THE TENDS OF CARTESIAN RATIONALISM

The great thinker from whom the basic ideas of what we shall call constructivist rationalism received their most complete expression was René Descartes. But white he refrained from drawing the conclusions from them for social and moral arguments, these were mainly elaborated by his slightly older (but much more long-lived) contemporary, Thomas Hobbes. Although Descartes' immediate concern was to establish criteria for the truth of propositions, these were inevitably also applied by his followers to judge the appropriateness and justification of actions. The 'radical doubt' which made him refuse to accept anything as true which could not be logically derived from explicit premises that were 'clear and distinct'! and therefore beyond possible doubt, deprived of validity all those rules of conduct which could not be justified in this manner. Although Descartes himself could escape the consequences by ascribing such rules of conduct to the design of an omniscient deity, for those among his followers to whom this no longer seemed an adequate explanation the acceptance of anything which was based merely on tradition and could not be fully justified on rational grounds appeared as an irrational superstition. The rejection as 'mere opinion' of all that could not be demonstrated to be true by his criteria became the dominant characteristic of the movement which he started.

Since for Descartes reason was defined as logical deduction from explicit premises, rational action also came to mean only such action as was determined entirely by known and demonstrable truth. It is almost an inevitable step from this to the conclusion that only what is true in this sense can lead to successful action, and that therefore everything to which man owes his achievements is a product of his reasoning thus conceived. Institutions and practices which have not been designed in this manner can be beneficial only by accident. Such became the characteristic attitude of Cartesian constructivism with its contempt for tradition, custom, and history in general. Man's reason alone should enable him to construct society anew.

This 'rationalist' approach, however, meant in effect a relapse into earlier, anthropomorphic modes of thinking. It produced a renewed propensity to ascribe the origin of all institutions of culture to invention or design, morals, religion and law, language and writing, money and the market, were thought of as having been deliberately constructed by somebody, or at least as owing whatever perfection they possessed to such design. This intentionalist or pragmatic account of history found its fullest expression in the conception of the formation of society by a social contract, first in Hobbes and then in Rousseau, who in many respects was a direct follower of Descartes. Even though their theory was not always meant as a historical account of what actually happened, it was always meant to provide a guideline for deciding whether or not existing institutions were to be approved as rational.

It is to this philosophical conception that we owe the preference which prevails to the present day for everything that is done 'consciously' or 'deliberately', and from it the terms 'irrational' or 'non-rational' derive the derogatory meaning they now have. Because of this the earlier presumption in favour of traditional or established institutions and usages became a presumption against them, and 'opinion' came to be thought of as 'mere' opinion—something not demonstrable or decidable by reason and therefore not to be accepted as a valid ground for decision.

Yet the basic assumption underlying the belief that man has achieved mastery of his surroundings mainly through his capacity for logical deduction from explicit premises is factually false, and any attempt to confine his actions to what could thus be justified would deprive him of many of the most effective means to success that have been available to him.

It is simply not true that our actions owe their effectiveness solely or chiefly to knowledge which we can state in words and which can therefore constitute the explicit premises of a syllogism. Many of the institutions of society which are indispensable conditions for the successful pursuit of our conscious aims are in fact the result of customs, habits or practices which have been neither invented nor are observed with any such purpose in view. We live in a society in which we can successfully orientate ourselves, and in which our actions have a good chance of achieving their aims, not only because our fellows are governed by known aims or known connections between means and ends, but because they are also confined by rules whose purpose or origin we often do not know and of whose very existence we are often not aware.

Man is as much a rule-following animal as a purpose-seeking one. And he is successful not because he knows why he ought to observe the rules which he does observe, or is even capable of stating all these rules in words, but because his thinking and acting are governed by rules which have by a process of selection been evolved in the society in which he lives, and which are thus the product of the experience of generations.

THE PERMANENT LIMITATIONS OF OUR FACTUAL KNOWLEDGE

The constructivist approach leads to false conclusions because man's actions are largely successful, not merely in the primitive stage but perhaps even more so in civilization, because they are adapted both to the particular facts which he knows and to a great many other facts he does not and cannot know. And this adaptation to the general circumstances that surround him is brought about by his observance of rules which he has not designed and often does not even know explicitly, although he is able to honour them in action. Or, to put this differently, our adaptation to our environment does not consist only, and perhaps not even chiefly, in an insight into the relations between cause and effect, but also in our actions being governed by rules adapted to the kind of world in which we live, that is, to circumstances which we are not aware of and which yet determine the pattern of our successful actions.

Complete rationality of action in the Cartesian sense demands complete knowledge of all the relevant facts. A designer or engineer needs all the data and full power to control or manipulate them if he is to organize the material objects to produce the intended result. But the success of action in society depends on more particular facts than anyone can possibly know. And our whole civilization in consequence rests, and must rest, on our *believing* much that we cannot *know* to be true in the Cartesian sense.

What we must ask the reader to keep constantly in mind throughout this book, then, is the fact of the necessary and irremediable ignorance on everyone's part of most of the particular facts which determine the actions of all the several members of human society. This may at first seem to be a fact so obvious and incontestable as hardly to deserve mention, and still less to require proof. Yet the result of not constantly stressing it is that it is only too readily forgotten. This is so mainly because it is a very inconvenient fact which makes both our attempts to explain and our attempts to influence intelligently the processes of society very much more difficult, and which places severe limits on what we can say or do about them. There exists therefore a great temptation, as a first approximation, to begin with the assumption that we know everything needed for full explanation or control. This provisional assumption is often treated as something of little consequence which can later be dropped without much effect on the conclusions. Yet this necessary ignorance of most of the particulars which enter the order of a Great Society is the source of the central problem of all social order and the false assumption by which it is provisionally put aside is mostly never explicitly abandoned but merely conveniently forgotten. The argument then proceeds as if that ignorance did not matter.

The fact of our irremediable ignorance of most of the particular facts which determine the processes of society is, however the reason why most social institutions have taken the form they actually have. To talk about a society about which either the observer or any of its members knows all the particular facts is to talk about something wholly different from anything which has ever existed—a society in which most of what we find in our society would not and could not exist and which, if it ever occurred, would possess properties we cannot even imagine.

I have discussed the importance of our necessary ignorance of the concrete facts at some length in an earlier book and will emphasize its central importance here mainly by stating it at the head of the whole exposition. But there are several points which require re-statement or elaboration. In the first instance, the incurable ignorance of everyone of whom I am speaking is the ignorance of particular facts which are or will become known to somebody and thereby affect the whole structure of society. This structure of human activities constantly adapts itself, and functions through adapting itself, to millions of facts which in their entirety are not known to anybody. The significance of this process is most obvious and was at first stressed in the economic field. As it has been said, 'the economic life of a non-socialist society consists of millions of relations or flows between individual firms and households. We can establish certain theorems about them, but we can never observe all.' The insight into the significance of our institutional ignorance in the economic sphere, and into the methods by which we have learnt to overcome this obstacle, was in fact the starting point for those ideas which in the present book are systematically applied to a much wider field. It will be one of our chief contentions that most of the rules of conduct which govern our actions, and most of the institutions which arise out of this regularity, are adaptations to the impossibility of anyone taking conscious account of all the particular facts which enter into the order of society. We shall see, in particular, that the possibility of justice rests on this necessary limitation of our factual knowledge, and that insight into the nature of justice is therefore denied to all those constructivists who habitually argue on the assumption of omniscience.

Another consequence of this basic fact which must be stressed here is that only in the small groups of primitive society can collaboration between the members rest largely on the circumstance that at any one moment they will know more or less the same particular circumstances. Some wise men may be better at interpreting the immediately perceived circumstances or at remembering things in remote places unknown to the others. But the concrete events which the individuals encounter in their daily pursuits will be very much the same for all, and they will act together because the events they know and the objectives at which they aim are more or less the same.

The situation is wholly different in the Great or Open Society where millions of men interact and where civilization as we know it has developed. Economics has long stressed the 'division of *labour*' which such a situation involves. But it has laid much less stress on the fragmentation of *knowledge,* on the fact that each member of society can have only a small fraction of the knowledge possessed by all, and that each is therefore ignorant of most of the facts on which the working of society rests. Yet it is the utilization of much more knowledge than anyone can possess, and therefore the fact that each moves within a coherent structure most of whose determinants are unknown to him, that constitutes the distinctive feature of all advanced civilizations.

In civilized society it is indeed not so much the greater knowledge that the individual can acquire, as the greater benefit he receives from the knowledge possessed by others, which is the cause of his ability to pursue an infinitely wider range of ends than merely the satisfaction of his most pressing physical needs. Indeed, a 'civilized' individual may be very ignorant, more ignorant than many a savage, and yet greatly benefit from the civilization in which he lives.

The characteristic error of the constructivist rationalists in this respect is that they tend to base their argument on what has been called the *synoptic delusion,* that is, on the fiction that all the relevant facts are known to some one mind, and that it is possible to construct from this knowledge of the particulars a desirable social order. Sometimes the delusion is expressed with a touching naïvetè by the enthusiasts for a deliberately planned society, as when one of them dreams of the development of 'the art of simultaneous thinking: the ability to deal with a multitude of related phenomena at the same time, and of composing in a single picture both the qualitative and the quantitative attributes of these phenomena.' They seem completely unaware that this dream simply assumes away the central problem which any effort towards the understanding or shaping of the order of society raises: our incapacity to assemble as a surveyable whole all the data which enter into the social order. Yet all those who are fascinated by the beautiful plans which result from such an approach because they are 'so orderly, so visible, so easy to understand', are the victims of the synoptic delusion and forget that these plans owe their seeming clarity to the planner's disregard of all the facts he does not know,

FACTUAL KNOWLEDGE AND SCIENCE

The chief reason why modern man has become so unwilling to admit that the constitutional limitations on his knowledge form a permanent barrier to the possibility of a rational construction of the whole of society is his unbounded confidence in the powers of science. We hear so much about the rapid advance of scientific knowledge that we have come to feel that all mere limitations of knowledge are soon bound to disappear. This confidence rests, however, on a misconception of the tasks and powers of science, that is, on the erroneous belief that science is a method of ascertaining particular facts and that the progress of its techniques will enable us to ascertain and manipulate all the particular facts we might want.

In one sense the saying that our civilization rests on the conquest of ignorance is of course a mere platitude. Yet our very familiarity with it tends to conceal from us what is most important in it: namely that civilization rests on the fact that we all benefit from knowledge which we do *not* possess, and one of the ways in which civilization helps us to overcome that limitation on the extent of individual knowledge is by conquering ignorance, not by the acquisition of more knowledge, but by the utilization of knowledge which is and remains widely dispersed among individuals. The limitation of knowledge with which we are concerned is therefore not a limitation which science can overcome. Contrary to a widely held belief, science consists not of the knowledge of particular facts; and in the case of very complex phenomena the powers of science are also limited by the practical impossibility of ascertaining all the particular facts which we would have to know if its theories were to give us the power of predicting specific events. The study of the relatively simple phenomena of the physical world, where it has proved possible to state the determining relations as functions of a few variables that can be easily ascertained in particular instances, and where as a consequence the astounding progress of disciplines concerned with them has become possible, has created the illusion that soon the same will also be true with regard to the more complex phenomena. But neither science nor any known technique enables us to overcome the fact that no mind, and therefore also no deliberately directed action, can take account of all the particular facts which are known to some men but not as a whole to any particular person.

Indeed, in its endeavour to explain and predict particular events, which it does so successfully in the case of relatively simple phenomena (or where it can at least approximately isolate 'closed systems' that are relatively simple), science encounters the same barrier of factual ignorance when it comes to apply its theories to very complex phenomena. In some fields it has developed important theories which give us much insight into the general character of some phenomena, but will never produce predictions of particular events, or a full explanation—simply because we can never know all the particular facts which according to these theories we would have to know in order to arrive at such concrete conclusions. The best example of this is the Darwinian (or Neo-Darwinian) theory of the evolution of biological organisms. If it were possible to ascertain the particular facts of the past which operated on the selection of the particular forms that emerged, it would provide a complete explanation of the structure of the existing organisms; and similarly, if it were possible to ascertain all the particular facts which will operate on them during some future period, it ought to enable us to predict future development. But, of course, we will never be able to do either, because science has no means of ascertaining all the particular facts that it would have to possess to perform such a feat.

There is another related misconception about the aim and power of science which it will be useful also to mention at this point. This is the belief that science is concerned exclusively with what exists and not with what could be. But the value of science consists largely in telling us what would happen if some facts were different from what they are. All the statements of theoretical science have the form of 'if, ... then' ... statements, and they are interesting mainly in so far as the conditions we insert in the 'if' clause are different from those that actually exist.

Perhaps this misconception has nowhere else been so important as in political science where it seems to have become a bar to serious consideration of the really important problems. Here the mistaken idea that science is simply a collection of observed facts has led to a confinement of research to the ascertainment of what is. While the chief value of *all* science is to tell us what the consequences would be if conditions were in some respects made different from what they are.

The fact that an increasing number of social scientists confine themselves to the study of what exists in some part of the social system does not make their results more realistic, but makes them largely irrelevant for most decisions about the future. Fruitful social science must be very largely a study of what is *not*: a construction of hypothetical models of possible worlds which might exist if some of the alterable conditions were made different. We need a scientific theory chiefly to tell us what would be the effects if some conditions were as they have never been before. All scientific knowledge is knowledge not of particular facts but of hypotheses which have so far withstood systematic attempts at refuting them.

THE CONCURRENT EVOLUTION OF MIND AND SOCIETY: THE ROLE OF RULES

The errors of constructivist rationalism are closely connected with Cartesian dualism, that is with the conception of an independently existing mind substance which stands outside the cosmos of nature and which enabled man, endowed with such a mind from the beginning, to design the institutions of society and culture among which he lives. The fact is, of course, that this mind is an adaptation to the natural and social surroundings in which man lives and that it has developed in constant interaction with the institutions which determine the structure of society. Mind is as much the product of the social environment in which it has grown up and which it has not made as something that has in turn acted upon and altered these institutions. It is the result of man having developed in society and having acquired those habits and practices that increased the chances of persistence of the group in which he lived. The conception of an already fully developed mind designing the institutions which made life in society possible is contrary to all we know about the evolution of man.

The cultural heritage into which man is born consists of a complex of practices or rules of conduct which have prevailed because they made a group of men successful but which were not adopted because it was known that they would bring about desired effects.

Man acted before he thought and did not understand before he acted. What we call understanding is in the last resort simply his capacity to respond to his environment with a pattern of actions that helps him to persist. Such is the modicum of truth in behaviourism and pragmatism, doctrines which, however, have so crudely oversimplified the determining relationships as to become more obstacles than helps to their appreciation.

'Learning from experience', among men no less than among animals, is a process not primarily of reasoning but of the observance, spreading, transmission and development of practices which have prevailed because they were successful—often not because they conferred any recognizable benefit on the acting individual but because they increased the chances of survival of the group to which he belonged. The result of this development will in the first instance not be articulated knowledge but a knowledge which, although it can be described in terms of rules, the individual cannot state in words but is merely able to honour in practice. The mind does not so much make rules as consist of rules of action, a complex of rules that is, which it has not made, but which have come to govern the actions of the individuals because actions in accordance with them have proved more successful than those of competing individuals or groups.

There is in the beginning no distinction between the practices one must observe in order to achieve a particular result and the practices one ought to observe. There is just one established manner of doing things, and knowledge of cause and effect and knowledge of the appropriate or permissible form of action are not distinct. Knowledge of the world is knowledge of what one must do or not do in certain kinds of circumstances. And in avoiding danger it is as important to know what one must never do as to know what one must do to achieve a particular result.

These rules of conduct have thus not developed as the recognized conditions for the achievement of a known purpose, but have evolved because the groups who practised them were more successful and displaced others. They were rules which, given the kind of environment in which man lived, secured that a greater number of the groups or individuals practising them would survive The problem of conducting himself successfully in a world only partially known to man was thus solved by adhering to rules which had served him well but which he did not and could not *know* to be true in the Cartesian sense.

There are thus two attributes of these rules that govern human conduct and make it appear intelligent which we shall have to stress throughout, because the constructivist approach denies implicitly that it can be rational to observe such rules. Of course in advanced society only some rules will be of this kind; what we want to emphasize is merely that even such advanced societies will in part owe their order to some such rules.

The first of these attributes which most rules of conduct originally possessed is that they are observed in action without being known to the acting person in articulated ('verbalised' or explicit) form. They will manifest themselves in a regularity of action which can be explicitly described, but this regularity of action is not the result of the acting persona being capable of thus stating them. The second is that such rules come to be observed because in fact they give the group in which they are practised superior strength, and not because this effect is known to those who are guided by them. Although such rules come to be generally accepted because their observation produces certain consequences, they are not observed with the intention of producing those consequences—consequences which the acting person need not know.

We cannot consider here the difficult question of how men can learn from each other such, often highly abstract, rules of conduct by example and imitation (or 'by analogy'), although neither those who set the examples nor those who learn from them may be consciously aware of the existence of the rules which they nevertheless strictly observe. This is a problem most familiar to us in the learning of language by children who are able to produce correctly most complicated expressions they have never heard before; but it occurs also in such fields as manners, morals and law, and in most skills where we are guided by rules which we know how to follow but are unable to state.

The important point is that every man growing up in a given culture will find in himself rules, or may discover that he acts in accordance with rules—and will similarly recognize the actions of others as conforming or not conforming to various rules. This is, of course, not proof that they are a permanent or unalterable part of 'human nature', or that they are innate, but proof only that they are part of a cultural heritage which is likely to be fairly constant, especially so long as they are not articulated in words and therefore also are not discussed or consciously examined.

THE FALSE DICHOTOMY OF 'NATURAL' AND 'ARTIFICIAL'

The discussion of the problems with which we are concerned was long hampered by the universal acceptance of a misleading distinction which was introduced by the ancient Greeks and from whose confusing effect we have not yet wholly freed ourselves. This is the division of phenomena between those which in modern terms are 'natural' and those which are 'artificial'. The original Greek terms, which seem to have been introduced by the Sophists of the fifth century B.C., were *physei*, which means 'by nature' and, in contrast to it, either *nomō*, best rendered as 'by convention', or *thesei*, which means roughly 'by deliberate decision'. The use of two terms with somewhat different meanings to express the second part of the division indicates the confusion which has beset the discussion ever since. The distinction intended may be either between objects which existed independently and objects which were the results of human *action,* or between objects which arose independently of, and objects which arose as the result of, human *design.* The failure to distinguish between these two meanings led to the situation where one author could argue with regard to a given phenomenon that it was artificial because it was the result of human action, while another might describe the same phenomenon as natural because it was evidently not the result of human design. Not until the eighteenth century did thinkers like Bernard Mandeville and David Hume make it dear that there existed a category of phenomena which, depending on which of the two definitions one adhered to, would fall into either the one or the other of the two categories and therefore ought to be assigned to a distinct third class of phenomena, later described by Adam Ferguson as 'the result of human action but not of human design'. These were the phenomena which required for their explanation a distinct body of theory and which came to provide the object of the theoretical social sciences.

But in the more than two thousand years during which the distinction introduced by the ancient Greeks has ruled thought almost unchallenged, it has become deeply engrained in concepts and language, in the second century A.D. a Latin grammarian, Aulus Gellius, rendered the Greek terms *physei* and *thesei* by *naturalis* and *positivus,* from which most European languages derived the words to describe two kinds of law.

There occurred later one promising development in the discussion of these questions by the medieval schoolmen, which led close to a recognition of the intermediate category of phenomena that were 'the result of human action but not of human design'. In the twelfth century some of those writers had begun to include under *naturalis* all that was not the result of human invention or a deliberate creation; and in the course of time it came to be increasingly recognized that many social phenomena fell into this category. Indeed, in the discussion of the problems of society by the last of the schoolmen, the Spanish Jesuits of the sixteenth century, *naturalis* became a technical term for such social phenomena as were not deliberately shaped by human will. In the work of one of them, Luis Molina, it is, for example, explained that the 'natural price' is so called because 'it results from the thing itself without regard to laws and decrees, but is dependent on many circumstances which alter it, such as the sentiments of men, their estimation of different uses, often even in consequence of whims and pleasures'. Indeed, these ancestors of ours thought and 'acted under a strong impression of the ignorance and fallibility of mankind', and, for instance, argued that the precise 'mathematical price' at which a commodity could be justly sold was only known to God, because it depended on more circumstances than any man could know, and that therefore the determination of the 'just price' must be left to the market.

These beginnings of an evolutionary approach were submerged, however, in the sixteenth and seventeenth centuries by the rise of constructivist rationalism, with the result that both the term 'reason' and the term 'natural law' completely changed their meaning. 'Reason', which had included the capacity of the mind to distinguish between good and evil, that is between what was and what was not in accordance with established rules, came to mean a capacity to construct such rules by deduction from explicit premises. The conception of natural law was thereby turned into that of a 'law of reason' and thus almost into the opposite of what it had meant. This new rationalist law of nature of Grotius and his successors, indeed, shared with its positivist antagonists the conception that all law was made by reason or could at least be fully justified by it, and differed from it only in the assumption that law could be logically derived from *a priori* premises, while positivism regarded it as a deliberate construction based on empirical knowledge of the effects it would have on the achievement of desirable human purposes.

THE RISE OF THE EVOLUTIONARY APPROACH

After the Cartesian relapse into anthropomorphic thinking on these matters a new start was made by Bernard Mandeville and David Hume. They were probably inspired more by the tradition of the English common law, especially as expounded by Matthew Hale, than by the law of nature. It came increasingly to be seen that the formation of regular patterns in human relations that were not the conscious aim of human actions raised a problem which required the development of a systematic social theory. This need was met during the second half of the eighteenth century in the field of economics by the Scottish moral philosophers, led by Adam Smith and Adam Ferguson while the consequences to be drawn for political theory received their magnificent formulations from the great seer Edmund Burke, in whose work we shall, however, seek in vain for a systematic theory. But while in England the development suffered a new setback from the intrusion of constructivism in the form of Benthamite utilitarianism, it gained a new vitality on the continent from the 'historical schools' of linguistics and law. After the beginnings made by the Scottish philosophers, the systematic development of the evolutionary aproach to social phenomena took place mainly in Germany through Wilhelm von Humboldt and F. C. von Savigny. We cannot consider here that development in linguistics, although for a long time it was the only field outside of economics where a coherent theory was achieved, and the extent to which since Roman times the theory of law has been fertilized by conceptions borrowed from the grammarians deserves to be better understood than it is. In the social sciences it was through Savigny's follower Sir Henry Maine that the evolutionary approach re-entered the English tradition. And in the great survey of 1883 of the methods of the social sciences by the founder of the Austrian school of economics, Carl Menger, the central position for all social sciences of the problem of the spontaneous formation of institutions and its genetic character was most fully restated on the continent. In recent times the tradition has been most fruitfully developed by cultural anthropology, at least some of whose leading figures are fully aware of this ancestry.

As the conception of evolution will play a central role throughout our discussion, it is important to clear up some misunderstandings which in recent times have made students of society reluctant to employ it. The first is the erroneous belief that it is a conception which the social sciences have borrowed from biology. It was in fact the other way round, and if Charles Darwin was able successfully to apply to biology a concept which he had largely learned from the social sciences, this does not make it less important in the field in which it originated. It was in the discussion of such social formations as language and morals, law and money, that in the eighteenth century the twin conceptions of evolution and the spontaneous formation of an order were at last clearly formulated, and provided the intellectual tools which Darwin and his contemporaries were able to apply to biological evolution. Those eighteenth-century moral philosophers and the historical schools of law and language might well be described, as some of the theorists of language of the nineteenth century indeed described themselves, as Darwinians before Darwin.

A nineteenth-century social theorist who needed Darwin to teach him the idea of evolution was not worth his salt. Unfortunately some did, and produced views which under the name of 'Social Darwinism' have since been responsible for the distrust with which the concept of evolution has been regarded by social scientists. There are, of course, important differences between the manner in which the process of selection operates in the cultural transmission that leads to the formation of social institutions, and the manner in which it operates in the selection of innate biological characteristics and their transmission by physiological inheritance. The error of 'Social Darwinism' was that it concentrated on the selection of individuals rather than on that of institutions and practices, and on the selection of innate rather than on culturally transmitted capacities of the individuals. But although the scheme of Darwinian theory has only limited application to the latter and its literal use leads to grave distortions, the basic conception of evolution is still the same in both fields.

The other great misunderstanding which has led to a discrediting of the theory of social evolution, is the belief that the theory of evolution consists of 'laws of evolution'. This is true at most in a special sense of the word 'law', and is certainly not true, as it is often thought, in the sense of a statement of a necessary sequence of particular stages or phases through which the process of evolution must pass and which by extrapolation leads to predictions of the future course of evolution. The theory of evolution proper provides no more than an account of a process the outcome of which will depend on a very large number of particular facts, far too numerous for us to know in their entirety, and therefore does not lead to predictions about the future. We are in consequence confined to 'explanations of the principle' or to predictions merely of the abstract pattern the process will follow.

The pretended laws of overall evolution supposedly derived from observation have in fact nothing to do with the legitimate theory of evolution which accounts for the process. They derive from the altogether different conceptions of the historicism of Comte, Hegel and Marx, and their holistic approach, and assert a purely mystical necessity that evolution must run a certain predetermined course. Although it must be admitted that the original meaning of the term 'evolution' refers to such an 'unwinding' of potentialities already contained in the germ, the process by which the biological and social theory of evolution accounts for the appearence of different complex structures does not imply such a succession of particular steps. Those to whom the concept of evolution implies necessary sequences of predetermined 'stages', or 'phrases', through which the development of an organism or a social institution must pass, are therefore justified in rejecting such a conception of evolution, for which there is no scientific warrant.

We will mention at this point only briefly that the frequent attempts made to use the conception of evolution, not merely as an explanation of the rise of rules of conduct, but as the basis of a prescriptive science of ethics, also have no foundation in the legitimate theory of evolution, but belong to those extrapolations of observed tendencies as 'laws of evolution' for which there is no justification. This needs saying here as some distinguished biologists who certainly understand the theory of evolution proper have been tempted into such assertions. It is our concern here, however, only to show that such abuses of the concept of evolution in subjects like anthropology, ethics, and also law, which have discredited it for a time, were based on a misconception of the nature of the theory of evolution; and that, if it is taken in its correct meaning, it still remains true that the complex, spontaneously formed structures with which social theory has to deal, can be understood only as the result of a process of evolution and that, therefore, here 'the genetic element is inseparable from the idea of theoretical sciences'.

THE PERSISTENCE OF CONSTRUCTIVISM IN CURRENT THOUGHT

It is difficult to appreciate fully the extent to which the constructivist fallacy has during the last three hundred years determined the attitudes of many of the most independent and courageous thinkers. The rejection of the accounts which religion gave of the source and grounds of validity of the traditional rules of morals and law led to the rejection of these rules themselves so far as they could not be rationally justified. It was to their achievement in thus 'freeing' the human mind that many of the celebrated thinkers of the period owe their fame. We can here illustrate this only by picking out almost at random a few characteristic instances.

One of the best known is, of course, Voltaire, whose views on the problem with which we shall be mainly concerned found expression in the exhortation, 'if you want good laws, burn those you have and make new ones'. Even greater influence was exercised by Rousseau; of him it has been well said that:

> There was even no law except law willed by living men—this was his greatest heresy from many points of view, including the Christian; it was also his greatest affirmation in political theory. … What he did, and it was revolutionary enough, was to undermine the faith of many people in the justice of the society in which they lived.

And he did so by demanding that 'society' should be just as if it were a thinking being.

The refusal to recognize as binding any rules of conduct whose justification had not been rationally demonstrated or 'made clear and demonstrative to every individual' becomes in the nineteenth century an ever recurring theme. Two examples will indicate the attitude. Early in that century we find Alexander Herzen arguing: 'You want a book of rules, while I think that when one reaches a certain age one ought to be ashamed of having to use one [because] the truly free man creates his own morality.' And quite in the same manner a distinguished contemporary positivist philosopher contends that 'the power of reason must be sought not in rules that reason dictates to our imagination, but in the ability to free ourselves from any kind of rules to which we have been conditioned through experience and traditions'.

The best description of this state of mind by a representative thinker of our time is found in the account given by Lord Keynes in a talk entitled 'My early beliefs'. Speaking in 1938 about the time thirty-five years before, when he himself was twenty, he says of himself and his friends:

> We entirely repudiated a personal liability on us to obey general rules. We claimed the right to judge every individual case on its merits, and the wisdom, experience, and self-control to do so successfully. This was a very important part of our faith, violently and aggressively held, and for the outer world it was our most obvious and dangerous characteristic. We repudiated entirely customary morals, conventions, and traditional wisdom. We were, that is to say, in the strict sense of the term, immoralists … we recognized no moral obligation, no inner sanction, to conform or obey. Before heaven we claimed to be our own judge in our own case.

To which he added: 'So far as I am concerned, it is too late to change. I remain, and always will remain, an immoralist.'

To anyone who has himself grown up before the First World War, it is obvious that this was then not an attitude peculiar to the Bloomsbury Group, but a very widespread one, shared by many of the most active and independent spirits of the time.

OUR ANTHROPOMORPHIC LANGUAGE

How deeply the erroneous constructivist or intentionalist interpretation pervades our thinking about the phenomena of society is seen when we consider the meaning of many of the terms which we have to use in referring to them. Indeed, most of the errors against which we shall have to argue throughout this book are so deeply built into our language that the use of established terms will lead the unwary almost necessarily to wrong conclusions. The language which we have to use has developed in the course of millennia when man could conceive of an order only as the product of design, and when he regarded as evidence of the action of a personal designer whatever order he discovered in the phenomena.

In consequence, practically all the terms that are available to us to describe such orderly structures or their functioning are charged with the suggestion that a personal agent has created them. Because of this they regularly lead to false conclusions.

To some extent this is true of all scientific vocabulary. The physical sciences no less than biology or social theory had to make use of terms of anthropomorphic origin. But the physicist who speaks of 'force' or 'inertia' or of a body 'acting' on another employs these terms in a generally understood technical sense not likely to mislead. But to speak of society as 'acting' at once conjures up associations which are very misleading.

We shall in general refer to this propensity as 'anthropomorphism', although the term is not wholly accurate. To be more exact we ought to distinguish between the even more primitive attitude which *personifies* such entities as society by ascribing to them possession of a mind and which is properly described as *anthropomorphism* or *animism,* and the slightly more sophisticated interpretation which ascribes their order and functioning to the *design* of some distinct agency, and which is better described as *intentionalism, artificialism,* or, as we do here, *constructivism.* However, these two propensities shade into each other more or less imperceptibly, and for our purposes we shall generally use 'anthropomorphism' without making the finer distinction.

Since practically the whole vocabulary available for the discussion of the spontaneous orders with which we shall be concerned possesses such misleading connotations, we must in some degree be arbitrary in deciding which words we shall use in a strictly non-anthropomorphic sense and which we shall use only if we want to imply intention or design. To preserve clarity, however, it is essential that with respect to many words we use them either for the results of deliberate constructions only, or for the results of spontaneous formation only, but not for both. Sometimes, however, as in the case of the term 'order', it will be necessary to use it in a neutral sense comprising both spontaneous orders and 'organizations' or 'arrangements'. The last two terms, which we shall use only for results of design, illustrate the fact that it is often as difficult to find terms which always imply design as it is to find those which do not suggest it. The biologist will generally without hesitation speak of 'organization' without implying design, but it would sound odd if he said that an organism not only had but was an organization or that it had been organized. The role that the term 'organization' has played in the development of modern political thought, and the meaning which modern 'organization theory' attaches to it, seem to justify in the present context a restriction of its meaning to results of design only.

Since the distinction between a made order and one which forms itself as a result of regularities of the actions of its elements will be the chief topic of the next chapter, we need not dwell upon it here any further. And in volume 2 we shall have to consider at some length the almost invariably confusing character of the little word 'social' which) because of its particularly elusive character, carries confusion into almost any statement in which it is used.

We shall find too that such current notions as that society 'acts' or that it 'treats', 're-wards', or 'remunerates' persons, or that it 'values' or 'owns' or 'controls' objects or services, or is 'responsible for' or 'guilty of' something, or that it has a 'will' or 'purpose', can be 'just' or 'unjust', or that the economy 'distributes' or 'allocates' resources, all suggest a false intentionalist or constructivist interpretation of words which might have been used without such a connotation, but which almost inevitably lead the user to illegitimate conclusions. We shall see that such confusions are at the root of the basic conceptions of highly influential schools of thought which have wholly succumbed to the belief that all rules or laws must have been invented or explicitly agreed upon by somebody. Only when it is wrongly assumed that all rules of just conduct have deliberately been made by somebody do such sophisms become plausible as that all power of making laws must be arbitrary, or that there must always exist an ultimate 'sovereign' source of power from which all law derives. Many of the age-old puzzles of political theory and many of the conceptions which have profoundly affected the evolution of political institutions are the product of this confusion. This is especially true of that tradition in legal theory which more than any other is proud of having fully escaped from anthropomorphic conceptions, namely legal positivism; for it proves on examination to be entirely based on what we have called the constructivist fallacy. It is actually one of the main offshoots of that rationalist constructivism which, in taking literally the expression that man has 'made' all his culture and institutions, has been driven to the fiction that all law is the product of somebody's will.

One more term whose ambiguity had a similar confusing effect on social theory, and particularly on some positivist theories of law, and which therefore ought to be briefly mentioned here, is the term 'function'. It is an almost indispensable term for the discussion of those self-maintaining structures which we find alike in biological organisms and in spontaneous social orders. Such a function may be performed without the acting part knowing what purpose its action serves. But the characteristic anthropomorphism of the positivist tradition has led to a curious perversion: from the discovery that an institution served a function the conclusion was drawn that the persons performing the function must be directed to do so by another human will. Thus the true insight that the institution of private property served a function necessary for the maintenance of the spontaneous order of society led to the belief that for this purpose a power of direction of some authority was required—an opinion even expressly laid down in the constitutions of some countries which were drawn up under positivist inspiration.

REASON AND ABSTRACTION

The aspects of the Cartesian tradition which we have described as constructivism are often also referred to simply as rationalism, and this is apt to give rise to a misunderstanding. It has, for instance, become customary to speak of its early critics, especially Bernard Mandeville and David Hume, as 'anti-rationalists' and this has conveyed the impression that these 'anti-rationalists' were less concerned to achieve the most effective use of reason than those who specially claimed the name of rationalists. The fact is, however, that the so-called anti-rationalists insist that to make reason as effective as possible requires an insight into the limitations of the powers of conscious reason and into the assistance we obtain from processes of which we are not aware, an insight which constructivist rationalism lacks. Thus, if the desire to make reason as effective as possible is what is meant by rationalism, I am myself a rationalist. If, however, the term means that conscious reason ought to determine every particular action, I am not a rationalist, and such rationalism seems to me to be very unreasonable. Surely, one of the tasks of reason is to decide how far it is to extend its control or how far it ought to rely on other forces which it cannot wholly control. It is therefore better in this connection not to distinguish between 'rationalism' and 'anti-rationalism' but to distinguish between a constructivist and an evolutionary, or, in Karl Popper's terms, a naïve and a critical rationalism.

Connected with the uncertain meaning of the term 'rationalism' are the opinions generally held about the attitude to 'abstraction' characteristic of 'rationalism'. The name is often even used to describe an undue addiction to abstraction. The characteristic property of constructivist rationalism, however, is rather that it is not content with abstraction—that it does not recognize that abstract concepts are a means to cope with the complexity of the concrete which our mind is not capable of fully mastering. Evolutionary rationalism, on the other hand, recognizes abstractions as the indispensable means of the mind which enable it to deal with a reality it cannot fully comprehend. This is connected with the fact that in the constructivist view 'abstractness' is conceived as a property confined to conscious thought or concepts, while actually it is a characteristic possessed by all the processes which determine action long before they appear in conscious thought or are expressed in language. Whenever a *type* of situation evokes in an individual a *disposition* towards a certain *pattern* of response, that basic relation which is described as 'abstract' is present. There can be little doubt that the peculiar capacities of a central nervous system consist precisely in the fact that particular stimuli do not directly evoke particular responses, but make it possible for certain classes or configurations of stimuli to set up certain dispositions towards classes of actions, and that only the superimposition of many such dispositions specify the particular action that will result. This 'primacy of the abstract', as I have called it elsewhere, will be assumed throughout this book.

Abstractness will here be regarded, therefore, not only as a property possessed to a greater or lesser degree by all (conscious or unconscious) mental processes, but as the basis of man's capacity to move successfully in a world very imperfectly known to him—an adaptation to his ignorance of most of the particular facts of his surroundings. The main purpose of our stress on the rules which govern our actions is to bring out the central importance of the abstract character of all mental processes.

Thus considered, abstraction is not something which the mind produces by processes of logic from its perception of reality, but rather a property of the categories with which it operates—not a product of the mind but rather what constitutes the mind. We never act, and could never act, in full consideration of all the facts of a particular situation, but always by singling out as relevant only some aspects of it; not by conscious choice or deliberate selection, but by a mechanism over which we do not exercise deliberate control.

It will perhaps be clear now that our constant stress on the non-rational character of much of our actions is meant not to belittle or criticize this manner of acting, but, on the contrary, to bring out one of the reasons why it is successful; and not to suggest that we ought to try fully to understand why we do what we do, but to point out that this is impossible; and that we can make use of so much experience, not because we possess that experience, but because, without our knowing it, it has become incorporated in the schemata of thought which guide us.

There are two possible misconceptions of the position taken which we must try to prevent. One derives from the fact that action which is guided by rules we are not aware of is often described as 'instinctive' or 'intuitive'. There is not much harm in these words except that both, and specially 'intuitive', usually refer to the perception of the particular and relatively concrete, while what we are here concerned with are capacities determining very general or abstract properties of the actions taken. As commonly used, the term 'intuitive' suggests an attribute not possessed by abstract rules which we follow in our actions, and for this reason it had better be avoided.

The other possible misunderstanding of our position is the impression that the emphasis we place on the non-conscious character of many of the rules which govern our action is connected with the conception of an unconscious or subconscious mind underlying the theories of psychoanalysis or 'depth-psychology'. But although to some extent the two views may aim at an explanation of the same phenomena, they are in fact wholly different. We shall not use, and in fact regard as unwarranted and false, the whole conception of an unconscious mind which differs from the conscious mind only by being unconscious, but in all other respects operates in the same, rational, goal-seeking manner as the conscious mind. Nothing is gained by postulating such a mystical entity, or by ascribing to the various propensities or rules which together produce the complex order we call mind any of the properties which the resulting order possesses. Psychoanalysis seems in this respect merely to have created another ghost which in turn is held to govern the 'ghost in the machine' of Cartesian dualism.

WHY THE EXTREME FORMS OF CONSTRUCTIVIST RATIONALISM REGULARLY LEAD TO A REVOLT AGAINST REASON

In conclusion of this introductory chapter some observations are in place on a phenomenon which transcends the scope of this book but which is of considerable importance for the understanding of its immediate concerns. We refer to the fact that the constructivist rationalism which knows no bounds to the applications of conscious reason has historically again and again given birth to a revolt against reason. Indeed, this development, in which an over-estimation of the powers of reason leads through disillusionment to a violent reaction against the guidance by abstract reason, and to an extolling of the powers of the particular will, is not in the least paradoxical, but almost inevitable.

The illusion that leads constructivist rationalists regularly to an enthronement of the will consists in the belief that reason can transcend the realm of the abstract and by itself is able to determine the desirability of particular actions. Yet it is always only in combination with particular, non-rational impulses that reason can determine what to do, and its function is essentially to act as a restraint on emotion, or to steer action impelled by other factors. The illusion that reason alone can tell us what we ought to do, and that therefore all reasonable men ought to be able to join in the endeavour to pursue common ends as members of an organization, is quickly dispelled when we attempt to put it into practice. But the desire to use our reason to turn the whole of society into one rationally directed engine persists, and in order to realize it common ends are imposed upon all that cannot be justified by reason and cannot be more than the decisions of particular wills.

The rationalist revolt against reason, if we may so call it, is usually directed against the abstractness of thought. It will not recognize that all thought must remain abstract to various degrees and that therefore it can never by itself fully determine particular actions. Reason is merely a discipline, an insight into the limitations of the possibilities of successful action, which often will tell us only what not to do. This discipline is necessary precisely because our intellect is not capable of grasping reality in all its complexity. Although the use of abstraction extends the scope of phenomena which we can master intellectually, it does so by limiting the degree to which we can foresee the effects of our actions, and therefore also by limiting to certain general features the degree to which we can shape the world to our liking. Liberalism for this reason restricts deliberate control of the overall order of society to the enforcement of such general rules as are necessary for the formation of a spontaneous order, the details of which we cannot foresee.

Perhaps nobody has seen this connection between liberalism and the insight into the limited powers of abstract thinking more clearly than that ultra-rationalist who has become the fountain head of most modem irationalism and totalitarianism, G. W. F. Hegel. When he wrote that 'the view which clings to abstraction is *liberalism,* over which the concrete always prevails and which always founders in the struggle against it', he truly described the fact that we are not yet mature enough to submit for any length of time to strict discipline of reason and allow our emotions constantly to break through its restraints.

The reliance on the abstract is thus not a result of an over-estimation but rather of an insight into the limited powers of our reason. It is the over-estimation of the powers of reason which leads to the revolt against the submission to abstract rules. Constructivist rationalism rejects the demand for this discipline of reason because it deceives itself that reason can directly master all the particulars; and it is thereby led to a preference for the concrete over the abstract, the particular over the general, because its adherents do not realize bow much they thereby limit the span of true control by reason. The hubris of reason manifests itself in those who believe that they can dispense with abstraction and achieve a full mastery of the concrete and thus positively master the social process, The desire to remodel society after the image of individual man, which since Hobbes has governed rationalist political theory, and which attributes to the Great Society properties which only individuals or deliberately created organizations can possess, leads to a striving not merely to be, but to make everything rational. Although we must endeavour to make society good in the sense that we shall like to live in it, we cannot make it good in the sense that it will behave morally. It does not make sense to apply the standards of conscious conduct to those unintended consequences of individual action which all the truly social represents, except by eliminating the unintended—which would mean eliminating all that we call culture.

The Great Society and the civilization it has made possible is the product of man's growing capacity to communicate abstract thought; and when we say that what all men have in common is their reason we mean their common capacity for abstract thought. That man uses this capacity largely without explicitly knowing the abstract principles which guide him, and does not understand all the reasons for allowing himself to be thus guided, has produced a situation in which the very over-estimation of those powers of reason of which man is conscious has led him to hold in contempt what has made reason as powerful as it is: its abstract character. It was the failure to recognize that abstractions help our reason go further than it could if it tried to master all the particulars which produced a host of schools of philosophy inimical to abstract reason—philosophies of the concrete, of 'life' and of 'existence' which extol emotion, the particular and the instinctive, and which are only too ready to support such emotions as those of race, nation, and class.

Thus constructivist rationalism, in its endeavour to make everything subject to rational control, in its preference for the concrete and its refusal to submit to the discipline of abstract rules, comes to join hands with irrationalism. Construction is possible only in the service of particular ends which in the last resort must be non-rational, and on which no rational argument can produce agreement if it is not already present at the outset.

CHAPTER 2

✦

TRUST AND TRADE

Leviathan

THOMAS HOBBES

CHAPTER XIII. OF THE NATURALL CONDITION OF MANKIND, AS CONCERNING THEIR FELICITY, AND MISERY

Nature hath made men so equall, in the faculties of body, and mind; as that though there bee found one man sometimes manifestly stronger in body, or of quicker mind then another; yet when all is reckoned together, the difference between man, and man, is not so considerable, as that one man can thereupon claim to himselfe any benefit, to which another may not pretend, as well as he. For as to the strength of body, the weakest has strength enough to kill the strongest, either by secret machination, or by confederacy with others, that are in the same danger with himselfe.

And as to the faculties of the mind, (setting aside the arts grounded upon words, and especially that skill of proceeding upon generall, and infallible rules, called Science; which very few have, and but in few things; as being not a native faculty, born with us; nor attained, (as Prudence) while we look after somewhat else) I find yet a greater equality amongst men, than that of strength. For Prudence, is but Experience; which equall time, equally bestowes on all men, in those things they equally apply themselves unto. That which may perhaps make such equality incredible, is but a vain conceipt of ones owne wisdome, which almost all men think they have in a greater degree, than the Vulgar; that is, than all men but themselves, and a few others, whom by Fame, or for concurring with themselves, they approve. For such is the nature of men, that howsoever they may acknowledge many others to be more witty, or more eloquent, or more learned; Yet they will hardly believe there be many so wise as themselves: For they see their own wit at hand, and other mens at a distance. But this proveth rather that men are in that point equall, than unequall. For there is not ordinarily a greater signe of the equall distribution of any thing, than that every man is contented with his share.

From Equality Proceeds Diffidence

From this equality of ability, ariseth equality of hope in the attaining of our Ends. And therefore if any two men desire the same thing, which neverthelesse they cannot both enjoy, they become enemies; and in the way to their End, (which is principally their owne conservation, and sometimes their delectation only) endeavour to destroy, or subdue one an other. And from hence it comes to passe, that where an Invader hath no more to feare, than an other mans single power; if one plant, sow, build, or possesse a convenient Seat, others may probably be expected to come prepared with forces united, to dispossesse, and deprive him, not only of the fruit of his labour, but also of his life, or liberty. And the Invader again is in the like danger of another.

From Diffidence Warre

And from this diffidence of one another, there is no way for any man to secure himselfe, so reasonable, as Anticipation; that is, by force, or wiles, to master the persons of all men he can, so long, till he see no other power great enough to endanger him: And this is no more than his own conservation requireth, and is generally allowed. Also because there be some, that taking pleasure in contemplating their own power in the acts of conquest, which they pursue farther than their security requires; if others, that otherwise would be glad to be at ease within modest bounds, should not by invasion increase their power, they would not be able, long time, by standing only on their defence, to subsist. And by consequence, such augmentation of dominion over men, being necessary to a mans conservation, it ought to be allowed him.

Againe, men have no pleasure, (but on the contrary a great deale of griefe) in keeping company, where there is no power able to over-awe them all. For every man looketh that his companion should value him, at the same rate he sets upon himselfe: And upon all signes of contempt, or undervaluing, naturally endeavours, as far as he dares (which amongst them that have no common power, to keep them in quiet, is far enough to make them destroy each other,) to extort a greater value from his contemners, by dommage; and from others, by the example.

So that in the nature of man, we find three principall causes of quarrel. First, Competition; Secondly, Diffidence; Thirdly, Glory.

The first, maketh men invade for Gain; the second, for Safety; and the third, for Reputation. The first use Violence, to make themselves Masters of other mens persons, wives, children, and cattell; the second, to defend them; the third, for trifles, as a word, a smile, a different opinion, and any other signe of undervalue, either direct in their Persons, or by reflexion in their Kindred, their Friends, their Nation, their Profession, or their Name.

Out of Civil States,

There Is Always Warre Of Every One Against Every One Hereby it is manifest, that during the time men live without a common Power to keep them all in awe, they are in that condition which is called Warre; and such a warre, as is of every man, against every man. For WARRE, consisteth not in Battell onely, or the act of fighting; but in a tract of time, wherein the Will to contend by Battell is sufficiently known: and therefore the notion of Time, is to be considered in the nature of Warre; as it is in the nature of Weather. For as the nature of Foule weather, lyeth not in a showre or two of rain; but in an inclination thereto of many dayes together: So the nature of War, consisteth not in actuall fighting; but in the known disposition thereto, during all the time there is no assurance to the contrary. All other time is PEACE.

The Incommodites of Such A War

Whatsoever therefore is consequent to a time of Warre, where every man is Enemy to every man; the same is consequent to the time, wherein men live without other security, than what their own strength, and their own invention shall furnish them withall. In such condition, there is no place for Industry; because the fruit thereof is uncertain; and consequently no Culture of the Earth; no Navigation, nor use of the commodities that may be imported by Sea; no commodious Building; no Instruments of moving, and removing such things as require much force; no Knowledge of the face of the Earth; no account of Time; no Arts; no Letters; no Society; and which is worst of all, continuall feare, and danger of violent death; And the life of man, solitary, poore, nasty, brutish, and short.

It may seem strange to some man, that has not well weighed these things; that Nature should thus dissociate, and render men apt to invade, and destroy one another: and he may therefore, not trusting to this Inference, made from the Passions, desire perhaps to have the same confirmed by Experience. Let him therefore consider with himselfe, when taking a journey, he armes himselfe, and seeks to go well accompanied; when going to sleep, he locks his dores; when even in his house he locks his chests; and this when he knows there bee Lawes, and publike Officers, armed, to revenge all injuries shall bee done him; what opinion he has of his fellow subjects, when he rides armed; of his fellow Citizens, when he locks his dores; and of his children, and servants, when he locks his chests. Does he not there as much accuse mankind by his actions, as I do by my words? But neither of us accuse mans nature in it. The Desires, and other Passions of man, are in themselves no Sin. No more are the Actions, that proceed from those Passions, till they know a Law that forbids them; which till Lawes be made they cannot know: nor can any Law be made, till they have agreed upon the Person that shall make it.

It may peradventure be thought, there was never such a time, nor condition of warre as this; and I believe it was never generally so, over all the world: but there are many places, where they live so now. For the savage people in many places of America, except the government of small Families, the concord whereof dependeth on naturall lust, have no government at all; and live at this day in that brutish manner, as I said before. Howsoever, it may be perceived what manner of life there would be, where there were no common Power to feare; by the manner of life, which men that have formerly lived under a peacefull government, use to degenerate into, in a civill Warre.

But though there had never been any time, wherein particular men were in a condition of warre one against another; yet in all times, Kings, and persons of Soveraigne authority, because of their Independency, are in continuall jealousies, and in the state and posture of Gladiators; having their weapons pointing, and their eyes fixed on one another; that is, their Forts, Garrisons, and Guns upon the Frontiers of their Kingdomes; and continuall Spyes upon their neighbours; which is a posture of War. But because they uphold thereby, the Industry of their Subjects; there does not follow from it, that misery, which accompanies the Liberty of particular men.

In Such a Warre, Nothing Is Unjust

To this warre of every man against every man, this also is consequent; that nothing can be Unjust. The notions of Right and Wrong, Justice and Injustice have there no place. Where there is no common Power, there is no Law: where no Law, no Injustice. Force, and Fraud, are in warre the two Cardinall vertues. Justice, and Injustice are none of the Faculties neither of the Body, nor Mind. If they were, they might be in a man that were alone in the world, as well as his Senses, and Passions. They are Qualities, that relate to men in Society, not in Solitude. It is consequent also to the same condition, that there be no Propriety, no Dominion, no Mine and Thine distinct; but onely that to be every mans that he can get; and for so long, as he can keep it. And thus much for the ill condition, which man by meer Nature is actually placed in; though with a possibility to come out of it, consisting partly in the Passions, partly in his Reason.

The Passions that Incline Men to Peace

The Passions that encline men to Peace, are Feare of Death; Desire of such things as are necessary to commodious living; and a Hope by their Industry to obtain them. And

Reason suggesteth convenient Articles of Peace, upon which men may be drawn to agreement. These Articles, are they, which otherwise are called the Lawes of Nature: whereof I shall speak more particularly, in the two following Chapters.

CHAPTER XIV. OF THE FIRST AND SECOND NATURALL LAWES, AND OF CONTRACTS

Right of Nature What

The RIGHT OF NATURE, which Writers commonly call Jus Naturale, is the Liberty each man hath, to use his own power, as he will himselfe, for the preservation of his own Nature; that is to say, of his own Life; and consequently, of doing any thing, which in his own Judgement, and Reason, hee shall conceive to be the aptest means thereunto.

Liberty What

By LIBERTY, is understood, according to the proper signification of the word, the absence of externall Impediments: which Impediments, may oft take away part of a mans power to do what hee would; but cannot hinder him from using the power left him, according as his judgement, and reason shall dictate to him.

A Law of Nature What

A LAW OF NATURE, (Lex Naturalis,) is a Precept, or generall Rule, found out by Reason, by which a man is forbidden to do, that, which is destructive of his life, or taketh away the means of preserving the same; and to omit, that, by which he thinketh it may be best preserved. For though they that speak of this subject, use to confound Jus, and Lex, Right and Law; yet they ought to be distinguished; because RIGHT, consisteth in liberty to do, or to forbeare; Whereas LAW, determineth, and bindeth to one of them: so that Law, and Right, differ as much, as Obligation, and Liberty; which in one and the same matter are inconsistent.

Naturally Every Man Has Right to Everything

And because the condition of Man, (as hath been declared in the precedent Chapter) is a condition of Warre of every one against every one; in which case every one is governed by his own Reason; and there is nothing he can make use of, that may not be a help unto him, in preserving his life against his enemyes; It followeth, that in such a condition, every man has a Right to every thing; even to one anothers body. And therefore, as long as this naturall Right of every man to every thing endureth, there can be no security to any man, (how strong or wise soever he be,) of living out the time, which Nature ordinarily alloweth men to live.

The Fundamental Law of Nature

And consequently it is a precept, or generall rule of Reason, "That every man, ought to endeavour Peace, as farre as he has hope of obtaining it; and when he cannot obtain it, that he may seek, and use, all helps, and advantages of Warre." The first branch, of which Rule, containeth the first, and Fundamentall Law of Nature; which is, "To seek Peace, and follow it." The Second, the summe of the Right of Nature; which is, "By all means we can, to defend our selves."

The Second Law of Nature

From this Fundamentall Law of Nature, by which men are commanded to endeavour Peace, is derived this second Law; "That a man be willing, when others are so too, as farre-forth, as for Peace, and defence of himselfe he shall think it necessary, to lay down this right to all things; and be contented with so much liberty against other men, as he would allow other men against himselfe." For as long as every man holdeth this Right, of doing any thing he liketh; so long are all men in the condition of Warre. But if other men will not lay down their Right, as well as he; then there is no Reason for any one, to devest himselfe of his: For that were to expose himselfe to Prey, (which no man is bound to) rather than to dispose himselfe to Peace. This is that Law of the Gospell; "Whatsoever you require that others should do to you, that do ye to them." And that Law of all men, "Quod tibi feiri non vis, alteri ne feceris."

What It Is to Lay Down a Right

To Lay Downe a mans Right to any thing, is to Devest himselfe of the Liberty, of hindring another of the benefit of his own Right to the same. For he that renounceth, or passeth away his Right, giveth not to any other man a Right which he had not before; because there is nothing to which every man had not Right by Nature: but onely standeth out of his way, that he may enjoy his own originall Right, without hindrance from him; not without hindrance from another. So that the effect which redoundeth to one man, by another mans defect of Right, is but so much diminution of impediments to the use of his own Right originall.

Renouncing (or) Transferring Right What; Obligation Duty Justice

Right is layd aside, either by simply Renouncing it; or by Transferring it to another. By Simply RENOUNCING; when he cares not to whom the benefit thereof redoundeth. By TRANSFERRING; when he intendeth the benefit thereof to some certain person, or persons. And when a man hath in either manner abandoned, or granted away his Right; then is he said to be OBLIGED, or BOUND, not to hinder those, to whom such Right is granted, or abandoned, from the benefit of it: and that he Ought, and it his DUTY, not to make voyd that voluntary act of his own: and that such hindrance is INJUSTICE, and INJURY, as being Sine Jure; the Right being before renounced, or transferred. So that Injury, or Injustice, in the controversies of the world, is somewhat like to that, which in the disputations of Scholers is called Absurdity. For as it is there called an Absurdity, to contradict what one maintained in the Beginning: so in the world, it is called Injustice, and Injury, voluntarily to undo that, which from the beginning he had voluntarily done. The way by which a man either simply Renounceth, or Transferreth his Right, is a Declaration, or Signification, by some voluntary and sufficient signe, or signes, that he doth so Renounce, or Transferre; or hath so Renounced, or Transferred the same, to him that accepteth it. And these Signes are either Words onely, or Actions onely; or (as it happeneth most often) both Words and Actions. And the same are the BONDS, by which men are bound, and obliged: Bonds, that have their strength, not from their own Nature, (for nothing is more easily broken then a mans word,) but from Feare of some evill consequence upon the rupture.

Not All Rights Are Alienable

Whensoever a man Transferreth his Right, or Renounceth it; it is either in consideration of some Right reciprocally transferred to himselfe; or for some other good he hopeth for thereby. For it is a voluntary act: and of the voluntary acts of every man, the object is some Good To Himselfe. And therefore there be some Rights, which no man can be understood by any words, or other signes, to have abandoned, or transferred. As first a man cannot lay down the right of resisting them, that assault him by force, to take away his life; because he cannot be understood to ayme thereby, at any Good to himself. The same may be sayd of Wounds, and Chayns, and Imprisonment; both because there is no benefit consequent to such patience; as there is to the patience of suffering another to be wounded, or imprisoned: as also because a man cannot tell, when he seeth men proceed against him by violence, whether they intend his death or not. And lastly the motive, and end for which this renouncing, and transferring or Right is introduced, is nothing else but the security of a mans person, in his life, and in the means of so preserving life, as not to be weary of it. And therefore if a man by words, or other signes, seem to despoyle himselfe of the End, for which those signes were intended; he is not to be understood as if he meant it, or that it was his will; but that he was ignorant of how such words and actions were to be interpreted.

CONTRACT WHAT

The mutuall transferring of Right, is that which men call CONTRACT.

There is difference, between transferring of Right to the Thing; and transferring, or tradition, that is, delivery of the Thing it selfe. For the Thing may be delivered together with the Translation of the Right; as in buying and selling with ready mony; or exchange of goods, or lands: and it may be delivered some time after.

Covenant What

Again, one of the Contractors, may deliver the Thing contracted for on his part, and leave the other to perform his part at some determinate time after, and in the mean time be trusted; and then the Contract on his part, is called PACT, or COVENANT: Or both parts may contract now, to performe hereafter: in which cases, he that is to performe in time to come, being trusted, his performance is called Keeping Of Promise, or Faith; and the fayling of performance (if it be voluntary) Violation Of Faith.

Free-gift

When the transferring of Right, is not mutuall; but one of the parties transferreth, in hope to gain thereby friendship, or service from another, or from his friends; or in hope to gain the reputation of Charity, or Magnanimity; or to deliver his mind from the pain of compassion; or in hope of reward in heaven. This is not Contract, but GIFT, FREEGIFT, GRACE: which words signifie one and the same thing.

Signes of Contract Expresse

Signes of Contract, are either Expresse, or By Inference. Expresse, are words spoken with understanding of what they signifie. And such words are either of the time Present, or Past; as, I Give, I Grant, I Have Given, I Have Granted, I Will That This Be Yours: Or of the future; as, I Will Give, I Will Grant; which words of the future, are called Promise.

Signes of Contract By Inference

Signes by Inference, are sometimes the consequence of Words; sometimes the consequence of Silence; sometimes the consequence of Actions; sometimes the consequence of Forbearing an Action: and generally a signe by Inference, of any Contract, is whatsoever sufficiently argues the will of the Contractor.

Free-gift Passeth by Words of the Present or Past

Words alone, if they be of the time to come, and contain a bare promise, are an insufficient signe of a Free-gift and therefore not obligatory. For if they be of the time to Come, as, To Morrow I Will Give, they are a signe I have not given yet, and consequently that my right is not transferred, but remaineth till I transferre it by some other Act. But if the words be of the time Present, or Past, as, "I have given, or do give to be delivered to morrow," then is my to morrows Right given away to day; and that by the vertue of the words, though there were no other argument of my will. And there is a great difference in the signification of these words, Volos Hoc Tuum Esse Cras, and Cros Dabo; that is between "I will that this be thine to morrow," and, "I will give it to thee to morrow:" For the word I Will, in the former manner of speech, signifies an act of the will Present; but in the later, it signifies a promise of an act of the will to Come: and therefore the former words, being of the Present, transferre a future right; the later, that be of the Future, transferre nothing. But if there be other signes of the Will to transferre a Right, besides Words; then, though the gift be Free, yet may the Right be understood to passe by words of the future: as if a man propound a Prize to him that comes first to the end of a race, The gift is Free; and though the words be of the Future, yet the Right passeth: for if he would not have his words so be understood, he should not have let them runne.

Signes Of Contract Are Words Both Of The Past, Present, and Future In Contracts, the right passeth, not onely where the words are of the time Present, or Past; but also where they are of the Future; because all Contract is mutuall translation, or change of Right; and therefore he that promiseth onely, because he hath already received the benefit for which he promiseth, is to be understood as if he intended the Right should passe: for unlesse he had been content to have his words so understood, the other would not have performed his part first. And for that cause, in buying, and selling, and other acts of Contract, A Promise is equivalent to a Covenant; and therefore obligatory.

Merit What

He that performeth first in the case of a Contract, is said to MERIT that which he is to receive by the performance of the other; and he hath it as Due. Also when a Prize is propounded to many, which is to be given to him onely that winneth; or mony is thrown amongst many, to be enjoyed by them that catch it; though this be a Free Gift; yet so to Win, or so to Catch, is to Merit, and to have it as DUE. For the Right is transferred in the Propounding of the Prize, and in throwing down the mony; though it be not determined to whom, but by the Event of the contention. But there is between these two sorts of Merit, this difference, that In Contract, I Merit by vertue of my own power, and the Contractors need; but in this case of Free Gift, I am enabled to Merit onely by the benignity of the Giver; In Contract, I merit at The Contractors hand that hee should depart with his right; In this case of gift, I Merit not that the giver should part with his right; but that when he has parted with it, it should be mine, rather than anothers. And this I think to be the meaning of that distinction of the Schooles, between Meritum Congrui, and Meritum Condigni. For God Almighty, having promised Paradise to those men (hoodwinkt with carnall desires,) that can walk through this world according to the Precepts, and Limits prescribed by him; they say, he that shall so walk, shall Merit Paradise Ex Congruo. But because no man can demand a right to it, by his own Righteousnesse, or any other power in himselfe, but by the Free Grace of God onely; they say, no man can Merit Paradise Ex Condigno. This I say, I think is the meaning of that distinction; but because Disputers do not agree upon the signification of their own termes of Art, longer than it serves their turn; I will not affirme any thing of their meaning: onely this I say; when a gift is given indefinitely, as a prize to be contended for, he that winneth Meriteth, and may claime the Prize as Due.

Covenants of Mutuall Trust, When Invalid

If a Covenant be made, wherein neither of the parties performe presently, but trust one another; in the condition of meer Nature, (which is a condition of Warre of every man against every man,) upon any reasonable suspition, it is Voyd; But if there be a common Power set over them bothe, with right and force sufficient to compell performance; it is not Voyd. For he that performeth first, has no assurance the other will performe after; because the bonds of words are too weak to bridle mens ambition, avarice, anger, and other Passions, without the feare of some coerceive Power; which in the condition of meer Nature, where all men are equall, and judges of the justnesse of their own fears cannot possibly be supposed. And therefore he which performeth first, does but betray himselfe to his enemy; contrary to the Right (he can never abandon) of defending his life, and means of living.

But in a civill estate, where there is a Power set up to constrain those that would otherwise violate their faith, that feare is no more reasonable; and for that cause, he which by the Covenant is to perform first, is obliged so to do.

The cause of Feare, which maketh such a Covenant invalid, must be alwayes something arising after the Covenant made; as some new fact, or other signe of the Will not to performe; else it cannot make the Covenant Voyd. For that which could not hinder a man from promising, ought not to be admitted as a hindrance of performing.

Right to the End, Containeth Right to the Means

He that transferreth any Right, transferreth the Means of enjoying it, as farre as lyeth in his power. As he that selleth Land, is understood to transferre the Herbage, and whatsoever growes upon it; Nor can he that sells a Mill turn away the Stream that drives it. And they that give to a man The Right of government in Soveraignty, are understood to give him the right of levying mony to maintain Souldiers; and of appointing Magistrates for the administration of Justice.

No Covenant with Beasts

To make Covenant with bruit Beasts, is impossible; because not understanding our speech, they understand not, nor accept of any translation of Right; nor can translate any Right to another; and without mutuall acceptation, there is no Covenant.

Nor with God without Speciall Revelation

To make Covenant with God, is impossible, but by Mediation of such as God speaketh to, either by Revelation supernaturall, or by his Lieutenants that govern under him, and in his Name; For otherwise we know not whether our Covenants be accepted, or not. And therefore they that Vow any thing contrary to any law of Nature, Vow in vain; as being a thing unjust to pay such Vow. And if it be a thing commanded by the Law of Nature, it is not the Vow, but the Law that binds them.

No Covenant, but of Possible and Future

The matter, or subject of a Covenant, is always something that falleth under deliberation; (For to Covenant, is an act of the Will; that is to say an act, and the last act, of deliberation;) and is therefore always understood to be something to come; and which is judged Possible for him that Covenanteth, to performe.

And therefore, to promise that which is known to be Impossible, is no Covenant. But if that prove impossible afterwards, which before was thought possible, the Covenant is valid, and bindeth, (though not to the thing it selfe,) yet to the value; or, if that also be impossible, to the unfeigned endeavour of performing as much as is possible; for to more no man can be obliged.

Covenants How Made Voyd

Men are freed of their Covenants two wayes; by Performing; or by being Forgiven. For Performance, is the naturall end of obligation; and Forgivenesse, the restitution of liberty; as being a retransferring of that Right, in which the obligation consisted.

Covenants Extorted by Feare Are Valide

Covenants entred into by fear, in the condition of meer Nature, are obligatory. For example, if I Covenant to pay a ransome, or service for my life, to an enemy; I am bound by it. For it is a Contract, wherein one receiveth the benefit of life; the other is to receive mony, or service for it; and consequently, where no other Law (as in the condition, of meer Nature) forbiddeth the performance, the Covenant is valid. Therefore Prisoners of warre, if trusted with the payment of their Ransome, are obliged to pay it; And if a weaker Prince, make a disadvantageous peace with a stronger, for feare; he is bound to keep it; unlesse (as hath been sayd before) there ariseth some new, and just cause of feare, to renew the war. And even in Common-wealths, if I be forced to redeem my selfe from a Theefe by promising him mony, I am bound to pay it, till the Civill Law discharge me. For whatsoever I may lawfully do without Obligation, the same I may lawfully Covenant to do through feare: and what I lawfully Covenant, I cannot lawfully break.

The Former Covenant to One, Makes Voyd the Later to Another

A former Covenant, makes voyd a later. For a man that hath passed away his Right to one man to day, hath it not to passe to morrow to another: and therefore the later promise passeth no Right, but is null.

A Mans Covenant Not to Defend Himselfe, Is Voyd

A Covenant not to defend my selfe from force, by force, is alwayes voyd. For (as I have shewed before) no man can transferre, or lay down his Right to save himselfe from Death, Wounds, and Imprisonment, (the avoyding whereof is the onely End of laying down any Right,) and therefore the promise of not resisting force, in no Covenant transferreth any right; nor is obliging. For though a man may Covenant thus, "Unlesse I do so, or so, kill me;" he cannot Covenant thus "Unless I do so, or so, I will not resist you, when you come to kill me." For man by nature chooseth the lesser evill, which is danger of death in resisting; rather than the greater, which is certain and present death in not resisting. And this is granted to be true by all men, in that they lead Criminals to Execution, and Prison, with armed men, notwithstanding that such Criminals have consented to the Law, by which they are condemned.

No Man Obliged To Accuse Himselfe

A Covenant to accuse ones Selfe, without assurance of pardon, is likewise invalid. For in the condition of Nature, where every man is Judge, there is no place for Accusation: and in the Civill State, the Accusation is followed with Punishment; which being Force, a man is not obliged not to resist. The same is also true, of the Accusation of those, by whose Condemnation a man falls into misery; as of a Father, Wife, or Benefactor. For the Testimony of such an Accuser, if it be not willingly given, is praesumed to be corrupted by Nature; and therefore not to be received: and where a mans Testimony is not to be credited, his not bound to give it. Also Accusations upon Torture, are not to be reputed as Testimonies. For Torture is to be used but as means of conjecture, and light, in the further examination, and search of truth; and what is in that case confessed, tendeth to the ease of him that is Tortured; not to the informing of the Torturers: and therefore ought not to have the credit of a sufficient Testimony: for whether he deliver himselfe by true, or false Accusation, he does it by the Right of preserving his own life.

The End of an Oath; The Forme of as Oath

The force of Words, being (as I have formerly noted) too weak to hold men to the performance of their Covenants; there are in mans nature, but two imaginable helps to strengthen it. And those are either a Feare of the consequence of breaking their word; or a Glory, or Pride in appearing not to need to breake it. This later is a Generosity too rarely found to be presumed on, especially in the pursuers of Wealth, Command, or sensuall Pleasure; which are the greatest part of Mankind. The Passion to be reckoned upon, is Fear; whereof there be two very generall Objects: one, the Power of Spirits Invisible; the other, the Power of those men they shall therein Offend. Of these two, though the former be the greater Power, yet the feare of the later is commonly the greater Feare. The Feare of the former is in every man, his own Religion: which hath place in the nature of man before Civill Society. The later hath not so; at least not place enough, to keep men to their promises; because in the condition of meer Nature, the inequality of Power is not discerned, but by the event of Battell. So that before the time of Civill Society, or in the interruption thereof by Warre, there is nothing can strengthen a Covenant of Peace agreed on, against the temptations of Avarice, Ambition, Lust, or other strong desire, but the feare of that Invisible Power, which they every one Worship as God; and Feare as a Revenger of their perfidy. All therefore that can be done between two men not subject to Civill Power, is to put one another to swear by the God he feareth: Which Swearing or OATH, is a Forme Of Speech, Added To A Promise; By Which He That Promiseth, Signifieth, That Unlesse He Performe, He Renounceth The Mercy Of His God, Or Calleth To Him For Vengeance On Himselfe. Such was the Heathen Forme, "Let Jupiter kill me else, as I kill this Beast." So is our Forme, "I shall do thus, and thus, so help me God." And this, with the Rites and Ceremonies, which every one useth in his own Religion, that the feare of breaking faith might be the greater.

No Oath, But by God

By this it appears, that an Oath taken according to any other Forme, or Rite, then his, that sweareth, is in vain; and no Oath: And there is no Swearing by any thing which the Swearer thinks not God. For though men have sometimes used to swear by their Kings, for feare, or flattery; yet they would have it thereby understood, they attributed to them

Divine honour. And that Swearing unnecessarily by God, is but prophaning of his name: and Swearing by other things, as men do in common discourse, is not Swearing, but an impious Custome, gotten by too much vehemence of talking.

An Oath Addes Nothing to the Obligation

It appears also, that the Oath addes nothing to the Obligation. For a Covenant, if lawfull, binds in the sight of God, without the Oath, as much as with it; if unlawfull, bindeth not at all; though it be confirmed with an Oath.

CHAPTER XV. OF OTHER LAWES OF NATURE

The Third Law of Nature, Justice

From that law of Nature, by which we are obliged to transferre to another, such Rights, as being retained, hinder the peace of Mankind, there followeth a Third; which is this, That Men Performe Their Covenants Made: without which, Covenants are in vain, and but Empty words; and the Right of all men to all things remaining, wee are still in the condition of Warre.

Justice and Injustice What

And in this law of Nature, consisteth the Fountain and Originall of JUSTICE. For where no Covenant hath preceded, there hath no Right been transferred, and every man has right to every thing; and consequently, no action can be Unjust. But when a Covenant is made, then to break it is Unjust: And the definition of INJUSTICE, is no other than The Not Performance Of Covenant. And whatsoever is not Unjust, is Just.

Justice And Propriety Begin With The Constitution of Common-wealth But because Covenants of mutuall trust, where there is a feare of not performance on either part, (as hath been said in the former Chapter,) are invalid; though the Originall of Justice be the making of Covenants; yet Injustice actually there can be none, till the cause of such feare be taken away; which while men are in the naturall condition of Warre, cannot be done. Therefore before the names of Just, and Unjust can have place, there must be some coercive Power, to compell men equally to the performance of their Covenants, by the terrour of some punishment, greater than the benefit they expect by the breach of their Covenant; and to make good that Propriety, which by mutuall Contract men acquire, in recompence of the universall Right they abandon: and such power there is none before the erection of a Common-wealth. And this is also to be gathered out of the ordinary definition of Justice in the Schooles: For they say, that "Justice is the constant Will of giving to every man his own." And therefore where there is no Own, that is, no Propriety, there is no Injustice; and where there is no coerceive Power erected, that is, where there is no Common-wealth, there is no Propriety; all men having Right to all things: Therefore where there is no Common-wealth, there nothing is Unjust. So that the nature of Justice, consisteth in keeping of valid Covenants: but the Validity of Covenants begins not but with the Constitution of a Civill Power, sufficient to compell men to keep them: And then it is also that Propriety begins.

Justice Not Contrary to Reason

The Foole hath sayd in his heart, there is no such thing as Justice; and sometimes also with his tongue; seriously alleaging, that every mans conservation, and contentment, being committed to his own care, there could be no reason, why every man might not do what he thought conduced thereunto; and therefore also to make, or not make; keep, or not keep Covenants, was not against Reason, when it conduced to ones benefit. He does not therein deny, that there be Covenants; and that they are sometimes broken, sometimes kept; and that such breach of them may be called Injustice, and the observance of them Justice: but he questioneth, whether Injustice, taking away the feare of God, (for the same Foole hath said in his heart there is no God,) may not sometimes stand with that Reason, which dictateth to every man his own good; and particularly then, when it conduceth to such a benefit, as shall put a man in a condition, to neglect not onely the dispraise, and revilings, but also the power of other men. The Kingdome of God is gotten by violence; but what if it could be gotten by unjust violence? were it against Reason so to get it, when it is impossible to receive hurt by it? and if it be not against Reason, it is not against Justice; or else Justice is not to be approved for good. From such reasoning as this, Succesfull wickednesse hath obtained the Name of Vertue; and some that in all other things have disallowed the violation of Faith; yet have allowed it, when it is for the getting of a Kingdome. And the Heathen that believed, that Saturn was deposed by his son Jupiter, believed neverthelesse the same Jupiter to be the avenger of Injustice: Somewhat like to a piece of Law in Cokes Commentaries on Litleton; where he sayes, If the right Heire of the Crown be attainted of Treason; yet the Crown shall descend to him, and Eo Instante the Atteynder be voyd; From which instances a man will be very prone to inferre; that when the Heire apparent of a Kingdome, shall kill him that is in possession, though his father; you may call it Injustice, or by what other name you will; yet it can never be against Reason, seeing all the voluntary actions of men tend to the benefit of themselves; and those actions are most Reasonable, that conduce most to their ends. This specious reasoning is nevertheless false.

For the question is not of promises mutuall, where there is no security of performance on either side; as when there is no Civill Power erected over the parties promising; for such promises are no Covenants: But either where one of the parties has performed already; or where there is a Power to make him performe; there is the question whether it be against reason, that is, against the benefit of the other to performe, or not. And I say it is not against reason. For the manifestation whereof, we are to consider; First, that when a man doth a thing, which notwithstanding any thing can be foreseen, and reckoned on, tendeth to his own destruction, howsoever some accident which he could not expect, arriving may turne it to his benefit; yet such events do not make it reasonably or wisely done. Secondly, that in a condition of Warre, wherein every man to every man, for want of a common Power to keep them all in awe, is an Enemy, there is no man can hope by his own strength, or wit, to defend himselfe from destruction, without the help of Confederates; where every one expects the same defence by the Confederation, that any one else does: and therefore he which declares he thinks it reason to deceive those that help him, can in reason expect no other means of safety, than what can be had from his own single Power. He therefore that breaketh his Covenant, and consequently declareth that he thinks he may with reason do so, cannot be received into any Society, that unite themselves for Peace and defence, but by the errour of them that receive him; nor when he is received, be retayned in it, without seeing the danger of their errour; which errours a man cannot reasonably reckon upon as the means of his security; and therefore if he be left, or cast out of Society, he perisheth; and if he live in Society, it is by the errours of other men, which he could not foresee, nor reckon upon; and consequently against the reason of his preservation; and so, as all men that contribute not to his destruction, forbear him onely out of ignorance of what is good for themselves.

As for the Instance of gaining the secure and perpetuall felicity of Heaven, by any way; it is frivolous: there being but one way imaginable; and that is not breaking, but keeping of Covenant.

And for the other Instance of attaining Soveraignty by Rebellion; it is manifest, that though the event follow, yet because it cannot reasonably be expected, but rather the contrary; and because by gaining it so, others are taught to gain the same in like manner, the attempt thereof is against reason. Justice therefore, that is to say, Keeping of Covenant, is a Rule of Reason, by which we are forbidden to do any thing destructive to our life; and consequently a Law of Nature.

There be some that proceed further; and will not have the Law of Nature, to be those Rules which conduce to the preservation of mans life on earth; but to the attaining of an eternall felicity after death; to which they think the breach of Covenant may conduce; and consequently be just and reasonable; (such are they that think it a work of merit to kill, or depose, or rebell against, the Soveraigne Power constituted over them by their own consent.) But because there is no naturall knowledge of mans estate after death; much lesse of the reward that is then to be given to breach of Faith; but onely a beliefe grounded upon other mens saying, that they know it supernaturally, or that they know those, that knew them, that knew others, that knew it supernaturally; Breach of Faith cannot be called a Precept of Reason, or Nature.

Covenants Not Discharged by the Vice of the Person to Whom Made

Others, that allow for a Law of Nature, the keeping of Faith, do neverthelesse make exception of certain persons; as Heretiques, and such as use not to performe their Covenant to others: And this also is against reason. For if any fault of a man, be sufficient to discharge our Covenant made; the same ought in reason to have been sufficient to have hindred the making of it.

Justice of Men, and Justice of Actions What

The names of Just, and Unjust, when they are attributed to Men, signifie one thing; and when they are attributed to Actions, another. When they are attributed to Men, they signifie Conformity, or Inconformity of Manners, to Reason. But when they are attributed to Actions, they signifie the Conformity, or Inconformity to Reason, not of Manners, or manner of life, but of particular Actions. A Just man therefore, is he that taketh all the care he can, that his Actions may be all Just: and an Unjust man, is he that neglecteth it. And such men are more often in our Language stiled by the names of Righteous, and Unrighteous; then Just, and Unjust; though the meaning be the same. Therefore a Righteous man, does not lose that Title, by one, or a few unjust Actions, that proceed from sudden Passion, or mistake of Things, or Persons: nor does an Unrighteous man, lose his character, for such Actions, as he does, of forbeares to do, for feare: because his Will is not framed by the Justice, but by the apparant benefit of what he is to do. That which gives to humane Actions the relish of Justice, is a certain Noblenesse or Gallantnesse of courage, (rarely found,) by which a man scorns to be beholding for the contentment of his life, to fraud, or breach of promise. This Justice of the Manners, is that which is meant, where Justice is called a Vertue; and Injustice a Vice.

But the Justice of Actions denominates men, not Just, but Guiltlesse; and the Injustice of the same, (which is also called Injury,) gives them but the name of Guilty.

Justice of Manners, and Justice of Actions

Again, the Injustice of Manners, is the disposition, or aptitude to do Injurie; and is Injustice before it proceed to Act; and without supposing any individuall person injured. But the Injustice of an Action, (that is to say Injury,) supposeth an individuall person Injured; namely him, to whom the Covenant was made: And therefore many times the injury is received by one man, when the dammage redoundeth to another. As when The Master commandeth his servant to give mony to a stranger; if it be not done, the Injury is done to the Master, whom he had before Covenanted to obey; but the dammage redoundeth to the stranger, to whom he had no Obligation; and therefore could not Injure him. And so also in Common-wealths, private men may remit to one another their debts; but not robberies or other violences, whereby they are endammaged; because the detaining of

Debt, is an Injury to themselves; but Robbery and Violence, are Injuries to the Person of the Common-wealth.

Nothing Done to a Man, by His Own Consent Can Be Injury

Whatsoever is done to a man, conformable to his own Will signified to the doer, is no Injury to him. For if he that doeth it, hath not passed away his originall right to do what he please, by some Antecedent Covenant, there is no breach of Covenant; and therefore no Injury done him. And if he have; then his Will to have it done being signified, is a release of that Covenant; and so again there is no Injury done him.

Justice Commutative, and Distributive

Justice of Actions, is by Writers divided into Commutative, and Distributive; and the former they say consisteth in proportion Arithmeticall; the later in proportion Geometricall. Commutative therefore, they place in the equality of value of the things contracted for; And Distributive, in the distribution of equall benefit, to men of equall merit. As if it were Injustice to sell dearer than we buy; or to give more to a man than he merits. The value of all things contracted for, is measured by the Appetite of the Contractors: and therefore the just value, is that which they be contented to give. And Merit (besides that which is by Covenant, where the performance on one part, meriteth the performance of the other part, and falls under Justice Commutative, not Distributive,) is not due by Justice; but is rewarded of Grace onely. And therefore this distinction, in the sense wherein it useth to be expounded, is not right. To speak properly, Commutative Justice, is the Justice of a Contractor; that is, a Performance of Covenant, in Buying, and Selling; Hiring, and Letting to Hire; Lending, and Borrowing; Exchanging, Bartering, and other acts of Contract.

And Distributive Justice, the Justice of an Arbitrator; that is to say, the act of defining what is Just. Wherein, (being trusted by them that make him Arbitrator,) if he performe his Trust, he is said to distribute to every man his own: and his is indeed Just Distribution, and may be called (though improperly) Distributive Justice; but more properly Equity; which also is a Law of Nature, as shall be shewn in due place.

The Fourth Law of Nature, Gratitude

As Justice dependeth on Antecedent Covenant; so does Gratitude depend on Antecedent Grace; that is to say, Antecedent Free-gift: and is the fourth Law of Nature; which may be conceived in this Forme, "That a man which receiveth Benefit from another of meer Grace, Endeavour that he which giveth it, have no reasonable cause to repent him of his good will." For no man giveth, but with intention of Good to himselfe; because Gift is Voluntary; and of all Voluntary Acts, the Object is to every man his own Good; of which if men see they shall be frustrated, there will be no beginning of benevolence, or trust; nor consequently of mutuall help; nor of reconciliation of one man to another; and therefore they are to remain still in the condition of War; which is contrary to the first and Fundamentall Law of Nature, which commandeth men to Seek Peace. The breach of this Law, is called Ingratitude; and hath the same relation to Grace, that Injustice hath to Obligation by Covenant.

The Fifth, Mutuall Accommodation, or Compleasance

A fifth Law of Nature, is COMPLEASANCE; that is to say, "That every man strive to accommodate himselfe to the rest." For the understanding whereof, we may consider, that there is in mens aptnesse to Society; a diversity of Nature, rising from their diversity of Affections; not unlike to that we see in stones brought together for building of an Aedifice. For as that stone which by the asperity, and irregularity of Figure, takes more room from others, than it selfe fills; and for the hardnesse, cannot be easily made plain, and thereby hindereth the building, is by the builders cast away as unprofitable, and troublesome: so also, a man that by asperity of Nature, will strive to retain those things which to himselfe are superfluous, and to others necessary; and for the stubbornness of his Passions, cannot be corrected, is to be left, or cast out of Society, as combersome thereunto. For seeing every man, not onely by Right, but also by necessity of Nature, is supposed to endeavour all he can, to obtain that which is necessary for his conservation; He that shall oppose himselfe against it, for things superfluous, is guilty of the warre that thereupon is to follow; and therefore doth that, which is contrary to the fundamentall Law of Nature, which commandeth To Seek Peace. The observers of this Law, may be called SOCIABLE, (the Latines call them Commodi;) The contrary, Stubborn, Insociable, Froward, Intractable.

The Sixth, Facility to Pardon

A sixth Law of Nature is this, "That upon caution of the Future time, a man ought to pardon the offences past of them that repenting, desire it." For PARDON, is nothing but granting of Peace; which though granted to them that persevere in their hostility, be not Peace, but Feare; yet not granted to them that give caution of the Future time, is signe of an aversion to Peace; and therefore contrary to the Law of Nature.

The Seventh, That in Revenges, Men Respect Only the Future Good

A seventh is, "That in Revenges, (that is, retribution of evil for evil,) Men look not at the greatnesse of the evill past, but the greatnesse of the good to follow." Whereby we are forbidden to inflict punishment with any other designe, than for correction of the offender, or direction of others. For this Law is consequent to the next before it, that commandeth Pardon, upon security of the Future Time. Besides, Revenge without respect to the Example, and profit to come, is a triumph, or glorying in the hurt of another, tending to no end; (for the End is alwayes somewhat to Come;) and glorying to no end, is vainglory, and contrary to reason; and to hurt without reason, tendeth to the introduction of Warre; which is against the Law of Nature; and is commonly stiled by the name of Cruelty.

The Eighth, Against Contumely

And because all signes of hatred, or contempt, provoke to fight; insomuch as most men choose rather to hazard their life, than not to be revenged; we may in the eighth place, for a Law of Nature set down this Precept, "That no man by deed, word, countenance, or gesture, declare Hatred, or Contempt of another." The breach of which Law, is commonly called Contumely.

The Ninth, Against Pride

The question who is the better man, has no place in the condition of meer Nature; where, (as has been shewn before,) all men are equall. The inequallity that now is, has been introduced by the Lawes civill. I know that Aristotle in the first booke of his Politiques, for a foundation of his doctrine, maketh men by Nature, some more worthy to Command, meaning the wiser sort (such as he thought himselfe to be for his Philosophy;) others to Serve, (meaning those that had strong bodies, but were not Philosophers as he;) as if Master and Servant were not introduced by consent of men, but by difference of Wit; which is not only against reason; but also against experience. For there are very few so foolish, that had not rather governe themselves, than be governed by others: Nor when the wise in their own conceit, contend by force, with them who distrust their owne wisdome, do they alwaies, or often, or almost at any time, get the Victory. If Nature therefore have made men equall, that equalitie is to be acknowledged; or if Nature have made men unequall; yet because men that think themselves equall, will not enter into conditions of Peace, but upon Equall termes, such equalitie must be admitted. And therefore for the ninth Law of Nature, I put this, "That every man acknowledge other for his Equall by Nature." The breach of this Precept is Pride.

The Tenth Against Arrogance

On this law, dependeth another, "That at the entrance into conditions of Peace, no man require to reserve to himselfe any Right, which he is not content should be reserved to every one of the rest." As it is necessary for all men that seek peace, to lay down certaine Rights of Nature; that is to say, not to have libertie to do all they list: so is it necessarie for mans life, to retaine some; as right to governe their owne bodies; enjoy aire, water, motion, waies to go from place to place; and all things else without which a man cannot live, or not live well. If in this case, at the making of Peace, men require for themselves, that which they would not have to be granted to others, they do contrary to the precedent law, that commandeth the acknowledgement of naturall equalitie, and therefore also against the law of Nature. The observers of this law, are those we call Modest, and the breakers Arrogant Men. The Greeks call the violation of this law pleonexia; that is, a desire of more than their share.

The Eleventh Equity

Also "If a man be trusted to judge between man and man," it is a precept of the Law of Nature, "that he deale Equally between them." For without that, the Controversies of men cannot be determined but by Warre. He therefore that is partiall in judgment, doth what in him lies, to deterre men from the use of Judges, and Arbitrators; and consequently, (against the fundamentall Lawe of Nature) is the cause of Warre.

The observance of this law, from the equall distribution to each man, of that which in reason belongeth to him, is called EQUITY, and (as I have sayd before) distributive justice: the violation, Acception Of Persons, Prosopolepsia.

The Twelfth, Equall Use of Things Common

And from this followeth another law, "That such things as cannot be divided, be enjoyed in Common, if it can be; and if the quantity of the thing permit, without Stint; otherwise Proportionably to the number of them that have Right." For otherwise the distribution is Unequall, and contrary to Equitie.

The Thirteenth, of Lot

But some things there be, that can neither be divided, nor enjoyed in common. Then, The Law of Nature, which prescribeth Equity, requireth, "That the Entire Right; or else, (making the use alternate,) the First Possession, be determined by Lot." For equall distribution, is of the Law of Nature; and other means of equall distribution cannot be imagined.

The Fourteenth, of Primogeniture, and First Seising

Of Lots there be two sorts, Arbitrary, and Naturall. Arbitrary, is that which is agreed on by the Competitors; Naturall, is either Primogeniture, (which the Greek calls Kleronomia, which signifies, Given by Lot;) or First Seisure.

And therefore those things which cannot be enjoyed in common, nor divided, ought to be adjudged to the First Possessor; and is some cases to the First-Borne, as acquired by Lot.

The Fifteenth, of Mediators

It is also a Law of Nature, "That all men that mediate Peace, be allowed safe Conduct." For the Law that commandeth Peace, as the End, commandeth Intercession, as the Means; and to Intercession the Means is safe Conduct.

The Sixteenth, of Submission to Arbitrement

And because, though men be never so willing to observe these Lawes, there may neverthelesse arise questions concerning a mans action; First, whether it were done, or not done; Secondly (if done) whether against the Law, or not against the Law; the former whereof, is called a question Of Fact; the later a question Of Right; therefore unlesse the parties to the question, Covenant mutually to stand to the sentence of another, they are as farre from Peace as ever. This other, to whose Sentence they submit, is called an ARBITRATOR. And therefore it is of the Law of Nature, "That they that are at controversie, submit their Right to the judgement of an Arbitrator."

The Seventeenth, No Man Is His Own Judge

And seeing every man is presumed to do all things in order to his own benefit, no man is a fit Arbitrator in his own cause: and if he were never so fit; yet Equity allowing to each party equall benefit, if one be admitted to be Judge, the other is to be admitted also; & so the controversie, that is, the cause of War, remains, against the Law of Nature.

The Eighteenth, No Man To Be Judge, That Has in Him Cause of Partiality

For the same reason no man in any Cause ought to be received for Arbitrator, to whom greater profit, or honour, or pleasure apparently ariseth out of the victory of one party, than of the other: for he hath taken (though an unavoydable bribe, yet) a bribe; and no man can be obliged to trust him. And thus also the controversie, and the condition of War remaineth, contrary to the Law of Nature.

The Nineteenth, of Witnesse

And in a controversie of Fact, the Judge being to give no more credit to one, than to the other, (if there be no other Arguments) must give credit to a third; or to a third and fourth; or more: For else the question is undecided, and left to force, contrary to the Law of Nature.

These are the Lawes of Nature, dictating Peace, for a means of the conservation of men in multitudes; and which onely concern the doctrine of Civill Society. There be other things tending to the destruction of particular men; as Drunkenness, and all other parts of Intemperance; which may therefore also be reckoned amongst those things which the

Law of Nature hath forbidden; but are not necessary to be mentioned, nor are pertinent enough to this place.

A Rule, by Which the Laws of Nature May Easily Be Examined

And though this may seem too subtile a deduction of the Lawes of Nature, to be taken notice of by all men; whereof the most part are too busie in getting food, and the rest too negligent to understand; yet to leave all men unexcusable, they have been contracted into one easie sum, intelligible even to the meanest capacity; and that is, "Do not that to another, which thou wouldest not have done to thy selfe;" which sheweth him, that he has no more to do in learning the Lawes of Nature, but, when weighing the actions of other men with his own, they seem too heavy, to put them into the other part of the ballance, and his own into their place, that his own passions, and selfe-love, may adde nothing to the weight; and then there is none of these Lawes of Nature that will not appear unto him very reasonable.

The Lawes of Nature Oblige in Conscience Alwayes,

But In Effect Then Onely When There Is Security The Lawes of Nature oblige In Foro Interno; that is to say, they bind to a desire they should take place: but In Foro Externo; that is, to the putting them in act, not alwayes. For he that should be modest, and tractable, and performe all he promises, in such time, and place, where no man els should do so, should but make himselfe a prey to others, and procure his own certain ruine, contrary to the ground of all Lawes of Nature, which tend to Natures preservation. And again, he that shall observe the same Lawes towards him, observes them not himselfe, seeketh not Peace, but War; and consequently the destruction of his Nature by Violence.

And whatsoever Lawes bind In Foro Interno, may be broken, not onely by a fact contrary to the Law but also by a fact according to it, in case a man think it contrary. For though his Action in this case, be according to the Law; which where the Obligation is In Foro Interno, is a breach.

The Laws of Nature Are Eternal;

The Lawes of Nature are Immutable and Eternall, For Injustice, Ingratitude, Arrogance, Pride, Iniquity, Acception of persons, and the rest, can never be made lawfull. For it can never be that Warre shall preserve life, and Peace destroy it.

And Yet Easie

The same Lawes, because they oblige onely to a desire, and endeavour, I mean an unfeigned and constant endeavour, are easie to be observed. For in that they require nothing but endeavour; he that endeavoureth their performance, fulfilleth them; and he that fulfilleth the Law, is Just.

The Science of These Lawes, Is the True Moral Philosophy

And the Science of them, is the true and onely Moral Philosophy. For Morall Philosophy is nothing else but the Science of what is Good, and Evill, in the conversation, and Society of mankind. Good, and Evill, are names that signifie our Appetites, and Aversions; which in different tempers, customes, and doctrines of men, are different: And divers men, differ not onely in their Judgement, on the senses of what is pleasant, and unpleasant to the tast, smell, hearing, touch, and sight; but also of what is conformable, or disagreeable to Reason, in the actions of common life. Nay, the same man, in divers times, differs from himselfe; and one time praiseth, that is, calleth Good, what another time he dispraiseth, and calleth Evil: From whence arise Disputes, Controversies, and at last War. And therefore so long as man is in the condition of meer Nature, (which is a condition of War,) as private Appetite is the measure of Good, and Evill: and consequently all men agree on this, that Peace is Good, and therefore also the way, or means of Peace, which (as I have shewed before) are Justice, Gratitude, Modesty, Equity, Mercy, & the rest of the Laws of Nature, are good; that is to say, Morall Vertues; and their contrarie Vices, Evill. Now the science of Vertue and Vice, is Morall Philosophie; and therfore the true Doctrine of the Lawes of Nature, is the true Morall Philosophie. But the Writers of Morall Philosophie, though they acknowledge the same Vertues and Vices; Yet not seeing wherein consisted their Goodnesse; nor that they come to be praised, as the meanes of peaceable, sociable, and comfortable living; place them in a mediocrity of passions: as if not the Cause, but the Degree of daring, made Fortitude; or not the Cause, but the Quantity of a gift, made Liberality.

These dictates of Reason, men use to call by the name of Lawes; but improperly: for they are but Conclusions, or Theoremes concerning what conduceth to the conservation and defence of themselves; whereas Law, properly is the word of him, that by right hath command over others. But yet if we consider the same Theoremes, as delivered in the word of God, that by right commandeth all things; then are they properly called Lawes.

CHAPTER XVI. OF PERSONS, AUTHORS, AND THINGS PERSONATED

A Person What

A PERSON, is he "whose words or actions are considered, either as his own, or as representing the words or actions of an other man, or of any other thing to whom they are attributed, whether Truly or by Fiction."

Person Naturall, and Artificiall

When they are considered as his owne, then is he called a Naturall Person: And when they are considered as representing the words and actions of an other, then is he a Feigned or Artificiall person.

The Word Person, Whence

The word Person is latine: instead whereof the Greeks have Prosopon, which signifies the Face, as Persona in latine signifies the Disguise, or Outward Appearance of a man, counterfeited on the Stage; and somtimes more particularly that part of it, which disguiseth the face, as a Mask or Visard: And from the Stage, hath been translated to any Representer of speech and action, as well in Tribunalls, as Theaters. So that a Person, is the same that an Actor is, both on the Stage and in common Conversation; and to Personate, is to Act, or Represent himselfe, or an other; and he that acteth another, is said to beare his Person, or act in his name; (in which sence Cicero useth it where he saies, "Unus Sustineo Tres Personas; Mei, Adversarii, & Judicis, I beare three Persons; my own, my Adversaries, and the Judges;") and is called in diverse occasions, diversly; as a Representer, or Representative, a Lieutenant, a Vicar, an Attorney, a Deputy, a Procurator, an Actor, and the like.

Actor, Author; Authority

Of Persons Artificiall, some have their words and actions Owned by those whom they represent. And then the Person is the Actor; and he that owneth his words and actions, is the AUTHOR: In which case the Actor acteth by Authority. For that which in speaking of goods and possessions, is called an Owner, and in latine Dominus, in Greeke Kurios; speaking of Actions, is called Author. And as the Right of possession, is called Dominion; so the Right of doing any Action, is called AUTHORITY. So that by Authority, is always understood a Right of doing any act: and Done By Authority, done by Commission, or Licence from him whose right it is.

Covenants by Authority, Bind the Author

From hence it followeth, that when the Actor maketh a Covenant by Authority, he bindeth thereby the Author, no lesse than if he had made it himselfe; and no lesse subjecteth him to all the consequences of the same. And therfore all that hath been said formerly, (Chap. 14) of the nature of Covenants between man and man in their naturall capacity, is true also when they are made by their Actors, Representers, or Procurators, that have authority from them, so far-forth as is in their Commission, but no farther.

And therefore he that maketh a Covenant with the Actor, or Representer, not knowing the Authority he hath, doth it at his own perill. For no man is obliged by a Covenant, whereof he is not Author; nor consequently by a Covenant made against, or beside the Authority he gave.

But Not the Actor

When the Actor doth any thing against the Law of Nature by command of the Author, if he be obliged by former Covenant to obey him, not he, but the Author breaketh the Law of Nature: for though the Action be against the Law of Nature; yet it is not his: but contrarily; to refuse to do it, is against the Law of Nature, that forbiddeth breach of Covenant.

The Authority Is To Be Shewne

And he that maketh a Covenant with the Author, by mediation of the Actor, not knowing what Authority he hath, but onely takes his word; in case such Authority be not made manifest unto him upon demand, is no longer obliged: For the Covenant made with the Author, is not valid, without his Counter-assurance. But if he that so Covenanteth, knew before hand he was to expect no other assurance, than the Actors word; then is the Covenant valid; because the Actor in this case maketh himselfe the Author. And therefore, as when the Authority is evident, the Covenant obligeth the Author, not the Actor; so when the Authority is feigned, it obligeth the Actor onely; there being no Author but himselfe.

Things Personated, Inanimate

There are few things, that are uncapable of being represented by Fiction. Inanimate things, as a Church, an Hospital, a Bridge, may be Personated by a Rector, Master, or Overseer. But things Inanimate, cannot be Authors, nor therefore give Authority to their Actors: Yet the Actors may have Authority to procure their maintenance, given them by those that are Owners, or Governours of those things. And therefore, such things cannot be Personated, before there be some state of Civill Government.

Irrational

Likewise Children, Fooles, and Mad-men that have no use of Reason, may be Personated by Guardians, or Curators; but can be no Authors (during that time) of any action done by them, longer then (when they shall recover the use of Reason) they shall judge the same reasonable. Yet during the Folly, he that hath right of governing them, may give Authority to the Guardian. But this again has no place but in a State Civill, because before such estate, there is no Dominion of Persons.

False Gods

An Idol, or meer Figment of the brain, my be Personated; as were the Gods of the Heathen; which by such Officers as the State appointed, were Personated, and held Possessions, and other Goods, and Rights, which men from time to time dedicated, and consecrated unto them. But idols cannot be Authors: for a Idol is nothing. The Authority proceeded from the State: and therefore before introduction of Civill Government, the Gods of the Heathen could not be Personated.

The True God

The true God may be Personated. As he was; first, by Moses; who governed the Israelites, (that were not his, but Gods people,) not in his own name, with Hoc Dicit Moses; but in Gods Name, with Hoc Dicit Dominus. Secondly, by the son of man, his own Son our Blessed Saviour Jesus Christ, that came to reduce the Jewes, and induce all Nations into the Kingdome of his Father; not as of himselfe, but as sent from his Father. And thirdly, by the Holy Ghost, or Comforter, speaking, and working in the Apostles: which Holy Ghost, was a Comforter that came not of himselfe; but was sent, and proceeded from them both.

A Multitude of Men, How One Person

A Multitude of men, are made One Person, when they are by one man, or one Person, Represented; so that it be done with the consent of every one of that Multitude in particular. For it is the Unity of the Representer, not the Unity of the Represented, that maketh the Person One. And it is the Representer that beareth the Person, and but one Person: And Unity, cannot otherwise be understood in Multitude.

Every One Is Author

And because the Multitude naturally is not One, but Many; they cannot be understood for one; but many Authors, of every thing their Representative faith, or doth in their name; Every man giving their common Representer, Authority from himselfe in particular; and owning all the actions the Representer doth, in case they give him Authority without stint: Otherwise, when they limit him in what, and how farre he shall represent them, none of them owneth more, than they gave him commission to Act.

An Actor May Be Many Men Made One by Plurality of Voyces

And if the Representative consist of many men, the voyce of the greater number, must be considered as the voyce of them all. For if the lesser number pronounce (for example) in the Affirmative, and the greater in the Negative, there will be Negatives more than enough to destroy the Affirmatives; and thereby the excesse of Negatives, standing uncontradicted, are the onely voyce the Representative hath.

Representatives, When the Number Is Even, Unprofitable

And a Representative of even number, especially when the number is not great, whereby the contradictory voyces are oftentimes equall, is therefore oftentimes mute, and uncapable of Action. Yet in some cases contradictory voyces equall in number, may determine a question; as in condemning, or absolving, equality of votes, even in that they condemne not, do absolve; but not on the contrary condemne, in that they absolve not. For when a Cause is heard; not to condemne, is to absolve; but on the contrary, to say that not absolving, is condemning, is not true. The like it is in a deliberation of executing presently, or deferring till another time; For when the voyces are equall, the not decreeing Execution, is a decree of Dilation.

Negative Voyce

Or if the number be odde, as three, or more, (men, or assemblies;) whereof every one has by a Negative Voice, authority to take away the effect of all the Affirmative Voices of the rest, This number is no Representative; because by the diversity of Opinions, and Interests of men, it becomes oftentimes, and in cases of the greatest consequence, a mute Person, and unapt, as for may things else, so for the government of a Multitude, especially in time of Warre.

Of Authors there be two sorts. The first simply so called; which I have before defined to be him, that owneth the Action of another simply. The second is he, that owneth an Action, or Covenant of another conditionally; that is to say, he undertaketh to do it, if the other doth it not, at, or before a certain time. And these Authors conditionall, are generally called SURETYES, in Latine Fidejussores, and Sponsores; and particularly for Debt, Praedes; and for Appearance before a Judge, or Magistrate, Vades.

PART II. OF COMMON-WEALTH

CHAPTER XVII. OF THE CAUSES, GENERATION, AND DEFINITION OF A COMMON-WEALTH

The End of Common-wealth, Particular Security

The finall Cause, End, or Designe of men, (who naturally love Liberty, and Dominion over others,) in the introduction of that restraint upon themselves, (in which wee see them live in Common-wealths,) is the foresight of their own preservation, and of a more contented life thereby; that is to say, of getting themselves out from that miserable condition of Warre, which is necessarily consequent (as hath been shewn) to the naturall Passions of men, when there is no visible Power to keep them in awe, and tye them by feare of punishment to the performance of their Covenants, and observation of these Lawes of Nature set down in the fourteenth and fifteenth Chapters.

Which Is Not To Be Had from the Law of Nature:

For the Lawes of Nature (as Justice, Equity, Modesty, Mercy, and (in summe) Doing To Others, As Wee Would Be Done To,) if themselves, without the terrour of some Power, to cause them to be observed, are contrary to our naturall Passions, that carry us to Partiality, Pride, Revenge, and the like. And Covenants, without the Sword, are but Words, and of no strength to secure a man at all. Therefore notwithstanding the Lawes of Nature, (which every one hath then kept, when he has the will to keep them, when he can do it safely,) if there be no Power erected, or not great enough for our security; every man will and may lawfully rely on his own strength and art, for caution against all other men. And in all places, where men have lived by small Families, to robbe and spoyle one another, has been a Trade, and so farre from being reputed against the Law of Nature, that the greater spoyles they gained, the greater was their honour; and men observed no other Lawes therein, but the Lawes of Honour; that is, to abstain from cruelty, leaving to men their lives, and instruments of husbandry. And as small Familyes did then; so now do Cities and Kingdomes which are but greater Families (for their own security) enlarge their Dominions, upon all pretences of danger, and fear of Invasion, or assistance that may be given to Invaders, endeavour as much as they can, to subdue, or weaken their neighbours, by open force, and secret arts, for want of other Caution, justly; and are rememdbred for it in after ages with honour.

Nor From the Conjunction of a Few Men or Familyes

Nor is it the joyning together of a small number of men, that gives them this security; because in small numbers, small additions on the one side or the other, make the advantage of strength so great, as is sufficient to carry the Victory; and therefore gives encouragement to an Invasion. The Multitude sufficient to confide in for our Security, is not determined by any certain number, but by comparison with the Enemy we feare; and is then sufficient, when the odds of the Enemy is not of so visible and conspicuous moment, to determine the event of warre, as to move him to attempt.

Nor from a Great Multitude, Unlesse Directed by One Judgement

And be there never so great a Multitude; yet if their actions be directed according to their particular judgements, and particular appetites, they can expect thereby no defence, nor protection, neither against a Common enemy, nor against the injuries of one another. For being distracted in opinions concerning the best use and application of their strength, they do not help, but hinder one another; and reduce their strength by mutuall opposition to nothing: whereby they are easily, not onely subdued by a very few that agree together; but also when there is no common enemy, they make warre upon each other, for their particular interests. For if we could suppose a great Multitude of men to consent in the observation of Justice, and other Lawes of Nature, without a common Power to keep them all in awe; we might as well suppose all Man-kind to do the same; and then there neither would be nor need to be any Civill Government, or Common-wealth at all; because there would be Peace without subjection.

And that Continually

Nor is it enough for the security, which men desire should last all the time of their life, that they be governed, and directed by one judgement, for a limited time; as in one Battell, or one Warre. For though they obtain a Victory by their unanimous endeavour against a forraign enemy; yet afterwards, when either they have no common enemy, or he that by one part is held for an enemy, is by another part held for a friend, they must needs by the difference of their interests dissolve, and fall again into a Warre amongst themselves.

Why Certain Creatures Without Reason, Or Speech, Do Neverthelesse Live In Society, Without Any Coercive Power

It is true, that certain living creatures, as Bees, and Ants, live sociably one with another, (which are therefore by Aristotle numbred amongst Politicall creatures;) and yet have no other direction, than their particular judgements and appetites; nor speech, whereby one of them can signifie to another, what he thinks expedient for the common benefit: and therefore some man may perhaps desire to know, why Man-kind cannot do the same. To which I answer,

First, that men are continually in competition for Honour and Dignity, which these creatures are not; and consequently amongst men there ariseth on that ground, Envy and Hatred, and finally Warre; but amongst these not so.

Secondly, that amongst these creatures, the Common good differeth not from the Private; and being by nature enclined to their private, they procure thereby the common benefit. But man, whose Joy consisteth in comparing himselfe with other men, can relish nothing but what is eminent.

Thirdly, that these creatures, having not (as man) the use of reason, do not see, nor think they see any fault, in the administration of their common businesse: whereas amongst men, there are very many, that thinke themselves wiser, and abler to govern the Publique, better than the rest; and these strive to reforme and innovate, one this way, another that way; and thereby bring it into Distraction and Civill warre.

Fourthly, that these creatures, though they have some use of voice, in making knowne to one another their desires, and other affections; yet they want that art of words, by which some men can represent to others, that which is Good, in the likenesse of Evill; and Evill, in the likenesse of Good; and augment, or diminish the apparent greatnesse of Good and Evill; discontenting men, and troubling their Peace at their pleasure.

Fiftly, irrationall creatures cannot distinguish betweene Injury, and Dammage; and therefore as long as they be at ease, they are not offended with their fellowes: whereas Man is then most troublesome, when he is most at ease: for then it is that he loves to shew his Wisdome, and controule the Actions of them that governe the Common-wealth.

Lastly, the agreement of these creatures is Naturall; that of men, is by Covenant only, which is Artificiall: and therefore it is no wonder if there be somewhat else required (besides Covenant) to make their Agreement constant and lasting; which is a Common Power, to keep them in awe, and to direct their actions to the Common Benefit.

The Generation of a Common-wealth

The only way to erect such a Common Power, as may be able to defend them from the invasion of Forraigners, and the injuries of one another, and thereby to secure them in such sort, as that by their owne industrie, and by the fruites of the Earth, they may nourish themselves and live contentedly; is, to conferre all their power and strength upon one Man, or upon one Assembly of men, that may reduce all their Wills, by plurality of voices, unto one Will: which is as much as to say, to appoint one man, or Assembly of men, to beare their Person; and every one to owne, and acknowledge himselfe to be Author of whatsoever he that so beareth their Person, shall Act, or cause to be Acted, in those things which concerne the Common Peace and Safetie; and therein to submit their Wills, every one to his Will, and their Judgements, to his Judgment. This is more than Consent, or Concord; it is a reall Unitie of them all, in one and the same Person, made by Covenant of every man with every man, in such manner, as if every man should say to every man, "I Authorise and give up my Right of Governing my selfe, to this Man, or to this Assembly of men, on this condition, that thou give up thy Right to him, and Authorise all his Actions in like manner." This done, the Multitude so united in one Person, is called a common-wealth, in latine civitas. This is the Generation of that great leviathan, or rather (to speake more reverently) of that Mortall God, to which wee owe under the Immortall God, our peace and defence. For by this Authoritie, given him by every particular man in the Common-Wealth, he hath the use of so much Power and Strength conferred on him, that by terror thereof, he is inabled to forme the wills of them all, to Peace at home, and mutuall ayd against their enemies abroad.

The Definition of a Common-wealth

And in him consisteth the Essence of the Common-wealth; which (to define it,) is "One Person, of whose Acts a great Multitude, by mutuall Covenants one with another, have made themselves every one the Author, to the end he may use the strength and means of them all, as he shall think expedient, for their Peace and Common Defence."

Soveraigne, and Subject, What

And he that carryeth this Person, as called soveraigne, and said to have Soveraigne Power; and every one besides, his subject.

The attaining to this Soveraigne Power, is by two wayes. One, by Naturall force; as when a man maketh his children, to submit themselves, and their children to his government, as being able to destroy them if they refuse, or by Warre subdueth his enemies to his will, giving them their lives on that condition. The other, is when men agree amongst themselves, to submit to some Man, or Assembly of men, voluntarily, on confidence to be protected by him against all others. This later, may be called a Politicall Common-wealth, or Common-wealth by Institution; and the former, a Common-wealth by Acquisition. And first, I shall speak of a Common-wealth by Institution.

What Is Seen and What Is Unseen

FREDERIC BASTIAT

1.1

In the economic sphere an act, a habit, an institution, a law produces not only one effect, but a series of effects. Of these effects, the first alone is immediate; it appears simultaneously with its cause; *it is seen*. The other effects emerge only subsequently; *they are not seen;* we are fortunate if we *foresee* them.

1.2

There is only one difference between a bad economist and a good one: the bad economist confines himself to the *visible* effect; the good economist takes into account both the effect that can be seen and those effects that must be *foreseen*.

1.3

Yet this difference is tremendous; for it almost always happens that when the immediate consequence is favorable, the later consequences are disastrous, and vice versa. Whence it follows that the bad economist pursues a small present good that will be followed by a great evil to come, while the good economist pursues a great good to come, at the risk of a small present evil.

1.4

The same thing, of course, is true of health and morals. Often, the sweeter the first fruit of a habit, the more bitter are its later fruits: for example, debauchery, sloth, prodigality. When a man is impressed by the effect *that is seen* and has not yet learned to discern the effects *that are not seen,* he indulges in deplorable habits, not only through natural inclination, but deliberately.

1.5

This explains man's necessarily painful evolution. Ignorance surrounds him at his cradle; therefore, he regulates his acts according to their first consequences, the only ones that, in his infancy, he can see. It is only after a long time that he learns to take account of the others."[2] Two very different masters teach him this lesson: experience and foresight. Experience teaches efficaciously but brutally. It instructs us in all the effects of an act by making us feel them, and we cannot fail to learn eventually, from having been burned ourselves, that fire burns. I should prefer, in so far as possible, to replace this rude teacher with one more gentle: foresight. For that reason I shall investigate the consequences of several economic phenomena, contrasting those *that are seen* with those *that are not seen.*

1. THE BROKEN WINDOW

1.6

Have you ever been witness to the fury of that solid citizen, James Goodfellow, when his incorrigible son has happened to break a pane of glass? If you have been present at this spectacle, certainly you must also have observed that the onlookers, even if there are as many as thirty of them, seem with one accord to offer the unfortunate owner the selfsame consolation: "It's an ill wind that blows nobody some good. Such accidents keep industry going. Everybody has to make a living. What would become of the glaziers if no one ever broke a window?"

1.7

Now, this formula of condolence contains a whole theory that it is a good idea for us to expose, *flagrante delicto,* in this very simple case, since it is exactly the same as that which, unfortunately, underlies most of our economic institutions.

1.8

Suppose that it will cost six francs to repair the damage. If you mean that the accident gives six francs' worth of encouragement to the aforesaid industry, I agree. I do not contest it in any way; your reasoning is correct. The glazier will come, do his job, receive six francs, congratulate himself, and bless in his heart the careless child. *That is what is seen.*

1.9

But if, by way of deduction, you conclude, as happens only too often, that it is good to break windows, that it helps to circulate money, that it results in encouraging industry in general, I am obliged to cry out: That will never do! Your theory stops at *what is seen.* It does not take account of *what is not seen.*

1.10

It is not seen that, since our citizen has spent six francs for one thing, he will not be able to spend them for another. *It is not seen* that if he had not had a windowpane to replace, he would have replaced, for example, his worn-out shoes or added another book to his library. In brief, he would have put his six francs to some use or other for which he will not now have them.

1.11

Let us next consider industry *in general*. The window having been broken, the glass industry gets six francs' worth of encouragement; *that is what is seen*.

1.12

If the window had not been broken, the shoe industry (or some other) would have received six francs' worth of encouragement; *that is what is not seen.*

1.13

And if we were to take into consideration *what is not seen,* because it is a negative factor, as well as *what is seen,* because it is a positive factor, we should understand that there is no benefit to industry *in general* or to *national employment* as a whole, whether windows are broken or not broken.

1.14

Now let us consider James Goodfellow.

1.15

On the first hypothesis, that of the broken window, he spends six francs and has, neither more nor less than before, the enjoyment of one window.

1.16

On the second, that in which the accident did not happen, he would have spent six francs for new shoes and would have had the enjoyment of a pair of shoes as well as of a window.

1.17

Now, if James Goodfellow is part of society, we must conclude that society, considering its labors and its enjoyments, has lost the value of the broken window.

1.18

From which, by generalizing, we arrive at this unexpected conclusion: "Society loses the value of objects unnecessarily destroyed," and at this aphorism, which will make the hair of the protectionists stand on end: "To break, to destroy, to dissipate is not to encourage national employment," or more briefly: "Destruction is not profitable."

1.19

What will the *Moniteur industriel* say to this, or the disciples of the estimable M. de Saint-Chamans, who has calculated with such precision what industry would gain from the burning of Paris, because of the houses that would have to be rebuilt?

1.20

I am sorry to upset his ingenious calculations, especially since their spirit has passed into our legislation. But I beg him to begin them again, entering *what is not seen* in the ledger beside *what is seen.*

1.21

The reader must apply himself to observe that there are not only two people, but three, in the little drama that I have presented. The one, James Goodfellow, represents the consumer, reduced by destruction to one enjoyment instead of two. The other, under the figure of the glazier, shows us the producer whose industry the accident encourages. The third is the shoemaker (or any other manufacturer) whose industry is correspondingly discouraged by the same cause. It is this third person who is always in the shadow, and who, personifying *what is not seen,* is an essential element of the problem. It is he who makes us understand how absurd it is to see a profit in destruction. It is he who will soon teach us that it is equally absurd to see a profit in trade restriction, which is, after all, nothing more nor less than partial destruction. So, if you get to the bottom of all the arguments advanced in favor of restrictionist measures, you will find only a paraphrase of that common cliché: *"What would become of the glaziers if no one ever broke any windows?"*

2. THE DEMOBILIZATION

1.22

A nation is in the same case as a man. When a man wishes to give himself a satisfaction, he has to see whether it is worth what it costs. For a nation, security is the greatest of blessings. If, to acquire it, a hundred thousand men must be mobilized, and a hundred million francs spent, I have nothing to say. It is an enjoyment bought at the price of a sacrifice.

1.23

Let there be no misunderstanding, then, about the point I wish to make in what I have to say on this subject.

1.24

A legislator proposes to discharge a hundred thousand men, which will relieve the taxpayers of a hundred million francs in taxes.

1.25

Suppose we confine ourselves to replying to him: "These one hundred thousand men and these one hundred million francs are indispensable to our national security. It is a sacrifice; but without this sacrifice France would be torn by internal factions or invaded from without." I have no objection here to this argument, which may be true or false as the case may be, but which theoretically does not constitute any economic heresy. The heresy begins when the sacrifice itself is represented as an advantage, because it brings profit to someone.

1.26

Now, if I am not mistaken, no sooner will the author of the proposal have descended from the platform, than an orator will rush up and say:

1.27

"Discharge a hundred thousand men! What are you thinking of? What will become of them? What will they live on? On their earnings? But do you not know that there is unemployment everywhere? That all occupations are oversupplied? Do you wish to throw them on the market to increase the competition and to depress wage rates? Just at the moment when it is difficult to earn a meager living, is it not fortunate that the state is giving bread to a hundred thousand individuals? Consider further that the army consumes wine, clothes, and weapons, that it thus spreads business to the factories and the garrison towns, and that it is nothing less than a godsend to its innumerable suppliers. Do you not tremble at the idea of bringing this immense industrial activity to an end?"

1.28

This speech, we see, concludes in favor of maintaining a hundred thousand soldiers, not because of the nation's need for the services rendered by the army, but for economic reasons. It is these considerations alone that I propose to refute.

1.29

A hundred thousand men, costing the taxpayers a hundred million francs, live as well and provide as good a living for their suppliers as a hundred million francs will allow: *that is what is seen.*

1.30

But a hundred million francs, coming from the pockets of the taxpayers, ceases to provide a living for these taxpayers and *their* suppliers, to the extent of a hundred million francs: *that is what is not seen.* Calculate, figure, and tell me where there is any profit for the mass of the people.

1.31

I will, for my part, tell you where the *loss* is, and to simplify things, instead of speaking of a hundred thousand men and a hundred million francs, let us talk about one man and a thousand francs.

1.32

Here we are in the village of A. The recruiters make the rounds and muster one man. The tax collectors make their rounds also and raise a thousand francs. The man and the sum are transported to Metz, the one destined to keep the other alive for a year without doing anything. If you look only at Metz, yes, you are right a hundred times; the procedure is very advantageous. But if you turn your eyes to the village of A, you will judge otherwise, for, unless you are blind, you will see that this village has lost a laborer and the thousand francs that would remunerate his labor, and the business which, through the spending of these thousand francs, he would spread about him.

1.33

At first glance it seems as if the loss is compensated. What took place at the village now takes place at Metz, and that is all there is to it. But here is where the loss is. In the village a man dug and labored: he was a worker; at Metz he goes through "Right dress!" and "Left dress!": he is a soldier. The money involved and its circulation are the same in both cases: but in one there were three hundred days of productive labor; in the other there are three hundreds days of unproductive labor, on the supposition, of course, that a part of the army is not indispensable to public security.

1.34

Now comes demobilization. You point out to me a surplus of a hundred thousand workers, intensified competition and the pressure that it exerts on wage rates. That is what you see.

1.35

But here is what you do not see. You do not see that to send home a hundred thousand soldiers is not to do away with a hundred million francs, but to return that money to the taxpayers. You do not see that to throw a hundred thousand workers on the market in this way is to throw in at the same time the hundred million francs destined to pay for their labor; that, as a consequence, the same measure that increases the *supply* of workers also increases the *demand;* from which it follows that your lowering of wages is illusory. You do not see that before, as well as after, the demobilization there are a hundred million francs corresponding to the hundred thousand men; that the whole difference consists in this: that before, the country gives the hundred million francs to the hundred thousand men for doing nothing; afterwards, it gives them the money for working. Finally, you do not see that when a taxpayer gives his money, whether to a soldier in exchange for nothing or to a worker in exchange for something, all the more remote consequences of the circulation of this money are the same in both cases: only, in the second case the taxpayer receives something; in the first he receives nothing. Result: a dead loss for the nation.

1.36

The sophism that I am attacking here cannot withstand the test of extended application, which is the touchstone of all theoretical principles. If, all things considered, there is a *national profit* in increasing the size of the army, why not call the whole male population of the country to the colors?

3. TAXES

1.37

Have you ever heard anyone say: "Taxes are the best investment; they are a life-giving dew. See how many families they keep alive, and follow in imagination their indirect effects on industry; they are infinite, as extensive as life itself."

1.38

To combat this doctrine, I am obliged to repeat the preceding refutation. Political economy knows very well that its arguments are not diverting enough for anyone to say about them: *Repetita placent;* repetition pleases. So, like Basile, political economy has "arranged" the proverb for its own use, quite convinced that, from its mouth, *Repetita docent;* repetition teaches.

1.39

The advantages that government officials enjoy in drawing their salaries are *what is seen.* The benefits that result for their suppliers are also *what is seen.* They are right under your nose.

1.40

But the disadvantage that the taxpayers try to free themselves from is *what is not seen,* and the distress that results from it for the merchants who supply them is *something further that is not seen,* although it should stand out plainly enough to be seen intellectually.

1.41

When a government official spends on his own behalf one hundred sous more, this implies that a taxpayer spends on his own behalf one hundred sous the less. But the spending of the government official is *seen,* because it is done; while that of the taxpayer *is not seen,* because—alas!—he is prevented from doing it.

1.42

You compare the nation to a parched piece of land and the tax to a life-giving rain. So be it. But you should also ask yourself where this rain comes from, and whether it is not precisely the tax that draws the moisture from the soil and dries it up.

1.43

You should ask yourself further whether the soil receives more of this precious water from the rain than it loses by the evaporation?

1.44

What is quite certain is that, when James Goodfellow counts out a hundred sous to the tax collector, he receives nothing in return. When, then, a government official, in spending these hundred sous, returns them to James Goodfellow, it is for an equivalent value in wheat or in labor. The final result is a loss of five francs for James Goodfellow.

1.45

It is quite true that often, nearly always if you will, the government official renders an equivalent service to James Goodfellow. In this case there is no loss on either side; there is only an exchange. Therefore, my argument is not in any way concerned with useful functions. I say this: If you wish to create a government office, prove its usefulness. Demonstrate that to James Goodfellow it is worth the equivalent of what it costs him by virtue of the services it renders him. But apart from this intrinsic utility, do not cite, as an argument in favor of opening the new bureau, the advantage that it constitutes for the bureaucrat, his family, and those who supply his needs; do not allege that it encourages employment.

1.46

When James Goodfellow gives a hundred sous to a government official for a really useful service, this is exactly the same as when he gives a hundred sous to a shoemaker for a pair of shoes. It's a case of give-and-take, and the score is even. But when James Goodfellow hands over a hundred sous to a government official to receive no service for it or even to be subjected to inconveniences, it is as if he were to give his money to a thief. It serves no purpose to say that the official will spend these hundred sous for the great profit of our *national industry;* the more the thief can do with them, the more James Goodfellow could have done with them if he had not met on his way either the extralegal or the legal parasite.

1.47

Let us accustom ourselves, then, not to judge things solely by *what is seen*, but rather by *what is not seen*.

1.48

Last year I was on the Finance Committee, for in the Constituent Assembly the members of the opposition were not systematically excluded from all committees. In this the framers of the Constitution acted wisely. We have heard M. Thiers say: "I have spent my life fighting men of the legitimist party and of the clerical party. Since, in the face of a common danger, I have come to know them and we have had heart-to-heart talks, I see that they are not the monsters I had imagined."

1.49

Yes, enmities become exaggerated and hatreds are intensified between parties that do not mingle; and if the majority would allow a few members of the minority to penetrate into the circles of the committees, perhaps it would be recognized on both sides that their ideas are not so far apart, and above all that their intentions are not so perverse, as supposed.

1.50

However that may be, last year I was on the Finance Committee. Each time that one of our colleagues spoke of fixing at a moderate figure the salaries of the President of the Republic, of cabinet ministers, and of ambassadors, he would be told:

1.51

"For the good of the service, we must surround certain offices with an aura of prestige and dignity. That is the way to attract to them men of merit. Innumerable unfortunate people turn to the President of the Republic, and he would be in a painful position if he were always forced to refuse them help. A certain amount of ostentation in the ministerial and diplomatic salons is part of the machinery of constitutional governments, etc., etc."

1.52

Whether or not such arguments can be controverted, they certainly deserve serious scrutiny. They are based on the public interest, rightly or wrongly estimated; and, personally, I can make more of a case for them than many of our Catos, moved by a narrow spirit of niggardliness or jealousy.

1.53

But what shocks my economist's conscience, what makes me blush for the intellectual renown of my country, is when they go on from these arguments (as they never fail to do) to this absurd banality (always favorably received):

1.54

"Besides, the luxury of high officials of the government encourages the arts, industry, and employment. The Chief of State and his ministers cannot give banquets and parties without infusing life into all the veins of the body politic. To reduce their salaries would be to starve industry in Paris and, at the same time, throughout the nation."

1.55

For heaven's sake, gentlemen, at least respect arithmetic, and do not come before the National Assembly of France and say, for fear that, to its shame, it will not support you, that an addition gives a different sum depending upon whether it is added from top to bottom or from bottom to top.

1.56

Well, then, suppose I arrange to have a navvy dig me a ditch in my field for the sum of a hundred sous. Just as I conclude this agreement, the tax collector takes my hundred sous from me and has them passed on to the Minister of the Interior. My contract is broken, but the Minister will add another dish at his dinner. On what basis do you dare to affirm that this official expenditure is an addition to the national industry? Do you not see that it is only a simple *transfer* of consumption and of labor? A cabinet minister has his table more lavishly set, it is true; but a farmer has his field less well drained, and this is just as true. A Parisian caterer has gained a hundred sous, I grant you; but grant me that a provincial ditchdigger has lost five francs. All that one can say is that the official dish and the satisfied caterer are *what is seen;* the swampy field and the excavator out of work are *what is not seen.*

1.57

Good Lord! What a lot of trouble to prove in political economy that two and two make four; and if you succeed in doing so, people cry, "It is so clear that it is boring." Then they vote as if you had never proved anything at all.

4. THEATERS AND FINE ARTS

1.58

Should the state subsidize the arts?

1.59

There is certainly a great deal to say on this subject pro and con.

1.60

In favor of the system of subsidies, one can say that the arts broaden, elevate, and poetize the soul of a nation; that they draw it away from material preoccupations, giving it a feeling for the beautiful, and thus react favorably on its manners, its customs, its morals, and even on its industry. One can ask where music would be in France without the Théâtre-Italien and the Conservatory; dramatic art without the Théâtre-Français; painting and sculpture without our collections and our museums. One can go further and ask whether, without the centralization and consequently the subsidizing of the fine arts, there would have developed that exquisite taste which is the noble endowment of French labor and sends its products out over the whole world. In the presence of such results would it not be the height of imprudence to renounce this moderate assessment on all the citizens, which, in the last analysis, is what has achieved for them their pre-eminence and their glory in the eyes of Europe?

1.61

To these reasons and many others, whose power I do not contest, one can oppose many no less cogent. There is, first of all, one could say, a question of distributive justice. Do the rights of the legislator go so far as to allow him to dip into the wages of the artisan in order to supplement the profits of the artist? M. de Lamartine said: "If you take away the subsidy of a theater, where are you going to stop on this path, and will you not be logically required to do away with your university faculties, your museums, your institutes, your libraries?" One could reply: If you wish to subsidize all that is good and useful, where are you going to stop on *that* path, and will you not logically be required to set up a civil list for agriculture, industry, commerce, welfare, and education? Furthermore, is it certain that subsidies favor the progress of the arts? It is a question that is far from being resolved, and we see with our own eyes that the theaters that prosper are those that live on their own profits. Finally, proceeding to higher considerations, one may observe that needs and desires give rise to one another and keep soaring into regions more and more rarefied"[3] in proportion as the national wealth permits their satisfaction; that the government must not meddle in this process, since, whatever may be currently the amount of the national wealth, it cannot stimulate luxury industries by taxation without harming essential industries, thus reversing the natural advance of civilization. One may also point out that this artificial dislocation of wants, tastes, labor, and population places nations in a precarious and dangerous situation, leaving them without a solid base.

1.62

These are some of the reasons alleged by the adversaries of state intervention concerning the order in which citizens believe they should satisfy their needs and their desires, and thus direct their activity. I confess that I am one of those who think that the choice, the impulse, should come from below, not from above, from the citizens, not from the legislator; and the contrary doctrine seems to me to lead to the annihilation of liberty and of human dignity.

1.63

But, by an inference as false as it is unjust, do you know what the economists are now accused of? When we oppose subsidies, we are charged with opposing the very thing that it was proposed to subsidize and of being the enemies of all kinds of activity, because we want these activities to be voluntary and to seek their proper reward in themselves. Thus, if we ask that the state not intervene, by taxation, in religious matters, we are atheists. If we ask that the state not intervene, by taxation, in education, then we hate enlightenment. If we say that the state should not give, by taxation, an artificial value to land or to some branch of industry, then we are the enemies of property and of labor. If we think that the state should not subsidize artists, we are barbarians who judge the arts useless.

1.64

I protest with all my power against these inferences. Far from entertaining the absurd thought of abolishing religion, education, property, labor, and the arts when we ask the state to protect the free development of all these types of human activity without keeping them on the payroll at one another's expense, we believe, on the contrary, that all these vital forces of society should develop harmoniously under the influence of liberty and that none of them should become, as we see has happened today, a source of trouble, abuses, tyranny, and disorder.

1.65

Our adversaries believe that an activity that is neither subsidized nor regulated is abolished. We believe the contrary. Their faith is in the legislator, not in mankind. Ours is in mankind, not in the legislator.

1.66

Thus, M. de Lamartine said: "On the basis of this principle, we should have to *abolish* the public expositions that bring wealth and honor to this country."

1.67

I reply to M. de Lamartine: From your point of view, *not to subsidize* is *to abolish,* because, proceeding from the premise that nothing exists except by the will of the state, you conclude that nothing lives that taxes do not keep alive. But I turn against you the example that you have chosen, and I point out to you that the greatest, the noblest, of all expositions, the one based on the most liberal, the most universal conception, and I can even use the word "humanitarian," which is not here exaggerated, is the exposition now being prepared in London, the only one in which no government meddles and which no tax supports.

1.68

Returning to the fine arts, one can, I repeat, allege weighty reasons for and against the system of subsidization. The reader understands that, in accordance with the special purpose of this essay, I have no need either to set forth these reasons or to decide between them.

1.69

But M. de Lamartine has advanced one argument that I cannot pass over in silence, for it falls within the very carefully defined limits of this economic study.

1.70

He has said:

> The economic question in the matter of theaters can be summed up in one word: employment. The nature of the employment matters little; it is of a kind just as productive and fertile as any other kind. The theaters, as you know, support by wages no less than eighty thousand workers of all kinds—painters, masons, decorators, costumers, architects, etc., who are the very life and industry of many quarters of this capital, and they should have this claim upon your sympathies!

1.71

Your sympathies? Translate: your subsidies.

1.72

And further on:

> The pleasures of Paris provide employment and consumers' goods for the pro-
> vincial departments, and the luxuries of the rich are the wages and the bread of
> two hundred thousand workers of all kinds, living on the complex industry of
> the theaters throughout the Republic, and receiving from these noble pleasures,
> which make France illustrious, their own livelihood and the means of providing
> the necessities of life for their families and their children. It is to them that you
> give the sixty thousand francs. [*Very good! Very good! Much applause.*]

1.73

For my part, I am forced to say: *Very bad! Very bad!* confining, of course, the burden of
this judgment to the economic argument which we are here concerned with.

1.74

Yes, it is, at least in part, to the workers in the theaters that the sixty thousand francs
in question will go. A few scraps might well get lost on the way. If one scrutinized the
matter closely, one might even discover that most of the pie will find its way elsewhere.
The workers will be fortunate if there are a few crumbs left for them! But I should like to
assume that the entire subsidy will go to the painters, decorators, costumers, hairdressers,
etc. *That is what is seen.*

1.75

But where does it come from? This is the *other side* of the coin, just as important to
examine as its *face.* What is the source of these 60,000 francs? And where *would they have
gone* if a legislative vote had not first directed them to the rue de Rivoli and from there to
the rue de Grenelle?*8 *That is what is not seen.*

1.76

Surely, no one will dare maintain that the legislative vote has caused this sum to hatch
out from the ballot box; that it is a pure addition to the national wealth; that, without this
miraculous vote, these sixty thousand francs would have remained invisible and impal-
pable. It must be admitted that all that the majority can do is to decide that they will be
taken from somewhere to be sent somewhere else, and that they will have one destination
only by being deflected from another.

1.77

This being the case, it is clear that the taxpayer who will have been taxed one franc will
no longer have this franc at his disposal. It is clear that he will be deprived of a satisfaction
to the tune of one franc, and that the worker, whoever he is, who would have procured this
satisfaction for him, will be deprived of wages in the same amount.

1.78

Let us not, then, yield to the childish illusion of believing that the vote of May 16 *adds*
anything whatever to national well-being and employment. It reallocates possessions, it
reallocates wages, and that is all.

1.79

Will it be said that for one kind of satisfaction and for one kind of job it substitutes satisfactions and jobs more urgent, more moral, more rational? I could do battle on this ground. I could say: In taking sixty thousand francs from the taxpayers, you reduce the wages of plowmen, ditchdiggers, carpenters, and blacksmiths, and you increase by the same amount the wages of singers, hairdressers, decorators, and costumers. Nothing proves that this latter class is more important than the other. M. de Lamartine does not make this allegation. He says himself that the work of the theaters is *just as* productive as, *just as* fruitful as, and not *more so* than, any other work, which might still be contested; for the best proof that theatrical work is not as productive as other work is that the latter is called upon to subsidize the former.

1.80

But this comparison of the intrinsic value and merit of the different kinds of work forms no part of my present subject. All that I have to do here is to show that, if M. de Lamartine and those who have applauded his argument have seen on the one hand the wages earned by those who supply the needs of the actors, they should see on the other the earnings lost by those who supply the needs of the taxpayers; if they do not, they are open to ridicule for mistaking a reallocation for a *gain*. If they were logical in their doctrine, they would ask for infinite subsidies; for what is true of one franc and of sixty thousand francs is true, in identical circumstances, of a billion francs.

1.81

When it is a question of taxes, gentlemen, prove their usefulness by reasons with some foundation, but not with that lamentable assertion: "Public spending keeps the working class alive." It makes the mistake of covering up a fact that it is essential to know: namely, that *public spending* is *always* a substitute for *private spending,* and that consequently it may well support one worker in place of another but adds nothing to the lot of the working class taken as a whole. Your argument is fashionable, but it is quite absurd, for the reasoning is not correct.

5. PUBLIC WORKS

1.82

Nothing is more natural than that a nation, after making sure that a great enterprise will profit the community, should have such an enterprise carried out with funds collected from the citizenry. But I lose patience completely, I confess, when I hear alleged in support of such a resolution this economic fallacy: "Besides, it is a way of creating jobs for the workers."

1.83

The state opens a road, builds a palace, repairs a street, digs a canal; with these projects it gives jobs to certain workers. *That is what is seen.* But it deprives certain other laborers of employment. *That is what is not seen.*

1.84

Suppose a road is under construction. A thousand laborers arrive every morning, go home every evening, and receive their wages; that is certain. If the road had not been authorized, if funds for it had not been voted, these good people would have neither found this work nor earned these wages; that again is certain.

1.85

But is this all? Taken all together, does not the operation involve something else? At the moment when M. Dupin pronounces the sacramental words: "The Assembly has adopted," ... do millions of francs descend miraculously on a moonbeam into the coffers of M. Fould and M. Bineau? For the process to be complete, does not the state have to organize the collection of funds as well as their expenditure? Does it not have to get its tax collectors into the country and its taxpayers to make their contribution?

1.86

Study the question, then, from its two aspects. In noting what the state is going to do with the millions of francs voted, do not neglect to note also what the taxpayers would have done—and can no longer do—with these same millions. You see, then, that a public enterprise is a coin with two sides. On one, the figure of a busy worker, with this device: *What is seen;* on the other, an unemployed worker, with this device: *What is not seen.*

1.87

The sophism that I am attacking in this essay is all the more dangerous when applied to public works, since it serves to justify the most foolishly prodigal enterprises. When a railroad or a bridge has real utility, it suffices to rely on this fact in arguing in its favor. But if one cannot do this, what does one do? One has recourse to this mumbo jumbo: "We must create jobs for the workers."

1.88

This means that the terraces of the Champ-de-Mars are ordered first to be built up and then to be torn down. The great Napoleon, it is said, thought he was doing philanthropic work when he had ditches dug and then filled in. He also said: "What difference does the result make? All we need is to see wealth spread among the laboring classes."

1.89

Let us get to the bottom of things. Money creates an illusion for us. To ask for co-operation, in the form of money, from all the citizens in a common enterprise is, in reality, to ask of them actual physical co-operation, for each one of them procures for himself by his labor the amount he is taxed. Now, if we were to gather together all the citizens and exact their services from them in order to have a piece of work performed that is useful to all, this would be understandable; their recompense would consist in the results of the work itself. But if, after being brought together, they were forced to build roads on which no one would travel, or palaces that no one would live in, all under the pretext of providing work for them, it would seem absurd, and they would certainly be justified in objecting: We will have none of that kind of work. We would rather work for ourselves.

Planning and the Rule of Law

FRIEDRICH A. HAYEK

Recent studies in the sociology of law once more confirm that the fundamental principle of formal law by which every case must be judged according to general rational precepts, which have as few exceptions as possible and are based on logical subsumptions, obtains only for the liberal competitive phase of capitalism.

—K. Mannheim

Nothing distinguishes more clearly conditions in a free country from those in a country under arbitrary government than the observance in the former of the great principles known as the Rule of Law. Stripped of all technicalities this means that government in all its actions is bound by rules fixed and announced before hand-rules which make it possible to foresee with fair certainty how the authority will use its coercive powers in given circumstances, and to plan one's individual affairs on the basis of this knowledge.[1]

---

1 According to the classical exposition by A. V. Dicey in *The Law of the Constitution* (8th ed., p. 198) the rule of law "means, in the first place, the absolute supremacy or predominance of regular law as opposed to the influence of arbitrary power, and excludes the existence of arbitrariness, of prerogative, or even of wide discretionary authority on the part of government". Largely as a result of Dicey's work the term has, however, in England acquired a narrower technical meaning which does not concern us here. The wider and older meaning of the concept of the rule or reign of law, which in England had become an established tradition which was more taken for granted than discussed, has been most fully elaborated, just because it raised what were there new problems, in the early nineteenth-century discussions in Germany about the nature of the Rechtsstaat.

Though this ideal can never be perfectly achieved, since legislators as well as those to whom the administration of the law is entrusted are fallible men, the essential point, that the discretion left to the executive organs wielding coercive power should be reduced as much as possible, is clear enough. While every law restricts individual freedom to some extent by altering the means which people may use in the pursuit of their aims, under the Rule of Law the government is prevented from stultifying individual efforts by ad hoc action. Within the known rules of the game the individual is free to pursue his personal ends and desires, certain that the powers of government will not be used deliberately to frustrate his efforts.

The distinction we have drawn before between the creation of a permanent framework of laws within which the productive activity is guided by individual decisions, and the direction of economic activity by a central authority, is thus really a particular case of the more general distinction between the Rule of Law and arbitrary government. Under the first the government confines itself to fixing rules determining the conditions under which the available resources may be used, leaving to the individuals the decision for what ends they are to be used. Under the second the government directs the use of the means of production to particular ends. The first type of rules can be made in advance, in the shape of formal rules which do not aim at the wants and needs of particular people. They are intended to be merely instrumental in the pursuit of people's various individual ends. And they are, or ought to be, intended for such long periods that it is impossible to know whether they will assist particular people more than others. They could almost be described as a kind of instrument of production, helping people to predict the behaviour of those with whom they must collaborate, rather than as efforts towards the satisfaction of particular needs.

Economic planning of the collectivist kind necessarily involves the very opposite of this. The planning authority cannot confine itself to providing opportunities for unknown people to make whatever use of them they like. It cannot tie itself down in advance to general and formal rules which prevent arbitrariness. It must provide for the actual needs of people as they arise and then choose deliberately between them. It must constantly decide questions which cannot be answered by formal principles only, and in making these decisions it must set up distinctions of merit between the needs of different people. When the government has to decide how many pigs are to be reared or how many buses are to be run, which coal mines are to operate, or at what prices boots are to be sold, these decisions cannot be deduced from formal principles, or settled for long periods in advance. They depend inevitably on the circumstances of the moment, and in making such decisions it will always be necessary to balance one against the other the interests of various persons and groups. In the end somebody's views will have to decide whose interests are more important; and these views must become part of the law of the land, a new distinction of rank which the coercive apparatus of government imposes upon the people.

*****

The distinction we have just used between formal law or justice and substantive rules is very important and at the same time most difficult to draw precisely in practice. Yet the general principle involved is simple enough. The difference between the two kinds of rules is the same as that between laying down a Rule of the Road, as in the Highway Code, and ordering people where to go; or, better still, between providing signposts and commanding people which road to take. The formal rules tell people in advance what action the state will take in certain types of situation defined in general terms, without reference to time and place or particular people. They refer to typical situations into which anyone may get and in which the existence of such rules will be useful for a great variety of individual purposes. The knowledge that in such situations the state will act in a definite way, or require people to behave in a certain manner, is provided as a means for people to use in making their own plans. Formal rules are thus merely instrumental in the sense that they are expected to be useful to yet unknown people, for purposes for which these people will decide to use them, and in circumstances which cannot be foreseen in detail. In fact, that we do not know their concrete effect, that we do not know what particular ends these rules will further, or which particular people they will assist, that they are merely given the form most likely on the whole to benefit all the people affected by them, is the most important criterion of formal rules in the sense in which we here use this term. They do not involve a choice between particular ends or particular people, because we just cannot know beforehand by whom and in what way they will be used.

In our age, with its passion for conscious control of everything, it may appear paradoxical to claim as a virtue that under one system we shall know less about the particular effect of the measures the state takes than would be true under most other systems and that a method of social control should be deemed superior because of our ignorance of its precise results. Yet this consideration is in fact the rationale of the great liberal principle of the Rule of Law. And the apparent paradox dissolves rapidly when we follow the argument a little further.

*****

This argument is two-fold; the first is economic and can here only briefly be stated. The state should confine itself to establishing rules applying to general types of situations, and should allow the individuals freedom in everything which depends on the circumstances of time and place, because only the individuals concerned in each instance can fully know these circumstances and adapt their actions to them. If the individuals are to be able to use their knowledge effectively in making plans, they must be able to predict actions of the state which may affect these plans. But if the actions of the state are to be predictable, they must be determined by rules fixed independently of the concrete circumstances which can neither be foreseen nor taken into account beforehand: and the particular effects of such actions will be unpredictable. If, on the other hand, the state were to direct the individual's actions so as to achieve particular ends, its action would have to be decided on the basis of the full circumstances of the moment and would therefore be unpredictable. Hence the familiar fact that the more the state "plans" the more difficult planning becomes for the individual.

The second, moral or political, argument is even more directly relevant to the point under discussion. If the state is precisely to foresee the incidence of its actions, it means that it can leave those affected no choice. Wherever the state can exactly foresee the effects on particular people of alternative courses of action, it is also the state which chooses between the different ends. If we want to create new opportunities open to all, to offer chances of which people can make what use they like, the precise results cannot be foreseen. General rules, genuine laws as distinguished from specific orders, must therefore be intended to operate in circumstances which cannot be foreseen in detail, and, therefore, their effect on particular ends or particular people cannot be known beforehand. It is in this sense alone that it is at all possible for the legislator to be impartial. To be impartial means to have no answer to certain questions—to the kind of questions which, if we have to decide them, we decide by tossing a coin. In a world where everything was precisely foreseen, the state could hardly do anything and remain impartial. But where the precise effects of government policy on particular people are known, where the government aims directly at such particular effects, it cannot help knowing these effects, and therefore it cannot be impartial. It must, of necessity, take sides, impose its valuations upon people and, instead of assisting them in the advancement of their own ends, choose the ends for them. As soon as the particular effects are foreseen at the time a law is made, it ceases to be a mere instrument to be used by the people and becomes instead an instrument used by the law-giver upon the people and for his ends. The state ceases to be a piece of utilitarian machinery intended to help individuals in the fullest development of their individual personality and becomes a "moral" institution—where "moral" is not used in contrast to immoral, but describes an institution which imposes on its members its views on all moral questions, whether these views be moral or highly immoral. In this sense the Nazi or any other collectivist state is "moral", while the liberal state is not.

Perhaps it will be said that all this raises no serious problem because in the kind of questions which the economic planner would have to decide he need not and should not be guided by his individual prejudices, but could rely on the general conviction of what is fair and reasonable. This contention usually receives support from those who have experience of planning in a particular industry and who find that there is no insuperable difficulty about arriving at a decision which all those immediately interested will accept as fair. The reason why this experience proves nothing is, of course, the selection of the "interests" concerned when planning is confined to a particular industry. Those most immediately interested in a particular issue are not necessarily the best judges of the interests of society as a whole. To take only the most characteristic case: when capital and labour in an industry agree on some policy of restriction and thus exploit the consumers, there is usually no difficulty about the division of the spoils in proportion to former earnings or on some similar principle. The loss which is divided between thousands or millions is usually either simply disregarded or quite inadequately considered. If we want to test the usefulness of the principle of "fairness" in deciding the kind of issues which arise in economic planning, we must apply it to some question where the gains and the losses are seen equally clearly. In such instances it is readily recognised that no general principle such as fairness can provide an answer. When we have to choose between higher wages for nurses or doctors and more extensive services for the sick, more milk for children and better wages for agricultural workers, or between employment for the unemployed or better wages for those already employed, nothing short of a complete system of values in which every want of every person or group has a definite place is necessary to provide an answer.

In fact, as planning becomes more and more extensive, it becomes regularly necessary to qualify legal provisions increasingly by reference to what is "fair" or "reasonable"; this means that it becomes necessary to leave the decision of the concrete case more and more to the discretion of the judge or authority in question. One could write a history of the decline of the Rule of Law, the disappearance of the Rechtsstaat, in terms of the progressive introduction of these vague formulae into legislation and jurisdiction, and of the increasing arbitrariness and uncertainty of, and the consequent disrespect for, the law and the judicature, which in these circumstances could not but become an instrument of policy. It is important to point out once more in this connection that this process of the decline of the Rule of Law had been going on steadily in Germany for some time before Hitler came into power, and that a policy well advanced towards totalitarian planning had already done a great deal of the work which Hitler completed.

There can be no doubt that planning necessarily involves deliberate discrimination between particular needs of different people, and allowing one man to do what another must be prevented from doing. It must lay down by a legal rule how well off particular people shall be and what different people are to be allowed to have and do. It means in effect a return to the rule of status, a reversal of the "movement of progressive societies" which, in the famous phrase of Sir Henry Maine, "has hitherto been a movement from status to contract". Indeed, the Rule of Law, more than the rule of contract, should probably be regarded as the true opposite of the rule of status. It is the Rule of Law, in the sense of the rule of formal law, the absence of legal privileges of particular people designated by authority, which safeguards that equality before the law which is the opposite of arbitrary government.

*****

A necessary, and only apparently paradoxical, result of this is that formal equality before the law is in conflict, and in fact incompatible, with any activity of the government deliberately aiming at material or substantive equality of different people, and that any policy aiming at a substantive ideal of distributive justice must lead to the destruction of the Rule of Law. To produce the same result for different people it is necessary to treat them differently. To give different people the same objective opportunities is not to give them the same subjective chance. It cannot be denied that the Rule of Law produces economic inequality—all that can be claimed for it is that this inequality is not designed to affect particular people in a particular way. It is very significant and characteristic that socialists (and Nazis) have always protested against "merely" formal justice, that they have always objected to a law which had no views on how well off particular people ought to be,[2] and that they have always demanded a "socialisation of the law", attacked the independence of judges, and at the same time given their support to all such movements as the Freirechtsschule which undermined the Rule of Law.

It may even be said that for the Rule of Law to be effective it is more important that there should be a rule applied always without exceptions, than what this rule is. Often the content of the rule is indeed of minor importance, provided the same rule is universally enforced. To revert to a former example: it does not matter whether we all drive on the left-or on the right-hand side of the road so long as we all do the same. The important thing is that the rule enables us to predict other people's behaviour correctly, and this requires that it should apply to all cases—even if in a particular instance we feel it to be unjust.

The conflict between formal justice and formal equality before the law on the one hand, and the attempts to realise various ideals of substantive justice and equality on the other, also accounts for the widespread confusion about the concept of "privilege" and its consequent abuse. To mention only the most important instance of this abuse—the application of the term privilege to property as such. It would indeed be privilege if, for example, as has sometimes been the case in the past, landed property were reserved to members of the nobility. And it is privilege if, as is true in our time, the right to produce or sell particular things is reserved to particular people designated by authority. But to call private property as such, which all can acquire under the same rules, a privilege, because only some succeed in acquiring it, is depriving the word privilege of its meaning.

The unpredictability of the particular effects, which is the distinguishing characteristic of the formal laws of a liberal system, is also important because it helps us to clear up another confusion about the nature of this system: the belief that its characteristic attitude is inaction of the state. The question whether the state should or should not "act" or "interfere" poses an altogether false alternative, and the term laissez-faire is a highly ambiguous and misleading description of the principles on which a liberal policy is based. Of course, every state must act and every action of the state interferes with something or other. But that is not the point. The important question is whether the individual can foresee the action of the state and make use of this knowledge as a datum in forming his own plans, with the result that the state cannot control the use made of its machinery, and that the individual knows precisely how far he will be protected against interference from others, or whether the state is in a position to frustrate individual efforts. The state controlling weights and measures (or preventing fraud and deception in any other way) is certainly acting, while

---

2   It is therefore not altogether false when the legal theorist of National Socialism, Carl Schmitt, opposes to the liberal Rechtsstaat (Le. the Rule of Law) the national-socialist ideal of the gerechte Staat (the just state)-only that the sort of justice which is opposed to formal justice necessarily implies discrimination between persons.

the state permitting the use of violence, for example, by strike pickets, is inactive. Yet it is in the first case that the state observes liberal principles and in the second that it does not. Similarly with respect to most of the general and permanent rules which the state may establish with regard to production, such as building regulations or factory laws: these may be wise or unwise in the particular instance, but they do not conflict with liberal principles so long as they are intended to be permanent and are not used to favour or harm particular people. It is true that in these instances there will, apart from the long-run effects which cannot be predicted, also be short-run effects on particular people which may be clearly known. But with this kind of laws the short-run effects are in general not (or at least ought not to be) the guiding consideration. As these immediate and predictable effects become more important compared with the long-run effects, we approach the border-line where the distinction, however, clear in principle, becomes blurred in practice.

*****

The Rule of Law was consciously evolved only during the liberal age and is one of its greatest achievements, not only as a safeguard but as the legal embodiment of freedom. As Immanuel Kant put it (and Voltaire expressed it before him in very much the same terms), "Man is free if he needs to obey no person but solely the laws". As a vague ideal it has, however, existed at least since Roman times, and during the last few centuries it has never been as seriously threatened as it is today. The idea that there is no limit to the powers of the legislator is in part a result of popular sovereignty and democratic government. It has been strengthened by the belief that so long as all actions of the state are duly authorised by legislation, the Rule of Law will be preserved. But this is completely to misconceive the meaning of the Rule of Law. This rule has little to do with the question whether all actions of government are legal in the juridical sense. They may well be and yet not conform to the Rule of Law. The fact that somebody has full legal authority to act in the way he does gives no answer to the question whether the law gives him power to act arbitrarily or whether the law prescribes unequivocally how he has to act. It may well be that Hitler has obtained his unlimited powers in a strictly constitutional manner and that whatever he does is therefore legal in the juridical sense. But who would suggest for that reason that the Rule of Law still prevails in Germany?

To say that in a planned society the Rule of Law cannot hold is, therefore, not to say that the actions of the government will not be legal or that such a society will necessarily be lawless. It means only that the use of the government's coercive powers will no longer be limited and determined by pre-established rules. The law can, and to make a central direction of economic activity possibly must, legalise what to all intents and purposes remains arbitrary action. If the law says that such a Board or Authority may do what it pleases, anything that Board or Authority does is legal—but its actions are certainly not subject to the Rule of

Law. By giving the government unlimited powers the most arbitrary rule can be made legal: and in this way a democracy may set up the most complete despotism imaginable.[3]

If, however, the law is to enable authorities to direct economic life, it must give them powers to make and enforce decisions in circumstances which cannot be foreseen and on principles which cannot be stated in generic form. The consequence is that as planning extends, the delegation of legislative powers to divers Boards and Authorities becomes increasingly common. When before the last war, in a case to which the late Lord Hewart has recently drawn attention, Mr. Justice Darling said "that Parliament had enacted only last year that the Board of Agriculture in acting as they did should be no more impeachable than Parliament itself", this was still a rare thing. It has since become an almost daily occurrence. Constantly the broadest powers are conferred on new authorities which, without being bound by fixed rules, have almost unlimited discretion in regulating this or that activity of the people.

The Rule of Law thus implies limits to the scope of legislation: it restricts it to the kind of general rules known as formal law, and excludes legislation either directly aimed at particular people, or at enabling anybody to use the coercive power of the state for the purpose of such discrimination. It means, not that everything is regulated by law, but, on the contrary, that the coercive power of the state can be used only in cases defined in advance by the law and in such a way that it can be foreseen how it will be used. A particular enactment can thus infringe the Rule of Law. Anyone ready to deny this would have to contend that whether the Rule of Law prevails today in Germany, Italy, or Russia, depends on whether the dictators have obtained their absolute power by constitutional means.[4]

*****

---

3 The conflict is thus not, as it has often been misconceived in nineteenth century discussions, one between liberty and law. As John Locke had already made clear, there can be no liberty without law. The conflict is between different kinds of law, law so different that it should hardly be called by the same name: one is the law of the Rule of Law, general principles laid down beforehand, the "rules of the game" which enable individuals to foresee how the coercive apparatus of the state will be used, or what he and his fellow-citizens will be allowed to do, or made to do, in stated circumstances. The other kind of law gives in effect the authority power to do what it thinks fit to do. Thus the Rule of Law could clearly not be preserved in a democracy that undertook to decide every conflict of interests not according to rules previously laid down, but "on its merits".

4 I another illustration of an infringement of the Rule of Law by legislation is the case of the bill of attainder, familiar in the history of this country. The form which the Rule of Law takes in criminal law is usually expressed by the Latin tag nulla poena sine lege—no punishment without a law expressly prescribing it. The essence of this rule is that the law must have existed as a general rule before the individual case arose to which it is to be applied. Nobody would argue that, when in a famous case in Henry VIII's reign Parliament resolved with respect to the Bishop of Rochester's cook "that the said Richard Rose shall be boiled to death without having the advantage of his clergy", this act was performed

Whether, as in some countries, the main applications of the Rule of Law are laid down in a Bill of Rights or a Constitutional Code, or whether the principle is merely a firmly established tradition, matters comparatively little. But it will readily be seen that whatever form it takes, any such recognised limitations of the powers of legislation imply the recognition of the inalienable right of the individual, inviolable rights of man.

It is pathetic, but characteristic of the muddle into which many of our intellectuals have been led by the conflicting ideals in which they believe, that a leading advocate of the most comprehensive central planning like Mr. H. G. Wells should at the same time write an ardent defence of the Rights of Man. The individual rights which Mr. Wells hopes to preserve would inevitably obstruct the planning which he desires. To some extent he seems to realise the dilemma, and we find therefore the provisions of his proposed "Declaration of the Rights of Man" so hedged about with qualifications that they lose all significance. While, for instance, his Declaration proclaims that every man "shall have the right to buy and sell without any discriminatory restrictions anything which may be lawfully bought and sold", which is admirable, he immediately proceeds to make the whole provision nugatory by adding that it applies only to buying and selling "in such quantities and with such reservations as are compatible with the common welfare". But since, of course, all restrictions ever imposed upon buying or selling anything are supposed to be necessary in the interest of the "common welfare", there is really no restriction which this clause effectively prevents, and no right of the individual that is safeguarded by it. Or, to take another basic clause, the Declaration states that every man "may engage in any lawful occupation" and that "he is entitled to paid employment and to a free choice whenever there is any variety of employment open to him". It is not stated, however, who is to decide whether a particular employment is "open" to a particular person, and the added provision that "he may suggest employment for himself and have his claim publicly considered, accepted or dismissed" shows that Mr. Wells is thinking in terms of an authority which decides whether a man is "entitled" to a particular position—which certainly means the opposite of free choice of occupation. And how in a planned world "freedom of travel and migration" is to be secured when not only the means of communication and currencies are controlled, but also the location of industries planned, or how the freedom of the press is to be safeguarded when the supply of paper and all the channels of distribution are controlled by the planning authority, are questions to which Mr. Wells provides as little answer as any other planner.

In this respect much more consistency is shown by the more numerous reformers who, ever since the beginning of the socialist movement, have attacked the "metaphysical" idea of individual rights and insisted that in a rationally ordered world there will be no individual rights but only individual duties. This, indeed, has become the much more common attitude of our so called progressives, and few things are more certain to expose one to the

---

under the Rule of Law. But while the Rule of Law had become an essential part of criminal procedure in all liberal countries, it cannot be preserved in totalitarian regimes. …

reproach of being a reactionary than if one protests against a measure on the grounds that it is a violation of the rights of the individual. Even a liberal paper like The Economist was a few years ago holding up to us the example of the French, of all people, who had learnt the lesson

> that democratic government no less than dictatorship must always [sic] have plenary powers in posse, without sacrificing their democratic and representative character. There is no restrictive penumbra of individual rights that can never be touched by government in administrative matters whatever the circumstances. There is no limit to the power of ruling which can and should be taken by a government freely chosen by the people and can be fully and openly criticised by an opposition.

This may be inevitable in wartime when, of course, even free and open criticism is necessarily restricted. But the "always" in the statement quoted does not suggest that The Economist regards it as a regrettable wartime necessity. Yet as a permanent institution this view is certainly incompatible with the preservation of the Rule of Law, and it leads straight to the totalitarian state. It is, however, the view which all those who want the government to direct economic life must hold.

How even a formal recognition of individual rights, or of the equal rights of minorities, loses all significance in a state which embarks on a complete control of economic life, has been amply demonstrated by the experience of the various Central European countries. It has been shown there that it is possible to pursue a policy of ruthless discrimination against national minorities by the use of recognised instruments of economic policy, without ever infringing the letter of the statutory protection of minority rights. This oppression by means of economic policy was greatly facilitated by the fact that particular industries or activities were largely in the hands of a national minority so that many a measure aimed ostensibly against an industry or class was in fact aimed at a national minority. But the almost boundless possibilities for a policy of discrimination and oppression provided by such apparently innocuous principles as "government control of the development of industries" have been amply demonstrated to all those desirous of seeing how the political consequences of planning appear in practice.

The Five Mysteries of Capital

HERNANDO DE SOTO

The key problem is to find out why that sector of society of the past, which I would not hesitate to call capitalist, should have lived as if in a bell jar, cut off from the rest; why was it not able to expand and conquer the whole of society? ... [Why was it that] a significant rate of capital formation was possible only in certain sectors and not in the whole market economy of the time?

—Fernand Braudel, *The Wheels of Commerce*

The hour of capitalism's greatest triumph is its hour of crisis. The fall of the Berlin Wall ended more than a century of political competition between capitalism and communism. Capitalism stands alone as the only feasible way to rationally organize a modern economy. At this moment in history, no responsible nation has a choice. As a result, with varying degrees of enthusiasm, Third World and former communist nations have balanced their budgets, cut subsidies, welcomed foreign investment, and dropped their tariff barriers.

Their efforts have been repaid with bitter disappointment. From Russia to Venezuela, the past half-decade has been a time of economic suffering, tumbling incomes, anxiety, and resentment; of "starving, rioting, and looting," in the stinging words of Malaysian prime minister Mahathir Mohamad. In a recent editorial the *New York Times* said, "For much of the world, the marketplace extolled by the West in the afterglow of victory in the Cold War has been supplanted by the cruelty of markets, wariness toward capitalism, and dangers of instability." The triumph of capitalism only in the West could be a recipe for economic and political disaster.

For Americans enjoying both peace and prosperity, it has been all too easy to ignore the turmoil elsewhere. How can capitalism be in trouble when the Dow Jones Industrial average is climbing higher than Sir Edmund Hillary? Americans look at other nations and see progress, even if it is slow and uneven. Can't you eat a Big Mac in Moscow, rent a video from Blockbuster in Shanghai, and reach the Internet in Caracas?

Even in the United States, however, the foreboding cannot be completely stifled. Americans see Colombia poised on the brink of a major civil war between drug-trafficking guerrillas and repressive militias, an intractable insurgency in the south of Mexico, and an important part of Asia's force-fed economic growth draining away into corruption and chaos. In Latin America, sympathy for free markets is dwindling: Support for privatization has dropped from 46 percent of the population to 36 percent in May 2000. Most ominously of all, in the former communist nations capitalism has been found wanting, and men associated with old regimes stand poised to resume power. Some Americans sense too that one reason for their decade-long boom is that the more precarious the rest of the world looks, the more attractive American stocks and bonds become as a haven for international money.

In the business community of the West, there is a growing concern that the failure of most of the rest of the world to implement capitalism will eventually drive the rich economies into recession. As millions of investors have painfully learned from the evaporation of their emerging market funds, globalization is a two-way street: If the Third World and former communist nations cannot escape the influence of the West, neither can the West disentangle itself from them. Adverse reactions to capitalism have also been growing stronger within rich countries themselves. The rioting in Seattle at the meeting of the World Trade Organization in December 1999 and a few months later at the IMF/World Bank meeting in Washington, D.C., regardless of the diversity of the grievances, highlighted the anger that spreading capitalism inspires. Many have begun recalling the economic historian Karl Polanyi's warnings that free markets can collide with society and lead to fascism. Japan is struggling through its most prolonged slump since the Great Depression. Western Europeans vote for politicians who promise them a "third way" that rejects what a French best-seller has labeled *L'Horreur économique*.

These whispers of alarm, disturbing though they are, have thus far only prompted American and European leaders to repeat to the rest of the world the same wearisome lectures: Stabilize your currencies, hang tough, ignore the food riots, and wait patiently for the foreign investors to return.

Foreign investment is, of course, a very good thing. The more of it, the better. Stable currencies are good, too, as are free trade and transparent banking practices and the privatization of state-owned industries and every other remedy in the Western pharmacopoeia. Yet we continually forget that global capitalism has been tried before. In Latin America, for example, reforms directed at creating capitalist systems have been tried at least four times since independence from Spain in the 1820s. Each time, after the initial euphoria, Latin Americans swung back from capitalist and market economy policies. These remedies are clearly not enough. Indeed, they fall so far short as to be almost irrelevant.

When these remedies fail, Westerners all too often respond not by questioning the adequacy of the remedies but by blaming Third World peoples for their lack of entrepreneurial spirit or market orientation. If they have failed to prosper despite all the excellent advice, it is because something is the matter with them: They missed the Protestant Reformation, or they are crippled by the disabling legacy of colonial Europe, or their IQs are too low. But the suggestion that it is culture that explains the success of such diverse places as Japan, Switzerland, and California, and culture again that explains the relative poverty of such equally diverse places as China, Estonia, and Baja California, is worse than inhumane; it is unconvincing. The disparity of wealth between the West and the rest of the world is far too great to be explained by culture alone. Most people want the fruits of capital—so much so that many, from the children of Sanchez to Khrushchev's son, are flocking to Western nations.

The cities of the Third World and the former communist countries are teeming with entrepreneurs. You cannot walk through a Middle Eastern market, hike up to a Latin American village, or climb into a taxicab in Moscow without someone trying to make a deal with you. The inhabitants of these countries possess talent, enthusiasm, and an astonishing ability to wring a profit out of practically nothing. They can grasp and use modern technology. Otherwise, American businesses would not be struggling to control the unauthorized use of their patents abroad, nor would the U.S. government be striving so desperately to keep modern weapons technology out of the hands of Third World countries. Markets are an ancient and universal tradition: Christ drove the merchants out of the temple two thousand years ago, and Mexicans were taking their products to market long before Columbus reached America.

But if people in countries making the transition to capitalism are not pitiful beggars, are not helplessly trapped in obsolete ways, and are not the uncritical prisoners of dysfunctional cultures, what is it that prevents capitalism from delivering to them the same wealth it has delivered to the West? Why does capitalism thrive only in the West, as if enclosed in a bell jar?

In this book I intend to demonstrate that the major stumbling block that keeps the rest of the world from benefiting from capitalism is its inability to produce capital. Capital is the force that raises the productivity of labor and creates the wealth of nations. It is the lifeblood of the capitalist system, the foundation of progress, and the one thing that the poor countries of the world cannot seem to produce for themselves, no matter how eagerly their people engage in all the other activities that characterize a capitalist economy.

I will also show, with the help of facts and figures that my research team and I have collected, block by block and farm by farm in Asia, Africa, the Middle East, and Latin

America, that most of the poor already possess the assets they need to make a success of capitalism. Even in the poorest countries, the poor save. The value of savings among the poor is, in fact, immense—forty times all the foreign aid received throughout the world since 1945. In Egypt, for instance, the wealth that the poor have accumulated is worth fifty-five times as much as the sum of all direct foreign investment ever recorded there, including the Suez Canal and the Aswan Dam. In Haiti, the poorest nation in Latin America, the total assets of the poor are more than one hundred fifty times greater than all the foreign investment received since Haiti's independence from France in 1804. If the United States were to hike its foreign-aid budget to the level recommended by the United Nations—0.7 percent of national income—it would take the richest country on earth more than 150 years to transfer to the world's poor resources equal to those they already possess.

But they hold these resources in defective forms: houses built on land whose ownership rights are not adequately recorded, unincorporated businesses with undefined liability, industries located where financiers and investors cannot see them. Because the rights to these possessions are not adequately documented, these assets cannot readily be turned into capital, cannot be traded outside of narrow local circles where people know and trust each other, cannot be used as collateral for a loan, and cannot be used as a share against an investment.

In the West, by contrast, every parcel of land, every building, every piece of equipment, or store of inventories is represented in a property document that is the visible sign of a vast hidden process that connects all these assets to the rest of the economy. Thanks to this representational process, assets can lead an invisible, parallel life alongside their material existence. They can be used as collateral for credit. The single most important source of funds for new businesses in the United States is a mortgage on the entrepreneur's house. These assets can also provide a link to the owner's credit history, an accountable address for the collection of debts and taxes, the basis for the creation of reliable and universal public utilities, and a foundation for the creation of securities (like mortgage-backed bonds) that can then be rediscounted and sold in secondary markets. By this process the West injects life into assets and makes them generate capital.

Third World and former communist nations do not have this representational process. As a result, most of them are undercapitalized, in the same way that a firm is undercapitalized when it issues fewer securities than its income and assets would justify. The enterprises of the poor are very much like corporations that cannot issue shares or bonds to obtain new investment and finance. Without representations, their assets are dead capital.

The poor inhabitants of these nations—five-sixths of humanity—do have things, but they lack the process to represent their property and create capital. They have houses but not titles; crops but not deeds; businesses but not statutes of incorporation. It is the unavailability of these essential representations that explains why people who have adapted every other Western invention, from the paper clip to the nuclear reactor, have not been able to produce sufficient capital to make their domestic capitalism work.

This is the mystery of capital. Solving it requires an understanding of why Westerners, by representing assets with titles, are able to see and draw out capital from them. One of the greatest challenges to the human mind is to comprehend and to gain access to those things we know exist but cannot see. Not everything that is real and useful is tangible and visible. Time, for example, is real, but it can only be efficiently managed when it is represented by a clock or a calendar. Throughout history, human beings have invented representational systems—writing, musical notation, double-entry bookkeeping—to grasp with the mind what human hands could never touch. In the same way, the great practitioners of capitalism, from the creators of integrated title systems and corporate stock to Michael Milken, were able to reveal and extract capital where others saw only junk by devising new ways to represent the invisible potential that is locked up in the assets we accumulate.

At this very moment you are surrounded by waves of Ukrainian, Chinese, and Brazilian television that you cannot see. So, too, are you surrounded by assets that invisibly harbor capital. Just as the waves of Ukrainian television are far too weak for you to sense them directly but can, with the help of a television set, be decoded to be seen and heard, so can capital be extracted and processed from assets. But only the West has the conversion process required to transform the invisible to the visible. It is *this* disparity that explains why Western nations can create capital and the Third World and former communist nations cannot.

The absence of this process in the poorer regions of the world—where two-thirds of humanity lives—is not the consequence of some Western monopolistic conspiracy. It is rather that Westerners take this mechanism so completely for granted that they have lost all awareness of its existence. Although it is huge, nobody sees it, including the Americans, Europeans, and Japanese who owe all their wealth to their ability to use it. It is an implicit legal infrastructure hidden deep within their property systems—of which ownership is but the tip of the iceberg. The rest of the iceberg is an intricate man-made process that can transform assets and labor into capital. This process was not created from a blueprint and is not described in a glossy brochure. Its origins are obscure and its significance buried in the economic subconscious of Western capitalist nations.

How could something so important have slipped our minds? It is not uncommon for us to know *how* to use things without understanding *why* they work. Sailors used magnetic compasses long before there was a satisfactory theory of magnetism. Animal breeders had a working knowledge of genetics long before Gregor Mendel explained genetic principles. Even as the West prospers from abundant capital, do people really understand the origin of capital? If they don't, there always remains the possibility that the West might damage the source of its own strength. Being clear about the source of capital will also prepare the West to protect itself and the rest of the world as soon as the prosperity of the moment yields to the crisis that is sure to come. Then the question that always arises in international crises will be heard again: Whose money will be used to solve the problem?

So far, Western countries have been happy to take their system for producing capital entirely for granted and to leave its history undocumented. That history must be recovered. This book is an effort to reopen the exploration of the source of capital and thus explain how to correct the economic failures of poor countries. These failures have nothing to do with deficiencies in cultural or genetic heritage. Would anyone suggest "cultural" commonalities between Latin Americans and Russians? Yet in the last decade, ever since both regions began to build capitalism without capital, they have shared the same political, social, and economic problems: glaring inequality, underground economies, pervasive mafias, political instability, capital flight, flagrant disregard for the law. These troubles did not originate in the monasteries of the Orthodox Church or along the pathways of the Incas.

But it is not only former communist and Third World countries that have suffered all of these problems. The same was true of the United States in 1783, when President George Washington complained about "banditti ... skimming and disposing of the cream of the country at the expense of the many." These "banditti" were squatters and small illegal entrepreneurs occupying lands they did not own. For the next one hundred years, such squatters battled for legal rights to their land and miners warred over their claims because ownership laws differed from town to town and camp to camp. Enforcing property rights created such a quagmire of social unrest and antagonism throughout the young United States that the Chief Justice of the Supreme Court, Joseph Story, wondered in 1820 whether lawyers would ever be able to settle them.

Do squatters, bandits, and flagrant disregard of the law sound familiar? Americans and Europeans have been telling the other countries of the world, "You have to be more like us." In fact, they are very much like the United States of a century ago when it too was an undeveloped country. Western politicians once faced the same dramatic challenges that leaders of the developing and former communist countries are facing today. But their successors have lost contact with the days when the pioneers who opened the American West were undercapitalized because they seldom possessed title to the lands they settled and the goods they owned, when Adam Smith did his shopping in black markets and English street urchins plucked pennies cast by laughing tourists into the mud banks of the Thames, when Jean-Baptiste Colbert's technocrats executed 16,000 small entrepreneurs whose only crime was manufacturing and importing cotton cloth in violation of France's industrial codes.

That past is many nations' present. The Western nations have so successfully integrated their poor into their economies that they have lost even the memory of how it was done, how the creation of capital began back when, as the American historian Gordon Wood has written, "something momentous was happening in the society and culture that released the aspirations and energies of common people as never before in American history." The "something momentous" was that Americans and Europeans were on the verge of establishing widespread formal property law and inventing the conversion process in that law that allowed them to create capital. This was the moment when the West crossed the demarcation line that led to successful capitalism—when it ceased being a private club and became a popular culture, when George Washington's dreaded "banditti" were transformed into the beloved pioneers that American culture now venerates.

***

The paradox is as clear as it is unsettling: Capital, the most essential component of Western economic advance, is the one that has received the least attention. Neglect has shrouded it in mystery—in fact, in a series of five mysteries.

THE MYSTERY OF THE MISSING INFORMATION

Charitable organizations have so emphasized the miseries and helplessness of the world's poor that no one has properly documented their capacity for accumulating assets. Over the past five years, I and a hundred colleagues from six different nations have closed our books and opened our eyes—and gone out into the streets and countrysides of four continents to count how much the poorest sectors of society have saved. The quantity is enormous. But most of it is dead capital.

THE MYSTERY OF CAPITAL

This is the key mystery and the centerpiece of this book. Capital is a subject that has fascinated thinkers for the past three centuries. Marx said that you needed to go beyond physics to touch "the hen that lays the golden eggs"; Adam Smith felt you had to create "a sort of waggon-way through the air" to reach that same hen. But no one has told us where the hen hides. What is capital, how is it produced, and how is it related to money?

THE MYSTERY OF POLITICAL AWARENESS

If there is so much dead capital in the world, and in the hands of so many poor people, why haven't governments tried to tap into this potential wealth? Simply because the evidence they needed has only become available in the past forty years as billions of people throughout the world have moved from life organized on a small scale to life on a large scale. This migration to the cities has rapidly divided labor and spawned in poorer countries a huge industrial-commercial revolution—one that, incredibly, has been virtually ignored.

THE MISSING LESSONS OF U.S. HISTORY

What is going on in the Third World and the former communist countries has happened before, in Europe and North America. Unfortunately, we have been so mesmerized by the failure of so many nations to make the transition to capitalism that we have forgotten how the successful capitalist nations actually did it. For years I visited technocrats and politicians in advanced nations, from Alaska to Tokyo, but they had no answers. It was a mystery. I finally found the answer in their history books, the most pertinent example being that of U.S. history.

THE MYSTERY OF LEGAL FAILURE: WHY PROPERTY LAW DOES NOT WORK OUTSIDE THE WEST

Since the nineteenth century, nations have been copying the laws of the West to give their citizens the institutional framework to produce wealth. They continue to copy such laws today, and obviously it doesn't work. Most citizens still cannot use the law to convert their savings into capital. Why this is so and what is needed to make the law work remains a mystery.

***

The moment is ripe to solve the problem of why capitalism is triumphant in the West and stalling practically everywhere else. As all plausible alternatives to capitalism have now evaporated, we are finally in a position to study capital dispassionately and carefully.

Who Protects the Consumer?

MILTON FRIEDMAN

I n recent years consumer advocacy has been something of a real growth industry. It has been sparked in this country, of course, by Ralph Nader, who played the same role in developing the consumer advocacy industry that Henry Ford played at a much earlier date—and with much greater benefit to the consumer, I may say—in developing the automobile industry. But since Ralph Nader has developed into a multinational conglomerate, he has had many imitators and many successors; and there has been a whole host of organizations and agencies that have developed supposedly to represent the consumer.

The old agencies—the ICC, FDA, SEC, CAB, FCC, FTC, FPC—have been supplemented by a host of new ones: the NHTSA, the OSHA, the OPA, the EEOC, the CPSC, the CFTC, the NTSP, and so on. Note that one of the effects of the increasing crowding of the spectrum has been that they have had to go from three alphabetical letters to four.

In 1975 there were at least twenty-seven major federal government regulatory agencies. They issued 60,000 pages of rules or proposed rules in the *Federal Register*. Their regulations occupied no less than 72,200 pages in the Code of Federal Regulations. I went to my bookshelf and measured what that would mean, and that turns out to be not a five-foot shelf of great books, but a literal twenty-four-foot shelf of not-so-great books.

The expenditures of these agencies on your behalf have literally tripled from $1.6 billion in 1970 to $4.7 billion in 1975 and, unless I am greatly mistaken, we ain't seen nothing yet.

Those are only the direct expenditures; those are what the government spends through the budget. They do not include the costs which those agencies have imposed on the rest of us in the form of the standards mandated on us. If you take the simplest example that is most familiar to all of us, the so-called antipollution and safety requirements on automobiles, those amount to about $500 to $1,000 worth on any automobile. If the government imposed a tax on each automobile of $500 and used the proceeds to pay directly for those items, that would appear in the Federal budget. But there is no economic difference whatsoever between that and the present situation in which you and I pay for them directly, but are forced to pay for them whether we want them or not. So the Federal budget figures are a gross underestimate.

Well, we have had this enormous growth, and we are continuing to have it, in these agencies in expenditures, in rules, in regulations. Is the consumer better protected as a result? Can he now settle back and say, "Well, now, I'm all taken care of, I can forget about that"? My thesis, and one I am going to try to persuade you of, is that the answer is a resounding no! That on the contrary these agencies, these regulations, these bureaucrats have not only picked our pockets but they have left us less well protected than we were before. When we as consumers really need help, we will find the self-styled consumer advocates conspicuous by their absence.

The banning of the cyclamates and the proposed ban on saccharin, some of these people would claim, is pro-consumer. But then if you ask them whom are you protecting the consumer against, the answer is clear: himself. They ere, they believe, pro-consumer by which they mean that they are forcing you to do what you would do of your own free will if you were as sensible and as smart as they are.

After all, the argument about saccharin and cyclamates is that they carry the risk of producing cancer. I have no competence whatsoever to question the scientific evidence on that; I wouldn't try to. But obviously the right way to handle it from the point of view of a believer in freedom is to let people know and let them make their own choice. Let everyone know what the risks are, saying they are one in ten million or one in a thousand—whatever may be the best evidence—have a Centre for Civil Society Liberty, Art & Culture Seminar free press. But then the question is: Ought you not be able to make your own choice?

I am saying that I don't believe that some people sitting in Washington ought to be able to make that judgment for me. That's my business. I belong to me, not to them. It's my life at stake.

And let me point out to you how utterly inconsistent and contradictory are the people involved in this. There's not a person in one of these consumer agencies who would deny for a moment that the smoking of cigarettes is a far greater source of death from cancer and from other diseases than even the most extreme figures you could put on cyclamates and saccharin. If it is right, if it is correct, if it is proper public policy to protect the consumer against himself with respect to saccharin or with respect to cyclamates, the same logic says it is proper policy to prohibit smoking of cigarettes.

I refer to cigarettes, but of course you realize that the same thing is true of booze. Again, there is overwhelming evidence that the consumption of alcohol causes far more human deaths both directly and indirectly through accidents on the highways than any conceivable effect from saccharin or from cyclamates. Indeed, there is no doubt whatsoever that if you could effectively prohibit drinking you would save more lives on the highways than by all of the so-called safety equipment on cars. The seat belts and air bags don't even hold a candle, in terms of the number of lives that would be saved, to the cessation of alcohol.

Needless to say, I am not in favor of prohibition. I'm not in favor of prohibition of alcohol; I'm not in favor of the prohibition of smoking; I'm not in favor of the prohibition of cyclamates or saccharin. I am simply in favor of letting everybody know what the risks are and letting everybody do what he, in the fullness of his own wisdom and judgment, wishes to do.

Let me emphasize that I'm not questioning the motives of the people involved. There's an old saying that you all know, about what it is that the road to hell is paved with. Intentions are one think; it's results we want to look at. Let me give you an even better quote and this is one from Justice Brandeis going back, I think, to the year 1928 or 1929 in one of the Supreme Court cases: "Experience should teach us to be most on our guard to protect liberty when the government's purposes are beneficial. Men born to freedom are naturally alert to repel invasion of their liberty by evilminded rulers. The greater dangers to liberty lurk in insidious encroachment by men of zeal, well-meaning but without understanding."

How can the consumer be protected? How is he protected? The clear answer, the answer that in my opinion cannot be denied, is that the most effective protection of the consumer is free competition, free competition at home and free trade throughout the world. It is the free market, the free private market, with free competition everywhere that is his best protector. The great danger to the consumer is from monopoly whether it be private or public. The great protection to the consumer is having alternative sources of supply. The thing that keeps the consumer from being exploited by Mr. X is that if Mr. X tried to charge him too much he can turn to Mr. Y.

People often say to me, why do you make such a big difference between private enterprise and government enterprise? What difference does it make whether you have a great big General Motors Corporation, it's a bureaucracy of the most extraordinary size, or whether you have a great big government corporation producing automobiles? Well it makes a big difference, and the difference is that there is no way in which General Motors can get a dollar from you unless you agree to hand it over. General Motors cannot send a policeman to pick your pocket, but the U.S. Government can, and as a result General Motors must serve your interests in a way which the U.S. Government as a whole, or a government agency, does not have to. It's the possibility of other competition. It's because if General Motors doesn't serve your interest, you can buy a Ford product or a Chrysler product, or you can buy a Volkswagen, or you can buy a Toyota. That's what prevents General Motors from exploiting you.

Let me emphasize: competition does not protect the consumer because businessmen are more softhearted than bureaucrats or because they are more altruistic or because Centre for Civil Society Liberty, Art & Culture Seminar they are more generous, but only because it is in the self-interest of the entrepreneur to protect the consumer. And on this subject let me quote to you from what the father of modern economics, Adam Smith, wrote 200 years ago in *The Wealth of Nations*.

"It is not from the benevolence of the butcher, the brewer, or the baker that we expect our dinner, but from their regard to their own selfinterest. We address ourselves not to their humanity but to their self-love and never talk to them of our own necessities but of their advantages. Nobody but a beggar chooses to depend chiefly upon the benevolence of his fellow citizens." So it's not from benevolence but from self-interest.

To return to the FDA, suppose it weren't there. What would prevent business from distributing adulterated products? It would be a very expensive thing to do. Consider the story that many of you have heard of a New Jersey firm which had been producing and marketing a high-quality soup product for fifty years very profitably. After fifty years of apparently safe operation, one case of adulterated or contaminated soup cans got out. That company very shortly went bankrupt. That's not a very sensible business practice.

What about the claim that the consumer cannot judge the quality of complex products, that he therefore requires the government's support and help? The market provides a very excellent answer. When it comes to complicated products, the consumer doesn't really trust his own judgment; he trusts the judgment of middlemen. Let me illustrate. No ordinary consumer is an expert about the quality of shirts, ties, shoes, goodness knows what. If one of them goes bad, if you find it's defective, do you go back to the shirt manufacturer? No, you go to the department store from which you bought it. The department store is acting as your middleman. Indeed, the reason the department store can exist and make money is because it can get the consumer to have confidence that the department store will sell him a good product for the price. In the same way you rely on a Sears Roebuck or a Montgomery Ward or a General Electric or a General Motors, not because they are altruistic but because it is in their self-interest to get the reputation and the standing which would be destroyed if they consistently turned out bad products.

What about the claim that consumers can be led by the nose by false advertising, the claim that people like John Kenneth Galbraith have done the most to promote? The simplest answer is that the consumer can't be. And if you don't believe it, ask Mr. Ford what happened to the Edsel, promoted by an enormously expensive advertising campaign—one of the great duds of all times. The fact is that the consumer ultimately is going to decide on the quality of the product he buys and not on the claims. On the contrary he is going to be put off by the claims.

Finally, and most important, does it pay enterprises to engage in false advertising? It's like the question of whether it pays them to produce shoddy products. Of course occasionally a fly-by-night outfit can make some money by fooling people. But you know,

Abraham Lincoln was absolutely right when he said many, many years ago, "You can fool some of the people all the time, you can fool all of the people some of the time, but you can't fool all of the people all of the time."

The profits of most enterprises depend on continuing customers; they don't depend on a one-time sale. And it is therefore in the longrun self-interest of the company to be sure that its advertising corresponds to the product it is selling. As I say, of course, there will always be some shoddy products, there will always be some quacks, there will always be some con artists. We've got to wait until the next world before we get rid of them. But we have to look at the real world.

I think that as consumers we are pretty good, if you leave us alone. But I think in our role as citizens we're terrible. And for good reason. If you're going to buy something every day it pays you to look into whether that's good or bad. If you are going to deal with the grocer daily, you'd better be pretty sure that he is a reasonably reliable grocer and that you'll get what you order and that he won't shortweight you or shortchange you.

But you may get to vote once a year—on what? On a long, long list of propositions, with very little relationship between your vote Centre for Civil Society Liberty, Art & Culture Seminar and what ultimately happens. How much time does it pay you to inform yourself about that?

It's just a waste of time and energy; you're not going to influence anything.

So it's understandable, in my opinion, why the individual is far better a consumer in his private capacity than he is as a citizen in his public capacity. And what we have to do from that point of view is to drive home that lesson and make individuals recognize the enormous importance of setting a limit to the powers that we grant to the government.

CHAPTER 3

✝

RESPONSIBILITY AND EXTERNALITIES

Politics

ARISTOTLE

Next let us consider what should be our arrangements about property: should the citizens of the perfect state have their possessions in common or not? This question may be discussed separately from the enactments about women and children. Even supposing that the women and children belong to individuals, according to the custom which is at present universal, may there not be an advantage in having and using possessions in common? Three cases are possible: (1) the soil may be appropriated, but the produce may be thrown for consumption into the common stock; and this is the practice of some nations. Or (2), the soil may be common, and may be cultivated in common, but the produce divided among individuals for their private use; this is a form of common property which is said to exist among certain barbarians. Or (3), the soil and the produce may be alike common.

When the husbandmen are not the owners, the case will be different and easier to deal with; but when they till the ground for themselves the question of ownership will give a world of trouble. If they do not share equally enjoyments and toils, those who labor much and get little will necessarily complain of those who labor little and receive or consume much. But indeed there is always a difficulty in men living together and having all human relations in common, but especially in their having common property. The partnerships of fellow-travelers are an example to the point; for they generally fall out over everyday matters and quarrel about any trifle which turns up. So with servants: we are most able to take offense at those with whom we most we most frequently come into contact in daily life.

These are only some of the disadvantages which attend the community of property; the present arrangement, if improved as it might be by good customs and laws, would be far better, and would have the advantages of both systems. Property should be in a certain sense common, but, as a general rule, private; for, when everyone has a distinct interest, men will not complain of one another, and they will make more progress, because every one will be attending to his own business. And yet by reason of goodness, and in respect of use, 'Friends,' as the proverb says, 'will have all things common.' Even now there are traces of such a principle, showing that it is not impracticable, but, in well-ordered states, exists already to a certain extent and may be carried further. For, although every man has his own property, some things he will place at the disposal of his friends, while of others he shares the use with them. The Lacedaemonians, for example, use one another's slaves, and horses, and dogs, as if they were their own; and when they lack provisions on a journey, they appropriate what they find in the fields throughout the country. It is clearly better that property should be private, but the use of it common; and the special business of the legislator is to create in men this benevolent disposition. Again, how immeasurably greater is the pleasure, when a man feels a thing to be his own; for surely the love of self is a feeling implanted by nature and not given in vain, although selfishness is rightly censured; this, however, is not the mere love of self, but the love of self in excess, like the miser's love of money; for all, or almost all, men love money and other such objects in a measure. And further, there is the greatest pleasure in doing a kindness or service to friends or guests or companions, which can only be rendered when a man has private property. These advantages are lost by excessive unification of the state. The exhibition of two virtues, besides, is visibly annihilated in such a state: first, temperance towards women (for it is an honorable action to abstain from another's wife for temperance's sake); secondly, liberality in the matter of property. No one, when men have all things in common, will any longer set an example of liberality or do any liberal action; for liberality consists in the use which is made of property.

Such legislation may have a specious appearance of benevolence; men readily listen to it, and are easily induced to believe that in some wonderful manner everybody will become everybody's friend, especially when some one is heard denouncing the evils now existing in states, suits about contracts, convictions for perjury, flatteries of rich men and the like, which are said to arise out of the possession of private property. These evils, however, are due to a very different cause—the wickedness of human nature. Indeed, we see that there is much more quarrelling among those who have all things in common, though there are not many of them when compared with the vast numbers who have private property.

Again, we ought to reckon, not only the evils from which the citizens will be saved, but also the advantages which they will lose. The life which they are to lead appears to be quite impracticable. The error of Socrates must be attributed to the false notion of unity from which he starts. Unity there should be, both of the family and of the state, but in some respects only. For there is a point at which a state may attain such a degree of unity as to be no longer a state, or at which, without actually ceasing to exist, it will become an inferior state, like harmony passing into unison, or rhythm which has been reduced to a single foot. The state, as I was saying, is a plurality which should be united and made into a community by education; and it is strange that the author of a system of education which he thinks will make the state virtuous, should expect to improve his citizens by regulations of this sort, and not by philosophy or by customs and laws, like those which prevail at Sparta and Crete respecting common meals, whereby the legislator has made property common. Let us remember that we should not disregard the experience of ages; in the multitude of years these things, if they were good, would certainly not have been unknown; for almost everything has been found out, although sometimes they are not put together; in other cases men do not use the knowledge which they have. Great light would be thrown on this subject if we could see such a form of government in the actual process of construction; for the legislator could not form a state at all without distributing and dividing its constituents into associations for common meals, and into phratries and tribes. But all this legislation ends only in forbidding agriculture to the guardians, a prohibition which the Lacedaemonians try to enforce already.

But, indeed, Socrates has not said, nor is it easy to decide, what in such a community will be the general form of the state. The citizens who are not guardians are the majority, and about them nothing has been determined: are the husbandmen, too, to have their property in common? Or is each individual to have his own? And are the wives and children to be individual or common. If, like the guardians, they are to have all things in common, what do they differ from them, or what will they gain by submitting to their government? Or, upon what principle would they submit, unless indeed the governing class adopt the ingenious policy of the Cretans, who give their slaves the same institutions as their own, but forbid them gymnastic exercises and the possession of arms. If, on the other hand, the inferior classes are to be like other cities in respect of marriage and property, what will be the form of the community? Must it not contain two states in one, each hostile to the other He makes the guardians into a mere occupying garrison, while the husbandmen and artisans and the rest are the real citizens. But if so the suits and quarrels, and all the evils which Socrates affirms to exist in other states, will exist equally among them. He says indeed that, having so good an education, the citizens will not need many laws, for example laws about the city or about the markets; but then he confines his education to the guardians. Again, he makes the husbandmen owners of the property upon condition of their paying a tribute. But in that case they are likely to be much more unmanageable and conceited than the Helots, or Penestae, or slaves in general. And whether community of wives and property be necessary for the lower equally with the higher class or not, and the questions akin to this, what will be the education, form of government, laws of the lower class, Socrates has nowhere determined: neither is it easy to discover this, nor is their character of small importance if the common life of the guardians is to be maintained.

Again, if Socrates makes the women common, and retains private property, the men will see to the fields, but who will see to the house? And who will do so if the agricultural class have both their property and their wives in common? Once more: it is absurd to argue, from the analogy of the animals, that men and women should follow the same pursuits, for animals have not to manage a household. The government, too, as constituted by Socrates, contains elements of danger; for he makes the same persons always rule. And if this is often a cause of disturbance among the meaner sort, how much more among high-spirited warriors? But that the persons whom he makes rulers must be the same is evident; for the gold which the God mingles in the souls of men is not at one time given to one, at another time to another, but always to the same: as he says, 'God mingles gold in some, and silver in others, from their very birth; but brass and iron in those who are meant to be artisans and husbandmen.' Again, he deprives the guardians even of happiness, and says that the legislator ought to make the whole state happy. But the whole cannot be happy unless most, or all, or some of its parts enjoy happiness. In this respect happiness is not like the even principle in numbers, which may exist only in the whole, but in neither of the parts; not so happiness. And if the guardians are not happy, who are? Surely not the artisans, or the common people. The Republic of which Socrates discourses has all these difficulties, and others quite as great.

Tragedy of the Commons

Garrett Hardin

n 1974 the general public got a graphic illustration of the "tragedy of the commons." in satellite photos of the earth. Pictures of northern Africa showed an irregular dark patch 390 square miles in area. Ground-level investigation revealed a fenced area inside of which there was plenty of grass. Outside, the ground cover had been devastated.

The explanation was simple. The fenced area was private property, subdivided into five portions. Each year the owners moved their animals to a new section. Fallow periods of four years gave the pastures time to recover from the grazing. The owners did this because they had an incentive to take care of their land. But no one owned the land outside the ranch. It was open to nomads and their herds. Though knowing nothing of Karl Marx, the herdsmen followed his famous advice of 1875: "To each according to his needs." Their needs were uncontrolled and grew with the increase in the number of animals. But supply was governed by nature and decreased drastically during the drought of the early 1970s. The herds exceeded the natural "carrying capacity" of their environment, soil was compacted and eroded, and "weedy" plants, unfit for cattle consumption, replaced good plants. Many cattle died, and so did humans.

The rational explanation for such ruin was given more than 170 years ago. In 1832 William Forster Lloyd, a political economist at Oxford University, looking at the recurring

Garrett Hardin, "Tragedy of the Commons," originally published in *Science*, Vol. 162, No. 3859; 13 December 1968, pp. 1243–1248. Copyright © 1968 by American Association for the Advancement of Science. Permission to reprint granted by the publisher. This excerpt is from Garrett Hardin, "Tragedy of the Commons." *The Concise Encyclopedia of Economics*. 2008. Library of Economics and Liberty. 19 July 2010. <http://www.econlib.org/library/Enc/TragedyoftheCommons.html>.

devastation of common (i.e., not privately owned) pastures in England, asked: "Why are the cattle on a common so puny and stunted? Why is the common itself so bare-worn, and cropped so differently from the adjoining inclosures?"

Lloyd's answer assumed that each human exploiter of the common was guided by self-interest. At the point when the carrying capacity of the commons was fully reached, a herdsman might ask himself, "Should I add another animal to my herd?" Because the herdsman owned his animals, the gain of so doing would come solely to him. But the loss incurred by overloading the pasture would be "commonized" among all the herdsmen. Because the privatized gain would exceed his share of the commonized loss, a self-seeking herdsman would add another animal to his herd. And another. And reasoning in the same way, so would all the other herdsmen. Ultimately, the common property would be ruined.

Even when herdsmen understand the long-run consequences of their actions, they generally are powerless to prevent such damage without some coercive means of controlling the actions of each individual. Idealists may appeal to individuals caught in such a system, asking them to let the long-term effects govern their actions. But each individual must first survive in the short run. If all decision makers were unselfish and idealistic calculators, a distribution governed by the rule "to each according to his needs" might work. But such is not our world. As James Madison said in 1788, "If men were angels, no Government would be necessary" (*Federalist*, no. 51). That is, if *all* men were angels. But in a world in which all resources are limited, a single nonangel in the commons spoils the environment for all.

The spoilage process comes in two stages. First, the nonangel gains from his "competitive advantage" (pursuing his own interest at the expense of others) over the angels. Then, as the once noble angels realize that they are losing out, some of them renounce their angelic behavior. They try to get their share out of the commons before competitors do.

In other words, every workable distribution system must meet the challenge of human self-interest. An unmanaged commons in a world of limited material wealth and unlimited desires inevitably ends in ruin. Inevitability justifies the epithet "tragedy," which I introduced in 1968.

Whenever a distribution system malfunctions, we should be on the lookout for some sort of commons. Fish populations in the oceans have been decimated because people have interpreted the "freedom of the seas" to include an unlimited right to fish them. The fish were, in effect, a commons. In the 1970s, nations began to assert their sole right to fish out to two hundred miles from shore (instead of the traditional three miles). But these exclusive rights did not eliminate the problem of the commons. They merely restricted the commons to individual nations. Each nation still has the problem of allocating fishing rights among its own people on a noncommonized basis. If each government allowed ownership of fish within a given area, so that an owner could sue those who encroach on his fish, owners would have an incentive to refrain from overfishing. But governments do not do that. Instead, they often estimate the maximum sustainable yield and then restrict fishing either to a fixed number of days or to a fixed aggregate catch. Both systems result in a vast overinvestment in fishing boats and equipment as individual fishermen compete to catch fish quickly.

Some of the common pastures of old England were protected from ruin by the tradition of stinting—limiting each herdsman to a fixed number of animals (not necessarily the same for all). Such cases are spoken of as "managed commons," which is the logical equivalent of socialism. Viewed this way, socialism may be good or bad, depending on the quality of the management. As with all things human, there is no guarantee of permanent excellence. The old Roman warning must be kept constantly in mind: *Quis custodiet ipsos custodes?* (Who shall watch the watchers themselves?)

Under special circumstances even an unmanaged commons may work well. The principal requirement is that there be no scarcity of goods. Early frontiersmen in the American colonies killed as much game as they wanted without endangering the supply, the multiplication of which kept pace with their needs. But as the human population grew larger, hunting and trapping had to be managed. Thus, the ratio of supply to demand is critical.

The scale of the commons (the number of people using it) also is important, as an examination of Hutterite communities reveals. These devoutly religious people in the northwestern United States live by Marx's formula: "From each according to his ability, to each according to his needs." (They give no credit to Marx, however; similar language can be found several places in the Bible.) At first glance Hutterite colonies appear to be truly unmanaged commons. But appearances are deceiving. The number of people included in the decision unit is crucial. As the size of a colony approaches 150, individual Hutterites begin to undercontribute from their abilities and overdemand for their needs. The experience of Hutterite communities indicates that below 150 people, the distribution system can be managed by shame; above that approximate number, shame loses its effectiveness.

If any group could make a commonistic system work, an earnest religious community like the Hutterites should be able to. But numbers are the nemesis. In Madison's terms, nonangelic members then corrupt the angelic. Whenever size alters the properties of a system, engineers speak of a "scale effect." A scale effect, based on human psychology, limits the workability of commonistic systems.

Even when the shortcomings of the commons are understood, areas remain in which reform is difficult. No one owns the Earth's atmosphere. Therefore, it is treated as a common dump into which everyone may discharge wastes. Among the unwanted consequences of this behavior are acid rain, the greenhouse effect, and the erosion of the Earth's protective ozone layer. Industries and even nations are apt to regard the cleansing of industrial discharges as prohibitively expensive. The oceans are also treated as a common dump. Yet continuing to defend the freedom to pollute will ultimately lead to ruin for all. Nations are just beginning to evolve controls to limit this damage.

The tragedy of the commons also arose in the savings and loan (S&L) crisis. The federal government created this tragedy by forming the Federal Savings and Loan Insurance Corporation (FSLIC). The FSLIC relieved S&L depositors of worry about their money by guaranteeing that it would use taxpayers' money to repay them if an S&L went broke. In effect, the government made the taxpayers' money into a commons that S&Ls and their depositors could exploit. S&Ls had the incentive to make overly risky investments, and depositors did not have to care because they did not bear the cost. This, combined with faltering federal surveillance of the S&Ls, led to widespread failures. The losses were "commonized" among the nation's taxpayers, with serious consequences to the federal budget.

Congestion on public roads that do not charge tolls is another example of a government-created tragedy of the commons. If roads were privately owned, owners would charge tolls and people would take the toll into account in deciding whether to use them. Owners of private roads would probably also engage in what is called peak-load pricing, charging higher prices during times of peak demand and lower prices at other times. But because governments own roads that they finance with tax dollars, they normally do not charge tolls. The government makes roads into a commons. The result is congestion.

ABOUT THE AUTHOR

The late Garrett Hardin was professor emeritus of human ecology at the University of California at Santa Barbara. He died in 2003.

FURTHER READING

Berkes, Fikret. *Common Property Resources.* London: Belhaven Press, 1989.

Hardin, Garrett. *Filters Against Folly.* New York: Viking-Penguin, 1985.

Hardin, Garrett. "Living on a Lifeboat." *BioScience* 24 (1974): 561–568.

Hardin, Garrett. "The Tragedy of the Commons." *Science* 162 (1968): 1243–1248.

Hardin, Garrett, and John Baden, eds. *Managing the Commons.* San Francisco: W. H. Freeman, 1977.

Hiatt, Howard H. *America's Health in the Balance.* New York: Harper and Row, 1987.

McCay, Bonnie J., and James M. Acheson, eds. *The Question of the Commons.* Tucson: University of Arizona Press, 1987.

McGoodwin, James R. *Crisis in the World's Fisheries.* Stanford: Stanford University Press, 1990.

Ostrom, Elinor. *Governing the Commons.* New York: Cambridge University Press, 1990.

Two Treatises of Government

BOOK II, CHAPTER 2: OF THE STATE OF NATURE

§ 4.

To understand political power aright, and derive it from its original, we must consider what estate all men are naturally in, and that is, a state of perfect freedom to order their actions, and dispose of their possessions and persons as they think fit, within the bounds of the law of Nature, without asking leave or depending upon the will of any other man.

A state also of equality, wherein all the power and jurisdiction is reciprocal, no one having more than another, there being nothing more evident than that creatures of the same species and rank, promiscuously born to all the same advantages of Nature, and the use of the same faculties, should also be equal one amongst another, without subordination or subjection, unless the lord and master of them all should, by any manifest declaration of his will, set one above another, and confer on him, by an evident and clear appointment, an undoubted right to dominion and sovereignty.

§ 5. This equality of men by Nature, the judicious Hooker looks upon as so evident in itself, and beyond all question, that he makes it the foundation of that obligation to mutual love amongst men on which he builds the duties they owe one another, and from whence he derives the great maxims of justice and charity. His words are:

"The like natural inducement hath brought men to know that it is no less their duty to love others than themselves, for seeing those things which are equal, must needs all have

John Locke, "Book 2, Chapters 2, 4, & 5," from *Two Treatises of Government*. Copyright in the Public Domain.

Two Treatises of Government | 147

one measure; if I cannot but wish to receive good, even as much at every man's hands, as any man can wish unto his own soul, how should I look to have any part of my desire herein satisfied, unless myself be careful to satisfy the like desire, which is undoubtedly in other men weak, being of one and the same nature: to have anything offered them repugnant to this desire must needs, in all respects, grieve them as much as me; so that if I do harm, I must look to suffer, there being no reason that others should show greater measure of love to me than they have by me showed unto them; my desire, therefore, to be loved of my equals in Nature, as much as possible may be, imposeth upon me a natural duty of bearing to themward fully the like affection. From which relation of equality between ourselves and them that are as ourselves, what several rules and canons natural reason hath drawn for direction of life no man is ignorant." (Eccl. Pol. i.)

§ **6.** But though this be a state of liberty, yet it is not a state of licence; though man in that state have an uncontrollable liberty to dispose of his person or possessions, yet he has not liberty to destroy himself, or so much as any creature in his possession, but where some nobler use than its bare preservation calls for it. The state of Nature has a law of Nature to govern it, which obliges every one, and reason, which is that law, teaches all mankind who will but consult it, that being all equal and independent, no one ought to harm another in his life, health, liberty or possessions; for men being all the workmanship of one omnipotent and infinitely wise Maker; all the servants of one sovereign Master, sent into the world by His order and about His business; they are His property, whose workmanship they are made to last during His, not one another's pleasure. And, being furnished with like faculties, sharing all in one community of Nature, there cannot be supposed any such subordination among us that may authorise us to destroy one another, as if we were made for one another's uses, as the inferior ranks of creatures are for ours. Every one as he is bound to preserve himself, and not to quit his station wilfully, so by the like reason, when his own preservation comes not in competition, ought he as much as he can to preserve the rest of mankind, and not unless it be to do justice on an offender, take away or impair the life, or what tends to the preservation of the life, the liberty, health, limb, or goods of another.

§ **7.** And that all men may be restrained from invading others' rights, and from doing hurt to one another, and the law of Nature be observed, which willeth the peace and preservation of all mankind, the execution of the law of Nature is in that state put into every man's hands, whereby every one has a right to punish the transgressors of that law to such a degree as may hinder its violation. For the law of Nature would, as all other laws that concern men in this world, be in vain if there were nobody that in the state of Nature had a power to execute that law, and thereby preserve the innocent and restrain offenders; and if any one in the state of Nature may punish another for any evil he has done, every one may do so. For in that state of perfect equality, where naturally there is no superiority or jurisdiction of one over another, what any may do in prosecution of that law, every one must needs have a right to do.

§ 8. And thus, in the state of Nature, one man comes by a power over another, but yet no absolute or arbitrary power to use a criminal, when he has got him in his hands, according to the passionate heats or boundless extravagancy of his own will, but only to retribute to him so far as calm reason and conscience dictate, what is proportionate to his transgression, which is so much as may serve for reparation and restraint. For these two are the only reasons why one man may lawfully do harm to another, which is that we call punishment. In transgressing the law of Nature, the offender declares himself to live by another rule than that of reason and common equity, which is that measure God has set to the actions of men for their mutual security, and so he becomes dangerous to mankind; the tie which is to secure them from injury and violence being slighted and broken by him, which being a trespass against the whole species, and the peace and safety of it, provided for by the law of Nature, every man upon this score, by the right he hath to preserve mankind in general, may restrain, or where it is necessary, destroy things noxious to them, and so may bring such evil on any one who hath transgressed that law, as may make him repent the doing of it, and thereby deter him, and, by his example, others from doing the like mischief. And in this case, and upon this ground, every man hath a right to punish the offender, and be executioner of the law of Nature.

§ 9. I doubt not but this will seem a very strange doctrine to some men; but before they condemn it, I desire them to resolve me by what right any prince or state can put to death or punish an alien for any crime he commits in their country? It is certain their laws, by virtue of any sanction they receive from the promulgated will of the legislature, reach not a stranger. They speak not to him, nor, if they did, is he bound to hearken to them. The legislative authority by which they are in force over the subjects of that commonwealth hath no power over him. Those who have the supreme power of making laws in England, France, or Holland are, to an Indian, but like the rest of the world—men without authority. And therefore, if by the law of Nature every man hath not a power to punish offences against it, as he soberly judges the case to require, I see not how the magistrates of any community can punish an alien of another country, since, in reference to him, they can have no more power than what every man naturally may have over another.

§ 10. Besides the crime which consists in violating the laws, and varying from the right rule of reason, whereby a man so far becomes degenerate, and declares himself to quit the principles of human nature and to be a noxious creature, there is commonly injury done, and some person or other, some other man, receives damage by his transgression; in which case, he who hath received any damage has (besides the right of punishment common to him, with other men) a particular right to seek reparation from him that hath done it. And any other person who finds it just may also join with him that is injured, and assist him in recovering from the offender so much as may make satisfaction for the harm he hath suffered.

§ 11. From these two distinct rights (the one of punishing the crime, for restraint and preventing the like offence, which right of punishing is in everybody, the other of taking reparation, which belongs only to the injured party) comes it to pass that the magistrate, who by being magistrate hath the common right of punishing put into his hands, can often, where the public good demands not the execution of the law, remit the punishment of criminal offences by his own authority, but yet cannot remit the satisfaction due to any private man for the damage he has received. That he who hath suffered the damage has a right to demand in his own name, and he alone can remit. The damnified person has this power of appropriating to himself the goods or service of the offender by right of self-preservation, as every man has a power to punish the crime to prevent its being committed again, by the right he has of preserving all mankind, and doing all reasonable things he can in order to that end. And thus it is that every man in the state of Nature has a power to kill a murderer, both to deter others from doing the like injury (which no reparation can compensate) by the example of the punishment that attends it from everybody, and also to secure men from the attempts of a criminal who, having renounced reason, the common rule and measure God hath given to mankind, hath, by the unjust violence and slaughter he hath committed upon one, declared war against all mankind, and therefore may be destroyed as a lion or a tiger, one of those wild savage beasts with whom men can have no society nor security. And upon this is grounded that great law of nature, "Whoso sheddeth man's blood, by man shall his blood be shed." And Cain was so fully convinced that every one had a right to destroy such a criminal, that, after the murder of his brother, he cries out, "Every one that findeth me shall slay me," so plain was it writ in the hearts of all mankind.

§ 12. By the same reason may a man in the state of Nature punish the lesser breaches of that law, it will, perhaps, be demanded, with death? I answer: Each transgression may be punished to that degree, and with so much severity, as will suffice to make it an ill bargain to the offender, give him cause to repent, and terrify others from doing the like. Every offence that can be committed in the state of Nature may, in the state of Nature, be also punished equally, and as far forth, as it may, in a commonwealth. For though it would be beside my present purpose to enter here into the particulars of the law of Nature, or its measures of punishment, yet it is certain there is such a law, and that too as intelligible and plain to a rational creature and a studier of that law as the positive laws of commonwealths, nay, possibly plainer; as much as reason is easier to be understood than the fancies and intricate contrivances of men, following contrary and hidden interests put into words; for truly so are a great part of the municipal laws of countries, which are only so far right as they are founded on the law of Nature, by which they are to be regulated and interpreted.

§ 13. To this strange doctrine—viz., That in the state of Nature every one has the executive power of the law of Nature—I doubt not but it will be objected that it is unreasonable for men to be judges in their own cases, that self-love will make men partial to themselves and their friends; and, on the other side, ill-nature, passion, and revenge will carry them too far in punishing others, and hence nothing but confusion and disorder will follow, and that therefore God hath certainly appointed government to restrain the partiality and violence of men. I easily grant that civil government is the proper remedy for the inconveniences of the state of Nature, which must certainly be great where men may be judges in their own case, since it is easy to be imagined that he who was so unjust as to do his brother an injury will scarce be so just as to condemn himself for it. But I shall desire those who make this objection to remember that absolute monarchs are but men; and if government is to be the remedy of those evils which necessarily follow from men being judges in their own cases, and the state of Nature is therefore not to be endured, I desire to know what kind of government that is, and how much better it is than the state of Nature, where one man commanding a multitude has the liberty to be judge in his own case, and may do to all his subjects whatever he pleases without the least question or control of those who execute his pleasure? and in whatsoever he doth, whether led by reason, mistake, or passion, must be submitted to? which men in the state of Nature are not bound to do one to another. And if he that judges, judges amiss in his own or any other case, he is answerable for it to the rest of mankind.

§ 14. It is often asked as a mighty objection, where are, or ever were, there any men in such a state of Nature? To which it may suffice as an answer at present, that since all princes and rulers of "independent" governments all through the world are in a state of Nature, it is plain the world never was, nor never will be, without numbers of men in that state. I have named all governors of "independent" communities, whether they are, or are not, in league with others; for it is not every compact that puts an end to the state of Nature between men, but only this one of agreeing together mutually to enter into one community, and make one body politic; other promises and compacts men may make one with another, and yet still be in the state of Nature. The promises and bargains for truck, etc., between the two men in Soldania, in or between a Swiss and an Indian, in the woods of America, are binding to them, though they are perfectly in a state of Nature in reference to one another for truth, and keeping of faith belongs to men as men, and not as members of society.

§ 15. To those that say there were never any men in the state of Nature, I will not oppose the authority of the judicious Hooker (Eccl. Pol. i. 10), where he says, "the laws which have been hitherto mentioned"—i.e., the laws of Nature—"do bind men absolutely, even as they are men, although they have never any settled fellowship, never any solemn agreement amongst themselves what to do or not to do; but for as much as we are not by ourselves sufficient to furnish ourselves with competent store of things needful for such a life as our Nature doth desire, a life fit for the dignity of man, therefore to supply those defects and imperfections which are in us, as living single and solely by ourselves, we are naturally induced to seek communion and fellowship with others; this was the cause of men uniting themselves as first in politic societies." But I, moreover, affirm that all men are naturally in that state, and remain so till, by their own consents, they make themselves members of some politic society, and I doubt not, in the sequel of this discourse, to make it very clear.

BOOK II, CHAPTER 4: OF SLAVERY

§ 21. The natural liberty of man is to be free from any superior power on earth, and not to be under the will or legislative authority of man, but to have only the law of Nature for his rule. The liberty of man in society is to be under no other legislative power but that established by consent in the commonwealth, nor under the dominion of any will, or restraint of any law, but what that legislative shall enact according to the trust put in it. Freedom, then, is not what Sir Robert Filmer tells us: "A liberty for every one to do what he lists, to live as he pleases, and not to be tied by any laws;" but freedom of men under government is to have a standing rule to live by, common to every one of that society, and made by the legislative power erected in it. A liberty to follow my own will in all things where that rule prescribes not, not to be subject to the inconstant, uncertain, unknown, arbitrary will of another man, as freedom of nature is to be under no other restraint but the law of Nature.

§ 22. This freedom from absolute, arbitrary power is so necessary to, and closely joined with, a man's preservation, that he cannot part with it but by what forfeits his preservation and life together. For a man, not having the power of his own life, cannot by compact or his own consent enslave himself to any one, nor put himself under the absolute, arbitrary power of another to take away his life when he pleases. Nobody can give more power than he has himself, and he that cannot take away his own life cannot give another power over it. Indeed, having by his fault forfeited his own life by some act that deserves death, he to whom he has forfeited it may, when he has him in his power, delay to take it, and make use of him to his own service; and he does him no injury by it. For, whenever he finds the hardship of his slavery outweigh the value of his life, it is in his power, by resisting the will of his master, to draw on himself the death he desires.

§ 23. This is the perfect condition of slavery, which is nothing else but the state of war continued between a lawful conqueror and a captive, for if once compact enter between them, and make an agreement for a limited power on the one side, and obedience on the other, the state of war and slavery ceases as long as the compact endures; for, as has been said, no man can by agreement pass over to another that which he hath not in himself—a power over his own life.

I confess, we find among the Jews, as well as other nations, that men did sell themselves; but it is plain this was only to drudgery, not to slavery; for it is evident the person sold was not under an absolute, arbitrary, despotical power, for the master could not have power to kill him at any time, whom at a certain time he was obliged to let go free out of his service; and the master of such a servant was so far from having an arbitrary power over his life that he could not at pleasure so much as maim him, but the loss of an eye or tooth set him free (Exod. 21.).

BOOK II, CHAPTER 5: OF PROPERTY

§ 24. Whether we consider natural reason, which tells us that men, being once born, have a right to their preservation, and consequently to meat and drink and such other things as Nature affords for their subsistence, or "revelation," which gives us an account of those grants God made of the world to Adam, and to Noah and his sons, it is very clear that God, as King David says (Psalm 115:16), "has given the earth to the children of men," given it to mankind in common. But, this being supposed, it seems to some a very great difficulty how any one should ever come to have a property in anything, I will not content myself to answer, that, if it be difficult to make out "property" upon a supposition that God gave the world to Adam and his posterity in common, it is impossible that any man but one universal monarch should have any "property" upon a supposition that God gave the world to Adam and his heirs in succession, exclusive of all the rest of his posterity; but I shall endeavour to show how men might come to have a property in several parts of that which God gave to mankind in common, and that without any express compact of all the commoners.

§ 25. God, who hath given the world to men in common, hath also given them reason to make use of it to the best advantage of life and convenience. The earth and all that is therein is given to men for the support and comfort of their being. And though all the fruits it naturally produces, and beasts it feeds, belong to mankind in common, as they are produced by the spontaneous hand of Nature, and nobody has originally a private dominion exclusive of the rest of mankind in any of them, as they are thus in their natural state, yet being given for the use of men, there must of necessity be a means to appropriate them some way or other before they can be of any use, or at all beneficial, to any particular men. The fruit or venison which nourishes the wild Indian, who knows no enclosure, and is still a tenant in common, must be his, and so his—i.e., a part of him, that another can no longer have any right to it before it can do him any good for the support of his life.

§ 26. Though the earth and all inferior creatures be common to all men, yet every man has a "property" in his own "person." This nobody has any right to but himself. The "labour" of his body and the "work" of his hands, we may say, are properly his. Whatsoever, then, he removes out of the state that Nature hath provided and left it in, he hath mixed his labour with it, and joined to it something that is his own, and thereby makes it his property. It being by him removed from the common state Nature placed it in, it hath by this labour something annexed to it that excludes the common right of other men. For this "labour" being the unquestionable property of the labourer, no man but he can have a right to what that is once joined to, at least where there is enough, and as good left in common for others.

§ 27. He that is nourished by the acorns he picked up under an oak, or the apples he gathered from the trees in the wood, has certainly appropriated them to himself. Nobody can deny but the nourishment is his. I ask, then, when did they begin to be his? when he digested? or when he ate? or when he boiled? or when he brought them home? or when he picked them up? And it is plain, if the first gathering made them not his, nothing else could. That labour put a distinction between them and common. That added something to them more than Nature, the common mother of all, had done, and so they became his private right. And will any one say he had no right to those acorns or apples he thus appropriated because he had not the consent of all mankind to make them his? Was it a robbery thus to assume to himself what belonged to all in common? If such a consent as that was necessary, man had starved, notwithstanding the plenty God had given him. We see in commons, which remain so by compact, that it is the taking any part of what is common, and removing it out of the state Nature leaves it in, which begins the property, without which the common is of no use. And the taking of this or that part does not depend on the express consent of all the commoners. Thus, the grass my horse has bit, the turfs my servant has cut, and the ore I have digged in any place, where I have a right to them in common with others, become my property without the assignation or consent of anybody. The labour that was mine, removing them out of that common state they were in, hath fixed my property in them.

§ 28. By making an explicit consent of every commoner necessary to any one's appropriating to himself any part of what is given in common. Children or servants could not cut the meat which their father or master had provided for them in common without assigning to every one his peculiar part. Though the water running in the fountain be every one's, yet who can doubt but that in the pitcher is his only who drew it out? His labour hath taken it out of the hands of Nature where it was common, and belonged equally to all her children, and hath thereby appropriated it to himself.

§ 29. Thus this law of reason makes the deer that Indian's who hath killed it; it is allowed to be his goods who hath bestowed his labour upon it, though, before, it was the common right of every one. And amongst those who are counted the civilised part of mankind, who have made and multiplied positive laws to determine property, this original law of Nature for the beginning of property, in what was before common, still takes place, and by virtue thereof, what fish any one catches in the ocean, that great and still remaining common of mankind; or what amber-gris any one takes up here is by the labour that removes it out of that common state Nature left it in, made his property who takes that pains about it. And even amongst us, the hare that any one is hunting is thought his who pursues her during the chase. For being a beast that is still looked upon as common, and no man's private possession, whoever has employed so much labour about any of that kind as to find and pursue her has thereby removed her from the state of Nature wherein she was common, and hath begun a property.

§ 30. It will, perhaps, be objected to this, that if gathering the acorns or other fruits of the earth, etc., makes a right to them, then any one may engross as much as he will. To which I answer, not so. The same law of Nature that does by this means give us property, does also bound that property too. "God has given us all things richly." Is the voice of reason confirmed by inspiration? But how far has He given it us "to enjoy"? As much as any one can make use of to any advantage of life before it spoils, so much he may by his labour fix a property in. Whatever is beyond this is more than his share, and belongs to others. Nothing was made by God for man to spoil or destroy. And thus considering the plenty of natural provisions there was a long time in the world, and the few spenders, and to how small a part of that provision the industry of one man could extend itself and engross it to the prejudice of others, especially keeping within the bounds set by reason of what might serve for his use, there could be then little room for quarrels or contentions about property so established.

§ 31. But the chief matter of property being now not the fruits of the earth and the beasts that subsist on it, but the earth itself, as that which takes in and carries with it all the rest, I think it is plain that property in that too is acquired as the former. As much land as a man tills, plants, improves, cultivates, and can use the product of, so much is his property. He by his labour does, as it were, enclose it from the common. Nor will it invalidate his right to say everybody else has an equal title to it, and therefore he cannot appropriate, he cannot enclose, without the consent of all his fellow-commoners, all mankind. God, when He gave the world in common to all mankind, commanded man also to labour, and the penury of his condition required it of him. God and his reason commanded him to subdue the earth—i.e., improve it for the benefit of life and therein lay out something upon it that was his own, his labour. He that, in obedience to this command of God, subdued, tilled, and sowed any part of it, thereby annexed to it something that was his property, which another had no title to, nor could without injury take from him.

§ 32. Nor was this appropriation of any parcel of land, by improving it, any prejudice to any other man, since there was still enough and as good left, and more than the yet unprovided could use. So that, in effect, there was never the less left for others because of his enclosure for himself. For he that leaves as much as another can make use of does as good as take nothing at all. Nobody could think himself injured by the drinking of another man, though he took a good draught, who had a whole river of the same water left him to quench his thirst. And the case of land and water, where there is enough of both, is perfectly the same.

§ 33. God gave the world to men in common, but since He gave it them for their benefit and the greatest conveniencies of life they were capable to draw from it, it cannot be supposed He meant it should always remain common and uncultivated. He gave it to the use of the industrious and rational (and labour was to be his title to it); not to the fancy or covetousness of the quarrelsome and contentious. He that had as good left for his improvement as was already taken up needed not complain, ought not to meddle with what was already improved by another's labour; if he did it is plain he desired the benefit of another's pains, which he had no right to, and not the ground which God had given him, in common with others, to labour on, and whereof there was as good left as that already possessed, and more than he knew what to do with, or his industry could reach to.

§ 34. It is true, in land that is common in England or any other country, where there are plenty of people under government who have money and commerce, no one can enclose or appropriate any part without the consent of all his fellow commoners; because this is left common by compact—i.e., by the law of the land, which is not to be violated. And, though it be common in respect of some men, it is not so to all mankind, but is the joint propriety of this country, or this parish. Besides, the remainder, after such enclosure, would not be as good to the rest of the commoners as the whole was, when they could all make use of the whole; whereas in the beginning and first peopling of the great common of the world it was quite otherwise. The law man was under was rather for appropriating. God commanded, and his wants forced him to labour. That was his property, which could not be taken from him wherever he had fixed it. And hence subduing or cultivating the earth and having dominion, we see, are joined together. The one gave title to the other. So that God, by commanding to subdue, gave authority so far to appropriate. And the condition of human life, which requires labour and materials to work on, necessarily introduce private possessions.

§ 35. The measure of property Nature well set, by the extent of men's labour and the conveniency of life. No man's labour could subdue or appropriate all, nor could his enjoyment consume more than a small part; so that it was impossible for any man, this way, to entrench upon the right of another or acquire to himself a property to the prejudice of his neighbour, who would still have room for as good and as large a possession (after the other had taken out his) as before it was appropriated. Which measure did confine every man's possession to a very moderate proportion, and such as he might appropriate to himself without injury to anybody in the first ages of the world, when men were more in danger to be lost, by wandering from their company, in the then vast wilderness of the earth than to be straitened for want of room to plant in.

§ 36. The same measure may be allowed still, without prejudice to anybody, full as the world seems. For, supposing a man or family, in the state they were at first, peopling of the world by the children of Adam or Noah, let him plant in some inland vacant places of America. We shall find that the possessions he could make himself, upon the measures we have given, would not be very large, nor, even to this day, prejudice the rest of mankind or give them reason to complain or think themselves injured by this man's encroachment, though the race of men have now spread themselves to all the corners of the world, and do infinitely exceed the small number was at the beginning. Nay, the extent of ground is of so little value without labour that I have heard it affirmed that in Spain itself a man may be permitted to plough, sow, and reap, without being disturbed, upon land he has no other title to, but only his making use of it. But, on the contrary, the inhabitants think themselves beholden to him who, by his industry on neglected, and consequently waste land, has increased the stock of corn, which they wanted. But be this as it will, which I lay no stress on, this I dare boldly affirm, that the same rule of propriety—viz., that every man should have as much as he could make use of, would hold still in the world, without straitening anybody, since there is land enough in the world to suffice double the inhabitants, had not the invention of money, and the tacit agreement of men to put a value on it, introduced (by consent) larger possessions and a right to them; which, how it has done, I shall by and by show more at large.

§ 37. This is certain, that in the beginning, before the desire of having more than men needed had altered the intrinsic value of things, which depends only on their usefulness to the life of man, or had agreed that a little piece of yellow metal, which would keep without wasting or decay, should be worth a great piece of flesh or a whole heap of corn, though men had a right to appropriate by their labour, each one to himself, as much of the things of Nature as he could use, yet this could not be much, nor to the prejudice of others, where the same plenty was still left, to those who would use the same industry.

Before the appropriation of land, he who gathered as much of the wild fruit, killed, caught, or tamed as many of the beasts as he could—he that so employed his pains about any of the spontaneous products of Nature as any way to alter them from the state Nature put them in, by placing any of his labour on them, did thereby acquire a propriety in them; but if they perished in his possession without their due use—if the fruits rotted or the venison putrefied before he could spend it, he offended against the common law of Nature, and was liable to be punished: he invaded his neighbour's share, for he had no right farther than his use called for any of them, and they might serve to afford him conveniencies of life.

§ 38. The same measures governed the possession of land, too. Whatsoever he tilled and reaped, laid up and made use of before it spoiled, that was his peculiar right; whatsoever he enclosed, and could feed and make use of, the cattle and product was also his. But if either the grass of his enclosure rotted on the ground, or the fruit of his planting perished without gathering and laying up, this part of the earth, notwithstanding his enclosure, was still to be looked on as waste, and might be the possession of any other. Thus, at the beginning, Cain might take as much ground as he could till and make it his own land, and yet leave enough to Abel's sheep to feed on: a few acres would serve for both their possessions. But as families increased and industry enlarged their stocks, their possessions enlarged with the need of them; but yet it was commonly without any fixed property in the ground they made use of till they incorporated, settled themselves together, and built cities, and then, by consent, they came in time to set out the bounds of their distinct territories and agree on limits between them and their neighbours, and by laws within themselves settled the properties of those of the same society. For we see that in that part of the world which was first inhabited, and therefore like to be best peopled, even as low down as Abraham's time, they wandered with their flocks and their herds, which was their substance, freely up and down—and this Abraham did in a country where he was a stranger; whence it is plain that, at least, a great part of the land lay in common, that the inhabitants valued it not, nor claimed property in any more than they made use of; but when there was not room enough in the same place for their herds to feed together, they, by consent, as Abraham and Lot did (Gen. 13:5), separated and enlarged their pasture where it best liked them.

And for the same reason, Esau went from his father and his brother, and planted in Mount Seir (Gen. 36:6).

§ 39. And thus, without supposing any private dominion and property in Adam over all the world, exclusive of all other men, which can no way be proved, nor any one's property be made out from it, but supposing the world, given as it was to the children of men in common, we see how labour could make men distinct titles to several parcels of it for their private uses, wherein there could be no doubt of right, no room for quarrel.

§ 40. Nor is it so strange as, perhaps, before consideration, it may appear, that the property of labour should be able to overbalance the community of land, for it is labour indeed that puts the difference of value on everything; and let any one consider what the difference is between an acre of land planted with tobacco or sugar, sown with wheat or barley, and an acre of the same land lying in common without any husbandry upon it, and he will find that the improvement of labour makes the far greater part of the value. I think it will be but a very modest computation to say, that of the products of the earth useful to the life of man, nine-tenths are the effects of labour. Nay, if we will rightly estimate things as they come to our use, and cast up the several expenses about them—what in them is purely owing to Nature and what to labour—we shall find that in most of them ninety-nine hundredths are wholly to be put on the account of labour.

§ 41. There cannot be a clearer demonstration of anything than several nations of the Americans are of this, who are rich in land and poor in all the comforts of life; whom Nature, having furnished as liberally as any other people with the materials of plenty— i.e., a fruitful soil, apt to produce in abundance what might serve for food, raiment, and delight; yet, for want of improving it by labour, have not one hundredth part of the conveniencies we enjoy, and a king of a large and fruitful territory there feeds, lodges, and is clad worse than a day labourer in England.

§ 42. To make this a little clearer, let us but trace some of the ordinary provisions of life, through their several progresses, before they come to our use, and see how much they receive of their value from human industry. Bread, wine, and cloth are things of daily use and great plenty; yet notwithstanding acorns, water, and leaves, or skins must be our bread, drink and clothing, did not labour furnish us with these more useful commodities. For whatever bread is more worth than acorns, wine than water, and cloth or silk than leaves, skins or moss, that is wholly owing to labour and industry. The one of these being the food and raiment which unassisted Nature furnishes us with; the other provisions which our industry and pains prepare for us, which how much they exceed the other in value, when any one hath computed, he will then see how much labour makes the far greatest part of the value of things we enjoy in this world; and the ground which produces the materials is scarce to be reckoned in as any, or at most, but a very small part of it; so little, that even amongst us, land that is left wholly to nature, that hath no improvement of pasturage, tillage, or planting, is called, as indeed it is, waste; and we shall find the benefit of it amount to little more than nothing.

§ 43. An acre of land that bears here twenty bushels of wheat, and another in America, which, with the same husbandry, would do the like, are, without doubt, of the same natural, intrinsic value. But yet the benefit mankind receives from one in a year is worth five pounds, and the other possibly not worth a penny; if all the profit an Indian received from it were to be valued and sold here, at least I may truly say, not one thousandth. It is labour, then, which puts the greatest part of value upon land, without which it would scarcely be worth anything; it is to that we owe the greatest part of all its useful products; for all that the straw, bran, bread, of that acre of wheat, is more worth than the product of an acre of as good land which lies waste is all the effect of labour. For it is not barely the ploughman's pains, the reaper's and thresher's toil, and the baker's sweat, is to be counted into the bread we eat; the labour of those who broke the oxen, who digged and wrought the iron and stones, who felled and framed the timber employed about the plough, mill, oven, or any other utensils, which are a vast number, requisite to this corn, from its sowing to its being made bread, must all be charged on the account of labour, and received as an effect of that; Nature and the earth furnished only the almost worthless materials as in themselves. It would be a strange catalogue of things that industry provided and made use of about every loaf of bread before it came to our use if we could trace them; iron, wood, leather, bark, timber, stone, bricks, coals, lime, cloth, dyeing-drugs, pitch, tar, masts, ropes, and all the materials made use of in the ship that brought any of the commodities made use of by any of the workmen, to any part of the work, all which it would be almost impossible, at least too long, to reckon up.

§ 44. From all which it is evident, that though the things of Nature are given in common, man (by being master of himself, and proprietor of his own person, and the actions or labour of it) had still in himself the great foundation of property; and that which made up the great part of what he applied to the support or comfort of his being, when invention and arts had improved the conveniences of life, was perfectly his own, and did not belong in common to others.

§ 45. Thus labour, in the beginning, gave a right of property, wherever any one was pleased to employ it, upon what was common, which remained a long while, the far greater part, and is yet more than mankind makes use of Men at first, for the most part, contented themselves with what unassisted Nature offered to their necessities; and though afterwards, in some parts of the world, where the increase of people and stock, with the use of money, had made land scarce, and so of some value, the several communities settled the bounds of their distinct territories, and, by laws, within themselves, regulated the properties of the private men of their society, and so, by compact and agreement, settled the property which labour and industry began. And the leagues that have been made between several states and kingdoms, either expressly or tacitly disowning all claim and right to the land in the other's possession, have, by common consent, given up their pretences to their natural common right, which originally they had to those countries; and so have, by positive agreement, settled a property amongst themselves, in distinct parts of the world;

yet there are still great tracts of ground to be found, which the inhabitants thereof, not having joined with the rest of mankind in the consent of the use of their common money, lie waste, and are more than the people who dwell on it, do, or can make use of, and so still lie in common; though this can scarce happen amongst that part of mankind that have consented to the use of money.

§ 46. The greatest part of things really useful to the life of man, and such as the necessity of subsisting made the first commoners of the world look after—as it doth the Americans now—are generally things of short duration, such as—if they are not consumed by use—will decay and perish of themselves. Gold, silver, and diamonds are things that fancy or agreement hath put the value on, more than real use and the necessary support of life. Now of those good things which Nature hath provided in common, every one hath a right (as hath been said) to as much as he could use; and had a property in all he could effect with his labour; all that his industry could extend to, to alter from the state Nature had put it in, was his. He that gathered a hundred bushels of acorns or apples had thereby a property in them; they were his goods as soon as gathered. He was only to look that he used them before they spoiled, else he took more than his share, and robbed others. And, indeed, it was a foolish thing, as well as dishonest, to hoard up more than he could make use of. If he gave away a part to anybody else, so that it perished not uselessly in his possession, these he also made use of. And if he also bartered away plums that would have rotted in a week, for nuts that would last good for his eating a whole year, he did no injury; he wasted not the common stock; destroyed no part of the portion of goods that belonged to others, so long as nothing perished uselessly in his hands. Again, if he would give his nuts for a piece of metal, pleased with its colour, or exchange his sheep for shells, or wool for a sparkling pebble or a diamond, and keep those by him all his life, he invaded not the right of others; he might heap up as much of these durable things as he pleased; the exceeding of the bounds of his just property not lying in the largeness of his possession, but the perishing of anything uselessly in it.

§ 47. And thus came in the use of money; some lasting thing that men might keep without spoiling, and that, by mutual consent, men would take in exchange for the truly useful but perishable supports of life.

§ 48. And as different degrees of industry were apt to give men possessions in different proportions, so this invention of money gave them the opportunity to continue and enlarge them. For supposing an island, separate from all possible commerce with the rest of the world, wherein there were but a hundred families, but there were sheep, horses, and cows, with other useful animals, wholesome fruits, and land enough for corn for a hundred thousand times as many, but nothing in the island, either because of its commonness or perishableness, fit to supply the place of money. What reason could any one have there to enlarge his possessions beyond the use of his family, and a plentiful supply to its consumption, either in what their own industry produced, or they could barter for like perishable, useful commodities with others? Where there is not something both lasting and scarce, and so valuable to be hoarded up, there men will not be apt to enlarge their possessions of land, were it never so rich, never so free for them to take. For I ask, what would a man value ten thousand or an hundred thousand acres of excellent land, ready cultivated and well stocked, too, with cattle, in the middle of the inland parts of America, where he had no hopes of commerce with other parts of the world, to draw money to him by the sale of the product? It would not be worth the enclosing, and we should see him give up again to the wild common of Nature whatever was more than would supply the conveniences of life, to be had there for him and his family.

§ 49. Thus, in the beginning, all the world was America, and more so than that is now; for no such thing as money was anywhere known. Find out something that hath the use and value of money amongst his neighbours, you shall see the same man will begin presently to enlarge his possessions.

§ 50. But, since gold and silver, being little useful to the life of man, in proportion to food, raiment, and carriage, has its value only from the consent of men—whereof labour yet makes in great part the measure—it is plain that the consent of men have agreed to a disproportionate and unequal possession of the earth—I mean out of the bounds of society and compact; for in governments the laws regulate it; they having, by consent, found out and agreed in a way how a man may, rightfully and without injury, possess more than he himself can make use of by receiving gold and silver, which may continue long in a man's possession without decaying for the overplus, and agreeing those metals should have a value.

§ 51. And thus, I think, it is very easy to conceive, without any difficulty, how labour could at first begin a title of property in the common things of Nature, and how the spending it upon our uses bounded it; so that there could then be no reason of quarrelling about title, nor any doubt about the largeness of possession it gave. Right and conveniency went together. For as a man had a right to all he could employ his labour upon, so he had no temptation to labour for more than he could make use of. This left no room for controversy about the title, nor for encroachment on the right of others. What portion a man carved to himself was easily seen; and it was useless, as well as dishonest, to carve himself too much, or take more than he needed.

Locke on Land and Labor

DANIEL RUSSELL

B read is the staff of life. So what makes its existence possible? Well, people make bread from the fruits of the land, so it takes two things to make bread: productive people and fruitful land. But what sort of contributions to our bread do land and labor make? Does one make a greater contribution to our bread? Do they make the same kind of contribution? John Locke raises these questions in the fifth chapter of the *Second Treatise of Government,* and argues that labor is by far the greater contributor to our bread than land is. This is an extraordinary claim: how can labor be more responsible for production than land is, since labor cannot produce anything by itself? Of what does labor contribute "more" than land does? How can labor be what creates usable things, since expending great effort on something is often neither necessary nor sufficient for making it more useful?

I argue that Locke's claim about labor is not only extraordinary, but also deeply insightful. My approach shall be threefold. First, I argue that a well-known criticism of Locke in G.A. Cohen's article, "Marx and Locke on Land and Labour," fails to grasp Locke's insight about labor, and fails in instructive ways. Second, I show what Locke's view of the nature of labor is, and why it is insightful. Finally, I show how this insight overcomes many of the most common, and most worrisome, objections to Locke's labor theory of value.

***

Daniel Russell, "Locke on Land and Labor," from *Philosophical Studies: An International Journal for Philosophy in the Analytic Tradition*, Vol. 117, No. 1/2; January 2004, pp. 303–325. Copyright © 2004 by Springer. Permission to reprint granted by the publisher.

It is important first to observe that Locke's labor theory of value is a theory of use-value, and not of exchange-value. The difference is that use-value is the value that something has for satisfying a need or desire, whereas *exchange*-value is the value at which something will exchange for other things;[1] a pencil, say, will have use-value if someone can write with it, and exchange-value if someone can sell or trade it. These types of value are related—usually people desire to trade for a thing because of its anticipated usefulness to them—but they still are different kinds of values. It is clear that Locke's labor theory concerns use-value rather than exchange-value, for several reasons.[2] For one thing, Locke's stated aim is to explain how labor affects the production of "the provisions serving to the support of human life" (*Second Treatise of Government* V, 37, emphasis added), that is, the use-value of land for producing useful goods; and he concludes that "the improvement of labour makes the far greater part of the value [of land]. I think it will be but a very modest computation to say, that of the products of the earth useful to the life of man nine tenths are the effects of labour (V, 40, emphasis added). And while Locke does say that labor can increase the exchange-value of land, he believes that it does so only because it directly increases the land's productivity.[3] It is labor's power to increase use-value, and the importance of that power, that is the concern of Locke's labor theory of value.[4]

Cohen argues that that theory relies on an absurd criterion for determining the relative contributions of labor and land to their joint yield.[5] Consider Locke's claim that

> the provisions serving to the support of human life produced by one acre of enclosed and cultivated land are (to speak much within compass) ten times more than those which are yielded by an acre of land of an equal richness lying waste in common … I have here rated the improved land very low, in making its product but as ten to one, when it is much nearer a hundred to one.[6]

To motivate this claim on Locke's behalf, Cohen offers what he calls the "subtraction criterion," which is a special case of the following general criterion for calculating the relative contributions of any two factors x and y to some joint yield:

$$\frac{(\text{yield of y given x})-(\text{yield of y})}{(\text{yield of y given x})} = C_x \text{ (contribution of x)}$$

We can then easily determine C_y as well, since $C_y = 1 - C_x$.[7] So suppose that some parcel of land yields 100 units of wheat with labor, and none without labor:[8]

$$\frac{(\text{yield of land given labor})-(\text{yield of land without labor})}{(\text{yield of land given labor})} = C_{labor}$$

Subtracting 0 units from 100 units and dividing the difference by 100 units gives us 1.0, or 100%, as C_{labor}, and so C_{land} will be 0%.

But notice what happens when we calculate C_{land} first, and then determine C_{labor}.[9] Obviously we cannot compare the yield of labor on land to the yield of labor *without* land, and so Cohen compares the yield of labor on land to the yield of the same labor on a different, *infertile* parcel of land, that is, land which makes no contribution to the process at all:

$$\frac{\text{(yield of labor on actual land)—(yield of labor on infertile land)}}{\text{(yield of labor on actual land)}} = C_{land}$$

If we suppose another 100-unit yield, then since the yield of labor on infertile land is 0 units, C_{land} turns out to be 100%—which is impossible if C_{labor} is also 100%![10] Labor and land, then, each turn out to contribute both everything and nothing to the yield. So the subtraction criterion is absurd, and so also, on Cohen's reading, is Locke's case for the greater contribution of labor.

But Locke is not committed to this absurd result, for a number of reasons. For one thing, Locke states explicitly that the plots of land compared are to be "of an equal *richness*" (V, 37, emphasis added), and is careful to restrict his comparisons to equally fertile lands, as when he compares the product of land that has been labored on with "the product of an acre of *as good land*, which lies waste" (V, 43, emphasis added).[11] And we have good reason to hold fertility constant in these kinds of comparisons. If we vary the fertility of the lands whose yields we are measuring, we may always artificially inflate the contribution of labor, simply by making the hypothetical parcel naturally poorer than the actual parcel. If fertility need not be constant in the calculation of C^{land}, then it need not be constant in the calculation of C_{labor} either, as each is an instance of the same criterion. This yields the following subtraction criteria:

$$\frac{\text{(yield of labor on land A)—(yield of labor on land B)}}{\text{(yield of labor on land A)}} = C_{landA}$$

and

$$\frac{\text{(yield of land A given labor on land A)—(yield of land B)}}{\text{(yield of land A given labor on land A)}} = C_{labor}$$

We can therefore inflate C_{labor} simply by making B poorer than A; in fact, we can make C_{landA} *negative* if we imagine B as more productive without labor than A is with labor, in which case A will have detracted from its own yield, and C_{labor} will be greater than 100%.

The comparisons that Cohen imagines are clearly meaningless, and so such factors as fertility *must* be held constant in comparisons of yields.

Moreover—and more important, philosophically—the labor on the actual parcel typically includes the very *selection* of that parcel, which is a considerable form of labor, indeed.[12] Obviously, one's labor on a plot of land does not begin only *after* the plot has been chosen, and so the labor on some imagined parcel will be crucially different from the labor on an actual parcel that one has chosen *because* of its fertility. And Locke is explicitly aware of the importance of selection:

> Where there is not some thing, both lasting and scarce, and so valuable to be hoarded up, there men will not be apt to enlarge their *possessions of land*, were it never so rich, never so free for them to take: for I ask, what would a man value ten thousand, or an hundred thousand acres of excellent *land*, ready cultivated, and well stocked too with cattle, in the middle of the inland parts of America, where he had no hopes of commerce with other parts of the world, to draw *money* to him by the sale of the product? It would not be worth the inclosing, and we should see him give up again to the wild common of nature, whatever was more than would supply the conveniences of life to be had there for him and his family. (V, 48, emphasis in original)

Some of the things, then, that go into selecting a piece of farming land are its location, its availability ("were it ... never so free for them to take"), *and its fertility* ("were it never so rich"). Since Locke does *not* allow fertility to vary between cases—and most reasonably so—it is patently clear that Locke does not hold the criterion that Cohen attributes to him. So Cohen's objection simply misfires.

But Locke is not off the hook yet. According to Cohen, Locke is trying "to answer something like the Shapley allocation problem," by determining "what different factors contribute to the product (in order, on that basis, to do some appropriate rewarding)";[13] and the point of answering that problem is to show what rewards such meritorious contributors could appropriately expect.[14] But notice that not only fertility of soil, but also good climate, location, and weather, absence of vermin and pests, and hence a fair measure of good fortune all make some contribution. Of course, the subtraction criterion could be rigged so as to hold these external factors constant, but that very rigging would only point out how much of the value of a parcel of land is not attributable to labor; in that case, a laborer could never be quite deserving enough to claim full title to his product. Hence, as Kristin Shrader-Frechette[15] points out, if Locke is trying to answer an allocation problem, then the fact that there is "some fraction of land value not created by human labor" may imply that "there is some fraction of property rights in land that cannot be appropriated from the commons,"[16] which, embarrassingly, is not the conclusion that Locke draws.

But Locke is not trying to solve an allocation problem. It's not simply that Locke does not accept the subtraction criterion that Cohen attributes to him, but that Locke does not accept any form of the subtraction criterion at all, because Locke's point in these passages is to deny the commensurability of the contributions of land and labor that the subtraction criterion—and the allocation problem—requires. The heart of Cohen's objection to Locke is his assumption that land and labor should be *commensurable*, contributing to the creation of goods in just the same way. This assumption is often motivated by the further assumption that Locke's concern is how labor establishes relative merit. As a result, many have come to think that, for Locke, labor is the same as "hard work" or effort, on the basis of which a laborer might be said to be deserving of reward. However, all three of these assumptions are false, and false for the same reason: the point of Locke's labor theory of use-value is to show that labor is a kind of agency that gives land direction with respect to our needs and purposes. Since land provides what can be given direction, while labor provides the direction itself, land and labor make *different kinds* of contributions to their joint yields. Moreover, on this view the point of understanding the nature of labor is to determine not who deserves what, but how our world comes to be so useful for us, rather than merely present to us;[17] and since the important point about labor is the direction it gives, it is not particularly important whether it does so with great effort or little. Cohen's objection and the many objections like it obscure the very heart of Locke's perspective on labor and value. And that perspective is worth winning back. Or so I shall argue now.

Locke realizes that land and labor are equally *necessary* for their joint yield, but he does not think that land and labor are equal *contributors* to the yield, or even the same *kind* of contributors. Consider the following passage:

> … all that the straw, bran, bread, of that acre of wheat, is more worth than the product of an acre of as good land, which lies waste, is all the effect of labour: for it is not barely the plough-man's pains, the reaper's and the thresher's toil, and the baker's sweat, is to be counted *into* the bread we eat; the labour of those who broke the oxen, who digged and wrought the iron and stones, who felled and framed the timber employed about the plough, mill, oven, or any other utensils, which are a vast number, requisite to this corn, from its being feed to be sown to its being made bread, must all be *charged on* the account of labour, and received as an effect of that: nature and the earth furnished only the almost worthless materials, as in themselves. It would be a strange *catalogue of things, that industry provided and made use of, about every loaf of bread*, before it came to our use, if we could trace them; iron, wood, leather, bark, timber, stone, bricks, coals, lime, cloth, dying drugs, pitch, tar, masts, ropes, and all the materials made use of in the ship, that brought any of the commodities made use of by any of the workmen, to any part of the work; all which it would be almost impossible, at least too long, to reckon up.[18]

Cohen takes this passage to represent an *ad hoc* attempt to shore up the subtraction criterion: it may take merely an hour's digging to turn a trickle of ten gallons of water per year into a flow of 1,000 gallons per year, but it is odd that so much value should be attributable to an almost negligible amount of labor. So Cohen concludes that Locke, being "obscurely aware" of this odd result, must focus on *large* amounts of labor, and that this is why Locke offer his "strange catalogue" of the many things that must be made to bring about a loaf of bread.[19]

But of course in Cohen's digging example Locke would tot up not only the digger's labor, but also the labor of the smith who forged the spade-head, the carpenter who lathed the handle, the toolmaker who joined them together, the cobbler who made the boots used to push the spade, and so on. Locke, then, would see little difference between his case and Cohen's, and Cohen sees a difference only because he is not on the same page as Locke about what labor is in the first place. Notice that what really strikes Locke in this passage is the ubiquity and variety of the labor that goes into bread: every loaf of bread has a history, and that history is a history of labor, of many wondrous kinds. To make bread, we need wheat, and therefore labor to cultivate and harvest it, and therefore labor to make tools, and therefore labor to collect ore and timber, and so on. Ultimately, our bread's lineage is traced back to the earth—to soil, seeds, iron, wood, and so on—but between a wild earth that *might* meet our needs, and the bread that actually *does*, is the labor of creative agents, a point that Locke underscores in section 41:

> There cannot be a clearer demonstration of any thing, than several nations of the *Americans* are of this, who are rich in land and poor in all the comforts of life; whom nature having furnished as liberally as any other people, with the materials of plenty, i.e. a fruitful soil, apt to produce in abundance, what might serve for food, raiment, and delight; yet for *want of improving it by labour*, have not one hundredth part of the conveniences we enjoy: and a king of a large and fruitful territory there, feeds, lodges, and is clad worse than a day-labourer in *England*. (emphasis in original)

While Locke has an impoverished view of life in the Americas, and a tragically narrow view of what counts as "good" use of land,[20] the point remains that between two worlds alike but for the difference in labor spent in them, it is labor that makes all the difference in the availability of useful goods in those worlds.

On the other hand, Cohen, like very many people, thinks of labor primarily as a kind of drudgery or hard work—"actual sweating toil," he calls it at one point.[21] But for Locke, what matters about labor is not how it is carried out (with difficulty, say). For Locke, the important fact about labor is that it makes a resource a resource, by giving materials the direction they have to have if they are to satisfy our needs.[22] For Locke, labor is a *directive principle*.

Locke's many examples of labor illustrate what it means for labor to be a directive principle. Consider his example of picking an apple from a tree (V, 28).[23] Here a person takes a raw material—an apple on a tree—and makes it a product that meets her needs, simply by picking it and making it available for consumption, that is, now useful in the right way. This is the simplest case of creating a resource—turning something that might meet a need into something that actually does—just by changing its location (cf. V, 48). A more complex case is that of a farmer growing crops (V, 37, 40, 43). Here, rather than gathering what happens to be available, the farmer makes the materials available in ways that make them more useful, by engineering the quantity, quality, variety, and location of the materials, thereby increasing their potential use-value. And this requires coordination with the activities of many others who are creating other resources—plows, mills, ovens, utensils, and so on—as Locke illustrates with the case of producing a loaf of bread (as well as wine, cloth, straw, and bran; V, 42–43), where the various activities, when coordinated, produce a further good.[24] This is a history of labor, and at every stage it is a matter of someone's making material into a resource. The difference between raw materials and resources is the direction that our agency—our labor—gives.

In particular, three theses demonstrate the history of labor that Locke says goes into our useful resources. One, as we have seen already, is that **selection is a kind of labor**. This is because labor is *goal-directed*: labor picks out things that can meet our needs—that is what labor is for. The plowman labors not only by plowing, but also by choosing the right kind of blade with which to plow. Farmers labor not only by growing crops, but also by growing them on fields within reach of users (cf. V, 48) and matching their crops to the land they have available.[25] Labor aims at goals and purposes that materials themselves do not aim at.[26] The materials *couldn't* aim at those goals, which are always changing, depending as they do on what people are doing: what is within reach depends on what portage services are provided; what is available depends on what is left unoccupied, or on offer; what is a good crop depends on what people need and desire, how much of it is already on offer, and what it is feasible to grow. Labor makes materials into resources by giving them the direction we need them to have, and it starts by deciding which materials to make into resources, and where, and when.[27]

I have been saying "often" and "usually"; there are, of course, exceptions to this thesis about selection. Sometimes a selection is a poor one for reasons that could not have been foreseen. Sometimes people get lucky, and unstop an oilfield without meaning to.[28] But these exceptions are instructive, because they illustrate a general feature of our world in their *very violation* of it. It calls for an explanation when a person labors and has nothing to show, or has something to show even though no one has labored for it. But laboring on something and then having something to show for it calls for no explanation. The issue is not that there are exceptions to the thesis that labor is a directive principle, but that it captures a general feature of our world that helps us get the most out of living together, despite exceptions to that thesis.[29]

A related thesis is that ***what can be a resource or not, depends on labor***. Land that is poor for producing wheat need not be poor, full stop; that depends on what else we can do with it.[30] It is tempting to think of materials, especially the ones we know how to make ready use of, as resources, just by themselves; indeed, insofar as the subtraction criterion assumes sameness of kind among contributions, it assumes that land is an active participant in the production of resources, of *just* the sort that labor is, so that things like land are, all by themselves, already resources. Of course, the material characteristics of a resource do make it fitted to the use we make of it; as Aristotle observed, it is the material properties of metal that suit it for saw-blades that cut wood—we cannot make a saw from wood or wool.[31] But a resource is a material that has been given a direction, and labor gives it that *direction*. Use-value does not inhere in materials;[32] rather, a material's inherent characteristics make it possible for labor to bring about use-value in it, and it is labor, then, that makes resources. Labor and materials both make necessary contributions to our resources, but their contributions are radically different in kind: labor is not one factor among the many that go into the production of some good, but the very special factor that directs, coordinates, and organizes all the other factors in order to meet goals that they cannot meet on their own. Locke's point is that some of bread's necessary conditions are quite different from others, since there is something special about *actually making it*.[33]

For this reason labor is not just "working" on something. Notice that in Locke's bread example the products of one activity are the materials of another—the miner's product becomes the smith's material, whose product in turn becomes the plowman's material, and so on—and all of these activities must converge to yield certain sorts of products, and yield them in the ways in which we need them.[34] In this example labor creates valuable resources because its very purpose is to produce not just anything, but *something that we can use*. Direction is the essence of labor; working in just any old way, then, will not be labor. This is not to define labor as, trivially, whatever happens to produce useful resources. But labor is, in general, what produces them, and that is what labor is for. And even the exceptional case of accidentally uncovering an oilfield counts as *good* luck only because people know how to use oil to meet needs; even luck requires the direction of agency. What is a resource depends on what people are doing, and so the aim of labor is to give materials the direction they need, given what people are doing.[35]

The third thesis is that ***external factors themselves are not all isolated from labor***. As we have seen, and as is obvious, successful farming depends on a number of factors, including such "external" factors as weather, pests, and climate—but of course labor often alters and responds to external factors. I cannot change the weather, but my labor might relocate me to a more hospitable climate, or it may change my plans so that they are better suited to the weather I cannot escape; I may live in a desert, but perhaps I can irrigate; I cannot make a hill a plain, but perhaps I can raise sheep on it, instead of corn; I may not need what can be raised on my land, but perhaps I can trade what I raise for what I do need. And so on. In general, whether some external factor will count as an impediment or not, depends mainly on how one is able to respond to it. The world does not come already divided into resources and impediments; it is up to labor to sort them out. Here too, then, labor is a directive principle.[36]

For all these reasons, it is a mistake to think of labor in terms of some quantitative contribution to a yield, the same in kind as the contributions of non-directing materials—an assumption built into the view that Locke is trying to solve an allocation problem.[37] Locke's point in saying that labor contributes more than land by ten-fold, or a hundred-fold, is to draw attention to just how *awesome* a contribution labor makes: labor does not merely produce more than fallow land does; labor and land differ by an order of magnitude. Labor is thus an entirely different *kind* of producer—it is, in a very real sense, the producer of goods in our world.[38]

* * *

Notice that, on Locke's view, labor is direction and *not* "exertion." The fact that giving materials this direction often requires exertion or "hard work" is an interesting fact about our existence, but it is not particularly important in the end with respect to the labor theory of use-value. We may be able to produce a stream from a trickle without *exertion*, but that does not mean that we may do so without *labor*. This sort of objection is simply beside the point. So too are very many of the stock objections to Locke's labor theory of value.

For instance, Robert Nozick asks us to imagine a world in which some people create valuable things "effortlessly, as the cartoon characters in *The Yellow Submarine* trail flowers in their wake"; why, he worries, should some "*cost*" to them, in exertion or effort, be tacked on as a necessary condition of their claim to have created those things?[39] Nozick therefore dismisses the labor theory of value as otiose. But on Locke's understanding of labor, the relevant difference between that imagined world and our own is not the difference in exertion or expenditure. The difference is that in the imagined world valuable things come into being, *according to regular patterns, without the need for any directive principle at all* to make them usable. Since in our world the very act of picking an apple up is necessary to make the apple usable, in that world apples would have to appear as by magic in one's stomach, at the right times, in the right amounts, and at the right stage of digestion. In order for resources to exist without labor, they would have to supply the direction we need them to take *all on their own*. Locke does not make exertion a necessary condition of creating useful things, but he does say that, as a rule, it takes *labor* to create useful things—and in our world, it does.[40]

It is here that Nozick's thought experiment is most telling: to imagine a world in which useful things come into being without any labor is to imagine a world that is itself an *agent*, capable of settings its own goals—goals which, fortuitously, lead it to meet all of our constantly shifting needs *for* us—and then doing what it must to realize those goals. And in fact that is how many people seem inclined to think of our world: if the history of a useful good is a history of labor giving materials direction, they will ask, then why shouldn't we say that it is *also* a history of the world offering up its resources for direction?[41] This line of thought, we should notice, is also implicit in the assumption that Locke's theory is an attempt to answer an allocation problem: since the attempt to determine the relative contributions to a joint yield assumes that the contributions are all of the same kind, determining the earth's contribution requires us to personify it, as one of the agents providing not merely the *materials* but the *direction* that those materials need in order for them to achieve the goals that the contributors share. Interestingly, the Shapely allocation problem was originally a problem about determining relative contributions of cooperating agents who act so as to realize some return for themselves—who engage, that is, in goal-directed activity.[42] Accordingly, recall that on the subtraction criterion we can determine the contribution of the land to the yield *in just the same way* that we determine the contribution of the laborer. Cohen's reading of Locke, then, obscures the key issue: land and labor do not contribute to a joint yield in the same way that two laboring agents do.

Labor, therefore, is essentially directive; and so it is not the same thing as exertion. In fact, exertion is not even a sufficient condition for labor. People sometimes worry that a thing need not become more useful, or may even become less useful, the more one works on it.[43] But we do not labor simply by *working* on something. Rather, since labor is a goal-oriented, directive principle, a crucial part of labor is knowing when to *cease* working on something. To invoke Aristotle again,[44] we might say that labor aims at a "mean," that is, at producing things in the right ways, at the right times, in the right amounts, in relation to the right interests, and so on. In this sense, a "mean" is valuable not because it achieves some quantity of something—a truckload of intricate widgets that no one knows how to use, say—but because it achieves something in the right ways, relative to our material needs.

Nor do we labor simply by working on just *anything*. People sometimes worry that if, as Locke says, laboring on something generates a claim to it, then laboring on, say, something that someone else already owns (such as one's neighbor's house), or something that no one can really own (such as the ocean),[45] should generate a claim to it as well, which is of course absurd. And quite generally, why should someone have any sort of claim against others as a result of producing something that no one wanted or requested?[46] But as we have seen a crucial part of labor is *selecting something appropriate* to labor on, and this includes determining when a thing is appropriately *available* to be labored on with an eye to staking a claim to it ("were it … never so free for them to take," V, 43).[47] As such, labor involves coordinating one's work with other people's activities, interests, projects, and claims. Labor is not doing, but directing by doing.

Nor is exertion a necessary condition of labor, or of producing useful resources by labor. If I were able to turn a trickle into a stream simply by wishing, my wishing would be the directive principle by which I create a more useable resource; in a world where wishes create resources, wishing is labor. The process by which an agent gives materials direction to become resources is, in the end, irrelevant. Where agents give direction, agents labor.

Of course, some people will refuse to call any act of so little effort a case of labor. The assumption that labor is or requires exertion is, I take it, usually tied to the view that labor is meant to be a basis of desert and reward—labor generates claims, the idea is, because hard work is thought to be meritorious.[48] For instance, although Cohen never explicitly says exactly what he takes labor to be, he clearly views labor as hard work, so that labor might be a way of demonstrating deserving through effort: if it's not difficult or strenuous or time-consuming, then it's not labor, or only a "mere whiff of labour,"[49] deserving no reward—and rewards, he maintains, are really the whole point of Locke's view. Consequently, he is puzzled by Locke's idea that gathering apples or acorns could count as "labor"—that seems too easy; if picking up acorns is labor, he says, then "*all* acting on the world" should count as labor.[50] Likewise, Lawrence Becker focuses on the unpleasantness of labor—that it involves "pains" (V, 34)—as the operant consideration in appropriations, since in this way labor can be taken as a basis of rewards.[51] Likewise, Shrader-Frechette argues that because one's labor is one's "pains," "Locke attests that those who labor are industrious and rational persons who, because of their initiative, merit the results of their labor."[52] So the key reason for identifying labor with hard work is the idea that, for Locke, labor is meant to be a basis of merit which gives claims to certain rewards.

However, there is simply no reason for such an association of merit and labor, as far as Locke is concerned. There certainly is no textual basis for doing so, since Locke has in fact nothing to say about merit, desert, or reward in his account of what labor generates. Surely the fact that he calls a person's labor his "pains" gives no suggestion of this; the point in that passage is simply that to appropriate something useful that someone else has created is morally equivalent to appropriate that person's agency without right:

> He that had as good left for his improvement, as was already taken up, needed not complain, ought not to meddle with what was already improved by another's labour: if he did, it is plain he desired the benefit of another man's pains, which he had no right to, and not the ground which God had given him in common with others to labour on, and whereof there was as good left, as that already possessed, and more than he knew what to do with, or his industry could reach to. (V, 34)

Locke bases the laborer's claim to the resource that his labor has produced on the fact of nature that it takes labor to produce resources from the materials available to us, and on the fact of morality that no one has the right to seize anyone else's labor (which, he argues, is morally equivalent to taking the output of someone's labor without consent). But I do not see in this or any passage that Locke says that when a person has worked hard, the rest of us owe it to him to give him some reward, namely the thing he has worked so hard on.

All he *does* say is that when a person has labored, the rest of us are forbidden from seizing the yield of his labor.[53] That hardly makes that yield the reward that the rest of us give him for being so industrious. More important, the hard-work-as-merit interpretation of Locke does injustice to his project, which is to determine what sorts of things make our world useful, and what modes of living together provide the best opportunities for those things to do so.[54] The question is not a *social* one—what I am owed because I've worked so hard or because I've invested my valuable labor,[55] or why I should deserve to have so much more than other people have.[56] The question is a *natural* one: what principles the world demands we observe if we are to avoid destitution and thrive in it.

On this way of understanding Locke's project, the focus is on what I think is exactly the right place: how we can live together in prosperity. This is why, before Locke ever turns his attention to property in the *Second Treatise*, he sets it down as foundational that "Every one, as he is *bound to preserve himself*, and not to quit his station willfully, so by the like reason, when his own preservation comes not into competition, ought he, as much as he can, *to preserve the rest of mankind*." … (II, 6, emphasis in original).[57] And what Locke notices is that labor is what tends, as a rule, to satisfy *both of these goals at once*. As people labor, materials become useful resources, and as the availability of these resources goes beyond what is needed for subsistence, more people come gradually to have more goods, more services, and more opportunities available to them. This idea too is clear in Locke's "strange catalogue": if I have the skill, means, and interest for becoming a baker, then I am better off when other people by their labor create the resources necessary for me to have the opportunity to support myself by baking. Of course, there is no guarantee that a person's most desired career will be made available by what other people are doing. But it is still the case that the ubiquity and variety of other people's labor is what makes careers that someone might desire available in the first place.[58]

It is because so many others have labored, and appropriated through their labor, that so many people can have projects far beyond mere subsistence. Indeed, for Locke the need to leave sufficient goods available to others is the best news about labor. For while it is true that when people acquire only what they need for personal subsistence, there tends to be enough at hand to go around (V, 33, 36), yet when people produce more than what they need in hopes of making profit (V, 36), the sum of available resources and opportunities actually tends to *increase*—because, Locke says, it is labor that makes resources in the first place:

> … [H]e who appropriates land to himself by his labour, *does not lessen, but increase* the common stock of mankind: for the provisions serving to the support of human life, produced by one acre of inclosed and cultivated land, are (to speak much within compass) ten times more than those which are yielded by an acre of land of an equal richness lying waste in common. And therefore he that incloses that land, and has a greater plenty of the conveniences of life from ten

acres, than he could have from an hundred left to nature, may truly be said to give ninety acres to mankind … I have here rated the improved land very low, in making its product as but ten to one, when it is much nearer an hundred to one … (V, 37, emphasis added)

Here some see merely an attempt to justify the benefits that some derive from a zero-sum game: since by my labor I appropriate, by my labor I leave others with that much less; since this activity is by its nature morally questionable, we had better have a story to exonerate those who engage in it. But on Locke's view labor, and appropriation through labor, is *positive*-sum,[59] in increments that add up to something huge over time. Labor explains why as generations pass free people tend to have more resources and opportunities, and better ones.[60] Labor is where enough and as good—or rather, more and better—comes from.[61] No exoneration is required.[62]

For Locke, labor is not the same as toil, exertion, effort, or strain. Labor is not the same as working on something. And labor is not particularly interesting as a basis of deserving. For Locke, labor is a directive principle. It is what enables us to meet our needs by giving the right kind of direction to materials that do not supply that direction for themselves. As such, the contribution of labor—of creativity and direction—to the resources we produce is unique, and different in kind from the contribution that materials make. The point is not allocations, rewards, or exoneration. The point is to find a way to live together. The demand for a directive principle is a reality of the world in which we must find a way to survive. And the difference between prosperity and destitution in our world, Locke finds, is the direction our labor gives our world.[63]

NOTES

1. Cf. G.A. Cohen (1995, p. 171).
2. See also Cohen (1995, pp. 178–182). Con. John Winfrey (1981, pp. 431–432); David Ellerman (1985, p. 294); and perhaps Karl Olivecrona (1974, p. 226), whose denying that gathering acorns increases their value leads me to think he probably does not have use-value in mind.
3. Of two parcels of land one of which is labored on and the other not, Locke says, the benefit mankind receives from the one in a year, is worth [51]. and from the other possibly not worth a penny. … It is labour then which puts the greatest part of value upon land, without which it would be scarcely worth anything: it is to that we owe the greatest part *of all its useful products* … (V, 43, emphasis added) Locke's point is that labor creates use-value ("all its useful products"), and is thus connected to increase in exchange-value (its "worth" in money) merely because its use-value is.
4. Moreover, as we shall see Locke takes a keen interest not only in the fact that labor has been expended on some good, but also in the *diversity* of the *kinds* of labor expended,

such as the fact that producing a loaf of bread requires the coordinated efforts of bakers, millers, blacksmiths, miners, lumberjacks, and so on (see V, 43); and while this diversity is significant for demonstrating the different kinds of use-value (useful flour, tools, ovens, etc.) that must be created in order to produce something like bread, it is irrelevant for determining how much bread is worth in exchange for other things. As Cohen notes (1995, pp. 171ff), Marx offers a labor theory of exchange-value, on which one need consider labor only as a "quantum," since exchange-value depends on *how much* labor, not *what kind* of labor, goes into a commodity.

5. Cohen (1995, pp. 165–194; see esp. pp. 179, 182–185);for the special emphasis that Cohen places on this criticism, see p. 182. As Cohen does (see pp. 175f), I shall confine myself to Locke's argument for the thesis that it is primarily labor that creates value; I shall not address here the question of what this thesis implies for a theory of property, nor the separate thesis that laboring on something is to "mix" one's labor with it.

6. V, 37, quoted by Cohen (1995, p. 179). Cohen also cites V, 36, 40, 41, 42, and 43 (p. 175, n. 20).

7. See Cohen's use of this feature (1995, p. 184). We should note that Cohen does not state the criterion in this purely general form, but he is clearly committed to it because he does assume that the subtraction criterion must be equally applicable to either of the variables examined in any particular application of the subtraction criterion, since Cohen assumes that the criterion applies both when <x, y> = <labor, land> and when <x, y> = <land, labor>; see pp. 179, 184.

8. See Cohen (1995, p. 179).

9. See Cohen (1995, p. 184).

10. Cohen (1995, p. 182f) cites, as a further counterintuitive result of the subtraction criterion, the fact that since (say) cowhide produces no shoes at all without labor, it follows on the subtraction criterion that the cowhide makes no contribution to the shoes yielded with labor.

11. Strangely, Cohen (1995, p. 179) quotes the passage in which Locke asserts the constancy of fertility, on the very page on which he first introduces the subtraction criterion.

12. This is, after all, why people enlist—at considerable expense—the services of realty agents.

13. Cohen (1995, p. 184f).

14. See Cohen (1995, p. 184f, nn. 35f).

15. Shrader-Frechette(1993, p. 215). See also Rolf Sartorius (1984, p. 200) for a similar worry.

16. I shall assume for the sake of argument that that conclusion follows. Actually, it is not clear to me how other people could claim a liberty-right to use some of the improved land on which a farmer has grown his crops (that is the point of making it still available in the commons), *simply because* the farmer had no control over the weather that allowed his crops to grow on that land. In fact, on this view no one (person or group)

could fully appropriate *anything*, even by mere gathering, since no one has control over the fair weather that allows him to go outside and gather, the air and sunshine that sustain him while he gathers, the cellular activities that keep his body going while he gathers, etc. How then people could ever eat (or drink, or breathe, or occupy space) without committing theft, since whatever one eats, one appropriates fully (as Locke noticed)? Moreover, since our farmer has no control over most of what makes his very existence possible, there seems to be no reason to allow the farmer, or anyone else, to exclude others from his person—no reason, that is, to allow him to be anything but a commons himself. For although his person was not initially in the commons, the land *with its improvements* was not what was initially in the commons, either; and if a lack of control over that land's fertility deprives him of title to that land, then he has no right to claim title to his own person, since he has no more control over what makes his existence and even his labor possible, and indeed he sustains them only by stealing from the commons. Feeding himself, then, must be understood as his tending that part of the commons that he is in a unique position to tend; otherwise it is theft. Of course, this follows only if we assume that one can rightfully appropriate only what labor can produce in the absence of all other factors—a bizarre assumption indeed, and in any case an assumption that Locke clearly does not hold, as he believes that labor is the greatest contributor, and not the sole contributor, to what one can rightfully appropriate. Locke surely need not hold that assumption in order to show that labor is what creates resources; for to show that, it is enough to show that among all those factors that go into producing a resource, only labor can rightly be said to *create* the resource. And this, I argue, is precisely Locke's position.

17. For Locke, labor does generate title, but that is not to say that labor does so because it is meritorious.

18. V, 43, emphasis in original. Scott Arnold reminds me of Leonard Read's colorful essay, "I, Pencil: My Family Tree as told by Leonard E. Read," in which a personified pencil enumerates all the people, skills, and resources required to make him—so many and diverse, he claims, that "*not a single person on the face of this earth knows how to make me.*"

19. Cohen (1995, pp. 181, 182, n. 33).

20. See note 22 for further discussion of this aspect of Locke's thought.

21. Cohen (1995, p. 173).

22. Notice that to think of labor as an organizing principle that gives materials direction relative to our needs and interests, is to think labor as something that uses the materials around us *in ways we can live with*. Interestingly, since Native Americans (it turns out) were doing exactly that, the means of removing Locke's blind-spot (as I think it is) with respect to Native Americans' use of land are in fact to be found within Locke's own theory. (Note also that Locke's conception(s) of waste must thus be revised, as well.) We should also notice that a value of land that is distinct from its use-value as fertile soil

is its value as the territory, the *home*, of people and their cultures, and as such people's interests are defined in part by the value that they place on their territory. Consequently, from the fact that other people might bring about a higher yield from the soil it will not follow, on appropriate Lockean principles, that that land is not already being given the right kind of direction it needs to meet the relevant needs and interests, since those interests—including territorial interests—are prior to the question of what will, in that context, count as labor. These seem just the right results to me, but I am unable to pursue them further here. See John Bishop (1997), who sketches a plausible Lockean case for native land rights; see also Herman Lebovics (1986, p. 577f). I have benefited here from conversations with Avery Kolers, Jay Price, Ben Rogers.

23. Locke there also considers gathering acorns as an equivalent case (and in V, 31), as well as cases of one's horse's eating grass, one's servant's cutting turfs, and digging ore oneself; in V, 29, taking a pitcherful of water from a fountain; in V, 30, killing a deer, catching a fish from the ocean, and pursuing a hare in the hunt; in V, 32–33, improving and cultivating land; in V, 33, taking a drink from a river. Thomas Mautner (1982, p. 263) makes a sharp distinction between labor as "doing"(e.g. gathering) and labor as "making," and argues that for Locke only the former is relevant to appropriation. While appropriation is not my topic in this paper, I think that the on the account of labor I develop on Locke's behalf in the rest of the paper, this distinction will appear much less important.

24. Unfortunately, Cohen focuses on the crops example, but is at a loss regarding the other two (see 1995, pp. 181, 75, respectively).

25. Likewise, as Arnold (1985, p. 100) points out, the very act by a capitalist of investing in one project rather than another is itself an entrepreneurial act.

26. This aspect of such cases goes unmentioned by Cohen, who speaks only of "amounts" of labor (e.g. 1995, p. 181).

27. And as we have seen, for this reason we cannot change level of fertility between two plots of land in imagination, and then simply assume that the labor invested in each will be the same nonetheless.

28. Is Cohen's "trickle" case also a case of mere good luck? Interestingly, Cohen is silent about whether any labor was involved in selecting one piece of land over another to dig on.

29. I have benefited here from correspondence with David Schmidtz.

30. Or to it; see the third thesis, below.

31. *Metaphysics* VI.I.4, 1044a28.

32. E.g., it is most implausible to say that the modern use-value of silica, say, inhered in it a century ago, before anyone had the interest or ability to create or use computer chips. See Jan Narveson (1998, p. 15).

33. I thank David Schmidtz for this way of putting the point.

34. Although I cannot pursue the issue here, I think that on this account of labor capital-ists can be said to labor, since they supply goods—financing—that others need, *when*

and where they need them, for production. See Arnold (1985) (see also 1987, p. 395) for an excellent discussion of capitalist and entrepreneurial activities as kinds of labor; see also Narveson (1998, p. 20f). In any case, this point demonstrates how activities can count as labor that do not involve manipulating materials, such as intellectual and creative activities, which are of course highly prevalent forms of labor in modern society; for they too are exercises of agency that give our world the direction that makes it a more beneficial place, practically, intellectually, and aesthetically. See also Narveson (1999, pp. 221–224), who says (p. 221), "We have what we have, material or otherwise, because a great number of people have applied their ingenuity to specific problems relevant to the satisfaction of human interests, ranging from hunger to sheer curiosity. The idea that wealth consists in the accumulation of a large mass of natural stuff is utterly wrong."

35. Narveson has made the point thus: "[T]he view of natural resources according to which they are, *just like that*, 'goods,' is fundamentally wrong-headed. As Karl Marx noted, nothing is any good for us except insofar as it has 'use-value'—serves someone's needs, desires, wants, interests, values. And it can *only* do that via knowledge of how to make it serve those values. ... Technology in the broad sense is, in short, a necessary condition of any natural items' having *any value at all*. This includes the human capacity to labor, which is interestingly distinctive only by virtue of embodying the cognitive output of its ingenious owners. ... There is no way to say how much of a 'resource' any hunk of mere stuff constitutes, absent technology. ... To call a resource 'natural' is to say, merely, that we know enough about it to see that finding and engaging in some primary processing activity might be worth engaging in" (Narveson 1998, pp. 14f, 21, emphasis in original). This point is tied, I take it, to Narveson's (1998, p. 19f) claim that "*All exchange is of services* ... [and] an orientation toward 'matter,' 'goods,' as the very point of the market is thus seen to be at base mistaken" (emphasis in original). I agree; but I cannot pursue the issue here.

36. Consider an analogous point in the case of language acquisition: although language can be successfully acquired by a mind only in the presence of certain external or environmental factors, nonetheless there is still something special about the role of the mind's structures and capacities that makes the mind the true "producer" of the languages kills that come about in it. I thank Jeff Hershfield for this analogy.

37. See esp. Cohen (1995, p. 185, n. 36).

38. Here again I am in agreement with Narveson (1998, p. 20): "Cohen touches on the question, What percentage of the value of valuable things is due to nature and what to labor? (as on pp. 182–185). But the question rests on a misconception. For in the only basically relevant sense, the answer is *100*% 'labor' (meaning, broadly, services). In another quite different sense, it is 0%, for nature too 'provides' everything: no nature, nothing to work on, nothing to do. But nature is 'dumb': it is just *there*, indifferent to our strivings, not a *participant* in economic activity. Only people, with their

intelligence, creative energies, and a great range of increasingly complicated interests, values, and needs, are responsible for *everything* on a market. "Narveson is right, and I have tried to argue that this is Locke's under-standing of labor and its contribution, too. Interestingly, what strikes Locke about humans is their creativity and agency: humans are not passive recipients of goods, but are active *creators* of goods, depending on what direction they give the raw "materials" life presents to them.

39. Nozick (1974, p. 175), emphasis in original.

40. How would property rights work in a world in which labor is unnecessary for the existence of usable goods? On my reading of Locke, he has no answer to give—and that seems to me to be exactly the right result.

41. I have benefited here from correspondence with Avery Kolers and Mark Michael.

42. "... [T]he Shapley value is presented as an answer to the question of what rewards owners of factors should expect, as a matter of fact, to get from *co-operation*" (Cohen 1995, p. 185, n. 35, emphasis added). Cohen notes that Locke's project differs from Shapley's in that Locke's is normative, but he sees no problem in moving from a comparison of people cooperating with each other to a comparison of land and farmers producing a yield, where such cooperation is missing.

43. I have benefited here from conversations with Jean Hampton and Anne Tarver.

44. See *Nicomachean Ethics* II.6, esp. 1106b21–23.

45. For the latter example, see Nozick (1974, p. 174).

46. See Becker (1976, p. 659) for a discussion of this worry of Proudhon's. Notice Proudhon's assumption that the claims that labor generates are claims *to rewards from others*; we shall return to this below.

47. This point is more than academic; e.g., we might wonder whether the improvements I make to my property, which increase the use-value of your property (as when I build an attractive park near your house, say), should therefore give me some stake in your property. This point was made during discussion of my paper at the Pacific Division meeting of the American Philosophical Association, 2003.

48. Consequently, on this view in a world where wishes create resources, there simply is no labor—after all, what is so impressive about simply *wishing*?

49. Cohen (1995, p. 185).

50. See Cohen (1995, p. 75), emphasis added.

51. Becker (1976, pp. 655, 659). See Judith Jarvis Thomson (1976) for a plausible reply.

52. See Shrader-Frechette (1993, p. 204), emphasis in original note.

53. Moreover, on Locke's view labor is a kind of agency; since, as I think, one's agency—what kind of direction one brings to the world—is essential to who one is, it makes perfect sense to say that someone who appropriates what I do and make is appropriating *me*. This brings out, in my view, a great deal of the force of the metaphor of "mixing" one's labor: to invest my labor in something is to invest *myself*—my *identity*—in it. I have benefited here from correspondence with David Schmidtz.

54. A crucial question indeed, if we need to know what makes material prosperity possible. Cohen (1995) has remarkably little to say about this question, aside from citing favorably the claim of Hal Varian (1975) that "market socialism" or "people's capitalism" is more productive than pure capitalism. However, Varian's "people's capitalism" forbids any exchange of goods—such as giving or bequeathing—except through the market. I wonder whether goods really would be so prolific in people's capitalism, since one of the major goals that shapes much of the rational direction we give to raw materials would, under that system, be completely removed (perhaps it is not surprising that Varian tends to treat labor as a quantum—of which some have "much," others "little"—rather than as goal-directed activity). Goods don't just "happen," and we cannot assume that they just will be there, no matter how people's abilities to use them are restricted. They are produced by directive activity, which aims at goals we have; and one of our central goals is the ability to give. Varian thinks that giving up certain rights of transfer may be a small price to pay for equal market opportunity. He does not say whether giving them up would jeopardize the creation of goods that are on such markets in the first place.

55. For the latter interpretation of Locke, see esp. Nozick (1974, p. 174).

56. Note Cohen's assumption that Locke's purpose is the devaluation of land as such (e.g. p. 183), and the justification of inequality in private property apparently for its own sake (pp. 176–178); see also Olivecrona (1974, pp. 231–233), who is cited approvingly by Mautner (1982, p. 263).

57. For this point I am indebted to a member of my audience at the Pacific Division meeting.

58. Nor should we suppose that we might take seriously the idea of a desired career or other project that is not shaped by what other people are doing and what is (and is likely to be) available.

59. Schmidtz discusses the idea of appropriation as positive-sum in 1998, Chapter 1.2 ("Why Isn't Everyone Destitute?") and 1990. See also Narveson (1999, pp. 220–224).

60. Cf. Narveson (1999, p. 222).

61. And it could not be otherwise, since what counts as "enough and as good" depends on the sorts of direction that materials do not give themselves.

62. I have benefited here from correspondence with David Schmidtz.

63. I have benefited greatly from comments by Scott Arnold, Mark LeBar, and Dave Schmidtz, and from conversations with Bob Feleppa, Jeff Hershfield, Jay Price, Ben Rogers, David Soles, Debby Soles, and Anne Tarver. I am also indebted to Nick Smith, to my audience at the 2003 Pacific Division Meeting of the American Philosophical Association, and to my commentator at the meeting, Mark Michael. All shortcomings in this paper remain wholly my own.

REFERENCES

Arnold, N.S. (1985): 'Capitalists and the Ethics of Contribution', *Canadian Journal of Philosophy* 15, 87–102.

Arnold, N.S. (1987): 'Why Profits are Deserved', *Ethics* 97, 387–402.

Becker, L.C. (1976): 'The Labor Theory of Property Acquisition', *Journal of Philosophy* 73, 653–664.

Bishop, J.D. (1997): 'Locke's Theory of Original Appropriation and the Right of Settlement in Iroquois Territory', *Canadian Journal of Philosophy* 27, 31 1–337.

Cohen, G.A. (1995): 'Marx and Locke on Land and Labour', in Cohen (ed.), *Self-Ownership, Freedom, and Equality* (pp. 165–194), Cambridge.

Ellerman, D.P. (1985): 'On the Labor Theory of Property', *Philosophical Forum* 16, 293–326.

Lebovics, H. (1986): 'The Uses of American in Locke's *Second Treatise of Government*', *Journal of the History of Ideas* 5, 65–78.

Locke, J. (1980): *Second Treatise of Government*, C.B. Macpherson (ed.), Hackett.

Mautner, T. (1982): 'Locke on Original Appropriation', *American Philosophical Quarterly* 19, 259–270.

Narveson, J. (1998): 'Libertarianism vs. Marxism: Reflections on G.A. Cohen's *Self-Ownership, Freedom and Equality*', Journal of Ethics 2, 1–26.

Narveson, J. (1999): 'Property Rights: Original Acquisition and Lockean Provisos', *Public Affairs Quarterly* 13, 205–227.

Nozick, R. (1974): *Anarchy, State, and Utopia*, Basic Books.

Olivecrona, K. (1974): 'Locke's Theory of Appropriation', *Philosophical Quarterly* 24, 220–234.

Read, L. (1956): 'I, Pencil: My Family Tree as told by Leonard E. Read', *The Foreman*.

Sartorius, R. (1984): 'Persons and Property', in R. Frey (ed.), *Utility and Rights* (pp. 196–214), University of Minnesota Press.

Schmidtz, D. (1990): 'When is Original Appropriation *Required?*', *Monist* 73, 504–518.

Schmidtz, D. (1998): 'Why Isn't Everyone Destitute?', in D. Schmidtz and R.E. Goodin (eds.), *Social Welfare and Individual Responsibility: For and Against* (pp. 24–43), Cambridge.

Shrader-Frechette, K. (1993): 'Locke and Limits on Land Ownership', *Journal of the History of Ideas* 54, 201–220.

Thomson, J. J. (1976): 'Property Acquisition', *Journal of Philosophy* 73, 664–666.

Varian, H. (1975): 'Distributive Justice, Welfare Economics, and the Theory of Fairness', *Philosophy and Public Affairs* 4, 223–247.

Winfrey, J.C. (1981): 'Charity versus Justice in Locke's Theory of Property', *Journal of the History of Ideas* 42, 423–438.

Department of Philosophy
  Wichita State Unviersity
  Wichita, KS 67260–0001
  USA
  E-mail: daniel.russell@wichita.edu

The Institution of Property

The evolution of property law is driven by an ongoing search for ways to internalize what economists call externalities: positive externalities associated with productive effort and negative externalities associated with misuse of commonly held resources.[1] If all goes well, property law enables would-be producers to enjoy the benefits of productive effort. It also enables people to insulate themselves from external costs associated with activities around the neighborhood. Property law is not perfect. To further reduce external costs that neighbors might otherwise impose on each other, people resort to nuisance and zoning laws, regulatory agencies, and so on, all with a view to supplementing and perfecting the critical role that property law plays in minimizing external costs.

Philosophers speak of the ideal of society as a cooperative venture for mutual advantage. To be a cooperative venture for mutual advantage, though, society must first be a setting in which mutually advantageous interaction is possible. In other words, borrowing a term from game theory, society must be a positive-sum game. What determines the extent to which society is a positive-sum game? This essay explains how property institutions convert negative-sum games to positive-sum games, setting the stage for society's flourishing as a cooperative venture.

---

1   A negative externality or external cost is a cost (of a decision or transaction) paid by bystanders who were not consulted and whose interests were not taken into account. A transaction may also, analogously, create positive externalities, that is, have external benefits.

The term "property rights" is used to refer to a bundle of rights that could include rights to sell, lend, bequeath, and so on. In what follows, I use the phrase to refer primarily to the right of owners to exclude nonowners. Private owners have the right to exclude nonowners, but the right to exclude is a feature of property rights in general rather than the defining feature of private ownership in particular. The National Park Service claims a right to exclude. Communes claim a right to exclude nonmembers. This essay does not settle which kind or which mix of public and private property institutions is best. Instead, it asks how we could justify *any* institution that recognizes a right to exclude.

1. ORIGINAL APPROPRIATION: THE PROBLEM

The right to exclude presents a philosophical problem. Consider how full-blooded rights differ from mere liberties. If I am at liberty to plant a garden, that means my planting a garden is permitted. That leaves open the possibility of you being at liberty to interfere with my gardening as you see fit. Thus, mere liberties are not full-blooded rights. When I stake a claim to a piece of land, though, I claim to be changing other people's liberties—canceling them somehow—so that other people no longer are at liberty to use the land without my permission. To say I have a right to the land is to say I have a right to exclude.

From where could such rights come? There must have been a time when no one had a right to exclude. Everyone had liberties regarding the land, but not rights. (Perhaps this does not seem obvious, but if no one owns the land, no one has a right to exclude. If no one has a right to exclude, everyone has liberties.) How, then, did we get from each person having a liberty to someone having an exclusive right to the land? What justifies original appropriation, that is, staking a claim to previously unowned resources?

To justify a claim to unowned land, people need not make as strong a case as would be needed to justify confiscating land already owned by someone else. Specifically, since there is no prior owner in original appropriation cases, there is no one from whom one can or needs to get consent. What, then, must a person do? Locke's idea was that any residual (perhaps need-based) communal claim to the land could be met if a person could appropriate it without prejudice to other people, in other words, if a person could leave "enough and as good" for others.[2] This so-called Lockean Proviso can be interpreted in many ways, but an adequate interpretation will note that this is its point: to license claims that can be made without making other people worse off.

We also should consider whether the "others" who are to be left with enough and as good include not just people currently on the scene but latecomers as well, including people not yet born. John Sanders asks, "What possible argument could at the same time require that the present generation have scruples about leaving enough and as good for one

---

2   See Locke (1960) chap. 5. Locke sometimes uses other locutions, such as "as much and as good."

another, while shrugging off such concern for future generations?"[3] Most theorists accept the more demanding interpretation. It fits better with Locke's idea that the preservation of humankind (which includes future generations) is the ultimate criterion by which any use of resources is assessed. Aside from that, we have a more compelling defense of an appropriation (especially in environmental terms) when we can argue that there was enough left over not just for contemporaries but also for generations to come.

Of course, when we justify original appropriation, we do not in the process justify expropriation. Some say institutions that license expropriation make people better off; I think our histories of violent expropriation are ongoing tragedies for us all. Capitalist regimes have tainted histories. Communist regimes have tainted histories. Indigenous peoples have tainted histories. Europeans look land from Algonquin tribes, and before that, Algonquin tribes took the same land from Iroquois tribes. We may regard those expropriations as the history of markets or governments or Christianity or tribalism or simply as the history of the human race. It makes little difference. This essay discusses the history of property institutions, not because their history can justify them, but rather because their history shows how some of them enable people to make themselves and the people around them better off without destroying their environment. Among such institutions are those that license original appropriation (and not expropriation).

2. ORIGINAL APPROPRIATION: A SOLUTION

Philosophical critics of private property often have claimed that justifying original appropriation is the key to justifying private property, frequently offering a version of Lockean Proviso as the standard of justification. Part of the Proviso's attraction for such critics was that it seemingly could not be met. Many critics conclude that the Proviso is, at least in the case of land appropriation, logically impossible to satisfy, and thus that (private) property in land cannot possibly be justified along Lockean lines.

The way Judith Thomson puts it, if "the first labor-mixer must literally leave as much and as good for others who come along later, then no one can come to own anything, for there are only finitely many things in the world so that every taking leaves less for others."[4] To say the least, Thomson is not alone:

"We leave enough and as good for others only when what we take is not scarce."[5]
"The Lockean Proviso, in the contemporary world of overpopulation and scarce resources, can almost never be met."[6]

---

3   Sanders (1987) 377.
4   Thomson (1990) 330.
5   Fried (1995) 230n.
6   Held (1980) 6.

"Every acquisition worsens the lot of others—and worsens their lot in relevant ways."[7]

The condition that there be enough and as good left for others could not of course be literally satisfied by any system of private property rights."[8]

"If the 'enough and as good' clause were a necessary condition on appropriation, it would follow that, in these circumstances, the only legitimate course for the inhabitants would be death by starvation … since *no* appropriation would leave enough and as good in common for others."[9]

And so on. If we take something out of the cookie jar, we *must* be leaving less for others. This appears self-evident. It has to be right. But it isn't right, for two reasons.

A. Appropriation Is Not a Zero-Sum Game

First, it is hardly impossible—certainly not logically impossible—for a taking to leave as much for others. We can at least imagine a logically possible world of magic cookie jars in which, every time you take out one cookie, more and better cookies take its place.

Second, the logically possible world I just imagined is the sort of world we actually live in. Philosophers writing about original appropriation tend to speak as if people who arrive first are luckier than those who come later. The truth is, first appropriators begin the process of resource creation; latecomers get most of the benefits. Consider America's first permanent English settlement, the Jamestown colony of 1607. (Or, if you prefer, imagine the lifestyles of people crossing the Bering Strait from Asia twelve thousand years ago.) Was their situation better than ours? How so? They were never caught in rush-hour traffic jams, of course. For that matter, they never worried about being overcharged for car repairs. They never awoke in the middle of the night to the sound of noisy refrigerators, leaky faucets, or even flushing toilets. They never wasted a minute at airports waiting for delayed flights. They never had to change a light bulb. They never agonized over the choice among cellular telephone companies. They never faced the prospect of a dentist's drill; after their teeth fell out, in their thirties, they could subsist for a while on liquids. Life was simple.

Philosophers are taught to say, in effect, that original appropriators got the good stuff for free. We have to pay for ugly leftovers. But in truth, original appropriation benefits latecomers far more than it benefits original appropriators. Original appropriation is a cornucopia of wealth, but mainly for latecomers. The people who got here first literally could not even have imagined what we latecomers take for granted. Our life expectancies exceed theirs by several *decades*.

Original appropriation diminishes the stock of what can be originally appropriated, at least in the case of land, but that is not the same thing as diminishing the stock of what can

---

7   Bogart (1985) 834.

8   Sartorius (1984) 210.

9   Waldron (1976) 325.

be owned.[10] On the contrary, in taking control of resources and thereby removing those particular resources from the stock of goods that can be acquired by original appropriation, people typically generate massive increases in the stock of goods that can be acquired by trade. The lesson is that appropriation typically is not a zero-sum but a positive-sum game. As Locke himself stressed, it creates the possibility of mutual benefit on a massive scale. It creates the possibility of society as a cooperative venture.

The point is not merely that enough is produced in appropriation's aftermath to compensate latecomers who lost out in the race to appropriate. The point is that being an original appropriator is not the prize. The prize is prosperity, and latecomers win big, courtesy of those who arrived first. If anyone had a right to be compensated, it would be the first appropriators.

B. The Commons Before Appropriation Is Not Zero-Sum Either

The second point is that the commons before appropriation is not a zero-sum game either. Typically it is a negative-sum game. Let me tell two stories. The first comes from the coral reefs of the Philippine and Tongan Islands.[11] People once fished those reefs with lures and traps, but then began bleach-fishing, which involves dumping bleach into the reefs. Fish cannot breathe sodium hypochlorite. Suffocated, they float to the surface, where they are easy to collect.[12]

The problem is, the coral itself is composed of living animals. The coral suffocates along with the fish, and the dead reef is no longer a viable habitat. (Another technique, blast-fishing, involves dynamiting the reefs. The concussion produces an easy harvest of stunned fish and dead coral.) Perhaps your first reaction is to say people ought to be more responsible. They ought to preserve the reefs for their children.

But that would miss the point, which is that individual fishermen lack the option of saving the coral for their children. Individual fishermen obviously have the option of not destroying it themselves, but what happens if they elect not to destroy it? What they want is for the reef to be left for their children; what is actually happening is that the reef is left for the next blast-fisher down the line. If a fisherman wants to have anything at all to give his children, he must act quickly, destroying the reef and grabbing the fish himself. It does

---

10   Is it fair for latecomers robe excluded from acquiring property by rules allowing original appropriation? Sanders (1987, 385) notes that latecomers "are *not* excluded from acquiring property by these rules. They are, instead, excluded from being the first to own what has not been owned previously. Is *that* unfair?"

11   Chesher (1985). Sec also Gomez, Alcala, and San Diego (1981), For a recent discussion of some of the legal issues pertaining to domestic conflicts between the fishing industry and the tourism industry's efforts to protect reefs with federal marine protected areas, see Craig (2008).

12   J. Madeleine Nash, "Wrecking the Reefs." *Time.* Sept. 30, 1996, 60–62, says fishermen currently pump 330.000 pounds of cyanide per year into Philippine reefs.

no good to tell fishermen to take responsibility. They are taking responsibility—for their children. Existing institutional arrangements do not empower them to lake responsibility in a way that would save the reef.

Under the circumstances, they are at liberty to not destroy the reef themselves, but they are not at liberty to do what is necessary to save the reef for their children. To save the reef for their children, fishermen must have the power to restrict access to the reef. They must claim a right to exclude blast-fishers. Whether they stake that claim as individuals or as a group is secondary, so long as they actually succeed in restricting access. One way or another, they must have, and must effectively exercise, a right to restrict access.

The second story comes from the Cayman Islands.[13] The Atlantic Green Turtle has long been prized as a source of meat and eggs. The turtles were a commonly held resource and were being harvested in an unsustainable way. In 1968, when by some estimates there were as few as three to five thousand left in the wild, a group of entrepreneurs and concerned scientists created Mariculture Ltd. (sold in 1976 and renamed Cayman Turtle Farm) and began raising and selling captivity-bred sea turtles. In the wild, as few as one-tenth of 1 percent of wild hatchlings survive to adulthood. Most are seized by predators before they can crawl from nest to sea. Cayman Farm, though, boosted the survival rate of captivity-bred animals to 50 percent or more. At the peak of operations, they were rearing over a hundred thousand turtles. They were releasing 1 percent of their hatchlings into the wild at the age of ten months, an age at which hatchlings have a decent chance of surviving to maturity.

In 1973, commerce in Atlantic green turtles was restricted by the Convention on International Trade in Endangered Species (CITES) and, in the United States, by the Fish and Wildlife Service, the Department of Commerce, and the Department of the Interior. Under the newly created Endangered Species Act, the United States classified the Atlantic green turtle as an endangered species, but Cayman Farm's business was unaffected, at first, because regulations pertaining to commerce in Atlantic green turtles covered only wild turtles, implicitly exempting commerce in captivity-bred animals. In 1978, however, the regulations were published in their final form, and although exemptions were granted for trade in captivity-bred animals of other species, no exemption was made for turtles. The company could no longer do business in the United States. Even worse, the company no longer could ship its products through American ports, so it no longer had access via Miami to world markets. The Cayman Farm exists today only to serve the population of the Cayman Islands themselves.[14]

---

13   I thank Peggy Fosdick at the National Aquarium in Baltimore for correspondence and documents. See also Fosdick and Fosdick (1994).

14   As later sections stress, privatization may be a key to avoiding commons tragedies, but it is not a panacea. In this case, there was concern that the farming of turtles would spur demand, and that rising demand would lead to rising prices, which would mean an increased poaching pressure on wild populations. This is unlikely. As a rule, the prices of scarce wild animals do not rise when people begin bringing

What do these stories tell us? The first tells us that we do not need to justify failing to preserve the commons in its pristine, original, unappropriated form, because preserving a pristine commons is not an option. Leaving our environment in the commons is not like putting our environment in a time capsule as a legacy for future generations. There are ways to take what we find in the commons and preserve it—to put it in a time capsule— but before we can put something in a time capsule, we have to appropriate it.[15]

C. Justifying the Game

Note a difference between justifying *institutions* that regulate appropriation and justifying particular *acts* of appropriation. Think of original appropriation as a game and of particular acts of appropriation as moves within the game. Even if the game is justified, a given move within the game may have nothing to recommend it. Indeed, we could say (for argument's sake) that any act of appropriation will seem arbitrary when viewed in isolation, and some will seem unconscionable. Even so, there can be compelling reasons for an institutional framework to recognize property claims on the basis of moves that would carry no moral weight in an institutional vacuum. Common law implicitly acknowledges morally weighty reasons for not requiring original appropriators to supply morally weighty reasons for their appropriations. Carol Rose argues that a rule of first possession, when the world is notified in an unambiguous way, induces discovery (and future productive activity) and minimizes disputes over discovered objects.[16] Particular acts of appropriation are justified not because they carry moral weight but because they are permitted moves within a game that carries moral weight.

Needless to say, the cornucopia of wealth generated by the appropriation and subsequent mobilization of resources is not an unambiguous benefit. Commerce made possible by original appropriation creates pollution, and other negative externalities as well. Further, there may be people who attach no value to the increases in life expectancy and other benefits that accompany the appropriation of resources for productive use. Some people may prefer a steady-state system that indefinitely supports their lifestyles as hunter-gatherers, untainted by the shoes, tents, fishing rods, and safety matches of

---

to market large quantities of farm-bred alternatives. One more likely danger, though, is that large-scale farms (salmon farms, cattle farms, etc.) breed disease and put wild as well as domestic populations at risk. As with any other new industry, there are always unanticipated problems and newly emerging externalities that need to be contained. See Davis (2007).

15   A private nonprofit organization, the Nature Conservancy, is pursuing such a strategy. Although not itself an original appropriator it has acquired over a billion dollars' worth of land in an effort to preserve natural ecosystems. Note that this includes habitat for endangered species that have no market value.

16   Rose (1985).

Western culture. If original appropriation forces such people to participate in a culture they want no part of, then from their viewpoint, the game does more harm than good.

Here are two things to keep in mind, though. First, as I said, the commons is not a time capsule. It does not preserve the status quo. For all kinds of reasons, quality of life could drop after appropriation. However, pressures that drive waves of people to appropriate are a lot more likely to compromise quality of life when those waves wash over an unregulated commons. In an unregulated commons, those who conserve pay the costs but do not get the benefits of conservation, while overusers get the benefits but do not pay the costs of overuse. An unregulated commons is thus a prescription for overuse, not for conservation.

Second, the option of living the life of a hunter-gatherer has not entirely disappeared. It is not a comfortable life. It never was. But it remains an option. There are places in northern Canada and elsewhere where people still live that way. As a bonus, those who opt to live as hunter-gatherers retain the option of participating in Western culture on a drop-in basis during medical emergencies, to trade for supplies, and so on. Obviously, someone might respond, "Even if the hunter-gatherer life is an option now, that option is disappearing as expanding populations equipped with advancing technologies claim the land for other purposes." Well, probably so. What does that prove? It proves that, in the world as it is, if hunter-gatherers want their children to have the option of living as hunter-gatherers, then they need to stake a claim to the territory on which they intend to preserve that option. They need to argue that they, as rightful owners, have a right to regulate access to it. If they want a steady-state civilization, they need to be aware that they will not find it in an unregulated commons. They need to exclude oil companies, for example, which would love to treat northern Canada as an unregulated commons.

When someone says appropriation does not leave enough and as good for others, the reply should be "compared to what?" Compared to the commons as it was? As it is? As it will be? Often, in fact, leaving resources *in the commons* does not leave enough and as good for others. The Lockean Proviso, far from forbidding appropriation of resources from the commons, actually requires appropriation under conditions of scarcity.

Removing goods from the commons stimulates increases in the stock of what can be owned and limits losses that occur in tragic commons. Appropriation replaces a negative-sum with a positive-sum game. Therein lies a justification for social structures enshrining a right to remove resources from the unregulated commons: when resources become scarce, we need to remove them if we want them to be there for our children. Or anyone else's.

3. WHAT KIND OF PROPERTY INSTITUTION IS IMPLIED?

I have defended appropriation of, and subsequent regulation of access to, scarce resources as a way of preserving (and creating) resources for the future. When resources are abundant, the Lockean Proviso permits appropriation; when resources are scarce, the Proviso requires appropriation. It is possible to appropriate without prejudice to future generations. Indeed, when the burden of common use begins to exceed a resource's ability to renew itself, leaving the resource in the commons is what would be prejudicial to future generations.

Private property enables people (and gives them an incentive) to take responsibility for conserving scarce resources. It preserves resources under a wide variety of circumstances. It is the preeminent vehicle for turning negative-sum commons into positive-sum property regimes. However, it is not the only way. Evidently, it is not always the best way, either. Public property is ubiquitous, and it is not only rapacious governments and mad ideologues who create it. It has a history of evolving spontaneously in response to real problems, enabling people to remove a resource from an unregulated commons and collectively take responsibility for its management. The following sections, discussing research by Martin Bailey, Harold Demsetz, Robert Ellickson, and Carol Rose, show how various property institutions help to ensure that enough and as good is left for future generations.

A. The Unregulated Commons

An unregulated commons need not be a disaster. An unregulated commons will work well enough so long as the level of use remains within the land's carrying capacity. However, as use nears carrying capacity, there will be pressure to shift to a more exclusive regime. For a real-world example of an unregulated commons evolving into a regime of private parcels as increasing traffic began to exceed carrying capacity, consider economist Harold Demsetz's classic account of how property institutions evolved among indigenous tribes of the Labrador peninsula. As Demsetz tells the story, the region's people had, for generations, treated the land as an open-access commons. The human population was small. There was plenty to eat. Thus, the patient of exploitation was within the land's carrying capacity.[17] The resource maintained itself. In that situation, the Lockean Proviso, on the previously discussed interpretation, was satisfied. Original appropriation would have been permissible, other things equal, but it was not required.

With the advent of the fur trade, though, the scale of hunting and trapping activity increased sharply. The population of game animals began to dwindle. The unregulated commons had worked for a while, but now the tribes were facing a classic "tragedy of the commons"[18] The tragedy of the commons is one version of a more general problem

---

17   This was not true everywhere. I have seen places where tribes hunted bison by stampeding whole herds over the edge of a cliff. (The Blackfoot name for one such place translates as "head-smashed-in buffalo jump.") So I accept Dukeminier and Krier's warning against forming "an unduly romantic image of Native American culture prior to the arrival of 'civilization.' There is considerable evidence that some American Indian tribes, rather than being natural ecologists who lived in respectful harmony with the land, exploited the environment ruthlessly by overhunting and extensive burning of forests" (1993, 62).

18   Hardin (1968) 1243. The cases described in previous sections are examples of the "tragedy of the commons" where unregulated access to a resource results in overuse by a population of users who lack the effective

of externalities. In this case, the benefits of exploiting the resource were internalized but the costs were not, and the arrangement was no longer viable. In response, tribe members began to mark out family plots. The game animals in question were small animals like beaver and otter that tend not to migrate from one plot to another. Thus, marking out plots of land effectively privatized small game as well as the land itself. In sum, the tribes converted the commons in nonmigratory fur-bearing game to family parcels when the fur trade began to spur a rising demand that exceeded the land's carrying capacity. When demand began to exceed carrying capacity, that was when the Lockean Proviso came not only to permit but to require original appropriation.

One other nuance of the privatization of fur-bearing game was that although the fur was privatized, the meat was not. There was still plenty of meat, so tribal law allowed people to hunt for meat on each other's land. Unannounced visitors could kill a beaver and take the meat, but had to leave the pelt, prominently displayed to signal that they had eaten and had respected the owner's right to the pelt. The new customs went to the heart of the matter, privatizing what had to be privatized, and leaving intact liberties people had always enjoyed with respect to other resources where unrestricted access had not yet become a problem.

B. The Communal Alternative[19]

We can contrast the unregulated or open-access commons with communes. A commune is a restricted-access commons. In a commune, property is owned by the group rather than by individual members. People as a group claim and exercise a right to exclude. Typically, communes draw a sharp distinction between members and nonmembers, and regulate access accordingly. Public property tends to restrict access by time of day or year. Some activities are permitted; others are prohibited.

Ellickson believes a broad campaign to abolish either private property or public and communal property would be ludicrous. Each kind of property serves social welfare in its own way. Likewise, every ownership regime has its own externality problems. Communal management leads to overconsumption and to shirking on maintenance and improvements, because people receive only a fraction of the value of their labor, and bear only a fraction of the costs of their consumption. To minimize these disincentives, a commune must monitor production and consumption activities.

In practice, communal regimes can lead to indiscriminate dumping of wastes, ranging from piles of unwashed dishes to ecological disasters that threaten whole continents. Privately managed parcels also can lead to indiscriminate dumping of wastes and to various

---

right to exclude other users and thus whose only rational alternative is to jump in and overuse while they can. See also Schmidtz and Willott (2003).

19   This essay discusses Ellickson's article in some detail. While I take little credit for the ideas in the next few sections, any errors are presumably mine.

other uses that ignore spillover effects on neighbors. One advantage of private property is that owners can buy each other out and reshuffle their holdings in such a way as to minimize the extent to which their activities bother each other. But it does not always work out so nicely, and the reshuffling itself can be a waste. There are transaction costs. Thus, one plausible social goal would be to have a system that combines private and public property in a way that reduces the sum of transaction costs and the cost of externalities.

4. LOCAL VERSUS REMOTE EXTERNALITIES

Is it generally best to convert an unregulated commons to smaller private parcels or to manage it as a commune with power to exclude nonmembers? It depends on what kind of problem the property regime is supposed to be solving. In particular, not all problems are of equal scale; some are more local than others. As a problem's scale changes, there will be corresponding changes in which responses are feasible and effective. An individual sheep eating grass in the pasture is what Ellickson and Demsetz would call a *small* event, affecting only a small area relative to the prevailing parcel size. If the commons is being ruined by small events, there is an easy solution: cut the land into parcels. We see this solution everywhere. If we can divide the land into parcels of a certain size, such that the cost of grazing an extra sheep is borne entirely by the individual owner who decides whether to graze the extra sheep, then we have internalized externalities and solved the problem. If we divide the pasture into private parcels, then what a particular sheep eats on a particular owner's pasture is no one else's concern. The grass is no longer a common pool.

For better or worse, events come in more than one size. For the sake of example, suppose six parcels are situated over a pool of oil in such a way that, via oil wells, each of the six owners has access to the common pool. The more wells individual owners sink, the more oil they can extract, up to a point. As the number of wellheads goes up, oil pressure per wellhead declines. Not only is the reserve of oil ultimately fixed, but the practically extractable reserve eventually begins to decline with the number of wells sunk. Past a point, we no longer have a situation in which what individual owners do on their property is of no concern to other owners.

Instead, the six owners become part of a *medium* event, a kind of problem that neighbors cannot solve simply by putting up fences. This kind of problem occurs when an event is too large to be contained on a single parcel, or does not have a precise and confined location, or migrates from one location to another. For one reason or another, the event is large enough that its effects spill over onto neighboring parcels.

In an unfenced commons, there is in effect only a single parcel, so the words "small," "medium," and "large" would refer simply to the radius over which the effects of an event are felt, that is, small, medium, or large parts of the whole parcel. In a regime that has been cut into smaller parcels, the more interesting distinction is between a small event that affects a single owner, a medium event that affects immediate neighbors, and a large event that affects remote parts of the community. When land is divided into parcels, whether an event is small, medium, or large will depend on the size of the parcels. Whether a regime succeeds in internalizing externalities will depend on whether it succeeds in carving out parcel sizes big enough to contain those events whose effects it is most crucial to internalize. In effect, if an individual owner's parcel size could be increased without limit, any event could be made "small."[20]

Ellickson says private regimes are clearly superior as methods for minimizing the costs of small and medium events. Regarding small events, the first point is that the external effects of small events are by definition vanishingly small. Neighbors do not care when we pick tomatoes on our own land; they do care when we pick tomatoes on their communal plot. In the former case, we are minding our own business; in the latter, we are minding theirs. (In effect, there are no small events on communal land. Everything we do affects our neighbors. Even doing nothing at all affects our neighbors, given that we could instead have been helping to tend the communal gardens.) The second point regarding small events concerns the cost of monitoring. To internalize externalities, whatever the property regime, owners must be able to monitor other would-be users and misusers. On a private parcel, though, it is only boundary crossings that need monitoring; guard dogs and motion sensors can handle that. By contrast, the monitoring needed in a commune involves evaluating whether workers are just going through the motions, whether they are taking more than their share, and so on. In sum, "detecting the presence of a trespasser is much less demanding than evaluating the conduct of a person who is privileged to he where he is."[21] Thus, the external cost of small events is lower on private parcels, and monitoring, while still required, is relatively cheap and relatively nonintrusive in a parcelized regime.

The effects of medium events tend to spill over onto one's neighbors, and thus can be a source of friction. Nevertheless, privatization has the advantage of limiting the number of people having to be consulted about how to deal with the externality, which reduces transaction costs. Instead of consulting the entire community of communal owners, each at liberty with respect to the affected area, one consults a handful of people who own parcels in the immediate area of the medium event. A further virtue of privatization is that disputes arising from medium events tend to be left in the hands of people in the immediate vicinity, who tend to have a better understanding of local conditions and thus are in a better position to devise resolutions without harmful unintended consequences. They are in a better position to foresee the costs and benefits of a medium event.[22]

When it comes to large events, though, there is no easy way to say which mix of private and public property is best. Large events involve far-flung externalities among people who do not have face-to-face relationships. The difficulties in detecting such externalities, tracing them to their source, and holding people accountable for them are difficulties

---

20   I have modified this discussion from that of the original essay, borrowing what first appeared in "Schmidtz and Willott (2003a)."

21   Ellickson (1993) 1327.

22   Ellickson (1993) 1331.

for any kind of property regime. It is no easy task to devise institutions that encourage pulp mills to take responsibility for their actions while simultaneously encouraging people downstream to take responsibility for their welfare, and thus to avoid being harmed by large-scale negative externalities. Ellickson says there is no general answer to the question of which regime best deals with them.

Large events will fall into one of two categories. Releasing toxic wastes into the atmosphere, for example, may violate existing legal rights or community norms. Or, such laws or norms may not yet be in place. Most of the problems arise when existing customs or laws fail to settle who (in effect) has the right of way. That is not a problem with parceling land per se but rather with the fact that key resources like air and waterways remain in a largely unregulated commons.

So, privatization exists in different degrees and takes different forms. Different forms have different incentive properties. Simply parceling out land or sea is not always enough to stabilize possession of resources that make land or sea valuable in the first place. Suppose, fish are known to migrate from one parcel to another. In that case, owners have an incentive to grab as many fish as they can whenever the school passes through their own territory. Thus, simply dividing fishing grounds into parcels may not be enough to put fishermen in a position to avoid collectively exceeding sustainable yields. It depends on the extent to which the sought-after fish migrate from one parcel to another, and on continuously evolving conventions that help neighbors deal with the inadequacy of their fences (or other ways of marking off territory). Clearly, then, not all forms of privatization are equally good at internalizing externalities. Privatization per se is not a panacea, and not all forms of privatization are equal.

There are obvious difficulties with how private property regimes handle large events. The nature and extent of the difficulties depends on details. So, for purposes of comparison, Ellickson looked at how communal regimes handle large events.

5. JAMESTOWN AND OTHER COMMUNES

The Jamestown Colony was North America's first permanent English settlement. It began in 1607 as a commune, sponsored by the London-based Virginia Company. Land was held and managed collectively. The colony's charter guaranteed to each settler an equal share of the collective product regardless of the amount of work personally contributed. Of the original group of 104 settlers, two-thirds died of starvation and disease before their first winter. New shiploads replenished the colony; the winter of 1609 cut the population from five hundred to sixty. Colonist William Simmons wrote, "It were too vile to say (and scarce to be believed) what we endured, but the occasion was only our own for want of providence, industry, and government, and not the barrenness and defect of the country, as is generally supposed."[23] In 1611, career soldier Thomas Dale (appointed by Governor Thomas Gates to administer martial law) arrived to find living skeletons bowling in the

---

23   Haile (1998) 340.

streets, waiting for someone else to plant the crops.[24] The settlers' main food source consisted of wild animals such as turtles and raccoons, which they hunted and ate by dark of night before neighbors arrived to demand equal shares.[25]

Colonist George Percy wrote that bad water accounted for many deaths, but most of the deaths were from "meere famine."[26] Archeologist Ivor Hume writes with wonder: "The James Fort colonists' unwillingness or inability to work toward their own salvation remains one of American history's great mysteries."[27] Newly arriving ship's crew members caught 7-foot sturgeon and oysters the size of dinner plates, and left their fishing gear with the colonists. How could colonists starve under such circumstances? Moreover, "Percy's recognition that bad water was the cause of many deaths leaves one asking why, then, nothing was done to combat its dangers. That foul water was bad for you had been known for centuries."[28]

In 1614, Thomas Dale (by now governor) had seen enough. He assigned 3-acre plots to individual settlers, which reportedly increased productivity at least sevenfold. (What colonist Captain John Smith actually said was "When our people were fed out of the common store, and laboured jointly together, glad was he could slip from his labour, or slumber over his taske he care not how, nay, the most honest among them would hardly

---

24   The word chosen by eyewitness George Percy was not skeletons but "anatomies" (Haile, 1998, 507). Eyewitness Ralph Hamor refers to Thomas Dale arriving at Jamestown, where "the most company were, amid their daily and usuall workes, bowling in the streetes." Dale declared marital law, conscripting these people to repair their buildings, plant corn, etc. (Hume 1994, 298).

25   As reported by CNN News, Sept. 13, 1996, on the occasion of the original fort's excavation.

26   Hume (1994) 159.

27   Hume (1994) 160.

28   Hume (1994) 160. Hume adds: "Although considering the geology of Jamestown Island, it would have been fruitless to try to reach sustained freshwater by digging wells, they were not to know that—but nobody even tried!" (161). Upon visiting the Jamestown excavation in 2007, I saw new diggings indicating that the colonists had indeed tried to dig a well, but Hume's point still holds. When the well project failed, the colonists seemed to give up. Just as inexplicably, they seem to have torn down sections of the fort to use as firewood, even though eyewitnesses described the edge of the forest as "within a stone's throw." Apart from the need for firewood, the forest should have been cut back anyway so as to secure the fort's perimeter.

take so much true paines in a weeke, as now for themselves they will doe in a day,") [29] The colony converted the rest of its land holdings to private parcels in 1619.[30]

Why go communal in the first place? Are there advantages to communal regimes? One advantage is obvious. Communal regimes can help people spread risks under conditions where risks are substantial and where alternative risk-spreading mechanisms, like insurance, are unavailable. The Virginia Company was sending settlers to a frontier where, without help, something as simple as a sprained ankle could be fatal. The only form of insurance available was, in effect, mutual insurance among the settlers, backed up by their ability to work overtime for less fortunate neighbors. But as communities build up capital reserves to the point where they can offer insurance, they tend to privatize, for insurance lets them secure a measure of risk spreading without having to endure the externalities that tend to afflict communal regimes.

A communal regime might also be an effective response to economies of scale in large-scale public works that are crucial in getting a community started. To build a fort, man its walls, dig wells, and so on, a communal economy is an obvious choice as a way of mobilizing the teams of workers needed to execute these urgent tasks. But again, as these tasks are completed and community welfare increasingly comes to depend on small events, the communal regime gives way to private parcels. At Jamestown, Plymouth, the Amana colonies, and Salt Lake, formerly communal settlers "understandably would switch to private land tenure, the system that most cheaply induces individuals to undertake small and medium events that are socially useful."[31] (The legend of Salt Lake says that the sudden improvement in the fortunes of once-starving Mormons occurred in 1848, when God sent seagulls to save

---

29 Quoted by Ellickson (1993) 1337. After visiting Jamestown in 2007, talking to four history buffs who work there, and reading scholarly work published since the first version of this essay (including Haile's extraordinary collection of eyewitness accounts), I now suspect that several factors exacerbated the communal charter's corrosive incentive effects. First, the Virginia Company intended to make a profit, so eventually skimming the produce of the colony was precisely the point. The colonists resented having been misled about how difficult life would be, and the idea of working harder than required for their own subsistence, largely to profit the lying fat cats who had put them in their plight to begin with, was intolerable. Second, the colonists wanted to go home, and had the idea that they could win a deadly fame of chicken. The idea, as reported by a horrified Thomas Dale, was: "We will weary out the Company at home in sending us provisions, and then, when they grow weary and see that we do not prosper here, they will send for us home. Therefore let us weary them out" (Haile, 1998, 779).

30 Under the new "Headright" system, settlers were given 50-acre plots, plus an additional 50 acres for each servant in their employ. So, they planted tobacco, harvested a crop, and used the money to return to England to recruit new servant/settlers. The recruiter collected the new settler's 50-acre grant. The new settler got transport to Virginia and some portion of the 50 acres, in return for working the recruiter's land for a few seasons while learning the essential skills. Recruiters thus began to cobble together large plantations, new recruits in turn became recruiters themselves, and Virginia's tobacco economy began to gallop.

31 Ellickson (1993) 1342.

them from plagues of locusts, at the same time they coincidentally were switching to private plots. Similarly, the Jamestown tragedy sometimes is attributed to harsh natural conditions, as if those conditions suddenly changed in 1614, multiplying productivity sevenfold while Governor Dale coincidentally was cutting the land into parcels.)

Of course, the tendency toward decentralized and individualized forms of management is only a (strong) tendency and, in any case, there are trade-offs. For example, what would be a small event on a larger parcel becomes a medium event under more crowded conditions. Loud music is an innocuous small event on a ranch but an irritating medium event in an apartment complex. Changes in technology or population density affect the scope or incidence of externalities. The trend, though, is that as people become aware of and concerned about a medium or large event, they seek ways of reducing the extent to which the event's cost is externalized. Social evolution is partly a process of perceiving new externalities and devising institutions to internalize them.

Historically, the benefits of communal management have not been enough to keep communes together indefinitely. Perhaps the most enduring and successful communes in human memory are the agricultural settlements of the Hutterites, dating back to the sixteenth-century Austria. They migrated to the Dakotas in the 1870s, then to Canada (to avoid compulsory military service during World War I). North American Hutterite communities now contain around forty thousand people (mostly on the Canadian prairies). Hutterites believe in a fairly strict sharing of assets. They forbid radio and television, to give one example of how strictly they control contact with the outside world.

Ellickson says Hutterite communities have three special things going for them:

A population cap: when a settlement reaches a population of 120, a portion of the community must leave to start a new community. The cap helps them retain a close-knit society.

Communal dining and worship: people congregate several times a day, which facilitates an intense monitoring of individual behavior and a ready avenue for supplying rapid feedback to those whose behavior deviates from expectations.

A ban on birth control: the average woman bears ten children (the highest documented fertility rate of any human population), which more than offsets the trickle of emigration.[32]

We might add that Hutterite culture and education leave people ill-prepared to live in anything other than Hutterite society, which accounts for the low emigration rate.

Ellickson discusses other examples of communal property regimes. But the most pervasive example of communal ownership in America, Ellickson says, is the family household. American suburbia consists of family communes nested within a network of open-access roadways. Family homes tacitly recognize limits to how far we can go in converting common holdings to individual parcels. Consider your living room. You could fully privatize, having one household member own it while others pay user fees. The fees could be used

---

32 Seth Mydans, "Hmong Refugees Import a Near Record Birthrate," *New York Times*, August 27, 1989, http://query.nytimes.com/gst/fullpage.html?sec=health&res=950DE7 D91631F934A1575BC0A96 F948260.

to pay family members or outside help to keep it clean. In some respects, it would be better that way. The average communal living room today, for example, is notably subject to overgrazing and shirking on maintenance. Yet we put up with it. No one charges user fees to household members. Seeing the living room degraded by communal use may be irritating, but it is better than treating it as one person's private domain.

Some institutions succeed while embodying a form of ownership that is essentially collective. History indicates, though, that members of successful communes internalize the rewards that come with that collective responsibility. In particular, they reserve the right to exclude nonmembers. A successful commune does not run itself as an open-access commons.

6. GOVERNANCE BY CUSTOM

Many commons (such as our living rooms) are regulated by custom rather than by government, so saying there is a role for common property and saying there is a role for government management of common property are two different things. As Ellickson notes, "Group ownership does not necessarily imply government ownership, of course. The sorry environmental records of federal land agencies and Communist regimes are a sharp reminder that governments are often particularly inept managers of large tracts."[33] Carol Rose tells of how, in the nineteenth century, public property was thought to be owned by society at large. The idea of public property often was taken to imply no particular role for government beyond whatever enforcement role is implied by private property. Society's right to such property was held to precede and supersede any claim by government. Rose says, "Implicit in these older doctrines is the notion that, even if a property should be open to the public, it does not follow that public rights should necessarily vest in an active governmental manager."[34] Sometimes, rights were held by an "unorganized public" rather than by a "governmentally organized public."[35]

Along the same lines, open-field agricultural practices of medieval times gave peasants exclusive cropping rights to scattered thin strips of arable land in each of the village fields. The strips were private only during the growing season, after which the land reverted to the commons for the duration of the grazing season.[36] Thus, ownership of parcels was usufructuary, in the sense that once the harvest was in, ownership reverted to the common herdsmen without negotiation or formal transfer.[37] The farmer had an exclusive claim to

---

33 Ellickson (1993) 1335.

34 Rose (1986) 720.

35 Rose (1986) 736.

36 Ellickson (1993) 1390.

37 For an excellent discussion of the issue of adverse possession, see Rose (1985). A "usufructuary" right is an entitlement that persists only so long as the owner is using an item for its customary purpose. For example, you establish a usufructuary right in a park bench by sitting on it, but you abandon that right when you leave.

the land only so long as he was using it for the purpose of bringing in a harvest. The scattering of strips was a means of diversification, reducing the risk of being ruined by small or medium events: small fires, pest infestations, and so on. The postharvest commons in grazing land exploited economies of scale in fencing and tending a herd. The scattering of strips also made it harder for a communal herdsman to position livestock exclusively over his own property, thus promoting more equitable distribution of manure (i.e., fertilizer).[38]

According to Martin Bailey, the pattern observed by Rose and Ellickson also was common among aboriginal tribes. That is, tribes that practiced agriculture treated the land as private during the growing season, and often treated it as a commons after the crops were in. Hunter-gatherer societies did not practice agriculture, but they, too, tended to leave the land in the commons during the summer when game was plentiful. It was during the winter, when food was most scarce, that they privatized. The rule among hunter-gatherers is that where group hunting's advantages are considerable, that factor dominates. But in the winter, small game is relatively more abundant, less migratory, and evenly spread. There was no "feast or famine" pattern of the sort one expects to see with big-game hunting. Rather, families tended to gather enough during the course of the day to get themselves through the day, day after day, with little to spare.[39]

Even though this pattern corroborates my own general thesis, I confess to being a bit surprised. I might have predicted that it would be during the harshest part of the year that families would band together and throw everything into the common pot in order to pull through. Not so. It was when the land was nearest its carrying capacity that they recognized the imperative to privatize.

Customary use of medieval commons was hedged with restrictions limiting depletion of resources. Custom prohibited activities inconsistent with the land's ability to recover.[40] In particular, the custom of "stinting" allowed the villagers to own livestock only in proportion to the relative size of their (growing season) land holdings. Governance by custom enabled people to avoid commons tragedies.[41]

Custom is a form of management unlike exclusive ownership by individuals or governments. Custom is a self-managing system for according property rights.[42] For example, custom governs rights-claims you establish by taking a place in line at a supermarket checkout counter. Rose believes common concerns often are best handled by decentralized, piecemeal, self-managing customs that tend to arise as needed at the local level.

---

38   Ellickson (1993) 1390.

39   Bailey (1992).

40   Rose (1986) 743.

41   Of course, no one thinks governance by custom automatically solves commons problems. Custom works when local users can restrict outsider access and monitor insider behavior, but those conditions are not always met, and tragedies like those discussed earlier continue to occur.

42   Rose (1986) 742.

So, to the previous section's conclusion that a successful commune does not operate as an open-access commons, we can add that a successful commune does not entrust its governance to a distant bureaucracy.

7. THE HUTTERITE SECRET

I argued that the original appropriation of (and subsequent regulation of access to) scarce resources is justifiable as a mechanism for preserving opportunities for future generations. There are various means of exclusive control, though. Some internalize externalities better than others, and how well they do so depends on the context. There is no single form of exclusive control that uniquely serves this purpose. Which form is best depends on what kind of activities are most prevalent in a community at any given time. It also depends on the extent to which public ownership implies control by a distant bureaucracy rather than by local custom.

As mentioned earlier, I have heard people say Jamestown failed because it faced harsh natural conditions. But communal (and noncommunal) settlements typically face harsh natural conditions. Jamestown had to deal with summer in Virginia. Hutterites dealt with winter on the Canadian prairie. It is revealing, not misleading, to compare Jamestown to settlements that faced harsher conditions more successfully. It also is fair to compare the two Jamestowns: the one before and the one immediately following Governor Dale's mandated privatization. What distinguished the first Jamestown from the second was not the harshness of the former's natural setting but rather the thoroughness with which it prevented people from internalizing externalities.

Michael Hechter considers group solidarity to be a function of (1) the extent to which members depend on the group and (2) the extent to which the group can monitor and enforce compliance with expectations that members will contribute to the group rather than free ride upon it.[43] On Hetchter's analysis, it is unsurprising that Hutterite communal society has been successful. Members are extremely dependent, for their upbringing leaves them unprepared to live in a non-Hutterite culture. Monitoring is intense. Feedback is immediate. But if that is the Hutterite secret, why did Jamestown fail? They, too, were extremely dependent on each other. They, too, had nowhere else to go. Monitoring was equally straightforward. Everyone knew who was planting crops (no one) and who was bowling (everyone). What was the problem?

The problem lay in the guarantee embedded in Jamestown charter. The charter entitled people to an equal share regardless of personal contribution, which is to say it ensure that individual workers would be maximally alienated from the fruits of their labors—that they would think of their work as disappearing into an open-access commons.

---

43   Hechter (1983) 21.

Robert Goodin says, "Working within the constraints set by natural scarcity, the greatest practical obstacle to achieving as much justice as resources permit is, and always has been, the supposition that each of us should cultivate his own garden."[44] However, Jamestown's charter did not suppose each of us should cultivate his own garden. It supposed the opposite. Colonists abided by the charter, and starved. Only a few years later, with a new charter, colonists were tending their own gardens, and thriving.

We should applaud institutions that encourage people to care for each other. But telling people they are required to tend someone else's garden rather than their own does not encourage people to care for each other. It does the opposite. It encourages spite. The people of Jamestown reached the point where they would rather die, bowling in the street, than tend the gardens of their free-riding neighbors, and die they did.

REFERENCES

Bailey, Martin J. 1992. Approximate Optimality of Aboriginal Property Rights. *Journal of Law and Economics.* 35: 183–98.

Bogart, J. H. 1985. Lockean Provisos and State of Nature Theories. *Ethics* 95: 828–36.

Chesher, R. 1985. Practical Problems in Coral Reef Utilization and Management: a Tongan Case Study. *Proceedings of the Fifth International Coral Reef Congress* 4: 213–24.

Davis, Frederick R. 2007. *The Man Who Saved Sea Turtles: Archie Carr and the Origins of Conservation Biology.* New York: Oxford University Press.

Demsetz, Harold. 1967. Toward a Theory of Property Rights. *American Economic Review.* (Papers & Proceedings) 57: 347–59.

Dukeminier, Jesse, and James E. Krier. 1993. *Property.* 3rd edn. Boston: Little, Brown.

Ellickson, Robert C. 1993. Property in Land. *Yale Law Journal* 102: 1315–1400.

Fosdick, Peggy, and Fosdick, Sam. 1994. *Last Chance Lost?* York, PA: Irvin S. Naylor Publishing.

Fried, Barbara. 1995. Wilt Chamberlain Revisited: Nozick's "Justice in Transfer" and the Problem of Market-Based Distribution. *Philosophy and Public Affairs* 24; 226–45.

Gomez, E.; A. Alcala; and A. San Diego. 1981. Status of Philippine Coral Reefs—1981. *Proceedings of the Fourth International Coral Reef Symposium* 1: 275–85.

Goodin, Robert E. 1985. *Protecting the Vulnerable: Toward a reanalysis of Our Social Responsibilities.* Chicago: University of Chicago Press.

Haile, Edward W. ed. 1998. *Jamestown Narratives: Eye Witness Accounts of the Virginia Colony, The First Decade, 1607–1617.* Champlain, Virginia: Roundhouse.

Hardin, Garrett. 1977. The Ethical Implications of Carrying Capacity. In G. Hardin and J. Baden, eds., *Managing the commons.* San Francisco: W. H. Freeman.

Hechter, Michael. 1983. A Theory of Group Solidarity. In Hechter, ed., *Microfoundations of Macrosociology.* Philadelphia: Temple University Press. 16–57.

---

44   Goodin (1985, 1) Good and I debate the issue at length in Schmidtz and Goodin (1998).

Held,Virginia. 1980. Introduction. In Held, ed., *Property, Profits, & Economic Justice*. Belmont: Wadsworth.

Hohfeld, Wesley. 1919. *Fundamental Legal Conceptions*. New Haven: Yale University Press.

Hume, Ivor N. 1994, *The Virginia Adventure*. Charlottesville: University of Virginia Press.

Locke, John. 1690. *Second Treatise of Government*. ed. P. Laslett. Cambridge: Cambridge University Press (reprinted 1960).

Nash, J. Madeleine. 1996. Wrecking the Reefs. *Time* (September 30): 60–2.

Rose, Carol. 1985. Possession as the Origin of Property. *University of Chicago Law Review*. 52: 73–88

Rose, Carol. 1986. The Comedy of the Commons: Custom, Commerce, and Inherently Public Property. *University of Chicago Law Review* 53: 711–87.

Sanders, John T. 1987. Justice and the Initial Acquisition of Private Property. *Harvard Journal of Law and Public Policy* 10: 367–99.

Sartorius, Rolf. 1984. Persons and Property. In Ray Frey, ed., *Utility and rights*. Minneapolis: University of Minnesota Press.

Schmidtz, David, and Robert E. Goodin. 1998. *Social Welfare and Individual Responsibility*. Cambridge: Harvard University Press.

Schmidtz, David, and Elizabeth Willott. 2003. "The Tragedy of the Commons," *Blackwell Companion to Applied Ethics*, ed. R.G. Frey & Christopher Wellman, 662–73. Oxford: Blackwell.

Schmidtz, David, and Elizabeth Willott. 2003a. "Reinventing the Commons: An African Case Study," *University of California at Davis Law Review* 36: 203–32.

Thomson, Judith Jarvis. 1990. *The Realm of Rights*. Cambridge: Harvard University Press.

Waldron, Jeremy. Enough and As Good Left For Others. *Philosophical Quarterly. 29* (1976) 319–28.

CHAPTER 4

✝

MUTUAL RESPECT AND EXPLOITATION

Sweatshops

Matt Zwolinski

Abstract: *This paper argues that sweatshop workers' choices to accept the conditions of their employment are morally significant, both as an exercise of their autonomy and as an expression of their preferences. This fact establishes a moral claim against interference in the conditions of sweatshop labor by third parties such as governments or consumer boycott groups. It should also lead us to doubt those who call for MNEs to voluntarily improve working conditions, at least when their arguments are based on the claim that workers have a moral right to such improvement. These conclusions are defended against three objections: 1) that sweatshop workers' consent to the conditions of their labor is not fully voluntary, 2) that sweatshops' offer of additional labor options is part of an overall package that actually harms workers, 3) that even if sweatshop labor benefits workers, it is nevertheless wrongfully exploitative.*

1. INTRODUCTION

For the most part, individuals who work in sweatshops choose to do so. They might not *like* working in sweatshops, and they might strongly desire that their circumstances were such that they did not have to do so. Nevertheless, the fact that they choose to work in sweatshops is morally significant. Taken seriously, workers' consent

Matt Zwolinski, "Sweatshops, Choice, and Exploitation," from *Business Ethics Quarterly: The Journal of the Society for Business Ethics*, Vol. 17, No. 4; October 2007, pp. 689–727. Copyright © 2007 by Philosophy Documentation Center. Permission to reprint granted by the publisher.
Footnotes deleted to save space. For a version with complete footnotes, visit The Freedom Center web site at the University of Arizona. (Google Freedom Center Arizona.) Click on "The 205 Store." As of the date of printing, the username for the file is "philosophy" and the password is "205".

to the conditions of their labor should lead us to abandon certain moral objections to sweatshops, and perhaps even to view them as, on net, a good thing.

This argument, or something like it, is the core of a number of popular and academic defenses of the moral legitimacy of sweatshops. It has been especially influential among economists, who point to the voluntary nature of sweatshop employment as evidence for the claim that Western governments ought not to restrict the importation of goods made by sweatshops (Anderson, 1996: 694), or that labor-rights organizations ought not to seek to change the law in countries which host sweatshops in order to establish higher minimum wages or better working conditions (Krugman, 1997; Maitland, 1996), or, finally, that consumer boycotts of sweatshop-produced goods are misguided (Kristof & Wudunn, 2000).

This paper seeks to defend a version of the argument above, while at the same time clarifying its structure and content. The first step is to understand how a worker's consent can have any moral weight at all. How does choice have the power (a 'moral magic,' as some have called it) to transform the moral and legal nature of certain interactions (Hurd, 1996)? I begin the paper in section two by exploring several ways in which choice can be morally transformative. I distinguish between autonomy-exercising and preference-evincing choice, and argue that while the latter has been given far more attention in the mostly consequentialist defenses of sweatshops, the former notion of consent, with its deontological underpinnings, is relevant as well. With this preliminary work accomplished, I then put forward in section three what I take to be the best reconstruction of the argument which seeks to base a moral defense of sweatshops on the consent of their workers. In section four, I explain how this argument undermines various proposals made by anti-sweatshop activists and academics. The remainder of the paper is devoted to a critical examination of this argument. I first examine, in section five, whether the morally transformative power of sweatshop workers' consent is undermined by a lack of voluntariness, failure of independence, or exploitation. My conclusion is that, at least in general, it is not. After having completed this discussion of the moral *weight* of consent in section five, I turn to considerations of its moral *force* in section 6. If consent makes sweatshop labor morally justifiable, what does that tell us about how businesses, consumers, and governments ought to act? And, perhaps more interestingly, if consent does *not* make sweatshop labor morally justifiable, what does *that* tell us? My position is that there is a large gulf between concluding that the activities of sweatshops are morally evil and concluding that sweatshop labor ought to be legally prohibited, boycotted, regulated, or prohibited by moral norms. To the extent that sweatshops do evil to their workers, they do so in the context of providing their workers with a financial benefit, and workers' eager readiness to consent to the conditions of sweatshop labor shows that they view this benefit as considerable. This fact leads to the ultimate practical conclusion of this paper, which is that there is a strong moral reason for third parties such as consumers and host and home country governments to refrain from acting in ways which are likely to deprive sweatshop workers of their jobs, and that both the policies traditionally promoted by anti-sweatshop activists (e.g., increasing the legal regulation of sweatshops, legally prohibiting the sale of sweatshop-produced goods, or subjecting such goods to economic boycott), and some more recent proposals by anti-sweatshop academics (i.e., voluntary self-regulation via industry-wide standards or universal moral norms) are subject to criticism on these grounds.

Before I begin with the main argument of the paper, however, I want to make a brief statement about the methodology by which that argument will proceed. Because there is such widespread disagreement among philosophers regarding what precise form a correct moral theory will have, I attempt to frame the argument of this paper in such a way that it remains valid given a wide range of conflicting assumptions about foundational moral questions, and to keep my assumptions on these matters as minimal as possible. This approach has its drawbacks. Those who are interested in approaching moral philosophy exclusively from the standpoint of one particular theory might find that theory given short shrift in this paper. And those who are interested in the foundations of moral theory will find little exploration of those topics here. I proceed in this manner not because I find such questions unimportant, but rather in order to be able to address a matter of broad social significance from a perspective that is relevant to as wide an audience as possible. In Rawlsian language, I hope that by avoiding commitment to any comprehensive moral doctrine, the argument of this paper might be part of an "overlapping consensus" of reasonable positions, finding support from not just one but a number of different more comprehensive moral theories.

2. THE MORAL MAGIC OF CHOICE

An agent's choice, or consent, is transformative insofar as it "alters the normative relations in which others stand with respect to what they may do" (Kleinig, 2001: 300). This transformation can affect both the moral and the legal claims and obligations of both the parties involved, and of third parties. Consent to sexual relations, for instance, can render permissible one's partner's otherwise impermissible sexual touching, and render it impermissible for third parties to interfere with the sexual activity to which one has consented. But the moral transformation to which choice gives rise can occur for various reasons. In this section, I will discuss two ways in which choice can be morally transformative, and argue that both are relevant to the case of sweatshop labor.

a. Autonomy-Exercising Choice

One way that choice can be morally transformative is if it is an exercise of an agent's autonomy. Sometimes we view the decisions of others as worthy of our respect because we believe that they reflect the agent's will, or because they stem from desires, goals and projects that are expressive the agent's authentic self. If so, this fact will often provide us with a reason for not interfering with the agent's action even if we think the consequences of her action will be bad for her, and even if we disagree with the reasoning that underlies her decision. I might believe my neighbor's religious practices to be based on an untrue faith, and ultimately detrimental to his financial, emotional, and spiritual well-being. Nonetheless, I am not entitled to compel my neighbor to abandon his religion, and this is not merely because the consequences of my interference would be worse for my neighbor than my doing nothing. Even if I could make him better off by compelling him to abandon his religion, and even if my coercion would have no other ill effects in the world, a respect for my neighbor's autonomy would still require me to abstain from such behavior.

Thus, one way that a worker's choice to accept the conditions of sweatshop labor can be morally transformative is if it is an exercise of autonomy. Such a choice can, I will argue, be morally transformative in certain respects even if it is not a *fully* autonomous one, and even if it does not achieve the full range of moral transformations that such a fully autonomous choice would yield. Specifically, I believe that a worker's autonomous choice to accept conditions of employment establishes a strong claim to freedom from certain sorts of interference by others, even if it fails to render the employment relationship a morally praiseworthy one. But how strong a claim to non-interference does it generate? And against which sorts of interference does it hold?

To take the first question first, it is of course true that not all autonomous choices generate claims to non-interference. But when the subject matter of the choice is of central importance to the agent's identity or core projects, it is plausible to suppose that autonomous choices do generate strong claims to liberty. And it is hard to deny that the choices made by potential sweatshop workers *are* of central importance in just this way. Sweatshop workers do not generally choose to work in order to gain some extra disposable income for luxuries, or simply to take pleasure in the activity of working. They work to survive, or to help their family survive, or so their children can gain an education and escape the misery of poverty that drove them to sweatshops in the first place. Choices such as these involve projects—one's own survival, one's role as a parent or a spouse—that are of central importance to most people's lives. Such choices, when made autonomously, deserve respect.

But what does respect amount to in this context? In the case of religious liberty, we think that the autonomous pursuit of religious practice generates a claim against certain sorts of interference with that practice by others. We might similarly hold, then, that the autonomous acceptance of sweatshop labor generates a claim against interference in carrying out the terms of their agreement, such as the kind that would be involved most obviously in an outright legal prohibition of sweatshop labor. But the idea that autonomous choice generates a claim to non-interference is one which stands in need of closer examination.

The analogy of religious practice is instructive. Note that even in the religious case, not *all* manifestations of religious practice are protected by a claim to noninterference, and not *all* kinds of interference, even those which involve the core aspects of religious practice, are prohibited. A religious believer who desires to murder a non-believer because his religion orders him to do so has *no* claim to freedom from interference in pursuit of this project. And even the ordinary religious desire to adhere to a certain structure of beliefs has no claim to freedom from the kind of interference that we classify as "persuasion." I cannot *force* you into abandoning your religious faith, but I can certainly try to talk you out of it.

I do not believe that the above qualifications pose a serious difficulty for the claim that the autonomous choice to accept sweatshop labor is entitled to a claim to noninterference. The reason the religious believer's desire to murder the non-believer is not entitled to any such claim is that the activity he wishes to engages in violates the rights of another. But those who worry about sweatshop labor are not typically worried that sweatshop workers are violating anyone else's rights. If anything, they worry that the rights of the sweatshop worker himself are being violated. But the fact that a worker loses some of his rights is a *consequence* of the autonomy of his choice, not an objection to it. One of the things that autonomous choices allow us to do is to waive certain claims that we might have had (in the case of workers, the claim not to be told what to do by others, or the claim to certain kinds of freedom of association, for instance). It is because we think it important to allow people to waive their rights in this way that we find autonomy to be such an important value, and why we believe it proper to respect autonomous choices—at least those which are largely self-regarding—with non-interference.

This is not to say that *all* sorts of interference with a sweatshop worker's choice are impermissible. To take some easy examples, it is of course permissible to use persuasion to try to get a sweatshop worker to not accept conditions of employment that you view as exploitative. And it is likewise permissible to start an ethically run MNE and to compete with the unethical sweatshop for its labor force. There are good reasons, both consequentialist and deontological, for refusing to view these sorts of actions as objectionable violations of workers' autonomy. But it *would* be immoral, I believe, to prevent contracts for sweatshop labor by legislative fiat. To do so would be to violate the autonomy of the workers who would have otherwise chosen to work in such conditions. And what it is immoral to do directly, it is also probably immoral to do indirectly. Laws which have the effect of preventing workers and sweatshops from freely contracting together—such as laws in the host country which raise the price of labor to a prohibitively high rate, or laws in countries that consume sweatshop labor which ban the importation of sweatshop-made goods—are thus also morally suspect.

b. Preference-Evincing Choice

Choices are more than a method of exercising autonomy. Choices also signal information about an agent's preferences. Significantly, this is true even when the choice is made under conditions of less than full autonomy. An agent faced with the gunman's threat of "your money or your life," for instance, still has a choice to make, even if it is only from among a range of options which has been illegitimately restricted by the gunman. And should the agent decide to hand over his wallet, this would tell us that among the two options he faces, as he understands them, he prefers giving his wallet to the gunman to losing his life. This might not be morally transformative in the same *way* as a fully autonomous choice would be, but surely it does *something* to change the moral landscape. Compare the following two cases:

> Accommodating Kidnapper: *A* kidnaps *B* and locks her in his basement. When mealtime arrives, *A* asks *B* which of two foods she would prefer to eat, and gives her whichever she requests.

> Curmudgeonly Kidnapper: *A* kidnaps *B* and locks her in his basement. When mealtime arrives, *A* asks *B* which of two foods she would prefer to eat, and gives her whichever one she does *not* request.

In both versions of the story, *A* illegitimately restricts *B*'s range of options. In neither case is *B*'s choice of meals fully autonomous. Still, it *is* a choice, and it seems clear that *B*'s making it will affect what *A* ought to do. Disregarding *B*'s preferences by giving her the meal that she least prefers is a wrong above and beyond the initial wrong of coercion. By choosing one meal over another, she has conveyed information about her preferences to *A*. And by giving her the meal she least prefers, *A* is knowingly acting in a way likely to make her worse off, and this is wrong. *B*'s choice is thus morally transformative, but in a way different from that described in the previous section. Here, the moral transformation occurs as a result of *B*'s choice providing *A* with information about *B*'s preferences. Knowing what somebody prefers often changes what one ought to do. It might not be wrong for me to serve fish to a guest about whom I know nothing. But if my guest tells me that she despises fish, serving it to her anyway would be (*ceteris paribus*) extremely disrespectful. By expressing preferences, choices thus transform the moral landscape.

In the mugging case, the victim's choice to hand over his wallet might not make the mugger's decision to take it a morally praiseworthy one, or even a morally permissible one. In *these* respects, therefore, his choice is *not* morally transformative. But there is another respect in which it is. It is transformative in that it renders impermissible certain attempts by other persons to interfere with his activity. A well-meaning busybody who attempted to prevent the victim from handing over his wallet, believing that death in such circumstances was surely better than dishonor, would be acting wrongly, and what makes the act wrong is that it goes against the victim's choice—whether that choice is fully autonomous or not.

In a similar way, then, a worker's choice to accept sweatshop labor can be morally transformative by signaling information about her preferences. A worker's choice to accept sweatshop labor shows that she prefers that kind of labor to any other alternative. Sweatshop labor might not be the kind of thing for which she has any *intrinsic* desire. But when all things are considered—her poverty, the wages paid by the sweatshop and that paid by alternative sources of employment, etc.—she prefers working there to anything else she might do.

And by expressing her preferences, her choice is morally transformative. To attempt to directly remove the option of sweatshop labor (or to act in ways which are likely to indirectly remove that option), while knowing that sweatshop labor is the most preferred option of many workers, is to knowingly act in a way which is likely to cause workers harm. Indeed, given that many potential sweatshop workers seem to express a *strong* preference for sweatshop labor over the alternatives, acting to remove that option is likely to cause them *great* harm. This is, *ceteris paribus*, wrong.

Sweatshop workers' choices can thus be morally transformative in two ways—by being exercises of their autonomy, or by being expressions of their preferences. Note that while both sorts of choice can be morally transformative, they achieve their respective transformations by calling attention to very different sorts of values or considerations. The proper response to an autonomy-exercising choice is one of *respect*, and this respect seems to counsel non-interference with the agent's choice even if we believe the consequences of interfering would be superior for the agent. Preference-evincing choices often give us reason for non-interference as well, but *only because* we think the consequences of doing so will be better in some respect for the agent. The expression of a choice for one thing over another is usually good evidence that one actually prefers that thing over the other, and it is, *ceteris paribus*, better for one to get what one wants.

With this understanding of the morally transformative power of choice in hand, we are now ready to turn to a closer look to the argument with which this paper began—an argument that seeks to base a moral defense of sweatshops on the consent of the workers.

3. THE ARGUMENT

1. Most sweatshop workers choose to accept the conditions of their employment, even if their choice is made from among a severely constrained set of options.
2. The fact that they choose the conditions of their employment from within a constrained set of options is strong evidence that they view it as their most-preferred option (within that set).
3. The fact that they view it as their most-preferred option is strong evidence that we will harm them by taking that option away.

4. It is also plausible that sweatshop workers' choice to accept the conditions of their employment is sufficiently autonomous that taking the option of sweatshop labor away from them would be a violation of their autonomy.
5. All else being equal, it is wrong to harm people or to violate their autonomy.
6. Therefore, all else being equal, it is wrong to take away the option of sweatshop labor from workers who would otherwise choose to engage in it.

I believe this argument (hereafter, "The Argument") captures and clarifies what lies behind many popular defenses of sweatshops. There are three things to note about it. The first is that, unlike popular defenses, The Argument clearly distinguishes two different ways in which workers' choices can serve to establish a claim of non-interference against those who act in ways that make sweatshop labor a nonoption—one based in respect for workers' autonomy (1, 4, 5, and 6) and another based in an obligation not to harm (1, 2, 3, 5 and 6). Unlike the standard economic defense of sweatshops, then, The Argument is not purely consequentialist in nature. Appeals to consequences are relevant in The Argument's appeal to the preference-evincing power of choice, which cautions us to avoid harming workers by frustrating their revealed preferences. But The Argument has a deontological foundation as well, which is brought out in its notion of autonomy-exercising choice. Here, The Argument counsels us to refrain from interfering in sweatshop workers' choices, not because that interference would frustrate preference-satisfaction, but because doing so would violate workers' autonomy in their choice of employment.

The second thing to note about The Argument is that, again unlike popular defenses, it is clear regarding the nature of the moral transformation that sweatshop workers' choices effect. Their choice establishes a claim of non-interference against those who might wish to prevent them from engaging in sweatshop labor, or make that labor more difficult to obtain. That is all that is claimed by The Argument. It does not attempt to show that workers' choices render the treatment bestowed on them by their employers morally praiseworthy. It does not even attempt to show that their choice renders such treatment morally *permissible*. And, finally, it does not establish an *insuperable* claim against interference. The Argument shows that harming sweatshop workers or violating their autonomy is wrong, but leaves open the possibility that these wrongs could be justifiable in certain circumstances. The Argument simply shifts the burden of proof on to those who wish to prohibit sweatshop labor to provide such justification.

The final thing to note about The Argument is that its success is extremely sensitive to a wide range of empirical facts. The truth of premise 1, for instance, hinges on whether people *do* in fact choose to work in sweatshops, and fails in cases of genuinely forced labor. The claim that we harm sweatshop workers' by removing what they see as their best option (premise 3) depends on particular facts about the nature of an individual's preferences and their relation to her well-being, and the claim that workers' choices are autonomous (premise 4) depends on the particular conditions under which the choice to accept sweatshop labor is made. This sensitivity to empirical facts means that we cannot determine *a priori* whether The Argument is successful. But this is as it should be. Sweatshops are a complicated phenomenon, and while philosophers have an important contribution to make to the conversation about their moral justifiability, it is only a partial contribution. For the complete picture, we need to supplement our moral theorizing with data from (at least) economists, psychologists, and social scientists. In this paper, I will draw on empirical data to support my argument where it is available. Since I am not well positioned to evaluate the soundness of such data, however, I will attempt to clearly signal when I appeal to it, and to indicate the way in which The Argument's success is or is not reliant on its veracity.

4. WHAT POLICIES DOES THE ARGUMENT OPPOSE?

The Argument's conclusion is that it is wrong to 'take away' the option of sweatshop labor from those who would otherwise choose to engage in it. But what exactly does it mean to take away the option of sweatshop labor? What sort of policies is The Argument meant to oppose?

a. Bans and Boycotts

The most obvious way in which the option of sweatshop labor can be 'taken away' is a legal ban on sweatshops or, more commonly, on the sale or importation of sweatshop-produced goods. The mechanism by which the former sort of ban removes the option of sweatshop labor is fairly obvious. But bans on the sale or importation of sweatshop goods can, if effective and large enough in scale, achieve the same results. If goods made in sweatshops cannot be sold, then it seems likely that sweatshops will stop producing such goods, and those who were employed in their production will be out of work. Economists and others have therefore criticized such bans as counterproductive in the quest to aid the working poor. As a result, neither sort of ban is defended by many anti-sweatshop scholars writing today, but many activists and politicians persist in their support of such measures. The Argument condemns them.

b. Legal Regulation

Bans on the importation or sale of sweatshop-produced goods take sweatshop jobs away from their workers by making their continued employment no longer economically viable for their employers. The increased legal regulation of sweatshops can accomplish the same effect for the same reason. Legal attempts to ameliorate working conditions in sweatshops by regulating the use of and pay for overtime, minimum wage laws, or workplace safety, for instance, raise the cost which sweatshops must incur to employ their workers. This cost is passed on to the MNE which, in turn, might decide once costs have passed a certain level, to move their operations to another country where labor is more productive or less heavily regulated.

Calls for the increased legal regulation of sweatshops are more common among both activists and academics alike. It is worth noting, though, that calls for the increased enforcement of existing regulations are likely to be indistinguishable in their effects. Many laws in the developing world which ostensibly regulate sweatshop activity are either poorly enforced or completely ignored. Sometimes the lack of enforcement is simply due to insufficient resources on the part of the enforcement agency. But sometimes it is a deliberate choice, since government officials want the tax revenue that MNEs bring to the country and worry that increasing the cost of doing business could lead those MNEs to stay away or leave. Calls for the enforcement of existing regulations do have the advantage over calls for new regulation in that such enforcement will help to promote the rule of law—a key value in both economic development and a healthy democracy. But in terms of their effect on workers' jobs, they are equally bad, and equally opposed by The Argument.

c. Voluntary Self-Regulation

Today, many of the most prominent academic critics of sweatshops focus their energy on calls for voluntary self-regulation on the part of MNEs and the sweat shops to which they subcontract. Their hope is that self-regulation can correct the moral failings of sweatshops while at the same time avoiding the unintended harms caused by the more heavy-handed attempts described above.

Nothing in The Argument is opposed to voluntary self-regulation as such. If, as The Argument was specifically formulated to allow, many of the activities of sweatshops are immoral, then they ought to change, and voluntary self-regulation will often be the best way to accomplish this change.

Furthermore, by providing concrete examples of 'positive deviancy'—cases where multinational enterprises have made changes to improve conditions for workers in their supply chain above and beyond those required by market pressures or the law—much of the recent scholarship on self-regulation has provided a valuable model for firms who wish to wish to begin making changes in the right direction.

There are, however, two significant causes for concern over the precise way in which the case for self-regulation has been made in the recent literature. First, to the extent that 'voluntary' self-regulation is to be accomplished by industry-wide standards, the regulation is really only voluntary for the industry as a whole. For any individual firm, compliance is essentially mandatory. Individual firms, then, are in much the same position as they would be under legal regulation, insofar as those who cannot afford to comply with the mandated standard would be forced to cut costs or alter their production in a way that could negatively affect the employment of sweatshop workers. Additionally, industry-wide standards serve as an impediment to the market's discovery process. By establishing *one* standard with which all firms must comply, this sort of approach discourages (and in some cases, prohibits) individual firms from experimenting with their own standards which might be better suited to the particular context in which they are operating.

The second and less well-recognized problem is that by making the case for self-regulation in terms of the *rights* workers have to certain forms of treatment and the *obligations* that MNEs have to ensure such treatment, supporters of 'voluntary' self-regulation end up putting too strong a demand on MNEs for the kind of reform they desire, while paying insufficient attention to ways of helping workers that fall short of their desired goal.

To see this problem more clearly, we can look at the recent work of Denis Arnold. The core philosophical argument of that work claims that workers have rights to freedom and well-being, and argues that these rights require MNEs to ensure that certain minimum conditions are met in their supply chain. As an example of the sort of specific obligation to which these general rights to freedom and well-being give rise, Arnold and Hartman state in a recent paper that "respect for the rights of workers to subsistence entails that MNEs and their suppliers have an obligation to ensure that workers do not live under conditions of overall poverty by providing adequate wages for a 48 h work week to satisfy both basic food needs and basic non-food needs" (Arnold & Hartman, 2005: 211).

Now, it cannot be doubted that it would be a morally praiseworthy thing for MNEs to ensure that their workers are given this level of treatment. But this is not what Arnold is claiming. He is claiming that MNEs have an *obligation* to provide this level of treatment—one that is grounded on workers' *rights*. This is making an extremely strong moral claim. Rights are generally thought to be 'trumps'—considerations which, when brought to bear on a decision, are supposed to override any competing claims. Respecting rights is non-optional.

But notice that while rights as such are non-optional, the right and corresponding obligation that Arnold endorses are conditional in an important way. Workers have a right to certain levels of minimum treatment, and MNEs have an obligation to provide it, *if* MNEs involve those workers in their supply chain. But nothing requires MNEs to do so. Workers have a right to adequate wages *if* MNEs contract with sweatshops to employ them. But MNEs are under no obligation to outsource labor in this way at all. And if the only morally permissible way to engage in such outsourcing is to incur heavy costs by seeing that workers receive the minimum level of wages, safety conditions and so forth demanded by Arnold et al., it is quite possible that many MNEs will choose *not* to do so.

Whether they would or not is, of course, an empirical question the resolution of which is beyond the scope of this paper. But merely noting the possibility highlights an odd feature of the logic of Arnold's position. Arnold is committed to claiming that:

1. It is morally permissible for MNEs not to outsource their labor to workers in the developing world at all.

2. It is not morally permissible for MNEs to outsource labor to workers in the developing world without meeting the minimum conditions set forth by Arnold's account of workers' rights.

But empirically, it seems plausible that

3. Sweatshop labor that falls short of meeting the minimum conditions set forth by Arnold's account of workers' rights can still be a net benefit to workers, relative to their other possible sources of employment.

And clearly,

4. MNEs which do not outsource their labor to workers in the developing world do not benefit those workers at all.

It follows that, on Arnold's view,

C1) It is morally permissible for MNEs not to benefit workers at all by not outsourcing their labor to workers in the developing world.

And

C2) It is morally impermissible for MNEs to benefit workers to some extent by outsourcing labor to workers in the developing world without meeting the minimum conditions set forth by Arnold's account of workers' rights.

This means, paradoxically, that according to Arnold's argument MNEs are more morally blameworthy for doing business with a sweatshop that pays less than adequate wages than for doing no business abroad at all, even if workers in the unethical sweatshop would prefer and freely choose their work over the option of no work at all. Indeed, elsewhere in their essay, Arnold and Hartman seem to explicitly embrace this point. They approvingly cite critics (one of whom includes Arnold himself) who argue that "regardless of the kinds of benefits that do or do not accrue from the use of sweatshops, it is simply morally impermissible to subject individuals to extended periods of grueling and mind-numbing labour in conditions that put their health and welfare at risk and which provide them with inadequate compensation" (210–11). But I do not think we should be so quick to declare as irrelevant the benefits that accrue to workers under conditions of labor which fall short of meeting the minimum standards demanded by Arnold. Labor which falls short of a living wage can still help a worker feed their family, educate their children, and generally make their lives better than they would have been without it. This is a morally significant benefit, and one our system of moral norms should at the very least *permit*, if not encourage.

Thus, while The Argument *does* not condemn voluntary self-regulation as such, it does condemn the claim that outsourcing labor to the developing world is only permissible if certain minimum standards are met. For we cannot simply assume that MNEs will continue to outsource labor to the developing world if the only conditions under which they may permissibly do so are ones in which the costs of outsourced labor are significantly higher than they are now. And without this assumption, our system of moral norms ought not to prohibit

MNEs from outsourcing labor in a way which falls short of meeting Arnold's standards, for to do so would be to deprive workers of the ability to engage in labor they would freely choose to accept, and thereby frustrate workers' choices and harm the very people we intended to help.

5. CHALLENGES TO THE ARGUMENT

I will discuss three potential vulnerabilities in The Argument. One potential vulnerability centers on premises 1, 2, and 4, and stems from possible failures of rationality and/or freedom (which I will group together as failures of voluntariness) in sweatshop workers' consent. The second is located in premise 3, and derives from a possibly unwarranted assumption regarding the independence of a potential worker's antecedent choice-set and the offer of employment by a sweatshop. A final criticism of The Argument is centered on the conclusion (6) and holds that even if everything in premises 1–5 is true, it nevertheless ignores a crucial moral consideration. That consideration is the wrongfulness of exploitation—for one can wrongfully *exploit* an individual even while one provides them with options better than any of their other available alternatives.

a. Failures of Voluntariness

The first premise states that sweatshop workers choose the conditions of their employment, even if that choice is made from among a severely constrained set of options. And undoubtedly, the set of options available to potential sweatshop workers is severely constrained indeed. Sweatshop workers are usually extremely poor and seeking employment to provide for the necessities of life, so prolonged unemployment is not an option. They lack the education necessary to obtain higher-paying jobs, and very often lack the resources to relocate to where better low-skill jobs are available. Given these dire economic circumstances, do sweatshop workers really make a "choice" in the relevant sense at all? Should we not say instead, with John Miller, that whatever "choice" sweatshop workers make is made only under the "coercion of economic necessity" (Miller, 2003: 97)? And would not such coercion undermine the morally transformative power of workers' choices?

I do not think so. The mugging case discussed in section two shows that while coercion may undermine *some* sorts of moral transformation effected by choice, it does not undermine *all* sorts. Specifically, the presence of coercion does not license third parties to disregard the stated preferences of the coerced party by interfering with their activity. After all, one of the main reasons that coercion is bad is because it reduces our options. The mugger in the case above, for instance, takes away our option of continuing our life and keeping our money, and limits our choices to two—give up the money or die. Poverty can be regarded as coercive because it, too, reduces our options. Poverty reduces the options of many sweatshop workers, for instance, to a small list of poor options—prostitution, theft, sweatshop labor, or starvation. This is bad. But removing one option from that short list—indeed, removing the *most preferred* option—does not make things any better for the worker. The coercion of poverty reduces a worker's options, but so long as he is still free to choose from among the set of options available to him, we will do him no favors by reducing his options still further. Indeed, to do so would be a *further* form of coercion, not a cure for the coercion of poverty.A related sort of criticism attempts to undermine the voluntariness of sweatshop workers' consent by pointing to their ignorance, or lack or rationality in making this decision. The relevant sort of ignorance could take two forms. Workers might lack knowledge about relevant alternatives such as better employment or chances to receive valuable education or training. Or they might not know various facts about employment conditions at the sweatshop—how dangerous it is, what their managers will be like, whether they will be able to unionize, and so forth. And even if workers have all the relevant knowledge, they might still fail to act rationally if they do not give this knowledge the proper weight in their deliberation. A worker might unreasonably devalue the risks associated with working in the proximity of toxic chemicals, or might over-value the benefit of her increased income.

To what extent does this objection undermine The Argument? It is almost certainly true that there are some, perhaps many, workers whose choice to accept the conditions of sweatshop labor is made irrationally, or in the absence of important relevant information. Some forms of information—such as the possibility of being raped by an abusive manager, or the possibility of miscarriage due to lack of medical treatment—might be especially difficult to foresee or appreciate antecedently to taking a job. But does it follow from this that it is, contrary to The Argument's conclusion, morally permissible to take away the option of sweatshop labor from those who would choose to engage in it?

There are two reasons to think not. First, just because some individuals make the choice to work in a sweatshop irrationally or ignorantly does not mean that *all* do so. It does not even begin to follow from this objection, therefore, that sweatshop labor should be removed as an option for *all* workers, unless it can be shown (a) that it is impossible to discriminate between those who are competent to freely accept sweatshop labor and those who are not, and (b) that the moral cost of allowing workers to consent to sweatshop labor ignorantly or irrationally is greater than the moral cost of prohibiting that choice for those who *are* competent.

Second, even if *all* workers who consent to the conditions of sweatshop labor were ignorant or irrational, it still does not necessarily follow that it is permissible to remove the option of sweatshop labor from them. This is because, as Janet Radcliffe Richards has noted in another context, "ignorance as such is not an irremediable state" (Radcliffe Richards, 1996: 380). It is a problem that can be addressed at a variety of levels—by individual managers, company policies, or legal rules that direct resources toward attempting to make sure that individuals have as much relevant information as possible available to them, along with the resources to deliberate properly over that information. This could be accomplished by modifying the content or enforcement of contract law to strengthen disclosure requirements, or by public education campaigns. If sweatshop workers are making decisions involuntarily, then it is at least possible that the correct response is to attack the involuntariness—not their decision-making capacity.

b. Failures of Independence

The intuitive pull of The Argument stems from the intuition that the offer of sweatshop labor can only improve the lot of potential workers. After all, sweatshops are only offering an additional option. Either this option is better than any of their available alternatives, in which case the workers are made better off, or it is not better than any of their available alternatives, in which case the workers are not made better off. But if they are not made better off, they are made no worse off, either—they can simply choose whatever option they would have selected in the absence of the sweatshop's offer. In neither case, then, does the offer of sweatshop labor make potential workers *worse* off.

Intuitive as this argument may be, it is only valid if the provision of an additional choice is the *only* way that sweatshops affect potential workers. But what if this assumption fails to hold? What if, in addition to offering jobs, sweatshops also close off other options that were previously available to potential workers? If this were the case, we could no longer conclude *a priori* that sweatshops make potential workers better off. The fact that an individual chooses to accept sweatshop labor might show that she prefers it to any of her *currently* available alternatives, but it does not show that she prefers it to any of the alternatives that were available to her *prior* to the introduction of sweatshops. Determining whether she is better or worse off would now require comparing the value of the opportunities provided by sweatshops to the value of the opportunities they foreclose. This makes any moral evaluation considerably more difficult.

How might sweatshops foreclose opportunities for potential workers? The most obvious possibility is that sweatshops might displace domestic producers. The multinational enterprises that contract with sweatshops are often in a position to eliminate competing firms in the host country. Sometimes they accomplish this by traditional economic competition due to economies of scale and superior technology. In other cases, however, host country governments are willing to grant special privileges to multinational enterprises in order to make their country a more "business-friendly" environment.

Another possibility is that sweatshops will suppress, often with the assistance of the host country government, efforts to unionize the labor force. A 2000 report by the El Salvadoran Ministry of Labor found that of the 229 *maquila* factories operating at the time, employing approximately 85,000 workers, not a single union existed with a collective contract. The reason is that any attempt to unionize was met with mass firings and subsequent blacklisting. In the case of El Salvador, these anti-unionization efforts were, in fact, a violation of national law. But this was insufficient to prevent their widespread violation, and many countries which host sweatshops lack even this formal legal protection.

The first approach eliminates alternative job possibilities directly, by putting the suppliers of those jobs out of business. Whether this makes workers better or worse off, of course, depends on whether the jobs provided by sweatshops are superior or inferior to the jobs they eliminate. This is difficult to assess, but we have at least two methods of doing so. First we can compare the wages paid by sweatshops with those paid by non-sweatshop host-country jobs. The economic research on this point, which I summarize in section 5.c.i, indicates that sweatshop jobs out-pay their domestic rivals by a significant margin. Second, we can look to see where workers choose to accept employment. On this point, even authors critical of sweatshops note that sweatshop labor is in high demand. Doris Hajewski notes, for instance, that on one day during her 2000 visit to a Nicaraguan free-trade zone, "about two dozen people lined up at 7:30 a.m. at the gates of the zone to apply for jobs. They line up every day" (Hajewski, 2000). This is not a perfect measure of worker-preference, but it is at least *prima facie* evidence of the greater desirability of sweatshop jobs.

The effect of the second approach on worker opportunities is less clear. If sweatshops deny workers the right to organize *within sweatshops* but have no effect on their ability to unionize elsewhere, then the offer of sweatshop labor really *is* independent, at least on this dimension, of other elements of potential workers' antecedent choice sets. Sweatshops are simply supplementing workers' antecedent choice set with an additional possibility of non-unionized labor. If, on the other hand, sweatshops are affecting workers' ability to unionize not only in the sweatshops themselves, but elsewhere in the domestic economy—perhaps by influencing national laws in a way that makes unionization more difficult—then the failure of independence is genuine, and The Argument, as stated, does not succeed. Still, this criticism only works in cases where the offer of a job is genuinely linked with the choice-diminishing activities of sweatshops. And this will not often be the case. For most workers, the choice-diminishing activities of sweatshops or their multinational partners will be a done deal. Such choice-diminishing activities are often co-incidental with the *introduction* of sweatshops into a country, but not with a sweatshop's offer of employment to any particular individual. For such individuals, the fact that it was sweatshops which diminished their range of opportunities is irrelevant. What are relevant are the options available to them *now*, and their choice to accept the conditions of sweatshop labor indicates that they view this option as preferable to any of the alternatives currently available to them. This is morally transformative, just as The Argument claims, and we should be wary of interfering in any labor agreement consented to by workers in such situations. Where this argument would give us possible license to interfere is in the introduction of sweatshops into the country. If workers can be made better off by our limiting MNEs' ability to collude with host country governments for lowered labor standards (perhaps through the mechanism of international law, or perhaps through import restrictions adopted unilaterally by foreign governments against non-compliant host countries), then we perhaps have reason to do so. But the mere fact of

MNE-host country government collusion does not demonstrate this by itself. In order to make this demonstration, we must compare the welfare of workers living under colluding governments with their expected welfare were collusion to be disallowed. If, in response to the prohibition on collusion, MNEs stop outsourcing, cut wages, reduce non-wage benefits, or shift outsourcing to other areas, then we might conclude that workers under the colluding government are better off, and that we therefore have good moral reason not to disallow such collusion.

c. Exploitation

One of the more common charges against sweatshops is that they exploit their workers. Such a charge, if true, might undermine our confidence in The Argument's conclusion by drawing our attention to a moral consideration ignored by it. But much depends on how we understand the concept of exploitation. Sometimes we use the term to refer to certain cases where *A* harms *B* and *A* benefits as a result. Allen Buchanan, for instance, defines exploitation as "the *harmful, merely instrumental utilization*" of an individual or her capacities for one's own advantage or ends (Buchanan, 1988: 87). A con artist who takes advantage of people's ignorance to sell them worthless stock, for instance, might be said to be exploiting them on this definition.

Upon reflection, however, it is clear that not all instances of exploitation are necessarily harmful. Consider the maritime case of *The Port of Caledonia and the Anna*. In this case, a vessel in distress sought assistance from a nearby tugboat. The tugmaster responded by offering a rope—but only for a payment of £1,000. The master of the vessel agreed to pay, but later sued and won (regaining £800 of the original £1,000) on the grounds that the bargain struck was "so unjust, so unreasonable that [the court] cannot allow it to stand" (Wertheimer, 1996: 40).

The appropriateness of this decision does not appear to turn on the claim that the owner of the vessel was *harmed*. Indeed, it does not seem appropriate to describe this as a case of harm at all. Philosophical definitions of the concept 'harm' vary, but all of them seem to have in common that being harmed involves some sort of setback to one's interests. In the current case, however, the result of the transaction was not to *set back* the interests of the vessel's owner, but to *advance* them. The owner of the vessel was much better off being rescued—even at a cost of £1,000—than he would have been had the tugmaster taken no action at all. The agreement to which they came, far from being harmful, was actually mutually beneficial, at least when compared to the alternative of no transaction at all. Relative to this alternative—where the tugmaster receives no money and the vessel in distress receives no rescue—both parties experience an increase in utility. This suggests that a proper understanding of exploitation will make room for mutually advantageous, as well as harmful, exploitative transactions.

In what ways might mutually beneficial transactions be wrongfully exploitative? There are various ways in which such a claim might be spelled out. One way is to say that though transactions such as that in the *Port of Caledonia* case are mutually beneficial, they are exploitative insofar as the benefits are unfairly distributed in some way. Any mutually beneficial exchange will be a positive-sum game, due to the differences in the values each party assigns to the objects of the exchange. In other words, mutually beneficial exchanges will create a *social surplus*—an amount of utility greater than that which existed prior to the exchange. But the way in which this social surplus is divided depends largely on the bargaining skill and position of the parties. One way of framing the claim that exchanges are exploitative, even if mutually beneficial, is thus to say that even though they benefit both parties, they do not benefit one of them *enough*. Alan Wertheimer, for example, offers an analysis of the *Port of Caledonia* case that runs as follows. While it is true that the owner of the vessel benefited (on net) by purchasing a rescue from the tug for £1,000—that is, he was better off accepting the tugmaster's offer than he would have been if the tugmaster had made no offer at all—he was nevertheless not made as well off as he should have been. He is not made as well off as he should have been because he *ought* to be rescued by the tug for a *reasonable* price (Wertheimer, 1996: 53). The tugmaster's threatened course of action—i.e., not rescuing the vessel if he was not paid £1,000—was thus not something he had a right to do. It is akin to a mugger's threatening to shoot you in the head unless you hand over to him everything in your wallet. In both cases, one party is threatening to violate the rights of another unless they agree to pay a certain sum. And while it is true that in both cases the extorted party is made better off by paying the sum *relative to the alternative of not paying and having their rights violated, this* is not the relevant comparison for determining whether the exchange was exploitative and morally objectionable. To determine whether a mutually beneficial exchange is exploitative, we must compare the gains made by the parties not (necessarily) to the baseline of no-exchange-at-all, but rather to the baseline in which each party acts within their rights with respect to the other, and ensure that parties are left at least as well off as they would be under *those* circumstances.

There are several ways in which concerns about exploitation might be relevant to an assessment of The Argument. The first has to do with the wages paid to sweatshop laborers. The second has to do with other conditions of the labor arrangement, such as safety conditions, overtime regulations, the right to unionize, and so on. I will look at wage agreements first.

i. Exploitative Wages

If sweatshops have an obligation to pay a living wage to sweatshop workers, or if they have an obligation to pay a wage which fairly divides the social surplus derived from the labor arrangement, then those who pay a wage below this level might be guilty of exploitation even if the worker benefits from the job relative to a baseline of no job at all. They might be guilty of exploitation because they are taking advantage of workers' vulnerability (their lack of better available options) in order to obtain agreement to an unjust wage contract. On this view, sweatshops that pay wages below a certain specified level (specified by a moral theory of just or fair wages) are in the same position as the tugmaster in the *Port of Caledonia* case. The agreement they strike with laborers is mutually beneficial, but it is not as beneficial as it *ought* to have been to the workers, since the sweatshops have an obligation to divide the beneficial surplus of the agreement more fairly.

Part of what we would need to do, then, in order to resolve the question of whether sweatshop wages are exploitative, is to develop a theory of just wages. I am not convinced that such a task is possible, and it is certainly not one I can hope to engage in here. For the sake of argument, however, let us assume that some such principle can be specified, and see what conclusions this supposition leads us to in the case of sweatshop labor.

It is important to begin this discussion by noting that the bulk of the empirical data suggest that wages paid by sweatshops are significantly higher than those paid by potential workers' other possible sources of employment. Aitken, Harrison, and Lipsey, for instance, show that wages paid by multinational firms are generally higher than wages paid by domestic firms in developing nations (Aitken, Harrison, & Lipsey, 1996), a fact which was cited by the Academic Consortium on International Trade (ACIT) in support of their claim that universities should exercise caution before signing on to Codes of Conduct that might have the effect of reducing American clothing firms use of labor in developing countries (ACIT, 2000). Furthermore, recent research has shown that sweatshop wages are higher regardless of whether they are paid by multinational firms or by domestic subcontractors—three to seven times as high as the national income in the Dominican Republic, Haiti, Honduras, and Nicaragua, for example (Powell & Skarbek, 2006). And if anything, these data probably tend to understate the extent to which sweatshop laborers out-earn other individuals in the developing world, as many of those other individuals work in either agriculture or the "informal economy," where wages (and other benefits) tend to be much lower, but numbers for which are not accounted for in the standard economic statistics (Maitland, 1996). Of course, these facts, by themselves, do not refute the charge of exploitation, since it is possible that while sweatshop wages are higher than wages earned by non-sweatshop laborers, the wages still represent an unfair division of the cooperative surplus generated by the employment arrangement. Perhaps sweatshops are taking advantage of the low wages paid by domestic industries in the developing world to reap exploitative profits by paying wages that are high enough to attract workers, but much lower than the firm could afford if they were willing to settle for a more reasonable level of profit. Resolving this question would require, in addition to a moral theory of just wages, an examination of the rate of profit made by MNEs who outsource the manufacture of products to third world sweatshops, compared with the profit-rates of non-outsourcing firms in the same industry, and firms in relevantly similar industries. If the profit rates of sweatshop-employing MNEs are significantly higher than other firms in the relevant comparison class, this would be some evidence for the claim that they are unfairly exploiting their workers.

For now, however, I want to leave the full resolution of these empirical questions to the economists, and return to an analysis of the concept of "exploitation." Suppose it turns out to be true that MNEs are earning an unusually high rate of profit from their use of sweatshop labor—high enough that they could afford to pay significantly higher wages without putting the firm at risk. Such firms could be said to be taking advantage of workers' vulnerability to benefit disproportionately from their labor agreements. Are they guilty of an objectionable form of exploitation? Are they acting in a blameworthy manner?

There is something rather odd about saying that they are. Recall that the form of exploitation with which we are concerned here is mutually advantageous exploitation. The charge against firms is not that they are *harming* workers, but that the benefit they gain from the transaction is disproportionate to that gained by the workers. But the firms are doing *something* to help. The wages they pay to workers make those workers better off than they used to be—even if it is not as well off as we think they ought to be made.

Do they have an obligation to do more? Consider the fact that most individuals do *nothing* to make Third-World workers better off. Are *they* blameworthy? As blameworthy as sweatshops? We need not suppose that such individuals do *nothing* charitable. Perhaps they spend their resources helping local causes, or global causes other than poverty-relief. My point is that it would be odd to blame MNEs for helping *some* when we blame individuals less (or not at all) for helping *none*.

The same point can be made comparing MNEs that outsource to Third-World sweatshops with businesses that do not. Take, for example, a US firm which could outsource production to the Third World, but chooses to produce domestically instead. Let us suppose that the firm, *qua* firm, does not donate any of its profits to the cause of Third-World poverty relief. Is such a firm blameworthy? Again, it would be odd to say that it was innocent, or *less* guilty than MNEs that outsource to sweatshops, when the latter does *something* to make workers in the Third World better off, while the former does *nothing*. Yet firms which do nothing in this way draw nothing like the ire drawn by firms which contract with sweatshops. This seems to suggest an incoherence between our understanding of the wrongfulness of exploitative wage agreements and our other moral judgments about duties to aid.

This same incoherence can be gotten at from a different direction. Sweatshops make the people who work for them better off. But there are a lot of people who are *not* made better off by sweatshops. They are not necessarily *harmed* by them; their position is simply unaffected one way or the other. Anyone who works in agriculture, for instance, or in the informal sector of the economy, will not benefit (directly) from the wages paid by sweatshops. Such individuals lack the skill or the opportunity to take advantage of the benefits that sweatshop labor offers. As a result, they tend to be much worse off in monetary terms than sweatshop workers. To illustrate: Ian Maitland notes that in 1996, workers in Nike's Indonesian plant in Serang earned the legal minimum wage of 5,200 rupiahs per day. By contrast, the typical agricultural worker earned only 2,000 rupiahs per day (Maitland, 1996: 599). Yet, most people do not fault Nike for doing *nothing* to improve the position of agricultural workers. Why, then, should they be faulted for doing *something* to improve the position of (some) urban workers?

The problem, then, is this. We criticize a firm for failing to benefit a certain group of individuals sufficiently, even though it benefits that group a little. But we do not fault other firms for failing to benefit that group at all, and we do not fault the firm in question for failing to benefit other, possibly much worse off groups, at all. What could justify this seeming disparity in our moral judgments?

Alan Wertheimer, though he does not endorse the intuition itself, suggests that there is a principle underlying many objections to exploitation. This principle, which he calls the "interaction principle," holds that "one has special responsibilities to those with whom one interacts beneficially that one would not have if one had chosen not to interact with them." To accept the interaction principle, Wertheimer says, is to reject the "non-worseness principle," which holds that "it cannot be morally worse for A to interact with B than not to interact with B if: (1) the interaction is better for B than non-interaction, (2) B consents to the interaction, (3) such interaction has no negative effects on others" (Wertheimer, 1996: 289–93). By adopting the interaction principle and rejecting the non-worseness principle, one could consistently hold that MNEs that outsource to sweatshops have a greater obligation to benefit workers in the developing world than do MNEs that do not.

In order to determine whether MNEs that outsource are wrongfully exploiting their workers, then, we must first determine whether the interaction principle is defensible. There seem to be two sorts of arguments that could be made in its defense in this context—one pragmatic in nature, the other stemming from deontological considerations about the nature of respect.

Pragmatically, we might suppose that MNEs have stronger or more demanding obligations to those with whom they are in close causal contact because they are in a better position to help such persons effectively. Perhaps they are more familiar with the needs of individuals with whom they are causally connected, or perhaps they are simply more able to interact with such individuals in a welfare-enhancing way. But note that what needs to be shown in the debate over sweatshops is not just that the relationship in which MNEs stand to their sweatshop laborers is one that gives rise to special obligations (i.e., obligations that are owed to some individuals but not others), but that it is one that gives rise to the *particular* special duty of monetary benefit. None of the facts about the MNE-laborer relationship seem to put MNEs in a better position to benefit workers in *that* way. One certainly needs to know certain details about a person before they can decide whether piano lessons, or a motorcycle, would benefit them. But money is not like these goods. Money is something like a primary good in Rawls's sense—it will help you achieve your ends, pretty much no matter what those ends happen to be (Rawls, 1971: 62). As a result, MNEs are in no better position to know that more money will benefit their workers than anybody else. Everybody knows this. Nor do they seem to be in any better position to *deliver* money to their workers. As supporters of Third-World poverty relief like Peter Unger point out, it takes only a few minutes to write a check to OXFAM or UNICEF, and with that simple action, money can be sent from anywhere in the world to aid individuals in any other part of the world.

Ruth Sample, in her recent work on exploitation, has suggested another way of defending the interaction principle (Sample, 2003). According to Sample, exploitation is a form of interaction that involves degrading and failing to respect the inherent value of another human being (Sample, 2003: 56–62). Neglect, on the other hand, is a kind of *non*-interaction. It is true that the consequences of neglect might sometimes be no different, or even worse than, the consequences of exploitation. But on Sample's account, there is something degrading and disrespectful about *treating* another person badly that is simply not there in cases of neglect, and this is why "we often regard exploitation as worse than neglect, even when the consequences of neglect are worse" (Sample, 2003: 60–61).

I am not convinced by Sample's argument. Sample is probably right to claim that we cannot account for subtle forms of wrongness inherent in exploitation by appeal to consequentialist considerations alone. But it is not clear that even a deontological approach will support the non-interaction principle. First, it is not clear that the sort of treatment to which sweatshops subject their workers is really disrespectful in the Kantian deontological sense of treating others as *mere* means. The sorts of wage agreements we are considering are the product of workers' consent. In forming these agreements employers are, of course, treating their employees in some respects as means—they are using workers' labor to benefit themselves. But a plausible, and common, interpretation of Kant's prohibition on treating people as mere means is that it rules out not *any* such use of other people—such treatment is ubiquitous and generally untroubling—but only those uses of other people that take place without their free consent. Further argument would be required to demonstrate that such agreements are degrading and disrespectful even in those cases where they are freely consented to. Second, even if low wage agreements are exploitative and disrespectful, I do not think that the sort of considerations Sample gives are sufficient to show that this treatment is *more disrespectful* than neglect. As Sample points out, neglect makes it easier for us to "lose sight of the value of other valuable beings" (Sample, 2003: 68). But this point counts against her position, not in favor of it. Exploitation involves "incomplete engagement" with another valuable being, but neglect involves a complete lack of engagement. Phenomenologically, then, neglect might *feel* less wrong to us, because we are not cognizant of the value we are neglecting. But if the persons we neglect are, as Sample points out, just as valuable as those with whom we are engaged, then it is hard to see how neglect could actually *be* less wrong. Similarly, if those we neglect are indeed as valuable as those with whom we are engaged, then it is also not clear how we come to acquire new obligations to persons just by virtue of being engaged with them. The value of persons is the same whether we are engaged with them or not, and if the value is the same, so too should be our call to respect that value.

There are no doubt other arguments that could be made in defense of the interaction principle. All I have tried to do here is to show that some of the more obvious ones are not successful. The burden of argument is thus on those who wish to criticize sweatshop wage agreements to provide a coherent defense of the interaction principle, and thereby show how sweatshops' marginal benefit to the poor of the developing world is worse than the complete lack of benefit that most of us provide.

ii. Other Exploitative Working Conditions

My comments in the last section might sound like they are aimed at undermining the moral weight of *all* claims of exploitation. But this was not my intent. I do, indeed, believe that claims of sweatshop wages being exploitative are implausible. But I think the case *can* be made that sweatshops wrongfully exploit their workers in other ways. Specifically, I think this can be said of various forms of psychological and/or physical abuse on the part of sweatshop managers, such as the case described by Denis Arnold and Norman Bowie of a pregnant female sweatshop worker who was threatened with termination if she sought medical assistance. Fearing for her job, she kept quiet even when she began hemorrhaging and eventually miscarried (Arnold & Bowie, 2003: 231).

What is the difference between cases of abuse such as this and low wages? Recall our discussion of the concept of exploitation, above. What makes an action exploitative, on that analysis, is that it involves some actual or threatened violation of the rights of the exploitee by the exploiter. In my discussion immediately above, I argued that we generally do not hold that those who provide *no* monetary benefit to poor in the developing world are thereby violating the rights of those poor. Since, however, providing no monetary benefit does not violate anyone's rights, and since a contract whereby sweatshops agree to provide *some* benefit does not in itself violate anyone's rights, it follows that such contracts are not exploitative.

Things are different when we switch our discussion from wages to other forms of treatment such as physical or emotional abuse. I do not think it is plausible that individuals in the developing world have a right to a certain level of monetary benefit. But this leaves open the possibility that there are some actions managers might take or threaten to take which *would* violate the employee's rights. For example, a mid-level manager who raped a female employee and warned her to keep quiet about it or else she would lose her job would be violating that employee's rights in raping her, and exploiting her by using his managerial power to cover up his crime.

My point here is not to provide a catalog of those actions which do and do not constitute exploitation on the part of sweatshops or their agents. My point, rather, is that one can consistently hold that certain forms of treatment by sweatshops of their workers are exploitative while denying that low wages are. Because I believe the concept of exploitation is best understood in terms of actual or threatened rights-violation, the precise nature of the line between those actions that constitute exploitation and those which do not will depend on one's theory of rights. In the last section, I gave my reasons in for thinking that low wages do not constitute a rights-violation. Rape, on the other hand, is likely to be condemned as a rights violation by any plausible moral theory. Between these fixed points, there is room for considerable complexity in the moral terrain, and reasonable disagreement between different moral theories.

Regardless of how we judge the moral merit of the various actions of sweatshops, or the label we choose to put on them, the question of what we should *do* about those actions remains separate, and this is a point worth stressing. Even if we concede that sweatshops do violate the rights of their employees, it will require further argument to justify third-party interference in the employment relationship. The Argument above gives us reason to think that sweatshop workers *prefer* and *voluntarily choose* the package of "employment plus rights-violation" to the package of "no employment plus no rights violation." This fact shifts the burden of proof onto those who wish to interfere with the employment relationship to show either why this preference/choice ought to be disregarded, or how their proposed regulation will do a better job satisfying workers preferences/choices than the current arrangement. In this spirit, let us now turn to questions of the moral force of sweatshop workers' consent.

6. CONCLUSION: MORAL WEIGHT VS. MORAL FORCE

In the end, I think that The Argument provides us with good reason to view the choice of workers to accept sweatshop labor as establishing a moral claim against certain sorts of interference with their freedom to conduct that labor. It does so by giving us reason to believe that those conditions of employment make the worker better off than she would have been without them, and by demonstrating that workers' choices to accept sweatshop labor are autonomous decisions worthy of our respect. This does not *necessarily* mean that employers are doing as much as they should be doing, from a moral point of view, to benefit those workers. Relative to a baseline of no job at all, a job with low wages and an emotionally abusive manager might be the best option available to many workers. But this does not morally justify the emotional abuse. Sweatshop workers' consent thus shows us that sweatshop employment is probably their best option, and that we will harm them if we take that option away. But it does not show us that the people who run sweatshops are morally virtuous, or that their actions are morally praiseworthy.

It is thus difficult to morally evaluate sweatshops *as such*. Much depends on the details of what the particular sweatshop under consideration is like, and upon the particular activities of the sweatshop one wishes to morally evaluate. Sometimes a more thorough evaluation *will* show the operations of the sweatshop to be praiseworthy. Considerations such as those discussed in the section on exploitative wages above, for instance, seem to show that MNEs which outsource and thereby provide wages to workers in the developing world—even if those wages are below the level of a "living wage"—*are* doing something morally praiseworthy. Compared to a firm which does not outsource at all, they are providing a great benefit to individuals who stand in great need of such benefit. Employers at the firm might be providing this benefit from purely selfish motives, and our judgment of their moral character would reflect this fact. But judgments of the virtue or viciousness of character can be separated from questions regarding the praiseworthiness or blameworthiness of actions, and our judgments of sweatshops should reflect this complexity.

So where does this leave us? Presumably, if we are interested in the moral evaluation of sweatshops, it is only because forming such an evaluation is a necessary step in deciding what we should *do* about them. So what moral force does our evaluation have?

The answer, I think, depends very much on which actors we are talking about. The reasons one has for responding to sweatshops in one way or another depend crucially on who one is. This is because different groups or individuals may have different knowledge of the wrongness, differing moral responsibility with regard to it, and differing abilities to intervene effectively.

The managers of sweatshops themselves, for instance, probably have the strongest reason to act by all three of these measures. They are more directly aware of the way in which workers are treated than any third party, they bear something very close to primary moral responsibility for that treatment, and are in the best position to change it. Insofar as economic, political, and other practical considerations make it possible, then, sweatshop managers ought to work to change conditions in sweatshops for the better, by refraining from physical and emotional abuse themselves, eliminating it among their subordinates, maintaining a safe and hospitable workplace, and so on.

Next to sweatshop managers, MNEs have probably the next strongest reason to act. As Arnold and Hartman have shown in their work on moral imagination and positive deviancy (Arnold & Hartman, 2003, 2005), MNEs are often in the best position to know about what needs to be done to improve labor conditions, and often have the power to make positive and creative changes. Experimentation with voluntary codes of conduct will provide a means for the market for labor in developing countries to itself develop, and will provide consumers with greater choices for ethically produced goods in the future. Caution needs to be taken, however, in both the methods and scope of change that MNEs seek to bring about. Requiring subcontractors to adhere to all local labor laws, for instance, could very well harm workers if the cost of that compliance is not shifted away from sweatshop workers themselves. And any shift from voluntary codes to talk of industry-wide standards or, even more broadly, to global human rights to certain standards, risks crowding out businesses that fall short of those standards even if the benefits they provide to their workers are considerable. MNEs may have the greatest power to do good, but they also have very close to the greatest power to harm.

The position of governments is much less clear. Governments have a reasonably good capacity to acquire knowledge of wrongdoing in sweatshops—at least in terms of general patterns of behavior. By utilizing their investigative powers, they can discover whether workers in a certain industry are routinely sexually abused, or intimidated, or paid as they should be. And host country governments probably have a significant moral responsibility with regard to the wrongful actions of sweatshops, insofar as they have a moral obligation to protect the welfare of their citizens. But do they have the capacity to intervene effectively?

This is a difficult question. We need to be especially careful in how we answer it when the wrongness with which we are concerned is the product of mutually beneficial exploitation. Even if, contrary to my arguments, the wages paid by sweatshops are wrongfully exploitative, this does not necessarily mean that governments should prohibit contracts that establish such wages by, for instance, legally mandating a minimum wage above the exploitative level. Whether they should do so depends on what the results of their interference would be. If, in the face of such a prohibition, sweatshops heaved a collective sigh and raised their wages to the government-mandated level, then the government action might be effective in preventing this form of wrongful exploitation. But if, instead, they shifted their operations to a lower-cost environment (to a country where exploitatively low wages are not legally prohibited, for instance), or if they shifted to an environment where they could obtain a higher quality of labor for the same price (as would no doubt occur if pressure was put to raise wages in the developing world to a point where the costs of employing such labor approached the cost of employing labor in the United States), then governments would have failed in their attempt to benefit their population. They would have prohibited the exploitation of their workers, but only at the cost of making their workers worse off. Host-country governments thus have a strong but defeasible reason to refrain from banning sweatshops, or from engaging in economic regulation that has the effect of preventing workers and sweatshops from freely agreeing to mutually beneficial labor contracts.

The case is much the same for foreign governments to which sweatshop-produced goods are exported as it is for host country governments, except that there may be even a greater case for non-intervention with the former. Governments in the developed world to which sweatshop-produced goods are exported are often pressured to reduce such imports in order to protect domestic jobs. But as I noted above, there exists a plausible moral case to be made in favor of outsourcing, since protectionist policies in the developed world tend to benefit those who, by global standards, are already extremely well off, at the expense of those who are badly off. Such governments are also often in a poor position to gain knowledge of the particular details of the sweatshop problem, or to effectively craft a response, thus making the worry of unintended harm to workers even more serious than it may be with host country governments.

Neither this paper, nor any purely philosophical paper, can hope to resolve the debate over what to do about sweatshops by itself. What I hope to have done instead is to show more clearly the sorts of moral issues that are at stake, and to show what kinds of questions remain to be answered before final resolution of the debate can occur. I have argued that considerations of exploitation and the allegedly non-autonomous nature of workers' consent to sweatshop labor do not give us reason, in general, to suppose that workers are being treated wrongly by sweatshops. And I have argued that even in those cases where we conclude that sweatshops *are* treating their workers wrongly, there is still good reason for governments and consumers to refrain from interfering in the conditions of sweatshop labor by means of increased legal/economic regulation or consumer boycotts. The Argument does not provide an unquestionable moral defense of sweatshops in all circumstances, but it does provide a hurdle which any proposed government action will have to surmount. Because workers' consent to sweatshop labor gives us *prima facie* reason to suppose that that labor benefits workers, governments need to show either that this *prima facie* belief is defeated by further evidence in some specific case *and* that their proposed regulation will benefit workers in the way they suppose, or at least (if the *prima facie* belief is not defeated) that their proposed regulation will benefit workers more than they benefit from the labor itself. If our concern is to respect workers, then we must respect their freedom to enter into even some contracts which we find morally objectionable, at least so long as their choices exhibit the morally transformative characteristics discussed in section 2 of this paper.

References

ACIT. (2000). ACIT Letter to University Presidents. from http://www.fordschool.umich.edu/rsie/acit/Documents/July29SweatshopLetter.pdf

Aitken, B., Harrison, A., & Lipsey, R. (1996). Wages and Foreign Ownership: A Comparative Study of Mexico, Venezuela, and the United States. *Journal of International Economics, 40,* 345–371.

Anderson, W. (1996). Kathie Lee's Children. *The Free Market,* 14(9).

Arnold, D. (2001). Coercion and Moral Responsibility. *American Philosophical Quarterly, 38*(1), 53–67.

Arnold, D., & Hartman, L. (2003). Moral Imagination and the Future of Sweatshops. *Business and Society Review, 108*(4), 425–461.

Arnold, D., & Hartman, L. (2005). Beyond Sweatshops: Positive Deviancy and Global Labour Practices. *Business Ethics: A European Review, 14*(3), 206–222.

Arnold, D., & Hartman, L. (2006). Worker Rights and Low Wage Industrialization: How to Avoid Sweatshops. *Human Rights Quarterly, 28*(3), 676–700.

Arnold, D., Hartman, L., & Wokutch, R. E. (2003). *Rising Above Sweatshops: Innovative Approaches to Global Labor Challenges.* Westport, Connecticut: Praeger.

Arnold, D. G. (2003). Exploitation and the Sweatshop Quandry. Business Ethics Quarterly, 13(2), 243–256.

Arnold, D. G., & Bowie, N. E. (2003). Sweatshops and Respect for Persons. Business Ethics Quarterly, 13(2), 221–242.

Arnold, D. G., & Bowie, N. E. (2007). Respect for Workers in Global Supply Chains: Advancing the Debate Over Sweatshops. *Business Ethics Quarterly, 17*(1), 135–145.

Bernstein, A. (2002, September 30). Remember Sweatshops? *Business Week.*

Brandt, R. (1979). *A Theory of the Good and the Right.* Oxford: Oxford University Press.

Brown, D. K., Deardorff, A. V., & Stern, R. M. (2004). The Effects of Multinational Production on Wages and Working Conditions in Developing Countries. In R. E. Baldwin & L. E. Winters (Eds.), *Challenges to Globalization: Analyzing the Economics.* Chicago: University of Chicago Press.

Buchanan, A. (1988). *Ethics, Efficiency, and the Market.* New York: Rowman and Littlefield.

Card, D., & Krueger, A. B. (1995). *Myth and Measurement: The New Economics of the Minimum Wage.* Princeton: Princeton University Press.

Dworkin, R. (1997). *Taking Rights Seriously.* Cambridge: Harvard University Press.

Feinberg, J. (1984). *Harm to Others.* Oxford: Oxford University Press.

Fischer, J. M., & Ravizza, M. (1998). *Responsibility and Control: A Theory of Moral Responsibility.* Cambridge: Cambridge University Press.

Frankfurt, H. (1988). Freedom of the Will and the Concept of a Person. In H. Frankfurt (Ed.), *The Importance of What We Care About.* Cambridge: Cambridge University Press.

Hajewski, D. (2000, December 29, 2000). *The Unsettling Price of Low-Cost Clothes.* Milwaukee Journal Sentinel.

Hartman, L., Shaw, B., & Stevenson, R. (2003). Exploring the Ethics and Economics of Global Labor Standards: A Challenge to Integrated Social Contract Theory. *Business Ethics Quarterly, 13*(2), 193–220.

Hayek, F. A. (1968). Competition as a Discovery Procedure. In *New Studies in Philosophy, Politics and Economics.* Chicago: University of Chicago Press.

Hurd, H. (1996). The Moral Magic of Consent. *Legal Theory, 2*(2), 121–146.

Klein, D. (1997). *Reputation: Studies in the Voluntary Elicitation of Good Conduct.* Ann Arbor: University of Michigan Press.

Kleinig, J. (2001). Consent. In L. Becker & C. Becker (Eds.), *Encyclopedia of Ethics* (2nd ed.). New York: Routledge.

Kristof, N. D., & Wudunn, S. (2000, September 24, 2000). Two Cheers for Sweatshops. *The New York Times.*

Krugman, P. (1997, March 21). In Praise of Cheap Labor. *Slate.*

Mackenzie, C., & Stoljar, N. (2000). *Relational Autonomy: Feminist Perspectives on Autonomy, Agency, and the Social Self.* Oxford: Oxford University Press.

Maitland, I. (1996). The Great Non-Debate Over International Sweatshops. In T. L. Beauchamp & N. E. Bowie (Eds.), *Ethical Theory and Business* (6th ed., pp. 593–605). Englewood Cliffes: Pretence Hall.

Merry, S. E. (1997). Rethinking Gossip and Scandal. In D. Klein (Ed.), *Reputation* (pp. 47–74). Ann Arbor: Michigan.

Meyers, C. (2004). Wrongful Beneficence: Exploitation and Third World Sweatshops. *Journal of Social Philosophy*, 35(3), 319–333.

Miller, J. (2003). Why Economists are Wrong about Sweatshops and the Antisweatshop Movement. *Challenge*(January/February), 93–122.

Morse, S. J. (2000). Uncontrollable Urges and Irrational People. *Virginia Law Review*, 88, 1025–1078.

Murray, J. (2003). The Global Context: Multinational Enterprises, Labor Standards, and Regulation. In L. Hartman, D. Arnold & R. E. Wokutch (Eds.), *Rising Above Sweatshops: Innovative Approaches to Global Labor Challenges* (pp. 27–48). Westport, Connecticut: Praeger.

Nagel, T. (1997). Equality and Priority. *Ratio, 10*, 202–221.

National Labor Committee. (2006). Support Grows for Anti-Sweatshop Legislation. Retrieved September 19, 2006, from http://www.nlcnet.org/live/article.php?id=120

Neumark, D., & Wascher, W. (1992). Employment Effects of Minimum and Subminimum Wages: Panel Data on State Minimum Wage Laws. *Industrial and Labor Relations Review, 46*(1), 55–81.

Neumark, D., & Wascher, W. (1994). Employment Effects of Minimum and Subminimum Wages: Reply to Card, Katz, and Krueger. *Industrial and Labor Relations Review, 47*(3), 497–512.

Neumark, D., & Wascher, W. (1996). The Effects of Minimum Wages on Teenage Employment and Enrollment: Evidence from Matched CPS Surveys. *Research in Labor Economics, 15*, 25–63.

Nickel, J. (2005). Who Needs Freedom of Religion? *Colorado Law Review, 76*, 909–933.

Nozick, R. (1969). Coercion. In S. Morgenbesser (Ed.), *Philosophy, Science and Method*. New York: St. Martin's Press.

Nozick, R. (1974). *Anarchy, State, and Utopia*. New York: Basic Books.

O'Neill, O. (1985). Between Consenting Adults. *Philosophy and Public Affairs, 14*(3), 252-277.

O'Neill, O. (1986). A Simplified Account of Kant's Ethics. In J. E. White (Ed.), *Contemporary Moral Problems* (4th ed.). New York: West Publishing Company.

Parfit, D. (1998). Equality and Priority. In A. Mason (Ed.), *Ideals of Equality*: Blackwell.

Powell, B. (2006). In Reply to Sweatshop Sophistries. *Human Rights Quarterly, 28*(4).

Powell, B., & Skarbek, D. (2006). Sweatshops and Third World Living Standards: Are the Jobs Worth the Sweat? *Journal of Labor Research, 27*(2).

Radcliffe Richards, J. (1996). Nephrarious Goings On: Kidney Sales and Moral Arguments. *Journal of Medicine and Philosophy, 21*, 375–416.

Rawls, J. (1971). *A Theory of Justice* (1st ed.). Cambridge: Belknap Press.

Rawls, J. (1993). *Political Liberalism*. New York: Columbia University Press.

Sample, R. (2003). *Exploitation: What it is and Why it's Wrong*. New York: Rowman and Littlefield.

SASL. (2001). Scholars Against Sweatshop Labor Statement. Retrieved September 12, 2006, from http://www.peri.umass.edu/SASL-Statement.253.0.html

Sollars, G. G., & Englander, F. (2007). Sweatshops: Kant and Consequences. *Business Ethics Quarterly, 17*(1), 115–133.

U.S. General Accounting Office, H. R. D. (1988). *Sweatshops in the U.S.: Opinions on Their Extent and Possible Enforcement Options*. Washington, D.C.

Unger, P. (1996). *Living High and Letting Die*. New York: Oxford University Press.

UNICEF. (1997). *State of the World's Children 1997*. Oxford.

Watson, G. (1975). Free Agency. *Journal of Philosophy, 72*, 205–220.

Wertheimer, A. (1996). *Exploitation*. Princeton: Princeton University Press.

Wertheimer, A. (2003). *Consent to Sexual Relations*. Cambridge: Cambridge University Press.

Wertheimer, A. (2005). Matt Zwolinski's "Choosing Sweatshops"—A Commentary.

Wertheimer, A. (2006). *Coercion*. Princeton: Princeton University Press.

Williams, N., & Mills, J. A. (2001). The Minimum Wage and Teenage Employment: Evidence from Time Series. *Applied Economics, 33*(3), 285–300.

Zwolinski, M. (2006). Sweatshops. In J. Ciment (Ed.), *Social Issues Encyclopedia*. New York: M.E. Sharpe.

Rational Choice and
Political Morality

GUIDO PINCIONE AND FERNANDO R. TESÓN

People frequently advance political proposals in the name of a goal while remaining apparently indifferent to the fact that those proposals, if implemented, would frustrate that goal. Theorists of "deliberative democracy" purport to avoid this difficulty by arguing that deliberation is primarily about moral not empirical issues. We reject this view (the moral turn) and propose a method (The Display Test) to check whether a political utterance is best explained by the rational ignorance hypothesis or by the moral turn: the speaker must be prepared to openly acknowledge the bad consequences of his political position. If he is, the position is genuinely moral; if he is not, the position evinces either rational ignorance or posturing. We introduce deontological notions to explain when the moral turn works and when it does not. We discuss and reject possible replies, in particular the view that a moral-political stance insensitive to consequences relies on a distribution of moral responsibility in evildoing. Finally, we show that even the must plausible candidates for the category of purely moral political proposals are best explained by the rational ignorance/posturing hypothesis, if only because enforcing morality gives rise to complex causal issues.

I. INTRODUCTION

Many public political proposals are arguably counterproductive. For example, people support minimum wage laws in the name of helping the poor, despite the fact that standard economics tells them that in many scenarios such laws

Guido Pincione and Fernando R. Tesón, "Rational Choice and Political Morality," from *Philosophy and Phenomenological Research*, Vol. LXXII, No. 1; January 2006, pp. 71–96. Copyright © 2006 by John Wiley & Sons, Inc. Published by International Phenomenological Society. Permission to reprint granted by the rights holder.

hurt the poor.[1] Even if it were *controversial* that minimum wage laws hurt the poor, there would be a self-defeating flavor in these utterances, for speakers would have to *qualify* their support for minimum-wage laws. Here we examine and reject a justification sometimes offered for speakers who ignore consequences: that those speakers are really advancing moral positions for which such empirical matters are irrelevant. The argument (which we call "the moral turn") runs as follows. Political disagreement is primarily moral in character.[2] Public debate on most political issues (regulatory policy, abortion, education, affirmative action, drug policy, and euthanasia) reflects a clash of values among different groups of citizens. In deliberation, citizens try to clarify, refine, and correct *moral* views. Moral views are not affected by citizens' ignorance of complex factual issues because those views are normative. Moreover, moral principles tell citizens in a relatively straightforward way what policies they ought to support in the public forum. Because the most frequent and important political disagreements are moral in character, citizens may fruitfully deliberate even if they lack incentives to investigate complex matters of fact. On this view, positions that apparently evince empirical ignorance are just respectable moral positions.

We reject this view. This article will show that relatively few political positions are genuine moral stances and that principles of political morality have by themselves no obvious implications for policy making. Most political issues have a causal structure. Because many people tend to overlook or ignore complex causal connections, they take the moral turn as a shortcut to a solution. Unfortunately, mainstream political philosophy in large part reinforces (or perhaps reflects) this pathology of public political discourse.

---

1.   Actually, standard economics predicts that such laws tend to hurt the worst off—typically, the unemployed who would otherwise earn the lowest salaries. See note 22 for some qualifications. For stylistic reasons, we refer to "the poor," meaning "the worst off."

2.   See Gutmann & Thomson, *Democracy* and *Disagreement* (Cambridge, Mass.: Harvard University Press, 1996), esp. pp. 11–51, and John Rawls, *Political Liberalism* (New York: Columbia University Press, 1991). Rawls's insistence that the stability of a just society depends on citizens using public reasons alone in political deliberation suggests that the most divisive and serious disagreements (what he calls conflicts among "comprehensive views") are moral in nature. This tendency to focus on moral disagreement is evident in Rawls's discussion of the ideal of democratic citizenship (pp. 216–220). In the same vein, Carlos Nino locates the value of democracy in the "moralization of people's preferences." See *The Constitution of Deliberative Democracy* (New Haven: Yale University Press, 1996) p. 107. Amy Gutmann and Dennis Thompson's opening sentence in their "Why Deliberative Democracy Is Different," *Social Philosophy and Policy,* Vol. 17, 2000, p. 161, reads: "In modem pluralist societies political disagreement often reflects moral disagreement, as citizens with conflicting perspectives on fundamental values debate the laws that govern their public life." A dissonant voice among those who favor deliberative practices is Phillip Pettit, who warns against the electoral incentives underlying moralistic politics. See Phillip Pettit, "Depoliticizing Democracy," *Ratio Juris,* volume 17, number 1, March 2004, pp. 52–65.

The average rational citizen will remain ignorant about politics, since his vote is for all practical purposes non-decisive, and reliable political information is usually quite costly to him. His expected utility from obtaining political information is usually negative.[3] The flip side of widespread citizens' ignorance is posturing: politicians and others stand to benefit from voicing truth-insensitive views as long as these are plausible to their audiences, given the latter's antecedent (ignorant) beliefs about how society works. On this view, rational ignorance and posturing are mutually reinforcing and give rise to many positions that are arguably counterproductive, such as widespread support for the minimum wage. This hypothesis predicts that the public will generally support proposals that look consequence-insensitive to better-informed observers.[4] We shall refer to this view as the discourse *failure (DF)* hypothesis.[5]

We will argue that discourse failure in politics affects many significant empirical and moral beliefs. The moral turn imports plausible traits of morality into areas of politics where they lose their appeal. More generally, we will argue that many important political controversies involve complex empirical matters, independently of whether they also involve matters of principle. In one natural sense, then, we will challenge all overmoralized views of politics.

There are two ways in which a speaker may disregard bad consequences of her proposal. First, someone who supports minimum-wage laws in the name of helping the poor, despite the fact that reliable economic theory tells her that minimum-wage laws will likely hurt the poor, seems to be arguing in a self-defeating way. Self-defeatingness is a particularly blatant case of inconsistency with goals embraced by the speaker, because the position advanced by the speaker defeats the very goals that she embraces. But a speaker may make a proposal that is inconsistent with valuable goals in a second, weaker sense. His proposal

---

3.   See Anthony Downs, *An Economic Theory of Democracy* (New York: Harper, 1957), especially part 111, pp. 207–76. The rational ignorance effect is well documented. See, for example, Larry M. Bartels, "Uninformed Votes: Information Effects in Presidential Elections," *American Journal of Political Science,* Vol. 40, No 1, February 1996, and Ilya Somin, "Voter Ignorance and the Democratic Ideal," *Critical Review,* Vol. 12, No. 4, Fall 1998, esp. pp. 416–419. Empirical research has even suggested that individuals, experts included, are often prone to invalid forms of inference. See the discussion and survey of relevant literature in Gerald Gaus, *Justificatory Liberalism* (New York: Oxford University Press, 1996), pp. 54–59. This innate propensity to err suggests that the task of becoming well informed is even more daunting than implied by Downs's formulation of the rational ignorance hypothesis.

4.   We first suggested what we now call "the DF hypothesis" in "Self-Defeating Symbolism in Politics," *The Journal of Philosophy,* Vol. 98, No. 12, December 2001, pp. 636–652. But the focus of our criticism there was Robert Nozick's symbolic account of the minimum-wage and other self-defeating proposals. See Robert Nozick, *The Nature of Rationality* (Princeton: Princeton University Press, 1993), pp. 26–35.

5.   We fully develop the idea of discourse failure in our *Rational Choice and Democratic Deliberation: A Theory of Discourse Failure* (Cambridge: Cambridge University Press, forthcoming June 2006).

may frustrate valuable goals (for himself or for his audience), including goals other than those in the name of which the speaker advances that proposal. Imagine someone who proposes protectionist measures for automakers in Detroit invoking the need to preserve jobs in that industry, and assume that such measures will effectively do that. To that extent, the proposal is not self-defeating in the stronger sense. However, given the theory of comparative advantages, the proposal predictably will harm other sectors of the economy, including many unskilled workers morally indistinguishable from the ones he is trying to protect.[6] We will use the term *counterproductive* to refer to positions suffering from either kind of inconsistency.

The moral turn recasts apparently counterproductive positions as moral. On this view, taking a stance on public policy primarily depends on moral considerations. Thus, if someone believes that the duty to help the poor overrides general welfare (a moral matter), this belief would settle the debate between supporters of minimum-wage laws and free marketeers in favor of the former.[7] People's political proposals would not be affected by

---

6.   Explanations of the law of comparative advantages can be found in any textbook on international economics. It was first formulated by David Ricardo in his *Principles of Political Economy.* 1817. See, generally, Animash Dixit and Victor Norman, *The Theory of International Trade* (Cambridge: Cambridge University Press, 1980). For a standard statement of the law, see Alan V. Deardorff, "The General Validity of the Law of Comparative Advantages," *Journal of Political Economy,* Vol. 88, 1980, pp. 941–957. Regarding empirical confirmation of the law, see James Harrigan, "Specialization and the Volume of Trade: Do the Data Obey the Laws?" working paper of the National Bureau of Economic Research, available at www.nber.org/papers, December 2001. A country has a comparative advantage in producing a good if its *opportunity cost* (i.e., the value of goods forgone) of doing so is lower than that of other countries. Standard trade theory predicts that countries will export goods in which they have a comparative advantage, and that free trade is a necessary condition for global efficiency. The law of comparative advantages entails that even nations lacking an *absolute* advantage in the production of any commodity (i.e., nations that cannot produce any good more cheaply than their trading partners) can gain from free trade if they concentrate on producing commodities for which they have *comparative* advantages (i.e., goods in which they had the smallest disadvantage in terms of forgone production). Most economists either accept the law of comparative advantages or qualify it for reasons (e.g., game-theoretical models of retaliatory tariffs) that are vastly more opaque and limited in scope than the protectionist arguments that we find in the political arena. Notice that a country C may possess a comparative advantage over country C^* in producing a good without having an absolute advantage over C^* in producing that good, that is, without producing it at a lower cost than C^*. Moreover, every nation has a comparative advantage in something, namely, that product for which it forgoes least value relative to the rest of the world.

7.   In their effort to show how moral principles have policy implications, Gutmann and Thompson extensively discuss whether the state ought to fund liver transplants for terminally ill indigents. They give an affirmative answer based on a *moral* reflection about basic opportunity. See *Democracy and Disagreement,* op. cit., pp. 201–229, esp. 220.

their ignorance. As a result, challenging public positions because they are counterproductive would overlook that such positions are often moral in nature.

This account of consequence-insensitive political discourse is particularly noticeable in theories of deliberative democracy,[8] but it is by no means confined to them. Non-utilitarian political philosophers sometimes seem to derive concrete political proposals from general moral theses alone. For example, Will Kymlicka describes liberal egalitarianism (as defended by John Rawls and Ronald Dworkin) as the doctrine seeking distributions that are sensitive to people's choices but not to factors outside their control.[9] But when he discusses the policy recommendations that follow from liberal egalitarianism, he presents as the only alternatives worth exploring the welfare state and "property-owning democracy" (i.e., a scheme that "seeks greater equality in the redistribution of property and skill endowments"[10]). More specifically, Kymlicka suggests that liberal egalitarians should be committed to "quite radical policies, such as affirmative action, basic income, employee self-ownership, 'stakeholding,' payment to homemakers, compensatory education investment, and so on."[11] The assumption here is that if you value distributions that are sensitive to people's choices but not to factors outside their control, you'd better limit the market in important ways. Kymlicka never considers whether free markets may realize liberal egalitarian values better than the alternatives he discusses.[12] And Kymlicka is not alone here. Another example is Simon Blackburn's discussion of Rawls's *A Theory of Justice in Ruling Passions*. Blackburn writes that Rawlsian ideal contractors would "choose a legal and economic system closely resembling those of modem western welfare-state democracies, with a substantial budget of freedoms under the law, and a substantial welfare floor." Interestingly, Blackburn criticizes Rawls for begging the question against, among others, the 'freemarketeer." Blackburn apparently excludes, then, the possibility of a Rawlsian

---

8. It is certainly a major theme in Gutmann and Thompson's *Democracy and Disagreement,* op. cit. A related theme in the literature on deliberative democracy is the connection between deliberation and moral truth or validity. See, e.g., Nino, op. cit.

9. Will Kymlicka, *Contemporary Political Philosophy: An Introduction,* 2d ed. (Oxford: Oxford University Press, 2001). Ch. 3.

10. R. Krouse and M.McPherson, "Capitalism, 'Property-Owning Democracy,' and the Welfare State," in Amy Gutmann (ed.), *Democracy and the Welfare State* (Princeton, N.J.: Princeton University Press, 1988), p. 84, cit. by Kymlicka, *Contemporary Political Philosophy: An Introduction,* op. *cit.,* p. 89.

11. Will Kymlicka, *Contemporary Political Philosophy: An Introduction,* p. 89.

12. To be sure, Kymlicka refers to the "New Right" as the view that wishes to cut back on the welfare state on the grounds that it rewards the lazy and incompetent, and suggests that liberal egalitarians should respond more adequately to this line of argument than they have done so far. But he does not address defenses of free markets on the grounds that they may help the poor. Ibid., pp. 92–96. See next note.

defense of free markets, i.e., a defense of free markets on the grounds that they best help the poor, and that helping the poor is paramount in a just society.[13]

Kymlicka and Blackburn must be assuming that the controversy between the supporter of state intervention and the supporter of free markets is essentially normative or evaluative in a sense that immunizes both positions against causal challenge. We can see the parties to this controversy as, say, imbued with different degrees of concern for the poor. If Kymlicka and Blackburn did not assume something like this, their policy proposals would not merely be obvious non sequiturs: their proposals might well frustrate the achievement of the stated goals.[14] Here the moral turn takes on a usual structure: policy proposals *are* held to be moral stances that *directly* derive from abstract values or principles of politi-

---

13. See Simon Blackburn, *Ruling Passions: A Theory of Practical Reasoning* (Oxford: Clarendon Press, 1998), pp. 273–274. Rawls himself has a more complex approach to this issue. On pp. 239–242 of *A Theory of Justice* (Cambridge, Mass.: Harvard University Press, rev. edition, 1999). He observes that his difference principle, according to which social and economic inequalities should work for the greatest benefit to the least advantaged, is agnostic about economic systems, thus allowing for the possibility that free markets be sometimes required by justice. But in the very next section he repeatedly refers to transfer payments and other redistributive devices as the institutional means to implement the difference principle (pp. 242–251.) It is unclear whether Rawls intends these remarks *to* be just examples of the requisite policies, but in any event they are remarks that have contributed to the dissemination of the reading indicated in the text. To be sure, Rawls rejects the "system of natural liberty" (roughly, a free market economy constrained by equal liberty and formal equality of opportunity) on the grounds that it "permits distributive shares to be improperly influenced by" natural talents and abilities, i.e., factors that are "arbitrary from a moral point of view" (pp. 62–63). Interpreters disagree, however, about the exact relationships between this argument against the free market and Rawls's appeal to the difference principle as a criterion *of* justice for society's basic institutions. This criterion prevents us from rejecting the system of natural liberty without an investigation into its distributive consequences. For opposing views on the relationships between these two themes in *A Theory of Justice*, see Kymlicka, op. cit., pp. 67–75, and Samuel Scheffler, "What Is Egalitarianism?" *Philosophy and Public Affairs*, Vol. 31, No. 1, Winter 2003, pp. 5–39. For an attempt to show that Rawls's theory, in conjunction with current economics, is generally friendly to free markets, see Loren E. Lomasky, "Libertarianism at Twin Harvard," *Social Philosophy and Policy*, Vol. 22, No. 1, Winter 2005, pp. 178–199.

14. Some influential economists claim that free markets best serve the poor. See, for example, Milton and Rose Friedman, *Free to Choose* (New York Harcourt, 2nd ed. 1990). For a recent, well-documented argument that the welfare state in the United States has in fact spawned poverty, and that the previous welfare provision through organized private charity better attended to the needs of the poor, see David Schmidtz, "Taking Responsibility," in David Schmidtz and Robert E. Goodin, *Social Welfare and individual Responsibility* (Cambridge: Cambridge University Press, 1998). For a discussion that emphasizes the shortsightedness and nationalism of usual defenses of the welfare state that invoke the plight of the poor, see Tyler Cowen, "Does the Welfare State Help the Poor?" *Social Philosophy* and *Policy*, Vol. 19, No. 1, Winter 2000, pp. 36–54. Our point is not that the Friedmans, Schmidtz, or Cowen are correct.

cal morality. It should be clear by now why the moral turn may be offered as a rival to the DF hypothesis to vindicate many consequence-insensitive political proposals that we find in ordinary political discourse. A *moral* commitment to benefiting the poor yields an *institutional* support for minimum wage laws (rather than, say, for free labor markets). The suggested upshot is that raising a charge of ignorance or posturing against these positions misses their moral character.

We claim that the DF hypothesis is superior to the moral turn as an account of ordinary political discourse that seems inattentive to relevant facts.

We will proceed in the following sequence. In section II, we propose a test (The Display Test) to find out whether a political proposal is genuinely moral or rather is attributable to rational ignorance or posturing; we use this test to show what is wrong with a version of the moral turn that rests on the idea of moral balancing. We then argue (Section III) that an unqualified appeal to deontological constraints fails The Display Test. In Section IV, we argue that a revised deontological model, based on the notion of direct involvement in evildoing, does account for both positive and negative results of The Display Test. In Section V, we criticize a version of the moral turn based on the notion of split responsibility. In section VI we present some examples that suggest how easy it is to underestimate the role of causal complexity in political argument, and, as a result, to make an unwarranted leap from principles or values to policies. Section VII shows that even the most plausible candidates for the category of purely moral political proposals are best explained by the DF hypothesis, if only because enforcing morality gives rise to complex causal issues. The last section summarizes our argument and presents a caveat on the scope of the DF hypothesis.

II. THE BALANCING MODEL AND THE DISPLAY TEST

The following example may be thought to support the moral turn. Suppose someone believes he ought to decrease the number of intentional killings in society. He also believes that the death penalty, through deterrence, would decrease intentional killings overall. However, he opposes capital punishment. He may believe that his behavior, and, by extension, the behavior of a just government, ought not to be informed by certain intentions, such as the intention to kill a human being. That the government not act on such an intention is for him an overriding imperative-no amount of good consequences (not even reduction in the total number of intentional killings) may override that constraint. This position is, in a sense, self-defeating, since this person (a) believes he has a duty to decrease the number of intentional killings in the world, and (b) believes his proposal does not decrease the number of intentional killings in the world. Yet, it is a quite reasonable position. Many people would say that this agent legitimately ignores facts he may regard **as**

Rather, we will argue that we should not jump from abstract principles of justice to policy conclusions without addressing opposing reasonable views about the empirical matters involved.

decisive in other contexts, because such facts lack enough purchase here. Why not think that this position illustrates the structure of many ostensibly counterproductive political positions? A genuine moral concern, rather than rational ignorance or posturing, might well motivate such positions. Just as the abolitionist can oppose the death penalty even if abolition would increase crime, so can the labor activist support the minimum wage even if it would cause unemployment. The intended upshot is that the discursive behavior of this abolitionist lends support to the moral turn.

This argument sounds plausible because an agent who endorses more than one principle may find himself under conflicting recommendations. If he chooses to follow one of those recommendations, he takes the principle that grounds it as overriding the competing principle. This agent has struck a balance between principles. Thus, the abolitionist believes that preventing the state from intentionally killing human beings is more important than decreasing the number of intentional killings overall. He might say that he wants to decrease the number of intentional killings but not at the cost of endorsing immoral behavior by the state. This position does not look unduly counterproductive. Similarly, people who support the rights of the criminal defendant typically do not invoke the need to reduce crime, even if they believe that crime ought to be reduced and know that stringent procedural rights will increase crime. The discursive behavior of these agents supports, then, the moral turn: the abolitionist's overriding moral commitments authorize him to ignore consequences he himself deplores.

But the capital-punishment example is not a good model for most counterproductive political positions. A sincere person should acknowledge, if need be, the bad consequences of the positions she endorses. Well-informed and sincere political speakers should publicly disclose those bad consequences. If the capital-punishment model is correct, they will not be embarrassed for doing so. Let us say that a speaker who is willing to disclose the bad consequences of a proposal meets The Display Test. More precisely: someone passes The Display Test if and only if he publicly acknowledges the downsides of his political proposal or, if he did not publicly acknowledge them, he would insist on the proposal if exposed to those downsides. For present purposes, we stipulate that a downside of a political proposal is any feature of it that, if disclosed, would likely reduce the audience's support for it. Such downsides are not only those outcomes that are *predictable* on the grounds of the most reliable theories available. They include, in addition, any non-negligible probability that the proposal will have bad effects, given the most reliable theories available. Those who pass The Display Test, then, do not publicly conceal or overlook the proposal's downsides; typically, they do not feel embarrassed by their recognition that it may frustrate some worthy goals. On the other hand, those who fail The Display Test are either ignorant or dishonest. They may be simply people who would withdraw their proposals if exposed to their downsides, in which case they are ignorant. Alternatively, they may conceal the problems with their proposal because they seek rhetorical advantages, as something different from winning the audience's informed approval. In that case, they are posturers who take advantage of the audience's rational ignorance. The Display Test is then clearly relevant to our investigation. We are trying to assess, remember, the merits of the DF hypothesis vis-8-vis the moral turn as accounts of apparently counterproductive political utterances. The Display Test helps us identify political stances that are genuinely animated by moral commitments, because the agent is willing to disclose those bad consequences that his moral commitments authorize him to accept (reluctantly, perhaps) as the price of doing the right thing.

We submit that the abolitionist meets The Display Test, while the protectionist and the supporter of minimum wage laws fail it. Imagine the abolitionist making the following statement: "I am committed to decreasing the number of intentional killings in society. I also believe that the state never ought to intentionally kill a human being. Under the circumstances, I can't achieve both goals. Since I believe that the first principle ought to *cede* when it conflicts with the second, I support the abolition of capital punishment. I regret to do this, since I know that I am supporting a measure that will increase the number of intentional killings in society." Although some people may reject this position, it is certainly reasonable, as we indicated. The agent is prepared to pay the price of increased crime in society for the sake of avoiding immoral behavior by the state, and to openly recognize that. The abolitionist, then, meets The Display Test.

This is not true of the supporter of minimum wage laws. Consider how she would defend her position in a manner analogous to the way the abolitionist did. She would say: "I am committed to helping the poor. I am also committed to using legal coercion to prevent employers from underpaying workers. Under the circumstances, I can't achieve both goals. Since I believe that the first principle ought to cede when it conflicts with the second, I sup-port minimum wage laws. I regret to do this, since I know that I am sup- porting measures that will hurt the poor."

Most of us would find this position bizarre. We would expect that a sup- porter of minimum wage laws would want to benefit, not hurt, the poor. We believe, that is, that supporting the minimum wage has an ineradicable causal component. This is why the typical[15] supporter of minimum wage laws fails The Display Test. Failing The Display Test in turn shows why the position cannot plausibly be portrayed as purely or mainly moral: as we have said, someone advancing a moral view that he actually holds is prepared to pay the cost of being moral, as it were. A *sincere* moral stance is transparent. To be sure, a defensible moral system may authorize us to lie in a typically narrow class of situations—the prohibition to lie may be overridden by other principles. But it is hard to see what more urgent or important moral principles lead political speakers to flunk The Display Test so often.

Four points about The Display Test. First, the capital-punishment and minimum wage examples may mislead us into thinking that satisfying The Display Test is a simple task. It

---

15. Bear in mind that we are testing the relative merits of the discourse failure hypothesis and the moral turn as analyses of public, non-academic, political discourse. We henceforth assume this qualification.

is precisely because the facts to be displayed are transparent only to those who are familiar with opaque social theories that people can so easily overlook or conceal them. Consider David Schmidtz's critique of Peter Unger's defense of a world in which "whenever well-off folks learn of people in great need, they promptly move to meet the need, almost no matter what the financial cost. *So,* at this later date, the basic needs of almost all the world's people will be met almost all the time."[16] Schmidtz writes (we quote *in extenso* because we find no way to improve on the *grace* and concision of his prose):

> Imagine what our community would be like if a lot of us voluntarily did as Unger asks. There were about five thousand people in the nearest town when I was growing up on a farm in Saskatchewan. Suppose farmers gave up that part of our crop we would have cashed in to buy movie tickets. The Towne Theater goes out of business. No big deal, perhaps. The half dozen employees seek work elsewhere, although suffice it to say that in a town of five thousand, opportunities are limited. Maybe they find work at the Princess or Lucky Cafés. Fine, but we are not done. We also stop cashing in grain for hamburgers at the café, instead sending that part of our crop abroad. The cafés close, over a dozen people are out of work. and we exceed our town's ability to find work for them. Unger says we would not have nice cars and nice homes … We send away that part of our crop that would have bought new cars. Fine. The car dealers and their employees are out of work. They no longer send money to foreign countries; nor do they support local merchants, critical services aside. The furniture shop and the clothing store shut down. They stop repaying business loans. Their employees stop making mortgage payments. Banks begin to foreclose on houses. There is no one to buy the houses, though, so the banks close too, and 1 don't know what happens to their employees. Perhaps they become refugees.[17]

Schmidtz's story is about people trying to do their moral duty. Political proposals are about creating *legal* duties—duties enforced by the state. Legal enforcement of the moral duties defended by Unger would arguably bring about even *worse* results, because legal enforcement has costs of its own, in addition to whatever moral costs are involved in the use of coercion (even to enforce morality). Those who propose such legal measures would meet The Display Test if, at the very least, they took the trouble to *address* the (types of) facts mentioned by Schmidtz—to say, that is, where he might have gone wrong. Assuming that the story told by Schmidtz is relevant to assess Unger's proposal (as it seems obvious

---

16.   Peter Unger, *Living High* and *Letting Die: Our Illusion of Innocence* (New York: Oxford University Press, 1996), p. 20.

17.   David Schmidtz, "Islands in a Sea of Obligation: Limits of the Duty to Rescue," *Law and Philosophy,* Vol. 19, No. 6, 2000, pp. 701–702.

to us that it is), those who advance this proposal while ignoring the story fail The Display Test. Or, more precisely: those who advance a political version of Unger's proposal while remaining silent about the kinds of facts mentioned by Schmidtz, or at least showing no willingness to indicate what is wrong with stories such as Schmidtz's, fail The Display Test.

Second, a comparative assessment of the DF hypothesis and the moral turn should look at *actual* political deliberation. This is so because we *are* trying to ascertain which of the two hypotheses best accommodates wide-spread cases of apparently counterproductive political discourse. Thus, in the minimum wage debate, one question relevant to the availability of the moral turn would be this: are union leaders and politicians who support minimum wage laws willing to publicly acknowledge that those laws hurt the poor, or at least that it is unclear whether they do so? It would be no counterexample to our critique of the moral turn the case of a philosopher or a social scientist who, in a scholarly seminar, puts forth a plausible case for minimum wage laws that includes a recognition that they may have bad consequences. In realistic politics, nobody is willing to make such concessions. Willingness to display those consequences of a proposal that others may take as reasons to reject it is surely relevant to determine whether that proposal is attributable to ignorance, posturing, or moral concerns.

Third, the fact that, in a natural sense, The Display Test heeds to the consequences of a political proposal does not commit us to utilitarianism. Someone may flunk The Display Test by failing to acknowledge consequences of his position that are inconsistent with the non-utilitarian political theory (Dworkinian, Nozickian, Rawlsian, among others) that he endorses. Thus, if I support a social program in the name of Rawls's difference principle, I should be sensitive to the fact (if it is a fact) that the program would worsen the situation of the worst-off groups. The point of The Display Test is to bring to the surface those consequences of a political proposal that the audience may take as morally relevant; it is not to suggest that the only relevant such consequences are those sanctioned by utilitarianism.

Fourth and finally, an agent may fail The Display Test even if, according to reliable social science, it is *unclear* whether his proposal will have bad consequences.[18] This will be

---

18. Some writers have argued that, because societies are too complex, social science cannot yield accurate predictions. *See,* e.g., Gerald Gaus, "Why All Welfare States (Including Laissez-Faire Ones) Are Unreasonable," *Social Philosophy and Policy,* Vol. IS (June 1998). pp. 1–33, and "Social Complexity and Moral Radicalism," unpublished. The connection between complexity and predictive unreliability was defended by Friedrich A. Hayek in "The Theory of Complex Phenomena," in Hayek, *Studies in Philosophy, Politics, and Economics* (London: The University of Chicago Press, 1967). pp. 22–42, reprinted, with added references, from Mario Bunge (ed.), *The Critical Approach to Science and Philosophy: Essays in Honor of K. R. Popper* (New York The Free Press, 1964). Recall that our formulation of The Display Test takes the uncertainty about the bad effects of a proposal as a downside of it. Predictive uncertainty would accordingly be evidence for the DF hypothesis, and against the moral turn. We should note, however, that *the* prevailing view holds that, while there is of course considerable predictive uncertainty in many

typically the case when public acknowledgement of the uncertainty would have rhetorical disadvantages. In order to meet The Display Test, those who propose minimum wage laws would have to be willing to acknowledge that *many* specialists argue that the laws will increase unemployment—academic consensus on this proposition was somewhat undermined only recently.[19] Since the typical supporter of minimum wage laws in actual deliberation does not say that it is at least uncertain whether the laws help the poor, he fails The Display Test. Of course, typical public support for minimum wage laws during the many decades when the pessimistic prediction went undisputed by economists flunked The Display Test and was, therefore, symptomatic of ignorance or posturing.

At this juncture someone may object to our insistence that, to avoid committing discourse failure, a speaker should acknowledge evidence against a proposal he utters in public. This requirement may be too demanding, because someone may have honestly formed a belief on the basis of available evidence yet be prepared to revise it in the light of strong evidence to the contrary. For example, a professional philosopher may have gathered enough evidence to subscribe to evolutionary biology but she may not be perfectly acquainted with all the problems attendant to the theory in the specialized literature. Nevertheless, she takes for granted evolutionary biology in her arguments on the philosophy of religion or ethics. To insist that this person express her opinion in a manner and

---

areas of the social sciences, we can *sometimes* tell what the *likely* effects of *some* policies will he on *suitably abstract* variables. For a classical statement of the view that radical skepticism about prediction in social science rests on confusions about the logical structure of prediction, see Ernest Nagel, *The Structure of Science: Problems in the Logic of Scientific Explanation* (New York: Harcourt, 1961), esp. pp. 459–473 and 503–520.

19. Mainstream economics predicts that minimum wages will have an adverse impact on employment. See, for example, Irving 8. Tucker, *Macroeconomics for Today* (Cincinnati, OH: Southwestern College Publishing, 1999), pp. 14, 90–92. There is an ongoing empirical controversy about the accuracy of that prediction. David Card and Alan B. Krueger present an empirical critique in "Minimum Wages and Employment: A Case Study of the Fast-Food Industry in New Jersey and Pennsylvania," *American Economic Review,* Vol. 84, No. 4 (Sep. 1994). pp. 772–793, at p. 772. For a reply on behalf of the standard view, see David Neumark and William Wascher, "Minimum Wages and Employment: A Case Study of the Fast-Food Industry in New Jersey and Pennsylvania: Comment," *American Economic Review,* Vol. 90, No. 5 (Dec. 2000). pp. 1362–1396, at p. 1363. Card and Krueger in turn reply in "Minimum Wages and Employment: A Case Study of the Fast-Food Industry in New Jersey and Pennsylvania: Reply," *American Economic Review,* Vol. 90, No. 5 (Dec. 2000), pp. 1397–1420. Even if the minimum wage had no definite impact on *employment,* recent literature argues that a *lower* minimum wage would arguably increase the *total income* of U.S. minimum-wage workers and help the worst off worker's family *escape poverty.* See Russell S. Sobel, "Theory and Evidence on the Political Economy of the Minimum Wage," *Journal of Political Economy,* Vol. 197, No. 4, 1999, at p. 782.

with a conviction commensurate with the evidence, the objector concludes, is to carry The Display Test too far.

We have two replies. First, we do not think that this person behaves like most people who keep silent about evidence against a political view they state in public. On the contrary, the distribution in the general population between opinions on each side of an issue is not commensurate with how strongly reliable social science supports each of them. Most people take a political stance, *not* because they have gathered enough evidence while not being completely acquainted with the relevant theories and data (as the objection suggests), but because they are rationally ignorant or have other truth-insensitive reasons to say what they say. The DF hypothesis better explains the discursive political behavior we observe.[20] Second, the philosopher in the evolutionary-theory example presumably would concede that the theory has problems, once she is shown those problems, so she would pass The Display Test. Recall that someone passes the test when he *would* be prepared to admit, or at least to address, the weaknesses of his view were he to become so informed. Whether politicians and other frequent users of political argument in non-academic contexts would be similarly sensitive to new information requires an empirical investigation that we cannot pursue here. But the systematic disharmony between the most widespread views among specialists (including their calls for agnosticism on some issues) and the most popular political proposals suggests a negative answer.[21]

III. THE DEONTOLOGICAL MODEL

When is it morally justifiable to ignore unpalatable consequences? On an influential view, a moral agent is committed to constraints on the pursuit of aggregate goals. Philosophers often use the language of rights to convey such constraints, and the terms *deontological ethics* or *Kantianism* to describe such positions. Rights-based moralities, unlike utilitarianism, hold that individuals ought to respect rights even when this is suboptimal from the point of view of welfare. Now welfare is not the only conceivable aggregate goal. An individual may have the goal of minimizing *rights violations,* no matter who commits them. Sometimes the achievement of this goal requires an agent to violate rights. For example, terrorists may credibly threaten someone with killing two innocents unless he kills one innocent. If this agent must not kill even in cases of this sort, he is under a *deontological constraint* on killing innocents. It might be thought that the idea of deontological constraints offers a better defense of the moral turn than that offered by the balancing model that was at work in the capital-punishment example. The overriding moral goal of the deontological agent is to refrain from bringing about states of affairs where *he* is killing innocents (even when bringing about such states of affairs minimizes the number of killings of innocents,

---

20. We extensively substantiate this claim in OUI *Rational Choice and Democratic Deliberation,* op. cit.

21. *See* our *Rational Choice and Democratic Deliberation,* op. cit.

whoever perpetrates them). In the terminology used by some philosophers, the agent in the terrorists example is governed by an *agent-relative* reason not to kill innocent [22] This reason contrasts with the *agent-neutral* reason to minimize the number of killings of innocents.[23] It may seem that this framework allows us to say that our agent-relative duty not to hurt specific poor people in specific ways (e.g., underpaying workers) prevails over everyone's (ourselves included) duty to refrain from hurting the poor. The suggestion is, then, that these positions lie beyond the reach of the DF hypothesis because, typically, deontological agents need not know complex facts and theories in order to discharge their duties. The victim of the terrorists' threat must only know how to avoid killing a particular agent—something that in most situations is very easy for him to know. He is prepared to tolerate the bad consequences of his choice (the terrorists' murder of the innocents).[24] If counterproductive proposals stem from such deontological concerns, then an agent may neglect relevant causal consequences while remaining rational, because he appropriately responds to his agent-relative reasons.

Moreover, if the deontological duty is negative (that is, a duty to refrain from doing something), the agent is trivially knowledgeable of the relevant facts. At least in ordinary settings, he knows, say, how to avoid killing a human being. By contrast, if his deontological

---

22. We are *characterizing* here deontological constraints, without taking sides on whether or how they can *justified*. The fact that deontological constraints are agent-relative need not imply that the justification of such constraints is agent-centered instead of victim-centered. On the justification issue, see the classic treatment by Bernard Williams, "A Critique of Utilitarianism," in J. J. C. Smart and Bernard Williams, *Utilitarianism: For & Against* (Cambridge: Cambridge University Press, 1973), esp. pp. 94–95. See also F. M. Kamm, *Morality. Mortality,* Vol. II (New York Oxford University Press, 1996), pp. 207–353; Thomas Nagel, *The View from Nowhere* (Oxford: Oxford University Press, 1986), ch. 9; Robert Nozick, *Anarchy,* State, and *Utopia,* op. cit., pp. 30–33; Samuel Scheffler, The *Rejection of Consequentialism,* rev. ed. (Oxford Clarendon Press, 1994); Horacio Spector, *Autonomy and Rights* (Oxford: Oxford University Press, 1992), ch. 5; and Eric Mack, "Deontic Restrictions Are Not Agent-Relative Restrictions," *Social Philosophy and Policy,* 15 (1998), pp. 61–83.

23. Some philosophers use the term *consequentialism* to refer to agent-neutral moralities. See, e.g., Derek Parfit, *Reasons and Persons* (Oxford Clarendon Press, 1985). pp. 26–27. We prefer not to use this term because it is sometimes meant to refer to utilitarianism, especially in contexts where utilitarianism is contrasted with rights-based theories. In any event, no substantive point *turns* on this terminological decision.

24. This formulation is not fully satisfactory, however. Saying that I do not kill somebody if I do not yield to a credible threat of killing others depends on the claim that the intervention of a third party displaces my responsibility for an evil outcome. In other words, someone may claim that I do kill those innocents when I refuse to yield to the threat. Our example in the text assumes the typical case in which the person who refuses to yield to the terrorists' threat answers to agent-relative reasons not to kill innocents in ways that do not require the intentional intervention of others.

duty is positive (typically, a duty to help others), he ordinarily needs to have more complex causal knowledge. Even so, he will be excused from understanding even more complex or remote consequences of his behavior. For example, I might recommend that the state help, here and now, poor schoolchildren by sending books to a public school. Arguably, this proposal will not be affected by rational ignorance, because the information state officials need to deliver the books is manageable. But the distinctive feature of this duty is that the donor may safely overlook how these acts of charity affect the poor overall (including how others will behave toward the poor). Typically, then, these agents will be neither irrational nor particularly ignorant. On this view, these positions are not counterproductive because deontological agents need not know complex facts and theories in order to discharge their duties.

However, the idea of deontological constraints is of no avail to downplay citizens' ignorance. Contexts in which deontological constraints are intuitively appealing are quite different from contexts in which counterproductive political behavior occurs. The victim of the terrorists' threat may justify his refusal to kill as follows: "I perfectly know that I could prevent two killings of innocents by killing this innocent. Faced with this tragic choice, I decide to follow the maxim never to kill an innocent person." Many of us would say that the soundness of this justification is *not* weakened by the agent's acknowledgement of the bad consequences of his decision. It is therefore reasonable for us to expect this agent to meet The Display Test.

Contrast this with an analogous defense that a supporter of minimum wage laws may offer: "I perfectly know that I could propose measures that help the poor by recommending that employers be allowed to pay lower salaries. Faced with this tragic choice, I decide to follow the maxim never to take public positions that tolerate *exploitation* of workers." On a natural reading of this position, the employer who underpays workers *wrongs* those very workers, in the sense that he hurts them in impermissible ways-he violates their rights, he exploits them.[25] So construed, the position is compatible with the belief that minimum wage laws hurt the pr in less objectionable ways. Avoiding exploitation is, on this view, more important than helping the poor.[26]

This agent believes that exploitation ought to be prevented even at the cost of creating unemployment or otherwise worsening the situation of the poor. His aim is to provide a moral defense of minimum wage laws that does not involve neglecting relevant facts.

---

25. Alternatively, the speaker may condemn exploitation because it promotes poverty. If *so,* since he believes that the measures he supports will hurt the poor, his position is incoherent. Or he may believe that the laws will have no definite impact on the poor. Our point stands too in this variant. We henceforth omit the qualification for stylistic reasons.

26. Remember that, in order to preempt explanations based on the DF hypothesis, the defender of the moral turn must claim that apparently counterproductive agents are *not* ignorant. In our example, the agent believes that minimum wage laws may well hurt the poor.

Indeed, he has eradicated the problematic causal component from that position. If political positions that look counterproductive can be rescued in this way, the moral turn would gain credibility vis-à-vis the DF hypothesis.

The problem here is that few citizens in *actual* political fora will accept a defense of the minimum wage formulated in this way. This position loses most of its appeal in any realistic deliberative setting once its proponents disclose its bad consequences, and for this reason in most cases it fails The Display Test. Most people regard someone who supports minimum wage laws while openly conceding that those laws may well hurt the poor as misguided at best. The public concession that minimum wage laws may well hurt the poor yet is needed to prevent exploitation is odd, and that is why no electoral platform of any ideological persuasion defends the minimum wage in *this* way.[27] By contrast, the DF model does no violence to these facts about political discourse.

We remain neutral on whether wages below some minimum are exploitative. Our point is that very few citizens advance that position in deliberative politics in ways that meet The Display Test. Most citizens regard proposals for minimum wage laws as sensitive to the plight of the poor. The balancing and deontological models we discussed are, then, overmoralized pictures of many counterproductive political positions. As such, they are unable to dispel the suspicion that those positions reflect ignorance or posturing.

IV. DIRECT INVOLVEMENT IN EVILDOING

We saw that the supporter of the minimum wage fails The Display Test while the abolitionist passes it. What explains this difference? Unless we offer a principled distinction between the two cases, those who take the moral turn may claim that the capital-punishment case models most ostensibly counterproductive political positions. If this move succeeds, most of the time people could safely advance counterproductive political positions. The fact that such positions are primarily moral would accordingly allow speakers to downplay unpalatable consequences of their proposals.

Let us compare the minimum wage example with the terrorists example. In the latter example the agent is concerned with his own involvement in evildoing, namely, intentionally killing an innocent. In contrast, in the minimum wage example the agent is not herself involved in evildoing, namely, underpaying workers. Her behavior is discursive. Since her personal involvement in evildoing is not at stake, she is not in this context

---

27. Most people who defend the minimum wage in the popular press on moral grounds deny that it causes unemployment. See, e.g., Peter Dreier and Kelly Candaele, "A Moral Minimum Wage," The *Nation*, December 6, 2004, available at www.thenation.com/doc.mhtrnl?i=20041220&s-&eier. The AFL-CIO's support of a minimum wage makes no reference to unemployment, nor does it hint at the argument in the text (that the minimum wage, while it hurts many people, should nonetheless be enacted to prevent exploitation.) See www.aflcio.org/youjobeconorny/minimum wagdta1kingpoints.cfm.

under deontological constraints on hurting the poor. Therefore, we would expect her to care about an aggregate outcome, namely, the overall effect of her proposal on the poor, including reducing the number of instances of what she calls "exploitation." Her position is best understood as grounded on an agent-neutral requirement (i.e., that the poor not *be* hurt) rather than on deontological constraints (i.e., that *she* not hurt the poor in specific ways), because, unlike the victim of the terrorist threat, hurting others (here: the poor, by underpaying them) is not among her options. Deontological constraints seem at home in the terrorists context, but quite unnatural here.

In contrast, the deontological model can accommodate the abolitionist case. The abolitionist who believes that intentionally killing human beings is wrong even for the sake of preventing further intentional killings will apply this judgment to the state. In his view, the state may never intentionally kill a human being, even for the sake of deterring murder, in much the same way as the person threatened by terrorists is governed by a deontological constraint on killing innocents. Both positions are coherent and plausible. By contrast, if the overriding concern of the critic of capital punishment were the minimization of intentional killings, *whoever* commits them, his position would sharply differ from that of the agent threatened by terrorists. For in this case his position would be this: "I oppose capital punishment in the name of the principle that mandates reducing the number of intentional killings, no matter who commits them. I believe that capital punishment, through deterrence, will reduce the number of intentional killings." This position is obviously incoherent.

While in the capital-punishment case the agent objects to killings perpetrated by the state, in the minimum wage *case* the agent objects to under-payment perpetrated by employers. Since in the latter case the state is not the agent who commits the underpayment, we tend to see its failure to enact minimum wage laws as less objectionable than the exploitation perpetrated by employers. The state might still be doing something objectionable-say, tolerating exploitation. However, we do not think that most people would support minimum wage laws even if they thought it wrong for the state to tolerate exploitation, should they learn about the bad consequences. The claim that we should not tolerate underpayment even when the predictable consequences are that more people will end up earning no salaries (or meager unemployment benefits) is unpersuasive to the ordinary citizen. Few proponents of this position will pass The Display Test, since most people feel that it does not make sense for someone to support minimum wages without thereby being committed to the welfare of the poor. Most of us expect the supporter of minimum wage laws to rely on an impersonal ethical viewpoint. She should be sensitive to evidence that the proposal she advances would, if implemented, hurt the poor. On the other hand, it does make sense for some-one who believes that the number of intentional killings ought to be reduced (even that the state ought to reduce it) to oppose capital punishment while publicly acknowledging that abolition will (regrettably) increase the number of intentional killings. Similarly, this analysis explains why civil libertarians can, without embarrassment, recognize some of the bad consequences that strengthening the protection of civil rights might produce, e.g., an increase in crime. For them, the protection of civil rights is an agent-relative concern of the state.

Another way of putting this is as follows. The act of tolerating immoral behavior does not itself instantiate that behavior. Suppose someone recommends invading North Korea on the grounds that millions of persons are suffering daily injustices at the hands of the government. If I oppose that recommendation on the grounds that the invasion would make things worse for the very victims it is intended to help, that obviously does not make me an accomplice in the injustices perpetrated by the North Korean government. Many people would regard my position as sensible, even though it entails tolerating injustice. This example shows that the nature of the reasons against tolerating evil is different from the nature of the reasons against evil-doing. Perhaps subjecting toleration of evil to an agent-neutral logic is the appropriate response to the fact that toleration is an attitude that relates to behavior by *others*. Of course, toleration of evil is sometimes an all-things-considered wrong, but not because the tolerator is violating the same agent-relative requirements that govern the evildoer. Rather, it is because the act of toleration has fallen short of independent, typically agent-neutral, moral requirements (imagine a state tolerating widespread spouse-beating, or some-one who tolerates burglars in her neighbor's house when she could safely prevent the burglary by calling the police).[28]

The same reasoning applies to the minimum wage laws example. The fact that I ought not to *exploit* workers no matter how many acts of exploitation by others I thereby forestall does not entail that I ought not to *tolerate* exploitation by others no matter how many acts of exploitation by others I thereby forestall. (Nor does it entail that I ought not to tolerate exploitation by others no matter how many *instances of tolerating exploitation* by others I thereby forestall.) The Display Test suggests that whether I ought to tolerate exploitation turns on agent-neutral considerations, e.g., whether I will be thereby minimizing exploitation (or what arguably makes it an evil, such as hurting the poor or increasing poverty). Deontological constraints govern the original immorality (the exploitative employer's), not third party's response to it, provided that such response does not instantiate the very action-type to which it responds. *Proposing* free labor markets does not *itself* violate a deontological constraint against exploitation. While my violating a deontological constraint places evil under what Thomas Nagel calls "the intensifying beam of my intentions,"[29] my proposing tolerance of evil intentionally done by others does not place my (discursive) be-

---

28. We do not go as far as to say that all instances of "tolerating *x*" are subject *to* an agent-neutral logic. Arguably, a state's obligation not to intervene (and so to tolerate tyranny in another state) holds even if that will result in a greater number of unlawful interventions by other states. For an argument that states *may* intervene *to* end tyranny, see Fernando R. Tesón. *Humanitarian Intervention: An Inquiry into LAW and Morality,* 3rd ed. (Ardsley, NY: Transnational Publishers, 2005).

29. Nagel, *The View From Nowhere,* op. cit., p. 180.

havior under such a beam. When I am not directly involved in a certain type of evildoing, it is natural for me to regard the evils of that type perpetrated by others as equally serious. The Display Test helps us disclose what the relevant consequences are in each context. If, in any realistic deliberative setting, people condemn under-payment because it hurts workers, the fact that most people who advocate the minimum wage fail to point out that it may well increase unemployment should surely count in any comparative assessment of the DF hypothesis and the moral turn.[30]

To be sure, sometimes the evil is so serious that the state should actively prevent it, even if by doing so the victims of evildoing will be hurt to a greater extent overall. Consider the claim that private racial discrimination ought to be banned even if it could be shown that the ban would hurt racial minorities overall. Supporting this ban may well be a compelling position even after computing the bad consequences of the ban, if any. Our point here is that The Display Test helps us see whether the moral turn is a plausible account of such positions. Proponents of the ban will pass The Display Test if they are prepared to openly acknowledge whatever bad consequences the ban may have. In this case, they think that the moral imperative not to tolerate racial discrimination outweighs those bad consequences. Conversely, if those who propose banning private racial discrimination are unwilling to talk about the possible unpalatable consequences of the ban or are merely misinformed about those consequences, they will flunk The Display Test. In these two latter cases, the DF model, rather than the moral turn, would provide the best explanation of their discursive behavior. The abolitionist's position is exceptional in that it forbids the state from intentionally killing persons irrespective of whether capital punishment prevents outcomes that are more serious from an impersonal point of view, including a greater number of intentional killings (perpetrated by other agents or the state itself). By the same token, core personal security rights prohibit government officials from exacting forced confessions, arresting persons without probable cause, and so on[31] irrespective of whether such prohibitions result in increased crime or other bad consequences, including more state misbehavior. We sometimes convey these ideas by talking about respecting persons, their inviolability, or their special status.[32] Both here and in the capital-punishment examples there is a special concern about the state violating rights, as opposed to minimizing rights violations.

---

30. Our argument is entirely independent of whether or not paying salaries below a certain threshold really amounts to exploitation or is otherwise unjust. It shows that even if underpayment violates deontological constraints, common-sense political morality does not place the state's tolerance, and a fortiori the agent's discursive behavior, under such constraints.

31. This duty of the state is different from the duty to protect individuals from each other. The design and enforcement of criminal legislation is arguably governed by appropriately weighed aggregative considerations (e.g., decreasing crime, optimizing retributive justice, or an appropriate mix of both).

32. The literature cited in note 24 elaborates on these notions.

But most political positions are *not* like this. Whether the state ought to enact minimum wage legislation, tariffs, or rent control laws is not a matter of *the state's* complying with deontological principles. In none of these cases is there an identifiable evil (such as intentionally killing an innocent was in the terrorists case) that the state ought to avoid perpetrating *itself*. We therefore find it natural for anyone, including state officials, to propose minimum wage legislation *in the name of helping the poor,* tariffs *in the name of reducing unemployment,* rent control laws in *the name of fighting homelessness.* Unlike the abolitionist's proposal, these proposals do not prohibit the state from doing the same kind of evil it is attempting to minimize. A fortiori, then, purely discursive political behavior is governed in these areas by an agent-neutral morality, since political discourse is even further removed from direct involvement in evildoing. In many areas of politics, the issue is, simply put, one of political craft: *how* to bring about good or just outcomes, as defined by a conception of social justice.

We conclude that many counterproductive political positions do not stem from genuine commitments to deontological principles. Such positions evince discourse failure. They look unattractive once their bad consequences are fully displayed. Their proponents contrast with the victim of the terrorists' threat, the abolitionist, or the civil libertarian, all of whom can, without embarrassment, disclose the bad consequences of their positions.

V. SPLIT RESPONSIBILITY

The moral turn may yet take on another form. Suppose again that a supporter of the minimum wage on behalf of the poor believes that the minimum wage would help the poor if employers were willing to cut down their profits to keep costs competitive while preserving employment. However, she predicts that employers will lay off workers in response to those laws. She might then say (a) that she has done her share for the cause of the poor, and (b) that she cannot take responsibility for the immoral autonomous behavior of others—employers in this case. Is there anything wrong with this position?[33]

Yes. The claim is that the state should impose minimum wages but permit layoffs. This speaker advocates the use of the coercive power of the state to force employers to pay higher salaries but is not prepared to support the use of that same power to prevent the consequence she predicts (layoffs) should markets be left otherwise unhampered. She is prepared to force employers to comply with their moral duty, but not to use force to prevent employers from bringing about outcomes that are arguably even worse for workers. One may wonder why this person does not support *both* a legal prohibition of unjust wages and a legal prohibition of layoffs. Of course, few people are prepared to

---

33. We are grateful to Seana Schiffrin for drawing our attention to this objection. She developed it in "Paternalism, Unconscionability Doctrine, and Accommodation," *Philosophy and Public Affairs*, Vol. 29, No. 3, July 2000, pp. *205–250*.

support both prohibitions. A prohibition of layoffs will arguably cause general hardship and thus violate the principle that we ought to help the poor. How many advocates of minimum wage laws would go as far as to prohibit employers from closing down their plants, sending money abroad, emigrating, and so forth? It seems safe to conjecture that, unlike the connection between the minimum wage and unemployment, the downsides attending those other measures will be transparent to most people, however (rationally) ignorant they are about other issues. This explains, we think, why so many people support minimum wage laws but not outright suppression of markets.

It might be objected that this speaker is not committed to endorsing such disastrous policies: she might reject a legal prohibition of layoffs precisely because of its bad effects. But it is odd for this person to appeal to economics at this juncture of the argument, given that she ignored it before. Recall that she would have contented herself with doing her share in alleviating the plight of the poor even though she had predicted that employers would not do their share. (She *must* have predicted that employers would not do their share if her behavior were to count as evidence for the moral turn rather than for the DF hypothesis.) She now predicts that outright suppression of markets will hurt the poor, i.e., she relies on economics to advise against such a policy. The problem with this is that there is no non-arbitrary juncture at which, to do one's share in helping the poor, one should reject the advice of economics and appeal to legal coercion. Why not use moral persuasion instead of legal coercion to get the employer to pay a just salary in the first place? On the other hand, it seems arbitrary to blame the employer for laying off workers and not the investor for not risking his capital (thereby helping to decrease the rate of unemployment) in a statist economy.

Moreover, what is this speaker's "share" in the social responsibility to help the poor? One may sensibly criticize the employer for underpaying workers yet refuse to recommend minimum wage *laws* (because, if enforced, they would hurt the poor). However, it does not seem sensible to go beyond moral judgment and recommend legal coercion when legal coercion (minimum wage laws) will predictably hurt the poor. An agent's "share" surely cannot be to recommend something that will hurt the poor, given how (according to her own beliefs) markets work. (Recall: if she does not believe that minimum wage laws hurt the poor *and* cannot dispel the economists' doubts on the claim that those laws help the poor, we could not attribute to moral commitments, rather than to ignorance or posturing, the insensitivity to consequences that pervades political discourse).[34] So someone who wants to do her share in helping the poor and believes that it is immoral to under-pay workers should simply urge employers to behave morally and hope that they

---

34. In other words, we intend to capture here the case of the speaker who believes, or does not know, that there are non-negligible *chances* that the consequences of her proposal will be even worse for the poor. As we indicated in Section 11, this person will flunk The Display Test as well. Here, as elsewhere, we do not introduce explicitly this qualification for stylistic reasons.

will do so. It is less defensible to advocate a ban on underpayment while believing that the consequences of the ban will be even worse for the poor.

VI. CAUSAL COMPLEXITY IN POLITICAL ARGUMENT

Other things being equal, the more complex the causal issues involved in the selection of public policies are, the more supported the DF hypothesis will be vis-à-vis the moral turn as an account of counterproductive political discourse. In this section, we briefly illustrate how easy it is to underestimate the role of such causal complexities.

It might be claimed that citizens disagree not only about the morality of capital punishment (where, as we saw, the policy implications are straight-forward), but also about abortion, euthanasia, affirmative action, drug policy, the place of religion in society, pornography, gay marriage, military intervention, and about many other issues that are distinctly moral in character. The suggested idea is that our analysis is limited to issues of economic policy, and perhaps a few others where the respective positions turn on complex facts. The minimum wage issue is one of such cases. Still, so the objection concludes, many important policy proposals straightforwardly derive from moral principles or values, in much the same way as opposition to capital punishment does.[35]

This view is overstated. Complex causal beliefs permeate most disputes in the political arena, including social issues ostensibly moral in character. In most cases, principles of political morality do not obviously lead to specific policies.[36] Suppose that two citizens agree that the state has a duty to mitigate poverty. One of them claims that strong private property rights will achieve that end. If the other citizen can convince her that private property rights will increase poverty, the first citizen would have to withdraw her earlier support. This is a causal, not moral controversy; it can only be settled by measuring the effects of strong property rights on poverty. Alternatively, the critic of property rights may oppose them on grounds of virtue: for him, say, private property promotes greed. This person would also make the defender of property rights retract from her position by convincing her that strong property rights would increase poverty. These possibilities illustrate the well-known fact that one can in principle (that is, were people willing to pass The Display Test) dissolve a political dispute by pointing to a causal mistake of an adversary who does not share one's values. What is less obvious is the extent to which the

---

35. As we saw, theorists of deliberative democracy tend to attribute disagreement about policies to moral disagreement. See notes 2 and 8.

36. There may well be *moral* complexity, in addition to causal complexity. If so, the scope of the DF hypothesis would be wider than suggested by the Downsian formulation of the rational ignorance effect. We will not pursue *this* line of argument here, but we do in *Rational Choice and Democratic Deliberation*, op. cit.

political proposals that citizens make are underdetermined by the moral positions they hold. Our discussion of Kymlicka's and Blackbum's views (section I) illustrates this fact.

There are, of course, purely moral positions. The abortion debate may be an example, because the relevant medical facts are not contested. Likewise, the euthanasia debate, at least in some versions of it, should be classified as a moral controversy. Sometimes it is unclear whether a controversy is moral or causal in nature. The debate over hate speech, for example, can be seen as a purely moral controversy in which supporters of hate-speech laws believe that it is simply wrong to allow certain insults to circulate in a society that respects human dignity and equality. Opponents may claim that free speech is a fundamental right that requires tolerance of unpopular and offensive utterances. Cast in these terms, this is a moral controversy. But if the supporter of hate-speech laws invokes the need to ensure that members of disadvantaged groups enjoy better opportunities, the controversy becomes causal.

Causal disagreement about public policies is large. It affects a significant number of controversies that, as shown by the above debate about property rights, involve a moral disagreement.[37] Even if citizens reached an "overlapping consensus" among divergent comprehensive moral views,[38] many empirical disagreements would remain, as the causal route to the goals laid down by comprehensive doctrines is far from obvious. Thus, Christian ethics (a comprehensive doctrine) tells people to help the poor—a goal that, if our analysis is right, many will pursue in counterproductive ways. Once we recognize how much political positions depend on complex causal relationships, we realize how pervasive the potential for ignorance and posturing is.[39]

Our point is not that citizens do not disagree about morality. Any defense of a public policy rests on moral as well as causal considerations. Yet many writers imply that set-

---

37. It may be objected that many important political issues do not involve causal complexities since they are about redressing past injustices. To that extent, those issues would be less affected by discourse failure. Yet political redress of injustice (as distinct perhaps from case-by-case, judicial reparation) requires complex causal analysis. Thus, whether affirmative action programs adequately redress disadvantages traceable to injustices perpetrated in the distant past is something that requires complex historical research. It also requires complex normative and empirical inquiry aimed at ascertaining whether affirmative action (rather than, say, monetary reparation to members of victimized groups) is the best way to remedy those injustices.

38. The ideas of overlapping consensus and comprehensive views are discussed by Rawls in *Political Liberalism,* op. cit., Lecture IV, pp. 133–172.

39. Politicians have an incentive to see moral issues everywhere, because it is easier to posture, to show that they stand for "what is right," than to try complex explanations that they know voters will not make the effort to learn and understand. We might speculate that the insistence in the literature on deliberative democracy on moral disagreement as the main divisive force in modem democracies stems from taking the politicians' overmoralization of politics too seriously.

tling the moral debate provides an easy path to the justification of a public policy. Were they right, they could hope to avoid the charge that much public debate is afflicted by discourse failure. But they are wrong. Complex causal claims are part and parcel of any sound defense of public policies.

VII. ENFORCEMENT AND CAUSATION

We have assumed, for the sake of argument, that certain political proposals, such as those advanced in the debate about euthanasia, are purely moral. By this we meant that those proposals are about the appropriate response of the law to the fact that euthanasia is morally permissible (or impermissible, as the case may be.) Thus, those who propose a ban on euthanasia typically believe that the ban is the appropriate moral response to the fact that euthanasia is morally wrong. This proposal is purely moral because it claims that a legal prohibition is the *morally* required *response* to the moral wrongness of euthanasia. It would be a mistake, however, to infer a moral requirement to ban X from the fact that X is immoral. Such inferences are vulnerable to challenges based on causal claims, and to that extent the DF hypothesis *can* explain their apparent insensitivity to relevant consequences. That extent is large indeed. Let us see why.

Because political deliberation concerns the adoption of binding public policies, i.e., laws, the facts that it should take as relevant differ from those that people should consider in their private capacities. Consider again euthanasia. I may face a difficult decision about whether or not to authorize termination of artificial life support of a relative. Whatever conclusions I reach, they cannot settle the question about whether or not to *legalize* euthanasia.

This is so because we may have good reasons not to criminalize euthanasia even if we think it wrong for us or others to perform euthanasia. Laws have all sorts of consequences that any responsible citizen will have to consider when deliberating and voting. One obvious such consequence is the use of public coercion-something that raises a host of independent moral issues. We do not have to think about those consequences in our private moral decisions. For example, the considerations relevant to someone's decision whether to become a prostitute are quite different from those relevant to legalizing or banning prostitution.

The corollary is far-reaching: even if we knew our moral duties, we would remain ignorant about many of the effects of legally enforcing those duties. The very fact that political discourse is geared toward public policy, that is, toward the use of state coercion, turns every moral dispute into a dispute that is, to an important extent, causal. Legislation has complex consequences, so it is usually insufficient to invoke the moral wrongness of an action as a reason to prohibit it. The prohibition in question may promote evil behavior or outcomes. For example, someone who advocates prohibition of drug use on moral grounds should be attentive to the fact that the prohibition may encourage criminal behavior that he also condemns, even if he believes that, other things being equal, the ban would be morally justified. Even legal perfectionists, i.e., people who want the state to coerce persons into leading virtuous lives, should accept this. Viewing the enforcement of morals as the main task of the law does not exempt one from causal analysis—unless, that is, legal perfectionism always overrides other moral concerns, such as mitigating poverty or reducing crime. Citizens should consider all the effects of the policies they are contemplating, and not just the answers to moral disputes posed in a legal vacuum. Here again, we can resort to The Display Test to determine the extent to which purely moral beliefs lead people to propose the legal enforcement of morality before audiences who would reject such measures if informed about their unpalatable consequences. The persistent divides that we witness in public debates on euthanasia, abortion, affirmative action, and the other social issues that philosophers use to study under the heading of applied ethics, along *with* the parties' reluctance to address facts that a typical audience would take to be against their proposals, are, again, best explained by the DF hypothesis. A version of the moral turn that appeals to the existence of purely moral positions ignores the fact that such positions often fail The Display Test.

VIII. SUMMARY

Let us recap. We assessed the relative merits of the moral turn and the DF hypothesis as accounts of political positions that seem insensitive to consequences. The moral turn regards such positions as moral in nature, in a sense that exempts citizens from causal inquiry. As against this view, we argued that typical counterproductive political positions would lose their appeal should their unpalatable consequences be disclosed. Most political disputes are causally complex and for this reason affected by rational ignorance and the forms of posturing that trade on it. We rejected, in particular, the attempt to ascribe counterproductive political speakers a belief in a distribution of distinct duties among various agents. This is untenable in areas of political morality where agent-neutral considerations are salient. Again, we rejected the idea of shared responsibility between political speakers and other agents (e.g., employers). The problem here is that the counterproductive speaker's selective sensitivity to causal analysis (of the sort found in economics, for example) is arbitrary. Indeed, citizens' ignorance and posturing are bound to affect even the attempt to use the law to enforce moral requirements. The enforcement of morality raises complex causal issues and moral concerns of its own. Given citizens' ignorance and the incentive to trade on it through various forms of posturing, public political morality should be seen as a narrower territory than overmoralized pictures of political discourse want us to believe.

The answer to political problems depends much less on matters of principle than political philosophers imply.[40]

---

40.   A caveat is in order. We have tried to show that the DF hypothesis is superior to the moral turn as an account of everyday political discourse, especially when public positions seem counterproductive. Our argument may not apply to many consequence-insensitive policy proposals advanced by philosophers and other scholars. Thus, by citing the works of Kymlicka, Blackburn, and Unger we meant to illustrate how widespread the moral turn is in contemporary political philosophy. In deriving controversial policy proposals from abstract principles of political morality, those writers have made, we suspect, a philosophical, not causal, mistake—they have taken for granted the moral turn. The moral turn may be so evident to some writers that they have not taken the trouble to defend it. Indeed, the moral turn has a good deal of initial plausibility, especially for people trained in contemporary moral theory. To that extent, they do not engage in discourse failure. The moral turn, when performed by scholars, may in many cases be a philosophical mistake of one of two kinds: either writers jump too easily from abstract principles to concrete political proposals, or they hastily portray as moral the political positions of the ordinary citizen. We suggested that the latter spring from the interaction between rational ignorance and posturing. While the plausibility of the moral turn explains its incidence among academics, which specific policies will be more popular among them can often be attributed to discourse failure. We offer a detailed defense of these suggestions in *Rational Choice and Democratic Deliberation*, op. cit.

The Paradox of Good Intentions

Jason Brennan

1. INTRODUCTION

In a famous address before a group of American activists, the former activist and missionary Ivan Illich said, "I am here to entreat you to use your money, your status and your education to travel in Latin America. Come to look, come to climb our mountains, to enjoy our flowers. Come to study. But do not come to help."[1] The title of Illich's speech is "To Hell with Good Intentions". Illich admonishes would-be do-gooders that despite their best intentions, many of them will do more harm than good. Illich says that all too often the glow of good intentions blinds us to the damage we do when we interfere with process and traditions we do not understand.

In this essay, I will illustrate how something like this criticism applies to contemporary egalitarian liberal political philosophy, in particular, the philosophy of John Rawls. Rawls is the most influential political philosopher of the past 50 years. Because of his influence, if Rawls made a mistake in the way he thinks about political institutions, then we are likely to see this mistake copied by many other philosophers. Readers won't need to know all the details of Rawls's political philosophy to follow the argument below. The problems I discuss below can potentially arise for anyone who seeks to move from advocating an abstract political philosophy to then advocating real world institutions in an attempt to realize that philosophy.

The most significant part of John Rawls's theory of justice (a theory of justice know as "justice as fairness"), is the difference principle. The difference principle requires that

Jason Brennan, "Rawls's Paradox," from *Constitutional Political Economy*, Vol. 18, No. 4; December 2007, pp. 287–299. Copyright © 2007 by Kluwer Academic Publishers. Published by Springer. Permission to reprint granted by the rights holder.

"social and economic inequalities be arranged so that they are ... to the greatest benefit of the least advantaged" ... (Rawls 1999:266) According to Rawls, in a just society, deviations from social and economic equalities are permitted only provided that such deviations maximize the social and economic goods received by the typical person in the least advantaged class in society. Rawls asserts that this is a fair solution to the problem of inequality because those who are least advantaged under this principle will be better off than under any other principle.

Political philosophers often argue that just institutions should aim to produce good results, and in particular, aim to produce these good results in a rather direct way. However, sometimes aiming to produce good results prevents us from actually achieving good results. Justice as fairness often appears to require that a society's basic structure must not merely satisfy the difference principle, but must *directly aim* to do so. The *basic structure* of a society consists of its "main political and social institutions and the way they fit together as one scheme of cooperation." (Rawls 2001:4) I will explain below why this appearance is not misleading; it is founded on deep theoretical concerns of Rawls. Yet by Rawls's own empirical premises—the very premises he uses to argue for the difference principle—in the long run, *directly aiming* to satisfy the difference principle would likely prevent the principle from being satisfied. There are good grounds for thinking that Rawls's suggested institutional mechanisms for helping the least advantaged will harm rather than help them. If satisfying the difference principle is important—a nonnegotiable point—it is incoherent that we would be required to aim directly to satisfy it at the cost of not satisfying it.

In order to show that this paradox exists in Rawls's theory, I first explain the distinction between *indirectly aiming to satisfy* a principle and *directly aiming to satisfy* it. Second, I examine Rawls's reasons for rejecting certain economic regimes. From this, I show that for Rawls, if a basic structure consistently satisfies the principles of justice as fairness but does not directly aim to do so, it is to be rejected as unjust, even if it far better satisfies the principles than any other basic structure. I then demonstrate, in the abstract, how this implies the paradox. Next, I show that this paradox is not merely hypothetical, but that the institutions Rawls endorses are in fact likely to undermine the aims of justice as he defines it. In the final section, the notion of publicity is explored as the probable fundamental basis of the paradox.

My goal isn't to criticize Rawls for the sake of Rawls exegesis. Rather, Rawls is the foremost representative of modern egalitarian liberalism. Modern egalitarian liberals often correctly identify the test of a flourishing society: the end or minimizing of domination, poverty, and medical want, and the spread of education, opportunity, peace, and full political autonomy. However, they quickly move from identifying the criteria of flourishing to concluding that a just society will enshrine these criteria as the immediate, direct goals by which it constructs its policy. Unfortunately, little effort is made to determine whether enshrining such goals is an aid, rather than an impediment, to achieving them. Living by the difference principle via Rawls's favored institutions is a way of enshrining concern for the poor, but it is not a way of helping them. That a society flourishes while living by a set of principles is a test of those principles. That a society has principles that directly aim at flourishing is a different matter. If we have to choose between success and symbolic concern for success, there is little to be said in favor of the latter.

2. AIMING AND SATISFYING

There are different ways of achieving an outcome. An outcome can be achieved either intentionally or unintentionally. When an outcome is achieved intentionally, it might be through direct or indirect means.

For example, suppose you think government should promote commerce. A government might attempt to promote commerce *directly*, by creating new corporations, offering subsidies and grants to businesses, providing tariff protections, and buying products, or *indirectly*, by providing a basic institutional framework (such as the rule of law, constitutional representative democracy, courts, and a well-functioning property rights regime).

Another example: Suppose you think government should promote the general welfare. The government might attempt to do this directly, but instituting welfare offices, offering subsidies and grants, providing a basic income, promoting employment, attempting macroeconomic adjustments, offering free healthcare, and the like. Alternatively, the government might achieve the goal *indirectly*, by providing a basic institutional framework (such as the rule of law, representative democracy, courts, and a well-functioning property rights regime) under which people will spontaneously act so as to promote the general welfare.

Suppose we think that society ought to have the goal of satisfying the difference principle. The idea of satisfying the difference principle is best expressed counterfactually. A society's basic structure satisfies the difference principle if and only there are no possible changes to the basic structure that would result in the least advantaged having more basic goods. Thus, if the representative person in the worst off class in a society has X amount of the basic goods (income, housing, social status, leisure, and so on), and all alternative basic structures provide her with either X or less than X, then that society's basic structure satisfies the difference principle.

A basic structure can unintentionally satisfy the difference principle. Regardless of what principle, if any, governs the distribution of holdings in that society, a society by no one's design or intention can meet the principle's required conditions. It is moreover possible for a basic structure consistently and stably to satisfy the difference principle, even though that is not the aim of that basic structure. A society might have principles such that its basic structure is designed with the intention of bringing about something else (e.g., the moral perfection of its members), but as the unintended result of background psychological and economic laws continually satisfy the difference principle.

A society's basic structure *aims to satisfy* the difference principle if and only if its basic structure is designed with the intention of satisfying the difference principle. When a society aims to satisfy a principle, its institutions track the principle and attempt adjustments for the explicit purpose of satisfying the principle.

Directly aiming at something is no guarantee of achieving it. E.g., in the familiar paradox of hedonism, the directly aiming for pleasure is what prevents the agent from getting pleasure. (Feinberg 2004:481) A person who single-mindedly pursues pleasure for its own sake, thinking everything else (science, art, friendship, sport, craft, industry, romance, self-expression, etc.) is intrinsically worthless, is likely to be frustrated. To derive pleasure from most activities, one must see those activities as intrinsically worthwhile. One does not normally enjoy playing tennis, for instance, until one sees tennis playing as valuable in itself and not a mere instrument for pleasure. One has to "get into the game," so to speak. If the hedonist is to succeed in living a maximally pleasurable life, she cannot treat activities and friends (in as much as a hedonist can have friends) like mere instruments. If one has the goal of being happy, one must achieve the goal through indirect means.

Directly aiming to achieve a goal can backfire in politics as well. For instance, governments often directly aim to produce higher wages for unskilled workers by increasing the minimum wage, thus making it illegal to hire workers at a lower wage rate. Though governments intend to increase wages this way, most economists think this strategy fails. Instead, it induces employers to hire fewer unskilled workers and thus creates unemployment. Employers won't hire a worker at a rate higher than the worker is worth to the employer. For instance, if the government mandated that philosophers could not be paid less than $1,000,000 a year, this wouldn't turn me into a millionaire. Instead, it would cause my university to fire me. Similarly, if you made a rule that said unskilled workers have to be paid $14/hour, then an unskilled worker whose labor is worth only $6/hour to his employer will be out of a job.

In contrast, if a government creates background institutions that lead to economic growth, this typically increases the wages of unskilled workers. In general, economic growth makes goods cheaper. Because goods are cheaper and easier to come by, an employer needs to pay workers more to induce them to work. An unskilled laborer in the U.S. today is paid vastly more than the same laborer in the U.S. 100 years ago. So, a government might do a better job of increasing the wage by pursuing the indirect route (i.e., helping to foster economic growth) than the direct route (i.e., by imposing minimum wage laws).

Rawls's political philosophy, we will see, has a problem analogous to the hedonic paradox or the problem with minimum wages. A theory that posited pleasure as the goal of all rational action and then demanded that we knowingly take a self-defeating strategy—failing to get pleasure for the sake of getting pleasure—is highly paradoxical. However, Rawls's theory, though it posits the satisfaction of the difference principle as one major goal of a basic structure, requires a counterproductive strategy. While satisfying the difference principle maybe a noble goal, Rawls's theory requires that we *directly* aim to satisfy it rather than indirectly aim, but by Rawls's own economic principles, this is likely to be self-defeating.

3. GUARANTEES AND AIMS

One of way of doing political philosophy holds that there is a division of labor between philosophers and social scientists. Once these principles are articulated, philosophers have done their job. They can then turn the principles over to social scientists, as it's the social scientist's job to determine what institutions actually realize those principles.

On this way of doing political philosophy, philosophers are supposed to remain (for the most part) agnostic about what institutions are worth promoting until social scientists have done their job. Suppose "justice as fairness" turns out to be the correct theory of justice. As far as philosophers know, it could turn out, from economics, political science, sociology, etc., that any number of kinds of political regimes could satisfy justice as fairness.

Some people interpret Rawls as doing political philosophy this way. This is not quite right. In fact, Rawls takes a strong stand regarding which types of social regime are compatible with his theory of justice. Rawls considers five types of social systems: laissez-faire capitalism, welfare-state capitalism, state socialism with a command economy, liberal democratic socialism, property-owning democracy. (Rawls 2001:136) Only the latter two systems are compatible with justice as fairness, and Rawls favors property-owning democracy. The fundamental reason Rawls rejects the two capitalist systems is that they do not (and he thinks cannot) aim to satisfy the principles of justice as fairness.

According to Rawls, laissez-faire capitalism *aims* at economic efficiency. (Rawls 1999:57, Rawls 2001:62) Laissez-faire capitalism requires only formal equality (equality in legal status) and does not directly aim to promote (it has "no effort to preserve") the fair value of political liberty or fair equality of opportunity.[2] (Rawls 1999:62) Rawls rejects laissez-faire capitalism because it *permits* huge income gaps to arise from morally arbitrary factors. (Rawls 1999:63) The language of permissibility is not accidental. Even if a given laissez-faire system were consistently to have a wealthier lower class than any other system, the system does not directly aim to make the least advantaged as well off as possible. As such, by *permitting* (if not necessarily causing in practice) inequality of opportunity, poverty, and so on, laissez-faire capitalism is disqualified. (Rawls 1999:62–65, Rawls 2001:136–137) Welfare state capitalism is rejected for similar reasons.

State socialism is rejected because it violates political rights and liberties and the fair value of those liberties. This brings us to property-owning democracy, which Rawls describes as an alternative to welfare-state capitalism. Property-owning democracies permit private ownership in the means of production; however, the government manipulates property rights and law to ensure that ownership is widespread rather than concentrated. The system attempts to satisfy the principles of justice as fairness not primarily by direct tax and transfer schemes, though such schemes will exist,[3] but through tax-financed education, training, and so on. Property-owning democracies have government-financed elections and provide numerous social services. (Rawls 2001:137–140) They attempt to avoid large concentrations of economic and bureaucratic power. From Rawls's earlier work on institutions, we can infer that a property-owning democracy will have various branches of government that aim to keep the price system competitive, that aim to stabilize resource use and sustain employment, that aim to secure the social minimum and adjust property rights in the attempt to satisfy the difference principle. (Rawls 1999: § 43) The property-owning democracy *directly aims* at satisfying the difference principle; its administrators make adjustments in the conscious effort to track the principle.

Rawls's way of thinking about regime-types is, on its face, somewhat bizarre. He thinks of regime-types as packages of aims and institutions. So, for instance, he thinks of capitalism as a set of institutions of a certain sort (free markets, open capital movement, private property) that aim for efficiency. But strictly speaking, institutions do not aim at anything. Capitalist institutions may or may not produce welfare, art, culture, or social justice, but regardless of what they produce, strictly speaking, they do not aim at anything. *People* aim at producing results when they advocate or implement institutions, but institutions do not aim at anything.

Thus, Rawls does not even consider the possibility that someone might advocate laissez faire or welfare state capitalism as a means to realizing Rawls's theory of justice. Someone might advocate welfare-state capitalism not because she takes economic efficiency as the highest value, but because she believes that given the constraints the real world imposes upon us and opportunities it provides, welfare-state capitalism will do the best job promoting social justice.

Still, Rawls thinks that capitalism institutions would be unjust—even if they did turned out to do the best job promoting the interests of the least advantaged—because they *permit* excessive inequalities. So, one problem with Rawls's way of doing political philosophy is that he wants legal guarantees built into regimes. He thinks just regimes must aim to produce justice, but he also thinks a society cannot aim to produce justice if it disposed to allow injustice to occur. However, what if being disposed to allow injustice to occur is actually one's best shot at achieving justice? What if being disposed to permit bad things to happen actually reduces the chances that bad things will happen?

Like many philosophers, Rawls tends to think that in order to achieve justice, we need to have legal guarantees that we will achieve it. But whether a legal guarantee is worth having is itself partly an empirical question. There is a difference between guaranteeing as rendering inevitable (as when an economist says doubling the minimum wage would guarantee rising unemployment) versus guaranteeing as expressing a firm intention. Clearly, *guaranteeing* something in the latter sense is no guarantee. Imagine a world where every time a government guarantees that people will achieve a given level of welfare, an evil demon makes sure (guarantees in the other sense) that people do not. In that world, if you wanted people to be well off, you wouldn't want to be issuing guarantees. You'd *permit* people to be badly off, because that would be their only chance to prosper in that demon-plagued world. Of course, we don't live in a world of evil demons, so perhaps that is irrelevant. By the same token, plenty of factors in this world can and do disrupt, corrupt, and pervert our best-laid plans and guarantees. Therefore, imagining a world devoid of corruption and of unintended consequences is no more relevant than imagining a world of evil demons. We have to *check* how the guaranteeing actually works in our world.

Suppose it happens, because of the laws of economics, political science, and so on, that in the real world, some form of capitalism always does a better job realizing justice as fairness than property-owning democracy. Rawls would then be committed to two claims. First, he would have to say that no social system is just, because those that satisfy the difference principle do not directly aim to do so, and those that directly aim to do so fail. Secondly, he would have to say that the systems that aim and fail are *morally superior* (i.e., more just) that systems that succeed without aiming. A property-owning democracy that fails to satisfy the difference principle can at least claim it is a token of a permissible type. Rawls seems to think the only way to *aim* to satisfy the difference principle is to have a property-owning democracy or liberal socialist regime so described.

However, it is not true that this is the only way to aim to satisfy the difference principle. Justice may require that we aim to satisfy the principle, but it does not require that we aim via direct methods (i.e., via the property-owning democracy). Rather, justice requires that we take whatever method of aiming, direct or indirect, that works.

When we think of individual moral agents, it is plausible to hold that people that aim at the right things but fail to achieve them are morally superior to those that unintentionally succeed in producing the good. Many theorists dispute this, but it is not obviously false. However, basic structures, states, and societies are not moral agents. It is far less plausible to think that if a certain goal is just, it is better for a basic structure to aim directly at it and consistently fail than to consistently succeed without directly aiming or aiming at all. We have to ask what the principles of justice are for. If, as Rawls thinks, they are for promoting our interests as free and politically equal members of society, we should stop valorizing the symbolism of direct aiming and get on with doing whatever actually makes us free and equal and promotes our interests.

4. DIRECTLY AIMING AT FAILURE

Rawls's argument for the difference principle crucially relies upon certain premises about economics and incentives. The reason that deviations from strict economic equality are justified, Rawls thinks, is that they are necessary in order to improve everyone's economic condition. Permitting inequalities generates incentives to those with better capabilities and greater ambition, who then turn the wheels of economic growth. Rawls himself states that attempting to satisfy the difference principle (or any other egalitarian principle) lowers incentives and interferes with efficient market allocations, such that economies that are more egalitarian will not grow as quickly as "unfair" economies. If these premises turn out to be problematic for Rawls, by undermining rather than supporting some of his conclusion, this does not mean that Rawls should just retract those premises. First, retracting these premises would remove the motivation behind the difference principle. The motivation behind the difference principle is that if we allow unequal slices of the social pie, this will tend to cause the pie to get bigger, and so everyone—even the person with the smallest slice—will get a bigger slice than she would have if slices had been more equal. Allowing unequal slices gives people an incentive to innovate and work harder—to cause economic growth. This growth tends to benefit everyone. Second, these premises about growth and inequality are accepted by all but a tiny minority of economists. So, it is not just that Rawls needs these premises in order to get to some of his conclusions, but also that these premises are true.

The society Rawls favors will be a property-owning democracy that, among other things, directly aims to satisfy the difference principle. It will be less efficient than capitalist societies that do not directly aim to satisfy the difference principle. Ceteris paribus, it will thus grow more slowly. (This is a claim Rawls himself accepts.) Rawls accepts this slower growth because he thinks that justice, not efficiency, is the first virtue of social institutions.

Imagine there are two societies, ParetoSuperiorland and Fairnessland. ParetoSuperiorland is some sort of capitalist society, divided roughly into three equally sized classes, with an income distribution of 10, 20, 40 income units from its bottom to upper class. Fairnessland initially is a mirror image of ParetoSuperiorland, with the same resources, human capital, and distribution of wealth. However, Fairnesslanders become convinced by reading Rawls's books, and thus introduce a basic structure that directly aims to satisfy justice as fairness via Rawls's preferred institutions. They determine, using immaculate counterfactual forecasting not yet available to our world's economists, that the difference principle is satisfied when the following distribution obtains: 15, 19, 24. Thus, at the moment that Fairnessland becomes a property-owning democracy, the poorest individuals in it are 50 percent wealthier than the poorest in ParetoSuperiorland.

Since ParetoSuperiorland, as Rawls claims, focuses on economic efficiency, its economy grows faster than Fairnessland's. Fairnessland works continually to maintain the 15–19–24 pattern, but since this work requires that its government interfere with the market's spontaneous allocations of resources, it retards growth. Such interference entails interrupting the information, incentive, and learning structure of the market, thus disrupting the operation of the equilibrium principles that generate efficiency and growth. Rawls has granted us all of this—these are his premises.

Fig. 1 maps the growth of the two economies. Suppose ParetoSuperiorland grows at 4 percent a year, while Fairnessland grows at 2 percent.[4] ParetoSuperiorland does not directly try to maximize the well-being of the worst off. For simplicity, let us stipulate that the real incomes of each class grow at the same rate (4% for ParetoSuperiorlanders,

Table 1. *Growth in Two Hypothetical Economic Regimes*

	ParetoSuperiorland			Fairnessland		
	Poor	Middle	Rich	Poor	Middle	Rich
1900	10	20	40	15	19	24
1901	10.4	20.8	41.6	15.3	19.4	24.5
1902	10.8	21.6	43.2	15.6	19.8	25.0
1925	26.7	53.3	106.6	24.6	31.2	39.4
1950	71.1	142.1	284.3	40.4	51.2	64.6
2000	505.1	1010.1	2020.2	108.7	137.7	173.9

2% for Fairnesslanders), though of course realistic income growth rates are much more dynamic. (Though see next page.) However, we have every reason to hold that the poor in ParetoSuperiorland will have higher growth rates than the poor in Fairnessland; no one realistically believes that under normal conditions only the rich benefit from growth. (Cowen 2002) Besides, the premise that growth is needed to benefit the poor is Rawls's own. Let us start at the year 1900 and see how the economies do over time.

Of course, the income of the higher classes does not matter for Rawls, since the difference principle requires us to focus on the least advantaged class only. Thus, even if the rich in ParetoSuperiorland enjoyed an even higher rate of growth, say 6%, that would not by itself be a count against that social structure.

After 25 years, the poor in ParetoSuperiorland, a society that does not try to bring about the difference principle, are richer than the poor are in Fairnessland. After 100 years, they are astoundingly richer. Yet ParetoSuperiorland is not eligible for consideration under justice as fairness—its basic structure is a token of a forbidden type. ParetoSuperiorland in principle *permits* its lowest class to be worse off than in Fairnessland. Still, the structures that embody this permission in fact benefit its "poor," certainly far more than directly aiming to satisfy the difference principle benefits the poor in Fairnessland.[5]

At what point do the least advantaged (and everyone else) in Fairnessland object that they were given a bad deal? It is perhaps always true at any given time that the condition of the least advantaged can be temporarily ameliorated by introducing some new basic structure that provides them with more resources. However, this move can also mean that over time the worst off will be worse off than they would be had nothing been done.

As an aside, note that starting sometime after 1925, if the two societies existed on the same world, we would begin to see rapid emigration from Fairnessland to ParetoSuperiorland. If Fairnesslanders were denied a right of exit, we would expect dissent and the desire for reform among its inhabitants. (In Rawls's theory, denying a right of exit would violate the first principle of justice.) If they were denied a right to exit, I suspect that Fairnesslanders will quickly lose their sense of justice and come to see their society as antagonistic to their conception of the good. In the year 2000 of our hypothetical model, Fairnesslanders could hardly boast that their society is one that takes the plight of the least advantaged seriously.

5. THE PARADOX IN REALITY

I have used a simplified model, one that relies only on Rawls's assumptions about economic growth. (One of the simplifications is to Rawls's benefit—it ignores the effects of class mobility over lifetime.) In this section, I offer some economic discussion of the issue to begin to substantiate Rawls's assumptions.

It certainly is true that growth does not guarantee a benefit to the poor—it is even compatible with harming them. However, historically, when growth harms the poor, it is usually because property rights regimes and the rule of law are not in place. (De Soto 2000, North 1990)

On the other hand, it is not to be *expected* that growth will harm the poor or fail to benefit them—quite the contrary, even if we get no guarantees. The biggest predictor and cause of increases in worker quality of life is capital accumulation, since this drives up the productivity of labor, and labor prices, like other prices, are determined by marginal productivity. World Bank economists David Dollar and Aart Kraay, after surveying 80 nations, found that on average when a country's real GDP grows at n% a year, the average income of the lowest quintile group and the per capita income grows at n% as well. (Dollar and Kraay 2002.)[6] I.e., they found that there is on average a 1:1 correspondence between growth in real GDP and the growth of the income of the poor. Additionally, this average is not merely a statistical artifact; most countries closely approximate the average. Thus, the simple model I used in §4 is apt.

More importantly, the *qualitative* difference in lifestyle and type of goods owned and consumed by rich and poor are much smaller now than 100 years ago. Income differences appear to misrepresent lifestyle differences. For instance, while the ratio between household income of the United States' top quintile and bottom quintile in 1995 was 14:1, the total *consumption* ratio (measured by expenditures on food, clothing, shelter, and so on) was a mere 4:1. Measured across individuals rather than households, the gap is only 2.3 to 1. It should be noted that higher income quintiles have more workers per household and work more hours per household. (Cox and Alm 17) Also, households at the poverty-line spend more than their official incomes. (Schmidtz and Goodin 1998:41) How is this possible? It is not because they accumulate massive debt. Rather, many such households include college students and young adults receiving cash from their parents, and retired seniors living off large savings but with little to no wage income.

Indeed, if we compare officially poor American households in 1994 to officially average American households in 1971, we find that the ownership of luxury goods (washing machines, air-conditioners, color televisions, etc.) is *higher* among poor families in 1994 than among average families in 1971. (Cox and Alm 15) It is informative to note that in the U.S., *individuals* who occupied the lowest income quintile in 1975 had an average increase of $25,322 in real income over the next 16 years, while those occupying the highest income quintile saw their real income rise only $3,974. (Schansberg 1996:8, Schmidtz and Goodin 1998:39) American poverty rates (which are defined and computed differently in the U.S. and Europe) have dropped to about 1/4 their 1929, pre-depression level. (Schmidtz and Goodin 1998:40)

Here is one way of driving home the potential effects of slower growth. The average growth rate in chained 2000 dollars of the U.S. real GDP from 1929 through 2004 was 3.559%.[7] As Rawls correctly contends, a property-owning democracy will have slower economic growth than a welfare-state capitalist society. Suppose Twin United States had, in that same period, become a property-owning democracy, and this had resulted in merely 1 point slower average growth, such that Twin United States' GDP grew at an average rate of 2.559%. (This is a charitable number, higher than the corresponding growth rate of most advanced European countries.) According to the Bureau of Economic Analysis, actual U.S. GDP, in 2000 dollars, was $10,841.9 billion in 2004. The GDP of Twin United States, with its slower average growth rate of 2.559%, would be approximately $5756.4 billion dollars. (At 2% average annual growth, its GDP would be less than $4000 billion.) Assuming that the Twin United States would have the same population as the real United States, its GDP per capita would be about that of Slovenia. It is doubtful that this would be favorable for the least advantaged of Twin United States, despite the difference principle. If Slovenia converted to the institutions of justice as fairness, this would be better for its poor than current American institutions, for all their manifest flaws? To be effective, redistribution needs resources to redistribute.

Thus far, all we have been considering are the bundle of goods regulated by the difference principle. It should be kept in mind, however, that the equal basic liberties and fair equality of opportunity principles have lexical priority over the difference principle. Perhaps European institutions, which are closer to Rawls's favored social system than American institutions, do worse in the long run than their American counterparts as measured by the difference principle. However, if a basic structure fails to satisfy the other principles, it is ruled out, and the difference principle is not even considered. Could European institutions receive a favorable verdict over the U.S. vis-à-vis the other principles?

Regarding the equal basic liberties principle, an uncommitted person who is neither Eurocentric or Americentric would likely answer that it is a tie. Citizens of North American and European countries have approximately the same degree of personal freedom, and while these freedoms are often abused (in different ways in different nations), there is no obvious winner. Perhaps, then, we should examine our hypothetical nations from the previous section. Whose citizens enjoy basic rights and liberties more, Fairnessland or ParetoSuperiorland? Maybe it is a tie. Maybe Fairnessland loses. After all, a property-owning democracy is more likely to fall prey to public choice problems and public predation than welfare state capitalism, which is in turn more likely to fall prey than laissez faire capitalism.

A basic conclusion of public choice theory is that as governments gain power and correspondingly have more to sell to would-be rent-seekers, the more these governments will sell. A laissez faire capitalist system, whatever its flaws, does not have many agencies worth capturing, but the property-owning democracy certainly does. According to Rawls, property-owning democracies attempt to avoid large concentrations of bureaucratic power, but public choice theory predicts that property-owning democracies are precisely susceptible to such concentrations on the grounds that it has more agencies worth capturing.[8] Regarding basic goods, rents most hurt the worker, *especially* the non-union laborer and the immigrant, because the economic fallout (i.e., the externalized costs) from rents mimics a regressive tax and because such workers have the least access to power. Regarding liberty, the property-owning democracy is a cause of public predation, which undermines the social union and causes public discord. In practice, Rawls's property-owning democracy would not function as intended. It is unfortunate and puzzling that while public choice theory rose to prominence over the years Rawls was writing, Rawls never considered the implications of the public choice for his theory.

We should ask how opportunities differ. Let us compare the U.S. to France and Germany. Official unemployment is chronically higher in the latter countries, and hidden unemployment (from make-work projects, etc.) may be even higher. (Hytti 2002) This is not a coincidence. A 2003 IMF study showed that replacing certain German policies with those of the U.S. would result in a 5 point drop in the unemployment rate and a 10% boost to GDP over 10 years. (IMF 2002:129) Had the U.S. not added a single retail (including fast food) job in the 1980s and 1990s, it would still have produced more new jobs than Germany, France, and Italy combined. (Garibaldi and Mauro 1999:12) Also, since 1989, the number of jobs in the highest earnings group, as defined by the Bureau of Labor Statistics, has grown about twice as fast in the U.S. as those of the lowest earning group. (Ilg and Haugen 2000) As for educational opportunity, despite the preponderance of tuition-free universities in Europe, the percentage of college-educated Americans age 25–64 is tends to be about double that of the wealthier European nations. (Cox and Alm 2000:98) While U.S. Department of Education and Bureau of Labor Statistics data indicate that 43.8% of 2002 high school graduates whose families are from the lowest income quintile started college in the fall, only 13% of their German counterparts did. (Bunderministerium für Bildung und Forschung 2003:204–205, U.S. Department of Education 2003:127) One might object that the German and American educational systems are different. Perhaps we are comparing apples and oranges, but even if so, we are still comparing fruits.

The preceding is merely a snapshot of the surrounding issues. However, it is evidence against Rawls's favored institutions. A full empirical and economic investigation of which types of institutions best satisfy Rawls's principles would require at least a book. Assessing the actual basic structures of various nations would require another. It is difficult to classify western nations under Rawls's categories of social systems. (E.g., Denmark has more extensive welfare state but also much freer markets than the United States. Is it thus more or less of a property-owning democracy than the U.S.? It's hard to say.) Germany, France, Italy, Sweden, Denmark, and the U.S. are all roughly described as welfare state capitalist, but with significant deviations toward property-owning democracy and to a lesser extent liberal socialism. They also each contain institutions that do not properly belong under any of those three systems. E.g., current imperialistic American military institutions seem to belong to an archaic mercantilist rather than a capitalist system.

6. THE IDEA OF PUBLICITY

Justice as fairness seems to require us to aim directly to satisfy principles even when doing so fails. One of the major reasons why direct, immediate aiming is important for Rawls is his conception of publicity. Thus, I will briefly explain the role of publicity in Rawls's theory.

Rawls advances a liberal theory of justice. Liberal societies, Rawls holds, have a sort of transparency in their aims. The use of political power must be justifiable to each citizen in reference to that citizen's reasonable moral beliefs. (Rawls 1995:xlvi) Justice must not merely be done, but *must be seen to be done for the sake of justice*. Because of this, just institutions must track and enforce compliance of Rawls principles, rather than permit deviance. Rawls advocates this view partly for reasons of stability, since citizens cannot have an adequate "sense of justice" (desire to conform to the law) unless they know the point of their institutions and what conception of justice the laws support. (Rawls 1999: §76 et passim) Also important is the need to avoid government house utilitarianism and other such doctrines that permit the government to deceive its citizens, e.g., by telling them the point of the laws is X when it is in fact Y. A society in which the principles of justice are known and shared by all is one that will lack false consciousness and ideology. (Rawls 2001:121–122) A politically liberal society, Rawls holds, will have a public conception of justice, a shared set of principles and values. (Rawls 1995:9) Principles of justice that would be effective at achieving society's shared goals provided they were not "publicly acknowledged" or "commonly known or believed" must be rejected. (Rawls 1995:69) However, all of these points are compatible with both direct and indirect methods of achieving Rawlsian aims.

No basic structure is considered just merely because it happens or even consistently happens to satisfy Rawls's principles–it must publicly aim to do so. Thus, if it turns out that a society that publicly lives by a different theory of justice happens to respect our basic liberties, is consistently better for the least advantaged than any other system, and consistently satisfies fair equality of opportunity, this society would still be considered unjust by Rawls.

Rawls argues for justice as fairness by having us imagine people coming to a bargaining table to choose principles of justice to govern society. He calls this bargaining situation the *original position*. In one recent formulation, the bargainers, known as the "parties", are to be thought of as our representatives. They choose principles for our sake. However, in order to make the bargain fair, Rawls places the parties under a veil of ignorance. This veil restricts the knowledge available to the parties about the citizens they represent (such as those citizens' sex, religion, social status, natural abilities, and economic class). This prevents any of the parties from possessing an unfair bargaining advantage. Rawls argues that in the original position, which he thinks embodies our common intuitive ideas of fairness, the principles of justice as fairness will be chosen.

If we care about the difference principle, maybe we must have a society that foregoes pursuing it directly in order to satisfy it. Perhaps, to keep the essence of Rawls, one could say that Rawls's principles should in fact be considered meta-principles, providing rules of recognition for the actual principles to govern a basic structure. In such a case, a basic structure would be just if and only if it follows those principles and has those aims, whatever they are (entitlement theory, perfectionism, utilitarian, etc.) that consistently satisfy the difference principle, fair equality of opportunity, and the principle of liberty. Rawls at least has the philosophical resources to make such a claim. (Rawls 1955) This would mean, however, that Rawls would have to treat market societies fairly, giving them honest consideration as candidates for just societies, rather than dismissing them out of hand.

7. CONCLUSION

Improving the plight of the worst off matters; so does pleasure. Yet, the way to obtain these things is not necessarily to aim directly at them. And in any case, aiming at them with a particular policy instrument is justified only in so far as the instrument works.

Rawls's assumption that one can do ideal theory first, and then look at compliance issues and how institutions actually work second, may be what leads him to the problems mentioned in this paper. Further empirical investigation may show us that the solution is to abandon some of Rawls's favored institutions even if we should keep his theory of justice. Alternatively, one might continue to defend the property-owning democracy by placing more weight on the notion of political equality and democratic participation. However, one of the main advantages of Rawls's theory was that it appeared to have taken the Marxist materialist critique seriously. (Cohen 1994) However, if the main reasons for accepting Rawls's favored institutions turn out not to be that they best benefit the least advantaged in material terms, but that they promote ideals of political participation, then the theory would seem to be answer more to Rousseau than Marx, as the theory would rest on controversial claims about the role of democratic participation in the good life.

ENDNOTES

1. URL = <http://www.swaraj.org/illich_hell.htm>.
2. The fair value of political liberty principle requires that citizens with similar abilities and motivation to use those abilities will have a roughly "equal chance of influencing the government's policy and of attaining positions of authority irrespective of their economic and social class." (Rawls 2001:46.) The fair equality of opportunity principle

requires that citizens with similar abilities and motivation will have a roughly equal chance of obtaining any job or position of prestige.

3. Just what taxation schemes are appropriate are up to the social sciences to determine. Rawls, however, believes that inheritance and bequest taxes will be needed, as well as either a progressive income tax, or, perhaps, a consumption tax. (Rawls 2001:160–161.)

4. I use 2 percent because it is a round number approximating (and better than) Sweden's average growth from 1970 to 1998. Sweden was on average 1 point lower in growth per annum than the OECD average from 1970 to 1998. In 1998, per capita income was 15% lower in Sweden than the average for the 23 richest countries. (OECD 1999). Sweden began an economic upturn in 1998, but this was caused by lowering tax rates, reducing the public sector size, reducing capital regulations, and other attempts to liberalize the economy. By contrast, Hong Kong, which is nearly always rated as the economically freest country in the world, had an average growth rate of over 6% from 1970 through 2000 (with about 4.4% average growth in the 1990s, despite having to suffer through the Asian financial crisis). (IMF 2001)

5. Moreover, Rawls cannot respond by saying that in such a case a society ought to have the entitlement theory's institutions right up until the point that the difference principle fails to be satisfied and then switch. Societies do not switch institutions so easily. The rule 'Follow the entitlement theory', followed in order to satisfy the difference principle, is not equivalent to the rule 'Follow the entitlement theory in order to satisfy the difference principle'. The paper that convinced me of this is Rawls 1955.

6. For a critique of earlier versions of (Dollar and Kraay 2002), see (Nye, Reddy, and Watkins 2002) and (Lükbar, Smith, and Weeks 2002).

7. Data taken from the Bureau of Economic Analysis, National Economic Accounts, http://www.bea.gov/bea/dn1.htm, with author's calculations.

8. In response, the defender of the property-owning democracy might claim that we need to equalize incomes so that no one will have a buying advantage to capture agencies. This misses the point. It is true that in countries with income inequality, wealthy groups (such as corporations and labor unions) buy a disproportionate share of the rents. They will also tend to bid up the prices of the rents, so that more money will be spent on rent-seeking. However, rent seeking does not decrease when incomes become more equal. Rent seeking occurs not because people have unequal amounts to pay for power, but because they have unequal amounts to gain from buying it. Benefits can be concentrated and costs diffused even when incomes are equal.

REFERENCES

Bundesministerium für Bildung und Forschung (2003) *Grund und Strukturdaten* 2001/2002. Berlin: Bundesministerium für Bildung und Forschung.

Cohen, J. (1994) "A More Democratic Liberalism", *Michigan Law Review 92*:1503–1546.

Cowen, T. (2002) "Does the Welfare State Help the Poor?", *Social Philosophy and Policy, 19*:36–54.

Cox, W. M., and Alm, R. (2000) *Myths of Rich and Poor*. New York: Basic Books.

De Soto, Hernando. (2000) *The Mystery of Capital*. New York: Basic Books.

Dollar, D. and Kraay, A. (2002) "Growth is Good for the Poor". *Journal of Economic Growth 7*:195–225.

Feinberg, J. (2004) "Psychological Egoism." In J. Feinberg and R. Shafer-Landau (Eds.) *Reason and Responsibility*. Belmont, CA: Thompson Learning.

Garibaldi, P., and Mauro, P. (1999) "Deconstructing Job Creation." IMF Working Paper No. 99/109 Available at SSRN: http://ssrn.com/abstract=880636

Hytti, H. (2002) "Miksi ruotsalaiset ovat sairaita mutta suomalaiset työttömiä?" [Why are the Swedes Sick but the Finns Unemployed?] Yhteiskuntapolitiikka. 76:333–344.

Ilg, R. E. and Haugen, S. E. (2000) "Earnings and Employment Trends in the 1990s." *Monthly Labor Review. 123*:21–33.

International Monetary Fund. (2001) *World Economic Outlook*. Washington, DC: International Monetary Fund.

International Monetary Fund. (2002) *World Economic Outlook: Trade and Finance*. Washington, DC: International Monetary Fund.

Lükbar, M., Smith, G., and Weeks, J. (2002) "Growth and the Poor: A Comment on Dollar and Kraay". *Journal of International Development, 14*:555–571.

North, D. (1990) *Institutions, Institutional Change, and Economic Performance*. Cambridge: Cambridge University Press.

Nye, H. L. M.., Reddy, S., and Watkins, K. (2002) "Dollar and Kraay on 'Trade, Growth, and Poverty'". International Development Associates IDEAS. Available at the Food and Agriculture Organization of the United Nations: http://www.fao.org/righttofood/kc/downloads/vl/en/details/214083.htm.

Organization for Economic Development and Cooperation. (1999) *National Accounts: Main Aggregates 1960/1998* 1999 Edition. Paris: Organization for Economic Cooperation and Development.

Rawls, J. (1955) "Two Concepts of Rules", *The Philosophical Review, 64*: 3–32.

Rawls, J. (1995) *Political Liberalism*. New York: Columbia University Press.

Rawls, J. (1999) *A Theory of Justice*. Cambridge, MA: Belknap Press.

Rawls, J. (2001) *Justice as Fairness: a Restatement*. Cambridge, MA: Belknap Press.

Schansberg, D. E. (1996) *Poor Policy*. Boulder: Westview Press.

Schmidtz, D,. and Goodin, R. (1998) *Social Welfare and Personal Responsibility*. Cambridge: Cambridge University Press.

United States Department of Education. (2003) *The Condition of Education 2002*. Washington, DC: United States Department of Education.

Wage Labor and Capital

KARL MARX

What is it that takes place in the exchange between the capitalist and the wage-labor?

The laborer receives means of subsistence in exchange for his labor-power; the capitalist receives, in exchange for his means of subsistence, labor, the productive activity of the laborer, the creative force by which the worker not only replaces what he consumes, but also gives to the accumulated labor a greater value than it previously possessed. The laborer gets from the capitalist a portion of the existing means of subsistence. For what purpose do these means of subsistence serve him? For immediate consumption. But as soon as I consume means of subsistence, they are irrevocably lost to me, unless I employ the time during which these means sustain my life in producing new means of subsistence, in creating by my labor new values in place of the values lost in consumption. But it is just this noble reproductive power that the laborer surrenders to the capitalist in exchange for means of subsistence received. Consequently, he has lost it for himself.

Let us take an example. For one shilling a laborer works all day long in the fields of a farmer, to whom he thus secures a return of two shillings. The farmer not only receives the replaced value which he has given to the day laborer, he has doubled it. Therefore, he has consumed the one shilling that he gave to the day laborer in a fruitful, productive manner. For the one shilling he has bought the labor-power of the day-laborer, which creates products of the soil of twice the value, and out of one shilling makes two. The day-laborer, on the contrary, receives in the place of his productive force, whose results he has just surrendered to the farmer, one shilling, which he exchanges for means of subsistence, which he consumes more or less quickly. The one shilling has therefore been consumed in a double manner—reproductively for the capitalist, for it has been exchanged for labor-power, which brought forth two shillings; unproductively for the worker, for it has been exchanged for means of subsistence which are lost for ever, and whose value he can obtain again only by repeating the same exchange with the farmer. Capital therefore presupposes wage-labor; wage-labor presupposes capital. They condition each other; each brings the other into existence.

Does a worker in a cotton factory produce only cotton? No. He produces capital. He produces values which serve anew to command his work and to create by means of it new values.

Capital can multiply itself only by exchanging itself for labor-power, by calling wage-labor into life. The labor-power of the wage-laborer can exchange itself for capital only by increasing capital, by strengthening that very power whose slave it is. Increase of capital, therefore, is increase of the proletariat, i.e., of the working class.

And so, the bourgeoisie and its economists maintain that the interest of the capitalist and of the laborer is the same. And in fact, so they are! The worker perishes if capital does not keep him busy. Capital perishes if it does not exploit labor-power, which, in order to exploit, it must buy. The more quickly the capital destined for production—the productive capital—increases, the more prosperous industry is, the more the bourgeoisie enriches itself, the better business gets, so many more workers does the capitalist need, so much the dearer does the worker sell himself. The fastest possible growth of productive capital is, therefore, the indispensable condition for a tolerable life to the laborer.

But what is growth of productive capital? Growth of the power of accumulated labor over living labor; growth of the rule of the bourgeoisie over the working class. When wage-labor produces the alien wealth dominating it, the power hostile to it, capital, there flow back to it its means of employment—i.e., its means of subsistence, under the condition that it again become a part of capital, that is become again the lever whereby capital is to be forced into an accelerated expansive movement.

To say that the interests of capital and the interests of the workers are identical, signifies only this: that capital and wage-labor are two sides of one and the same relation. The one conditions the other in the same way that the usurer and the borrower condition each other.

As long as the wage-laborer remains a wage-laborer, his lot is dependent upon capital. That is what the boasted community of interests between worker and capitalists amounts to.

If capital grows, the mass of wage-labor grows, the number of wage-workers increases; in a word, the sway of capital extends over a greater mass of individuals.

Let us suppose the most favorable case: if productive capital grows, the demand for labor grows. It therefore increases the price of labor-power, wages.

A house may be large or small; as long as the neighboring houses are likewise small, it satisfies all social requirement for a residence. But let there arise next to the little house a palace, and the little house shrinks to a hut. The little house now makes it clear that its inmate has no social position at all to maintain, or but a very insignificant one; and however high it may shoot up in the course of civilization, if the neighboring palace rises in equal or even in greater measure, the occupant of the relatively little house will always find himself more uncomfortable, more dissatisfied, more cramped within his four walls.

An appreciable rise in wages presupposes a rapid growth of productive capital. Rapid growth of productive capital calls forth just as rapid a growth of wealth, of luxury, of social needs and social pleasures. Therefore, although the pleasures of the laborer have increased, the social gratification which they afford has fallen in comparison with the increased pleasures of the capitalist, which are inaccessible to the worker, in comparison with the stage of development of society in general. Our wants and pleasures have their origin in society; we therefore measure them in relation to society; we do not measure them in relation to the objects which serve for their gratification. Since they are of a social nature, they are of a relative nature.

But wages are not at all determined merely by the sum of commodities for which they may be exchanged. Other factors enter into the problem. What the workers directly receive for their labor-power is a certain sum of money. Are wages determined merely by this money price?

In the 16th century, the gold and silver circulation in Europe increased in consequence of the discovery of richer and more easily worked mines in America. The value of gold and silver, therefore, fell in relation to other commodities. The workers received the same amount of coined silver for their labor-power as before. The money price of their work remained the same, and yet their wages had fallen, for in exchange for the same amount of silver they obtained a smaller amount of other commodities. This was one of the circumstances which furthered the growth of capital, the rise of the bourgeoisie, in the 18th century.

Let us take another case. In the winter of 1847, in consequence of bad harvest, the most indispensable means of subsistence—grains, meat, butter, cheese, etc.—rose greatly in price. Let us suppose that the workers still received the same sum of money for their labor-power as before. Did not their wages fall? To be sure. For the same money they received in exchange less bread, meat, etc. Their wages fell, not because the value of silver was less, but because the value of the means of subsistence had increased.

Finally, let us suppose that the money price of labor-power remained the same, while all agricultural and manufactured commodities had fallen in price because of the employment of new machines, of favorable seasons, etc. For the same money the workers could now buy more commodities of all kinds. Their wages have therefore risen, just because their money value has not changed.

The money price of labor-power, the nominal wages, do not therefore coincide with the actual or real wages—i.e., with the amount of commodities which are actually given in exchange for the wages. If then we speak of a rise or fall of wages, we have to keep in mind not only the money price of labor-power, the nominal wages, but also the real wages.

But neither the nominal wages—i.e., the amount of money for which the laborer sells himself to the capitalist—nor the real wages—i.e., the amount of commodities which he can buy for this money—exhausts the relations which are comprehended in the term wages.

Wages are determined above all by their relations to the gain, the profit, of the capitalist. In other words, wages are a proportionate, relative quantity.

Real wages express the price of labor-power in relation to the price of commodities; relative wages, on the other hand, express the share of immediate labor in the value newly created by it, in relation to the share of it which falls to accumulated labor, to capital.

The Ethics of Price Gouging

MATT ZWOLINSKI

Abstract: *Price gouging occurs when, in the wake of an emergency, sellers of a certain necessary goods sharply raise their prices beyond the level needed to cover increased costs. Most people think that price gouging is immoral, and most states have laws rendering the practice a civil or criminal offense. The purpose of this paper is to explore some of the philosophic issues surrounding price gouging, and to argue that the common moral condemnation of it is largely mistaken. I will make this argument in three steps, by rebutting three widely held beliefs about the ethics of price gouging: 1) that laws prohibiting price gouging are morally justified, 2) that price gouging is morally impermissible behavior, even if it ought not be illegal, and 3) that price gouging reflects poorly on the moral character of those who engage in it, even if the act itself is not morally impermissible.*

1. INTRODUCTION

I n 1996, Hurricane Eran struck North Carolina, leaving over a million people in the Raleigh-Durham area without power. Without any way of refrigerating food, infant formula, or insulin, and without any idea of when power would be restored, people were desperate for ice, but existing supplies quickly sold out. Four young men from Goldsboro, which was not significantly affected by the storm, rented refrigerated trucks, bought 500 bags of ice for $1.70 per bag, and drove to Raleigh. The price they charged for the ice was $12 per bag—more than seven times what they paid for it.

This kind of behavior is often referred to as "price gouging." Many states, North Carolina included, prohibit it by law. And even when it is not legally prohibited, it is generally thought to be exploitative and immoral. The purpose of this paper is to explore the philosophic issues surrounding price gouging, and to argue that the common moral condemnation of it is largely mistaken. I will make this argument in three steps, by rebutting three widely held beliefs about the ethics of price gouging: 1) that laws prohibiting price gouging are morally justified, 2) that price gouging is morally impermissible behavior, even if it ought not be illegal, and 3) that price gouging reflects poorly on the moral character of those who engage in it, even if the act itself is not morally impermissible. The core of my argument will be that standard cases of price gouging provide great benefit to those in desperate need, that they tend to lack the morally objectionable features often ascribed to them such as coercion and exploitation, and that attempts to prohibit the practice will harm individuals who are already vulnerable and can least afford to bear further harm.

The argument of this paper is an exercise in non-ideal theory. Much of what bothers us about price gouging, I suspect, is the fact that it takes place in a social context where the background political and economic institutions are less than fully just. Many people object to the inequality which pervades the distribution of wealth and social services in the United States, and worry that price gouging either exploits or exacerbates that inequality. The real problem, such people might say, is not price gouging itself but the more fundamental issue of an unjust basic structure. I do not wish to deny that questions about the basic structure are important. But they cannot be the only questions that are important. If our basic structure is unjust, then we still need to decide how individuals should act, and how particular policies should be formulated, in the context of our unjust society. Part of what we should be doing, to be sure, is trying to make the basic structure more just. But assuming that this goal will not be achieved immediately, we still need to decide what to do about price gouging here and now.

Before we can proceed to the normative arguments about price gouging, however, we will need to arrive at a more precise understanding of the concept than that which we are given by common usage. Specifically, we will want an analysis which makes clear how cases of price gouging differ from the kind of ordinary market price hikes which are not even prima facie morally objectionable. Section two will undertake this analysis. Section three will begin the normative argument by attempting to show that laws prohibiting price gouging are morally unjustified and ought to be repealed. Section four will go further and argue that most, though not all, cases of price gouging are at least morally permissible, if not morally praise-worthy. An implication of this position is that individuals have reason to reject calls to voluntarily refrain from price gouging where it is not prohibited by law. Finally, section five will argue that price gouging does not necessarily reflect poorly on the character of those who engage in it. Some people who engage in price gouging no doubt will do it from bad motives or disreputable characters, but the mere fact that they engage in price gouging is not evidence for this conclusion.

2. THE CONCEPT OF PRICE GOUGING

A fruitful place to begin a conceptual analysis of price gouging is with the language of the statutes which prohibit it. At present, there is no Federal anti-gouging legislation, though one bill specifically focused on gasoline has passed the House and is currently pending in the Senate. Approximately thirty-four states, however, have laws against price gouging, a survey of which reveals that gouging is generally defined in terms of three elements. See Appendix A for a detailed overview of these laws.

1. Period of Emergency: Almost all anti-gouging laws specify that they apply only to actions taken during times of disaster or emergency.
2. Necessary Items: Most laws further specify that their restrictions apply only to certain classes of items, generally those which are necessary for survival or for coping with serious problems caused by the disaster. California, for instance, is typical in limiting its scope to items which are "consumer food items or goods, goods or services used for emergency cleanup, emergency supplies, medical supplies, home heating oil, building materials, housing, transportation, freight, and storage services, or gasoline or other motorfuels."
3. Price Ceilings: The definitive feature of anti-gouging laws is the limit they set on the maximum price that can be charged for specified goods. Such limits are set either by prohibitions on "unreasonable," "excessive" or "unconscionable" price increases, or by specific limits on the percentage increase in price allowed after the onset of the emergency. In the most extreme laws, the maximum allowable percentage increase is set at zero.

This preliminary analysis leaves a number of important questions unresolved, such as what ought to count as an emergency, which kinds of items are "necessary," and which of the varying methods of determining unacceptable price hikes should be employed. These complexities will be explored to some extent in the remainder of this paper. For the most part, however, the argument that follows will be broad enough that the differences between various conceptions of price gouging will not matter. Any conception of price gouging which fits the general outline above is vulnerable to the kinds of criticism that I will make below.

It is worth noting the heavy strain of moralistic language running through the various anti-gouging statutes. The vast majority of state statutes define the act of price gouging in terms of normative concepts such as "unreasonable" or "unconscionable." And both

Arkansas and California claim in the preamble to their laws that their restrictions are necessary in order to prevent merchants from taking "unfair advantage" of consumers. These facts, along with the very name for the activity (one usually finds the verb "gouging" in conjunction with the direct object "eyes") suggest that the concept of price gouging is moralized—part of what we mean in saying that someone is engaged in price gouging is that they are doing something wrong. To avoid settling the substantive question of the morality of price gouging by definition, however, I propose that we understand the wrongness of price gouging in a prima facie sense. Thus, I suggest that we understand price gouging as a practice in which prices on certain kinds of necessary items are raised in the wake of an emergency to what appear to be unfair or exploitatively high levels.

Whatever its defects in terms of lack of precision, this definition should serve to narrow the focus of our normative investigation. For, note what this definition does not include. It does not say that price gouging involves deception, misinformation, or the use of force against consumers, nor do these claims play any role in the standard arguments against price gouging. In the discussion that follows, then, we shall focus on cases where these factors are not present. We shall do this in order to discover whether there is anything objectionable in price gouging per se, and not just with extraneous factors or behaviors which might or might not accompany it.

3. THE MORAL STATUS OF LAWS AGAINST PRICE GOUGING

The argument in this section is designed to show that laws against price gouging are morally unjustified. That is, it attempts to show that we do not have all-things-considered good moral reasons to pass, maintain, or support such laws, and that we do have all-things-considered good moral reason to repeal them. Moreover, it is designed to show that such laws are unjustified whatever one might think about the moral status of price gouging itself. Even if price gouging is morally reprehensible, there is good reason not to prohibit it by law.

One difficulty with anti-gouging laws is that there is no unproblematic way of defining the practice of price gouging for legal purposes. Laws which prohibit "un-conscionable" or "unreasonable" exchanges, for instance, present serious problems of interpretation and predictability given the difficulty of assigning clear and shared meanings to these terms. Even those whose full-time occupation is interpreting, applying, and working with the law have grave difficulty understanding precisely what these terms mean. There is little hope, then, that ordinary merchants or individuals who begin selling goods for the first time in the wake of a disaster will be able to form a clear understanding of what the law requires of them. Without such an understanding, these individuals will be unable to predict how the law will respond to their behavior, and unable to plan their economic activity accordingly. This is objectionable both on grounds of efficiency and fairness.

Laws which prohibit price increases above a specified level (including zero) fare better on the dimension of clarity, but run into other difficulties as a result of the inflexible nature of the limits they set. Many such laws, for instance, take no account of increased costs which the sellers might face as a result of the same disaster which put their customers in difficulty. This raises problems from both fairness and consequentialist perspectives. In terms of fairness, it is not clear why the merchant should be forced to absorb the increased costs in order to benefit her customers, especially if we think that those merchants exercised good foresight and responsibility in obtaining a ready stock of goods which might be necessary in the case of a disaster. It is true that we might plausibly think that society as a whole bears some responsibility for protecting its members in time of crisis, but placing the whole of this responsibility on one class of persons seems an affront to fairness. In addition, the consequences of not allowing merchants to make up for increased costs are likely to be bad—for merchants, of course, but for customers as well. For, while the statutes under consideration punish selling items at above a certain specified level of price, they do not punish those who choose not to sell at all. Rather than continuing to sell needed goods such as generators, then, merchants might respond to anti-gouging statutes by closing up shop altogether. Because of the law, merchants will lose out on potential profits and customers will lose out on the opportunity to decide for themselves whether the goods they could have bought would have been worth the higher price.

Some statutes try to avoid these difficulties by allowing price increases above the specified cap if the increased price is directly attributable to increases in cost borne by the seller. But even here, problems persist. For, most states which do allow such an exception limit the kinds of costs which can be taken into account to either increased costs imposed by the merchant's supplier or increased costs of labor and material in the merchant's provision of the goods. And this limitation of relevant costs seems arbitrary. Why, for instance, should there be no account made for increased risk faced by the merchant in remaining open for business during time of disaster? Surely an increased risk of damage or theft is a factor that merchant sought to be able to consider in deciding whether the benefits of doing business in a post-disaster context outweigh the costs, and is a reasonable consideration in favor of raising one's prices. But risk is not the only sort of cost neglected by anti-gouging laws. Such laws also fail to take account of the various opportunity costs that the merchant might face in continuing to do business in the area, rather than shifting her capital to other less dangerous and more profitable markets. From an economic perspective, opportunity costs and costs imposed by risk can be just as burden someone the seller as standard monetary costs, so there is no obvious reason why one special category of costs should be privileged above others (Buchanan, 1999). But the law is often a clumsy instrument for achieving morally precise outcomes, and here as elsewhere, I suspect, it prefers to look only at those elements of the situation which are easily measurable—costs of products, labor and material. Lawmakers are thus faced with a dilemma. A narrow focus on easily measurable costs might be necessary in order to craft a law that can be enforced and understood, but this clarity can only be accomplished at the cost of failing to take account of all the relevant costs faced by the merchants to whom the restrictions apply.

Even if these practical difficulties could be overcome, however, there would still remain a decisive moral consideration against anti-gouging laws. The main reason why such laws are morally unjustified is that they prohibit mutually beneficial exchange in a way that makes those who are already vulnerable even worse off.

Whatever else one might think about price gouging, the standard cases—those not involving deception, misinformation, or other extraneous factors—are clearly beneficial to both parties participating in the exchange. Even if the price they are being charged is exceptionally high and more than consumers would ideally like to pay, the fact that they are willing to pay it shows that they nevertheless value the good they are purchasing more than the money they are giving up for it. And assuming they are not misinformed, deceived, or irrational, there is no reason to think that they are wrong in assigning these relative values. Not only will the exchange satisfy their subjective preferences, but there is every reason to think that it will make them better off from an objective point of view as well. The goods that they are purchasing are, after all, genuinely important. And while the price of generators might rise dramatically in the wake of a disaster which knocks out power to a certain population, so too does the need people have for generators. Their willingness to pay the higher price is a reflection of this increased need, and not the product of mistake or irrationality.

Of course, one might insist that consumers are not benefitting enough from the exchange. Perhaps merchants have a moral duty of beneficence to sell needed goods to consumers at something less than the market-clearing price. Or perhaps there is some moral notion of a "fair" price which price-gouging merchants are violating. One could grant all that has been said above, in other words, and still hold that merchants who charge the market-clearing price for necessary goods in the wake of a disaster are exploiting their customers.

I am not convinced by the accounts of exploitation on which such an argument would rely, and will have more to say about this in the next section. For our present purposes, however, we can grant the wrongfulness of this kind of exploitation and simply point out that this wrongfulness is insufficient warrant for prohibiting price gouging by law. For many of the very same concerns which underlie our objection to exploitation also count against any attempt to prohibit mutually beneficial but exploitative exchanges.

If, for instance, we object to exploitation because it sets back the interests of the exploited person, we can note that the prohibition of price gouging sets back their interests even more. To see this, we need simply to think about how anti-gouging laws work. When such laws have any effect at all, it is because they require merchants to sell goods at below the market-clearing price. The market-clearing price is the price at which the quantity supplied is equal to the quantity demanded. If prices are set above the market-clearing price, there will be insufficient demand for merchants to sell all their goods, and a surplus will result. If, on the other hand, prices are set below the market-clearing price as anti-gouging statutes require, there will be too much demand for available supply. There will, in other words, be a shortage of the relevant goods. This point is established both by widely accepted economic theory, and by experiences with price caps such as those established during the oil crisis of the late 1970s. The existence of shortages, in turn, means that many consumers who would like to buy goods—even at the illegal market-clearing price—will be unable to do so. Because they are prevented from engaging in the economic exchanges they desire, they are made worse off. And because the goods affected by price gouging laws are necessary goods that are especially important for their health and well-being, they are probably made significantly worse off.

If, on the other hand, one's reasons for objecting to exploitation are of a de-ontological rather than a consequentialist nature, then a parallel argument can be made regarding the relevant deontological considerations. Exploitation might plausibly be argued to manifest a lack of respect for the personhood of those who are exploited. But laws against price gouging both manifest and encourage similar or greater lack of respect. They manifest a lack of respect for both merchants and customers by preventing them from making the autonomous choice to enter into economic exchanges at the market-clearing price. They send the signal, in effect, that your decision that this exchange is in your best interest is unimportant, and that the law will decide for you what sorts of transactions you are allowed to enter into. And they encourage a lack of respect for buyers by making it more likely that their needs will be neglected by those who are in a position to help them." This is because anti-gouging laws lead to shortages not just in the literal sense in which the supply is completely consumed with leftover demand unsatisfied, but also in a broader sense in which others who could supply the needed goods choose not to. The world never literally runs out of ice, generators, or sandbags in the wake of disaster. Such goods exist, and could be brought to the people who need them if those who possessed them were sufficiently motivated to do so. And whatever our moral attitude toward the fact might be, it is nevertheless a fact that the potential for high profits is one of the most effective ways available of so motivating individuals. Laws which prohibit the reaping of such high profits lead many individuals who would have done something to help to do nothing instead. As a result, disaster victims' needs are not exploited, but they are not satisfied either. They are simply ignored. This is a less obvious way of failing to value the humanity of such per-sons, but it is a failure nonetheless, and one which I am sure most persons would be willing to trade for the disrespect involved in mutually beneficial exploitation, if given the choice.

Before moving on to a moral evaluation of price gouging itself, there is one complica-tion regarding the consequentialist case against anti-gouging laws. That case assumes that anti-gouging laws will prohibit mutually beneficial exchanges, and this seems to be an a priori truth. But the argument also assumes that prohibiting mutually beneficial exchanges will make consumers worse off, and this is more properly seen as an empirical hypothesis than an issue of pure economic logic. Suppose that price gouger 5 holds a monopoly on good G in a given area. And suppose further that the lowest price that 5 would be willing to accept for G is X, whereas the highest price that buyer B would be willing to pay for G would be Z (where Z> X). In the absence of anti-gouging restrictions, the market-clearing price will be very close to Z. With carefully crafted anti-gouging laws, however, it is possible to set the maximum legally permissible price at something closer to X. The law would simply need to know the value of X and set the maximum legal price of G at X. Since S is still willing to sell G at X, and B of course is willing to buy G at X, such laws could conceivably reduce the price which B must pay for G, without destroying S's incentive to supply B with G. Anti-gouging laws could thus, at least in principle, function as strategic mechanisms for reducing disparities in the distribution of cooperative surplus. But while this result is possible in theory, in practice the epistemic hurdles involved arriving at knowledge of X for all goods G and all sellers S seem utterly insurmountable.

In summary, this section has argued that laws against price gouging are subject to several important objections. First, anti-gouging laws face a dilemma in the way they define the offense. Laws which define gouging in terms of "unconscionable" or "exploitative" prices do a good job capturing the nature of the moral opposition to price gouging, but are so vague that there is little chance that market actors will be able to predict which prices would be illegal and which would not. This is both unfair and inefficient. On the other hand, laws which seek to resolve this vagueness by setting clear limits on permissible price increases wind up being excessively rigid and prohibiting not only morally objectionable increases (say, those due to pure greed) but morally unobjectionable ones as well (those due to the supplier's attempt to recoup increased costs due to risk or opportunity costs). Finally, even if anti-gouging laws could be crafted in such a way as to avoid this dilemma, they would still face a decisive objection insofar as they prohibit mutually beneficial exchanges between sellers and buyers, and moreover prohibit them for buyers who stand in desperate need of precisely this kind of beneficial exchange. Anti-gouging laws thereby cause great harm to precisely the people who can afford it least. For all these reasons, I conclude that even if price gouging is in some way immoral, laws against the practice ought to be repealed.

4. THE MORAL STATUS OF PRICE GOUGING ITSELF

The last section accepted, arguendo, that the activity of price gouging is immoral. This section seeks to challenge that assumption by showing that price gouging is, at least in many cases, morally permissible. To make this argument I will set forth and rebut two arguments against the moral permissibility of price gouging, and then set forth two positive arguments in support of its moral permissibility. Throughout, my strategy will be to show both that there is more that is morally praiseworthy in price gouging than we might expect, and that much of what has been labeled morally questionable about the practice is either less objectionable or less unique to the practice of price gouging than has been supposed. Thus, the claim I wish to defend in this section is not that all cases of price gouging are morally permissible. Rather, it is that many cases of price gouging lack morally objectionable features and have much that is morally praiseworthy, and that when these conditions are met, we should view price gouging as morally permissible.

a. Against the Permissibility of Gouging—Coercion

The first concern one might have about price gouging is that it is objectionably coercive. Philosophical accounts of coercion vary, so it is difficult to provide a one-size-fits-all refutation of this claim. Nevertheless, before turning to a more thorough examination of the charge, we can note that most cases of price gouging have three features that, together, appear to undermine concerns about coercion on almost any understanding of that concept. First, most buyers in price gouging cases consent to the exchange. Second, most cases of price gouging do not involve deceit, lack of information, or irrationality on the buyers' part. Taken together, these two facts support, though they do not yet conclusively establish, the claim that buyers enter into the exchange voluntarily. Finally, unlike standard cases of coercion, the harm which threatens to befall the victim is not caused by the alleged perpetrator (the price gouger) but rather by the disaster or emergency from which the buyer is trying to recover. Relative to the baseline of no exchange at all, the gouger's proposal stands to improve the lot of the buyer, not to worsen it.

Still, even granting all this, there are two remaining ways in which one could make the case that price gouging is coercive, both of which involve different ways of understanding the "baseline" to which the buyer's situation is to be compared in order to determine whether she is being subjected to non-coercive offer or a coercive threat. The first way is to assume that the seller has a moral obligation to supply the good to the buyer at less than the market-clearing price, and to understand coercion as defined relative to a moralized baseline (Wertheimer, 2006: 206–11). If we make these assumptions, then the seller's proposal to "take it or leave it" at the market-clearing price is more like a threat than an offer, since what the seller is doing is threatening to violate a moral obligation by which she is bound—the obligation to provide the good to the person in need at a reasonable (less than market-clearing) price. This line of thought seems to be what underlies the claim that proposals are coercive when the alternatives to accepting it are flatly unacceptable or incompatible with "the minimum conditions of a worthwhile life" (Raz, 1982: 112; Raz, 1986: 148–57). For, if such arguments are meant to show that the person making the proposal is acting coercively, and not merely that the person to whom the proposal is made is being coerced (perhaps by the storm, or by her need),then this will presumably have to be grounded in a claim that the person making the proposal has an obligation not to take advantage of the victim's vulnerability by making her proposal on such unfavorable terms, i.e., that her proposal is more like a threat than an offer.

The problem with this line of argument is that it seems to mask what is really a concern about exploitation as a concern about coercion. Intuitively, the difference between threats and offers is that threats reduce options while offers enhance them. And equally intuitively, the actions of price gougers—especially the sort of price gougers described in the story at the opening of this paper—appear to enhance rather than to reduce the options of disaster victims. Thus, I think we should conclude that the proposals which gougers make to buyers are genuinely offers and not coercive threats, but this will leave open the possibility that they are wrongfully exploitative offers. I will address this concern in the next section.

The second remaining way of making the case for the coercive nature of gougers' proposals is to define coercion relative to a non-moralized baseline of statistical normalcy. On such an understanding, A's proposal would count as coercive if and only if it makes the consequences of B's not doing X worse than they would be in the normal course of events. To slightly alter an example from Alan Wertheimer, suppose that B asks A, a physician, to treat his illness. A is charitable physician who normally treats all patients at no cost. In this case, however, A, seeing that B is desperate, says that he will treat JB'S illness if and only if B gives him $100.

On the statistical test, A's actions constitute coercion because his actions make the consequences of ß's not paying $100 much worse than they would normally be. Similarly, then, we might hold that if B could normally buy ice for $1.70 per bag, and A proposes to sell the only remaining ice for $12 per bag, then A's proposal is coercive insofar as it makes the consequences of B's not paying $12 much worse than they would normally be. As I see it, there are several responses to this line of argument. Much will depend, of course, on how we understand the "normalcy" condition in this analysis. We might conclude, for instance, that the charge of gouging could be applied to long-standing merchants who increase their prices in the wake of a disaster, but not to "entrepreneurs" like the ones described at the beginning of this paper, since it is only from the former that buyers could have ever obtained ice for $1.70 in the first place. Or we might instead deny that the price which individuals would normally be charged in a non-disaster situation is the appropriate test for what they should be charged in an emergency where shortages exist—that what is normal in context X is an appropriate standard for what is coercive in context Y.

There is probably some truth in both of these responses to this argument, but the most fundamental response is simply that the statistical test is an inappropriate test for the presence of coercion. Nozick's counterexample to this theory seems devastating: if A beats B, his slave, each morning on a regular basis, and one day offers to stop beating him if and only if B does X, it seems clear that A is wrong-fully coercing B (Nozick, 1969: 450). But on the statistical test, A is not coercing B, since he is not proposing to make the consequences of B's not doing X worse than they would normally be. This seems clearly wrong. Hence, examples like this demonstrate that our intuitions are strongly driven by moralized understandings of the baseline by which coercion is to be defined. And this, as I have said, leads us back to what is really a concern about exploitation, not coercion.

b. Against the Permissibility of Gouging—Exploitation

The second and much more prevalent concern about price gouging is that it is wrongfully exploitative. We have already examined the concept and possible moral wrongness of mutually beneficial exploitation in section two of this paper. The core of this concern is that it is unfair for sellers to take advantage of buyers' vulnerability in order to derive disproportionate benefit to themselves, even if buyers are benefitting from the exchange as well.

There are, however, some puzzles about the wrongness of mutually beneficial exploitation, at least when it is supposed to lead us to think that there is something especially wrong with acts of price gouging, as compared with the actions of most non-gougers.

The puzzles have to do with an incoherence in our thinking about what morality requires of us in terms of aiding those in distress. On the one hand, to the extent that we hold that price gougers are guilty of mutually beneficial exploitation, we hold that they are acting wrongly even though their actions bring some benefit to disaster victims. On the other hand, many of us do nothing to relieve the suffering of most disaster victims, and we generally do not view ourselves as acting wrongly in failing to provide this benefit—or, at least, we do not view ourselves as acting as wrongly as price gougers. How can it make sense to hold these two attitudes simultaneously?

The puzzle is one way of bringing out what Wertheimer calls the "nonworseness claim." That claim holds that in cases where A has a right not to transact with B, and where transacting with B is not worse for B than not transacting with B at all, then it cannot be seriously wrong for A to engage in this transaction, even if its terms are judged to be unfair by some external standard (Wertheimer, 1996: 189).

From a consequentialist moral framework, the nonworseness claim seems obviously true. But the point is meant to have traction for deontological theories as well. B's need places a claim on A for help, then it is puzzling how it could be worse by any moral standard—respect for persons, responsiveness to moral reasons, and so on—for A to provide some help than it is for him to provide none. On the face of it, those who ignore the needs of the vulnerable altogether treat them with less respect than those who do something to help.

But not all are convinced by this claim. Those who reject it typically do so on the grounds that there are special moral constraints that apply to our interactions with others if we choose to interact with them, but which do not have anything to say about those who choose not to interact at all. We can spell out this idea more precisely with the following three claims: (1) in some situations A has special moral reasons to provide certain benefits to B if A and B interact in mutually beneficial and consensual ways, (2) A would not have had those moral reasons had A not chosen to interact with B, and (3) this is true even if B is better off as a result of interacting with A regardless of whether these additional benefits are provided. Alan Wertheimer has called this idea the "interaction principle," and some form of it seems necessary for rejecting the nonworseness claim. But what reasons can be given in support of the interaction principle?

While she does not address the principle by this name, Ruth Sample provides one argument in support of the interaction principle. According to Sample, the core wrongness of exploitation lies in the fact that it is a form of treatment which "degrades or fails to respect the inherent value" of the person with whom one is interacting (Sample, 2003: 57). The inherent value of others, according to Sample, "makes a claim on us," and when we exploit them, we fail to honor that claim (Sample, 2003: 57). We fail to do this by "neglecting what is necessary for that person's well-being or flourishing," by "taking advantage of an injustice done to him," or by "commodifying, or treating as a fungible object of market exchange, an aspect of that person's being that ought not be commodified" (Sample, 2003: 57). Because hers is non-consequentialist account. Sample holds, it cannot be defeated by appeal to the nonworseness principle. For there is a difference, she claims, between exploitative interaction and mere neglect. Neglect is "simply not interacting with another person when we could do so" (Sample, 2003: 60). Neglect might be morally wrong, as when we ignore a person suffering from malnutrition. but there is nevertheless a basic distinction between treatment and nontreatment which "motivate[s] our idea that exploitation is particularly bad" compared to neglect (Sample, 2003: 61, emphasis added).

I have criticized Sample's argument in more detail elsewhere (Zwolinski, 2007: 709–10). The basic problems with applying it to the standard cases of price gouging are two. First, it is not clear that charging market-clearing prices in a time of shortage is really disrespectful in the necessary sense. One can admit that the inherent value of other human beings makes a moral claim on us while disputing that claim requires us to sell scarce goods at below the market-clearing price. This is especially true if we broaden our focus from a single instance of a purportedly exploitative transaction to the broader market of which that exchange is but one small part. Selling one unit of a good to an individual at below the market-clearing price might be a way of honoring the value of that individual, but what about the value of all the other individuals in the market? Ex hypothesi there are not enough units of the good to satisfy everyone's demands, so some people's needs will go unmet. Rejecting consequentialism does not allow one to avoid the problems of scarcity and the trade-offs it requires. I will have more to say later about how charging the market-clearing price can be compatible with respect for persons. Here it is sufficient to note that the charge of its disrespectfulness has not been sufficiently established.

The second problem with Sample's account lies in its contrast between exploitation and neglect. Sample holds that the former is disrespectful in a way which makes it particularly bad compared to the latter. But it is not clear why this should be so. As Sample points out, what respect for others requires from us is not universal beneficence of a Singerian sort. Rather, it requires "limited but positive engagement" with others" (Sample, 2003: 67). Sample infers from this that those who neglect others have often simply "[lost] sight of the value of other valuable beings," whereas those who engage exploitatively with others are coming face to face with others' value but "flouting" the requirement of respect (Sample, 2003: 68). But it is a mistake to read this much about agents' motivations from their behaviors. Neglect might be the product of simply not having others' value at the forefront of one's mind, and in such cases neglect might be less disrespectful than certain forms of exploitation. We usually blame someone less severely who does the wrong thing because they are distracted, compared to someone who does wrong with full clarity and focus of intention. But neglect can also be a conscious choice. When we know of others' suffering and have the ability to relieve it but do not, we are making a choice. When we know of others' suffering and choose not to think about it—to change the channel either literally or figuratively—we are similarly making a choice. This choice might sometimes be justified—indeed, given the never-ending cycle of suffering in the world, it has to be sometimes justified if we are to live normal lives. But a justified choice is still a choice, and it is a mistake to simply lump those who make it in with those who are non-culpably uninformed or unable to help.

Likewise, it is a mistake to assume that all those who are engaged in price gouging are "flouting" the value of other persons in a way which makes their action worse than conscious neglect. Price gouging might not express beneficence towards others, as would an act of charitable donation, but it is at least a partial engagement with the value of others, unlike neglect, which ignores that value altogether. Price gougers treat their fellow human beings as traders, rather than as brothers and sisters in the Kingdom of Ends. But to treat someone as a trader is still a far cry more respectful than treating him as an object. And it is more respectful, too, than treating him as an insignificance.

Even if one accepts some version of the interaction principle, however, its application to the case of price gouging is not without substantial difficulties. For it is not at all clear how we should understand the nature of the "interaction" which is alleged to give rise to new obligations on the part of the seller. Does the fact that A owns a store which sells generators in the town where B lives entail that A has "interacted" with B and as such has special moral obligations to relieve B's suffering in the wake of a disaster by supplying her with a generator at a less than market-clearing price? Does it matter whether B was previously a customer of A's? What about someone who, like the men in the story with which this paper began, makes their first foray into arbitrage by bringing needed goods from out of town and selling them to disaster victims with whom they have never done business before? Is the fact that they interact with the sellers at the time of the sale sufficient to generate special moral obligations, or does there need to be some pre-existing interaction?

Regardless of the way in which these questions of detail are settled, appeals to an interaction principle in cases such as these raise a difficult question of fairness given the burdens they impose on sellers. This point can be made clear by reflecting on an analogy with cases of easy rescue. It is natural to think that where A can rescue B at little or no cost, A has a moral obligation to do so. But the validity of this intuition is cast into some doubt when we consider the broader context of A's interaction with B. Suppose it is the case that (1) A is under no obligation to interact with B in the first place, (2) A's interaction with B makes B better off, even when A does not satisfy the moral obligation of rescue, (3)

A and B interact consensually, (4) A's interaction with B violates no independent moral constraints, and (5) A would not consent to interacting with B if A knows that he would be bound by amoral obligation to rescue if he chooses to do so. If these conditions are met, then theories which subject A to a moral obligation to rescue B on condition of their interaction seem to suffer from both a defect of unfairness and a serious internal tension. A's interaction with B is supererogatory, done with B's consent, violates no independent moral constraints, and benefits B. Why, then, should the interaction itself place A under new moral obligations toward B, beyond those to which A and B mutually agree? On the face of it, it seems unfair to burden A with this extra requirement given that he is already doing more than is morally required of him. If, however, one wishes to claim that the additional moral burden on A is not unfair, perhaps because B's great need is of such tremendous moral weight, then it is not clear why one should agree with (1) above. If B's being rescued is that important why hold that A can blamelessly avoid rescuing B simply by refusing to interact with B in the first place? The claim that A is under no obligation to interact with B at all seems, at the very least, in tension with what must be supposed about the moral importance of B's being rescued in order to support the belief that A would be under a moral obligation to rescue B should A and B choose to interact.

This argument of this section is meant to cast doubt on the claim that price gouging is wrongfully exploitative, but it has not decisively demonstrated that the argument is without merit. My argument against the wrongfulness of mutually beneficial exploitation is an inconsistency argument—it is meant to show that there is something inconsistent about condemning mutually beneficial exploitation in the form of price gouging more than we blame those who do nothing at all to help victims of disaster. One way of avoiding this inconsistency would be to blame price gougers less, but we could resolve it equally well by blaming those who do nothing more. My argument in this section, then, does not show that price gouging is not wrong—it only shows that considerations of exploitation do not establish it as being especially wrong in the way that most of us view it as bring prior to philosophical reflection.

c. Prices and Allocative Efficiency

We turn now from rebutting arguments against the moral permissibility of price gouging to setting out arguments in favor of it. The first argument has to do with the allocative function of prices in a market economy. When functioning properly, markets tend to allocate resources toward their most valued uses. Those who value a good more will be willing to pay a higher price for it than those who value it less. If everyone bids for items in proportion to the value it holds for them, each item will go to the person who values it most. But this only happens if prices are allowed to adjust freely in response to changes in supply and demand. If prices are not allowed to rise above a exogenously specified level, there will be no way of discriminating between those who value goods more highly than the level reflected by that price, no way of using higher prices to ration scarce supply, and needs that could have been satisfied will go unmet. Indeed, the most urgent needs may go unmet precisely because the scarce resources were sold at a price too low to exclude consumers whose need was not urgent.

Of course, in a less than perfectly competitive market allocative efficiency is only a tendency, and not an absolute law. If you don't have enough money, or if you're not thinking rationally, or if you're not in the right place at the right time, or if you simply don't know about the opportunity to purchase some good, the market won't allocate it to you no matter how much you value it.

I will have more to say below about the implications of the ways in which real world markets fall short of the ideal of perfect competition. For now, it is enough to note that the mere tendency toward allocative efficiency is morally significant. Scarcity is a ubiquitous fact in markets and decision making, but in the wake of a disaster it is a fact which looms especially large. Without electricity to power their refrigerators, for example, lots of people will have lots of different uses for ice. Some of those uses will be trivial—someone will want ice merely to keep her beer cold. Other uses will be more serious—a diabetic wants ice to keep her insulin safely stored. But there will not be enough ice to satisfy all potential uses. Some method must be used to ration the available supply. The real question is not whether the price system is a perfect mechanism for allocating goods to their most valued use, but whether it is better than the available alternatives.

It might seem that there is one obviously superior alternative—making individualized judgments about the need and/or desert of prospective buyers, and selling to those who measure highest on those morally relevant characteristics. Since the argument for relying on prices is simply that ability to pay correlates with what we take to be a morally significant characteristic—the extent to which an individual values the good—we could do better by assessing the morally relevant characteristic directly, and distributing on that basis.

There is more than a grain of truth to this argument, and I suspect it underlies much of our discomfort with price gouging and, more generally, the use of prices to allocate scarce resources. No parent would distribute food to his children—even in an emergency—on the basis of ability to pay. I doubt that most people would treat even their neighbors this way. Why, then, should it be acceptable as a system of distribution more generally?

The answer has to do with several important differences between these kinds of relationships and the kinds of relationships usually involved in price gouging. First, most plausible moral views hold that we have special duties toward our families, friends, and neighbors. We might have imperfect or perfect duties of care, for instance, which conflict with and override our liberty to profit from selling them scarce resources. Furthermore, and more significantly for this argument, we are in a better position to know the morally relevant characteristics of those with whom we are in close association. This sort of consideration is easy for us as philosophers to lose sight of. After all, in philosophic arguments and thought experiments we can stipulate the morally relevant characteristics and take them as a given. In practice, however, discerning which characteristics are morally significant and which are not is considerably more difficult. And, importantly, our ignorance of moral significance is itself morally significant, for it suggests that one of the criteria by which our actual practices should be evaluated is how well they work in a world where we do not operate with all the relevant moral knowledge. In some contexts our ignorance will be less of a factor than it is in others. It is relatively easy for me to know my neighbor's needs, character, and so on. But even with my neighbors my epistemic state is significantly inferior to that which characterizes my relation to my family. And the four men from Goldsboro with whom this paper began had essentially no way of knowing anything about the people to whom they were distributing their ice. Furthermore, if we are to take recent evidence from moral psychology seriously, it appears that individuals are not as skilled or consistent in assessing the morally relevant characteristics of others as we might like to believe.

We are often swayed by what in a more objective light we would view as morally irrelevant characteristics, such as race, sex, or affective display. The choice, then, is not between imperfect allocation by prices versus perfect allocation by moral merit. All our distributive options are imperfect. Sometimes the imperfections of market prices will be more significant than those of individualized judgment, and sometimes the opposite will be true. The point of this section is not to argue that price gouging is permissible in all cases. Rather, it is to argue that in many cases of price gouging, charging the market-clearing price will tend to allocate goods in a way that tracks (albeit imperfectly) what we think are morally significant characteristics like intensity of need. When it does, and when we have no alternatives available which better satisfy out moral obligations, we have good reason to view price gouging as morally permissible.

Furthermore, in those cases where price gouging produces something short of a morally ideal allocation, the best response might not be to try to prohibit or condemn price gouging, but to alter the institutional rules under which it takes place. If, for instance, one's concern with price gouging is that antecedent inequalities of wealth will lead to the rich getting the goods and the poor being left with nothing, the none could address this by either attacking the inequality of wealth directly through social welfare policies or, perhaps more plausibly, having governmental agencies purchase scarce and necessary goods at market prices and provide those goods at a subsidized rate or free of charge to those in need. This latter approach was taken by the city of Boston, with apparent success, during a shortage of flu vaccines in 2004 (*Boston Globe*, 2004). By setting up clear "rules of the game" and allowing market actors to operate freely within those rules, these approaches take advantage of market efficiencies without raising concerns over distributional inequality.

d. The Signaling Function of Prices

The final argument in support of the permissibility of price gouging draws on Hayek's work on the information-conveying function of the price system." For Hayek, as for others in the Austrian tradition of economics, the imperfect nature of market competition is a crucially important fact for understanding the nature of markets." It is precisely because we do not live in a competitive equilibrium where supply is precisely equal to demand that prices and market competition are important. In the real world, as opposed to the world of equilibrium models, facts are constantly changing. People's desires change, the quantity and quality of available resources change, and so on. When this happens, the natural reaction of prices is to change accordingly. In so doing, prices convey information to market actors about the new relative supply and demand of goods, and at the same time provide them with an incentive to alter their behavior in light of that new information.

In the case of price gouging, the higher prices charged for ordinary goods serve as a signal to both consumers and suppliers of that good. We have already seen, in the section above, how prices can serve as a signal to consumers. To illustrate the theoretical point with a real-world example, however, we can look at the case of hotels in Florida which were charged with price gouging in the wake of Hurricane Charley. According to charges filed by the state Attorney General, one hotel in West Palm Beach charged three individuals a rate of over $100 per night for a room, more than double their advertised rate of less than $50 per night. "Families putting their lives back together," the Attorney General wrote, "should not have to worry about price gouging" (Crist, 2004).

But the higher prices did more than simply increase the profits of the hotel owner. They also sent a signal to consumers to economize, and in so doing helped many families. The lower the price of hotel rooms, the higher people's demand for them. As prices increased, people looked for other ways to satisfy their needs. As one commentator pointed out, a family that might have chosen to rent separate rooms for parents and children at $50 per night will be more likely to rent only one room at the higher price, and a family whose home was damaged but in livable condition might choose to tough it out if the cost of hotel room is $100 rather than $50 (Sowell, 2004). Thus, while the increase in price does not literally increase the supply of hotel rooms, it increases the available supply—as a result of consumers' economizing behavior, more hotel rooms are available to individuals and families who need them most.

Prices also send signals to increase supply in more direct ways." If ice can be bought for $1.70 per bag in Goldsboro and sold for $12 in Raleigh, this tells people that Raleigh needs Goldsboro's ice, and that there is a substantial profit to be made in getting it there. Prices convey information about where there is high demand for goods, and supply a built-in incentive for individuals to meet that demand. The four men discussed at the beginning of this paper were probably not moved to drive to Raleigh by altruistic motives. But in doing so, they did something to help alleviate the shortage of ice that Raleigh was facing. And if they hadn't been arrested for price gouging, others who heard about the profits they were making presumably would have followed suit. As more people brought needed supplies to Raleigh, competition would cause the price to decrease, and a new and lower equilibrium would be approximated.

The lesson we can draw from Hayek's insight is that markets are dynamic, and that our moral intuitions often fail to consider this dynamism. When we think about price gouging we often imagine a small, fixed supply of resources being distributed among a group of people. If a high price is charged, the rich will get the goods, and the rest won't. From all appearances, those who bought ice from the four men in Raleigh were in a zero-sum game with each other—one could win only if another lost—and the price gougers were taking advantage of this vulnerability. This seems to violate the most basic of moral standards—if we were desperately in need of ice, we would not want others to profit from our misery. In a static world, price gouging seems to be a clear-cut violation of the Golden Rule.

But here, as with many other cases involving markets, our intuitive moral response is driven too much by what we can visualize, and not enough by what is harder to see." It is easy for us to visualize the zero-sum relation between the individuals fighting over a small immediate supply of ice. It is more difficult for us to see the way in which the market forces at work in that scenario operate to increase supply and to spur the discovery and improvisation of substitutes, such that what is zero-sum in the microcosm is positive-sum in the macrocosm. The quantity of a resource available in a market can shrink or grow, and the most important factor in effecting this change is the resource's price. Indeed, the fact that a resource commands a high price in a market is an essential step in bring-ing additional supply to that market. Holding prices low, voluntarily or by regulation, may seem to achieve justice in the microcosm, but it does so at the cost of keeping the microcosm static, and preventing the influx of supply that would alleviate concerns about unfairly high prices in the market as a whole. Market competition is a process, and the high short-term prices charged by gougers are just one step in that a process—a step that is indispensible to the incentives for discovery and entrepreneurship which move markets closer to a state where people's needs are more widely met.

e. Emergencies and Market Failure

Before moving on to explore the ways in which price gouging reflects on an agent's moral character, it is worth pausing to consider an obvious line of objection to the arguments of the preceding two sections. The defense of price gouging that I have just presented is based on certain empirical and theoretical claims about the effective operation of markets. And while those claims might have merit in the ordinary, day-to-day operation of the market, it is not so obvious that they continue to hold in cases of emergency. And since it is only in such emergency conditions that price gouging becomes an issue, what reason do we have to suppose that market mechanisms will be effective in situations where individuals are operating on a possibly very short time horizon, with imperfect information, high transaction costs, and with a possibly very small number of sellers?

By the neoclassical standard of perfect competition, markets in emergency situations are rife with market failures. But the model of perfect competition is not the only way of thinking about the virtues of markets, and is probably not the most illuminating way of thinking about them in emergency contexts. In such contexts, a model which focuses on competition as a process rather than as an equilibrium state is likely to be more helpful. Israel Kirzner's presentation of the Austrian theory of the market process, for instance, defines competition as the "rivalrous activities of market participants trying to win profits by offering the market better opportunities than are currently available" (Kirzner, 1979: 9). Note that this kind of competition, unlike the competition of the neoclassical model, occurs not in spite of the fact that equilibrium has not been reached, but precisely because equilibrium has not been reached. It is by the process of competition that we move from states of greater disequilibrium to states of lesser disequilibrium. In other words, no progress toward equilibrium could be made unless the current allocation of resources is flawed in some way. Competition, for Kirzner and others in the Austrian school, is a discovery process in which new opportunities are sought out, and in which the potential for pure entrepreneurial profit spurs individuals and firms to discover errors in the ways that others are currently deciding to use scarce resources (Hayek, 1968).

To illustrate, while it is true that market actors in a state of emergency will not have access to perfect information, this at most shows that the outcomes of market processes will fall short of the theoretical ideal of perfect competition." But this does not mean that competitive forces are doing no significant work. As Vernon Smith and others have demonstrated experimentally, markets can achieve equilibrium or near-equilibrium outcomes even when none of the actors in those markets have perfect information or act perfectly rationally." Even in the absence of perfect information there are still market pressures, which place a premium on the discovery of new and better ways of using scarce resources to satisfy demand. Buyers will still buy a greater quantity of a good at a lower price, and sellers will still sell a greater quantity at a higher price. Gaps in information will thus result in increased expenses or decreased profits, while advantages in information will lead to entrepreneurial profit. Even in a state of great disequilibrium and market imperfection, market pressures will thus still have an equilibrating effect. This, presumably, is why the four men described at the beginning of this essay charged only $12 per bag. What prevented them from charging, say, $40 instead was presumably not altruism, but the realization that $40 was more than the market would bear. The higher the price, the greater the incentive would have been for individuals to make do with existing substitute goods, or to innovate new substitutes, and the greater the incentive would have been for other individuals to supply the same good more cheaply. The equilibrating tendencies of the market are not instantaneous, but neither are they completely negated in the face of emergency.

Much will depend, however, on the nature of the emergency involved. In a natural disaster the effects of which persist for several days or weeks, there is time for information to spread, for individuals from non-affected areas to marshal resources, and for the process of competition to work. In other sorts of emergencies, though, the notion of a "market" seems entirely misplaced. Take the simple thought experiment often used to illustrate the nature of wrongful exploitation. A is drowning in a lake, and B rows by on the only boat in sight. B offers to give A a ride to shore if A is willing to sign a contract (which B has brought along in anticipation of just such an occasion) pledging to sign over the deed to his house in exchange. In this example, it is clear that B's price does little to promote the value of allocative efficiency. There is no one else fighting for a spot in ß's boat. If A doesn't get in, B will simply leave it empty. Moreover, in this case, there is no doubt in B's mind about which allocation of resources would best promote overall welfare or moral goodness however defined. A needs the extra seat more than B needs to keep it empty, and there is no need to rely on the information-conveying function of prices to tell him this. And, finally, while it is logically possible to make the argument that B's exploitatively expensive rescue will lead others to increase the supply of rescues over the long run (C, D, and E, upon hearing the story behind B's fancy new house, invest in houseboats and start patrolling nearby lakes looking for drowning victims to exploit), the appeal to the signaling function of prices in this context looks more like a pathetically thin rationalization of individual greed than a genuine justification. In this kind of emergency, then, none of the standard moral justifications of market processes are present, and the worry about morally objectionable exploitation looms large. Price gouging in this sort of situation, then,ought to be regarded as morally impermissible—what is clearly morally required in this situation is rescue at a fair price, even if what exactly constitutes a fair price is not itself entirely clear. But not all emergencies will look like this. And in cases of emergency where the normal market processes can still be expected to produce morally admirable outcomes, and in which alternative institutional or individual arrangements for achieving better outcomes (however defined) are not present, then there is still a strong case for the moral permissibility of price gouging.

5. PRICE GOUGING AND MORAL CHARACTER

Even those who are swayed by the arguments above might feel that there must still be something morally objectionable about those who engage in price gouging. Perhaps the practice should not be prohibited by law. And perhaps the act of gouging itself is not per se morally objectionable. But the fact that there are good arguments to be made for the moral permissibility of price gouging in certain cases does not mean that those who actually engage in the practice are motivated by these considerations. In other words, the common moral condemnation of price gougers as greedy, callous, and selfish might be absolutely correct.

It is, however, a bit of a puzzle why one might think that engaging in a morally permissible activity would constitute evidence of an immoral character. If an action is morally permissible, then what can one's performing that action say about one's character other than that one is disposed to perform morally permissible actions? Still, many find arguments of this sort convincing. Immanuel Kant, for instance,thought that non-human animals did not have moral status, and hence that there was nothing wrong per se with treating them as mere means to one's own ends. Still, even Kant thought there was something wrong with people who inflict gratuitous suffering on animals. What was wrong with them, however, was not merely that they were causing animals to suffer, but that in doing so they betrayed a defect in their character. The kind of people who inflict gratuitous suffering on animals, Kant reasoned, tend to also be the kind of people who inflict gratuitous suffering on human beings. Hence, even though there's nothing morally wrong with causing animals to suffer in itself, people who do so thereby demonstrate that they are likely to do other things which are morally wrong—viz., causing human beings to suffer (Kant, 1994, p. 106).

Kant's reasoning points us in the direction of one way in which engaging in morally permissible behavior might betray a morally vicious character. We should notice, though, that Kant's reasoning is only valid on the assumption that moral character operates in a fairly "coarse-grained" way. After all, it certainly seems as though there is a fairly sharp and obvious distinction to be made between hurting animals and hurting human beings, such that even if one had a disposition to engage in the former sort of activity, one might lack the disposition to engage in activity of the latter sort. If, however, our dispositions are so coarse-grained that they cannot track the relatively fine-grained distinctions between different the different targets on which cruelty might be inflicted, then it is possible that there will be what Nozick calls an "undesirable moral spillover" between actions of one sort and actions of another.'" On this scenario, our options are less like a "disposition to hurt animals"versus a "disposition to hurt human beings," and more like a "disposition to hurt living things" or not. One who hurts animals is expressing a disposition of this latter coarse-grained sort, and this, on the Kantian account, makes him liable to do somethings which are morally permissible (hurting non-human animals) but also to do some things which are morally impermissible (hurting human beings).

As it so happens, Kant was mostly correct when it comes to people who inflict needless suffering on animals. But notice that his argument rests inescapably on empirical premises. Whether our dispositions are fine- or coarse-grained is aquestion for empirical psychologists to resolve, not one which can be settled from the philosopher's armchair. And there's no reason to suppose that the answers psychologists return will be of a tidy or uniform sort. Human beings might be very poor at drawing distinctions between different instances of inflicting pain, but very good at drawing distinctions between, say, different ways of expressing falsehoods (most people, I would suppose, are unlike Kant in recognizing a rather stark moral difference between lying on one's resume about one's educational background and lying to a murderer at one's doorstep about the location of his intended victim).

It is similarly an empirical question, then, whether the motivations which drive people to engage in price gouging are sufficiently coarse-grained that they will, as a tendency or as an inexorable psychological law, drive them to engage in morally impermissible acts as well. A disposition to charge market-clearing prices for necessary items to desperate people might also be a disposition to engage in acts of fraud or coercion against the vulnerable when one can make a profit by doing so. But then again, it might not.

None of this is meant to dispute the intuition with which this section began—that some people who engage in price gouging do so from morally despicable motives. This is a real possibility, and indeed could be the reality in a majority of cases. All I want to argue here is that the fact that a person engages in price gouging is not sufficient evidence to conclude that she has a bad moral character. Assuming the arguments in section four regarding the moral permissibility of price gouging are correct (or even just assuming that people believe them to be correct), the activity of price gouging is compatible with a number of different moral motivations. Some might engage in the activity because they care only about their own profit, and engage in price gouging for this reason alone. Others, however, might care both about their own wealth and the suffering of others, and believe that charging the market-clearing price will contribute to both these ends. We would properly condemn the former sort of gouger as having insufficient regard for the well-being of others. But what about the latter sort? A gouger of this kind is not a moral saint—he does not do all that is possible in order to help those in need without any regard to his own interest. But neither, it seems, is he necessarily morally vicious. He bases his decision partly on his own interests and those of his family, but also on consideration for the needs of others and what he not unreasonably behaves will best serve those needs. His moral character, while perhaps not exemplary, is at least decent.

Perhaps, though, we will want to say that moral virtue requires more than merely doing what is morally permissible. The Aristotelian *phroimos* doesn't simply do the bare minimum that morality permits. Someone who fully instantiates all the virtues such as justice, beneficence, and liberality, we tend to think, would be disposed to charge less than the market-clearing price, even if charging the market-clearing price passes the threshold of moral permissibility. Such an individual would still allow himself some profit, since nothing in the traditional Aristotelian account of virtues requires that he give his own interest no weight or even less weight than the interests of others. But he could, we think, reap a reasonable rate of profit while still charging far less than what the market would bear.

To a large extent, I think this is an accurate account of how the fully virtuous person would act. After all, the justification I have given in this paper of relying on market prices is, in large part, that they are a useful heuristic for achieving moral good. If the *phronimos* can achieve that good directly, by allocating resources to those who need/deserve/merit them most, and if he can find ways other than high prices to channel increased supply to the area, then he has good moral reason to do so. So should we ordinary mortals try to do as the phronimos would do? Two considerations must be kept in mind in answering this question, though they pull us in opposite directions. On the one hand, we should keep in mind that the decision-procedure which would be ideal if we were fully virtuous, fully informed, and fully rational, is not necessarily the decision-procedure that is ideal for us as we are. Call this an attitude of epistemic humility. Relying on the imperfect heuristic of market prices might very well do more good than trying to make decisions based on full considerations of the morally relevant facts, at least when we are largely ignorant of those facts. On the other hand, just as we should keep in mind that our decisions can be led astray by our ignorance of the relevant facts, so too should we keep in mind that they can be led astray by our biases. In particular, it is important to bear in mind our bias toward rationalizing those actions which serve our own self-interest. Most of us, unfortunately, will probably not look too hard for counter arguments when we're told that seeking maximum profit for ourselves will do more good for others than charging less. While there is a case, then, to be made for charging the market-clearing price, we should never be too sanguine about thinking that this case applies to us in our situation. Most of us are simply too willing to fool ourselves into thinking that it does, regardless of the facts.

6. CONCLUSION

In this paper, I have presented a qualified defense of price gouging. I have done so by arguing for three claims. First, I argued that even if price gouging is immoral, it ought not to be prohibited by law. Existing laws against price gouging either fail to provide clear guidance to sellers or fail to take account of all the morally significant reasons which could underlie a price increase, and it is difficult to see how laws could be reformed to avoid this dilemma. Furthermore, any legal prohibition of price gouging will create disincentives for individuals to engage in economic activity which helps those made vulnerable by emergencies. Because laws which prohibit price gouging thus harm vulnerable buyers and are unfair or unclear to sellers, they are immoral and should be repealed. Second, I argued that price gouging is, at least oftentimes, morally permissible. Price gouging is not inherently coercive, and if it is exploitative at all it is so in a way which makes it difficult to see why it is wrong (or, at least, more wrong than the actions of those who do nothing to help victims of emergencies). Moreover, price gouging can serve morally admirable goals by promoting an efficient allocation of scarce and needed resources, and by creating economic signals which will lead to increases in the supply of needed goods available to desperate populations. When it does so, I have claimed that we have good reason to think of price gouging as morally permissible. Finally, I argued that even though those who engage in price gouging might do so from morally despicable motives or characters, we cannot assume that all of them do so, since there are morally virtuous (or at least morally acceptable) motives which might drive individuals to engage in the practice as well.

REFERENCES

Aquinas, T. (1918). *Summa Theologica*. London: R.T. Washbourne.

Barry, B. (1986). Lady Chatterley's Lover and Doctor Fischer's Bomb Party: Liberalism, Pareto-Optimality, and the Problem of Objectionable Preferences. In J. Elster & A. Hylland (Eds.), *Foundations of Social Choice Theory*. Cambridge: Cambridge University Press.

Bastiat, F. (1995). What is Seen and What is Not Seen. In G. B. de Huszar (Ed.), *Selected Essays on Political Economy*. Irvington-on-Hudson, NY Foundation for Economic Education.

Bowie, N. E. (1988). Fair Markets. *Journal of Business Ethics, 7*, 89–98.

Bowie, N. E., & Werhane, P. (2005). *Management Ethics*. Malden, MA: Blackwell.

Buchanan, J. (1999). *Cost and Choice: An Inquiry in Economic Theory*. Indianapolis: Liberty Fund.

City Seeks to Buy Excess Flu Vaccine (2004, October 15). *Boston Globe*, p. B2, from http://www.boston. com/news/local/massachusetts/articles/2004/10/15/6_accused_of_rmv_permit_scheme/

Crist, C. (2004). Attorney General Charges Two Florida Hotels With Price Gouging Retrieved November 27, 2007, from http://myfloridalegal.com/___852562220065EE67.nsf/0/A15CA1 08ECBF1DDE85256EF30054D0FC?Open&Highlight=0,gouging,palm,beach

Cullity, G. (2006). *The Moral Demands of Affluence*. Oxford: Oxford University Press.

Dressler, J. (2006). *Understanding the Criminal Law* (4th ed.). Newark: LexisNexis.

Farnsworth, E. A. (1982). *Contracts*. Boston: Little Brown and Company.

Federal Trade Commission (2006). Investigation of Gasoline Price Manipulation and Post-Katrina Gasoline Price Increases Retrieved August 29, 2007, from http://www.ftc.gov/reports/060518 PublicGasolinePricesInvestigationReportFinal.pdf

Feinberg, J. (1983). Legal Paternalism. In R. Sartorius (Ed.), *Paternalism*. Minneapolis: University of Minnesota Press.

Feinberg, J. (1986). *Harm to Self*. New York: Oxford University Press.

Frankfurt, H. (1973). Coercion and Moral Responsibility. In T. Honderich (Ed.), *Essays on Freedom of Action*. London: Routledge Kegan Paul.

Fuller, L. (1964). *The Morality of Law*. New Haven: Yale University Press.

Gode, D. K., & Sunder, S. (1993). Allocative Efficiency of Markets with Zero-Intelligence Traders: Markets as a Partial Substitute for Individual Rationality. *Journal of Political Economy, 101*(1), 119–137.

Gorr, M. (1986). Toward a Theory of Coercion. *Canadian Journal of Philosophy, 16*(383–406).

Haidt, J. (2001). The Emotional Dog and its Rational Tail: A Social Intuitionist Approach to Moral Judgment. *Psychological Review, 108*, 814–834.

Haidt, J., Koller, S. H., & Dias, M. G. (1993). Affect, culture, and morality, or is it wrong to eat your dog? . *Journal of Personality and Social Psychology, 65*(4), 613–628.

Hayek, F. A. (1944). *The Road to Serfdom*. Chicago: University of Chicago Press.

Hayek, F. A. (1968). Competition as a Discovery Procedure. In F. A. Hayek (Ed.), *New Studies in Philosophy, Politics, Economics, and the History of Ideas*. Chicago: University of Chicago Press.

Hayek, F. A. (1980). The Use of Knowledge in Society. In F. Hayek (Ed.), *Individualism and Economic Order* (pp. 77–91). Chicago: University of Chicago Press.

Kahneman, D., & Tversky, A. (1982). *Judgment Under Uncertainty: Heuristics and Biases* Cambridge: Cambridge University Press.

Kamm, F. (2006). *Intricate Ethics*. Oxford: Oxford University Press.

Kant, I. (1991). *The Metaphysics of Morals* (M. Gregor, Trans.). New York: Cambridge University Press.

Kirzner, I. (1979). *The Perils of Regulation: A Market Process Approach*. Coral Gables: University of Miami School of Law, Law and Economics Center.

Kirzner, I. (1996). *The Meaning of Market Process: Essays in the Development of Modern Austiran Economics*. New York: Routledge.

Leff, A. A. (1967). Unconscionability and the Code: The Emperor's New Clause. *University of Pennsylvania Law Review, 115*.

Mayer, R. (2007). What's Wrong with Exploitation? *Journal of Applied Philosophy, 24*(2), 137–150.

Meyers, C. (2004). Wrongful Beneficence: Exploitation and Third World Sweatshops. *Journal of Social Philosophy, 35*(3), 319–333.

Miller, R. (2004). Beneficence, Duty and Distance. *Philosophy and Public Affairs, 32*(4), 357–383.

Munger, M. (2007). They Clapped: Can Price Gouging Laws Prohibit Scarcity? Retrieved June 12, 2007, from http://www.econlib.org/LIBRARY/Columns/y2007/Mungergouging.html

Murphy, L. (2003). *Moral Demands in Nonideal Theory*. Oxford: Oxford University Press.

Nozick, R. (1969). Coercion. In S. Morgenbesser (Ed.), *Philosophy, Science and Method*. New York: St. Martin's Press.

Nozick, R. (1974). *Anarchy, State, and Utopia*. New York: Basic Books.

O'Driscoll, G., & Rizzo, M. (1996). *The Economics of Time and Ignorance*. New York: Routledge.

Rapp, G. (2005-2006). Gouging: Terrorist Attacks, Hurricanes, and the Legal and Economic Aspects of Post-Disaster Price Regulation *Kentucky Law Journal, 94*.

Rawls, J. (1971). *A Theory of Justice* (1st ed.). Cambridge: Belknap Press.

Raz, J. (1982). Liberalism, Autonomy, and the Politics of Neutral Concern. In P. French (Ed.), *Midwest Studies in Philosophy* (Vol. VIII). Minneapolis: University of Minnesota Press.

Raz, J. (1986). *The Morality of Freedom*. Oxford: Oxford University Press.

Sample, R. (2003). *Exploitation: What it is and Why it's Wrong*. New York: Rowman and Littlefield.

Samuelson, P., & Nordhaus, W. (1998). *Economics*. Boston: Irwin McGraw-Hill.

Schmidtz, D. (2000). Islands in a Sea of Obligation: Limits of the Duty to Rescue. *Law and Philosophy, 19*(6), 683–705.

Schmidtz, D. (2006). *Elements of Justice*. Cambridge: Cambridge University Press.

Simmons, A. J. (1993). *On the Edge of Anarchy*: Princeton.

Singer, P. (1972). Famine, Affluence, and Morality. *Philosophy and Public Affairs, 1*(1), 229–243.

Skarbek, D. (2008). Market Failure and Natural Disaster: A Reexamination of Anti-Gouging Laws. *Public Contract Law Journal, 37*(4), 709–718.

Skarbek, D., & Skarbek, B. (2008). The Price is Right!: How Price Gouging Laws Delay Post-Disaster Recovery. Unpublished manuscript. Santa Clara University.

Smith, V. (1982). Market as Economizers of Information: Experimental Examination of the "Hayek Hypothesis". *Economic Inquiry, 20*(2), 165–179.

Sollars, G. G., & Englander, F. (2007). Sweatshops: Kant and Consequences. *Business Ethics Quarterly, 17*(1), 115–133.

Sowell, T. (2004, September 28). 'Price Gouging' in Florida. *Jewish World Review* Retrieved November 15, 2007, from http://www.jewishworldreview.com/cols/sowell091404.asp

Wertheimer, A. (1996). *Exploitation*. Princeton: Princeton University Press.

Wertheimer, A. (2006). *Coercion*. Princeton: Princeton University Press.

Zimmerman, D. (1981). Coercive Wage Offers. *Philosophy and Public Affairs, 10*(2), 121–145.

Zwolinski, M. (2007). Sweatshops, Choice, and Exploitation. *Business Ethics Quarterly, 17*(4).

CHAPTER 5

✛

SELF-RESPECT AND ALIENATION

The Wealth of Nations

Book 5, Chapter 1, Article 2

ADAM SMITH

In some cases the state of the society necessarily places the greater part of individuals in such situations as naturally form in them, without any attention of government, almost all the abilities and virtues which that state requires, or perhaps can admit of. In other cases the state of the society does not place the part of individuals in such situations, and some attention of government is necessary in order to prevent the almost entire corruption and degeneracy of the great body of the people.

V.1.178

In the progress of the division of labour, the employment of the far greater part of those who live by labour, that is, of the great body of the people, comes to be confined to a few very simple operations, frequently to one or two. But the understandings of the greater part of men are necessarily formed by their ordinary employments. The man whose whole life is spent in performing a few simple operations, of which the effects are perhaps always the same, or very nearly the same, has no occasion to exert his understanding or to exercise his invention in finding out expedients for removing difficulties which never occur. He naturally loses, therefore, the habit of such exertion, and generally becomes as stupid and ignorant as it is possible for a human creature to become. The torpor of his mind renders him not only incapable of relishing or bearing a part in any rational conversation, but of conceiving any generous, noble, or tender sentiment, and consequently of forming any just judgment concerning many even of the ordinary duties of private life. Of the great and extensive interests of his country he is altogether incapable of judging, and unless very particular pains have been taken to render him otherwise, he is equally incapable of defending his country in war. The uniformity of his stationary life naturally corrupts the courage of his mind, and makes him regard with abhorrence the irregular, uncertain, and adventurous life of a soldier. It corrupts even the activity of his body, and renders him incapable of exerting his strength with vigour and perseverance in any other employment than that to which he has been bred. His dexterity at his own particular trade seems, in this manner, to be acquired at the expence of his intellectual, social, and martial virtues. But in every improved and civilized society this is the state into which the labouring poor, that is, the great body of the people, must necessarily fall, unless government takes some pains to prevent it.

V.1.179

It is otherwise in the barbarous societies, as they are commonly called, of hunters, of shepherds, and even of husbandmen in that rude state of husbandry which precedes the improvement of manufactures and the extension of foreign commerce. In such societies the varied occupations of every man oblige every man to exert his capacity and to invent expedients for removing difficulties which are continually occurring. Invention is kept alive, and the mind is not suffered to fall into that drowsy stupidity which, in a civilized society, seems to benumb the understanding of almost all the inferior ranks of people. In those barbarous societies, as they are called, every man, it has already been observed, is a warrior. Every man, too, is in some measure a statesman, and can form a tolerable judgment concerning the interest of the society and the conduct of those who govern it. How far their chiefs are good judges in peace, or good leaders in war, is obvious to the observation of almost every single man among them. In such a society, indeed, no man can well acquire that improved and refined understanding which a few men sometimes possess in a more civilized state. Though in a rude society there is a good deal of variety in the occupations of every individual, there is not a great deal in those of the whole society. Every man does, or is capable of doing, almost every thing which any other man does, or is capable of doing. Every man has a considerable degree of knowledge, ingenuity, and invention: but scarce any man has a great degree. The degree, however, which is commonly possessed, is generally sufficient for conducting the whole simple business of the society. In a civilized state, on the contrary, though there is little variety in the occupations of the greater part of individuals, there is an almost infinite variety in those of the whole society. These varied occupations present an almost infinite variety of objects to the contemplation of those few, who, being attached to no particular occupation themselves, have leisure and inclination to examine the occupations of other people. The contemplation of so great a variety of objects necessarily exercises their minds in endless comparisons and combinations, and renders their understandings, in an extraordinary degree, both acute and comprehensive. Unless those few, however, happen to be placed in some very particular situations, their great abilities, though honourable to themselves, may contribute very little to the good government or happiness of their society. Notwithstanding the great abilities of those few, all the nobler parts of the human character may be, in a great measure, obliterated and extinguished in the great body of the people.

Alienation

Estranged Labour

KARL MARX

||XXII||

We have proceeded from the premises of political economy. We have accepted its language and its laws. We presupposed private property, the separation of labor, capital and land, and of wages, profit of capital and rent of land—likewise division of labor, competition, the concept of exchange value, etc. On the basis of political economy itself, in its own words, we have shown that the worker sinks to the level of a commodity and becomes indeed the most wretched of commodities; that the wretchedness of the worker is in inverse proportion to the power and magnitude of his production; that the necessary result of competition is the accumulation of capital in a few hands, and thus the restoration of monopoly in a more terrible form; and that finally the distinction between capitalist and land rentier, like that between the tiller of the soil and the factory worker, disappears and that the whole of society must fall apart into the two classes—*property owners* and propertyless *workers*.

Political economy starts with the fact of private property; it does not explain it to us. It expresses in general, abstract formulas the *material* process through which private property actually passes, and these formulas it then takes for *laws*. It does not *comprehend* these laws—i.e., it does not demonstrate how they arise from the very nature of private property. Political economy throws no light on the cause of the division between labor and capital, and between capital and land. When, for example, it defines the relationship of wages to profit, it takes the interest of the capitalists to be the ultimate cause, i.e., it takes for granted what it is supposed to explain. Similarly, competition comes in everywhere. It is explained from external circumstances. As to how far these external and apparently accidental circumstances are but the expression of a necessary course of development, political economy teaches us nothing. We have seen how exchange itself appears to it as an accidental fact. The only wheels which political economy sets in motion are *greed*, and the *war amongst the greedy—competition*.

Precisely because political economy does not grasp the way the movement is connected, it was possible to oppose, for instance, the doctrine of competition to the doctrine of monopoly, the doctrine of craft freedom to the doctrine of the guild, the doctrine of the division of landed property to the doctrine of the big estate—for competition, freedom of the crafts and the division of landed property were explained and comprehended only as accidental, premeditated and violent consequences of monopoly, of the guild system, and of feudal property, not as their necessary, inevitable and natural consequences.

Now, therefore, we have to grasp the intrinsic connection between private property, greed, the separation of labor, capital and landed property; the connection of exchange and competition, of value and the devaluation of man, of monopoly and competition, etc.—the connection between this whole estrangement and the *money* system.

Do not let us go back to a fictitious primordial condition as the political economist does, when he tries to explain. Such a primordial condition explains nothing; it merely pushes the question away into a grey nebulous distance. The economist assumes in the form of a fact, of an event, what he is supposed to deduce—namely, the necessary relationship between two things—between, for example, division of labor and exchange. Thus the theologian explains the origin of evil by the fall of Man—that is, he assumes as a fact, in historical form, what has to be explained.

We proceed from an actual economic fact.
The worker becomes all the poorer the more wealth he produces, the more his production increases in power and size. The worker becomes an ever cheaper commodity the more commodities he creates. The *devaluation* of the world of men is in direct proportion to the *increasing value* of the world of things. Labor produces not only commodities; it produces itself and the worker as a *commodity*—and this at the same rate at which it produces commodities in general.

This fact expresses merely that the object which labor produces—labor's product—confronts it as *something alien*, as a *power independent* of the producer. The product of labor is labor which has been embodied in an object, which has become material: it is the *objectification* of labor. Labor's realization is its objectification. Under these economic conditions this realization of labor appears as *loss of realization* for the workers[18]; objectification as *loss of the object and bondage to it;* appropriation as *estrangement*, as *alienation*.

So much does the labor's realization appear as loss of realization that the worker loses realization to the point of starving to death. So much does objectification appear as loss of the object that the worker is robbed of the objects most necessary not only for his life but for his work. Indeed, labor itself becomes an object which he can obtain only with the greatest effort and with the most irregular interruptions. So much does the appropriation of the object appear as estrangement that the more objects the worker produces the less he can possess and the more he falls under the sway of his product, capital.

All these consequences are implied in the statement that the worker is related to the *product of labor* as to an *alien* object. For on this premise it is clear that the more the worker spends himself, the more powerful becomes the alien world of objects which he creates over and against himself, the poorer he himself—his inner world—becomes, the less belongs to him as his own. It is the same in religion. The more man puts into God, the less he retains in himself. The worker puts his life into the object; but now his life no longer belongs to him but to the object. Hence, the greater this activity, the more the worker lacks objects. Whatever the product of his labor is, he is not. Therefore, the greater this product, the less is he himself. The *alienation* of the worker in his product means not only that his labor becomes an object, an *external* existence, but that it exists *outside him*, independently, as something alien to him, and that it becomes a power on its own confronting him. It means that the life which he has conferred on the object confronts him as something hostile and alien.

||XXIII||

Let us now look more closely at the *objectification*, at the production of the worker; and in it at the *estrangement,* the loss of the object, of his product.

The worker can create nothing without *nature,* without the *sensuous external world.* It is the material on which his labor is realized, in which it is active, from which, and by means of which it produces.

But just as nature provides labor with [the] *means of life* in the sense that labor cannot *live* without objects on which to operate, on the other hand, it also provides the *means of life* in the more restricted sense, i.e., the means for the physical subsistence of the *worker* himself.

Thus the more the worker by his labor *appropriates* the external world, sensuous nature, the more he deprives himself of the *means of life* in two respects: first, in that the sensuous external world more and more ceases to be an object belonging to his labor—to be his labor's *means of life*; and, second, in that it more and more ceases to be a *means of life* in the immediate sense, means for the physical subsistence of the worker.

In both respects, therefore, the worker becomes a servant of his object, first, in that he receives an *object of labor*, i.e., in that he receives *work*, and, secondly, in that he receives *means of subsistence*. This enables him to exist, first as a worker; and second, as a *physical subject.* The height of this servitude is that it is only as a *worker* that he can maintain himself as a *physical subject* and that it is only as a *physical subject* that he is a worker.

(According to the economic laws the estrangement of the worker in his object is expressed thus: the more the worker produces, the less he has to consume; the more values he creates, the more valueless, the more unworthy he becomes; the better formed his product, the more deformed becomes the worker; the more civilized his object, the more barbarous becomes the worker; the more powerful labor becomes, the more powerless becomes the worker; the more ingenious labor becomes, the less ingenious becomes the worker and the more he becomes nature's slave.)

Political economy conceals the estrangement inherent in the nature of labor by not considering the **direct** *relationship between the* **worker** (labor) *and production.* It is true that labor produces for the rich wonderful things—but for the worker it produces privation. It produces palaces—but for the worker, hovels. It produces beauty—but for the worker, deformity. It replaces labor by machines, but it throws one section of the workers back into barbarous types of labor and it turns the other section into a machine. It produces intelligence—but for the worker, stupidity, cretinism.

The direct relationship of labor to its products is the relationship of the worker to the objects of his production. The relationship of the man of means to the objects of production and to production itself is only a *consequence* of this first relationship—and confirms it. We shall consider this other aspect later. When we ask, then, what is the essential relationship of labor we are asking about the relationship of the *worker* to production.

Till now we have been considering the estrangement, the alienation of the worker only in one of its aspects, i.e., *the worker's relationship to the products of his labor.* But the estrangement is manifested not only in the result but in the *act of production*, within the *producing activity*, itself. How could the worker come to face the product of his activity as a stranger, were it not that in the very act of production he was estranging himself from himself? The product is after all but the summary of the activity, of production. If then the product of labor is alienation, production itself must be active alienation, the alienation of activity, the activity of alienation. In the estrangement of the object of labor is merely summarized the estrangement, the alienation, in the activity of labor itself.

What, then, constitutes the alienation of labor?

First, the fact that labor is *external* to the worker, i.e., it does not belong to his intrinsic nature; that in his work, therefore, he does not affirm himself but denies himself, does not feel content but unhappy, does not develop freely his physical and mental energy but mortifies his body and ruins his mind. The worker therefore only feels himself outside his work, and in his work feels outside himself. He feels at home when he is not working, and when he is working he does not feel at home. His labor is therefore not voluntary, but coerced; it is *forced labor*. It is therefore not the satisfaction of a need; it is merely a *means* to satisfy needs external to it. Its alien character emerges clearly in the fact that as soon as no physical or other compulsion exists, labor is shunned like the plague. External labor, labor in which man alienates himself, is a labor of self-sacrifice, of mortification. Lastly, the external character of labor for the worker appears in the fact that it is not his own, but someone else's, that it does not belong to him, that in it he belongs, not to himself, but to another. Just as in religion the spontaneous activity of the human imagination, of the human brain and the human heart, operates on the individual independently of him—that is, operates as an alien, divine or diabolical activity—so is the worker's activity not his spontaneous activity. It belongs to another; it is the loss of his self.

As a result, therefore, man (the worker) only feels himself freely active in his animal functions—eating, drinking, procreating, or at most in his dwelling and in dressing-up, etc.; and in his human functions he no longer feels himself to be anything but an animal. What is animal becomes human and what is human becomes animal.

Certainly eating, drinking, procreating, etc., are also genuinely human functions. But taken abstractly, separated from the sphere of all other human activity and turned into sole and ultimate ends, they are animal functions.

We have considered the act of estranging practical human activity, labor, in two of its aspects. (1) The relation of the worker to the *product of labor* as an alien object exercising power over him. This relation is at the same time the relation to the sensuous external world, to the objects of nature, as an alien world inimically opposed to him. (2) The relation of labor to the *act of production* within the *labor* process. This relation is the relation of the worker to his own activity as an alien activity not belonging to him; it is activity as suffering, strength as weakness, begetting as emasculating, the worker's *own* physical and mental energy, his personal life—for what is life but activity?—as an activity which is turned against him, independent of him and not belonging to him. Here we have *self-estrangement,* as previously we had the estrangement of the *thing*.

||XXIV||

We have still a third aspect of *estranged labor* to deduce from the two already considered.

Man is a species-being, not only because in practice and in theory he adopts the species (his own as well as those of other things) as his object, but—and this is only another way of expressing it—also because he treats himself as the actual, living species; because he treats himself as a *universal* and therefore a free being.

The life of the species, both in man and in animals, consists physically in the fact that man (like the animal) lives on organic nature; and the more universal man (or the animal) is, the more universal is the sphere of inorganic nature on which he lives. Just as plants, animals, stones, air, light, etc., constitute theoretically a part of human consciousness, partly as objects of natural science, partly as objects of art—his spiritual inorganic nature, spiritual nourishment which he must first prepare to make palatable and digestible—so also in the realm of practice they constitute a part of human life and human activity. Physically man lives only on these products of nature, whether they appear in the form of food, heating, clothes, a dwelling, etc. The universality of man appears in practice precisely in the universality which makes all nature his *inorganic* body—both inasmuch as nature is (1) his direct means of life, and (2) the material, the object, and the instrument of his life activity. Nature is man's *inorganic* body—nature, that is, insofar as it is not itself human body. Man *lives* on nature—means that nature is his body, with which he must remain in continuous interchange if he is not to die. That man's physical and spiritual life is linked to nature means simply that nature is linked to itself, for man is a part of nature.

In estranging from man (1) nature, and (2) himself, his own active functions, his life activity, estranged labor estranges the *species* from man. It changes for him the *life of the species* into a means of individual life. First it estranges the life of the species and individual life, and secondly it makes individual life in its abstract form the purpose of the life of the species, likewise in its abstract and estranged form.

For labor, *life activity, productive life* itself, appears to man in the first place merely as a means of satisfying a need—the need to maintain physical existence. Yet the productive life is the life of the species. It is life-engendering life. The whole character of a species, its species-character, is contained in the character of its life activity; and free, conscious activity is man's species-character. Life itself appears only as a *means to life*.

The animal is immediately one with its life activity. It does not distinguish itself from it. It is *its life activity*. Man makes his life activity itself the object of his will and of his consciousness. He has conscious life activity. It is not a determination with which he directly merges. Conscious life activity distinguishes man immediately from animal life activity. It is just because of this that he is a species-being. Or it is only because he is a species-being that he is a conscious being, i.e., that his own life is an object for him. Only because of that is his activity free activity. Estranged labor reverses the relationship, so that it is just because man is a conscious being that he makes his life activity, his *essential being*, a mere means to his *existence*.

In creating a *world of objects* by his personal activity, in his *work upon* inorganic nature, man proves himself a conscious species-being, i.e., as a being that treats the species as his own essential being, or that treats itself as a species-being. Admittedly animals also produce. They build themselves nests, dwellings, like the bees, beavers, ants, etc. But an animal only produces what it immediately needs for itself or its young. It produces one-sidedly, whilst man produces universally. It produces only under the dominion of immediate physical need, whilst man produces even when he is free from physical need and only truly produces in freedom therefrom. An animal produces only itself, whilst man reproduces the whole of nature. An animal's product belongs immediately to its physical body, whilst man freely confronts his product. An animal forms only in accordance with the standard and the need of the species to which it belongs, whilst man knows how to produce in accordance with the standard of every species, and knows how to apply everywhere the inherent standard to the object. Man therefore also forms objects in accordance with the laws of beauty.

It is just in his work upon the objective world, therefore, that man really proves himself to be a *species-being*. This production is his active species-life. Through this production, nature appears as *his* work and his reality. The object of labor is, therefore, the *objectification of man's species-life*: for he duplicates himself not only, as in consciousness, intellectually, but also actively, in reality, and therefore he sees himself in a world that he has created. In tearing away from man the object of his production, therefore, estranged labor tears from him his *species-life*, his real objectivity as a member of the species and transforms his advantage over animals into the disadvantage that his inorganic body, nature, is taken from him.

Similarly, in degrading spontaneous, free activity to a means, estranged labor makes man's species-life a means to his physical existence.

The consciousness which man has of his species is thus transformed by estrangement in such a way that species[-life] becomes for him a means.

Estranged labor turns thus:

(3) *Man's species-being,* both nature and his spiritual species-property, into a being *alien* to him, into a *means* of his *individual existence*. It estranges from man his own body, as well as external nature and his spiritual aspect, his *human* aspect.

(4) An immediate consequence of the fact that man is estranged from the product of his labor, from his life activity, from his species-being, is the *estrangement of man* from *man*. When man confronts himself, he confronts the *other* man. What applies to a man's relation to his work, to the product of his labor and to himself, also holds of a man's relation to the other man, and to the other man's labor and object of labor.

In fact, the proposition that man's species-nature is estranged from him means that one man is estranged from the other, as each of them is from man's essential nature.

The estrangement of man, and in fact every relationship in which man [stands] to himself, is realized and expressed only in the relationship in which a man stands to other men.

Hence within the relationship of estranged labor each man views the other in accordance with the standard and the relationship in which he finds himself as a worker.

||XXV||

We took our departure from a fact of political economy—the estrangement of the worker and his production. We have formulated this fact in conceptual terms as *estranged, alienated* labor. We have analyzed this concept—hence analyzing merely a fact of political economy.

Let us now see, further, how the concept of estranged, alienated labor must express and present itself in real life.

If the product of labor is alien to me, if it confronts me as an alien power, to whom, then, does it belong?

To a being *other* than myself.

Who is this being?

The *gods*? To be sure, in the earliest times the principal production (for example, the building of temples, etc., in Egypt, India and Mexico) appears to be in the service of the gods, and the product belongs to the gods. However, the gods on their own were never the lords of labor. No more was *nature*. And what a contradiction it would be if, the more man subjugated nature by his labor and the more the miracles of the gods were rendered superfluous by the miracles of industry, the more man were to renounce the joy of production and the enjoyment of the product to please these powers.

The *alien* being, to whom labor and the product of labor belongs, in whose service labor is done and for whose benefit the product of labor is provided, can only be *man* himself.

If the product of labor does not belong to the worker, if it confronts him as an alien power, then this can only be because it belongs to some *other man than the worker*. If the worker's activity is a torment to him, to another it must give *satisfaction* and pleasure. Not the gods, not nature, but only man himself can be this alien power over man.

We must bear in mind the previous proposition that man's relation to himself becomes for him *objective* and *actual* through his relation to the other man. Thus, if the product of his labor, his labor objectified, is for him an *alien, hostile*, powerful object independent of him, then his position towards it is such that someone else is master of this object, someone who is alien, hostile, powerful, and independent of him. If he treats his own activity as an unfree activity, then he treats it as an activity performed in the service, under the dominion, the coercion, and the yoke of another man.

Every self-estrangement of man, from himself and from nature, appears in the relation in which he places himself and nature to men other than and differentiated from himself. For this reason religious self-estrangement necessarily appears in the relationship of the layman to the priest, or again to a mediator, etc., since we are here dealing with the intellectual world. In the real practical world self-estrangement can only become manifest through the real practical relationship to other men. The medium through which estrangement takes place is itself *practical*. Thus through estranged labor man not only creates his relationship to the object and to the act of production as to powers that are alien and hostile to him; he also creates the relationship in which other men stand to his production and to his product, and the relationship in which he stands to these other men. Just as he creates his own production as the loss of his reality, as his punishment; his own product as a loss, as a product not belonging to him; so he creates the domination of the person who does not produce over production and over the product. Just as he estranges his own activity from himself, so he confers upon the stranger an activity which is not his own.

We have until now considered this relationship only from the standpoint of the worker and later on we shall be considering it also from the standpoint of the non-worker.

Through *estranged, alienated labor*, then, the worker produces the relationship to this labor of a man alien to labor and standing outside it. The relationship of the worker to labor creates the relation to it of the capitalist (or whatever one chooses to call the master of labor). *Private property* is thus the product, the result, the necessary consequence, of *alienated labor*, of the external relation of the worker to nature and to himself.

Private property thus results by analysis from the concept of *alienated labor*, i.e., of *alienated man*, of estranged labor, of estranged life, of *estranged* man.

True, it is as a result of the *movement of private property* that we have obtained the concept of *alienated labor* (*of alienated life*) in political economy. But on analysis of this concept it becomes clear that though private property appears to be the reason, the cause of alienated labor, it is rather its consequence, just as the gods are *originally* not the cause but the effect of man's intellectual confusion. Later this relationship becomes reciprocal.

Only at the culmination of the development of private property does this, its secret, appear again, namely, that on the one hand it is the *product* of alienated labor, and that on the other it is the *means* by which labor alienates itself, *the realization of this alienation*.

This exposition immediately sheds light on various hitherto unsolved conflicts.

(1) Political economy starts from labor as the real soul of production; yet to labor it gives nothing, and to private property everything. Confronting this contradiction, Proudhon has decided in favor of labor against private property. We understand, however, that this apparent contradiction is the contradiction of *estranged labor* with itself, and that political economy has merely formulated the laws of estranged labor.

We also understand, therefore, that *wages* and *private property* are identical. Indeed, where the product, as the object of labor, pays for labor itself, there the wage is but a necessary consequence of labor's estrangement. Likewise, in the wage of labor, labor does not appear as an end in itself but as the servant of the wage. We shall develop this point later, and meanwhile will only draw some conclusions.

||XXVI||

An enforced *increase of wages* (disregarding all other difficulties, including the fact that it would only be by force, too, that such an increase, being an anomaly, could be maintained) would therefore be nothing but better *payment for the slave*, and would not win either for the worker or for labor their human status and dignity.

Indeed, even the *equality of wages*, as demanded by Proudhon, only transforms the relationship of the present-day worker to his labor into the relationship of all men to labor. Society would then be conceived as an abstract capitalist.

Wages are a direct consequence of estranged labor, and estranged labor is the direct cause of private property. The downfall of the one must therefore involve the downfall of the other.

(2) From the relationship of estranged labor to private property it follows further that the emancipation of society from private property, etc., from servitude, is expressed in the *political* form of the *emancipation of the workers*; not that *their* emancipation alone is at stake, but because the emancipation of the workers contains universal human emancipation—and it contains this because the whole of human servitude is involved in the relation of the worker to production, and all relations of servitude are but modifications and consequences of this relation.

Just as we have derived the concept of *private property* from the concept of *estranged, alienated labor* by *analysis*, so we can develop every *category* of political economy with the help of these two factors; and we shall find again in each category, e.g., trade, competition, capital, money only a *particular* and *developed* expression of these first elements.

Critique of the Gotha Programme

KARL MARX

First part of the paragraph: "Labor is the source of all wealth and all culture."

Labor is *not the source* of all wealth. *Nature* is just as much the source of use values (and it is surely of such that material wealth consists!) as labor, which itself is only the manifestation of a force of nature, human labor power. The above phrase is to be found in all children's primers and is correct insofar as it is implied that labor is performed with the appurtenant subjects and instruments. But a socialist program cannot allow such bourgeois phrases to pass over in silence the *conditions* that lone give them meaning. And insofar as man from the beginning behaves toward nature, the primary source of all instruments and subjects of labor, as an owner, treats her as belonging to him, his labor becomes the source of use values, therefore also of wealth. The bourgeois have very good grounds for falsely ascribing *supernatural creative power* to labor; since precisely from the fact that labor depends on nature it follows that the man who possesses no other property than his labor power must, in all conditions of society and culture, be the slave of other men who have made themselves the owners of the material conditions of labor. He can only work with their permission, hence live only with their permission.

Let us now leave the sentence as it stands, or rather limps. What could one have expected in conclusion? Obviously this:

"Since labor is the source of all wealth, no one in society can appropriate wealth except as the product of labor. Therefore, if he himself does not work, he lives by the labor of others and also acquires his culture at the expense of the labor of others."

Instead of this, by means of the verbal river "and since," a proposition is added in order to draw a conclusion from this and not from the first one.

Second part of the paragraph: "Useful labor is possible only in society and through society."

According to the first proposition, labor was the source of all wealth and all culture; therefore no society is possible without labor. Now we learn, conversely, that no "useful" labor is possible without society.

One could just as well have said that only in society can useless and even socially harmful labor become a branch of gainful occupation, that only in society can one live by being idle, etc., etc.—in short, once could just as well have copied the whole of Rousseau.

And what is "useful" labor? Surely only labor which produces the intended useful result. A savage—and man was a savage after he had ceased to be an ape—who kills an animal with a stone, who collects fruit, etc., performs "useful" labor.

Thirdly, the conclusion: "Useful labor is possible only in society and through society, the proceeds of labor belong undiminished with equal right to all members of society."

A fine conclusion! If useful labor is possible only in society and through society, the proceeds of labor belong to society—and only so much therefrom accrues to the individual worker as is not required to maintain the "condition" of labor, society.

In fact, this proposition has at all times been made use of by the champions of the *state of society prevailing at any given time*. First comes the claims of the government and everything that sticks to it, since it is the social organ for the maintenance of the social order; then comes the claims of the various kinds of private property, for the various kinds of private property are the foundations of society, etc. One sees that such hollow phrases are the foundations of society, etc. One sees that such hollow phrases can be twisted and turned as desired.

The first and second parts of the paragraph have some intelligible connection only in the following wording:

"Labor becomes the source of wealth and culture only as social labor", or, what is the same thing, "in and through society".

This proposition is incontestably correct, for although isolated labor (its material conditions presupposed) can create use value, it can create neither wealth nor culture.

But equally incontestable is this other proposition:

"In proportion as labor develops socially, and becomes thereby a source of wealth and culture, poverty and destitution develop among the workers, and wealth and culture among the nonworkers."

This is the law of all history hitherto. What, therefore, had to be done here, instead of setting down general phrases about "labor" and "society", was to prove concretely how in present capitalist society the material, etc., conditions have at last been created which enable and compel the workers to lift this social curse.

In fact, however, the whole paragraph, bungled in style and content, is only there in order to inscribe the Lassallean catchword of the "undiminished proceeds of labor" as a slogan at the top of the party banner. I shall return later to the "proceeds of labor," "equal right," etc., since the same thing recurs in a somewhat different form further on.

2. "In present-day society, the instruments of labor are the monopoly of the capitalist class; the resulting dependence of the working class is the cause of misery and servitude in all forms."

This sentence, borrowed from the Rules of the International, is incorrect in this "improved" edition.

In present-day society, the instruments of labor are the monopoly of the landowners (the monopoly of property in land is even the basis of the monopoly of capital) *and* the capitalists. In the passage in question, the Rules of the International do not mention either one or the other class of monopolists. They speak of the "monopolizer of the means of labor, that is, *the sources of life.*" The addition, "sources of life," makes it sufficiently clear that land is included in the instruments of labor.

The correction was introduced because Lassalle, for reasons now generally known, attacked *only* the capitalist class and not the landowners. In England, the capitalist class is usually not even the owner of the land on which his factory stands.

3. "The emancipation of labor demands the promotion of the instruments of labor to the common property of society and the co-operative regulation of the total labor, with a fair distribution of the proceeds of labor."

"Promotion of the instruments of labor to the common property" ought obviously to read their "conversion into the common property;" but this is only passing.

What are the "proceeds of labor"? The product of labor, or its value? And in the latter case, is it the total value of the product, or only that part of the value which labor has newly added to the value of the means of production consumed?

"Proceeds of labor" is a loose notion which Lassalle has put in the place of definite economic conceptions.

What is "a fair distribution"?

Do not the bourgeois assert that the present-day distribution is "fair"? And is it not, in fact, the only "fair" distribution on the basis of the present-day mode of production? Are economic relations regulated by legal conceptions, or do not, on the contrary, legal relations arise out of economic ones? Have not also the socialist sectarians the most varied notions about "fair" distribution?

To understand what is implied in this connection by the phrase "fair distribution", we must take the first paragraph and this one together. The latter presupposes a society wherein the instruments of labor are common property and the total labor is co-operatively regulated, and from the first paragraph we learn that "the proceeds of labor belong undiminished with equal right to all members of society."

"To all members of society"? To those who do not work as well? What remains then of the "undiminished" proceeds of labor? Only to those members of society who work? What remains then of the "equal right" of all members of society?

But "all members of society" and "equal right" are obviously mere phrases. The kernel consists in this, that in this communist society every worker must receive the "undiminished" Lassallean "proceeds of labor".

Let us take, first of all, the words "proceeds of labor" in the sense of the product of labor; then the co-operative proceeds of labor are the *total social product*.

From this must now be deducted: *First*, cover for replacement of the means of production used up. *Second*, additional portion for expansion of production. *Third*, reserve or insurance funds to provide against accidents, dislocations caused by natural calamities, etc.

These deductions from the "undiminished" proceeds of labor are an economic necessity, and their magnitude is to be determined according to available means and forces, and partly by computation of probabilities, but they are in no way calculable by equity.

There remains the other part of the total product, intended to serve as means of consumption.

Before this is divided among the individuals, there has to be deducted again, from it: *First*, the general costs of administration not belonging to production. This part will, from the outset, be very considerably restricted in comparison with present-day society, and it diminishes in proportion as the new society develops. *Second*, that which is intended for the common satisfaction of needs, such as schools, health services, etc. From the outset, this part grows considerably in comparison with present-day society, and it grows in proportion as the new society develops. *Third*, funds for those unable to work, etc., in short, for what is included under so-called official poor relief today.

Only now do we come to the "distribution" which the program, under Lassallean influence, alone has in view in its narrow fashion—namely, to that part of the means of consumption which is divided among the individual producers of the co-operative society.

The "undiminished" proceeds of labor have already unnoticeably become converted into the "diminished" proceeds, although what the producer is deprived of in his capacity as a private individual benefits him directly or indirectly in his capacity as a member of society.

Just as the phrase of the "undiminished" proceeds of labor has disappeared, so now does the phrase of the "proceeds of labor" disappear altogether.

Within the co-operative society based on common ownership of the means of production, the producers do not exchange their products; just as little does the labor employed on the products appear here as the *value* of these products, as a material quality possessed by them, since now, in contrast to capitalist society, individual labor no longer exists in an indirect fashion but directly as a component part of total labor. The phrase "proceeds of labor", objectionable also today on account of its ambiguity, thus loses all meaning.

What we have to deal with here is a communist society, not as it has *developed* on its own foundations, but, on the contrary, just as it *emerges* from capitalist society; which is thus in every respect, economically, morally, and intellectually, still stamped with the birthmarks of the old society from whose womb it emerges. Accordingly, the individual producer receives back from society—after the deductions have been made—exactly what he gives to it. What he has given to it is his individual quantum of labor. For example, the social working day consists of the sum of the individual hours of work; the individual labor time of the individual producer is the part of the social working day contributed by him, his share in it. He receives a certificate from society that he has furnished such-and-such an amount of labor (after deducting his labor for the common funds); and with this certificate, he draws from the social stock of means of consumption as much as the same amount of labor cost. The same amount of labor which he has given to society in one form, he receives back in another.

Here, obviously, the same principle prevails as that which regulates the exchange of commodities, as far as this is exchange of equal values. Content and form are changed, because under the altered circumstances no one can give anything except his labor, and because, on the other hand, nothing can pass to the ownership of individuals, except individual means of consumption. But as far as the distribution of the latter among the individual producers is concerned, the same principle prevails as in the exchange of commodity equivalents: a given amount of labor in one form is exchanged for an equal amount of labor in another form.

Hence, *equal right* here is still in principle—*bourgeois right*, although principle and practice are no longer at loggerheads, while the exchange of equivalents in commodity exchange exists only on the average and not in the individual case.

In spite of this advance, this equal right is still constantly stigmatized by a bourgeois limitation. The right of the producers is *proportional* to the labor they supply; the equality consists in the fact that measurement is made with an *equal standard*, labor.

But one man is superior to another physically, or mentally, and supplies more labor in the same time, or can labor for a longer time; and labor, to serve as a measure, must be defined by its duration or intensity, otherwise it ceases to be a standard of measurement. This *equal* right is an unequal right for unequal labor. It recognizes no class differences, because everyone is only a worker like everyone else; but it tacitly recognizes unequal individual endowment, and thus productive capacity, as a natural privilege. It is, therefore, a right of inequality, in its content, like every right. Right, by its very nature, can consist only in the application of an equal standard; but unequal individuals (and they would not be different individuals if they were not unequal) are measurable only by an equal standard insofar as they are brought under an equal point of view, are taken from one definite side only—for instance, in the present case, are regarded *only as workers* and nothing more is seen in them, everything else being ignored. Further, one worker is married, another is not; one has more children than another, and so on and so forth. Thus, with an equal performance of labor, and hence an equal in the social consumption fund, one will in fact receive more than another, one will be richer than another, and so on. To avoid all these defects, right, instead of being equal, would have to be unequal.

But these defects are inevitable in the first phase of communist society as it is when it has just emerged after prolonged birth pangs from capitalist society. Right can never be higher than the economic structure of society and its cultural development conditioned thereby.

In a higher phase of communist society, after the enslaving subordination of the individual to the division of labor, and therewith also the antithesis between mental and physical labor, has vanished; after labor has become not only a means of life but life's prime want; after the productive forces have also increased with the all-around development of the individual, and all the springs of co-operative wealth flow more abundantly—only then then can the narrow horizon of bourgeois right be crossed in its entirety and society inscribe on its banners: From each according to his ability, to each according to his needs!

I have dealt more at length with the "undiminished" proceeds of labor, on the one hand, and with "equal right" and "fair distribution", on the other, in order to show what a crime it is to attempt, on the one hand, to force on our Party again, as dogmas, ideas which in a certain period had some meaning but have now become obsolete verbal rubbish, while again perverting, on the other, the realistic outlook, which it cost so much effort to instill into the Party but which has now taken root in it, by means of ideological nonsense about right and other trash so common among the democrats and French socialists.

Quite apart from the analysis so far given, it was in general a mistake to make a fuss about so-called distribution and put the principal stress on it.

Any distribution whatever of the means of consumption is only a consequence of the distribution of the conditions of production themselves. The latter distribution, however, is a feature of the mode of production itself. The capitalist mode of production, for example, rests on the fact that the material conditions of production are in the hands of nonworkers in the form of property in capital and land, while the masses are only owners of the personal condition of production, of labor power. If the elements of production are so distributed, then the present-day distribution of the means of consumption results automatically. If the material conditions of production are the co-operative property of the workers themselves, then there likewise results a distribution of the means of consumption different from the present one. Vulgar socialism (and from it in turn a section of the democrats) has taken over from the bourgeois economists the consideration and treatment of distribution as independent of the mode of production and hence the presentation of socialism as turning principally on distribution. After the real relation has long been made clear, why retrogress again?

The Idea and Ideal of Capitalism

GERALD GAUS

1. CAPITALISM, BUSINESS AND ETHICS

Consider a stylized contrast between medical and business ethics. Both fields of applied ethics focus on a profession whose activities are basic to human welfare. Both enquire into obligations of professionals, and the relations between goals intrinsic to the profession and ethical duties to others and to the society. I am struck, however, by a fundamental difference: whereas medical ethics takes place against a background of almost universal consensus that the practice of medicine is admirable and morally praiseworthy, the business profession is embedded within the framework of firms in a capitalist market economy, and for the last century and a half there has been sustained debate about the moral and economic justifiability of such an economy. To be sure, even under socialism there might be an "ethics of socialist managers," and there would be some overlap between such an ethic and contemporary business ethics. Nevertheless, many of the characteristic problems of business ethics—e.g., what are the obligations of a corporation to its shareholders?—arise only in the context of a private property-based market economy.

This raises a deep problem for business ethics: can one develop an account of ethical practices for an activity (i.e., business) while ignoring that the context in which this activity occurs (i.e., capitalism) is morally controversial? It is as if the work in medical ethics proceeded in the midst of widespread disagreement whether medicine was a good thing. Another way of thinking about the problem is: if one teaches business ethics, does this commit you to accepting that business can be ethical? And doesn't this commit you to accepting that capitalism is justifiable?[1] I suspect that this is a serious problem for many teachers of business ethics. Many were trained in academic philosophy, and within academic philosophy there are many who think—or at least suspect—that capitalism is basically unjust, or perhaps that only a greatly modified capitalism would be acceptable. The great economist, John Maynard Keynes articulated a view that is probably shared by many teachers of business ethics:

> For my part I think that capitalism, wisely managed, can probably be made more efficient for attaining economic ends than any alternative system yet in sight, but that in itself it is in many ways extremely objectionable. Our problem is to work out a social organisation which shall be as efficient as possible without offending our notions of a satisfactory way of life.[2]

Indeed, many teachers and students of business ethics may not even incline as far as Keynes in thinking that capitalism can be made acceptable: in the end, Keynes was more a liberal reformer than a radical critic of capitalism.

If the practice of business ethics is embedded in a capitalist economic system, students and teachers of business ethics should have an appreciation of what a relatively pure form of capitalism would look like. We can then begin to think about what would be required for its justification. Knowing that, we will then be in a position to reflect on whether we think there can be truly ethical business practices. If, after seeing what a pure form of capitalism would be, and what would be required for its justification, a student or teacher of business ethics concludes that such justification is not to be had, then her task is basically Keynes's: to determine what, if any, alteration of this system retains the important benefits of capitalist business while conforming to her notion of "a satisfactory way of life." Perhaps, reflecting on contemporary versions of capitalism she will decide that the current versions depart from the pure form, and because of that they are consistent with her notion of a satisfactory way of life; then again, it is possible that contemporary capitalism is objectionable just because it departs too much from the pure form.

My task in this chapter is to sketch what I see as the elements of a pure form of capitalism, and to indicate some of the ways that proponents of capitalism have sought to justify these elements. The rather vague idea of "capitalism" is better grasped if we analyze it into distinct elements. And each element might be justified in different ways. As the reader will see, I believe that once we reflect on the elements of capitalism we will see that Keynes and many others have woefully underestimated its power as an ideal way to organize economic—and indeed many social—relations. However, my main aim is not to defend capitalism as an ideal, but to analyze capitalism into its constitutive elements. This will not only allow us to better understand the context in which business occurs, but it will help the reader to better identify just what aspect of capitalism, if any, offends her notion "of a satisfactory way of life." This chapter, then, is not so much an essay *in* business ethics as it is an essay on the foundations of the very practice of business and business ethics—the idea of a capitalist economic order.

2. PRIVATE PROPERTY

Maximally Extensive Feasible Property Rights: Capitalist Ownership

Classical debates about the justifiabiity of capitalism, and especially the contrast between capitalism and communism, focused on the right to private property. John Stuart Mill (a defender of a modified version of capitalism) and Karl Marx (the most famous critic of all) supposed that capitalism is essentially defined by a system that relies on private property rights, and so they thought that the rejection of capitalism just *is* the rejection of private property. "Communism is the positive abolition of private property," wrote Marx.[3] The *complete* abolition of private property has rarely been advocated. In Plato's ideal republic, it is true, the ruling class were to live under complete communism—including communism of wives—but that is an extreme view indeed.[4] Even Soviet Communism recognized personal private property in the form of consumer goods such as clothes, household items, and books. Perhaps, then, capitalism requires private property in non-personal goods—we might think that capitalism is characterized by the private ownership of capital goods (i.e., goods required for the production of other goods). Although there is something to this, throughout almost all of human history capital goods such as tools and farm equipment have been privately owned, yet we wouldn't want to say that capitalism has been the dominant mode of production throughout all human history.[5] Just what is the relation between capitalism and private property?

The ideal of capitalism—that is, a pure version of capitalism—is characterized by *maximally extensive feasible property rights* along two different dimensions. The *first* dimension concerns the extent of an individual's ownership right or, as philosophers often put it, the extent of the bundle of rights that make up a person's property. Most scholars today conceive of property in terms of a set of rights that might vary. For Alf to have *full private property rights* over *P*, Alf must have:[6]

- The right to use *P* as he wishes so long as this is not harmful to others or their property;
- The right to exclude others from using *P*;
- The right to manage: Alf may give permission to any others he wishes to use *P*, and determine how it may be used by them;
- The right to compensation: If someone damages or uses *P* without Alf's consent, Alf has a right to compensation for the loss of *P*'s value from that person.
- The rights to destroy, waste or modify: Alf may destroy *P*, waste it or change it.

- The right to income: Alf has a right to the financial benefits of forgoing his own use of *P* and letting someone else use it.
- Immunity from expropriation: *P* (or any part of *P*) may not be made the property of another or the government without Alf's consent, with the exception of a few items such as taxation.
- Liability to execution: *P* may be taken away from Alf by authorized persons for repayment of a debt.
- Absence of term: Alf's rights over *P* are of indefinite duration.
- Rights to rent and sale (transfer rights): Alf may temporarily or permanently transfer all or some of his rights over *P* to anyone he chooses.

To say that someone who holds these rights over *P* has maximally extensive feasible property rights over *P* is to say that his control over *P* is as complete as possible (the maximal claim) given the like control of others over their property (the feasibility claim). If we drop the feasibility requirement we can give Alf an even more extensive control over *P*: he might have the right to use his property in ways that harm others, or has no liability to execution. But this increase in his control would limit others' control over their property. If Alf has the right to use his property in ways harmful to others, their use of their property will be impaired. If Alf is free from liability to execution, he can avoid paying compensation when he damages the property of others. So we can think of the above as approaching the maximally extensive control of Alf over *P* consistent with the like control of others over their property.

Maximally extensive feasible property rights is part of an ideal, pure conception of capitalism. Real world economic systems, even those that we would all agree are appropriately deemed "capitalist," may limit Alf's control over *P* by limiting, or even removing, some of these rights. Zoning laws limit the uses to which Alf may put his property; historical district regulations limit his rights to destroy, waste or modify his residence; business licensing laws limit his ability to transfer his property; laws setting a maximum interest rate limit his right to an income. Sometimes, however, real-world systems actually expand these rights. A long-established public policy has been to limit the extent to which consumers can claim rights to compensation against harm from certain public utilities; thus the utilities have less liability than other property owners.[7] All these are rightly seen as ways of qualifying full capitalist ownership of some people. It is clear, though, that as these qualifications accumulate, we are apt to wonder whether the remaining property rights are sufficiently extensive to provide the basis for capitalism. And certainly some of these rights are more fundamental to capitalism than others. The rights to use, to exclude, to income, to modify, to manage, to transfer, to compensation and immunity from expropriation are basic to a capitalist order. An economic system that is based on some qualifications on them may still be recognizably capitalist: one that drastically curtails any of them over a wide range of property begins to loose its capitalist character. A system that does not generally recognize the rights to income or to transfer, for example, may be said to have a sort of private property, but not capitalist property.

The right against expropriation raises deep questions about the justifiability of taxation. Non-consensual takings of property limit or abridge this right; if such takings are extensive, the resulting system will be far from the capitalist ideal.[8] As John Locke insisted, if government may legitimately take away people's property without their consent, "this would be in effect to leave them no *Property* at all."[9] Given this, the most extreme capitalist position is "anarcho-capitalism," which maintains that, because all taxation is non-consensual, government is inherently illegitimate.[10] Locke took a more moderate view. Though he held that government may not raise taxes without the people's consent, insofar as a legitimate legislature rests on the consent of the governed, taxation approved by a representative legislature does not constitute an expropriation, and so is not a violation of property rights.[11] Thus the famous rallying cry of the American Revolution—"No taxation without representation!"—expresses a strong commitment to capitalist property rights. Only if government is organized in a certain way can its taxes, which take a citizen's property, be legitimate.[12]

Maximally Extensive Feasible Property Rights: What Can Be Owned

One dimension along which the ideal of capitalism endorses maximally extensive feasible property rights is, then, the extent of the bundle of rights one has over *P*. The other dimension concerns the range of objects[13] over which one can have property rights. The capitalist ideal is to extend as far as possible the range of things that are privately owned. Of course under the capitalist ideal, consumer and productive goods are privately owned. So too are natural resources. Recently advocates of capitalism have argued that many of our environmental problems stem from the *absence* of private property rights over such resources. Many environmental problems concern what are called "common pool resources," which are characterized by (1) relatively open ("public") access and (2) private consumption. Clean air and fresh water are common pool resources: they are accessible to everyone but consumed privately. The "tragedy of the commons" arises in situations in which individuals (or groups) make individually rational decisions about how much of the relevant resource (e.g., water, air) to consume that, collectively, leads to the over-harvesting of that resource and depleting its sustainable capacity.[14] Pollution is a prime example of a common pool problem: over-use of the air's ability to dissipate waste gasses leads to the depletion of that ability. When goods remain in the common pool, if some restrain their current consumption (e.g., fish less) while others do not, those who restrain themselves will not only end up with less today, but very likely will have no more in the future: those who do not restrain themselves may well over-harvest the resource, depleting future stocks. If so, no one has an incentive to restrain themselves today and all will over-harvest. Most of our worst resource depletion problems—the ability of the atmosphere to absorb carbon dioxide, fresh air, fresh water, fisheries, coral reefs, wild animals—stem from *lack* of private property rights. When a resource is privately owned, the owner will be confident that she will benefit from her restraint on present use: she will reap less today but she will gain the benefit—future sustainable yields. As David Schmidtz has convincingly argued, only if resources are taken out of the common pool will depletions be minimized. As he tellingly puts it, "leaving goods in the common practically ensures their destruction."[15] When dealing with resources that cannot be renewed such as petroleum, capitalist ownership induces efficient pricing (see section 3, below), which in turn encourages both search for additional supplies and alternative technologies.

Advocates of the capitalist ideal thus have sought to extend as far as feasible the range of objects subject to private property rights. This includes maximal rights over one's body and labor, so that one is free to sell any services to others that do not harm third parties (again, one's use of one's property does not uncontroversially extend to harmful uses). Although Marx sometimes saw private property as characteristic of capitalism, at other times he stressed that capitalism's truly distinctive feature was the "commodification of labor": that labor itself is a commodity to be bought and sold like any other good.[16] This "commodification" of labor and services is embraced by capitalism: defenders of capitalism not only endorse the sale of labor in the usual contexts, but may also support—even strongly support—more controversial applications such as the right to sell sexual services in the form of prostitution, sell pornography, create clubs with strippers, and so on. The terms "sex industry" and "workers in the sex industry" expresses this "commodification" of sexual services. Indeed, many friends of capitalism push the "commodification" even further, arguing for property rights in body parts, and thus for the right to sell parts of one's body such as a kidney[17]—or, more radically, any body part. The upshot of this conception of capitalism is a "permissive society": in "competitive capitalism … the businessman will make money by catering to for whatever it is people wish to do—by providing pop records, or nude shows, or candyfloss."[18] At the extreme, this leads some advocates of capitalism to allow that an individual may transfer the property over himself to another, becoming a slave or a source of many body parts for research and transplantation.[19]

Justifying Capitalist Property Rights

The space of capitalist property. I have been describing a regime of maximally extensive feasible property rights; as Figure 1 shows, there are numerous regimes of property that lie between such a regime (point A) and communism (point D):

One might speculate that, say current American capitalism is closer to point C than to A, the capitalist ideal: the range of things that can be owned is quite extensive (though certainly not maximal—think of the absence of property over heroin, certain sexual services, and kidneys), but ownership rights are qualified in numerous ways (licensing regulations, environmental regulations, health and safety rules, and so on). On the other hand, John

FIGURE 1

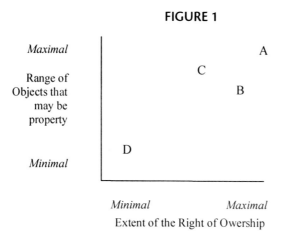

Extent of the Right of Ownership

Stuart Mill seemed to support a system closer to B: something like full property rights over what can be owned but significant limitations on what should be owned. For Mill, the justification of private property—that people deserve the fruits of their labor—does not apply to land: "No man made the land. It is the original inheritance of the whole species."[20]

To justify a non-pure regime of capitalist property rights, then, is to justify a system of property rights somewhere *in the neighbourhood* of point A. To justify the capitalist ideal is to justify the sort of maximally extensive feasible property rights *at* A. Although we cannot even begin to fully survey the arguments that have been advanced to justify such extensive property rights, it will help to get some idea of why advocates of capitalism have thought property rights approaching point A can be justified. I consider briefly two important lines of justification advanced by political philosophers (I turn to economists in section 3).

Self-ownership. Perhaps the most influential justification holds that (1) to be a free person is to have maximally extensive feasible property rights over oneself and (2) there is some mechanism that allows these extensive self-ownership rights to yield extensive rights over objects in the world. For Locke, one's property is not just one's "estates" but one's "life," "liberty," and "person."[21] In this sense we are self-owners, and our ownership over parts of the world is an extension of our self-ownership. For Locke, when a person mixes his labor (which is his property) with unowned parts of the world, he can extend his property in his person to include those parts of the world. This type of view was by no means unique to Locke. As Stephen Buckle shows in his study of the natural law theories of property, Hugo Grotius, Samuel Pufendorf, and Locke all insisted on an intimate connection between a person's rights and what "belongs" to her. This idea of what belongs to a person or her *"suum"* concerns a set of "essential possessions": life, limbs, and liberty. Thus understood, says Buckle, the *suum* is "what naturally belongs to a person because none of these things can be taken away without injustice."[22] Now, crucially, natural law theorists held that one's *suum* could be—indeed, if we are to survive, must be—extended into the world. As Buckle says, concerning Locke, "[t]he property in one's own person thus has a dynamic quality, in that it needs to grow to survive—it requires the acquisition of certain things. The *suum* must be extended—'mixed' with things—in order to be maintained."[23] Thus by extending one's *suum* into the external world—in Locke's theory, by mixing one's labor with parts of the world—external private property in goods is generated. External ownership involves property rights over things that are as extensive as property rights over oneself: they are an extension of the attributes of personhood itself.

If the self-ownership argument is to justify the sort of extensive capitalist property rights we have been analyzing, (1) it must be shown that the extension process applies a suitably wide range of objects and (2) that these new property rights are characterized by the full bundle of capitalist rights. Both of these tasks look daunting. As Buckle notes, at the heart of self-ownership theories such as Locke's was the idea that our right of self-ownership is inalienable: we have property in our own person, but no right to destroy or waste it.[24] But if one's property rights over one's self constitutes less than full capitalist property, it is hard to see how one's extension of this right of self-ownership creates full capitalist property rights: the extended property rights would be more complete than the property right on which they are based. Moreover, if the point of the extension of one's *suum* is to provide for our maintenance, then it seems that this process could not justify property rights that would ultimately be harmful to us, such as property rights over heroin or alcohol. To be sure, some advocates of the self-ownership view have insisted that a pure self-ownership doctrine would accord us full capitalist property rights over our body and labor.[25] An implication of this position would be that others would have a right of execution over your body for purpose of compensation and non-payment of debts—a radical view.

Agency Justifications. A more adequate justification of maximally extensive property seeks to derive them from the very idea of agency. Loren Lomasky, for example, argues that persons, understood as pursuers of projects, have a natural and important interest in possessing things:

> Persons … have a natural interest in having things. The relation of *having* is conceptually more basic and not to be confused with a *property right*. It amounts to the actual ability to employ some object in the furtherance of one's designs and does not presuppose the existence of any structure of rights. Having *I* and enjoying property rights in *I* are conceptually and empirically distinguishable … However, these are not two unrelated concepts. It is because of a person's interests in having objects that there is an interest in being accorded property rights.[26]

Thus, as Lomasky understands them, property rights protect one's possession of things. "Property rights demarcate a moral space within which what one has is marked as immune from predation."[27] Such morally secure possession is required for successful project pursuit.

The crucial task for the agency justification is to move from a general argument that *some* property is necessary for agency to a defense of *maximally extensive* property rights. The agency argument has an easier time than self-ownership accounts in showing that our rights of ownership should approximate full property rights (our first dimension of capitalist property rights): agency requires that one be able to control parts of the world as part of one's projects, and full capitalist property maximizes control. But can it also be shown that the agency justification leads to the desirability of maximal property rights over the other dimension—the things over which one can have property? This looks more dubious. The key, it would seem, is to show that (1) agency is a great, perhaps the supreme value and (2) to limit what parts of the world a person may own, or what services she may sell, always to some extent limits her agency and so (3) it takes a extremely strong case, in terms of competing values, to justifiably set a limit on what can be owned, or what services can be sold. Thus, for example, an advocate of the agency justification may object to John Rawls's suggestion that one's interest in agency is adequately advanced by a system that grants private property over personal items but prohibits it over productive goods.[28] Such a socialist system prohibits "capitalist acts between consenting adults"[29]—and that looks like a significant limitation on the types of projects that one is free to pursue.

3. CAPITALISM AND MARKETS

Markets and Efficient Property: Full Capitalist Property Rights

To fully understand why capitalism endorses maximally extensive property rights we need to turn from philosophic justifications to the analysis of the market and efficiency. In his classical paper on "The Problem of Social Cost" R.M. Coase showed that, regardless of the initial distribution of property rights, if there are no transaction costs, free exchange in the market yields an efficient outcome.[30] Consider an example. As we all know, there is a great demand for solar panels in the West; environmentalists, those concerned about global warming, and those interested in national energy independence all are urging increased use of solar power. Now the production of solar panels requires polysilcon, but manufacturing polysilcon produces toxic waste. In western countries this waste is recycled; in China, however, recycling technologies are not well developed, and recycling is not required by law.[31] Waste is either stored or, after minimal reprocessing, released into the environment. It is estimated that to recycle the waste would increase the cost of Chinese polysilcon by somewhere between 50 to 400%. It is disputed how great the resulting pollution is, but it is safe to say that enough waste leaks on to adjoining land to severely curtail agriculture on surrounding farms. Suppose, as does Coase, that we ignore transaction and bargaining costs; and simply focus on the Polysilcon Factory and say, the group of Affected Farmers. The Polysilcon Factory clearly produces what economists call a *negative externality* on the Affected Farmers: its productive activity negatively impacts their livelihood. Now if the Polysilcon Factory does not take this negative impact into account it has an incentive to produce polysilcon up to the point where its marginal costs equal its marginal benefits: that is, up to the point where its costs for producing another ton of polysilcon equals the profits of doing so. (That this is so is a standard axiom of economics.) If the Polysilcon Factory is at a level of production such that the benefits of producing another ton of polysilcon exceed the total costs of producing that unit, it clearly has an incentive to produce that additional ton; if it is at the point where the total costs of producing another ton of polysilcon exceed the benefits of producing that unit, it clearly has an incentive *not* to produce that ton. But the problem for society is that at the point at which the Polysilcon Factory's marginal costs equal *its* marginal benefits, the *total social costs* will have exceeded the total social benefits. This is because the Polysilcon Factory does not take into account the costs imposed on the Affected Framers; if it considers these costs in its calculations, it would have ceased production at a lower level of output (at an extreme, zero).

To see this better, let us assume some figures. Suppose that a Polysilcon Factory would incur a one-time cost of $500,000 to build an improved storage facility that would not leak on to neighboring properties: suppose such a facility would last 20 years, so the yearly cost is roughly $25,000. Now assume that the pollution causes a collective loss of $40,000 a year to the Affected Farmers. Even if there is no law against the pollution, an efficient result can still be achieved: the Farmers can pay the Factory $25,000 a year to build the improved facility. They will be $15,000 a year better off, and the factory will be no worse off (if they pay $26,000, both will be better off than in the current situation). It is important that this "theorem" applies regardless of how the property rights are divided between the two parties. An efficient outcome can be reached whether the Factory has a right to pollute or the Farmers have a right that it not pollute. Suppose that there is indeed a law against pollution, but to totally stop pollution would require a much larger expenditure, say $10,000,000; suppose the Factory could not afford to pay this and would close down. Assume that the Farmers still suffer a total loss of $25,000 a year and that the Farmers have the right to bring suit against the Factory. Now it is efficient for the Factory to pay the Farmers something more than $25,000 a year not to bring suit. This would be better for both the Farmers and the Factory than shutting down the Factory.

According to Coase, then, in the absence of transaction and bargaining costs, parties to activities with negative externalities will agree to some efficient allocation of resources regardless of the initial distribution of property rights. Coase's theorem challenges one of the main principled justifications for government activity. In the absence of a perfect scheme of property rights that fully internalizes costs and benefits (i.e., an economic actor reaps the full benefits, but also pays the full costs, of his activity), it has been widely argued that government action is necessary to regulate the "market failure" that results from externalities (when an actor imposes costs on another that are not considered in his calculations). But Coase argues that, at least ideally, market transactions can solve the problem of externalities and get us to efficient outcomes (though the actual costs involved in negotiation, etc. may preclude this, and then government action may be required as a second-best strategy). But—and this is the important point—if markets are to approach efficient outcomes in which people are compensated for externalities, people must have extensive rights to make agreements. Restrictions on to what they can agree to—what trades they can make, what aspects of their rights they can transfer to others, how they can use their property, and so on—will undermine efficiency and the possibility of mutual benefit. Suppose that the Factory is doing $1,000,000 damage to the Farmers, but that strict enforcement of the pollution code would raise the price of Factory's polysilcon by 200%, which would drive it out of business. It would obviously be mutually beneficial for the Factory and the Framers to agree to, say, a payment to the Farmers of $1,500,000 a year: both would be better off than if the factory closed. If such agreements are precluded—if the parties cannot trade their rights in these ways—then the efficient outcome may not be possible. Thus we see how full capitalist ownership rights are conducive to efficiency—and "efficiency" is simply a term for mutual benefit. Unless each is free to trade her rights as she sees fit, opportunities for mutually beneficial exchanges will be blocked.

Markets, Mutual Benefit, and Mutual Respect

The account I have been stressing conceives of markets as arenas of mutual benefit. The idea that exchange is generally mutually beneficial is at the heart of what we might call that capitalist view of social life (and most of modern economics). In contrast, in the eyes of many opponents of capitalist markets, market exchanges are what game theorists call "zero-sum" transactions: for every gain by one party, there is a corresponding loss by another. The market is seen as a realm of dog-eat-dog competition: some win by devouring others, but the devoured lose. For every one who eats there is someone who is eaten. In the words of a former French prime minister, "What is the market? It is the law of the jungle, the law of nature."[32] Capitalism rejects this conflict-ridden view of social life and the market. If I possess two bottles of beer, and you posses two slices of pizza, an exchange of a slice of pizza for a bottle of beer will make us both better off.[33] As Adam Smith saw it, our propensity to "truck, barter and exchange one thing for another"[34] is at the root of mutual benefit, and the growth of wealth.

> Give me that which I want and you shall have this which you want, is the meaning of every such offer; and it is in this manner that we obtain from one another the far greater part of those good offices which we stand in need of. It is not from the benevolence of the butcher, the brewer, or the baker, that we

expect our dinner, but from their regard to their own interest. … Nobody but a beggar chooses to depend chiefly on the benevolence of his fellow-citizens.[35]

In commenting on this passage Stephen Darwall stresses that, though certainly it is about mutual advantage, it presumes far more than mere self-interested agency. Smith stresses that exchange relations presuppose agents who conceive of each other of having distinct points of view, which demand respect. "Smith evidently thinks of exchange as an interaction in which both parties are committed to various normative presuppositions, for example, that the exchange is made by free mutual consent, that neither party will simply take what the other has. … Both parties must presume that the other is dealing fairly."[36] Market transactions are built on a foundation of trust and a type of mutual respect: without that, we are apt to invade for gain (a true zero-sum interaction) rather than trade for mutual gain.

As Smith famously shows, markets both rely on, and provide the main impetus to, the division of labor. If someone is a butcher, another a brewer, and another a baker, an immensely greater amount of food and drink is available than if each is her own butcher, brewer, and baker. According to David Hume, this is the very essence of society: "By the partition of employments, our ability encreases."[37] Indeed, for Hume market relations are even more basic than property or justice: the rules of property and justice evolve out of market relations based on the division of labor. As cooperation proceeds, conventions arise about the terms of our cooperative interactions—hence the genesis of our principles of justice.

Are Market Exchanges Always Beneficial?

A fundamental claim of capitalism, then, is that markets respect full private property rights and allow for mutual benefit among independent agents. We have been assuming that each of the parties to the exchange has full information about what they are exchanging. Economists generally assume that both parties to an exchange are equally informed; only recently has there been a sustained interest in how asymmetric information can affect market transactions.[38] To the extent that one party does not know what he is buying, we can no longer suppose that market exchanges are truly mutually beneficial. Of course classical exponents of the market economy insisted that mutual gain through markets presupposed the absence of fraud and force (recall the idea that markets are based on trust and a sort of mutual respect), but the problems of asymmetric information run deeper.

A related problem is asymmetric bargaining power. One of the main justifications for labor laws regulating hours and factory conditions in the early part of twentieth century was that employers and workers had asymmetric bargaining power, so that workers were forced to accept disadvantageous bargains. This line of analysis is more complex and controversial than it first appears. Hardly any bargains are made from equality of bargaining power, yet the fact that some need the bargain more than others does not show that the exchange is not mutually beneficial. On the other hand, in extreme cases unequal bargaining power can undermine the moral legitimacy of market outcomes. As Robert Nozick, a staunch defender of capitalism argued, "a person may not appropriate the only water hole in a desert and charge what he will. Nor may he charge what he will if he possesses one, and unfortunately it happens that all the water holes in the desert dry up but his."[39] Under these conditions an offer of a glass of water for all your property would be a *coercive offer*: an offer that exploits one's bargaining power and simply cannot be refused.[40] Instead of mutual advantage we have a sort of exploitation of those in great need.

Thus far we have been considering the conditions under which an individual market transaction is genuinely mutually beneficial. But it might be objected that a *series* of market transactions, each of which is unobjectionable, may have an outcome in which some (i.e., the workers) have no real choices, and so their freedom and self-ownership is undermined. Nozick appears to deny this:

> Consider the following example. Suppose that there are twenty-six women and twenty-six men each wanting to get married. For each sex, all of that sex agree on the same ranking of the twenty-six members of the opposite sex in terms of desirability of marriage partners: call them *A* to *Z*, and *A* to *Z* respectively in decreasing preferential order. *A* and *A* voluntarily choose to get married, each preferring the other to any other partner. *B* would most prefer to marry *A*, and *B* would most prefer to marry *A*, but by their choices *A* and *A* have removed these options. When *B* and *B* marry, their choices are not made nonvoluntary merely by the fact that there is something else they would rather do. This other most preferred option requires the cooperation of others who have chosen, as is their right, not to cooperate. ... This contraction of the range of options continues down to *Z* and *Z*, who face a choice between marrying the other or remaining unmarried.[41]

Nozick argues that *Z* and *Z* are still free to choose whether or not to get married, despite their extremely restricted range of options. After all, the others have simply chosen other partners, a decision that was fully within their rights. *Z* and *Z* are not unfree simply because no one has chosen them. Nozick goes on to insist that this same reasoning applies to workers who may face extremely restricted employment options: their freedom and self-ownership have not been undermined by the legitimate choices of others. Suppose a business ethics teacher at a small college complains that she is not free to move to some other position because no one wishes to give her a job—Nozick insists she is perfectly free, the problem is that her services simply are not desired by any other institution. G. A. Cohen disagrees: he believes that a series of legitimate choices can lead to an outcome that undermines the freedom of some and so some are forced to accept offers.[42] Suppose that each person in a community acts within their rights to erect a fence on their property, preventing others from crossing it. Now also suppose that Alf is surrounded by such fences, and can no longer leave his property. Betty makes an offer: half his wealth for free passage through her property. Do we really want to say that, as a result of a series of legitimate choices, Alf's self-ownership and freedom have not been compromised? It seems that they have been.

A defender of markets must, I think, show that the overall effect of markets, far from radically decreasing options, is to increase them, providing a greater range of choice. [43] To be sure, just what we mean by a greater range of choice is open to various interpretations: it might mean simply how many options a person has, how many options a person values, the breadth of options (not simply a lot of options to do basically similar things), and so on. These are difficult issues in the philosophy of freedom. However, on almost any interpretation, modern capitalist-like market economies have astronomically increased people's range of options. Consider Eric Beinhocker's comparison of two tribes: the Yanomamö, a tribe living along the Orinoco River between Brazil and Venezuela, and the New Yorkers, a tribe living on Hudson River along the border of New York and New Jersey. The Yanomamö have an average income of $90 a year, the New Yorker $36,000:

> But it is not just the absolute level of income that makes the New Yorkers so wealthy: it is also the incredible variety of things their wealth can buy. Imagine you had the income of a New Yorker, but you could only spend it on things in the Yanomamö economy. If you spent your $36,000 fixing up your mud hut, buying the best clay pots in the village, and eating the finest Yanomamö cuisine, you would be extraordinarily wealthy by Yanomamö standards, but you would still feel far poorer than a typical New Yorker with his or her Nike sneakers, televisions and vacations in Florida. The number of economic choices the average New Yorker has is staggering. The Wal-Mart near the JFK Airport has over 100,000 different items in stock, there are over 200 television channels offered on cable TV, Barnes and Noble lists over 8 million titles, the local supermarket has 275 varieties of breakfast cereal, the typical department store offers 150 types of lipstick, and there are over 50,000 restaurants in New York City alone. [44]

Beinhocker points out that the 400-fold difference in income does not even begin to estimate the difference in options; the New Yorker, he estimates, has an order of 10^{10} more choices—an astronomical number. [45] And with these consumer choices come occupational, educational, and religious ones as well. When we compare capitalist modern market economies with simple non-market economies (and Soviet-type planned economies), what is striking is not simply the difference in the absolute level of wealth, but in the range of options—the jobs one can perform, the goods one can consume, the lives one can have.

Markets and Efficiency: The Extent of Property

As we have already seen in the case of common pool resources, extending the range of things that can be privately owned is of fundamental importance if our aim is to ensure efficient sustainable use. Efficiency is also nearly always enhanced when services are privately rather than publicly provided. There is evidence of the greater efficiency of private over public ownership in, among other things, airlines, banks, municipal bus services, cleaning services, debt collection, fire protection, hospitals, housing insurance claims processing, military aircraft repair, ocean tanker maintenance, preschool education, garbage collection, removal of abandoned vehicles, slaughterhouses and weather forecasting.[46]

Hayek provides one of the most compelling arguments for extending as far as possible the range of things subject to private ownership. As Hayek understands a modern society, each individual has her own projects and plans (think again of the agency justification in section 2); whether she is successful depends on whether she can mesh her plans with those of others.[47] If plans come into constant conflict, people will find their aims and projects frustrated. Two things are needed for this meshing. First, there must be settled rules of conduct that allow each to anticipate the actions of others: repeated interventions by government to change regulations and the rules of the market undermine our ability to anticipate others. Second, however, we require knowledge: we need to know what others are doing. If we are to efficiently pursue our own goals we must have an idea of whether the resources necessary for our plans are being demanded by others, whether others will be interested in the outputs of our plans and projects, and so on. But how can we know that? Modern society is literally composed on hundreds of millions of people; the knowledge required for meshing the plans of these great societies is of an incredible magnitude.

> The economic problem of society is thus not merely a problem of how to allocate "given" resources—if "given" is taken to mean given to a single mind which deliberately solves the problem set by these "data." It is rather a problem of how to secure the best use of resources known to any of the members of society, for ends whose relative importance only these individuals know. Or, to put it briefly, it is a problem of the utilization of knowledge which is not given to anyone in its totality.[48]

The problem is this: each of us has both personal and local knowledge not generally available to others, and yet the success of our plans often depends on knowing the personal and local knowledge of others. Personal knowledge consists of one's knowledge of one's own plans and goals. Local knowledge is "the knowledge of the particular circumstances of time and place. It is with respect to this that practically every individual has some advantage over all others because he possesses unique information of which beneficial use might be made, but of which use can be made only if the decisions depending on it are left to him or are made with his active cooperation."[49] I wish to employ my local knowledge to exploit those possibilities of which I know. But for me to successfully do this requires that I know about events in far off places that might affect my plans: what do others want, what alternative uses do they have for resources, what local new possibilities do they see that I don't? How can I possibly know all this? Now—and here is Hayek's great contribution—this knowledge of remoter events is conveyed by the price system. The relative prices for goods do not tell us why goods are wanted, or why they are in short supply: it is a summary measure conveying just the crucial information—that others want the good, or that they are having a hard time getting hold of enough. "The marvel [of the market] is that in a case like that of a scarcity of one raw material, without an order being issued, without more than perhaps a handful of people knowing the cause, tens of thousands of people whose identity could not be ascertained by months of investigation, are made to use the material or its products more sparingly; i.e., they move in the right direction."[50] The market, then, sums up the local and personal knowledge of actors across the world, and converts it into the crucial information that each of us must have so that we can use our own local and personal knowledge to efficiently satisfy our aims. If, though, the market is to convey as much information as possible about the plans, resources, and opportunities, as many resources as possible must be subject to the price mechanism. To take something out of the market limits the spread of information about it, impairing the effectiveness of plans throughout the market.

Consider the use of central city streets. In most large metropolitan areas, streets in the central business district are jammed: it is very difficult for anyone to make reasonable progress in their journeys. It is the perfect case where plans fail to mesh: in fact, they often gridlock. The system does not tend to promote efficient outcomes: the increased demand for city streets does not sufficiently raise the price, which would induce people to use alternative methods of transport, or simply avoid the central city. To be sure, as congestion becomes horrible, there is some movement to other modes of transport or avoiding the city center, but it is very difficult to gauge what are the relative costs or benefits. The problem is that use of city streets is not a tradable good, and so no price emerges. This could be remedied by a system in which those who placed a higher value on using central city streets could pay others not to use them. Transactions costs, though, would be extraordinarily high in this case. A more realistic proposal that would tend toward efficiency would be to auction a limited number of permits to use central city streets. Those who place more value on using the streets would pay more and, if these permits could be traded, those who lost out on the auction could buy permits from others: we would then have a useful social signal about how much value people place on using non-jammed streets. Moving yet further away from a market solution, cities might follow London in placing a fee on using city center streets. This limits congestion, but the price does not provide much information about how much people value using the streets, since it is set by a central authority and not by market interactions.

The "Commodification" Objection to a Market with Extensive Property Rights

"The market," Cass Sunstein tells us, "is typically the sphere for use."[51] The things bought and sold on the market are typically commodities. But humans also have a wide range of non-use values such as friendship, life, health, enlightenment. They are not only different goods, they are valued in different ways: friends—true ones, at any rate—do not value each other because of their use to each other. Or, according to Elizabeth Anderson's somewhat different analysis, sometimes "higher" and "lower" valued goods cannot really be compared, and if they cannot be compared, they cannot be traded, for the market "commensurates" goods: it scores all goods on a common, monetary, scale of value.

> Two goods are incomparable in intrinsic worth if they are not candidates for the same mode of valuation. One good is of incomparably higher worth than another if it is worthy of a higher mode of valuation than the other—worthy of love, awe, respect or honor beyond what is owed to persons in general, worthy of respect beyond the consideration owed to animals, worthy of consideration beyond mere use. ... [O]ne way to express this difference in demands is to prohibit tradeoffs between states of affairs concerning the goods that express a lower kind of valuation for the higher good than it merits.[52]

Thus, argue critics, because markets turn all goods into mere tradable commodities, they violate our sense of value.

When thinking about these matters, it is important to be careful how we relate the idea of "price" (or "economic value") to our wider notions of what is valuable. Consider two "commodities" that in some ways appear of widely different types: Norman Rockwell's 1943 "Rosie the Riveter" and an endowed chair in Philosophy. Rockwell's painting has sold for almost five million dollars; a fully endowed chair in Philosophy costs between three and four million. If price is meant to sum up the total values of the "Rosie the Riveter" and a chair in philosophy, and if to accept the market is to accept that "Rosie the Riveter" is, overall, more valuable than a philosophy professorship, then the market certainly would do violence to *my* values. There is more to values than that. But it is not—or at least it shouldn't be—a claim of friends of market that price fully captures what we mean by the "value" of two "commodities." Ideally, the market price of X indicates the amount of resources the marginal buyer is willing to allocate to secure X. I can, and do, hold that the philosophy professorship is more valuable than "Rosie the Riveter," and in so saying I do not claim that there has been a market failure. We do not all place the same value on each commodity: that is precisely why trades take place. It is our differences, not agreements, in valuations that underlie market exchange. If we all valued everything to the same extent, no one would trade her goods for anyone else's. As Hayek stressed, it makes no sense to say that the market price is *the* value of anything; market prices are the result of our differences in how we value goods.[53] The mistaken idea that goods in the market that have equal prices must have equal value inherent in them, and so the market exchange somehow expresses—or purports to express—the true value of goods, is at the heart of the Marxist criticism of markets (see further section 4).[54]

4. THE HIERARCHICAL, PROFIT-MAXIMIZING FIRM

The Master–Servant Relation

It might seem that once we have described a market based on maximally extensive property rights we have completed our task of characterizing the capitalist ideal. Not so. In his *Principles of Political Economy*—the most influential economic text of the nineteenth century—John Stuart Mill sketches an *alternative* to capitalism that embraces both private property and markets. Mill endorsed the private ownership of firms, but not firms in which some were hired and were required to obey the instructions of the owners—the "master."

> Hitherto there has been no alternative for those who lived by their labour, but that of labouring either each for himself alone, or for a master. But the civilizing and improving influences of association, and the efficiency and economy of production on a large scale, may be obtained without dividing the producers into two parties with hostile interests and feelings, the many who do the work being mere servants under the command of the one who supplies the funds, and having no interest of their own in the enterprise except to earn their wages with as little labour as possible. ... [T]here can be little doubt that the status of hired labourers will gradually tend to confine itself to the description of workpeople whose low moral qualities render them unfit for anything more independent: and that the relation of masters and workpeople will be gradually superseded by partnership, in one of two forms: in some cases, association of the labourers with the capitalist; in others, and perhaps finally in all, association of labourers among themselves.[55]

As workers become better educated and more public-spirited, Mill argued, the master/servant relation characteristic of the capitalist firm will be replaced by a regime of worker cooperatives: worker-owned firms that compete in the market. The idea was that workers would be collective owners of the firms and democratically decide important strategic matters, though-day-to-day operations would still be directed by a manger instructing workers what to do—but a manger that could be dismissed by the workers. Thus the worker cooperatives were privately held firms in a competitive market economy without the master-servant relation (in which the owners are masters and the workers simply hired servants). Unfortunately for this view, the worker cooperative movement barely outlived Mill; worker cooperatives appear to have succumbed to the greater efficiency of capitalist firms based on the master-servant relation.[56]

Hierarchy and Efficiency

Why did Mill's hope for the future—firms owned by the workers and, ultimately, managed by them, succumb to traditional capitalist firms in which, either, the owner managed the firm and hired workers as his "servants," or (see below) the owners hired managers, who in turn instructed the workers about what to do, when to do it, and so on? As we have seen, Coase had a fundamental impact on our thinking about markets, property and efficiency. Another of his papers fundamentally changed our thinking about "The Nature of the Firm."[57] Coase agrees with Mill: the "master and servant" relation is fundamental to the capitalist firm (it is widely thought that this relation is at least partly constitutive of capitalism).[58] This, of course, is a hierarchical, authority, relation: those who own (or at the behest of the owners, who manage) make the decisions about what is to be produced, how, by whom, etc. The job of the workers is to do as they are instructed by their "boss." Coase and his followers show that organization via such an authority relation reduces transaction costs. Transactions organized through the market and its price mechanism entail, for instance, negotiating costs and information costs: we must find out who is selling a product, whether we wish to pay his price, and so on. Typically these costs are not so great as to make market exchange inefficient; however in some cases the negotiations would be quite costly. Suppose that one is building a new computer. One might buy all the components in the market, but perhaps one's aim is to design a new computer. This would involve a new motherboard unit, a video display that works well with it, effective power sources, and so on. Now these new units must work well together, and this may require constant cooperation by the individual design teams (focusing on the motherboard, display, etc.) as they are building the unit. If so, it may greatly reduce transaction costs to have a central coordinator who directs each specialist team and their activities, giving them design parameters so that the designs work well together. And so one may organize a hierarchical firm. The firm, then, is a way to decrease some transaction costs. In this sense the hierarchical firm is an engine of efficiency.[59]

The "Socialist" Character of the Capitalist Firm

The division of labor in the market is based on individual producers and consumers, each contracting with each other; one's reward is directly based on one's production of what others want. The division of labor in the firm is very different. It is based on a central coordinator—the boss—who decides the relevant targets, and then designs systems that divide up tasks in order to achieve the goals. Of course the boss may seek input and feedback from her subordinates, but this is up to her. Those with authority make plans and instruct the "servants" how to go about implementing them. The values *within* the firm are in many ways the opposite of the values *between* participants in the market: whereas the latter stress independence, contract, and reward based satisfaction of demand, the former stresses the values of leadership, teamwork (directed by leaders), tasks based on instruction from above, and reward based on the boss's evaluation of the subordinates' usefulness to the firm.

It is interesting that the values within the firm were attractive to many communists. N. I. Bukharin and Evgenii Preobrazhensky sought to organize all of society as one large factory. They wrote in their *ABC of Communism*:

> We must know in advance how much labour to assign to the various branches of industry; what products are required and how much of each it is necessary to produce; how and where machines must be provided. These and similar details must be thought out beforehand, with approximate accuracy at least; and the work must be guided in accordance with calculations. ... Without a general plan, *without a general directive system*, and without careful calculation and book-keeping, there can be no organization. But in the communist social organization, there is such a plan.[60]

Just as a factory manager seeks to organize and plan production, so too, it was thought, must communist planners organize and plan production for the entire economy. Thus early communists had great regard for capitalist techniques of production *within* enterprises; it was the "anarchy" of the market that provoked their deepest ire.[61]

Because most people in capitalist societies spend their lives within large corporations, in non-profit organizations such as universities, or in government service, we arrive at the surprising conclusion that most people in capitalist societies spend their lives in organizations whose values are in many ways more "socialist" than "capitalist." This is an important theme in Hayek's work. In large organizations subordinates expect to be rewarded according to their merit: they were given tasks to perform and if, on some set of criteria, they performed well, they merit a higher pay. As Hayek points out, this is very different than reward in the market: "Reward for merit is reward for obeying the wishes of others in what we do, not compensation for the benefits we have conferred upon them by doing what we thought best."[62] In the market one's reward *does* depend on how much others benefit from your action; and a good deal of luck may be involved in this. An entrepreneur may gain because she was in the right place and the right time, and so able to perceive a way to satisfy others' wants. In the market two entrepreneurs may have tried equally hard, done everything in their power, and one entirely fail and the other be a great success. It is not the case that such luck is simply about the way a "deliberate gamble" works out: the luck may be that the entrepreneur's local situation was such that she had possibilities of gain that were simply unknowable by others.[63]

Because most of us spend most of our time in organizations not informed by market values, when we come to politics—where market outcomes are often the subject of debate—we tend to apply our "socialist" (i.e., non-market) values to market outcomes. For example, in contemporary political philosophy one of the most influential doctrines of distributive justice is that property should track the distinction between "choice and chance": although one should be held responsible for one's choices, one should not be held responsible for what results from mere brute chance.[64] Distributive justice, it is said, should compensate people for bad brute luck.[65] This claim resonates with all of us who have spent our life within large organizations: if things go wrong for us and it was through no fault of our own, then we insist that this does not detract from our merit, or the rewards we are due from our bosses. "It was simply bad luck" is a relevant reply in one's end-of-the-year review. But, as Hayek points out, this makes no sense in the market, which in many ways runs by brute luck. Entrepreneurs are confronted by options many of which are not of their own devising; efficiency is promoted by them taking advantage of this "brute luck" (a sort of local knowledge) to satisfy additional wants and aims.[66] To "compensate" entrepreneurs for their bad luck (not having the same local knowledge as others) would undermine the very core of the market as a device for generating information. For the market to function, differential local knowledge must crucially enter into an entrepreneur's profits. In Hayek's eyes the upshot of this is a certain moral instability of capitalism: most people in capitalist economic systems have moral views about justice and distribution that they apply to the market, and are destructive of the very economic prosperity on which all depend.

What Is the Aim of the Capitalist Firm?

Ever since Marx it has been said that a constitutive characteristic of capitalism is the profit-maximizing firm.[67] Given that the capitalist ideal is based on full property rights, this cannot be literally true: a full owner can do anything he wishes with his property. Think of the familiar story of the *Christmas Carol.*[68] The firm of Scrooge and Marley was profit-maximizing with a vengeance: the *only* thing that Scrooge and Marley ever cared about was maximizing their profit. On the other hand, the firm at which Scrooge apprenticed as a lad, run by Mr. Fezziwig, moderated profit maximization with special kindness to its employees. Now it does not seem that Fezziwig's firm departs from any of the core commitments of capitalism: Fezziwig owned his firm and competed in the market. Still there is something right about identifying Scrooge and Marley as the "more" capitalist firm. After all, Fezziwig cannot go too far in ignoring profitability: if he runs his firm simply as a way to be kind to employees, it will fail. If Fezziwig's costs are too high he will be out-competed—consumers will not buy his product; if his returns are too low, he will not be able to loan funds from banks. (Indeed, he does go out of business in the 1951 movie version.) So we might think of Fezziwig as compromising the firm's profitability with his concern for his employees.[69] Scrooge and

Marley can run their firm simply and purely as a way to maximize profit, and that will not cause it to fail. Market competition does reward firms that excel at earning profits.

In contrast to Dickens's Victorian-era capitalism, in which firms are often privately owned by those who manage them, modern-era large capitalist firms are largely owned by shareholders, and their shares are very often publicly traded. And they are managed by non-owners, or at most by partial owners. This raises a host of difficult issues about what the aim of such firms should be.[70] Instead of owner-managers, we are confronted by a world composed of principals and agents: the managers of the firm are agents of the principals, the shareholders. This leads to a host of possible complications and problems: agents may pursue aims not approved by principals, and which are not in the principals' interests—a possibility that simply did not arise in owner-managed firms.[71] We cannot explore these difficult issues here, but one thing seems clear: in anything approaching the capitalist ideal, the shareholders own the firm, and it is their wishes and interests that should guide the agents. Capitalism, we have seen, is based on full ownership: if the firm is not managed according to the wishes or interests of the shareholders, their ownership rights are abridged. Apart from contractual obligations and basic market norms of fair-dealing (see section 3), the interests of employees *as such*—simply as "stakeholders" in the firm—are not ultimate aims of mangers in an ideal capitalist order. Of course the shareholders may desire that such stakeholders be accorded consideration: like modern Fezziwigs, they may compromise some profit in order to improve the lot of their non-owning stakeholders. But when firms are publicly traded, conveying this information to prospective investors may be costly and difficult. In capitalist economies there is a presumption that managers are the agents of the shareholders: firms that have included non-owners among their principals run the risk of misleading potential investors about their ownership rights.

Profit

But what is profit? In his important essay on the concept of profit, James Child remarks that there is no accepted understanding of the concept.[72] One remarkable feature of debates about profit is that to friends of capitalism "profit" has strongly positive connotations, while to critics it is a strongly pejorative term. Hayek argues that intellectuals, from Aristotle to Bertrand Russell and Albert Einstein, all misunderstand the idea, a misunderstanding summed up by the slogan "Production for use, not for profit."[73] This common attitude to profit derives from seeing economics as an engineering problem: knowing what people want and what resources are available, the problem is to maximize the production of goods to maximize the satisfaction of wants. But, as we saw in section 3, Hayek stressed that economics is precisely the study of how wants are satisfied when no one knows everyone's wants, no single person knows all the available resources, or the possible ways to satisfy these (largely unknown) wants. The "search for profit" by the entrepreneur is the probing of the entrepreneur "beyond known uses and ends" in order to best satisfy the "*multiplicity* of human ends."[74]

In contrast, for Marx "profit and wages remain in inverse proportion": profits come out of the possible wages of laborers.[75] For Marx the key to profit under capitalism is that in the market the exchange value of a commodity is determined by its cost of production, in particular by the amount of labor it takes to produce a good.[76] Because capitalist markets treat the ability to labor as itself a commodity, it too has an exchange value—the amount of labor it takes to produce a unit (e.g., an hour) of the ability to work (or, we might say, "labor power"). The key to understanding capitalism, Marx insists, is that labor power is "a source not only of value, but of more value than it has itself."[77] The price of a unit of (say, a day's) labour power is the amount of labor it takes to produce it; suppose it take four hours of labor to produce a day's worth of labor power. This would include all the labor that goes into the worker's food for the day, his clothes for the day, supporting his family for the day, and so on. But the worker labors ten hours a day and so creates ten hours of value; the price of his labor power was four hours of labor. The six hours of surplus value—that which the worker creates above and beyond the cost of producing his ability to work for the day—is the source of profit. Hence profit directly comes out of what the worker produced and, in other systems of production, might have constituted his reward for his work. For Marx, profit is a sort of theft.

Child proposes that these different attitudes toward profit derive from the two opposed attitudes toward exchange that we observed in section 3: exchange as a zero-sum versus positive sum, cooperative, interaction. If exchange is viewed as zero-sum, then one party's profits must come out of the other party. If we focus on the firm and the sale of labor power, the capitalist's profits must be someone's loss—the workers'. Where else could profits come from? In contrast, on the positive sum view, "*One makes profits by benefiting those one transacts with, while benefiting oneself.*"[78] … Capitalism insists that the pursuit of profit is not only socially useful, but benefits all parties to the exchange.

5. CONCLUSION

In this chapter I have sketched the elements of the capitalist ideal: maximally extensive property rights, efficient markets employing such rights, and hierarchical firms run in the interest of the owners. I have focused here on an ideal or pure version of capitalism: real-world systems often described as "capitalist" modify one or more of these elements. To know one's attitude to capitalism is to know one's evaluation of these elements: someone who strongly supports them all is a fervent defender of capitalism. Others may advance criticisms of one or more elements, and so approve of a modified form of capitalism. As one rejects more elements, either on moral or economic grounds, one begins to move to a non-capitalist economic system. The question for teachers and students of business ethics is whether their evaluation of the elements still endorses a recognizably capitalist business firm. If not, they are confronted with problem with which we began: studying the ethics of an organization embedded in a system that we ought not to have.

NOTES

1. Or perhaps business ethics is some sort of theory of the morally second-best: it instructs one how to act ethically in a morally unjustifiable context. Is that what business ethics does?

2. John Maynard Keynes, "The End of Laissez-Faire," in his *Essays in Persuasion* (London: Macmillan, 1972), p. 294.

3. Karl Marx, *Economic and Philosophic Manuscripts of 1844,* in *Marx/Engels Collected Works* (London: Lawrence & Wishart, 1975–2002), vol. 4, p. 293. Compare John Stuart Mill, *Principles of Political Economy with Some of Their Applications to Social Philosophy,* in *The Collected Works of John Stuart Mill,* edited by J.M. Robson (Toronto: University of Toronto Press, 1977), vol. 2, Book II, chap. 1.

4. Plato, *The Republic,* in *The Dialogues of Plato* translated into English with Analyses and Introductions by B. Jowett, 3rd edition revised and corrected (Oxford University Press, 1892), pp. 106ff.

5. On this point see Jürg Niehans, *A History of Economic Theory: Classic Contributions, 1720–1980* (Baltimore: Johns Hopkins University Press, 1990), p. 143.

6. This list draws on A.M. Honoré, "Ownership" in *Oxford Essays in Jurisprudence,* edited by A. G. Guest (Oxford: Clarendon Press, 1961), pp. 107–47; and Frank Snare, "The Concept of Property," *AmericanPhilosophical Quarterly,* vol. 9 (April 1972), pp. 200–206. For an excellent and accessible discussion, seeLawrence C. Becker, *Property Rights: Philosophical Foundations* (London: Routledge & Kegan Paul,1977), chapter. 2.

7. See Paul Finn, "Public Function—Private Action: A Common Law Dilemma," in *Public and Private in Social Life,* edited by S.I. Benn and G.F. Gaus (New York: St. Martin's Press, 1983): 93–111.

8. The now-classic work on this matter is Richard A. Epstein, *Takings: Private Property and the Power of Eminent Domain* (Cambridge, MA: Harvard University Press, 1985).

9. John Locke, *Second Treatise of Government,* edited by Peter Laslett (Cambridge: Cambridge UniversityPress, 1960), section 139. Emphasis in original.

10. See David Friedman, *The Machinery of Freedom* (New York: Harper and Row, 1973); Murray Rothbard,"Society without a State," in *NOMOS XIX: Anarchism,* edited by J. Roland Pennock and John W. Chapman (New York: New York University Press, 1978), pp. 191–207.

11. Locke, *Second Treatise,* section 142. On the range of anti-taxation anarcho-capitalist views, see Eric Mack and Gerald F. Gaus, "Classical Liberalism and Libertarianism: the Liberty Tradition," in *The Handbook of Political Theory,* edited by Gerald F. Gaus and Chandran Kukathas (London: Sage, 2004), pp. 115–142.

12. For a contemporary criticism of this view, see Liam Murphy and Thomas Nagel, *The Myth of Ownership: Taxes and Justice* (New York: Oxford University Press, 2002). I respond to some of their main claims in my "Proto-Ownership Rights and the Requirements of Justice," *Social Philosophy & Policy,* forthcoming.

13. I use "objects" broadly here to include financial instruments, such as mortgages.

14. See Garret Hardin, "The Tragedy of the Commons," in his *Managing the Commons*, (New York: W.H. Freeman, 1977).

15. David Schmidtz, *The Limits of Government: An Essay on the Public Goods Argument* (Boulder, CO: Westview Press, 1991), p. 21.

16. Karl Marx, *Capital*, vol. I in *Marx/Engels Collected Works*, vol. 35, chapter. 6.

17. See James Stacey Taylor, *Stakes and Kidneys: Why Markets in Human Body Parts Are Morally Imperative* (Aldershot, UK: Ashgate, 2005). Cf. Stephen R. Munzer, "An Uneasy Case Against Property Rights in Body Parts," *Social Philosophy & Policy*, vol. 11 (Summer, 1994): 259–86. I do not mean to suggest that only friends of the capitalist ideal support such markets.

18. Samuel Brittan, *A Restatement of Economic Liberalism* (Atlantic Highlands, NJ: Humanities Press, 1988), p. 1.

19. See Robert Nozick, *Anarchy, State and Utopia* (New York: Basic Books, 1974), p. 331.

20. Mill, *Principles of Political Economy*, book 2, chapter 2, section 6. Emphasis added.

21. Locke, *Second Treatise*, sections 27, 123.

22. Stephen Buckle, *Natural Law and the Theory of Property* (Oxford: Clarendon Press, 1991), p. 29.

23. Buckle, *Natural Law and the Theory of Property*, p. 171. Buckle argues for the applicability of the concept of *suum* to Locke's theory on pp. 168–74. See also A. John Simmons, *The Lockean Theory ofRights* (Princeton: Princeton University Press, 1992), pp. 226–27.

24. Buckle, *Natural Law and the Theory of Property*, pp. 191.

25. Nozick, *Anarchy, State and Utopia*, p. 58.

26. Loren E. Lomasky, *Persons, Rights and the Moral Community* (New York: Oxford University Press,1987), pp. 120–21. Emphasis in original.

27. Lomasky, *Persons, Rights and the Moral Community*, p. 121.

28. John Rawls, *Justice as Fairness: A Restatement*, edited by Erin Kelly (Cambridge, MA: Harvard University Press, 2001), pp. 136ff. I have in mind here Rawls's support of "liberal (democratic) socialism."

29. Nozick, *Anarchy, State and Utopia*, p. 163.

30. See Ronald Coase, "The Problem of Social Cost," *Journal of Law and Economics*, vol. 3 (1960): 1–44. My explication follows Dennis Mueller, *Public Choice III* (Cambridge: Cambridge University Press, 2003), pp. 27–30.

31. See Ariana Eunjung Cha, "Solar Energy Firms Leave Waste Behind in China," *Washington Post*, March 9, 2008, page A1.

32. Edouard Balladur quoted in Martin Wolf, *Why Globalization Works* (New Haven: Yale University Press, 2004), p. 4.

33. For an explanation of this notion of allocative efficiency, see my *On Philosophy, Politics, and Economics* (Belmont, CA: Thomson Wadsworth, 2008), chap. 3.

34. Adam Smith, *An Inquiry Into the Nature and Causes of the Wealth of Nations*, edited by W.B. Todd (Indianapolis: Liberty Fund, 1981), book I, chapter 2, paragraph 1.

35. Smith, *The Wealth of Nations*, book I, chapter 2, paragraph 2.

36. Stephen Darwall, *The Second-person Standpoint: Morality, Respect, and Accountability* (Cambridge: Harvard University Press, 2006), p. 47.

37. David Hume, *A Treatise of Human Nature*, second edition, edited by L. A. Selby-Bigge and P. H. Nidditch (Oxford: Oxford University Press, 1978), book 3, part 2, section 2, paragraph 3.

38. See Todd Sandler, *Economic Concepts for the Social Sciences* (Cambridge: Cambridge University Press,2001), chapter 7.

39. Nozick, *Anarchy, State and Utopia*, p. 180.

40. Joel Feinberg, *The Moral Limits of the Criminal Law*, vol. 3, *Harm to Self* (New York: Oxford University Press, 1986), p. 250.

41. Nozick, *Anarchy, State and Utopia*, p. 263.

42. See G. A. Cohen, *Self-Ownership, Freedom and Equality* (Cambridge: Cambridge University Press, 1995), pp. 35–37.

43. See Eric Mack, "Self-ownership, Marxism, and Egalitarianism, Part II: Challenges to the Self-ownership Thesis," *Politics, Philosophy and Economics,* vol. 1 (June 2002): 237–76, pp. 243ff.

44. Eric D. Beinhocker, *The Origin of Wealth* (Cambridge: Harvard Business School Press, 2006), p. 9.

45. Beinhocker, *The Origin of Wealth*, p. 9.

46. Charles Wolff, Jr., *Markets or Governments: Choosing between Imperfect Alternatives* (Cambridge, MA:MIT Press, 1993), Appendix B

47. See Hayek, *Law, Legislation and Liberty*, vol. 1, *Rules and Order* (Chicago: University of Chicago Press, 1973), p. 99.

48. F.A. Hayek "The Use of Knowledge in Society," *American Economic Review* 35 (September 1945), pp.519–520.

49. Hayek "The Use of Knowledge in Society," p. 522.

50. Hayek "The Use of Knowledge in Society," p. 527.

51. Cass R. Sunstein, *Free Markets and Social Justice* (Oxford: Oxford University Press, 1997), p. 94.

52. Elizabeth Anderson, *Values in Ethics and Economics* (Cambridge, MA: Harvard University Press, 1993), p. 70.

53. Hayek, *The Mirage of Social Justice*, p. 76.

54. Marx, *Capital,* vol. 1, part I, chapter 1, section 1.

55. Mill, *Principles*, book 4, chapter 7, section 4.

56. For an excellent analysis of cooperative production, see P.J.D. Wiles, *Economic Institutions Compared* (New York: Wiley, 1977), chapter 6. See also Oliver E. Williamson's analysis of the "Peer Group" systemin *The Economic Institutions of Capitalism* (New York: Free Press, 1985), pp. 217ff.

57. Coase, *The Firm, The Market and the Law*, chapter 2.

58. See, for example, Talcott Parsons's "Introduction" to Max Weber, *The Theory of Social and Economic Organization*, translated by A. M. Henderson and Talcott Parsons (New York: Free Press, 1947), p. 51; Niehaus, *A History of Economic Theory*, p. 144; Karl Marx, *Capital*, chapter 14, section 5.

59. See Williamson, *The Economic Institutions of Capitalism*.

60. Nikolai Bukharin and Evgenii Preobrazhensky, *The ABC of Communism,* quoted in Michael Ellman, *Socialist Planning* (Cambridge: Cambridge University Press, 1979), p. 9. Emphasis added.

61. See Bukharin and Preobrazhensky's views on the "anarchy of production" in Ellman, *Socialist Planning*, p. 8. See also Marx, *Capital,* chap. 14, section. 4.

62. F.A. Hayek, *The Constitution of Liberty* (London: Routledge and Kegan Paul, 1960), p. 100.

63. On the distinction between "option" luck and "brute" luck, see Ronald Dworkin, *Sovereign Virtue: The Theory and Practice of Equality* (Cambridge, MA: Harvard University Press, 2000), pp. 73ff

64. Dworkin, *Sovereign Virtue*, pp. 287ff.

65. Whether *good* brute luck should be compensated for is a matter of disagreement. See Peter Vallentyne, "Self-Ownership and Equality: Brute Luck, Gifts, Universal Dominance and Leximin," in *Real Libertarianism Assessed*, edited by Andrew Reeve and Andrew Williams (New York: Palgrave Macmillan, 2003): 29–52.

66. Indeed, believing that one's property is deserved, Hayek says, encourages "an air of self-righteousness." Hayek, *Law, Legislation and Liberty*, vol. 2, *The Mirage of Social Justice* (Chicago: University of Chicago Press, 1976), p. 74.

67. See, for example, Niehans, *A History of Economic Theory*, p. 144.

68. Charles Dickens, *A Christmas Carol* in *Five Christmas Novels* (New York: Heritage Press, 1939).

69. See Wiles, *Economic Institutions Compared*, p. 67.

70. For complexities, see Wiles, *Economic Institutions Compared*, pp. 69–70.

71. On economic analyses of principal-agent relations, see Sandler, *Economic Concepts for the Social Sciences*, pp. 120.

72. James W. Child, "Profit: The Concept and its Moral Features," *Social Philosophy & Policy*, vol. 15 (Summer 1998): 243–82, pp. 243.

73. F. A. Hayek, *The Fatal Conceit*, edited by W.W. Bartley III (Chicago: University of Chicago Press, 1988), p. 104.

74. Hayek, the *Fatal Conceit*, pp. 104–05.

75. Karl Marx, "Wage Labour and Capital" ("The general law that determines the rise and fall of wages and profit") in *Marx/Engels Collected Works,* vol. 9.

76. Marx, *Capital,* part I, chapter 1, sections 1–3; part 2, chapter 6.

77. Marx, *Capital,* part 3, chapter 8, section 2. Emphasis in original.

78. Child, "Profit," p. 282. Emphasis in original.

BIBLIOGRAPHY

Anderson, Elizabeth. *Values in Ethics and Economics*. Cambridge, MA: Harvard University Press, 1993.

Brittan, Samuel. *A Restatement of Economic Liberalism*. Atlantic Highlands, NJ: Humanities Press, 1988.

Buchanan, Allen. *Ethics, Efficiency and the Market*. Oxford: Clarendon Press, 1986.

Buckle, Stephen. *Natural Law and the Theory of Property*. Oxford: Clarendon Press, 1991.

Child, James W. "Profit: The Concept and its Moral Features," *Social Philosophy & Policy*, vol. 15 (Summer 1998): 243–82.

Coase, R. H. *The Firm, the Market and the Law*. Chicago: University of Chicago Press, 1998.

Cohen, G. A. *Self-Ownership, Freedom and Equality*. Cambridge: Cambridge University Press, 1995.

Gaus, Gerald F. *On Philosophy, Politics and Economics*. Belmont, CA: Thomson Wadsworth, 2008.

Heath, Joseph. "Business Ethics Without Stakeholders," *Business Ethics Quarterly*, vol. 16 (2006): 533–557.

Hayek, F. A. *Law, Legislation and Liberty*. Chicago: University of Chicago Press, 1973–1979, three vols.

Mack, Eric and Gerald F. Gaus, "Classical Liberalism and Libertarianism: the Liberty Tradition." In *The Handbook of Political Theory*, edited by Gerald F. Gaus and Chandran Kukathas. London: Sage, 2004, pp. 115–142.

Marx, Karl. *Capital*, edited by Friedrich Engels, translated by Samuel Moore and Edward Avling. London: W. Glaisher, 1909.

Mill, John Stuart. *Principles of Political Economy with Some of Their Applications to Social Philosophy* in *The Collected Works of John Stuart Mill*, edited by J. M. Robson. Toronto: University of Toronto Press, 1977, vols. 2 and 3.

Nozick, Robert. *Anarchy, State and Utopia*. New York: Basic Books, 1974.

Schmidtz, David. *The Elements of Justice*. Cambridge, UK: Cambridge University Press, 2006.

Smith, Adam. *An Inquiry into the Nature and Causes of the Wealth of Nations*, edited by R. H. Campbell and A. S. Skinner. Indianapolis, IN: Liberty Press, 1981, two vols.

Waldron, Jeremy. *The Right to Private Property*. Oxford: Clarendon Press, 1988.

Wiles, P.J.D. *Economic Institutions Compared*. New York: Wiley, 1977.

Wolff, Charles, Jr. *Markets of Governments: the Choice between Imperfect Alternatives*, second edition. Cambridge, MA: MIT Press, 1994.

Williamson, Oliver E. *The Economic Institutions of Capitalism*. New York: Free Press, 1985.

CHAPTER 6

✝

ORDER AND INCENTIVES

Man of System
Theory of Moral Sentiments

The love of our country seems, in ordinary cases, to involve in it two different principles; first, a certain respect and reverence for that constitution or form of government which is actually established; and secondly, an earnest desire to render the condition of our fellow-citizens as safe, respectable, and happy as we can. He is not a citizen who is not disposed to respect the laws and to obey the civil magistrate; and he is certainly not a good citizen who does not wish to promote, by every means in his power, the welfare of the whole society of his fellow-citizens.

In peaceable and quiet times, those two principles generally coincide and lead to the same conduct. The support of the established government seems evidently the best expedient for maintaining the safe, respectable, and happy situation of our fellow-citizens; when we see that this government actually maintains them in that situation. But in times of public discontent, faction, and disorder, those two different principles may draw different ways, and even a wise man may be disposed to think some alteration necessary in that constitution or form of government, which, in its actual condition, appears plainly unable to maintain the public tranquillity. In such cases, however, it often requires, perhaps, the highest effort of political wisdom to determine when a real patriot ought to support and endeavour to re-establish the authority of the old system, and when he ought to give way to the more daring, but often dangerous spirit of innovation.

Amidst the turbulence and disorder of faction, a certain spirit of system is apt to mix itself with that public spirit which is founded upon the love of humanity, upon a real fellow-feeling with the inconveniencies and distresses to which some of our fellow-citizens may be exposed. This spirit of system commonly takes the direction of that more gentle public spirit; always animates it, and often inflames it even to the madness of fanaticism. The leaders of the discontented party seldom fail to hold out some plausible plan of reformation which, they pretend, will not only remove the inconveniencies and relieve the distresses immediately complained of, but will prevent, in all time coming, any return of the like inconveniencies and distresses. They often propose, upon this account, to new-model the constitution, and to alter, in some of its most essential parts, that system of government under which the subjects of a great empire have enjoyed, perhaps, peace, security, and even glory, during the course of several centuries together. The great body of the party are commonly intoxicated with the imaginary beauty of this ideal system, of which they have no experience, but which has been represented to them in all the most dazzling colours in which the eloquence of their leaders could paint it. Those leaders themselves, though they originally may have meant nothing but their own aggrandizement, become many of them in time the dupes of their own sophistry, and are as eager for this great reformation as the weakest and foolishest of their followers. Even though the leaders should have preserved their own heads, as indeed they commonly do, free from this fanaticism, yet they dare not always disappoint the expectation of their followers; but are often obliged, though contrary to their principle and their conscience, to act as if they were under the common delusion. The violence of the party, refusing all palliatives, all temperaments, all reasonable accommodations, by requiring too much frequently obtains nothing; and those inconveniencies and distresses which, with a little moderation, might in a great measure have been removed and relieved, are the man whose public spirit is prompted altogether by humanity and benevolence, will respect the established powers and privileges even of individuals, and still more those of the great orders and societies, into which the state is divided. Though he should consider some of them as in some measure abusive, he will content himself with moderating, what he often cannot annihilate without great violence. When he cannot conquer the rooted prejudices of the people by reason and persuasion, he will not attempt to subdue them by force; but will religiously observe what, by Cicero, is justly called the divine maxim of Plato, never to use violence to his country no more than to his parents. He will accommodate, as well as he can, his public arrangements to the confirmed habits and prejudices of the people; and will remedy as well as he can, the inconveniencies which may flow from the want of those regulations which the people are averse to submit to. When he cannot establish the right, he will not disdain to ameliorate the wrong; but like Solon, when he cannot establish the best system of laws, he will endeavour to establish the best that the people can bear.

The man of system, on the contrary, is apt to be very wise in his own conceit; and is often so enamoured with the supposed beauty of his own ideal plan of government, that he cannot suffer the smallest deviation from any part of it. He goes on to establish it completely and in all its parts, without any regard either to the great interests, or to the strong prejudices which may oppose it. He seems to imagine that he can arrange the different members of a great society with as much ease as the hand arranges the different pieces upon a chess-board. He does not consider that the pieces upon the chess-board have no other principle of motion besides that which the hand impresses upon them; but that, in the great chess-board of human society, every single piece has a principle of motion of its own, altogether different from that which the legislature might cause to impress upon it. If those two principles coincide and act in the same direction, the game of human society will go on easily and harmoniously, and is very likely to be happy and successful. If they are opposite or different, the game will go on miserably, and the society must be at all times in the highest degree of disorder.

Some general, and even systematical, idea of the perfection of policy and law, may no doubt be necessary for directing the views of the statesman. But to insist upon establishing, and upon establishing all at once, and in spite of all opposition, every thing which that idea may seem to require, must often be the highest degree of arrogance. It is to erect his own judgment into the supreme standard of right and wrong. It is to fancy himself the only wise and worthy man in the commonwealth, and that his fellow-citizens should accommodate themselves to him and not he to them. It is upon this account, that of all political speculators, sovereign princes are by far the most dangerous. This arrogance is perfectly familiar to them. They entertain no doubt of the immense superiority of their own judgment. When such imperial and royal reformers, therefore, condescend to contemplate the constitution of the country which is committed to their government, they seldom see any thing so wrong in it as the obstructions which it may sometimes oppose to the execution of their own will. They hold in contempt the divine maxim of Plato, and consider the state as made for themselves, not themselves for the state. The great object of their reformation, therefore, is to remove those obstructions; to reduce the authority of the nobility; to take away the privileges of cities and provinces, and to render both the greatest individuals and the greatest orders of the state, as incapable of opposing their commands, as the weakest and most insignificant.

Price-Fixing
The Wealth of Nations

ADAM SMITH

P eople of the same trade seldom meet together, even for merriment and diversion, but the conversation ends in a conspiracy against the public, or in some contrivance to raise prices. It is impossible indeed to prevent such meetings, by any law which either could be executed, or would be consistent with liberty and justice. But though the law cannot hinder people of the same trade from sometimes assembling together, it ought to do nothing to facilitate such assemblies; much less to render them necessary.

A regulation which obliges all those of the same trade in a particular town to enter their names and places of abode in a public register, facilitates such assemblies. It connects individuals who might never otherwise be known to one another, and gives every man of the trade a direction where to find every other man of it.

A regulation which enables those of the same trade to tax themselves in order to provide for their poor, their sick, their widows and orphans, by giving them a common interest to manage, renders such assemblies necessary.

An incorporation not only renders them necessary, but makes the act of the majority binding upon the whole. In a free trade an effectual combination cannot be established but by the unanimous consent of every single trader, and it cannot last longer than every single trader continues of the same mind. The majority of a corporation can enact a bye-law with proper penalties, which will limit the competition more effectually and more durably than any voluntary combination whatever.

The pretence that corporations are necessary for the better government of the trade, is without any foundation. The real and effectual discipline which is exercised over a workman, is not that of his corporation, but that of his customers. It is the fear of losing their employment which restrains his frauds and corrects his negligence. An exclusive corporation necessarily weakens the force of this discipline. A particular set of workmen must then be employed, let them behave well or ill. It is upon this account, that in many large incorporated towns no tolerable workmen are to be found, even in some of the most necessary trades. If you would have your work tolerably executed, it must be done in the suburbs, where the workmen having no exclusive privilege, have nothing but their character to depend upon, and you must then smuggle it into the town as well as you can.

The Use of Knowledge in Society

Friedrich A. Hayek

I

What is the problem we wish to solve when we try to construct a rational economic order?

On certain familiar assumptions the answer is simple enough. *If* we possess all the relevant information, *if* we can start out from a given system of preferences, and *if* we command complete knowledge of available means, the problem which remains is purely one of logic. That is, the answer to the question of what is the best use of the available means is implicit in our assumptions. The conditions which the solution of this optimum problem must satisfy have been fully worked out and can be stated best in mathematical form: put at their briefest, they are that the marginal rates of substitution between any two commodities or factors must be the same in all their different uses.

This, however, is emphatically *not* the economic problem which society faces. And the economic calculus which we have developed to solve this logical problem, though an important step toward the solution of the economic problem of society, does not yet provide an answer to it. The reason for this is that the "data" from which the economic calculus starts are never for the whole society "given" to a single mind which could work out the implications and can never be so given.

The peculiar character of the problem of a rational economic order is determined precisely by the fact that the knowledge of the circumstances of which we must make use never exists in concentrated or integrated form, but solely as the dispersed bits of

Friedrich A. Hayek, "The Use of Knowledge in Society," from *The American Economic Review*, Vol. 35, Issue 4; September 1945, pp. 519–530. Copyright © 1945 by American Economic Association. Permission to reprint granted by the publisher.

incomplete and frequently contradictory knowledge which all the separate individuals possess. The economic problem of society is thus not merely a problem of how to allocate "given" resources—if "given" is taken to mean given to a single mind which deliberately solves the problem set by these "data." It is rather a problem of how to secure the best use of resources known to any of the members of society, for ends whose relative importance only these individuals know. Or, to put it briefly, it is a problem of the utilization of knowledge not given to anyone in its totality.

This character of the fundamental problem has, I am afraid, been rather obscured than illuminated by many of the recent refinements of economic theory, particularly by many of the uses made of mathematics. Though the problem with which I want primarily to deal in this paper is the problem of a rational economic organization, I shall in its course be led again and again to point to its close connections with certain methodological questions. Many of the points I wish to make are indeed conclusions toward which diverse paths of reasoning have unexpectedly converged. But as I now see these problems, this is no accident. It seems to me that many of the current disputes with regard to both economic theory and economic policy have their common origin in a misconception about the nature of the economic problem of society. This misconception in turn is due to an erroneous transfer to social phenomena of the habits of thought we have developed in dealing with the phenomena of nature.

II

In ordinary language we describe by the word "planning" the complex of interrelated decisions about the allocation of our available resources. All economic activity is in this sense planning; and in any society in which many people collaborate, this planning, whoever does it, will in some measure have to be based on knowledge which, in the first instance, is not given to the planner but to somebody else, which somehow will have to be conveyed to the planner. The various ways in which the knowledge on which people base their plans is communicated to them is the crucial problem for any theory explaining the economic process. And the problem of what is the best way of utilizing knowledge initially dispersed among all the people is at least one of the main problems of economic policy—or of designing an efficient economic system.

The answer to this question is closely connected with that other question which arises here, that of *who* is to do the planning. It is about this question that all the dispute about "economic planning" centers. This is not a dispute about whether planning is to be done or not. It is a dispute as to whether planning is to be done centrally, by one authority for the whole economic system, or is to be divided among many individuals. Planning in the specific sense in which the term is used in contemporary controversy necessarily means central planning—direction of the whole economic system according to one unified plan. Competition, on the other hand, means decentralized planning by many separate persons. The half-way house between the two, about which many people talk but which few like when they see it, is the delegation of planning to organized industries, or, in other words, monopoly.

Which of these systems is likely to be more efficient depends mainly on the question under which of them we can expect that fuller use will be made of the existing knowledge. And this, in turn, depends on whether we are more likely to succeed in putting at the disposal of a single central authority all the knowledge which ought to be used but which is initially dispersed among many different individuals, or in conveying to the individuals such additional knowledge as they need in order to enable them to fit their plans with those of others.

III

It will at once be evident that on this point the position will be different with respect to different kinds of knowledge; and the answer to our question will therefore largely turn on the relative importance of the different kinds of knowledge; those more likely to be at the disposal of particular individuals and those which we should with greater confidence expect to find in the possession of an authority made up of suitably chosen experts. If it is today so widely assumed that the latter will be in a better position, this is because one kind of knowledge, namely, scientific knowledge, occupies now so prominent a place in public imagination that we tend to forget that it is not the only kind that is relevant. It may be admitted that, so far as scientific knowledge is concerned, a body of suitably chosen experts may be in the best position to command all the best knowledge available—though this is of course merely shifting the difficulty to the problem of selecting the experts. What I wish to point out is that, even assuming that this problem can be readily solved, it is only a small part of the wider problem.

Today it is almost heresy to suggest that scientific knowledge is not the sum of all knowledge. But a little reflection will show that there is beyond question a body of very important but unorganized knowledge which cannot possibly be called scientific in the sense of knowledge of general rules: the knowledge of the particular circumstances of time and place. It is with respect to this that practically every individual has some advantage over all others in that he possesses unique information of which beneficial use might be made, but of which use can be made only if the decisions depending on it are left to him or are made with his active cooperation. We need to remember only how much we have to learn in any occupation after we have completed our theoretical training, how big a part of our working life we spend learning particular jobs, and how valuable an asset in all walks of life is knowledge of people, of local conditions, and special circumstances. To know of and put to use a machine not fully employed, or somebody's skill which could be better utilized, or to be aware of a surplus stock which can be drawn upon during an interruption of supplies, is socially quite as useful as the knowledge of better alternative techniques. And the shipper who earns his living from using otherwise empty or half-filled journeys of tramp-steamers, or the estate agent whose whole knowledge is almost exclusively one of temporary opportunities, or the *arbitrageur* who gains from local differences of commodity prices, are all performing eminently useful functions based on special knowledge of circumstances of the fleeting moment not known to others.

It is a curious fact that this sort of knowledge should today be generally regarded with a kind of contempt, and that anyone who by such knowledge gains an advantage over somebody better equipped with theoretical or technical knowledge is thought to have acted almost disreputably. To gain an advantage from better knowledge of facilities of communication or transport is sometimes regarded as almost dishonest, although it is quite as important that society make use of the best opportunities in this respect as in using the latest scientific discoveries. This prejudice has in a considerable measure affected the attitude toward commerce in general compared with that toward production. Even economists who regard themselves as definitely above the crude materialist fallacies of the past constantly commit the same mistake where activities directed toward the acquisition of such practical knowledge are concerned—apparently because in their scheme of things all such knowledge is supposed to be "given." The common idea now seems to be that all such knowledge should as a matter of course be readily at the command of everybody, and the reproach of irrationality leveled against the existing economic order is frequently based on the fact that it is not so available. This view disregards the fact that the method by which such knowledge can be made as widely available as possible is precisely the problem to which we have to find an answer.

IV

If it is fashionable today to minimize the importance of the knowledge of the particular circumstances of time and place, this is closely connected with the smaller importance which is now attached to change as such. Indeed, there are few points on which the assumptions made (usually only implicitly) by the "planners" differ from those of their opponents as much as with regard to the significance and frequency of changes which will make substantial alterations of production plans necessary. Of course, if detailed economic plans could be laid down for fairly long periods in advance and then closely adhered to, so that no further economic decisions of importance would be required, the task of drawing up a comprehensive plan governing all economic activity would appear much less formidable.

It is, perhaps, worth stressing that economic problems arise always and only in consequence of change. So long as things continue as before, or at least as they were expected to, there arise no new problems requiring a decision, no need to form a new plan. The belief that changes, or at least day-to-day adjustments, have become less important in modern times implies the contention that economic problems also have become less important. This belief in the decreasing importance of change is, for that reason, usually held by the same people who argue that the importance of economic considerations has been driven into the background by the growing importance of technological knowledge.

Is it true that, with the elaborate apparatus of modern production, economic decisions are required only at long intervals, as when a new factory is to be erected or a new process to be introduced? Is it true that, once a plant has been built, the rest is all more or less mechanical, determined by the character of the plant, and leaving little to be changed in adapting to the ever-changing circumstances of the moment?

The fairly widespread belief in the affirmative is not, so far as I can ascertain, borne out by the practical experience of the business man. In a competitive industry at any rate—and such an industry alone can serve as a test—the task of keeping cost from rising requires constant struggle, absorbing a great part of the energy of the manager. How easy it is for an inefficient manager to dissipate the differentials on which profitability rests, and that it is possible, with the same technical facilities, to produce with a great variety of costs, are among the commonplaces of business experience which do not seem to be equally familiar in the study of the economist. The very strength of the desire, constantly voiced by producers and engineers, to be able to proceed untrammeled by considerations of money costs, is eloquent testimony to the extent to which these factors enter into their daily work.

One reason why economists are increasingly apt to forget about the constant small changes which make up the whole economic picture is probably their growing preoccupation with statistical aggregates, which show a very much greater stability than the movements of the detail. The comparative stability of the aggregates cannot, however, be accounted for—as the statisticians seem occasionally to be inclined to do—by the "law of large numbers" or the mutual compensation of random changes. The number of elements with which we have to deal is not large enough for such accidental forces to produce stability. The continuous flow of goods and services is maintained by constant deliberate adjustments, by new dispositions made every day in the light of circumstances not known the day before, by B stepping in at once when A fails to deliver. Even the large and highly mechanized plant keeps going largely because of an environment upon which it can draw for all sorts of unexpected needs; tiles for its roof, stationery for its forms, and all the thousand and one kinds of equipment in which it cannot be self-contained and which the plans for the operation of the plant require to be readily available in the market.

This is, perhaps, also the point where I should briefly mention the fact that the sort of knowledge with which I have been concerned is knowledge of the kind which by its nature cannot enter into statistics and therefore cannot be conveyed to any central authority in statistical form. The statistics which such a central authority would have to use would have to be arrived at precisely by abstracting from minor differences between the things, by lumping together, as resources of one kind, items which differ as regards location, quality, and other particulars, in a way which may be very significant for the specific decision. It follows from this that central planning based on statistical information by its nature cannot take direct account of these circumstances of time and place and that the central planner will have to find some way or other in which the decisions depending on them can be left to the "man on the spot."

V

If we can agree that the economic problem of society is mainly one of rapid adaptation to changes in the particular circumstances of time and place, it would seem to follow that the ultimate decisions must be left to the people who are familiar with these circumstances, who know directly of the relevant changes and of the resources immediately available to meet them. We cannot expect that this problem will be solved by first communicating all this knowledge to a central board which, after integrating *all* knowledge, issues its orders. We must solve it by some form of decentralization. But this answers only part of our problem. We need decentralization because only thus can we ensure that the knowledge of the particular circumstances of time and place will be promptly used. But the "man on the spot" cannot decide solely on the basis of his limited but intimate knowledge of the facts of his immediate surroundings. There still remains the problem of communicating to him such further information as he needs to fit his decisions into the whole pattern of changes of the larger economic system.

How much knowledge does he need to do so successfully? Which of the events which happen beyond the horizon of his immediate knowledge are of relevance to his immediate decision, and how much of them need he know?

There is hardly anything that happens anywhere in the world that *might* not have an effect on the decision he ought to make. But he need not know of these events as such, nor of *all* their effects. It does not matter for him *why* at the particular moment more screws of one size than of another are wanted, *why* paper bags are more readily available than canvas bags, or *why* skilled labor, or particular machine tools, have for the moment become more difficult to acquire. All that is significant for him is *how much more or less* difficult to procure they have become compared with other things with which he is also concerned, or how much more or less urgently wanted are the alternative things he produces or uses. It is always a question of the relative importance of the particular things with which he is concerned, and the causes which alter their relative importance are of no interest to him beyond the effect on those concrete things of his own environment.

It is in this connection that what I have called the economic calculus proper helps us, at least by analogy, to see how this problem can be solved, and in fact is being solved, by the price system. Even the single controlling mind, in possession of all the data for some small, self-contained economic system, would not—every time some small adjustment in the al-location of resources had to be made—go explicitly through all the relations between ends and means which might possibly be affected. It is indeed the great contribution of the pure logic of choice that it has demonstrated conclusively that even such a single mind could solve this kind of problem only by constructing and constantly using rates of equivalence (or "values," or "marginal rates of substitution"), *i.e.*, by attaching to each kind of scarce resource a numerical index which cannot be derived from any property possessed by that particular thing, but which reflects, or in which is condensed, its significance in view of the whole means-end structure. In any small change he will have to consider only these quantitative indices (or "values") in which all the relevant information is concentrated; and, by adjusting the quantities one by one, he can appropriately rearrange his dispositions without having to solve the whole puzzle *ab initio*, or without needing at any stage to survey it at once in all its ramifications.

Fundamentally, in a system where the knowledge of the relevant facts is dispersed among many people, prices can act to coordinate the separate actions of different people in the same way as subjective values help the individual to coordinate the parts of his plan. It is worth contemplating for a moment a very simple and commonplace instance of the action of the price system to see what precisely it accomplishes. Assume that somewhere in the world a new opportunity for the use of some raw material, say, tin, has arisen, or that one of the sources of supply of tin has been eliminated. It does not matter for our purpose—and it is very significant that it does not matter—which of these two causes has made tin more scarce. All that the users of tin need to know is that some of the tin they used to consume is now more profitably employed elsewhere, and that, in consequence they must economize tin. There is no need for the great majority of them even to know where the more urgent need has arisen, or in favor of what other needs they ought to husband the supply. If only some of them know directly of the new demand, and switch resources over to it, and if the people who are aware of the new gap thus created in turn fill it from still other sources, the effect will rapidly spread throughout the whole economic system and influence not only all the uses of tin, but also those of its substitutes and the substitutes of these substitutes, the supply of all the things made of tin, and their substitutes, and so on; and all his without the great majority of those instrumental in bringing about these substitutions knowing anything at all about the original cause of these changes. The whole acts as one market, not because any of its members survey the whole field, but because their limited individual fields of vision sufficiently overlap so that through many intermediaries the relevant information is communicated to all. The mere fact that there is one price for any commodity—or rather that local prices are connected in a manner determined by the cost of transport, etc.—brings about the solution which (it is just conceptually possible) might have been arrived at by one single mind possessing all the information which is in fact dispersed among all the people involved in the process.

VI

We must look at the price system as such a mechanism for communicating information if we want to understand its real function—a function which, of course, it fulfils less perfectly as prices grow more rigid. (Even when quoted prices have become quite rigid, however, the forces which would operate through changes in price still operate to a considerable extent through changes in the other terms of the contract.) The most significant fact about this system is the economy of knowledge with which it operates, or how little the individual participants need to know in order to be able to take the right action. In abbreviated form, by a kind of symbol, only the most essential information is passed on, and passed on only to those concerned. It is more than a metaphor to describe the price system as a kind of machinery for registering change, or a system of telecommunications which enables individual producers to watch merely the movement of a few pointers, as an engineer might watch the hands of a few dials, in order to adjust their activities to changes of which they may never know more than is reflected in the price movement.

Of course, these adjustments are probably never "perfect" in the sense in which the economist conceives of them in his equilibrium analysis. But I fear that our theoretical habits of approaching the problem with the assumption of more or less perfect knowledge on the part of almost everyone has made us somewhat blind to the true function of the price mechanism and led us to apply rather misleading standards in judging its efficiency. The marvel is that in a case like that of a scarcity of one raw material, without an order being issued, without more than perhaps a handful of people knowing the cause, tens of thousands of people whose identity could not be ascertained by months of investigation, are made to use the material or its products more sparingly; *i.e.*, they move in the right direction. This is enough of a marvel even if, in a constantly changing world, not all will hit it off so perfectly that their profit rates will always be maintained at the same constant or "normal" level.

I have deliberately used the word "marvel" to shock the reader out of the complacency with which we often take the working of this mechanism for granted. I am convinced that if it were the result of deliberate human design, and if the people guided by the price changes understood that their decisions have significance far beyond their immediate aim, this mechanism would have been acclaimed as one of the greatest triumphs of the human mind. Its misfortune is the double one that it is not the product of human design and that the people guided by it usually do not know why they are made to do what they do. But those who clamor for "conscious direction"—and who cannot believe that anything which has evolved without design (and even without our understanding it) should solve problems which we should not be able to solve consciously—should remember this: The problem is precisely how to extend the span of our utilization of resources beyond the span of the control of any one mind; and, therefore, how to dispense with the need of conscious control and how to provide inducements which will make the individuals do the desirable things without anyone having to tell them what to do.

The problem which we meet here is by no means peculiar to economics but arises in connection with nearly all truly social phenomena, with language and most of our cultural inheritance, and constitutes really the central theoretical problem of all social science. As Alfred Whitehead has said in another connection, "It is a profoundly erroneous truism, repeated by all copy-books and by eminent people when they are making speeches, that we should cultivate the habit of thinking what we are doing. The precise opposite is the case. Civilization advances by extending the number of important operations which we can perform without thinking about them." This is of profound significance in the social field. We make constant use of formulas, symbols and rules whose meaning we do not understand and through the use of which we avail ourselves of the assistance of knowledge which individually we do not possess. We have developed these practices and institutions by building upon habits and institutions which have proved successful in their own sphere and which have in turn become the foundation of the civilization we have built up.

The price system is just one of those formations which man has learned to use (though he is still very far from having learned to make the best use of it) after he had stumbled upon it without understanding it. Through it not only a division of labor but also a coordinated utilization of resources based on an equally divided knowledge has become possible. The people who like to deride any suggestion that this may be so usually distort the argument by insinuating that it asserts that by some miracle just that sort of system has spontaneously grown up which is best suited to modern civilization. It is the other way round: man has been able to develop that division of labor on which our civilization is based because he happened to stumble upon a method which made it possible. Had he not done so he might still have developed some other, altogether different, type of civilization, something like the "state" of the termite ants, or some other altogether unimaginable type. All that we can say is that nobody has yet succeeded in designing an alternative system in which certain features of the existing one can be preserved which are dear even to those who most violently assail it—such as particularly the extent to which the individual can choose his pursuits and consequently freely use his own knowledge and skill.

VII

It is in many ways fortunate that the dispute about the indispensability of the price system for any rational calculation in a complex society is now no longer conducted entirely between camps holding different political views. The thesis that without the price system we could not preserve a society based on such extensive division of labor as ours was greeted with a howl of derision when it was first advanced by von Mises twenty-five years ago. Today the difficulties which some still find in accepting it are no longer mainly political, and this makes for an atmosphere much more conducive to reasonable discussion. When we find Leon Trotsky arguing that "economic accounting is unthinkable without market relations"; when Professor Oscar Lange promises Professor von Mises a statue in the marble halls of the future Central Planning Board; and when Professor Abba P. Lerner rediscovers Adam Smith and emphasizes that the essential utility of the price system consists in inducing the individual, while seeking his own interest, to do what is in the general interest, the differences can indeed no longer be ascribed to political prejudice.

The remaining dissent seems clearly to be due to purely intellectual, and more particularly methodological, differences.

A recent statement by Professor Joseph Schumpeter in his *Capitalism, Socialism, and Democracy* provides a clear illustration of one of the methodological differences which I have in mind. Its author is pre-eminent among those economists who approach economic phenomena in the light of a certain branch of positivism. To him these phenomena accordingly appear as objectively given quantities of commodities impinging directly upon each other, almost, it would seem, without any intervention of human minds. Only against this background can I account for the following (to me startling) pronouncement. Professor Schumpeter argues that the possibility of a rational calculation in the absence of markets for the factors of production follows for the theorist "from the elementary proposition that consumers in evaluating ('demanding') consumers' goods *ipso facto* also evaluate the means of production which enter into the production of these goods."[1]

Taken literally, this statement is simply untrue. The consumers do nothing of the kind. What Professor Schumpeter's *"ipso facto"* presumably means is that the valuation of the factors of production is implied in, or follows necessarily from, the valuation of consumers' goods. But this, too, is not correct. Implication is a logical relationship which can be meaningfully asserted only of propositions simultaneously present to one and the same mind. It is evident, however, that the values of the factors of production do not depend solely on the valuation of the consumers' goods but also on the conditions of supply of the various factors of production. Only to a mind to which all these facts were simultaneously known would the answer necessarily follow from the facts given to it. The practical problem, however, arises precisely because these facts are never so given to a single mind, and because, in consequence, it is necessary that in the solution of the problem knowledge should be used that is dispersed among many people.

---

1. J. Schumpeter, *Capitalism, Socialism, and Democracy* (New York; Harper, 1942), p. 175. Professor Schumpeter is, I believe, also the original author of the myth that Pareto and Barone have "solved" the problem of socialist calculation. What they, and many others, did was merely to state the conditions which a rational allocation of resources would have to satisfy, and to point out that these were essentially the same as the conditions of equilibrium of a competitive market. This is something altogether different from showing how the allocation of resources satisfying these conditions can be found in practice. Pareto himself (from whom Barone has taken practically everything he has to say), far from claiming to have solved the practical problem, in fact explicitly denies that it can be solved without the help of the market. See his *Manuel d'économie pure* (2d ed., 1927), pp. 233–34. The relevant passage is quoted in an English translation at the beginning of my article on "Socialist Calculation: The Competitive 'Solution,' " in *Economica*, New Series, Vol. VIII, No. 26 (May, 1940), p. 125.

The problem is thus in no way solved if we can show that all the facts, *if* they were known to a single mind (as we hypothetically assume them to be given to the observing economist), would uniquely determine the solution; instead we must show how a solution is produced by the interactions of people each of whom possesses only partial knowledge. To assume all the knowledge to be given to a single mind in the same manner in which we assume it to be given to us as the explaining economists is to assume the problem away and to disregard everything that is important and significant in the real world.

That an economist of Professor Schumpeter's standing should thus have fallen into a trap which the ambiguity of the term "datum" sets to the unwary can hardly be explained as a simple error. It suggests rather that there is something fundamentally wrong with an approach which habitually disregards an essential part of the phenomena with which we have to deal: the unavoidable imperfection of man's knowledge and the consequent need for a process by which knowledge is constantly communicated and acquired. Any approach, such as that of much of mathematical economics with its simultaneous equations, which in effect starts from the assumption that people's *knowledge* corresponds with the objective *facts* of the situation, systematically leaves out what is our main task to explain. I am far from denying that in our system equilibrium analysis has a useful function to perform. But when it comes to the point where it misleads some of our leading thinkers into believing that the situation which it describes has direct relevance to the solution of practical problems, it is high time that we remember that it does not deal with the social process at all and that it is no more than a useful preliminary to the study of the main problem.

The Soul of Classical Liberalism

JAMES M. BUCHANAN

... the bizarre fact that alone among the great political currents, liberalism has no ideology.

—Anthony de Jasay

During the ideologically dark days of the 1950s, my colleague Warren Nutter often referred to "saving the books" as the minimal objective of likeminded classical liberals. F. A. Hayek, throughout a long career, effectively broadened that objective to "saving the ideas." In a certain sense, both of these objectives have been achieved: the books are still being read, and the ideas are more widely understood than they were a half-century ago.

My thesis here is that, despite these successes, we have, over more than a century, failed to "save the soul" of classical liberalism. Books and ideas are, of course, necessary, but alone they are not sufficient to ensure the viability of effectively free societies.

I hope that my thesis provokes interest along several dimensions. I shall try to respond in advance to the obvious questions. What do I mean by the soul of classical liberalism? And what is intended when I say that there has been a failure to save that soul during the whole socialist epoch? Most important, what can, and should, be done now by those of us who call ourselves classical liberals?

James M. Buchanan, "The Soul of Classical Liberalism," from *The Independent Review: A Journal of Political Economy*, Vol. 5, No. 1; Summer 2000, pp. 111–119. Copyright © 2000 by The Independent Institute. Permission to reprint granted by the publisher.

The Soul of Classical Liberalism | 377

SCIENCE, SELF-INTEREST, AND SOUL

George Bush, sometime during his presidency, derisively referred to "that vision thing" when someone sought to juxtapose his position with that of his predecessor, Ronald Reagan. He meant the "shining city on a hill," the Puritan image that Reagan invoked to call attention to the American ideal; that image, and others like it, were foreign to Bush's whole mind-set. He simply did not understand what Reagan meant and totally failed to appreciate why the image resonated so successfully in public attitudes. In a sense, we can say that Ronald Reagan was tapping into and expressing a part of the American soul beyond George Bush's ken.

The example is helpful even if it applies to a specific, politically organized, temporally restricted, and territorially defined society. The critical distinction between those whose window on reality emerges from a comprehensive vision of what might be and those whose window is pragmatically limited to current sense perceptions is made clear in the comparison. We may extend and apply a similar comparison to the attitudes of and approaches taken by various spokesmen and commentators to the extended order of social interaction described under the rubric of classical liberalism.

Note that I do not go beyond those persons who profess adherence to the policy stances associated with the ideas emergent from within this framework, policy stances summarized as support for limited government, constitutional democracy, free trade, private property, rule of law, open franchise, and federalism. My focus is on the differences among these adherents, and specifically on the differences between those whose advocacy stems from an understanding of the very soul of the integrated ideational entity and those whose advocacy finds its origins primarily in the results of scientific inquiry and the dictates of enlightened self-interest.

The larger thesis is that classical liberalism, as a coherent set of principles, has not secured, and cannot secure, sufficient public acceptability when its vocal advocates are limited to the second group. Science and self-interest, especially as combined, do indeed lend force to any argument. But a vision of an ideal, over and beyond science and self-interest, is necessary, and those who profess membership in the club of classical liberals have failed singularly in their neglect of this requirement. Whether or not particular proponents find their ultimate motivations in such a vision is left for each, individually, to decide.

I have indirectly indicated the meaning of my title. Dictionary definitions of soul include "animating or vital principle" and "moving spirit," attributes that would seem equally applicable to persons and to philosophical perspectives. Perhaps it is misleading, however, to refer to "saving" the soul so defined, whether applied to a person or a perspective. Souls are themselves created rather than saved, and the absence of an animating principle implies only the presence of some potential for such creation rather than a latent actuality or spent force.

The work of Adam Smith, along with that of his philosophical predecessors and successors, created a comprehensive and coherent vision of an order of human interaction that seemed to be potentially approachable in reality, at least sufficiently so to offer the animating principle or moving spirit for constructive institutional change. At the same time, and precisely because it is and remains potentially rather than actually attainable, this vision satisfies a generalized human yearning for a supraexistent ideal. Classical liberalism shares this quality with its archrival, socialism, which also offers a comprehensive vision that transcends both the science and self-interest that its sometime advocates claimed as characteristic features. That is to say, both classical liberalism and socialism have souls, even if those motivating spirits are categorically and dramatically different.

Few would dispute the suggestion that an animating principle is central to the whole socialist perspective. But many professing classical liberals have seemed reluctant to acknowledge the existence of what I have called the soul of their position. They seem often to seek exclusive "scientific" cover for advocacy, supplementing it occasionally by reference to enlightened self-interest. They seem somehow to be embarrassed to admit, if indeed they even recognize the presence of, the underlying ideological appeal that classical liberalism as a comprehensive weltanschauung can possess. Although this aloof stance may offer some satisfaction to the individuals who qualify as cognoscenti, there is an opportunity loss in public acceptance as the central principles are promulgated to the nonscientific community.

EVERY MAN HIS OWN ECONOMIST

In this respect, political economists are plagued by the presence of the "every man his own economist" phenomenon. Scientific evidence, on its own, cannot be made convincing; it must be supplemented by persuasive argument that comes from the genuine conviction that can be possessed only by those who do understand the soul of classical liberalism. True, every man thinks of himself as his own economist, but every man also retains an inner yearning to become a participant in the imagined community, the virtual utopia, that embodies a set of abstract principles of order.

It is critically important to understand why classical liberalism needs what I call a soul, and why science and self-interest are not, in themselves, sufficient. Hard scientists, the physicists or the biologists, need not concern themselves with the public acceptability of the findings of their analyses and experiments. The public necessarily confronts natural reality, and to deny this immediately sensed reality is to enter the room of fools. We do not observe many persons trying to walk through walls or on water.

Also, and importantly, we recognize that we can utilize modern technological devices without any understanding of their souls, the organizing principles of their operation. I do not personally know or need to know the principle on which the computer allows me to put the words on the page.

Compare this stance of ignorance and awed acceptance before the computer with that of an ordinary participant in the economic nexus. The latter may, of course, simply respond to opportunities confronted, as buyer, seller, or entrepreneur, without so much as questioning the principles of the order of interaction that generates such opportunities. At another level of consciousness, however, the participant must recognize that this order is, in itself, artifactual, that it emerges from human choices made within a structure that must somehow be subject to deliberative change through human action. And even if a person might otherwise remain quiescent about the structure within which he carries out his ordinary affairs, he will everywhere be faced with pervasive reminders offered by political agitators and entrepreneurs motivated by their own self-interest.

It is only through an understanding of and appreciation for the animating principles of the extended order of market interaction that an individual who is not directly self-interested may refrain from expressive political action that becomes the equivalent of efforts to walk through walls or on water (for example, support for minimum wage laws, rent controls, tariffs, quotas, restrictive licensing, price supports, or monetary inflation). For the scientist in the academy, understanding such principles does, or should, translate into reasoned advocacy of classical liberal policy stances. But, for the reasons noted, the economic scientists by themselves do not possess either the formal or the informal authority to impose on others what may seem to be only their own opinions. Members of the body politic, the citizenry at large, must also be brought into the ranks. And they cannot, or so it seems to me, become sophisticated economic scientists, at least in large enough numbers. The expectation that the didactic skills of the academic disciplinarians in economics would make scientists of the intelligentsia, the "great unwashed," or all those in between was an expectation grounded in a combination of hubris and folly.

WHEN POLITICAL ECONOMY LOST ITS SOUL

What to do? This challenge remains even after the manifest collapse of socialism in our time. And it is in direct response to this challenge that I suggest invoking the soul of classical liberalism, an aesthetic-ethical-ideological potential attractor, one that stands independent of ordinary science, both below the latter's rigor and above its antiseptic neutrality.

I am admittedly in rhetorical as well as intellectual difficulty here, as I try to articulate my intuitively derived argument. Perhaps I can best proceed by historical reference. Classical political economy, in the early decades of the nineteenth century, particularly in England, did capture the minds of many persons who surely did not qualify even as amateur scientists in the still-developing science of economics. The "soul" of classical liberalism somehow came through to provide a vision of social order that was sufficient to motivate support for major institutional reform. The repeal of the Corn Laws changed the world.

After midcentury, however, the soul or spirit of the movement seems to have lost its way. The light did not fail in any manner akin to the collapse of the socialist ideal in our time. But the light of classical liberalism was dimmed, put in the shadows, by the emergent attraction of socialism. From the middle of the nineteenth century onward, classical liberals retreated into a defensive posture, struggling continuously against the reforms promulgated by utilitarian dreamers who claimed superior wisdom in discovering routes to aggregate happiness, as aided and abetted by the Hegel-inspired political idealists, who transferred personal realization to a collective psyche and away from the individual. The soul of socialism, even in contradiction to scientific evidence, was variously successful in capturing adherents to schemes for major institutional transformation.

VISION AND "SOCIAL" PURPOSE

What I have called the soul of a public philosophy is necessarily embedded in an encompassing vision of a social order of human interaction—a vision of that which might be, and which as such offers the ideal that motivates support for constructive change. The categorical difference between the soul of classical liberalism and that of socialism is located in the nature of the ideal and the relation of the individual to the collective. The encompassing vision that informs classical liberalism is described by an interaction of persons and groups within a rule-bound set of behavioral norms that allow each person or agent to achieve internally defined goals that are mutually achievable by all participants. And, precisely because those goals are internal to the consciousness of those who make choices and take actions, the outcomes produced are not either measurable or meaningful as "social" outcomes. There is, and can be, no social or collective purpose to be expected from the process of interaction; only private purposes are realized, even under the idealized operation of the structure and even if collectivized institutions may be instruments toward such achievements. To lay down a "social" purpose, even as a target, is to contradict the principle of liberalism itself, the principle that leaves each participant free to pursue whatever it is that remains feasible within the limits of the legal-institutional parameters.

The soul about which I am concerned here does involve a broad, and simple, understanding of the logic of human interaction in an interlinked chain of reciprocal exchanges among persons and groups. As noted previously, however, this logical understanding need not be scientifically sophisticated. It must, however, be basic understanding accompanied by a faith, or normative belief, in the competence of individuals to make their own choices based on their own valuation of the alternatives they confront. Can a person properly share the soul of classical liberalism without sharing the conviction that values emerge only from individuals? In some ultimate sense, is classical liberalism compatible with any transcendental ordering of values? My answer is no, but I also recognize that a reconciliation of sorts can be effected by engaging in epistemological games.

Classical liberals themselves have added confusion rather than clarity to the discussion when they have advanced the claim that the idealized and extended market order produces a larger "bundle" of valued goods than any socialist alternative. To invoke the efficiency norm in so crude a fashion as this, even conceptually, is to give away the whole game.

Almost all of us are guilty of this charge, because we know, of course, that the extended market does indeed produce the relatively larger bundle, by any measure. But attention to any aggregative value scale, even as modified to Adam Smith's well-being of the poorer classes or to John Rawls's share for the least advantaged, conceals the uniqueness of the liberal order in achieving the objective of individual liberty. To be sure, we can play good defense even in the socialists' own game. But by so doing we shift our own focus to that game rather than our own, which we as classical liberals must learn to play on our own terms, as well as getting others involved. Happily, a few modern classical liberals are indeed beginning to redraw the playing fields as they introduce comparative league tables that place emphasis on measuring liberty.

HEAT AND LIGHT

As I recall, it was A. C. Pigou, the founder of neoclassical welfare economics, who remarked that the purpose of economics and economists was that of providing heat rather than light, presumably to citizens-consumers as ultimate users. What I understood Pigou to be saying was that the economist's role is strictly functional, like the roles of dentists, plumbers, or mechanics, and that we could scarcely expect either ourselves or others to derive aesthetic pleasure from what we do. He seemed to be suggesting that nothing in economics can generate the exhilaration consequent upon revelation of inner truths.

Empirically, and unfortunately, Pigou may have been correct, especially in relation to the political economy and economists of the twentieth century. The discipline as practiced and promulgated has been drained of its potential capacity to offer genuine intellectual adventure and excitement in the large. This characteristic was only partially offset during the decades of the Cold War, when the continuing challenge of socialism offered Hayek and a relatively small number of his peers a motivation deeper and more comprehensive than that of the piddling puzzle-solving that economics has become. Absent the socialist challenge, what might evoke a sense of encompassing and generalized understanding? And, further, what may be required to bring forth such a sense in those who, themselves, can never be enrolled among the ranks of the professionally trained scientists?

Let me return to Ronald Reagan and his "shining city on a hill." What was the foundational inspiration that motivated that metaphor for an idealized American society? Reagan could not solve the simultaneous equations of general-equilibrium economics. But he carried with him a vision of a social order that might be an abstraction but which embodied elements that contained more light than heat. This vision, or that of classical liberalism generally, is built on the central, and simple, notion that "we can all be free." Adam Smith's "simple system of natural liberty," even if only vaguely understood, can enlighten the spirit, can create a soul that generates a coherence, a unifying philosophical discipline, that brings order to an internal psyche that might otherwise remain confused.

A motivating element is, of course, the individual's desire for liberty from the coercive power of others—an element that may be almost universally shared. But a second element is critically important: the absence of desire to exert power over others. In a real sense, the classical liberal stands in opposition to Thomas Hobbes, who modeled persons as universal seekers of personal power and authority. But Hobbes failed, himself, to share the liberal vision; he failed to understand that an idealized structure of social interaction is possible in which no person exerts power over another. In the idealized operation of an extended market order, each person confronts a costless exit option in each market, thereby eliminating totally any discretionary power of anyone with whom such a person might exchange. Coercion by another person is drained out; individuals are genuinely "at liberty."

Of course, this characterization is an idealization of any social order that might exist. But, as an ideal, such an imagined order can offer the exciting and normatively relevant prospect of a world in which all participants are free to choose.

Much has been made of the American spirit or soul as influenced by the availability of the territorial frontier during the first century of the United States' historical experience. Why was the frontier important? The proper economic interpretation of frontier lies in its guarantee of an exit option, the presence of which dramatically limits the potential for interpersonal exploitation. There has been a general failure to recognize that the effectively operating market order acts in precisely the same way as the frontier; it offers each participant exit options in each relationship.

The classical liberal can be philosophically self-satisfied, because he has seen the light, because he has come to understand the underlying principle of the social order that might be. It is not at all surprising that those who seem to express the elements of the soul of classical liberalism best are those who have experienced genuine conversion from the socialist vision. I entitled my lecture in the Trinity University series "Born Again Economist."[1] In that lecture I tried to summarize my experience in 1946 at the University of Chicago, where exposure to the teachings of Frank Knight and Henry Simons converted me to classical liberalism from the ranks of flaming socialism, and in a hurry. For me, there was light not heat on offer at Chicago. I cannot, personally, share in an experience that does not include the creation of my classical liberal soul. I remain puzzled by how it would feel never to have seen the light, to have understood all along what the liberal vision embodies but without the excitement of the experience.

---

1 "Born Again Economist," in *Lives of the Laureates: Ten Nobel Economists*, edited by William Breit (Cambridge, Mass.: MIT Press, 1990), pp. 163–80.

CONSTITUTIONALISM AGAIN

A necessary critical step is to draw back from a stance of active advocacy in the discussion of policy alternatives as confronted in ordinary politics. There is, of course, a liberal position on almost any of the alternatives. But classical liberals do, indeed, "get their hands dirty" when they engage with the policy wonks within the political game as played. Again, the distraction of debate works against focus on the inclusive structure—"the constitution"—within which the debates are allowed to take place and from which decisions are forthcoming.

Political "victory" on a detail of legislative policy (for example, rent control) or even electoral success by those who, to an extent, espouse the relevant principles (for example, Thatcher or Reagan) is likely to produce an illusion that classical liberalism, as an underlying philosophical basis for understanding, informs public attitudes. Classical liberals who do have an appreciation of the soul of the whole two-century enterprise quite literally went to sleep during the decade of the 1980s, especially after the death of socialism both in idea and in practice. The nanny-state, paternalist, mercantilist, rent-seeking regimes in which we now live emerged from the vacuum in political philosophy.

The task of the political economist as classical liberal is not that of demonstrating specifically to the citizenry that coercively imposed price and wage controls cause damages that exceed any possible benefits. Of course, such specific demonstration is strictly within recognized competence. But a distinction must be made between exemplary use of the analysis and its use merely as a contribution to the ongoing political argument.

I am not suggesting that attention should be limited to the design and presentation of all-inclusive political packages whose implementation would amount to major and dramatic changes in the basic constitutional structure. Politics, for the most part, proceeds in a piecemeal fashion. What I am suggesting is that the relevant arguments in support of particular proposals for change are those that emphasize conformity with the *integrating philosophy of the liberal order*, that locate the proposals in the larger context of the *constitution of liberty* rather than in some pragmatic utilitarian calculus. The italicized words, which served as the title of F. A. Hayek's magnum opus, call to mind Hayek's own behavior. To my knowledge, Hayek did not engage his intellectual enemies, whether in America, Britain, Austria, or Germany, on particular policy matters. Instead, his emphasis was always on grounding the arguments in an internally coherent philosophical position. In effect, Hayek was, from the outset, engaged in constitutional dialogue.

In establishing the Mont Pelerin Society in 1947, Hayek called for a return to first principles, for a renewed discourse in political philosophy—a discourse that would preserve and recreate what we may properly call the soul of classical liberalism.

The organizational and intellectual bankruptcy of socialism in our time has not removed the relevance of the Hayekian imperative. At a certain level, the public and the intellectual elites may indeed now possess a somewhat better abstract understanding of the organizing principles of extended market order. Hayek and other classical liberals have "saved the ideas." But an awesome gap continues to separate such abstract and generalized understanding from philosophical coherence in practical political reform. There must emerge a public awareness of the continuing relevance of the limits of collective action, even in the absence of any integrated ideological thrust toward social control.

If politics is allowed to become little more than a commons on which competing coalitions seek mutual exploitation, potential value is destroyed and liberty is lost just as surely as in the rigidities of misguided efforts at collective command. Who, indeed, can be expected to be motivated to support such "politics as competition for the commons"? Where is the dream? Perhaps resurrection of the soul of classical liberalism is beyond realistic hopes for the twenty-first century. But those of us who think that we have glimpsed the shining city have a moral obligation to proceed as if that society, of which Adam Smith, James Madison, and F. A. Hayek (and, yes, Ronald Reagan) dreamed, can become reality.

ACKNOWLEDGMENTS

A previous version of this article was presented at the Mont Pelerin Society Regional Meeting, Potsdam, Germany, October 1999. A revised and shortened version was published as "Saving the Soul of Classical Liberalism," *Wall Street Journal*, January 1, 2000, p. 29. I am indebted to Yong J. Yoon for helpful comments.

CHAPTER 7

✣

EQUALITY AND MUTUAL ADVANTAGE

Are Freedom and Equality Compatible?

G. A. COHEN

The first man who, having enclosed a piece of land, took it into his head to say, 'This is mine', and found people simple enough to believe him, was the true founder of civil society. The human race would have been spared endless crimes, wars, murders, and horrors if someone had pulled up the stakes or filled in the ditch and cried out to his fellow men, 'Do not listen to this impostor! You are lost if you forget that the fruits of the earth belong to everyone, and the earth to no one!'

—Jean-Jacques Rousseau, *Discourse on Inequality*

I INTRODUCTION

Two kinds of response to Nozick were contrasted in Chapter 3. In the first, a premiss that equality of condition is morally mandatory is used to reject his starting point, the thesis of self-ownership. But this first response (so I claimed) has the defect that the idea of self-ownership enjoys an initial appeal which so swiftly derived a rejection of it will not undermine. (In Chapter 10 I hope to undermine it in the more painstaking way that I think is necessary.)

In light of the poverty of that first response, a second response was projected (see Chapter 3, p. 71), which proceeds in two stages. First, it is shown that self-ownership does not justify an inegalitarian scramble for raw worldly resources: this first stage of the second response was completed, with success, in Chapter 3. The second stage of the

G. A. Cohen, "Are Freedom and Equality Compatible?," from *Policy: A Journal of Public Policy and Ideas*, Vol. 19, No. 3; Spring 2003, pp. 92–115. Copyright © 1995 by Cambridge University Press. Permission to reprint granted by the publisher.

projected response is pursued in the present chapter. Here, once again, equality of condition is not put as a premiss, and the principle of self-ownership is not rejected, on that or any other basis. Instead, one strives to reconcile self-ownership with equality (or not too much inequality) of condition, by constructing an economic constitution which combines self-ownership with an egalitarian approach to raw worldly resources. The strategy is to concede to libertarianism its attractive thesis, which is its assertion of each person's rights over his own being and powers, while attacking its implausible one, which is its view of the original moral relationship between people and things, the moral relationship, that is, between people and things which have not as yet been acted on by people.

The desired economic constitution respects both self-ownership and equality of worldly resources. Any such constitution would be opposed both by Nozick and other entitlement theorists on the one hand, and by John Rawls and Ronald Dworkin on the other. For both ranges of theorists are unwilling to distinguish as sharply as the stated strategy does between the moral status of ownership of external resources and the moral status of ownership of persons. Nozick endows people's claims to legitimately acquired external resources with the moral quality that belongs, so he believes, to people's ownership of themselves, and Rawls and Dworkin treat people's personal powers as subject, albeit with important qualifications,[1] to the same egalitarian principles of distribution that they apply, less controversially, to external wherewithal. The suggested intermediate position, to be reflected in the desired constitution, is with Nozick and against Rawls and Dworkin in its affirmation (or at least non-denial) of self-ownership, but with Rawls and Dworkin and against Nozick in subjecting the distribution of non-human resources to egalitarian appraisal.

One conclusion of this chapter is that no constitution that is truly intermediate in the described sense is capable of ensuring equality of condition. It follows that the two-stage response to Nozick rehearsed in the second paragraph of this chapter is not, in fact, a viable one. An intermediate constitution would preserve self-ownership but equalize rights in worldly resources. The present chapter examines two ways of achieving that latter equalization. One is by placing all external resources under the joint ownership of everyone in society, with each having a veto over what is to be done with them. That regime, together with self-ownership, indeed ensures equality of condition, but the joint ownership element deprives the self-ownership with which it is combined of its intended effect, which is the provision of autonomous self-governance. For people can do (virtually) nothing without using parts of the external world. If, then, they require the leave of the community to use it, then, effectively (as opposed to formally, or juridically), they do not own themselves, since they can do nothing

---

1   Rawls and Dworkin assert a certain sovereignty of persons over themselves in their affirmation of political and other liberties, such as choice of career, and granting those liberties has distributive implications. nothing without communal authorization. Accordingly, no constitution that prescribes this first way of equalizing rights in external resources is truly intermediate.

without communal authorization. Accordingly, no constitution that prescribes this first way of equalizing rights in external resources is truly intermediate.

But, if the contrast between effective and merely formal self-ownership upsets the described attempt to design an intermediate constitution, it also generates a serious problem for libertarians. For the propertyless proletarian who cannot use means of production without a capitalist's leave suffers a lack of effective self-ownership. It follows, as I argue in section 6 below, that, since libertarians regard proletarianhood as consistent with all the rights that they think people have, the self-ownership that they defend is much thinner and far less attractive than it appears, at first sight, to be.

Another way of equalizing rights in external resources is by distributing an equal amount of them to each person. Then each, if self-owning, could do with his share as he pleases. This yields a truly intermediate constitution, at any rate initially, but one that, I argue, fails to secure the equality of condition that socialists prize. I conclude that socialists must reject self-ownership, and I show how to reject it in Chapter 10.

II RETURNS TO ABILITY AND INABILITY UNDER JOINT OWNERSHIP

2. In Chapter 3, I questioned Nozick's blithe assumption that 'virgin' things may be regarded as quite unowned and therefore (virtually) up for grabs; one scarcely need share that assumption even if one accepts that people are full owners of themselves. Now, a radical alternative to the view that things are, in their native state, quite unowned, is to regard them as jointly or collectively owned by all persons. In this section, I study an attempt to combine such a conception of the original moral relationship between people and things with the principle of self-ownership. I inquire into the upshot of uniting self-ownership with joint ownership of the external world, with a view to shedding some light on the distributive effect of self-ownership in a world whose parts are not open to unilateral privatization.

For the sake of simplicity, imagine a society of two people, who are called Able and Infirm, after their respective natural endowments. Each owns himself and both jointly own everything else. (It is immaterial, here, how these rules of ownership are enforced. We can imagine that a suitably powerful external authority (e.g., God) enforces them.) With suitable external resources, Able can produce life-sustaining and life-enhancing good, but Infirm has no productive power at all. We suppose that each is rational, self-interested, and mutually disinterested (devoid, that is, of spite, benevolence, and all other motivations into which the welfare of others enters essentially),[2] and we ask what scheme of production and distribution they will agree on. We thereby investigate the reward which self-owned ability would command in one kind of world without private property.

---

2   The point of these familiar stipulations is to trace what reflects the structure of rights as such, apart from special generosity or malice.

Now, what Able and Infirm get depend not only on their own powers and decisions but also on what the world is like, materially speaking. Five mutually exclusive and jointly exhaustive possible material situations, not all of which are interesting, may readily be distinguished:

i. Able cannot produce per day what is needed for one person for a day, so Able and Infirm both die.

ii. Able can produce enough or more than enough for one person, but not enough for two. Infirm lets Able produce what he can, since only spite or envy would lead him not to.[3] Able lives and Infirm dies.

iii. Able can produce just enough to sustain both himself and Infirm. So Infirm forbids him to produce unless he produces that much. Able consequently does, and both live at subsistence.

iv. If Able produces at all, then the amount he produces is determined independently of his choice, and it exceeds what is needed to sustain both Able and Infirm. They therefore bargain over the distribution of a fixed surplus. The price of failure to agree (the 'threat point') is no production, and, therefore, death for both.

v. Again, Able can produce a surplus, but now, more realistically, he can vary its size, so that Able and Infirm will bargain not only, as in (iv), over who gets how much, but also over how much will be produced.

The interesting cases are (iv) and (v), in which bargains will be struck[4] It is a controversial question, in the relevant philosophical and economic literature, what one should expect the outcome of such bargaining to be. But it seems clear that the inputs to the bargaining process will be the utility functions of Able and Infirm, including the disutility of labour for Able and the disutility of infirmity for Infirm. What will matter, in other and less technical words, is their preferences, what they like and dislike, and how much. And the crucial point is that Able's talent will not, just as such, affect how much he gets. If the exercise of his talent is irksome to him, then he will indeed get additional compensation, but only because he is irked, not because it is his labour which irks him. In short, he gets nothing extra just because it is he, and not Infirm, who does the producing. Infirm controls one necessary condition of production (relaxing his veto over use of the land), and Able controls two, but that gives Able no bargaining advantage. If a good costs $101, and you have one hundred of the dollars and I only one of them, then, if we are both rational

---

3   Alternatively, and on the assumption that each must eat in the evening to be alive the next day. Infirm allows Able to work for a day on condition that, at the end of it, a lottery decides who gets the food. If Infirm wins. Able dies and Infirm lives one day more than he would if Able wins (and then lives out his span).

4   I am supposing that it is not open to Able to wait until Infirm dies in order to become the sole owner of everything: assume that he would himself die no later than Infirm does in the absence of production. (Recall that the land is jointly owned, so that production by Able requires Infirm's permission.)

and self-interested, you will not get a greater share of the good if we buy it jointly just because you supply so much more of what is required to obtain it.

Here, then, joint world ownership prevents self-ownership from generating an inequality to which egalitarians would object. And, while the Able and Infirm story is an extremely special one in several respects, the particular point that talent as such yields no extra reward even under self-ownership where there is also joint ownership of external resources is, I believe, generalizable. (I do not say that no inequality repugnant to egalitarians can arise in the Able/Infirm situation, but only that either there will be no such inequality, or its source will not be Able's ownership of his own powers, but the influence of the parties' utility functions on the outcome of the bargaining process. One cannot guarantee that no inequality repugnant to egalitarians will arise, if only because different egalitarians favour different equalities, and it is extremely unlikely that all of them will emerge from the bargaining process.)

3. In section 41 shall describe a seemingly fatal objection to the argument of section 2, and one from which, as I try to show in section 6, we can learn a great deal. But here, somewhat digressively, I develop a relatively minor objection to the argument, and one which is rather difficult to assess, because of controversial questions about the concept of rationality.

The objection questions the claim that self-ownership has no unequalizing effect in a jointly owned world. The following model may be used to develop the objection.

Consider two sets of equally able fanners. Members of the first set, the Joint fanners, own all the land jointly. Members of the second set, the Mixed fanners, each own some land privately, in varying amounts, but in no case enough to live off, and they also jointly own a further tract of land Land fertility is such that the material position for each set of farmers is a multi-person version of either (iv) or (v) of section 2: more than enough to keep everyone alive is available, if all the farmers work all the soil. If I am right in section 2, then the upshots of bargaining among Joint and among Mixed farmers should be identical whenever production possibilities are the same in the two cases, because private ownership of tracts of land insufficient to sustain life confers no more bargaining leverage than private ownership of nothing but talent alone does, where the rest of what is required for life-sustaining production is jointly owned.

The objection is that a Mixed farmer could threaten to destroy (part of) his private plot, whereas no one can threaten to destroy anything which is held jointly. If such threats would be credible, then it seems that privately well-endowed Mixed farmers could assert leverage over their privately less well-endowed cousins. And, if they could do so, then so could Able in the case, not excluded above, in which he has it in his power to let (part of) his talent decay. What is unclear, because of difficulties in the concept of rationality, is whether such a Schellingian[5] threat would be credible, and, therefore, effective, under the assumption that everyone is rational. If it would be, then those with greater power

---

5   See Thomas Schelling, *Strategy of Conflict.*

to produce could get more in a jointly owned world for reasons which go beyond the consideration that their labour might be irksome to them.

But this objection to the argument of section 2 is, as I said, relatively minor, even if it is sound. One reason why it is minor is that it achieves purchase only in the rather peculiar case in which Able can indeed diminish his own productive power. But a more important reason for considering the objection secondary is that no libertarian would want to defeat the Able/Infirm argument (for the consistency of equality and self-ownership) on so adventitious a basis. He would want, instead, to overcome it by pressing the more fundamental objection to which I now turn.

4. Whatever should be said about the objection of section 3, there remains a deeper and seemingly fatal objection to the lesson drawn in section 2 from the Able/Infirm story. That lesson is that, without denying self-ownership, and without affirming equality of condition as an underived principle, one may move towards a form of equality of condition by insisting on joint ownership of the external world. And the seemingly fatal objection is that to affirm joint ownership of the world is, as the story of Able and Infirm might be thought to show, inconsistent with achieving the purpose and expected effect of self-ownership. What is the point of my owning myself if I can do nothing without the agreement of others? Do not Able and Infirm jointly own not only the world but also, in effect, each other? Would they not bargain exactly as they do if, instead of being self-owning, each was jointly owned by both? Does not joint world ownership entitle a person to prohibit another's wholly harmless use of an external resource, such as taking some water from a superabundant stream,[6] and is it not, therefore, inconsistent with the most minimal effective self-ownership (and independently indefensible to boot)? It looks as though the suggested form of external resource equality, namely, joint world ownership, renders nugatory the self-ownership with which we had hoped to combine it. Self-ownership is not eliminated, but it is rendered useless, rather as it is useless to own a corkscrew when you are forbidden access to bottles of wine.

There are two possible replies to the objection that self-ownership is useless when it is combined with joint ownership of the world. The first, which is explored in section 5, is to argue that joint world ownership does not, in fact, deprive self-ownership of all use, since, to put the point crudely, economics isn't everything. The second reply, which I regard as both correct and very important, and which is mounted in section 6, is to accept that joint world ownership renders self-ownership merely formal, while showing that present polemical purposes do not require it to be anything more than that.

5. The first reply says that people have vital interests in matters other than production and the distribution of its fruits, matters on which joint world ownership might have no, or only a reduced, bearing. It would then be false that joint world ownership would render individual self-ownership useless.

---

6   See Chapter 3, p. 77 above.

But this reply seems to be incompatible with the fact that all human action requires space, which is jointly owned if the world is.[7] (Even the mental activity of an immobile agent requires the space he occupies.) Or, if that is thought far-fetched, then consider, instead, that all human action requires nourishment, which requires food, which comes from the external world. It seems to follow that collective control over what anyone may do with the external world affects every department of life, and not just the domain of production. It looks, indeed, as though joint world ownership fully determines the entire outcome, whatever may be laid down officially about who owns whose powers.[8]

There is, perhaps, one 'action' which could be performed without the permission of others in a jointly owned world as long as there is self-ownership, and possibly not without it, namely, letting oneself die: in the absence of self-ownership one has noncontractual obligations which might forbid letting oneself die. (I speak of letting oneself die rather than of (other forms of) suicide, since active suicide might require external resources, and letting oneself die is achieved by refraining from using any.) But even this suggestion may be incorrect, since the world's joint owners might be thought to have the right to forbid one to die on the ground, for example, that one's dead body might pollute some of the world's resources.

6. But now let us recall our polemical task, which is to address Robert Nozick's contention that honouring people's self-ownership requires extending to them a freedom to live their own lives which is incompatible with the equality of condition prized by socialists. The recently suggested response to that contention was that self-ownership is, contrary to what Nozick says, compatible with equality of condition, since the inequality which Nozick defends depends on adjoining to self-ownership an inegalitarian principle of external resource distribution, which need not be accepted. When, instead, self-ownership is combined with joint ownership of the world, its tendency to generate inequality is removed.

The section 4 objection to that response was that the resource distribution under joint world ownership renders the self-ownership with which it is officially combined merely formal. But that objection would, for immediate polemical purposes, be laid to rest, if it

---

7   On the importance of space as a resource, see my *Karl Marx's Theory of History*, pp. 50–2. For strong claims about the relationship between freedom and rights over space, see H.M. Steiner, "Individual Liberty," pp. 44.

8   If, that is, the joint world ownership is itself substantive rather than merely official. For consider a regime in which a person A owns both himself and everyone else, with all other resources being in joint ownership. Then either that joint ownership remains substantive (because A's ownership of everyone is substantively consistent with the exercise of rights over things), in which case the statement in the text applies; or the joint world ownership itself lacks substance (because all 'rights' over things by owned persons belong, substantially, to the owner of those persons). I provisionally conclude, pending further possible counter-examples, that joint world ownership fully determines the outcome, rendering other provisions merely official, except for the case, if there is one, where it is itself merely official.

could be shown that the self-ownership defended by Nozick is itself merely formal, for he could not then maintain that self-ownership necessitates inequality of condition (since the Able/Infirm model shows that merely formal self-ownership does not do that).

To be sure, Nozick would like us to think, what he evidently himself thinks, that the self-ownership which he favours is more than merely formal. In Chapter III of Anarchy, State, and Utopia he pleads that each person should be free to live his own life, a desideratum which is supposed to be secured by the rights constituting Nozickian self-ownership.[9] But Nozick also thinks that the most abject proletarian—call him Z[10]—who must either sell his labour power to a capitalist or die, enjoys the relevant rights.[11] And if that is so, then Nozick could not object that Able's self-ownership is merely formal, since, whether or not it is indeed merely formal, it is not less consequential than Z's.

If Able and Z lack self-ownership, in an effective sense, then that is because neither can do anything without the agreement of Infirm and the capitalist, respectively. But they are, nevertheless, different from chattel slaves. For while each can do nothing without another's agreement, it is also true that there is nothing which either need do without his own agreement: neither Infirm nor the capitalist has rights of sheer command that are not grounded in a prior contract to obey. By contrast, the slave's master may unilaterally determine what the slave must do.

The resulting dilemma for Nozick is severe. Either capitalism does not confer consequential self-ownership, since Z's self-ownership is not robust enough to qualify as such; or, if it does so qualify, then genuine self-ownership allows the enforcement of equality of condition, since Able's self-ownership is at least as robust as Z's, and no inequality follows from self-ownership in the Able/Infirm world.

Notice, moreover, that both Able and Infirm are in one respect far better placed than Z is. For each of Able and Infirm must strike an agreement with the other in order to survive, and, since both are rational and self-interested, it follows that the survival of each is assured (in a world abundant enough to sustain two people on the labour of one). By contrast, no capitalist need strike an agreement with Z in order to survive,[12] and Z's very survival is, therefore, not guaranteed.

To put the main point differently: Nozick says that a propensity to inequality is unavoidable when people are allowed to live their own lives. Yet he must hold that, despite

---

9 See *Anarchy*, pp. 28–35 (on side constraints) and pp. 42–5, 48–51 (on leading one's own life).

10 After ibid., pp. 262–4.

11 Z is abject because he owns no private property, and he will therefore contract, on adverse terms, with someone who does own some, if he can find a propertied person willing to contract with him. His predicament might be thought dire, but Nozick does not think that he has (in general) a just grievance: see Chapter 3 above, pp. 85–6.

12 Some would question this contrast between the capitalist and the worker. I defend it in section 13 of Chapter 13 ('The Structure of Proletarian Unfreedom') of *History, Labour and Freedom*.

the constraints on his life choices, and despite his adverse power position vis-a-vis others, Z leads his own life. But it then follows that Nozick is wrong that, when people lead their own lives, equality of condition cannot be guaranteed, since Able and Infirm lead their own lives at least as much as Z does, and the constitution under which they live guarantees a certain equality of condition.[13]

I have said (see Chapter 3, p. 70 above) that it is a strength in Nozick's position that the thesis of self-ownership is inherently appealing. But what exactly, we should now ask, possesses appeal for us? What, in this conceptual region, do we feel moved to insist that people should enjoy? Is it (i) self-ownership as such, the bare bourgeois freedom which distinguishes the most abject proletarian from a slave; or is it (ii) the more substantive circumstance of control over one's life? If (i) is the right answer, then we win both the polemic against Nozick and the larger struggle to reconcile socialist equality with liberty. But I think that most of us believe that people should have more effective sovereignty over themselves than either Able or the proletarian enjoy. This does not, of course, rescue Nozick. On the contrary: whereas it seemed that it was a virtue in libertarianism that it affirms self-ownership, it now turns out that self-ownership as such, in the absence of further enfranchisement, has no special attraction. But it is also true, for similar reasons, that socialists should not favour joint world ownership. They must seek another way of achieving equality of condition, one that supports greater autonomy than joint world ownership allows.

We can now draw three conclusions. First, the tale of Able and Infirm shows that strict socialist equality is compatible with the freedom that defenders of capitalism boast that everyone has in capitalist society, since that freedom is nothing more than formal self-ownership, and formal self-ownership obtains in the world of Able and Infirm.

Second, although it indeed turns out that the freedom of which Nozick speaks can be reconciled with equality, that is only because it is a very confined freedom, and it remains to be shown that equality can be reconciled with a freedom more worthy of the name.

Such freedom—and this is the third conclusion—is not self-ownership, but autonomy, the circumstance of genuine control over one's own life. Universal self-ownership with the world up for grabs fails to ensure autonomy, since it tends to produce proletarians, who lack it. Universal self-ownership does not, indeed, produce proletarians when it is conjoined with joint ownership of external resources, but the latter breaches autonomy in a different way. I shall argue, later, that the right conclusion is that, for real freedom, or autonomy, to prevail, there have to be restrictions on self-ownership,[14] and that is ironical, since it is autonomy that attracts us to self-ownership, through a disastrous misidentification. The very thing that makes the self-ownership thesis attractive should actually make

---

13 For a challenge to the parallel between Able and Z, see Jan Narveson, *The Libertarian Idea*, pp. 71–3. For excellent defence of it, see Grant Brown, review of Narveson's book, pp. 442–3.

14 See Chapter 10, section 3 below.

us spurn self-ownership. But I now proceed to expound, and reject, a different attempt to secure equality of condition, which combines self-ownership with an egalitarian dispensation over external resources of a kind other than joint ownership.

III THE STEINER CONSTITUTION

7. A third economic constitution, different from both Nozick's and the one described in section 2 above, combines self-ownership with private ownership of initially equal parts of the world's resources. Unlike joint ownership, which forbids a Nozickian formation of unequal private property by placing all resources under collective control, the new proposal, which I shall call the Steiner constitution,[15] institutes private property from the start, but it forbids the inegalitarian Nozickian scramble by privatizing resources in an initially equal division. The Steiner constitution is not Ronald Dworkin's well-known economic constitution, which Dworkin calls 'Equality of Resources', since Steiner equalizes external resources only, whereas Dworkin also favours an equalizing compensation for inequality of personal talent.[16] In fact, and as we shall see in section 9, Dworkin contends, in my view unsuccessfully, that a constitution of the Steiner type is incapable of consistent justification.

At first blush, joint ownership and equal division look to be equally egalitarian ways of treating external resources, but, whether or not they really are both egalitarian, and equally so, their outcomes are utterly different. Consider, again, Infirm and Able. Suppose that Steiner is in force, so that each owns an equal amount of land. Suppose, further, that Able could work both plots of land and thereby produce more than enough to sustain both himself and Infirm, and that Able can also produce at least enough to sustain himself by working his own land only. Then Able's precontractual 'threat-point' would be much higher than Infirm's: Infirm's would be death, but Able's would be whatever standard of living he could achieve by working his own land only. If, then, Able contracts to support Infirm in return for some of the product of working Infirm's land, he is likely to supply Infirm with his subsistence only, since he has Infirm over a barrel. And if the product Able could keep for himself after tilling Infirm's land is not, in his view, worth the additional labour he must spend to get it, then

---

15   I so name it because it is Hillel Steiner's solution to the problem of justice in distribution when the issue of successive generations, which I do not address here, is set aside. See Steiner's 'The Natural Right to the Means of Production', pp. 48–9, and his superb 'Capitalism, Justice and Equal Starts', passim. The latter article is particularly relevant to and against Ronald Dworkin's claim—see part IV below—that the Steiner constitution lacks coherent motivation.

16   I do not know whether Dworkin thinks that the equalizing compensation ought, if possible, to be complete. The following pages of 'Equality of Resources' suggest more than one answer to that question: pp. 299,301,327,337.

Able will let Infirm die.[17] So in this case, and, no doubt, generally, joint ownership is kinder than equal division to the less able. Note, further, that Infirm would fare even worse under Lockean common ownership.[18] Common ownership would allow Able to till as much land as he wished without giving Infirm anything, and, unlike the Steiner constitution, it would endow Infirm with nothing to offer Able in return for Able's support.

Notice that, under many circumstances, equal division will generate capitalism. If people's talent and/or luck are sufficiently unequal, relatively high fliers may so transform their original shares that they can profitably hire others to work on them at wages superior to what those others could glean from working their own resources. Low fliers will then have reason to sell their shares to their more fortunate brethren and become their wage labourers.[19] By contrast, joint ownership turns into capitalism only if every joint owner agrees that it should, or agrees to an equal (or other) division out of which capitalism develops. And capitalist societies which develop out of an initially equal division will tend to display more inequality (or display the same inequality sooner) than those capitalist arrangements with joint ownership in their prehistory, even if both sorts will also tend to display less inequality than those growing out of Nozickian appropriation.

Unlike joint ownership, equal division does not guarantee subsistence for Infirm, even when that is materially possible,[20] and it therefore contradicts a basic welfare state principle. Equal division under self-ownership must therefore be unacceptable to anyone who believes in even a minimally demanding principle of equality of condition, and it might therefore be argued that equal division does not, in fact, respect the egalitarian intuition about external resources.[21] But, however that maybe, self-ownership together with equal

---

17   I suppose, once again (see footnote 4 above), that Able may not wait until Inform dies in order to pick up his share. (Perhaps Infirm forestalls that by designating his land as his burial plot.)

18   At least if we ignore the First Treatise of Government (see especially paras. 41,42), which can be interpreted as laying a duty on Able to support Infirm. For more on that, see the critique of James Tully at Chapter 7, section 11 below.

19   There is less tendency to such an upshot when the greater talent of more productive people cannot be developed, and / or exercised to differentially productive effect, except as a result of a division of labour in which less productive people are essential participants. But socialists and left-wing liberals are inclined to exaggerate the extent to which that is likely to be so.

20   As it is in scenarios iii–v (but not i and ii) in section 2 above.

21   For an implicit claim to that effect, see the axiomatization of self-ownership with external resource equality offered by John Roemer in his 'Public Ownership'. I must emphasize 'might' in the text because I do not believe that Roemer demonstrates that external resources are unequally distributed in the Steiner constitution. They patently are equally distributed, and some (at least) of Roemer's axioms therefore lack generality, as conditions on self-ownership and external resource equality, even if they are true of particular ways of achieving that conjunction. In an unpublished paper which I will send to anyone who asks for it, I show that axioms 3, 5 and 6 (Land Monotonicity, Technological Monotonicity and Self-Ownership

division will not yield the equality of condition prized by socialists. And, since joint ownership, which might yield that equality, rules out the substantive personal rights definitive of effective self-ownership, a constitution of the sort I described in section 1, combining self-ownership (in something more than name) with equality of worldly resources and securing equality of condition, has not been discovered here.

For a set of statements urging some such dependence of the more on the less productive, see William Galston, Justice and the Human Good, pp. 207, 211–12; and two authors he quotes: David Miller, Social Justice, pp. 105–6; and Leonard Hobhouse, The Elements of Social Justice, pp. 140–1. Part of the claim is nicely put by Bishop Latour in Willa Gather's Death Comes for the Archbishop. Latour says to his friend, the excellent cook, Father Joseph Vaillant: 'I am not deprecating your individual talent, Joseph ... but, when one thinks of it, a soup like this is not the work of one man. It is the result of a constantly refined tradition. "There are nearly one thousand years of history in this soup' (p. 39). For a persuasive attempt to block inferences which socialists might wish to draw from Bishop Latour's observation, see Nozick, Anarchy, p. 95.

I believe, moreover, that no such constitution is to be discovered: no egalitarian rule regarding external resources alone will, together with self-ownership, deliver equality of outcome, except, as in the case of joint ownership, at an unacceptable sacrifice of autonomy. There is a tendency in self-ownership to produce inequality, and the only way to nullify that tendency (without expressly abridging self-ownership) is through a regime over external resources which is so rigid that it excludes exercise of independent rights over oneself.

8. A comparative examination of the convertibility into one another of equal division (ED) and joint ownership (JO) constitutions supports the view that, self-ownership is to be maintained, then ED is the preferable form of external resource equality. What follows is not intended as a case for ED over JO tout court, though some of it might also be so viewed, but only for ED over JO given that people are regarded as sovereign over their own powers.

Where there is unanimous preference for the other constitution, either of JO and ED may readily be converted into the other. If everyone under JO wants ED, they will simply divide the jointly owned resources. And if everyone under ED wants JO, they will simply pool what they separately own. Neither system has a convertibility advantage over the other under unanimous preference for the alternative system, when transaction costs are ignored (as they surely should be at the present level of reflection). But what if some but not all under ED want JO, or some but not all under JO want ED?

---

of Skill, respectively, see, further, footnote 25 below) lack the stated generality. I distinguish in that paper respects in which Roemer's construction is successful from the particular respect, mentioned here, in which it fails.

Under ED the some who want JO will not get it. They will not, that is, get full joint ownership of everything by everybody, since some will keep their separate shares. But those who want JO could join with all those who want to join with them in a less than comprehensive joint ownership: call it VJO (V for voluntary). Now, not all of those who want JO will want VJO as much as they do JO, or even at all. Do they therefore have a grievance against the ED starting point? Can they say that those who want ED get what they want but those who want JO do not? No, for the proper parallel to someone who wants comprehensive JO is someone who wants comprehensive ED, and he is not guaranteed what he wants under ED either (since ED makes VJO possible). If those who want JO go into VJO, then neither they nor those who want comprehensive ED get what they want But both groups fail to get what they want because others make choices which a believer in self-ownership must endorse their right to make.

If, on the other hand, there is JO at the beginning, then it persists as long as just one person wants it to, and that seems inconsistent with regarding the others as self-owners, in an effective sense. One could, of course, begin with a JO under which any of the n joint owners would be entitled to leave with 1/nth of total external resources. But, when transaction costs are ignored, to add such an entitlement to JO is to assimilate it to ED: JO with the right to contract out is, for practical purposes, equivalent to ED (since ED permits each to contract into JO or VJO).

The conclusion seems to be that, if one begins with a commitment to both self-ownership and equality of external resources, and one has to choose between JO and ED, then the natural way to realize external resources equality is through ED rather than through JO. To go for JO would probably reflect a belief, prejudicial to self-ownership, that people should be endowed with rights which enable them to benefit from (the fruits of) the personal powers of others.

IV DWORKIN ON STEINER

9. The Steiner constitution unites self-ownership with an equal division of external resources (only), and therefore implements what Ronald Dworkin calls 'the starting gate theory of justice', which he wrongly supposes may readily be dismissed.[22]

Before I address Dworkin's case against the starting gate theory, it will be useful to relate the concerns of the present chapter to those of his magisterial diptych on the theme of equality.[23] The Dworkin articles define a distinction between equality of welfare, which Dworkin rejects, and equality of resources, which he favours. That distinction is orthogonal to the one which has exercised me here, which is between personal and worldly endowments. An egalitarian view of wordly resources may be attached to an egalitarian view of

---

22   See Dworkin, 'Equality of Resources', pp. 309–10.

23   I refer to the two-part essay which appeared in *Philosophy and Public Affairs* for 1981.

	Welfare egalitarianism	Resources egalitarianism
with respect to all resources	comprehensive welfare egalitarianism (e.g., as described by Dworkin)	comprehensive resources egalitarianism (e.g., as espoused by Dworkin)
with respect to external resources	partial welfare egalitarianism (e.g., as axiomatized by Roemer)	partial resources egalitarianism only (e.g., as espoused by Steiner)

personal powers, or, instead, as in Steiner, to a view which represents them as self-owned. If one takes, as Dworkin does, a doubly egalitarian view, then one may, as he shows, develop that view either as an egalitarianism of welfare or as an egalitarianism of (all) resources. Whichever way one develops the comprehensively egalitarian view, no one owns anything as of basic moral right, and relations among things and persons are arranged so that either welfare or share in total resources is equalized. But if, like Steiner, one restricts one's egalitarianism to worldly resources, then, too, one might develop the egalitarian component either as an egalitarianism of resources or as an egalitarianism of welfare. The first alternative is to divide the external resources themselves equally[24] and then let people do what they want with them. The second alternative, to wit, welfare egalitarianism with respect to external resources only, might seem incoherent (since external resources produce no—or only a negligible—stream of utility dissociable from the result of applying talent to them), but John Roemer has provided an arresting axiomatic sketch of it.[25]

Thus, Dworkin's distinction between welfare and resources egalitarianism, and my distinction between comprehensive egalitarianism and egalitarianism with respect to external resources only, generate, when they are put together, the following four-fold classification of views:

Dworkin emphasizes the distinction separating the columns of the above table, but he gives short shrift to the distinction which separates its rows. He does not bring the bottom row into clear focus, and he therefore does not deal successfully with its right-hand side, which is tantamount to what he calls the 'starting gate theory', a theory whose fairly obvious rationale eludes him. The starting gate theory 'holds that justice requires equal initial resources' and 'laissez-faire thereafter'. It says that 'if people start in the same circumstances and do not cheat or steal from one another, then it is fair that people keep what they gain through their own skill'. This, says Dworkin, is 'hardly a coherent political theory at all'. It

---

24   For example, by means of the auction described by Dworkin at pp. 286–90 of 'Equality of Resources'.

25   See footnote 21 above. Two of Roemer's axioms are (1) Land Monotonicity: nobody's welfare declines if all retain the same skill as before and the amount of land increases and (2) Self-Ownership of Skill' if A has at least as much skill as B, then he has at least as much welfare as B.

is 'an indefensible combination of very different theories of justice': for Dworkin, an initial equality is justifiable if and only if it is justifiable to preserve equality throughout.

But Dworkin misunderstands the motivation for the starting gate theory. He is wrong that the laissez-faire component depends on 'some version of the Lockean theory that people acquire property by mixing their labour with goods or something of that sort', and that a similar approach should, therefore, apply at the beginning, that consistency requires Lockean or Nozickian acquisition then, rather than an equal division of resources. It is, I shall argue, false that 'the moment when the immigrants first land is … an arbitrary point in their lives at which to locate any one-shot requirement that they each have an equal share of any available resources'.[26]

The laissez-faire component in the starting gate theory cannot be grounded in Locke's theory that people acquire property by mixing their labour with things, since starting gate's laissez-faire begins only once all external resources have been distributed, and it is then too late to acquire title in something by mixing one's labour with it. Labour mixture secures title, for Locke, only in what is not yet owned, and there is nothing unowned with which to mix one's labour once the initial equal division of external resources has been effected.

Dworkin represents Locke as holding that labour secures title because it joins what the labourer works on to something he already owns, to wit, his labour. I think that is a correct exegesis of Locke. But some think that, for Locke, labouring on something makes it one's own not (only) for the stated reason, but when and because, by labouring on it, one thereby enhances its value. And some such consideration might indeed be used to justify the laissez-faire component in the starting gate theory. But one who drew upon it would not, I shall argue, be thereby committed against an initial equal division.

Note that what I shall call the 'value argument' is truly different from the argument from labour mixture, even though many (and sometimes, perhaps, Locke) are prone to confuse the two. If the justification of your ownership of what you have laboured on is that your labour is in it, then you do not own it because you have enhanced its value, even if what deserves to be called 'labour' necessarily creates value. And, for the value argument, it is the conferring of value itself, not the labour by which it is conferred, which is essential: if you magically enhanced something's value without labouring, but, say, by wishing that it was more valuable, then, on the value argument, you would be entitled to whatever that argument justifies you in having.

Locke's principal labour mixture paragraphs do not, in my view, invoke the consideration that labour enhances the value of that to which it is applied. And Karl Olivecrona maybe right that when, in later paragraphs, Locke does bring value enhancement to the fore, he is not trying to justify the initial appropriation of private property.[27] According to Olivecrona, Locke is there, instead, justifying the extensive inequality of goods that comes

---

26 All quotations in the foregoing two paragraphs are from 'Equality of Resources', p. 309.
27 See his 'Locke's Theory of Appropriation', pp. 231–3.

to obtain long after original appropriation has ceased. Locke's justification of it is that almost all of the value of what is now so unequally distributed is due not to any unequal initial appropriating but to the labour which followed long after initial appropriation.[28]

So construed—not, that is, as a justification for original appropriation—the value argument might indeed be used to justify the inequality generated by laissez-faire, the justification of it being that labour is responsible for (almost all of) the value difference in which that inequality inheres. But it is perfectly consistent to propound that defence of laissez-faire inequality while yet insisting on an equal division at the outset of the resources for whose value no one's labour is responsible. Indeed, if labour's value-creating power is the basic justification of the inequality brought about by laissez-faire, then an initial equal division of external resources is not merely consistent with, but also a natural prelude to, laissez-faire, since no one creates the value of raw natural resources.

To conclude: if what matters about labour is that it annexes something already owned to something unowned, then labour plays no part in justifying the laissez-faire component in the starting gate theory, since, on that theory, everything is already owned once laissez-faire begins. And if what matters about labour is that it adds value, then that might indeed justify the laissez-faire component, but without having inegalitarian implications for the distribution of raw resources. To be sure, one might contrive a (not very good) argument for original appropriation by reference to labour's value-creating power,[29] but one is not committed to endorsing such an argument when one justifies inequalities which arise after appropriation by arguing that labour brought them about. It is, then, false that the theory of Lockean acquisition (or whatever other theory of justice in acquisition is supposed to justify the laissez-faire component in a starting gate theory) can have no less force in governing the initial distribution than it has in justifying title through talent.[30]

Now, the true foundation of the starting gate theory is the contrast between persons and worldly resources as possible objects of rights and egalitarian dispensation. It is reasonable to think, with respect to external resources that have not been acted upon by anyone, that no one has more right to them than anyone else does, and that equal rights in them should therefore be instituted. But it is not so evidently reasonable to suppose, similarly, that no one has, to begin with, more right than anyone else over the powers of given people. And if you also think that each individual has the right to decide what to do with his own powers, and you (surely not inconsistently) combine that thought with external resources egalitarianism, then the upshot is the 'starting gate theory'.

The fundamental distinction for the starting gate theory is not between what is appropriate at the beginning and what is appropriate later. The theory gets framed that way only on the supposition that all external resources are to hand at the outset. If that is false,

---

28   For more on Locke on labour's value-creating power, see Chapter 7, sections 6–10 below.

29   See, Chapter 7, footnote 37, below.

30   Dworkin, 'Equality of Resources', p. 309.

and some of them come forward later, by rising out of the sea, or as a consequence of exploration, then the so-called (and essentially misnamed) starting gate theory requires a supplementary equal division rather than a Nozickian free-for-all. 'The moment when the immigrants first land' is not, therefore, 'an arbitrary point' at which to insist on equality. It is unarbitrary in virtue of the auxiliary assumption that all the external resources that will ever exist are already available.

The combination of initial equality and subsequent unequalizing competition which, Dworkin claims, 'cannot hold together a political theory', makes sense, he thinks, in the game of Monopoly, 'whose point is to allow luck and skill a highly circumscribed and, in the last analysis, arbitrary role'.[31] Now, whatever Dworkin means (I find the statement baffling) when he says that part of the point of Monopoly is to allow skill to play an arbitrary role, consider instead a different game, which models the 'starting gate theory' rather more accurately, and indeed gives it its name, to wit, some sort of track race. One may find a political theory which takes that as a suitable model for distributive justice repugnant. One may think that the Coes and Ovetts and Chamberlains in the game of life should not receive high rewards because of their God- or nature-given talents. But then one must contend with intelligible qualms about people's rights over their own powers, which Dworkin ignores. The normative stance of the left would be easier to sustain if the starting gate theory were simply incoherent. But it is not.[32]

---

31 Ibid., p. 310.

32 It is curious that Dworkin should object to the starting gate theory on the ground that it distinguishes an initial just distribution from later distributions justified as voluntary transformations of that initial one, since his own theory of justice, equality of resources, has the same structure. Readers familiar with the 'Equality of Resources' article will understand that if people do not differ in their intangible personal resources, then what follows the auction's equal division of external resources is, precisely, laissez-faire. Nor does Dworkin's theory articulate itself in that two-stage starting-gate-like way only in the special case in which intangible resources are equal. A structurally identical dichotomous articulation also holds in the more general case in which a redistributive tax scheme (modelled on a scheme insuring against low talent endowment) precedes pure market process. So Dworkin's privileged starting point is no less (and no more) arbitrary than Steiner's. What divides their theories is nothing to do with temporal structure, but the content of the initial quality. Dworkin characterizes the starting gate theory as urging that (this was quoted at p. 107 above) 'if people start in the same circumstances, and do not cheat or steal from one another, then it is fair that people keep what they gain through their own skill' ('Equality of Resources', p. 309). But if we read 'circumstances' in the extended fashion (which includes internal resources) in which Dworkin uses that term (see ibid., p. 302), then he himself affirms the quoted statement.

406 | Creating Wealth

V CONCLUSION

10. It is a familiar right-wing claim that freedom and equality are conflicting ideals, and that, to the extent that they conflict, freedom should be preferred to equality. Some rightists regret that, as they suppose, equality has to be rejected, whereas other see no harm in that.

Most leftists reply either that there is no real conflict between equality and freedom, when both are properly conceived, or that, to the extent that there indeed is one, freedom should give way to equality, since justice demands equality, and justice comes before all other political values.

This chapter has been about equality and freedom, and its author is one kind of leftist. But I have not tried to show that there is no conflict between equality and freedom for leftists to worry about: that large question has gone unaddressed here. What I have shown, instead, is that there is no conflict between equality and what the libertarian Right calls freedom. For, under joint ownership of the world's resources, everyone has the rights constituting self-ownership—which is the libertarian Right's conception of freedom—without prejudice to the maintenance of equality of condition.

VI RETROSPECT

I now offer a summary of the pair of chapters that come to an end here, which some readers may find useful.

One way of doing philosophy well is to assemble premises which even opponents will not want to deny, and by dint of skill at inference, to derive results which opponents will indeed want to deny but which, having granted the premises, they will be hard pressed to deny. The trick is to go from widely accepted premises to controversial conclusions. It is, of course, no trick at all to go from premises which are themselves controversial to controversial conclusions.

Now some critics of Robert Nozick dismiss his work as belonging to the second category just distinguished. Thomas Nagel, for example, avers, in his review of Anarchy, State, and Utopia, that Nozick's strongly inegalitarian conclusions are boringly unsurprising in light of the strongly inegalitarian premises with which he begins.[33] But I believe that Nozick can be presented more sympathetically than that, and that he needs to be so presented in order that we may understand the otherwise unaccountable allure of his ideas.

Nagel thinks what he does about Nozick because[34] he shares Nozick's view that freedom is antithetical to equality, the difference between these thinkers being that Nagel does not regard the antithesis as a reason for rejecting equality wholesale. Being less disposed to regard freedom and equality as incompatible, I am less inclined to treat Nozick's

---

33   See his 'Libertarianism Without Foundations', especially p. 193.

34   See Chapter 2, subsection 2e above.

inegalitarian conclusions as a rewrite of his (would-be) freedom-affirming premisses. Let me, then, say how I think Nozick gets from the latter to the former, and, then, in what ways his progress can be blocked.

Nozick aims to defend the inequality that makes socialists angry and liberals uneasy by exploiting the commitment to freedom which is common to socialists, liberals, and rightists of the Nozick free-market supporting kind. There exist other kinds of rightists, such as Roger Scruton, who affect scepticism about freedom itself, but, whatever impact they have achieved on contemporary upper middle-brow intellectual culture, they do not, like Nozick, disturb socialists and liberals intellectually, precisely because they do not pretend to build their edifice on shared normative foundations.

But how does Nozick go from freedom to inequality? He departs from essentially two premisses, the first of which is that no one should be a slave, in whole or in part, to anyone else. No one, that is, may rightfully be owned by anyone else, but each is, rightfully, a self-owner. And, since I am not a slave, but a sovereign self-owner, then you may not co-opt my services when I have not contracted to supply them. If you had the right to command them independent of contract, then I would be, to that extent, your slave. It supposedly follows that a welfare state, in which, for example, quadriplegics are sustained by income extracted from the able-bodied on pain of coercive sanction, involves the partial slavery of some to others. It involves, so Nozick would contend, exactly that subordination of some to others to which socialists object when they plead against the power of capitalists over workers. Yet that is a legitimate power, being the fruit of contract, whereas no contract is involved as background to the service which the welfare state demands.

We may summarize this first part of Nozick's argument as follows:

1. No one is to any degree the slave of anyone else. Therefore
2. No one is owned, in whole or in part, by anyone else. Therefore
3. Each person is owned by himself. Therefore
4. Each person must be free to do as he pleases, if[35] he does not harm anyone else: he is not required to help anyone else.

Now the conclusion just stated does not by itself legitimate extensive inequality of distribution. For inequality to begin to form, people must have rights not over themselves but over external things, and no such rights can be excogitated from the foregoing argument. In order to establish them, Nozick needs a further premiss, a second premiss, and that is the premiss to which I now turn.

---

35   Not 'if and only if', since some harmings do not violate self-ownership, just as some damages to your property do not violate your rights in it. The issue of which harms are permissible, and which not, is addressed in section 6 of chapter 9 below.

Whereas Nozick's first premiss is about people and their powers, his second premiss ((5), below) is about everything else and its powers, which is to say that it is about nature and about the unmodified resources of nature. These, for Nozick, are, antecedently to anyone's actions or labour on them, not owned by anyone. They pre-dated the appearance of human beings in the world, and while each human being is born with the natural rights over himself implied by the first premiss, none is born with any natural rights over things. Accordingly, any rights which anyone establishes in things must derive from exercises of rights over himself.[36] And the way, in particular, that original rights in things are formed is through each person's entitlement to appropriate any amount of raw resources if (see (4), which is a consequence of (1)) he does not thereby harm anyone (including in 'anyone' not only those who exist when he appropriates but also anyone who comes later). Non-harming appropriation is simply a case in point of the 'natural liberty endorsed in (4).

So the second premiss is:

5. The external world, in its native state, is not owned, in whole or in part, by anyone. And (5), together with (4), enables inference of:
6. Each person may gather to himself unlimited quantities of natural resources if he does not thereby harm anyone.

The next step requires a view about what it means to harm somebody by appropriating an unowned natural resource. Nozick's answer is that it is to make him worse off than he would have been had the resource not been appropriated at all. But unappropriated resources, like common land, tend to be used less productively, for organizational and incentive reasons, than resources that have been taken into secure private control and that are therefore transformable for private gain. It is relatively easy to obtain sufficient benefit from private exploitation of resources that appropriators will have enough to compensate others for the latter's loss of access to them. Non-appropriators will not then be worse off than they would have been had the resources not been appropriated. Along these lines, the comprehensive privatization of almost everything, by those who are quick enough to privatize before others do, is readily justified. Some, who form what we may call a proletariat, will have been too slow or will have been born too late to privatize anything, but they will not be relevantly worse off, so they have no just grievance to press. In sum, (6) enables inference of:

7. Unequal quantities of natural resources may become, with full legitimacy, privately owned by a section of the population.

---

36 On the plausible principle that a creature lacking certain rights could acquire them only as a result of exercises of rights by a creature (for example, as in this case, itself) that already has rights of some kind.

Now if each owns himself, in the sense of (4), and the resources of the external world are monopolized by a section of the population, the resulting economy will, on ordinary assumptions about human motivation (which is to say, on the assumption that people are not extraordinarily altruistic), exhibit extensive inequality of condition, on any view of what equality of condition is, be it equality of income, or of utility, or of need satisfaction or whatever. So (4) and (7) yield the desired conclusion, which is that:

8. Extensive inequality of condition is unavoidable, or avoidable only on pain of violating people's rights to themselves and to things.

Now, there are (at least) three ways of resisting the foregoing line of argumentation, each of which is featured in this book. The first is to challenge the derivation of (4) from (1), and, more generally, to subject the rhetoric of self-ownership to critical scrutiny: that will be the task of Chapter 10 below. But I think that it is interesting and important that we can resist Nozick in two decisive ways which involve no rejection of the self-ownership idea. One is to challenge his notion of harm, by means of which he passes from (6) to (7). One can question the test Nozick uses for determining whether an appropriation of private property harms someone, and argue, against him, that the fact that a person is no worse off than he would have been had the resource not been privately appropriated at all does not show that he is not harmed, since he may nevertheless be far worse off than he would have been had the resource not been appropriated by whoever actually appropriated it: that was the burden of section 3 of Chapter 3 above. And the other way of objecting to Nozick without questioning the idea of self-ownership is to challenge his second premiss, (5), the premiss that the external world is originally unowned. It is, of course, legally speaking, originally unowned, but we are here discussing not its original legal condition, but its original moral condition. (If we were discussing legal, as opposed to moral, truth, then the claim that people own themselves would also be evidently false.) One may, then, press against Nozick an alternative view of the original moral relationship between people and things, under which we regard nature as, from the start, collectively owned by everyone. If that different conception of rights over the world is united with the principle of self-ownership, extensive inequality of condition is avoidable: and that was a principal claim of the chapter that ends here.

Equal Respect and Equal Shares

DAVID SCHMIDTZ

I. INTRODUCTION

We are all equal, sort of. We are not equal in terms of our physical or mental capacities. Morally speaking, we are not all equally good. Evidently, if we are equal, it is not in virtue of our actual characteristics, but despite them. Our equality is of a political rather than metaphysical nature. We do not expect people to be the same, but we expect differences to have no bearing on how people ought to be treated as citizens. Or when differences do matter, we expect that they will not matter in the sense of being a basis for class distinction. We admire tenacity, talent, and so on, but do not take such features to entitle their bearers to be treated as "upper class." Neither are people who are relatively lacking in these features obliged to tolerate being treated as "lower class." As a society, we have made moral progress. Such progress consists in part of progress toward political and cultural equality.

Have we also made progress toward *economic* equality? If so, does that likewise count as moral progress? Some people have more than others. Some earn more than others. Do these things matter? In two ways, they could. First, we may care about differences in wealth and income on humanitarian grounds; that is, we may worry about some people having less not because less is less but because less sometimes is not enough. Second, we may care on grounds of justice; that is, we may think people would not have less if some injustice had not been done.[1]

What provokes such concerns? One provocation is conceptual: philosophical thought experiments, and so on. We imagine how the world would be in some idealized hypothetical situation, and then ask whether departures from the ideal are unjust, and if so, how they might be redressed. A second provocation is empirical: statistical reports on income inequality, and so on. Statistics paint a picture of how the world actually is, and how unequal it is. We are left wondering whether such inequality is acceptable, and if not, what to do about it.

This essay examines these two provocations. In response to concerns of a conceptual nature, Section II offers a limited defense of distribution according to a principle of "equal shares," explaining how and why even nonegalitarians can and should respect egalitarian concerns and make room for them even in otherwise nonegalitarian theories of justice. As Section III notes, though, "equal shares" is only one way of expressing egalitarian concern. The connection between equal treatment and justice may be essential, but the connection between equal treatment and equal shares is not. Sections IV and V reflect on why the rule of first possession limits attempts to distribute according to principles (not only egalitarian principles) of justice. Finally, in response to empirical concerns, Section VI examines recent studies of income distribution in the United States.

Undoubtedly, egalitarians will think I have not made *enough* room for egalitarian concern. After all, if an egalitarian is someone who thinks many economic goods should be distributed equally, and redistributed as often as needed so that shares remain equal, then at the end of the day, I am not an egalitarian. I am, however, a kind of pluralist. Justice is about giving people their due; if we are not talking about what people are due, then we are not talking about justice. On the other hand, what people are due is a complex, multifaceted, context-sensitive matter. There is a place for equal shares.

II. ON BEHALF OF EQUAL SHARES

Political theorist Bruce Ackerman's essay "On Getting What We Don't Deserve" is a short, engaging dialogue that captures the essence of egalitarian concern about the justice of differences in wealth and income.[2] Ackerman imagines you and he are in a garden. As

---

1 Some worry about differences in wealth because they believe such differences eventually become differences in political power. (Whether such concerns justify increasing or decreasing the amount of political power that eventually gets put up for sale is a separate question, touched on at the end of this essay.) This worry could be made to fit quite nicely into either of the above two reasons for concern about inequality, or we could call it a third, separate reason.

2 Bruce A. Ackerman, "On Getting What We Don't Deserve," *Social Philosophy and Policy* 1, no. 1 (1983): 60–70. My discussion of Ackerman borrows from David Schmidtz, "Finders, Keepers?" *Advances*

Ackerman tells the story, you see two apples on a tree and swallow them in one gulp while an amazed Ackerman looks on. Ackerman then asks you, as one human being to another, shouldn't I have gotten one of those apples?

Should he? If so, why? Why only one? What grounds our admittedly compelling intuition that Ackerman should have gotten one—exactly one—of those apples? Notably, Ackerman explicitly rejects the idea that his claim to an apple is based on need, signaling that his primary concern is not humanitarian. Instead, Ackerman's view is that the point of getting one apple is that one apple would have been an equal share. Equal shares is a moral default. Morally speaking, distribution by equal shares is what we automatically go to if we cannot justify anything else. As Ackerman sees it, to give Ackerman an equal share is to treat him with respect. In Ackerman's garden, at least, to say he does not command an equal share is to say he does not command respect.

Is Ackerman right? Looking at the question dispassionately, there are several things to say on behalf of equal shares as an allocation rule, even if we reject Ackerman's presumption in favor of it. In Ackerman's garden, equal shares has the virtue of not requiring further debate about who gets the bigger share. No one has reason to envy anyone else's share. When we arrive all at once, equal shares is a cooperative, mutually advantageous, mutually respectful departure from the status quo (in which none of us yet has a share of the good to be distributed). In short, equal shares is easy. We call it "splitting the difference," and often it is a pleasant way of solving our distributional problem. In the process, we not only solve the problem, but offer each other a kind of salute. In Ackerman's garden, it is an obvious way to divide things and get on with our lives—with no hard feelings at worst, and at best with a sense of having been honored by honorable people.

These ideas may not be equality's foundation, but they are among equality's virtues. Crucially, even nonegalitarians can appreciate that they are virtues. Thus, while critics may say Ackerman is assuming the egalitarianism for which he is supposed to be arguing, the virtues just mentioned beg no questions. Even from nonegalitarian perspectives, then, there is something to be said for equal shares. Therefore, whatever conception of justice we ultimately entertain, we can agree there is a place in a just society for dividing certain goods into equal shares. In particular, when we arrive at the bargaining table more or less at the same time, for the purpose of dividing goods to which no one has made a prior claim, we are in a situation where equal shares is a way of achieving a just distribution.

It may not be the only way. For example, we could flesh out the thought experiment in such a way as to make bargainers' unequal needs more salient than their equality as citizens. But it is one way.

---

in Austrian Economics 5 (1998): 277–89; and David Schmidtz and Robert Goodin, *Social Welfare and Individual Responsibility* (New York: Cambridge University Press, 1998). For a skeptical response to Ackerman's thought-experiment methodology from an egalitarian perspective, see James K. Galbraith, "Raised on Robbery," *Yale Law and Policy Review* 18, no. 2 (2000): 387–404.

III. AN EGALITARIAN CRITIQUE OF EQUAL SHARES

Yet there are times when following the equal-shares principle—paying people the same wage, say—would fail to show others equal respect. Suppose an employer routinely expects more work, or more competent work, from one employee than from another, but sees no reason to pay them differently. In such cases, the problem is not raw wage differentials so much as a lack of proportion in the relations between contribution and compensation. The lack of proportion is one kind of unequal treatment. And unequal treatment, and the lack of respect it signals, is what people resent.

Children often are jealous when comparing their shares to those of their siblings—or, a bit more precisely, when comparing shares doled out by their parents. Why? Because being given a lesser share by their parents signals to them that they are held in lower esteem. They tend to feel differently about having less than their richest neighbor, because so long as no one is deliberately assigning them smaller shares, no one is sending a signal of unequal esteem.[3] Here, too, the problem is departures from equal respect rather than from equal shares. Equal shares is not the same as equal respect, and is not always compatible with it.[4] "Unequal pay for equal work" is offensive, but so is "equal pay for unequal work."

Intuitively, we all believe some people deserve more than others. This belief, though, is ambiguous. If I have better opportunities than you do, and as a result acquire more than you do, do I deserve more? Egalitarians will say no. The ambiguity is this: I do not deserve "more than you do" *under this description* because there never was a fair competition between us to determine which of us deserves more. Therefore, I do not deserve to have a central distributor maintain any particular ratio between your reward and mine. Nevertheless, notice what this leaves open. I may well deserve X while you deserve Y, on the basis of my working hard for X and your working hard for Y as we live our separate lives, with nothing in this story even suggesting that $X = Y$. Therefore, even if we were right to suppose that a central distributor would have no basis for judging us to be of unequal

---

3   As children grow up, we expect them to resent their siblings less rather than resent their neighbors more, but this expectation is not always met. A well-known philosopher once complained to me about airline deregulation, not because of safety or quality of service or anything like that, but because it made her unsure of whether she was getting the lowest possible price. She had paid $300 for her ticket, and for all she knew the person beside her paid $200 for the same ticket. I speculated that before deregulation, both tickets would have cost $700. She answered, in a passionate voice, "But at least you knew!" Knew what? Obviously, there was nothing humanitarian in this kind of egalitarianism. This philosopher is not alone. A neighbor of mine recently said she would rather pay $20 for a blanket at K-Mart than pay $8 for the same blanket in the nearby border town of Nogales, because at K-Mart you know everyone is paying the same price, whereas in Nogales, someone else might be getting the same blanket for $6.

4   As David Gauthier expresses a related point, "impartial practices respect people as they are, the inequalities among them as well as the equalities." See David Gauthier, *Morals by Agreement* (Oxford: Oxford University Press, 1986), 270.

merit, and thus could be denounced for deliberately assigning unequal shares, we could still be wrong to infer that the shares we respectively deserve are equal.

Accordingly, there is a difference between unequal treatment and unequal shares. Unequal treatment presupposes treatment; unequal shares do not. If we are being *treated* unequally, then there is someone whom we can ask to justify treating us unequally. It would make sense for an egalitarian such as Ackerman to insist on this. Moreover, in Ackerman's garden, your grabbing both apples arguably is a token of unequal treatment. But what if Ackerman arrives several years after you have grabbed both apples and turned the garden into an orchard? Nonsimultaneous arrival complicates the case, making it harder to see the grab as a token of treatment at all, unequal or otherwise. Suffice it to say, we can be committed to denouncing unequal treatment without being committed to denouncing every unequal outcome as if it were a result of unequal treatment. Ackerman presumes the moral default (in a very general way) is equal shares. Even if, as seems likely, Ackerman is wrong, this is no reason to give up on the idea that the moral default is equal *treatment*.

A. Equal worth and equal treatment

Suppose we have a certain moral worth that is not affected by our choices. That is, although we may live in a morally heroic way or a morally depraved way, how we live makes no difference as far as this moral worth is concerned: there is nothing we can do to make ourselves more or less worthy. If this were true, then we might all, as it happens, be of equal worth.

Now suppose instead that along certain dimensions our moral worth can be affected by our choices. In certain respects, that is, some of our choices make us more or less worthy. In this case, if in certain respects our choices affect our worth over time, it is unlikely that there will ever be a time when we are all of equal worth in those respects.

None of this is a threat to egalitarianism, because only a caricature of egalitarianism would presume that all of us are equally worthy along all dimensions. Instead, part of the point of the liberal ideal of political equality is to foster conditions under which we will tend to make choices that augment rather than diminish our worth along dimensions where worth depends on choice. Liberal political equality is not premised on the false hope that under ideal conditions, we all turn out to be equally worthy. It presupposes only a classically liberal optimism regarding the kind of society that results from putting people (all people, so far as this is realistically feasible) in a position to choose worthy ways of life.

B. Equality and oppression

Humanitarianism is concerned with how people fare. Egalitarianism is concerned with how people fare relative to each other. So says philosopher Larry Temkin. Humanitarians, he says, favor equality *solely* as a means to helping the worse off, and given the choice between redistribution from the better off to the worse off, and identical gains for the worse off with equal, or even greater, gains for the better off, they would see no reason to favor the former over the latter. ... But such people are not egalitarians in my sense if their concerns would be satisfied by a system in which the poor had access to quality care, but the rich had even greater access to much better care.[5]

Accordingly, what distinguishes egalitarianism from humanitarianism is that a humanitarian would never compromise the care offered to the poor merely to greatly worsen the care offered to the rich, whereas an egalitarian at least sometimes would.[6] Temkin, himself an egalitarian, says the problem with humanitarianism is that it is not concerned with equality.[7] In Temkin's words, "As a plausible analysis of what the egalitarian really cares about, ... humanitarianism is a nonstarter."[8]

Philosopher Elizabeth Anderson responds, "Those on the left have no less reason than conservatives and libertarians to be disturbed by recent trends in academic egalitarian thought."[9] Academic egalitarians, she thinks, have lost sight of why equality matters.[10] Thus, she criticizes philosopher Richard Arneson for saying, "The concern of distributive justice is to compensate individuals for misfortune. ... Distributive justice stipulates that the lucky should transfer some or all of their gains due to luck to the unlucky."[11] Along with Arneson, Anderson classifies Gerald Cohen and John Roemer as welfare egalitarians.[12]

---

5   Larry S. Temkin, *Inequality* (New York: Oxford University Press, 1993), 8.

6   One of Temkin's contributions to the literature is his discussion of what he calls "the Slogan": "One situation cannot be better than another unless there is someone for whom it is better" (ibid., 248). The Slogan's point is to separate true egalitarians (who would say a more equal distribution can be better even when there is no one for whom it is better) from true humanitarians (who would deny this). Temkin, an egalitarian, says the Slogan is false (ibid., 249).

7   Ibid., 246.

8   Ibid., 247.

9   Elizabeth S. Anderson, "What is the Point of Equality?" *Ethics* 109, no. 2 (1999): 288.

10   Terry L. Price reaches a similar conclusion in Terry L. Price, "Egalitarian Justice, Luck, and the Costs of Chosen Ends," *American Philosophical Quarterly* 36, no. 4 (1999): 267–78.

11   Richard J. Arneson, "Rawls, Responsibility, and Distributive Justice," in Maurice Salles and John A. Weymark, eds., *Justice, Political Liberalism, and Utilitarianism: Themes from Harsanyi* (Cambridge: Cambridge University Press, in press), quoted in Anderson, "What Is the Point of Equality?" 290. For a later work in which Arneson abandons egalitarianism in favor of what he calls sufficientarianism, see Richard J. Arneson, "Why Justice Requires Transfers to Offset Income and Wealth Inequalities," in this volume.

12   For a sustained and circumspect—yet uncompromising—defense of a related kind of egalitarianism, see the more recent Tom Christiano, "Arguing for Equality of Condition" (manuscript).

She contrasts this group with those who advocate equalizing resources rather than welfare, such as Ronald Dworkin, Eric Rakowski, and Philippe Van Parijs.[13] Despite differences between these thinkers, what their works collectively show, Anderson says, is that "[r]ecent egalitarian writing has come to be dominated by the view that the fundamental aim of equality is to compensate people for undeserved bad luck."[14] Anderson, though, thinks that "[t]he proper negative aim of egalitarian justice is not to eliminate the impact of brute luck from human affairs, but to end oppression."[15] Egalitarianism's proper aim, she claims, is to enable us "to live together in a democratic community, as opposed to a hierarchical one."[16]

Anderson says that "democratic equality's principles of distribution neither presume to tell people how to use their opportunities nor attempt to judge how responsible people are for choices that lead to unfortunate outcomes. Instead, it avoids bankruptcy at the hands of the imprudent by limiting the range of goods provided collectively and expecting individuals to take personal responsibility for the other goods in their possession."[17] In contrast, Anderson argues, academic egalitarianism gains some undeserved credibility because we assume anything calling itself egalitarian must also be humanitarian. But although she is an egalitarian herself, Anderson says we cannot assume this connection.[18] Moreover, the academic egalitarian's reasons for granting aid are disrespectful. When redistribution's purpose is to make up for someone's being less capable than others (due to bad luck in the natural lottery), the result in practice is that "[p]eople lay claim to the resources of egalitarian redistribution in virtue of their inferiority to others, not in virtue of their equality to others."[19] Political equality has no such consequence. In the nineteenth century, when women began to present themselves as having a right to vote, they were presenting themselves not as needy inferiors but as autonomous equals—not as having a right to equal shares but as having a right to equal treatment.

We can draw two conclusions from all this. First, egalitarianism cannot afford to define itself by contrast with humanitarianism. No conception of justice can afford that. Second, egalitarians and nonegalitarians can agree that a kind of political equality is called for even when equal shares as a distributive principle is not. Thus, to the conclusion that a pluralistic theory of justice can make some room for equal shares, we can add that a pluralistic theory can make room for a second kind of equality as well, a specifically political kind.

---

13   Anderson, "What Is the Point of Equality?" 293.

14   Ibid., 288.

15   Ibid.

16   Ibid., 313.

17   Ibid., 289.

18   Ibid.

19   Ibid., 306.

C. Equality and meritocracy

Very roughly, a regime is meritocratic to the extent that people are judged on the merits of their performance. A pure meritocracy is hard to imagine, but any regime is bound to have meritocratic elements. A corporation is meritocratic insofar as it ties promotions to performance, and departs from meritocracy insofar as it ties promotions to seniority. A society is meritocratic insofar as, within it, people are paid what their work is worth. In short, in meritocracies, rewards track performance. The important point is that rewards actually track performance; it is neither necessary nor sufficient that anyone *intends* for them to do so. A corporation's culture of meritocracy is often partially a product of deliberate design, but a corporation (or especially, a whole society) can be meritocratic in some ways without anyone deciding it ought to be.

The idea of meritocracy is vague, to be sure, yet precise enough for academic egalitarians to see conflict between equality and meritocracy. Thus, philosopher Norman Daniels says that claims of merit derive from considerations of efficiency and cannot support stronger notions of desert.[20] Furthermore, regarding job placement, "the meritocrat is committed, given his concern for productivity, to distributing at least some goods, the jobs themselves, in accordance with a morally arbitrary distribution of abilities and traits."[21] Daniels concludes, "Unfortunately, many proponents of meritocracy have been so concerned with combating the lesser evil of non-meritocratic job placement that they have left unchallenged the greater evil of highly inegalitarian reward schedules. One suspects that an elitist infatuation for such reward schedules lurks behind their ardor for meritocratic job placement."[22]

Daniels's view exemplifies what Anderson calls academic egalitarianism, but liberalism also has an older, nonacademic tradition within which equal respect and meritocracy go hand in hand.[23] We see people as commanding equal respect qua citizens or human beings, but not as commanding equal respect in every respect. Egalitarians and nonegalitarians alike appreciate that genuine respect has meritocratic elements, and thus to some extent tracks how people distinguish themselves as they develop their differing potentials in different ways.[24]

---

20 Norman Daniels, "Merit and Meritocracy," *Philosophy and Public Affairs* 7, no. 3 (1978): 207.

21 Ibid., 222.

22 Ibid.

23 I mean to be speaking here of the liberal tradition in a quite general way, rather than of classical or modern variations on the theme. To put it in terms of stylized history, I mean liberalism as it developed in Europe and America in reaction to monarchy in particular and to social hierarchy in general. For that matter, even the socialist tradition once was in part a meritocratic reaction to a social hierarchy that prevented working classes from being able to earn fair wages.

24 For a good discussion of this issue, see Richard J. Arneson, "What, if Anything, Renders All Humans Morally Equal?" in Dale Jamieson, ed., *Singer and His Critics* (Oxford: Blackwell Publishers, 1999), 103–28. Temkin too makes room for merit, saying, "I think deserved inequalities are not bad *at all*.

Daniels says the "abilities and traits" that individual people are "morally arbitrary," but I say that if we care about what people contribute to our society, then traits that enable people to contribute are not arbitrary. Those traits make people who they are and define what people aspire to be, at least in societies that respect those traits. We encourage people to work hard and contribute to society by truly respecting people who work hard, not by insisting that hard work is morally arbitrary while conceding a need to fake respect in hope of conditioning people to work harder. Incentive structures work better when we see them not merely as incentive structures but also as structures that recognize merit.

For practical purposes, certain kinds of egalitarian and meritocratic elements often go together. As a broad empirical generalization, wherever we find a substantial degree of political equality, we also find a substantial degree of economic meritocracy. Far from being antithetical, the two ideas are symbiotic. A central facet of the traditional liberal ideal of equal opportunity is a call for removing arbitrary political or cultural barriers to economic mobility. After the fact, we need not and do not attach the same value to what people produce. (Obviously, people themselves are not indifferent to whether their plans pan out one way rather than another. If our inventions work, we attach more value to them than we would have if they had not, and we expect the market to do likewise.) Before the fact, though, traditional liberals want people—all people—to be as free as possible to pursue their dreams. That is to say, the equal-opportunity element of liberal tradition placed the emphasis on improving opportunities, not equalizing them.[25] The ideal of "equal pay for equal work," within the tradition from which that ideal emerged, has more in common with the ideal of meritocracy, and with the kind of equal respect built into the concept of meritocracy, than with equal shares per se.

In passing, note that meritocracy is not a synonym for market society. Meritocrats could say the marketplace's meritocratic tendencies are too weak; great talent too often goes unrecognized and unrewarded. Egalitarians could say such tendencies are too strong;

Rather, what is objectionable is some being worse off than others *through no fault of their own*" (Temkin, *Inequality*, 17). Unfortunately, the sort of room Temkin tries to make has an awkward consequence. If Bill has more than me because he does better work, then according to the quotation's first sentence the inequality is deserved and therefore not bad at all; at the same time, though, I am worse off through no fault of my own, which is objectionable according to the quotation's second sentence.

25   Interestingly, Richard Miller says "people are pervasively victimized by social barriers to advancement in any reasonably efficient capitalist economy. … On the other hand, in an advanced industrial setting, some reasonably efficient capitalist system is best for everyone who is constrained by justice" as Miller conceives of it. There is nothing inconsistent about this, although it "depends on facts that would sadden most observers of the modern industrial scene, saddening different observers for different reasons: Central planning does not work, yet traditional socialists were right in most of their charges of capitalist inequality." Richard Miller, "Justice as Social Freedom," in Rodger Beehler, David Copp, and Béla Szabados, eds., *On the Track of Reason: Essays in Honor of Kai Nielsen* (Boulder, CO: Westview, 1992), 38.

Daniels seems to worry that rewards for satisfying millions of customers are larger than they should be. Underlying both complaints is the more fundamental fact that markets react to performance only in the form in which said performance is *brought to market*. So long as Emily Dickinson kept her poetry secret, the marketplace had no opinion about its merits. The marketplace tends to reward a particular kind of performance—namely, wealth-creating performance—and tends to reward that kind of performance in a particular way—namely, with wealth, or sometimes with fame and glory.[26] Markets create time and space within which people can afford hobbies; they can write poetry, if that is what pleases them, without having to worry about whether that particular activity is putting dinner on the table. But the marketplace generally does not judge, and does not reward, what people do with the space they reserve for nonmarket activities.

Let me stress that my remarks about the consistency of, and even synergy between, equality and meritocracy are offered in defense of the proposition that there is room within a pluralistic conception of justice for elements of egalitarianism. If, contrary to fact, it really were true that we had to make a choice between equality and meritocracy, it would be like choosing between egalitarianism and humanitarianism. When egalitarianism allows itself to be contrasted with humanitarianism, it begins to look monstrous. It likewise would be monstrous to reject a system not because it *fails* to recognize and reward merit, but precisely because it succeeds.

D. Pure distribution is rare

In the real world, almost nothing we do is purely distributive. To take from one and give to another does not only alter a distribution. It also alters the degree to which products are controlled by their producers. To redistribute under real-world conditions, we must alienate producers from their products. This alienation was identified as a problem by Marx, and ought to be regarded as a problem from any perspective.

In a world bound to depart systematically from egalitarian ideals, egalitarian philosophy can encourage these alienated and alienating attitudes, although egalitarian philosophy is not unique in this respect. As noted by Anderson, academic egalitarians tend to see luck as a moral problem. A purist meritocrat, though, would agree, saying success should not be mere luck, but ought to be earned. So, if meritocratic ideals had the actual effect of encouraging feelings of alienation in a world bound to depart systematically from meritocratic ideals, that would be regrettable. The general point here is that even when an uncompromisingly radical philosophy is attractive on its face, the psychological baggage that goes with it need not be. A theory of justice can deafen us to the cost of alienating

---

26   On this topic, I regard as essential reading Tyler Cowen, *In Praise of Commercial Culture* (Cambridge, MA: Harvard University Press, 1998); and Tyler Cowen, *What Price Fame?* (Cambridge, MA: Harvard University Press, 2000).

producers from their product. It deafens us by telling us what we want to hear: that the product should be distributed in accordance with our dream, not the producers'.

Defenders of redistribution sometimes try to justify ignoring this cost. A familiar move is to deny that people are producers. On this account, natural endowments produce. Characters produce. Persons do not. A person's character "depends in large part upon fortunate family and social circumstances for which he can claim no credit,"[27] and therefore, at least theoretically, there is a form of respect we can have for people even while giving them no credit for the effort and talent they bring to the table.

So the story goes. One basic problem with it is that the form of respect it posits is not the kind that brings producers to the table, and therefore that form of respect is, from any perspective, deficient. It is not the kind of respect that human beings value; it is not the kind that makes societies work.

Anderson notes, as many have noted, that egalitarians "regard the economy as a system of cooperative, joint production," in contrast with "the more familiar image of self-sufficient Robinson Crusoes, producing everything all by themselves until the point of trade."[28] She goes on to say that we ought to "regard every product of the economy as

---

27   John Rawls, *A Theory of Justice* (Cambridge, MA: Harvard University Press, 1971), 104. No one has done more than Rawls in recent generations to rekindle philosophical interest in liberal egalitarianism. Rawls's approach is to set aside as morally arbitrary everything that makes people unequal: that they have unequal talents, that some have better characters than others, that they have differing hopes and dreams, and so on. Crucially, and rather incredibly, he sets aside that some people have done more than others. All of these things, he says, are arbitrary from a moral point of view (ibid., sec. 17). Having done all this, it could hardly be news if the resulting conclusion turned out to have an egalitarian flavor. Many of Rawls's moderate and mainstream readers have been offended by Rawls's apparent denigration of everything that makes a person a person, and by what they see as egalitarianism taken to absurd extremes. But I think these reactions miss the fundamental point. The Rawlsian exercise does not surprise readers by coming to extreme yet plausible egalitarian conclusions. On the contrary, what is newsworthy is that the result is not a strict form of egalitarianism. Even if we resolve to ignore everything that makes people unequal, and indeed everything that individuates them as persons, the door remains wide open for unequal shares. *This* is Rawls's signature contribution. If we understand Rawls in this way, then this essay's objective is complementary to Rawls's. That is, where Rawls argues that even if we stack the deck in favor of egalitarianism, we still find substantial room for unequal shares, I argue that even for beings as unequal in morally nonarbitrary ways as we are, there remains significant room within a pluralistic theory of justice for important elements of egalitarianism.

28   Anderson, "What Is the Point of Equality?" 321. In passing, the Crusoe image is indeed familiar, even if only in the works of liberalism's communitarian critics. In fact, the classical liberal view is that the legacy of free association is community, not atomic isolation. Humans have been organizing themselves into communities since long before there was any such thing as what we now call the state. See Loren Lomasky, "Nozick on Utopias," in David Schmidtz, ed., *Robert Nozick* (New York: Cambridge

jointly produced by everyone working together."[29] By way of response, we all understand that Anderson's article is the product of a system of cooperative, joint production. We all know she did not produce it by herself. Yet we also understand that it is her article, and we would be furious were we to learn that Ackerman had walked into her office one day and said, "Shouldn't I get half of that article?" We do not start "from scratch." Rather, we build upon work already done. We weave our contribution into an existing fabric of contributions. We contribute at the margin (as an economist would put it) to the system of cooperative production, and, within limits, we are seen as owning our contributions, however humble they may be. This is *why* people continue to contribute, and this in turn is why we continue to have a system of cooperative production.

The most crucial point, perhaps, is that there is something necessarily and laudably historical about simply respecting the abilities that people bring to the table. We need not always dig around for evidence (or worse, stipulate) that people are products of nature and nurture and therefore ineligible for moral credit. Neither must we think of our trading partners as Robinson Crusoes. Often, we simply give them credit, and often simply giving them credit is the essence of treating them as persons rather than as mere confluences of historical forces.

When we do choose to reflect on the historical background of any particular ongoing enterprise, it is appropriate to feel grateful to Thomas Edison and all those people who actually did help to make the current enterprise possible. It would be inappropriate (that is, disrespectful to people like Edison) to feel similarly grateful to people who did not actually do anything to help make the current enterprise possible. (To my mind, one of the most perfectly incredible facts about political philosophy is that, given the premise that thousands of people contribute to the tide of progress that puts individuals in a position to do what they do, we go on to debate whether the appropriate response is to honor those who did contribute or to take their money and give it to those who did not.) When particular people literally contribute to joint projects, they ought to feel grateful to each other and collectively proud of their joint achievement. However, they need not feign agnosticism about the specifics of each partner's contribution in cases where (as it usually works) they are keenly aware of the nature and value of what particular partners have contributed.

Of course, there is much to be said for acknowledging how lucky we are to live within this particular "system of cooperative, joint production" and for respecting what makes it work. My point is only (and my guess is that Anderson would agree) that the room we make for these attitudes must leave room for acknowledging complementary considerations: the kind that bring producers to the table, and the kind involved in treating individual flesh-and-blood workers with genuine respect.

University Press, 2001); and Christopher Morris, *An Essay on the Modern State* (Cambridge: Cambridge University Press, 1998).

29   Anderson, "What Is the Point of Equality?" 321.

IV. EQUAL SHARES VERSUS FIRST POSSESSION

In Section II, I attributed to Ackerman the view that "equal shares" is a moral default, the distribution rule we automatically go to if we cannot justify anything else. Needless to say, that is not how we actually do it. For various resources in the real world, the principle we go to if we cannot justify anything else is one invoking first possession. If you walk into the cafeteria carrying two apples, we do not begin to discuss how to allocate them. If the apples are in your hand, their allocation normally is not our business.

Ackerman, though, rejects the rule of first possession. He says that "the only liberty worthy of a community of rational persons is a liberty each is ready and willing to justify in conversation with his fellow questioners. To ground rights on first possession is at war with this ideal."[30] But if this is so, why is first possession ubiquitous? In Ackerman's garden, we are offended when you grab both apples. Why is the real world so different—so different that if Ackerman were to walk up to you in the cafeteria and say, "Shouldn't I get half of your lunch?" we would be offended by Ackerman's behavior, not yours?

Evidently, there is some difficulty in generalizing from Ackerman's thought experiment. Why? The main reason why Ackerman's point does not generalize is that in the real world we do not begin life by dividing a sack of apples that somehow, on its own, made its way to the bargaining table. Instead, we start with resources that some people have helped to produce and others have not, resources already possessed and in use by some people as others arrive on the scene. Contractarian frameworks like Ackerman's depict everyone as getting to the bargaining table at the same time; it is of fundamental moral importance that the world is not like that.

In a world where virtually everything at the table is there because someone brought it to the table, it is easy for equal respect and equal shares to come apart. In a world like that—a world like ours—to respect people is to acknowledge what they bring to the table, to respect the talent and effort manifest in what they bring, and to respect the hopes and dreams that lead them to bring what they do. But to respect them in this way is to respect their contributions as *theirs*.

A. Respect in a world of nonsimultaneous arrival

Why do property regimes around the world and throughout history consistently operate on a principle of first possession rather than one of equal shares? The reason, I suppose, starts with the fact that in the real world people arrive at different times. When people arrive at different times, equal shares no longer has the intuitive salience it had in the case of simultaneous arrival. When someone has gotten there first and is peacefully trying to put his or her discovery to use, trying to grab a piece of the action, even if only an equal piece, is not a peaceful act. It is not a respectful act. If Ackerman were to enter a corner

---

30 Ackerman, "On Getting What We Don't Deserve," 63.

grocery and begin discussing how to allocate whatever he can find in the cash register, as if the shopkeeper were merely another party to the discussion, he would not be treating the shopkeeper with respect. Here is a thought experiment: in a world where Ackerman was not obliged to respect prior possession, how long would shops remain open for business?

Academic lawyer Carol Rose says that a legal rule that confers the status of owner upon the first person unambiguously taking possession of a given object induces discovery.[31] By inducing discovery, the rule induces future productive activity. A second virtue of such a rule is that it minimizes disputes over discovered objects.[32] In short, it enables shopkeepers to make a living in peace.[33]

Recall Ackerman's previous claim: "[T]he only liberty worthy of a community of rational persons is a liberty each is ready and willing to justify in conversation with his fellow questioners. To ground rights on first possession is at war with this ideal." Simply dismissing the other side as at war with the ideal of rational conversation, as Ackerman does here, is itself at war with the ideal of rational conversation. The truth, for millennia, has been that failing to respect prior possession is the stuff of war in an absolutely literal way. Moreover, the central place of prior possession is not a cultural artifact. Virtually any animal capable of locomotion understands at some level that if you ignore the claim of an animal that got there first, you are not treating it with respect.

B. Xenophobia

An overlooked virtue of first possession is that it lets us live together without having to view newcomers as a threat, whereas a rule of equal shares does not. If we were to regard every

---

31 Carol Rose, "Possession As the Origin of Property," *University of Chicago Law Review* 52, no. 1 (1985): 73–88.

32 Note that the person who establishes first possession need not acquire unconditional permanent ownership. The kind of ownership one establishes by being the first to register a *patent*, for example, is temporally limited. Alternatively, a *usufructuary* right is a particular kind of ownership that lasts only so long as the owned object is being used for its customary purpose. Thus, for example, the first person to grab a particular park bench acquires a right to use that seat for its customary purpose, but only so long as he or she occupies the bench. When the person gets up and leaves the park, the bench reverts to its previous unclaimed status.

33 Needless to say, history is filled with irreparable injustices, which often boil down to failures to respect claims of those who were there first. The ubiquitous phenomenon of respect for prior possession is mostly an in-group phenomenon. Human groups tend not to respect claims of other groups unless those other groups are capable of defending their claims in battle. So, nothing said by Rose or by me is meant to imply that prior possession has in fact been consistently respected. On the contrary, aboriginal peoples around the world consistently have been brutally subjugated. Had prior possession been respected, many of human history's most tragic episodes would not have happened.

newcomer as having a claim to an equal share of our holdings, the arrival of newcomers would be inherently threatening. Imagine another thought experiment: A town has one hundred people. Each has a lot that is one hundred feet wide. Every time someone new shows up, we redraw property lines. Each lot shrinks by the amount needed to make room for the new person's equal share. Question: how friendly will this town be? Even now, in our world, people who see the world in zero-sum terms tend to despise immigrants. The point is not that xenophobia has moral weight, of course, but rather that it is real, a variable we want to minimize if we can. Recognizing first possession helps, compared to redistributing according to an equal-shares principle. To say the least, it would not help to tell people that newly arriving immigrants have a right to an equal share. At first, members of the community would clamor for a wall to stop people from getting in. Eventually, the point of the wall would be to stop people from getting out.

Likewise, apropos Ackerman's assertion that a liberty is worthy only if we are each ready and willing to justify it in conversation, imagine a world in which the title to your property was perpetually contingent on your ability to defeat all challengers in debate. In any remotely successful community, quite a lot of the structure of daily life literally goes without saying and needs no argument; this enables people to take quite a lot for granted and allows them to pour their energy into production rather than self-defense, verbal or otherwise.

The central role played by prior possession in any viable culture, across human history, is a problem for egalitarianism, although not uniquely for egalitarianism. Meritocracy is equally in a position of having to defer somewhat to a norm of respecting prior possession. A viable culture is a web of positive-sum games, but a game is positive-sum only if players are willing to take what they have as their starting point and carry on from there. A viable conception of justice takes *this* (along with other prerequisites of positive-sum games) as its starting point.

V. THE ZERO-SUM PERSPECTIVE

The obvious moral problem with first possession, of course, is that those who arrive later do not get an equal share. Is that fair? It depends. Exactly how bad is it to be a latecomer? Egalitarian thought experiments such as Ackerman's are zero-sum games. In such models, first possession leaves latecomers with nothing. When you, the first appropriator, grab both apples (or even one, for that matter), you leave less for Ackerman or anyone else who comes along later. Your grab is a preface to pure consumption. Thus, as philosopher Hillel Steiner has noted, in the same way that first-comers would see newcomers as a threat under an equal-shares regime, newcomers would see first-comers as a threat under a regime of first possession.[34] Or at least, newcomers would see first-comers as a threat if it really were true that in a first-possession regime it is better to arrive early than late.

But this is not true. One central fact about a regime of first possession is that over time, as a rule, it is far better to arrive late than early. It would be unusual to meet people in a developed nation who are not substantially more wealthy than their grandparents were at a comparable age. We have unprecedented wealth today precisely because our ancestors got here first, cleared the land, and began the laborious process of turning society into a vast network of cooperative ventures for mutual advantage. In the real world, original appropriation typically is a preface to production, and then to mutually advantageous commerce with widely dispersed benefits. It is not a zero-sum game. First possessors pay the price of converting resources to productive use. Latecomers reap the benefits.[35] We occasionally should remind ourselves that in the race to appropriate, the chance to be a first appropriator is not the prize. The prize is prosperity, and latecomers win big, courtesy of the toil of those who got there first.

So, when someone asks why entrepreneurs should get to keep the whole value of what they produce, the answer is that they don't. To some people, this will seem obvious. Yet there are some who really do see the world in zero-sum terms. To them, when you grab an apple in Ackerman's garden and start planting apple seeds, it is analytic that no one else will ever benefit from all those future harvests.

A. Structural unemployment

The zero-sum perspective is most tempting when viewing the labor market. Thus, philosopher Robert Goodin can say, "If there are a thousand people looking for work and only one job, one can get work only on condition that the remainder do not. That one person succeeds in getting a job, far from proving that all could, actually precludes others from doing so."[36] Goodin admits labor markets are not really like that, yet he does not retract the claim. Citing philosopher G. A. Cohen, Goodin says, "Marxian economics provides reasons for believing that precisely that is true of the proletarian in any capitalist economy."[37] That is, "If the structure of the situation is such that one can succeed only

---

34   Hillel Steiner, conversation with author, September 24, 2000.

35   For a state-of-the-art discussion of this issue, see John T. Sanders, "Projects and Property," in Schmidtz, ed., *Robert Nozick*. See also David Schmidtz, "The Institution of Property," *Social Philosophy and Policy* 11, no. 2 (1994): 42–62.

36   Schmidtz and Goodin, *Social Welfare and Individual Responsibility*, 126.

37   Ibid., 126 n.

on condition that not all do, then the freedom of the one is perfectly consistent with the 'unfreedom' of the many."[38] This is what has come to be called "structural" unemployment.

Some will see Goodin as stating a necessary truth: when two people apply for the same job, it is as if there were only one apple in Ackerman's garden. Others will say that in developed economies, the salient ratio is not (or not only) the number of jobs per *job-seeker* but the number of jobs per *month*. The former ratio leads people to misinterpret the supply of jobs as a stock rather than as a flow. If the unemployment rate is 10 percent, that does not mean one-tenth of the population is doomed to unemployment. For many, what it means is that their number is called less often than it would be if the rate were lower—unless there is genuine structural unemployment, as in countries where, for example, women are legally or culturally barred from working. But what creates structural unemployment is structure, not the rate of flow in the labor market.

B. Markets are not auctions

If society were a zero-sum game, then the only way for some to have more would be for others to have less. When we see society as actually like this, we are tempted to believe the argument that when some people have more dollars, they bid up prices of whatever is available for purchase, thereby out competing cash-poor people and making them worse off. This is an interesting and rhetorically powerful idea. It would even be true in a society where people acquire paper dollars from a central distributor without having done anything to create the stock of wealth for which those paper dollars are supposed to be a receipt. But now contrast this zero-sum picture with a generally more realistic picture of market society. If I acquire more dollars by contributing more goods and services to the economy, then my participation in the economy is not inflationary. On the contrary, insofar as people give me paper dollars in exchange for goods and services I bring to market, the process by which I acquire dollars has a deflationary impact, for the result of my contribution is that there now are more goods and services in circulation with no corresponding increase in the number of paper dollars in circulation. The net impact of the process by which I amass paper dollars is that *prices fall*, unless the money

---

38   Ibid., 126. Cohen considers the proletariat free to remain or not remain proletarian workers in the following sense: The proletariat is like a group of people locked in a room. There is a key, but it will work only for the first person who uses it. "Each is free to seize the key and leave. But note the conditional nature of his freedom. He is free not only *because* none of the others tries to get the key, but *on condition* that they do not (a condition which, in this story, is fulfilled)." G. A. Cohen, "The Structure of Proletarian Unfreedom," *Philosophy and Public Affairs* 12, no. 1 (1983): 11. Cohen's article is wonderfully provocative. It is easy to see how someone could see it as realistically describing the kind of "key to success" we have when seeking work, although I am not sure whether Cohen himself meant it this way.

supply is increased to keep pace with the increased volume of goods and services in circulation.

Many people, though, continue to be swayed (if not downright blinded) by arguments premised on the assumption that for some to have more, others must have less. For some reason, this assumption is unshaken by everyday observation of people acquiring wealth not by subtracting it from a fixed stock, but by adding goods and services to the economy.

C. Sexism

Goodin's odd picture of what it is like to participate in an economy is implicit in arguments of theorists who occasionally propose, as a way of redressing our society's sexist bias, that mothers be paid a wage simply for being mothers. This too begins with an interesting and rhetorically powerful idea: When men go to the factory and women stay home to manage the household, they both work really hard. The men get paid. Why don't the women?

Here is one answer. The problem is not that the market does not recognize *women*, but that it does not recognize what is *not brought to market*. Suppose a farmer raises a crop while his wife raises children. Is it sexist that only the man's labor earns money? To test the hypothesis, imagine a farmer saying to prospective customers, "My wife and I have two things for sale: first, the fact that we are growing a crop, and second, the fact that we are raising six kids." Would prospective customers volunteer to pay the farmer for raising crops, but not for raising children?

If they would, that might suggest a sexist bias. But they would not. Their response would be, "Just show us what you have for sale. If your crop or your day-care services are for sale, we're interested. When your kids have goods of their own for sale, we'll be interested. But if what you want is to be paid to consume your own crop and raise your own kids, then in all seriousness, we have children of our own to feed. By the way, would you be better off if the king took your money to feed our kids and took our money to feed yours? Would your daughters be better off if women were expected to maximize their family's slice of the redistributive pie by having more babies than they otherwise would want? Would that end sexism?"

When people say women should be paid to raise their own children, it is as if a farmer demanded to be paid for raising a crop without actually having brought anything to market. It is to fail to grasp what is involved in exchanging value for value. It is a mistake to criticize markets for failing to commodify children. Commodifying children would be catastrophic for everyone, but especially for women. If we want to keep making progress toward the kind of society in which men and women can flourish as political equals, we need to find another way.

VI. ABOUT EMPIRICAL STUDIES

I close with observations about the other major source of provocation mentioned at the outset—namely, empirical studies of income inequality.[39] Although I am a professor of economics by joint appointment, I am at heart a philosopher. I trust conceptual arguments. I do not want to win arguments I do not deserve to win, and when the terrain is conceptual, I trust myself to know where I stand. I do not feel this way about statistics. This section's main purpose is not to settle some empirical issue, but simply to show how easily numbers create false impressions.

For example, studies of income distribution typically separate populations into quintiles according to household income. While each quintile for household income contains 20 percent of all households by definition, as of 1997 the United States's bottom quintile contained only 14.8 percent of individual persons, whereas the top quintile contained 24.3 percent. Households in the bottom quintile averaged 1.9 persons and 0.6 workers, compared to 3.1 persons and 2.1 workers in the top.[40] So, one major source of income inequality among households is that some contain more wage-earners than others. If we look at raw data comparing household incomes in the top and bottom quintiles, we will not see this, and will be misled.

We can be misled in another way when studying changes in household income in a society where the number of wage-earners per household is falling. When the number of wage-earners per household falls, average *household* income can fall even as *individual* incomes rise. If two people live in a typical college-student household today versus three in a household a generation ago, this will show up in our statistics as a fall in the bottom quintile's average income. Yet in such cases, household income falls because the individuals are more wealthy, not less, which is why they now can afford to split the rent with fewer people.[41]

It is easy to dig up a study showing that average wages fell by, say, 9 percent between 1975 and 1997, if that is what we want to hear. If not, it is equally easy to verify that such studies are based upon a discredited way of correcting for inflation (in addition, these studies ignore factors such as the burgeoning of fringe benefits) and that when we use more currently accepted ways of correcting for inflation, the corrected numbers show average wages rising 35 percent between 1975 and 1997.[42] In 1996, a panel of five

---

39   See Tyler Cowen, "Does the Welfare State Help the Poor?" in this volume for a discussion of the relatively more accurate picture painted when we measure inequality of consumption rather than income.

40   Robert Rector and Rea S. Hederman, *Income Inequality: How Census Data Misrepresent Income Distribution* (Washington, DC: Heritage Foundation, 1999).

41   Edward Wolff notes that it is easy to contrive size-adjusted family-income equivalents. But my point is that Census Bureau data—the standard source for almost any study you will read on U.S. income inequality—is not in fact corrected in this way.

42   Both figures are in Floyd Norris, "Sorry, Wrong Numbers: So Maybe It Wasn'tthe Economy," *New York Times*, December 1, 1996, sec. 4, p. 1. The first number is based on the standard consumer price index at the time. The second number was supplied by Leonard Nakamura, an economist with the

economists, commissioned by the Senate Finance Committee and chaired by Michael Boskin, concluded that the consumer price index overstates inflation by about 1.1 percent per year (perhaps as little as 0.8 percent; perhaps as much as 1.6 percent).[43] If the figure of 1.1 percent is correct, then "instead of the stagnation recorded in official statistics, a lower inflation measure would mean that *real* median family income grew from 1973 to 1995 by 36 percent." [44]

If there is one thing I would like readers to take away as the message of this section, it would not be a number. It would be the following picture. An income distribution is a bunch of people occupying steps on a staircase.[45] Pessimists use numbers to show that the bottom step is where it always has been. Even worse, they claim, the staircase has begun to stretch. The top now climbs higher than it once did, thereby increasing the gap between the top and bottom steps, that is, between the rich and poor. Optimists use the same numbers to show that people who once stood on the lower steps have moved up. While there are still people at the bottom, many belong to a younger generation whose time to move up is still coming. From a "snapshot" perspective, the picture is one of stagnation, but to people actually living these lives, the staircase is a moving escalator, lifting people to heights that did not exist when their grandparents were children. This perspective—which treats life in the way people actually live it—is a picture of incremental improvement.

I am not asking you to be an optimist. The message, instead, is that the pessimistic perspective is, at very best, only one way of being realistic. At bottom, the profound truth of the matter may be, as philosopher Richard Miller once remarked to me, that there is a place for a Democratic sort of emphasis on complaining about where some of us had to

---

Federal Reserve Bank of Philadelphia. Recent reports from the U.S. Census Bureau and the Bureau of Labor Statistics contain punishingly technical discussions of alternative ways of calculating inflation.

Edward Wolff provides the first, negative number in Edward Wolff, "The Stagnating Fortunes of the Middle Class," in this volume. In a conversation in September 2000 regarding a draft of that essay, Wolff admitted that his numbers were based upon a discredited method of adjusting for inflation. He rejected the idea that he should adjust his numbers, though, because, as he put it, "we can debate endlessly about the exact nature of the required adjustment, but it wouldn't be productive." When I noted that all he needed to do was correct his data by whatever measure he considered reasonable, and that his own best judgment would thereby be shown to be incompatible with his thesis that the middle class is stagnating, Wolff appeared indifferent.

43 "Statistical Guessing Game," *Economist*, December 7, 1996, 25.

44 David Gergen, "Flying in an Economic Fog," *U.S. News and World Report*, September 8, 1997, 104 (emphasis added). See also Michael Boskin et al., *Toward a More Accurate Measure of the Cost of Living: Final Report to the Senate Finance Committee*, available on-line at http://www.ssa.gov/history/reports/boskinrpt.html.

45 I borrow this metaphor from Stephen Rose, "Is Mobility in the United States Still Alive?" *International Review of Applied Economics* 13, no. 3 (1999): 417–36.

start, and also a place for a Republican sort of emphasis on accepting our starting point as a starting point and making the best of it.

A. Inequality and age in the United States

Statistics seem to indicate that the rich are getting richer. The income gap between the top quintile and other quintiles has, by some measures, been growing. What does this mean? For the sake of reference, when we divide households into income quintiles, the income cutoffs as of 1999 are as follows:

Lowest quintile: Zero to $17,262
Second quintile: $17,263 to $32,034
Third quintile: $32,035 to $50,851
Fourth quintile: $50,852 to $79,454
Top quintile: $79,455 and up[46]

Household income at the 80th percentile is thus 4.6 times household income at the 20th percentile. Compare this to the median household incomes of different age groups, as of 1999:

$24,031 when the head of the household is under 25
$43,309 when the head of the household is between ages 25 and 34
$54,993 when the head of the household is between ages 35 and 44
$65,303 when the head of the household is between ages 45 and 54
$54,249 when the head of the household is between ages 55 and 64[47]

Like the gaps between the quintiles, gaps between age groups appear to be increasing. Where earnings had once begun to trail off as workers entered their forties, earnings now continue to rise as workers reach their fifties, only then beginning to drop as early retirements start to cut into average earnings. Economist Michael Cox and journalist Robert Alm report that "[i]n 1951, individuals aged 35 to 44 earned 1.6 times as much as those aged 20 to 24, on average. By 1993, the highest paid age group had shifted to the 45 to 54-year-olds, who earned nearly 3.1 times as much as the 20 to 24-year-olds." [48]

---

46 This data is from U.S. Census Bureau, *Money Income in the United States: 1999* (Washington, DC: U.S. Government Printing Office, 2000), table 13.

47 This data is from ibid., table 4.

48 Michael Cox and Robert Alm, "By Our Own Bootstraps" (annual report of the Federal Reserve Bank of Dallas, published in 1995).

The numbers seem to say that the top quintile cannot be characterized as a separate caste of aristocrats. To some extent, the quintiles appear to be constituted by ordinary median people at different ages.[49] So, when we read that median income at the 80th percentile has jumped by 46 percent in real dollar terms between 1967 and 1999,[50] we should entertain the likelihood that for many people living at the 20th percentile, that jump represents increasing opportunity for them, not just for some separate elite. It represents what many reasonably hope to earn as they reach the age when people like them take their turn composing the top quintile. Again, the fact that 45-to 54-year-olds are doing much better today, thereby widening the gaps between income quintiles, appears to be good news for a lot of people, not only for people currently in that age group.[51]

Even if the lowest quintile has not been getting richer over time, this does not mean that the group of people flipping burgers a generation ago is still today stuck flipping burgers. Rather, the implication is that when this year's crop of high school graduates flips burgers for a year, they will get paid roughly what their parents were paid when they were the same age, doing the same things. (What else would we expect?) Again, if today's bottom 20 percent is no richer than the bottom 20 percent was a generation ago, the upshot is that the lowest-paying *jobs* do not pay much more than they ever did, not that the people who once held those jobs still hold them today.

Although the lowest-paying jobs may not pay much more now than they ever did, we know many low-pay workers did not remain low-pay workers. "Individuals in the lowest income quintile in 1975 saw, on average, a $25,322 rise in their real income over the sixteen years from 1975 to 1991. Those in the highest income quintile had a $3,974

---

49   Richard Miller has referred me to a study estimating that the proportion of income inequality that is due to age inequality is 28 percent for men and 14 percent for women. See Gary Burtless, *A Future of Lousy Jobs? The Changing Structure of U.S. Wages* (Washington, DC: Brookings Institution, 1990). That is a substantial proportion, although I am a bit surprised, given the income statistics for 1999 just cited in the text. Given that average income for household heads aged 45 to 54 is now 2.7 times that for household heads under 25, I might guess the proportion of income inequality due to age inequality in 1999 was higher than the numbers cited by Burtless.

50   U.S. Census Bureau, *Money Income in the United States: 1999*, table C.

51   Martin Feldstein lists several reasons for rapid rises in income at the top of the distribution: there are more people with advanced educations; there has been an increase in entrepreneurial activity, with many new businesses being created; highly paid professionals are working longer hours; and the cost of capital is declining, reducing perceived risks of investment and entrepreneurial activity. See Martin Feldstein, "Overview" (comments delivered at symposium on income inequality hosted by the Federal Reserve Bank of Kansas City, Jackson Hole, WY, August 1998), available on-line at http://www.kc.frb. org/PUBLICAT/SYMPOS/1998/S98feldstein.pdf.

increase in real income, on average." [52] How could people who had been in the bottom quintile gain over six times as much as people who had been in the top one? Assuming the numbers indicate something real, my conjecture would be that, again, what we call income quintiles are, to some extent, different age groups. Over sixteen years, people who had in 1975 made up a large part of the top quintile edged into retirement while younger people who had made up a large part of the bottom quintile in 1975 hit their peak earning years. This is only a conjecture, but it would explain why those who had composed the bottom quintile gained substantially more over sixteen years than those who had composed the top did.

B. While the rich get richer

Ideally, we want to know two things. First, are people doing better than their parents were doing at the same age? Second, do people do better as they get older? The answer to each of these crucial questions appears to be yes in general, although obviously I do not mean to suggest everyone is doing well. Still, in general, the numbers seem to say that it is not only the already rich who are getting richer. There are many more people *getting* rich. In 1967, only 3.2 percent of U.S. households were making the equivalent of $100,000 in 1999 dollars. By 1999, the number had risen to 12.3 percent. For whites, the increase was from 3.4 to 12.9 percent; for blacks, the increase was from 1.0 to 6.1 percent.[53] So, if we ask why the top quintile made further gains between 1967 and 1999, it apparently would be incorrect to explain the change by saying that a small cadre of people had a lot of money in 1967 and that by 1999 that same cadre had pulled even farther ahead. On the contrary, what seems to explain the burgeoning wealth of the top quintile is that millions upon millions of people joined the ranks of the rich. These people were not rich when they were younger. Their parents were not rich. But they are rich today.

In "America's Rags-to-Riches Myth," journalist Michael M. Weinstein says Americans "cling to the conceit that they have unrivaled opportunity to move up." [54] But the conceit, Weinstein says, is merely that. Yet Weinstein is aware that the U.S. Treasury Department's Office of Tax Analysis found that of people in the bottom income quintile in 1979, 65 percent moved up two or more quintiles by 1988. Eighty-six percent jumped at least one quintile.[55] Are these findings unique? There is room for skepticism, here as elsewhere. But no, the finding is not unique. Using independent data from the Michigan Panel Study of

---

52   Cox and Alm, "By Our Own Bootstraps," 8, citing Institute for Social Research, *A Panel Study of Income Dynamics* (Ann Arbor, MI: Institute for Social Research, 1989). The numbers are in 1993 dollars.

53   This data is from U.S. Census Bureau, *Money Income in the United States: 1999*, table B–2.

54   Michael M. Weinstein, "America's Rags-to-Riches Myth," *New York Times*, February 18, 2000, A28.

55   U.S. Department of the Treasury, Office of Tax Analysis, "Household Income Changes over Time: Some Basic Questions and Facts," *Tax Notes*, August 24, 1992.

Income Dynamics, Cox and Alm's study tracked a different group occupying the lowest quintile in 1975, and saw 80.3 percent of the group move up two or more quintiles by 1991. Ninety-five percent moved up at least one quintile. Furthermore, 29 percent moved from the bottom quintile to the top quintile between 1975 and 1991.[56] In absolute terms (that is, in terms of income gains in real dollar terms), the improvement is even larger. In absolute terms, 39.2 percent of those in the bottom quintile in 1975 had, by 1991, moved to where the top quintile *had been* in 1975. Only 2.3 percent remained at a living standard equal to that of 1975's lowest quintile.[57]

These studies do *not* show us to be a nation of people lifting ourselves out of poverty "by our own bootstraps," though, because not everyone with a low income is from a poor background. Many low-income people are students who receive substantial family support. We should not infer from Cox and Alm's study that family background does not matter.[58]

Researchers Daniel McMurrer, Mark Condon, and Isabell Sawhill say:

> Overall, the evidence suggests that the playing field is becoming more level in the United States. Socioeconomic origins today are less important than they used to be. Further, such origins have little or no impact for individuals with a college degree, and the ranks of such individuals continue to increase. This growth in access to higher education represents an important vehicle for expanding opportunity. Still, family background continues to matter. While the playing field may be becoming more level, family factors still significantly shape the economic outcomes of children.[59]

---

56   Cox and Alm, "By Our Own Bootstraps," 8, citing Institute for Social Research, *A Panel Study of Income Dynamics.*

57   Cox and Alm, "By Our Own Bootstraps," 8, citing Institute for Social Research, *A Panel Study of Income Dynamics.*

58   I thank Richard Miller for a helpful discussion and references, including Thomas L. Hungerford, "U.S. Income Mobility in the Seventies and Eighties," *Review of Income and Wealth* 39, no. 4 (1993): 403–17. As we would expect, Hungerford finds less movement in his seven-year studies than we see in the nine-year and sixteen-year studies by the U.S. Treasury Department and U.S. Federal Reserve Bank. Hungerford also finds that between his 1969–76 and 1979–86 studies, upward mobility decreased somewhat for the bottom five deciles, while increasing somewhat for the sixth, seventh, and eighth (ibid., 407). Isabel V. Sawhill and Daniel P. McMurrer compare several studies on income mobility and find a rough consensus that about 40 percent of those in the bottom quintile at a given point in time move up in ten years; after twenty years, about 50 percent have moved up. Isabell V. Sawhill and Daniel P. McMurrer, "Economic Mobility in the United States" (report published by the Urban Institute, December 1996), available on-line at http://www.urban.org/oppor/opp_031b.html.

59   Daniel P. McMurrer, Mark Condon, and Isabel V. Sawhill, "Intergenerational Mobility in the United States" (report published by the Urban Institute, May 1997), available on-line at http://www.

A related issue: we have looked at the upward mobility of individuals, but we find less mobility in studies tracking households. Researchers Greg Duncan, Johanne Boisjoly, and Timothy Smeeding estimate that if we were to look at household rather than individual mobility, we would see that 47 percent of those in the bottom quintile in 1975 were still there in 1991. (Actually, they refer to the bottom quintile as "the poor," which is an increasingly untenable equation as the percentage of households officially in poverty continues to drop.) Twenty percent moved to the distribution's top half, and 6 percent moved to the top quintile.[60]

These numbers suggest household mobility is quite substantial; nevertheless, there apparently is a big difference between individual upward mobility and household upward mobility. Why would that be? Imagine a household with two teenagers, circa 1975. Two studies track this household. One study tracks household members as individuals, and finds that sixteen years later the teenagers' incomes have risen several quintiles. A second study tracking the original household as a household finds that the household lost the summer wages the now-departed teenagers earned while living at home and attending college. When the teenagers left home, they disappeared from the second study because the households they went on to form did not exist when the study began in 1975. That is, a longitudinal study tracking 1975 households ignores individuals who grow up, move out, form new households, and move up after 1975. Given the same data, a longitudinal study of circa-1975 households paints a picture of modest progress while a longitudinal study of circa-1975 individuals suggests volcanic upward mobility. Which picture is more realistic?

Duncan et al. do not reveal the basis of their estimates. I have no reason to doubt them, but it is interesting that Duncan et al. mention later in their article that their data set, drawn from the Michigan Panel Study, "is designed to be continuously representative of the nonimmigrant population as a whole."[61] I presume they have reasons for excluding immigrants, yet I would wager that immigrant households are more upwardly mobile than nonimmigrant households. Immigrant and nonimmigrant individuals may not differ much, relatively speaking, since they all start with teenage incomes and then move up. Households, though, are another matter, since if we exclude immigrant households, we are excluding households that are not established but are instead in a position like that of individual teenagers: they have little wealth and little income, for now, but they came here to work and make a major move up as a household. A focus on households already lends itself to an understatement of income mobility, compared to studies that focus on tracking

---

urban.org/oppor/opp_4b.htm.

60   Greg Duncan, Johanne Boisjoly, and Timothy Smeeding, "How Long Does It Take for a Young Worker to Support a Family?" *NU Policy Research* 1, no. 1 (1996). *NU Policy Research* is an on-line journal; the essay is available at http://www.northwestern.edu/IPR/ publications/nupr/nuprv01n1/duncan.html.

61   Ibid.

individuals. Excluding immigrant households presumably increases the magnitude of that relative understatement.

Again, I do not mean to say that the study by Duncan et al. is especially flawed. On the contrary, it is not. Like any other study, it is potentially informative, and potentially misleading. It offers not simply numbers, but interpretations of numbers. Any study of income mobility begins with key decisions about what the researchers are looking for. Different studies measure different things, and no one is to blame for that.

Weinstein simply dismisses Cox and Alm's study of individuals on the ground that many people who moved up were people who were students when the study began. Of course students make up a big part of the bottom quintile, and of course they move up, Weinstein says, but so what? "This upward mobility of students hardly answers the enduring question: How many grown-ups are trapped in low-paying jobs?" Weinstein answers his own question by saying, "The answer is, a lot." [62] Oddly, though, the only evidence he offers that "a lot" of grown-ups are trapped is a study of poverty among children. To that study we now turn.

C. Children

In their study, economists Peter Gottschalk and Sheldon Danziger separated children into quintiles according to family income.[63] Their data, Weinstein reports, shows that "[a]bout 6 in 10 of the children in the lowest group—the poorest 20 percent—in the early 1970's were still in the bottom group 10 years later. ... No conceit about mobility, real or imagined, can excuse that unconscionable fact."[64]

Since Weinstein relies solely on Gottschalk and Danziger, I checked the original study. Gottschalk and Danziger were studying American children that were 5 years old or younger when their ten-year studies began—ten years later, the children were still children.[65] What we appear to have, then, is a cohort of mostly young couples with babies, about 40 percent of whom had moved into higher quintiles ten years later. Is this percentage bad? Out of context, it looks neither bad nor good. Has any society ever done better?

Yes. It turns out at least one society has done better: the United States itself. The figure cited by Weinstein is the result from the first decade of a two-decade study. Weinstein

---

62   Weinstein, "America's Rags-to-Riches Myth."

63   Peter Gottschalk and Sheldon Danziger, "Income Mobility and Exits from Poverty of American Children, 1970–1992" (study prepared for UNICEF's International Child Development Centre, 1999), available on-line at http://ideas.uqam.ca/ideas/data/Papers/ bocbocoec430.html. The paper is also in Bruce Bradbury, Stephen P. Jenkins, and John Micklewright, eds., *The Dynamics of Child Poverty in Industrialized Nations* (Cambridge: Cambridge University Press, 2001).

64   Weinstein, "America's Rags-to-Riches Myth."

65   Gottschalk and Danziger, "Income Mobility and Exits from Poverty," 4.

presents the figure from the 1970s (only 43 percent moving up) as an indictment of America today, neglecting to mention that the study's corresponding figure from the 1980s was 51 percent. Although the two figures come from the same table in Gottschalk and Danziger's paper, Weinstein evidently felt the more up-to-date number and the upward trend were not worth mentioning.

A further thought: At the end of the Gottschalk-Danziger studies, the parents of the studied children are (generally) in their early thirties, still ten years away from the time when they become most upwardly mobile. And of course, the kids are still thirty years away from the time when they become most upwardly mobile. So, the Gottschalk-Danziger studies end at a point where I would have predicted it would be too soon for there to be much evidence of upward mobility.

I myself would have been one of those kids they are talking about. I grew up on a farm in Saskatchewan. We sold the farm when I was 11 and moved to the city, where Dad became a janitor and Mom became a cashier in a fabric shop. Even before we left the farm, we had already moved up in absolute terms—we got indoor plumbing when I was about 3 years old—but we would still have been in the bottom quintile. Even after we got a flush toilet, water had to be delivered by truck, and it was so expensive that we flushed the toilet only once a day—and it served a family of eight. Thirty-five years later, my household income is in the top 5 percent of the overall distribution. Had I been part of Gottschalk and Danziger's study, though, Weinstein would have been professing to be outraged by the "unconscionable" fact that when I was 10 years old, I had not yet made my move.

In my case, the problem with childhood poverty was not lack of money. Money was never a problem. Even the toilet was not really a problem. Lack of knowledge was a problem. Lack of educated role models was a problem. (My parents received sixth-grade educations. I did not know what a university was until we moved to the city.) I suspect that the Internet notwithstanding, the big obstacles I faced continue to be big obstacles for poor kids today.

Let us return to the study. As I said, I would have predicted that we would see precious little evidence of upward mobility in a study that ends before subjects reach their mid-teens. But let us take a look. According to Gottschalk and Danziger, among children in bottom-quintile families that received welfare payments in the early 1970s, 2.3 percent were in households that rose beyond the second quintile by the early 1980s. Bottom-quintile children living in single-parent families had a 6.4 percent chance of being in a household that moved beyond the second quintile.[66] Unsurprisingly, one-adult households brought in less income than two-adult households at both points in time, and therefore we find them in the bottom two quintiles. How bad is that? The poverty rate in the United

---

66   Ibid., 8.

States continues to fall and was most recently measured at 11.8 percent,[67] which means that being in the bottom two quintiles—the bottom 40 percent—is not the synonym for "being poor" that it once was.[68]

If there is a problem here, it appears to have less to do with differences in income and wealth per se and more to do with single parenthood (and I do not pretend to know how to solve that problem). Economist Robert Lerman estimates that half the increase in income inequality observed in the late 1980s and early 1990s was due to an increase in the number of single-parent households.[69] According to Gottschalk and Danziger, there is a big difference between being poor and white and being poor and black: blacks are more likely to stay in the bottom quintile. I am reluctant to quarrel with Gottschalk and Danziger here, and yet, according to their own numbers, the result of their ten-year study begun in 1971 is that "black children had a *higher* chance than white children of escaping poverty if they made the transition from a single-parent family to a 2-parent family by the end of the decade (67.9 versus 42.6 percent)."[70] Looking at results of the second study, begun in 1981, we find the chance of a child escaping poverty (actually, the bottom quintile) upon moving from a single-parent to a two-parent family improving to 87.8 percent for blacks and 57.6 percent for whites.[71]

---

67 U.S. Census Bureau, *Poverty in the United States: 1999* (Washington, DC: U.S. Government Printing Office, 2000), table A. The poverty threshold varies with the size of the household (and, less intuitively, with the age of the household's members). For 1999, the official poverty threshold for a household consisting of two adults under age 65 was $11,214.

U.S. Census Bureau, "Poverty Thresholds: 1999," in U.S. Census Bureau, *March Current Population Survey: 1999* (Washington, DC: U.S. Government Printing Office, 2000).

68 Furthermore, being officially below the poverty threshold does not entail material hardship. There are truly suffering people out there, but in the United States they are a small percentage of the total population. According to a U.S. Department of Agriculture survey, only one-third of 1 percent of U.S. households reported a child skipping a meal due to lack of food in 1994–95. Of households *below the poverty level*, only 3.5 percent reported having a child who needed medical care or surgery but did not get it. The original sources of this data are U.S. Department of Agriculture, *Household Food Security in the United States in 1995: Summary Report of the Food Security Measurement Project* (Washington, DC: U.S. Department of Agriculture, 1997); and Centers for Disease Control, National Center for Health Statistics, *Access to Health Care* (Washington, DC: U.S. Government Printing Office, 1997). See also Robert E. Rector, Kirk A. Johnson, and Sarah E. Youssef, "The Extent of Material Hardship and Poverty in the United States," *Review of Social Economy* 57, no. 3 (1999): 351–87.

69 Robert I. Lerman, "The Impact of the Changing U.S. Family Structure on Child Poverty and Income Inequality," *Economica* 63, no. 250 (1996): 119–39.

70 Gottschalk and Danziger, "Income Mobility and Exits from Poverty," 11.

71 Ibid., table 6.

The numbers seem to say that race is not the problem; again, coming from a single-parent family is the problem. However, in the 1980s, whites were nearly three times as likely as blacks to make that move from single-parent to two-parent families (which represents a closing of what had been a fourfold gap in the 1970s).[72] Furthermore, black children are more likely to be in a single-parent setting in the first place. As of 1998, the percentage of out-of-wedlock births was 21.9 percent for non-Hispanic whites and 69.3 percent for blacks.[73] I trust even hardcore egalitarians will agree that what is bad about these numbers is how high they are, not how unequal they are.

In the 1980s, Gottschalk and Danziger say, the overall probability that a child would escape poverty was higher than it was in the 1970s, although the improvement was not significant.[74] For the record—using their numbers—the chance of escaping poverty improved from 43.2 percent to 51.2 percent.[75] Oddly, when Gottschalk and Danziger say that an eight-point swing is not significant, they do not hasten to clarify what this means. What they do not say is that although the change appears huge, they did not collect enough data to be able to call the improvement *statistically* significant.[76] Uncritical readers such as Weinstein are left to infer that there was no improvement.

Gottschalk and Danziger say that "only one demographic group (children in two parent families) shows a significant decline in the probability of remaining poor."[77] (What a discouraging thought—that we have reached a point where children in two-parent families are "only one demographic group.") Within that group, the chance of escaping poverty improved from 47 percent in the 1970s to 65 percent in the 1980s. Again, there is something so odd here that I am left not knowing what to think: the authors acknowledge the massively improved prospects of "children of two parent families" parenthetically, as if that class were a small anomaly that does not bear on their contention that the probability of escaping poverty has not significantly improved.

Finally, recall that we are talking about the chance of escaping poverty (more accurately, the bottom quintile) before leaving the 10–15 age bracket. If we sought deliberately to design an experiment guaranteed to show no evidence of vertical mobility, we could hardly do better. Yet what Gottschalk and Danziger's numbers say is that nearly two-thirds of poor kids in unbroken homes escape poverty before earning their first paycheck. If

---

72   Ibid., table 7.

73   National Center for Health Statistics, "Births: Final Data for 1998," available on-line at http://www.cdc.gov/nchs/data/nvsr/nvsr48/nvs48_3.pdf.

74   Gottschalk and Danziger, "Income Mobility and Exits from Poverty," 9.

75   Ibid., table 4.

76   For the classic warning against equating statistical significance with significance in the ordinary sense of the term, see Deirdre N. McCloskey, *The Rhetoric of Economics*, 2ded. (Madison: University of Wisconsin Press, 1998).

77   Ibid., 10.

Gottschalk and Danziger's numbers are right, then it is fact, not myth: these kids live in a land of opportunity.

Are growing differences in wealth and income a problem? Maybe so, in some respects. Nothing said here proves otherwise. The truly obvious problem, though, is more specific. In general, in the United States, poor people not only can but typically do move up—it is kids from broken homes who have a problem.

D. The political problem

One might argue that the problem of inequality is fundamentally caused by a lack of political will to "soak" the rich. We can imagine asking young poor people whether it is to their advantage for us to raise marginal rates on the tax brackets they are hoping to move into. It is possible they will say yes, but it is equally possible that the tax hike would take a bigger bite out of their ambitions than out of rich people's wallets. (This last claim may be very hard to imagine for people who grew up in middle-class homes and never saw working-class life as an option, but a "What's the point?" sentiment was common among people with whom I grew up at a time when marginal tax rates were higher.)

Would "soaking the rich" lead to greater equality? The answer, obviously, is that it depends on how the tax revenues would be distributed. The current U.S. federal budget is 1.7 trillion dollars. If we were to distribute that kind of money among the 14.8 percent of people who make up the poorest 20 percent of American households—roughly forty million people—we would already have enough to give a little over $40,000 to each person. A family of four would receive over $160,000. Of course, nothing remotely like that is happening. Why not? At least a part of the story is that the federal government has other priorities, and always will. We might suspect the problem cannot be solved by giving the government more money. After all, gaps between rich and poor apparently widened in tandem with rising federal budgets.

We can hope that as the rich get richer, more money will trickle down to the poor. We can also hope that as federal budgets grow, money will trickle down to the poor. But the rich have been getting richer, and federal budgets have grown. So, if the trickle down is not working now, perhaps it never will. In particular, as federal budgets grow, we would expect to reach a point (if we have not already done so) where the trickle down would come to a halt, or even reverse itself. The reason is that as budgets grow, it becomes increasingly worthwhile for special interest groups to fight for control of those budgets at the expense of the politically disenfranchised. If unequal concentrations of political power can be thought of as a beast, then government budgets are part of what feeds that beast and gives it reason to live. Although it is beyond the scope of this essay, my guess is that an effective coalescing of will and ability to help people avoid or at least cope with single parenthood and other pressing problems is more likely to occur in those local nongovernmental organizations whose budgets are small enough and whose governance is transparent enough to be less inviting to political opportunists.[78]

VII. SUMMARY

As economist Amartya Sen says, "[E]very normative theory or social arrangement that has at all stood the test of time seems to demand equality of *something*." [79] It is worth adding, though, that by the same token every theory, including egalitarian theories, countenances inequality as well. An egalitarian is a person who embraces one kind of unequal treatment as the price of securing equality of (what he or she considers) a more important kind.

There is a place for equal shares. Paradigmatically, there is a place for the principle of equal shares when we arrive simultaneously at the bargaining table to distribute goods to which no one has any prior claim. It would be a thankless task to try to construct a complete catalog of cases where equal shares is most salient. Suffice it to say that we can ask what the virtues of equal shares would be in a given context, were we to assess the principle without begging the question; that is, were we to assess the principle by reference to moral considerations that do not presuppose the principle. This is how we can try to make room for any given principle of justice within a pluralist theory.[80]

Equal respect is among the most basic of moral desiderata. Equal respect or equal treatment may be analytically built into the concept of justice even if equal shares is not. The idea of giving people their due is the basic concept of justice, not merely a contested conception. And the idea of giving people their due is hard to separate (at least at the most abstract level) from an ideal of equal treatment.

However, it would be a mistake to think that a commitment to treat people with equal respect entails a *general* commitment to make sure they have equal shares. In the marketplace, at least, meritocracy can embody one way of implementing a conception of equal treatment. Historically, "equal pay for equal work" has been seen this way within the liberal tradition.

First possession arguably is not a principle of justice at all, yet it plays a central role in any viable society. It is one of the signposts by which we navigate in a social world. We can question the principle in theory (and in theory it probably is easier to attack than to defend), but we do not and cannot question the principle in our daily practice. We would be lost without it.

---

78   But see the chapter on mutual aid in Schmidtz and Goodin, *Social Welfare and Individual Responsibility*.

79   Amartya Sen, *Inequality Reexamined* (Cambridge, MA: Harvard University Press, 1992), 12–13.

80   Or so I argue in the larger work (David Schmidtz, *The Elements of Justice*) of which this essay will be a part.

Empirically, it can be hard to know what to make of recent income trends. We are barraged by numbers, or by interpretations thereof, and people skilled at gathering numbers are not always so skilled at interpreting them. If I were to do serious empirical work, I would ask why people today generally look forward to standards of living almost beyond the imagination of their ancestors from a century ago. (Life expectancy, for example, has nearly doubled.) I would ask who has been left behind by this burgeoning of real prosperity and why, and what can be done about it. I would not assume that all problems have solutions, nor that all solutions are worth their costs. Optimist that I am, I assume we can do better. Realist that I am, I know we could do worse.

Philosophy and Economics, University of Arizona

Freedom as a Political Ideal

STEVEN WALL

I. INTRODUCTION

I shall assume that a well-ordered state is one that promotes the freedom of its subjects. My question is what is the kind of freedom that the state ought to promote? This question is different from the question of what freedom is. It might be thought, for example, that freedom consists in the autonomous pursuit of valuable goals and projects, but that the state cannot directly promote this freedom. On this view, the state would not be able to make its citizens free. However, it might be able to do things that make it easier or more likely for them to be free. The freedom that the state promotes might be merely an aspect of or a condition for the freedom that really matters.

A political ideal of freedom tells us what kind of freedom the state ought to promote. If the ideal is sound, and if a state successfully promotes the kind of freedom that this political ideal identifies, then the state will have done all that it can do to promote the freedom of its subjects, even if some of its subjects remain substantially unfree. My purpose in this essay is to articulate and defend a particular ideal of political freedom. This ideal holds that the state ought to promote and sustain an environment in which its subjects are best able to carry out their plans and to form new ones. The freedom-supportive state, on the ideal

*I would like to thank Ellen Frankel Paul and fellow contributors to this volume for their helpful comments and suggestions.

that I shall offer, is the state that best enables its subjects to plan their lives, whatever their plans might be.

II. POLITICAL FREEDOM AND PERSONAL AUTONOMY

Political freedom is valuable because of its contribution to the freedom of individual persons. Here I shall assume, but will not defend, the claim that individual freedom is best understood in terms of personal autonomy.[1] I shall also assume a particular understanding of autonomy. An autonomous life is one in which a person charts his own course through life, fashioning his character by self-consciously choosing projects and assuming commitments from a wide range of eligible alternatives, and making something out of his life according to his own understanding of what is valuable and worth doing. So described, autonomy is a distinctive ideal. It applies to a person's whole life or to large stretches of it.

To realize autonomy, one needs several things. One needs at least (1) the capacity to form complex intentions and to sustain commitments, (2) the independence necessary to chart one's own course through life and to develop one's own understanding of what is valuable and worth doing, (3) the self-consciousness and vigor necessary to take control of one's affairs, and (4) access to an environment that provides one with a wide range of valuable options.[2] Elements (1) and (3) refer to mental capacities and virtues. Element (2) refers to one's relations with other persons who could exercise power over one. Element (4) refers to the environment in which one lives.

I shall argue that the state should be primarily concerned with the second and fourth elements. A freedom-supportive state is one that protects the independence of its subjects and ensures that they have access to a wide range of valuable options. The reason for limiting the concern of the state to elements (2) and (4) is that the state is generally not an effective instrument for cultivating mental capacities and virtues.[3] When the state attempts to improve individuals' psychologies or remove intra-personal barriers, it is likely to do more harm than good. The state that attempts to make its subjects masters of themselves will

---

1   Many writers distinguish freedom from autonomy. They hold that freedom applies to particular options, whereas autonomy refers to the way in which a person leads his life over time. See, for example, Joel Feinberg, *Harm to Self* (Oxford: Oxford University Press, 1986), 62–68. I do not deny that this distinction can serve some theoretical purposes. But, because my concern in this essay is with what a state should do to assist persons in leading free lives, I shall not insist on the distinction here.

2   I discuss each of these requirements in greater detail in Steven Wall, *Liberalism, Perfectionism, and Restraint* (Cambridge: Cambridge University Press, 1998), 127–61.

3   There are a few things that the state can effectively do in this regard. For example, it can do its best to ensure that all children receive an adequate education. But even here there are serious limits to what the state can do. Whether a child receives the kind of education that he needs to live an autonomous life depends more on what his parents do than what his state does.

likely just end up oppressing them.[4] This is not to say that the lack of certain psychological capacities or the presence of certain internal constraints do not diminish or undermine autonomy. They clearly do. My argument here simply recognizes the limits of the state's power to promote freedom.

This is why a political ideal of freedom should not be identified with freedom itself. The freedom that the state should promote and protect is valuable and important, but it is a only part of and a condition for the freedom that really matters.[5] It should now be clear why a state that does all that it can and should do in promoting freedom may exercise authority over some individuals who remain substantially unfree. Their failure to be free is not *its* failure.

III. THREE PROBLEMS

What kind of freedom should the state promote? What kind of freedom-supportive environment should it strive to create and sustain? A political ideal of freedom provides answers to these questions. But, of course, there are rival ideals of political freedom. How should we decide between them?

I suggest that any satisfactory political ideal of freedom must respond well to three problems. I shall refer to these problems as *the problem of integrity, the problem of pluralism,* and *the problem of unacceptable implications.* We may be able to decide between rival political ideals of freedom by assessing how well each responds to these problems. This, at any rate, is the approach that I shall take in this essay.[6]

The three problems require explanation. *The problem of integrity* is the problem of showing how political freedom is a distinct ideal, one that is not reducible to some other ideal and one that is capable of conflicting with other values. There is a temptation in political philosophy to make freedom compatible with all that is valuable. When this temptation is not resisted, freedom becomes a master value that subsumes all that is thought to be valuable. Likewise, there is a temptation to reduce freedom to some other value or ideal, since doing so provides a ready explanation for why freedom is valuable. For example, it

---

4   Here I follow Isaiah Berlin, *Four Essays on Liberty* (Oxford: Oxford University Press, 1969), 131–34; and Philip Pettit, *A Theory of Freedom: From the Psychology to the Politics of Agency* (Oxford: Oxford University Press, 2001), 127. As Berlin notes, "many of the nationalist, communist, authoritarian and totalitarian creeds of our day" have been informed by a view of freedom as self-mastery (144).

5   The freedom that the state promotes may be valuable for its own sake, in addition to its contribution toward what I have been calling "the freedom that really matters"; but I shall not consider this possibility in this essay. I shall assume that the primary reason why political freedom is valuable is that it contributes to the autonomy of those who enjoy it.

6   Naturally, I believe that these three problems are especially important ones, even if they are not the only ones that confront an account of political freedom.

is sometimes claimed that a freedom-supportive state is a state that treats its subjects with equal concern and respect.[7] Such a claim threatens to reduce political freedom to equality.

An adequate account of political freedom must not succumb to these temptations. Political freedom is one ideal that a state should be concerned with. Promoting political freedom may conflict with other values that the state should also be concerned with, such as security, equality, or excellence. The best state is not necessarily the state that best promotes and sustains political freedom.[8] The problem of integrity, then, is to explain the value of political freedom without claiming too much or too little for it. If too much is claimed for it, then it will not give us a clear target at which the state could aim. If too little is claimed for it, then political freedom will direct us toward some other ideal or value to which it is reducible.

The second problem, *the problem of pluralism*, refers to the fact that political freedom can be reduced or diminished by different factors. Sometimes theorists attempt to show that there is only one freedom-reducing factor—such as physical obstruction—and that all other (purported) freedom-reducing factors are really just instances of this one factor. Below I shall argue that this is a mistake. And if it is a mistake, then an important problem must be faced. Assuming that there exists a plurality of freedom-reducing factors, each of which is not reducible to the others, then how should these factors be combined or aggregated into one overall measure of political freedom? If one state does a good job of minimizing one freedom-reducing factor, and another state does a worse job of minimizing this factor, but a better job of minimizing others, then how are we to decide which state is better in terms of promoting political freedom? The need to find satisfactory answers to these questions is the problem of pluralism.

The problem of unacceptable implications is the most straightforward of the three problems. Theoretical discussions of individual freedom notoriously give rise to troubling paradoxes.[9] The same is true of political freedom. The problem of unacceptable implications concerns how to avoid or at least diminish the force of these paradoxes. An account of political freedom that has strongly counterintuitive implications is one that should not be accepted. For example, if an account of political freedom yields the judgment that a state that engages in an enormous amount of coercive interference in the lives of its

---

7   See Ronald M. Dworkin, "What Is Equality? Part 3: The Place of Liberty," *Iowa Law Review* 73 (1987): 1–54.

8   I shall make no attempt in this essay to assess how important political freedom is compared to other values that the state can promote or protect, such as security, equality, or excellence.

9   These paradoxes result from the fact that there exists a range of highly plausible, but mutually inconsistent, judgments about freedom. For example, the judgment that a person who hands over his money at gunpoint does not perform a free act conflicts with the judgment that a person cannot be unfree to perform an act that he actually does. For discussion of a number of these paradoxes see Christine Swanton, *Freedom: A Coherence Theory* (Indianapolis, IN: Hackett, 1992).

subjects is one that scores well in terms of political freedom, then we should reject this account. The difficulty is that each account of political freedom will give rise to its own set of counter-intuitive implications.

The ideal of political freedom that I shall propose and defend in Section VI relates judgments of freedom to the opportunities that persons have to plan their lives. As such, this ideal is vulnerable to the objection that a state can make its subjects "more free" by getting them to change or simplify their plans. Thus, on this objection, subjects of *Brave New World* might paradoxically turn out to be living in a free state.[10] Obviously, this would be an unacceptable implication. For my ideal of political freedom to be at all plausible, I shall need to explain why it does not have this implication.

There are likely other problems that are relevant to assessing rival ideals of political freedom. But the problems of integrity, pluralism, and unacceptable implications are central problems. A satisfactory ideal of political freedom must be able to present freedom as a distinct value, show how different freedom-reducing factors can be combined in overall judgments of a free state, and show how the account of political freedom that it offers can avoid grossly unacceptable implications.

IV. RIVAL IDEALS

Keeping these problems in mind, I now consider two important ideals of political freedom that rival the one that I shall be defending. I refer to these rival ideals as *freedom as noninterference* and *freedom as nondomination*.[11] The selection of these two ideals for discussion is motivated in part by their importance and in part by what can be learned from them. As we shall begin to see in the next section, a better ideal of political freedom is one that builds upon the insights of both of these rival ideals while avoiding the problems that they encounter.[12]

Let us start with freedom as noninterference, an ideal that has deep roots in the liberal tradition of political thought. Adherents of this ideal view interference as the primary threat to freedom. A freedom-supportive state, they hold, will be one that does a good job

---

10　See Berlin, introduction to *Four Essays on Liberty*, lii.

11　For discussions of freedom as noninterference, see Berlin, *Four Essays on Liberty*; David Miller, "Constraints on Freedom," *Ethics* 94 (1984): 66–86; and Jan Narveson, *The Libertarian Idea* (Philadelphia: Temple University Press, 1988), chaps. 2, 4. For discussions of freedom as nondomination see Philip Pettit, *Republicanism: A Theory of Freedom and Government* (Oxford: Oxford University Press, 1997), chaps. 2–3; and Pettit, *A Theory of Freedom*, chaps. 6–7.

12　A third important and influential ideal of political freedom, one that I shall not discuss here, identifies a freedom-supportive state with the state that best promotes civic participation. I criticize this radical democratic view of political freedom in detail in Steven Wall, "Radical Democracy, Personal Freedom, and the Transformative Potential of Politics," *Social Philosophy and Policy* 17, no. 1 (2000): 225–54.

of reducing interference. However, to understand exactly what this means, we must clarify the concept of interference. If a state offers its citizens a subsidy to visit natural parks, then in one sense this subsidy may be an act of interference, but not in a sense relevant to freedom as noninterference.[13] Likewise, if a person offers me unwanted advice, then he may be interfering with my affairs; but, here too, not in a sense relevant to freedom as noninterference. Thus, judgments of interference taken from ordinary language are not identical to judgments of interference as this phrase relates to political freedom. We therefore need to analyze the sense of interference in question.[14] I propose the following account: *A interferes with B if A hinders B from doing what B would have done in the absence of A's action.* And I propose that we say that to hinder someone from doing something is either to prevent him from doing it or to make it more costly for him to do it. According to this definition, acts of interference either remove options from people or increase the costs to them of choosing the options that remain open.

This construal of interference is formulated with certain threats to freedom in mind. Coercive directives are the primary means by which agents of the state (but not only agents of the state) interfere with the lives of others. An ideal of political freedom should accordingly put the focus on coercive directives. Offering bribes or giving advice may in some circumstances plausibly be said to reduce the freedom of those who are targeted by such efforts,[15] but for the purpose of assessing political freedom, we can put such cases to one side.

A more difficult issue concerns whether interference must be intentional. If *A* hinders *B* by mistake, has *A* interfered with *B*? The focus on coercion suggests that interference is the result of intentional action. But perhaps this is too restrictive.[16] If I am unable to carry out some plan because an obstacle has been put in my path, then I may have been interfered with, irrespective of whether the obstacle was deliberately placed in my path or whether its placement was an unintended consequence of human action. Let us say, then, that *A* hinders *B* if *A* either does so intentionally or does so in a way for which it makes sense for *B* to ask *A* for a justification for his action. If this is correct, then not every obstacle placed in my path will be an interference, but sometimes I will be interfered with even when no one intended to do so.

---

13 But in this example will not the subsidy itself have been raised by coercive interference? Not necessarily. If we like, we can stipulate that the subsidy is raised from revenues from the state's voluntary lottery.

14 I draw here on my discussion in Steven Wall, "Freedom, Interference, and Domination," *Political Studies* 49, no. 2 (2001): 216–30.

15 For discussion see Harry G. Frankfurt, "Coercion and Responsibility," in Ted Honderich, ed., *Essays on Freedom of Action* (London: Routledge and Kegan Paul, 1973); and J. P. Day, "Threats, Offers, Law, Opinion, and Liberty," *American Philosophical Quarterly* 14, no. 4 (1977): 257–72.

16 David Miller, "Constraints on Freedom," *Ethics* 92, no. 4 (1983): 66–86.

Many other difficult issues remain. Manipulation is a freedom-reducing form of interference, but it does not remove options or increase the cost of pursuing them. Instead, it distorts the way in which persons decide which options they want to pursue. Nevertheless, we can say that, in common with coercive directives, manipulation hinders a person from doing what he would have done in the absence of such interference. A more difficult problem concerns how property rights relate to or condition acts of interference. If the police prevent me from trespassing on your land, then the state has interfered with me. But it surely matters whether or not you have legitimate property rights to the land in question.[17] A full account of interference must address this matter, but I shall pass over it here.

As sketchy as these remarks are, they go some way toward giving content to the ideal of freedom as noninterference. According to this ideal, a freedom-supportive state will reduce or minimize interference. It will strive to establish an environment in which its subjects are able to pursue their plans free from interference and coercion by others. Those who adhere to the ideal of freedom as noninterference need not think that the state should never interfere in order to promote other values. They might think that other values should sometimes take precedence over political freedom, but when this occurs they will view it as imposing a cost, even if they think that it is a cost worth paying.[18]

So described, freedom as noninterference captures some of the truth about political freedom, but it is not a sound ideal. Before discussing the problems that it encounters, I want to introduce the second ideal that I mentioned above—freedom as nondomination.[19] Domination can take the form of interference, but, importantly, it is not reducible to it. *A* can dominate *B* without interfering with him, and *A* can interfere with *B* without dominating him. So the goal of reducing domination can diverge from the goal of reducing interference. Freedom as nondomination holds that the former goal is the one that a freedom-supportive state should pursue.

But what exactly is domination? In the sense relevant to political freedom, it refers to the condition or status of living at the mercy of another. Consider the case of a slave. A slave is distinguished from a nonslave by the slave's complete lack of independence. He lives his life utterly subject to the arbitrary will of his master. Importantly, the slave

---

17   When you talk with the police, you might say that I am interfering with you because I am trespassing on your land. This suggests that in order to identify acts of interference we need first to have specified who has rights to what. I return to this point in Section VII below.

18   See Berlin, introduction to *Four Essays on Liberty*, liii–liv.

19   The leading contemporary proponent of freedom as nondomination is Pettit. My discussion of domination draws on, but does not perfectly follow, his account of this concept. See Pettit, *Republicanism*; and Pettit, *A Theory of Freedom*. Pettit follows Quentin Skinner, *Liberty Before Liberalism* (Cambridge: Cambridge University Press, 1998), in holding that this ideal of political freedom has deep roots in the civic republican tradition of political thought.

remains a slave even if his master allows him, for the most part, to do as he pleases. A slave is still a slave even when he has a liberal master.

Slavery, of course, is an extreme instance of domination. Less extreme instances abound in everyday life. A woman lives under the dominating eye of her husband. A junior member of a firm does not speak his mind to his senior colleagues. And a small business owner is paralyzed by the fact that his government may, at any moment, arbitrarily confiscate his economic assets. Each of these subjects lives, to a lesser or greater extent, under the arbitrary control of others. Notice, moreover, that in each of these examples, the dominated person need not be "interfered with" by those who dominate him. The woman may never be interfered with by her husband because she realizes how to please him. The junior member of the firm may learn to hold his tongue and the business owner may never be interfered with because his government does not confiscate his assets. Thus, domination does not require actual interference. This is why domination can occur in the absence of interference.[20]

Reflection on these examples suggests the following general account. Domination is a condition that exists within a social relationship when one party is subject to the arbitrary power of another. We can measure the intensity of domination along four main dimensions: (1) How extensive is the power that is exercised within the relationship? (2) How predictable is its exercise? (3) To what extent is this power subject to checks? And (4) how easy is it for the dominated party to exit the relationship?

The first and fourth dimensions are reasonably clear, but the second and third require comment. When someone rules in an arbitrary manner, he often does so capriciously. For instance, we call a government arbitrary when it rules by decree and not according to the rule of law. One important element of arbitrary power, then, is unpredictable rule.[21] But this cannot be the whole story about such power. To see why, consider this example: an abusive husband rules over his wife in strict accordance with a set of rules that he has formulated. Here we have a case of domination that does not involve submission to the

---

20   Domination can occur in the absence of interference, but might it be reducible to expected interference? The idea that it can be is defended by Ian Carter in his *A Measure of Freedom* (Oxford: Oxford University Press, 1999), 237–45. On Carter's view, the dominated agent is unfree because there is a high probability that he will be interfered with if he acts or attempts to act in a number of ways that are open to him. But this reduction of domination to expected interference fails to explain why unpredictable interference is worse (from the standpoint of freedom) than predictable interference. Two agents who confront the same amount of expected interference might differ in their freedom if one is able to predict the interference, whereas the other is not. This is true, at least, on the view of political freedom that I shall defend below in the text, a view that understands freedom in terms of the nonobstruction of planning.

21   See Jeremy Waldron, "The Rule of Law in Contemporary Liberal Theory," *Ratio Juris* 2, no. 1 (1989): 79–96.

capricious will of another. The husband's behavior is predictable and consistent.[22] So, if the wife in this example is dominated, and if domination is to be understood in terms of being subject to the arbitrary will of another, then there must be more to arbitrary rule than capricious rule.

What then is the additional element? The answer is to be found in the kind of vulnerability involved in being subject to domination. The dominated person's ability to make her own decisions about her life depends crucially on the will of another. In our example, the dominated wife lives her life under the watchful eye of her husband. Even if she is able to predict his behavior, she remains subject to his rules, not her own. Moreover, she is not in a position to force him to change his rules so that they are more acceptable to her. The power that he exercises over her is arbitrary in the sense that she has no way to make it track her interests.[23] Much power that is arbitrary in this sense is also capricious and unpredictable. But power can be arbitrary, even if it is not exercised capriciously, so long as those who are subject to it have no way to check it or to force it to take account of their interests.[24]

A fully adequate account of domination would need to provide some way to integrate or balance the four different dimensions that I listed above (the extent of power exercised, its degree of predictability, the extent of checks upon it, and its degree of avoidability). But I shall not attempt this integration here. I hope that these brief remarks on domination suffice to give us a reasonably clear picture of the ideal of freedom as nondomination. This ideal rightly views the state as a (potentially) very dangerous, dominating agent. After all, states claim the authority to rule every aspect of our lives. States often rule in unpredictable and arbitrary ways, and the costs of exiting our relationship with them are extremely high. Accordingly, proponents of freedom as nondomination typically view a freedom-supportive state as one that exercises a minimum of arbitrary power. If you are to be politically free, they insist, you "must not fall into a condition of political subjection or dependence, thereby leaving yourself open to the danger of being forcibly or coercively deprived by your government of your life, liberty, and estates."[25]

Beyond the goal of reducing the arbitrary power of the state, and in some tension with this end, freedom as nondomination directs the state to combat domination within civil society. As the above examples suggested, many forms of domination exist within

---

22   I am assuming here that the husband does not frequently and unpredictably change the set of rules that he strictly adheres to in dominating his wife.

23   See Pettit, *A Theory of Freedom*, 134.

24   Ibid. Pettit describes arbitrary rule as rule that is "not forced to track the interferee's avowable interests and that typically reflects the interests or perceptions of the interferer." But this does not capture the other element of arbitrariness—namely, subjection to the unpredictable or capricious will of another. And this other element is, as we shall see, important to assessing political freedom.

25   Skinner, *Liberty Before Liberalism*, 69–70.

nonpolitical, social relationships. Thus, on the nondomination view of political freedom, a freedom-supportive state not only must minimize its own arbitrary power, but also must seek to create and sustain an environment in which the arbitrary power of others is also minimized.

V. POLITICAL FREEDOM AND ITS VALUE

I have been discussing two rival ideals of political freedom, freedom as noninterference and freedom as nondomination. I now want to argue that, despite their genuine attractions, neither ideal is adequate. One reason for this is that each ideal exposes inadequacies in the other. To see this, consider the following two archetypal governments.[26]

> *The Arbitrary Liberal Government*: This is a government that interferes in the lives of its subjects much less often and with much less intensity than the governments of almost all modern states. For the most part, its massive regulatory powers remain underutilized. But this government is not freedom-supportive. It rules by administrative fiat, and its regulations are not rationally consistent or predictable. As a result, its subjects have great difficulty planning their lives. They never know what their government is going to do next.

> *The Nonarbitrary Illiberal Government*: This is a government that is constrained by well-designed constitutional checks and balances. It governs in strict accordance with the rule of law. And it governs in a manner that does a reasonably good job of tracking the interests of those who are subject to its power. Nonetheless, the government is illiberal in the sense that it interferes with its subjects to a much greater degree than do the governments of almost all modern states. It regulates a wide range of activities, for example, prohibiting smoking and drinking, enforcing dietary restrictions and exercise requirements, and nationalizing schools and hospitals.

These examples represent ideal types. Most arbitrary governments are not liberal, and most nonarbitrary governments do not interfere with their subjects to such an extreme extent. But the examples, while not fully realistic, raise an important question. From the standpoint of political freedom, which is worse, the arbitrary liberal government or the nonarbitrary illiberal government?

To answer this question confidently we would need to know much more about the details of these two governments. But this should not distract us here. The point of the

---

26 I have discussed slightly different versions of these examples elsewhere. See Wall, "Freedom, Interference, and Domination," 220–24.

question is that an adequate ideal of political freedom should give us some way of thinking about how to answer it. It should help us to think about which is worse from the standpoint of political freedom, arbitrary power or illiberal interference. Neither freedom as noninterference nor freedom as nondomination help us to approach this question. Or, to put the point more precisely, each does so in a way that is too easy. If proponents of freedom as noninterference judge the arbitrary liberal government to be freedom-supportive simply because it seldom interferes, then they are clearly missing something important. Such a judgment would be an unacceptable implication of their view. Likewise, if proponents of freedom as nondomination judge the nonarbitrary illiberal government to be freedom-supportive, simply because it does not act arbitrarily, then they too are missing something important. Such a judgment would be an unacceptable implication of their view.

Can these self-indicting judgments be resisted? Do proponents of these ideals have the resources to account for the archetypical governments that I have presented?[27] If the answer is no, then we have good reason to look for a third ideal of political freedom. Before drawing this conclusion, however, I shall discuss an important reply available to proponents of these ideals.[28] The reply attempts to take the sting out of the examples.

Not infrequently writers draw a distinction between freedom and its value. They sometimes ask rhetorically, What is the value of freedom if one lives in conditions in which one cannot exercise it or enjoy it?[29] If I live in a state that has an ideal set of rules for governing the free transfer of property, but I own nothing myself, then what is the value of this freedom to me? Drawing on this distinction, a proponent of freedom as noninterference might argue that the arbitrary liberal government is deficient not because it reduces political freedom, but because it diminishes its value. In the same spirit, the proponent of freedom as nondomination might say the same thing about the nonarbitrary illiberal

---

27   Some might be tempted to view these two governments not over time, but at particular points in time. When asked which government is worse from the standpoint of political freedom, some might interpret this as a series of questions about the two governments at different time-slices. If one does this, then at many points in time one will have to conclude that the arbitrary liberal government is a model government in terms of political freedom. Indeed, on the time-slice view, one will not be able to discriminate between arbitrary and nonarbitrary governments that engage in the same amount of interference at a given point in time. This is to miss something important. A plausible ideal of political freedom should be able to explain both why interference reduces freedom and why arbitrary interference is more freedom-reducing than nonarbitrary interference.

28   I shall not attempt to anticipate every possible reply that proponents of these ideals could make to my archetypal governments. By discussing (what I consider to be) the strongest reply that is available to such proponents, I hope to cast some doubt on the plausibility of these ideals. This will fall short of a decisive refutation, but it should provide some motivation for the search for an alternative, and I hope better, ideal of political freedom.

29   See Berlin, introduction to *Four Essays on Liberty*, xlv–xlvi.

government. Both types of proponents might then conclude that a freedom-supportive state is the state that promotes *both* political freedom and its value.

This reply has the effect of dramatically reducing the distance between the two rival ideals of freedom as noninterference and freedom as non-domination. The two camps will converge in their judgments if the following occurs: (1) it is agreed that the freedom-supportive state should be as concerned with promoting the value of political freedom as it is concerned with promoting political freedom itself; and (2) the proponent of freedom as noninterference concedes that being subject to arbitrary power reduces the value of freedom, while the proponent of freedom as non-domination admits that even nonarbitrary interference reduces the value of freedom. The difference between the two sides will reduce to a disagreement over how to distinguish between actual freedom-reducing factors and factors that merely condition freedom's value. But proponents of both sets of ideals will converge on what is important, namely, what a freedom-supportive state should be promoting.

However, in all likelihood, proponents of these rival ideals would want to insist on some priority rule for ranking the promotion of freedom above the promotion of its value. Depending on the priority rule proposed, this ranking would enable proponents of the respective ideals to arrive at different judgments about the freedom-supportive state. The difference between freedom as noninterference and freedom as non-domination would then boil down to a difference in emphasis. Proponents of the former would insist that reducing interference is more important than reducing domination, while the latter would insist on the opposite.

Drawing a distinction between freedom and its value does indeed appear to take the sting out of the examples that I have presented. Does it overcome the problem of unacceptable implications, however, and uphold the integrity of political freedom as a distinct ideal? Notice that if both political freedom and its value are to be promoted, then a freedom-supportive state has two goals, not one. This is a problem. Recall that in investigating the ideal of political freedom, we are not attempting to identify the full range of justified state action. Perhaps a good state will promote both political freedom and its enjoyment, as well as other valuable goals. We are now, however, seeking to understand only what a freedom-supportive state ought to promote. It should promote political freedom. It need have no other goal. Indeed, the pursuit of other goals—such as the goal of increasing the value of political freedom—may compete against or conflict with the goal of promoting political freedom. We do well, then, to keep these two goals distinct. In seeking to avoid the counterintuitive judgments of my two example governments, the reply that a freedom-supportive state promotes both political freedom and its value obscures this important point.

Those who would press the reply might now object that my representation here mischaracterizes what they are saying. They might say that noninterference and the value of noninterference, or, alternatively, non-domination and the value of nondomination, are constituent parts of a single value. This value is what political freedom is. Accordingly, the freedom-supportive state has only one goal, which is the promotion of political freedom so understood.

This rejoinder, however, generates its own problems. To begin with, it threatens to compromise the integrity of freedom as a political ideal. Interference and domination are not the only factors that condition the enjoyment of freedom. A number of other factors, such as residing in a country with a clean environment, plausibly condition the value or enjoyment of freedom. Should such factors be counted as constituent elements of freedom as a political ideal? If we say yes, then political freedom starts to resemble a master value encompassing all or most of what a state might reasonably be in the business of promoting.[30] This would amount to, or come close to, denying that political freedom is a distinct ideal, thus succumbing to the problem of integrity. While laws that protect clean air may be a good thing (and may enhance the enjoyment of political freedom), we should not say that the state promotes political freedom when it passes these laws.

Of course, proponents of freedom as noninterference and freedom as nondomination might insist that only interference or domination count as constituent elements of political freedom. Other factors that condition its value, they might say, are not included within it. This would rescue their respective ideals from the problem of integrity, but it would do so at the price of being ad hoc. Once factors that condition the value of freedom are included within the value itself, then we are owed an explanation for why some factors get included and others do not. Proponents of the two ideals have not provided any such explanation, and it is unclear how they might do so. But even if they can offer the needed explanation, a second problem lies in wait. If political freedom includes two components non-interference and nondomination—then how should we decide which component is more important? Should we say, for example, that one component takes lexical priority over the other? This seems doubtful. If the state has a choice between greatly reducing interference or slightly reducing exposure to domination, then even a proponent of freedom as nondomination should allow that the state should reduce the interference.

This suggests that on any plausible view of political freedom, the two components must be balanced against one another. But to explain how this should be done we need a priority rule or a standard to guide us. Without such a rule or standard, we will not be able to make reasonably determinate judgments about the promotion of political freedom. When confronted with a choice between an arbitrary liberal government or a nonarbitrary illiberal government, we will not be able to say which is worse from the standpoint of political freedom. Working from within either freedom as noninterference or freedom as nondomination, we may be able to say which of these governments does worse in compromising freedom and which does worse in reducing its value, but we will not be able to say which government is worse overall.

---

30   Pettit argues for a wide range of public policies by appealing to the value or enjoyment of nondomination. In his eyes, a freedom-supportive state should be in the business of doing most of what a state might reasonably do. See Pettit, *Republicanism*, chap. 5.

The problem, here, is what I earlier termed the problem of pluralism. If political freedom consists of different components, then we need to know how to establish a proper measure for the components in arriving at overall judgments of political freedom. It is important to see that this problem is a theoretical problem. We may be able to avoid the problem in some practical contexts. For example, if a state in a given set of circumstances cannot do much to reduce interference, but can do very much to reduce domination, then the problem that I am now calling attention to would not be particularly troubling. A freedom-supportive state in these circumstances should act to reduce domination rather than attempt to reduce interference, and this judgment holds true whether we view freedom as nondomination or as noninterference.

Notwithstanding this point, the problem of pluralism is not, first and foremost, a problem of applied political theory. It is a problem that concerns the theoretical structure of our judgments about political freedom. An account of political freedom that identifies a plurality of freedom-reducing factors, but offers no guidance as to how they should be integrated into overall judgments of political freedom is, other things being equal, less satisfactory than one that can guide us.

I contend that neither proponents of freedom as noninterference nor proponents of freedom as nondomination have the resources to overcome the problem of pluralism. When seeking to avoid the counterintuitive implications that are forced upon them by the examples of an arbitrary liberal government and a nonarbitrary illiberal government, proponents may be tempted to appeal to the distinction between political freedom and its value. However, if they do this, then their accounts of political freedom will fare poorly with respect to the problem of integrity, or the problem of pluralism, or both. We have ample reason, therefore, to investigate whether a third ideal of political freedom might be able to incorporate the good insights of both freedom as noninterference and freedom as nondomination, while avoiding the difficulties that these rival ideals encounter. Let us turn now to this task.

VI. FREEDOM AND PLANNING

I have already intimated that the ideal of political freedom that I wish to defend centers on the ability of persons to plan their lives. Lacking a concise name for this ideal, I shall employ the somewhat cumbersome appellation *freedom as the nonobstruction of planning*. According to this ideal, a freedom-supportive state promotes and sustains an environment in which its subjects are best able to carry out their plans and to form new ones.

I need to explain what I mean, here, by planning, and why it is reasonable to think that there is an intimate connection between planning and political freedom. Planning is one kind of practical activity. It can be contrasted with other kinds of practical activity, such as the kind of activity that we engage in when we act from impulse.[31] Typically, planning is a process that involves setting for oneself a goal (or goals), deliberating about which actions to take in order to achieve the goal(s), reaching a judgment that certain actions should be undertaken in the pursuit of the goal(s), and forming intentions to carry out those actions. So described, planning involves committing oneself to undertake future actions. Planning is the way we actively control and shape our lives.

Plans and the process of forming them can be simple or complex, limited or comprehensive. (Some plans might affect the freedom of others, but I shall address that concern in Section VII.) I might plan to take a walk this afternoon. This plan is simple and limited. The steps that I need to take in order to fulfill it are relatively few, and the impact that it will have on my life as a whole will be very modest. Alternatively, I might plan to become a physician. This plan is complex and comprehensive. The steps that I need to take in order to fulfill it will be many and will require a good deal of ongoing deliberation on my part. The impact of this plan on my life will be substantial. If I seriously adopt and pursue a comprehensive plan and fail to achieve it, then, other things being equal, my life will be significantly affected for the worse. The reason for this is that comprehensive plans, like the plan of pursuing a career in medicine, have a hierarchical structure. They embed a plurality of simpler and more limited plans. In planning to become a physician, I might plan to pursue one line of study rather than another, or I might plan to start a family later rather than sooner. Failure to achieve one's comprehensive plan often casts a shadow over the simpler and more limited plans that were embedded within it.

Much more could be said about plans and the role that they play in our lives;[32] but these brief remarks should suffice for present purposes. It should be clear that persons are planning agents. Even those persons who lead relatively spontaneous lives are distinguished not by the absence of plans, but by the lack of enduring, stable, comprehensive plans in their lives. It should also be clear that planning is integral to autonomy. We take charge of our affairs and chart our own course through life by adopting and pursuing plans.[33] This,

---

31 Practical activity terminates in intentional action, but not all intentional action is well described in terms of forming plans and carrying them out. For a more detailed discussion of practical activity, see Christine Swanton, *Freedom: A Coherence Theory*, 49–60.

32 See Michael E. Bratman, *Intention, Plans, and Practical Reason* (Cambridge, MA: Harvard University Press, 1987).

33 Could one live an autonomous life without any plans? I doubt it. One might resolve never to commit oneself to any future course of action, preferring instead to always "live in the present." But this would itself be a kind of plan. Even if one could somehow avoid making plans altogether, I suspect that one's life would be so lacking in narrative structure that it would be wrong to call it autonomous. This

in turn, suggests why it is reasonable to think that there is an intimate connection between planning and freedom. To lead a free life, we must be able to form plans and to take steps to carry them out.

Building on this idea, the ideal of political freedom that I am now recommending holds that a freedom-supportive state should sustain and promote an environment in which its subjects are best able to plan their lives. But now, it may be asked, why emphasize the obstruction of planning when assessing political freedom? After all, as we have seen, interference and domination also reduce political freedom. Moreover, a person can be interfered with or subjected to domination even if he is not forming or pursuing any plan at all.

The response to the question comes in two parts. First, the main reason why interference and domination reduce political freedom is that they both obstruct the ability of persons to plan their lives. Interference diminishes our freedom by closing off or raising the costs of options that are relevant to our plans. Domination diminishes our freedom by subjecting us to the arbitrary will of another, which in turn hinders our ability to plan our lives by leaving us vulnerable to the often unpredictable power of the dominator. The root explanation, then, for why both interference and domination are freedom-reducing factors is that they both are important and effective means by which agents can and do obstruct the plans of others. For this reason, an ideal of political freedom should put the focus on the obstruction of planning rather than on interference or domination. The former idea subsumes the latter two.

Second, while it remains true that it is possible to interfere with or dominate a person without obstructing his plans (think, for example, of the person who forcibly prevents me in a given situation from acting on an impulse), this possibility is not particularly important for judgments of political freedom. The reason for this is that if a state sustains and promotes an environment in which its subjects are best able to plan their lives, then this will also be an environment in which interference and domination are minimized. For, at least generally speaking, the state is not in a position to know when acts of interference or domination impede the plans of persons and when they do not do so. A law that criminalizes gambling may hinder some individuals from giving in to the impulse to gamble, but the law will also almost certainly hinder some who have made gambling a part of their plans. Since the state cannot effectively target the former group while excluding the latter group, then a state that wishes to promote freedom will not pass the law.

This is true, as I just allowed, only generally speaking. There are exceptions. But consideration of the exceptions strengthens, rather than weakens, the plausibility of freedom as the nonobstruction of planning. To see this, consider laws that require a short waiting period before one is allowed to purchase a firearm. It is not unreasonable to think that these laws do a good job of interfering with those who are moved to buy firearms on

---

is one reason why I characterized autonomy (see Section II above) in terms of the manner in which, and circumstances under which, we form complex intentions and sustain commitments.

impulse, without significantly obstructing those whose plans include owning a firearm. Such laws are good examples of how a state can engage in interference without obstructing the plans of those who are interfered with. But laws that only restrict those who are acting on impulse, and do not obstruct the plans of anyone, are not plausible candidates for being judged as laws that reduce freedom. Indeed, a strong case can be made that such laws can actually increase freedom by preventing people from acting in ways that they would not act if they were not in the grip of an impulse. The extent to which this is true is not something that I shall explore here. My point is that even when the state interferes with or dominates its subjects, but does not obstruct their plans (and it can only do this in exceptional cases), its action does not plausibly reduce their freedom.[34]

It is worth pausing now to consider an important objection. Some will claim that freedom as the nonobstruction of planning fails to account adequately for the freedom associated with spontaneous intentional action.[35] Consider, for instance, a character whom we can call "the spontaneous man." This is a person who believes that he acts most authentically when he acts without deliberation or planning of any sort. The spontaneous man might concede that his ability to engage in the kind of spontaneous activity that he prizes is best protected by a state that sustains an environment in which persons are best able to form and execute their plans. But he might object that an ideal of political freedom that is characterized in terms of the nonobstruction of planning would fail to give the freedom that he prizes its due.

Several replies can be made to the spontaneous man. First, as I mentioned above, even those individuals who lead relatively spontaneous lives must engage in some planning to lead the lives that they want to lead. A spontaneous decision to paint in the afternoon typically requires either that one plan to get materials that are needed to paint, or that one previously had planned to have materials around in case one spontaneously decides to paint. As I have stressed, it is a mistake to identify all plans with highly structured, long-term commitments. Second, if the spontaneous man values his spontaneous activity, then if he is rational he should take steps to ensure that he can successfully engage in it. For example, he should avoid assuming long-term responsibilities. This, ironically, requires a good deal of planning.

These replies go some distance toward responding to the objection raised by the spontaneous man. However, a determined proponent of this objection will insist that the obstruction of purposive, spontaneous activity still is not fully accounted for by the ideal of political freedom that I am defending. Does this objection give us good reason to revise my

---

34   Recall here the assumption in Section II above that freedom is best understood in terms of personal autonomy. On alternative understandings of freedom the point in the text might not be plausible. For example, if freedom were best understood in terms of the satisfaction of desire, then such laws would plausibly reduce freedom.

35   I thank Keith Lehrer and James Stacey Taylor for helping me to see the force of this objection.

account? At this point it is necessary to recall some of the assumptions that I made earlier in this essay. I assumed that freedom is best understood in terms of personal autonomy. I also assumed a particular understanding of personal autonomy, one that identifies the autonomous life with a life of freely chosen projects and commitments. If this understanding of autonomy is essentially correct, then it is appropriate to give planning agency the kind of prominence that I have given it here. Autonomous persons are planning agents, and their plans are integral to their autonomy. A full response to the spontaneous man, accordingly, requires a defense of this understanding of autonomy.

I shall not attempt to provide this defense here.[36] But if it can be given, then freedom as the nonobstruction of planning will emerge as a highly plausible ideal of political freedom. This ideal not only explains why and how interference and domination reduce freedom, but also implies that neither interference nor domination, per se, reduce freedom. They reduce freedom only to the extent that they obstruct planning.[37] Yet, as important as these points are, they do not exhaust the case for freedom as the nonobstruction of planning over its rival ideals. An important issue remains to be discussed.

As we saw in Section V, the ideals of freedom as noninterference and freedom as nondomination run into the problem of pluralism once they attempt to respond to my two examples of the arbitrary liberal government and the nonarbitrary illiberal government. By introducing the distinction between freedom and its value, proponents of these ideals of freedom can explain why both of these governments are not freedom-supportive, but in doing so, these proponents incur the problem of balancing freedom and its value. To achieve this balance in a non ad hoc way, proponents of both ideals need to appeal to some rule or standard to provide guidance on how the balancing should be done. Neither group of proponents, I suggested, has the resources to provide such a standard.

It should now be fairly clear that freedom as the nonobstruction of planning does not confront this problem. Since the ideal recognizes that both interference and domination are freedom-reducing factors, it does not have any difficulty accounting for the examples of arbitrary liberal government and nonarbitrary illiberal government. Nor do I need to invoke the suspect distinction between freedom and its value in order to judge either sort of government. Finally, the ideal does not lack a standard for balancing the relative importance of interference and domination in making judgments about political freedom. The standard it uses is the degree or extent to which these freedom-reducing factors obstruct the ability of persons to plan their lives. Indeed, reference to this standard enables us to address the question that neither freedom as noninterference nor freedom as nondomination

---

36   For some defense, see Wall, *Liberalism, Perfectionism, and Restraint*, 127–61.

37   This is not to say that they are objectionable only when they obstruct planning. Freedom is just one value. Interference and domination may be bad for reasons other than the role that they play in reducing freedom.

is able to approach satisfactorily: What is worse from the standpoint of political freedom, the arbitrary liberal government or the nonarbitrary illiberal government?

I do not mean to say that proponents of freedom as the nonobstruction of planning can answer this question without exercising judgment or without knowing more about the concrete details of these respective governments. The point is simply that this ideal provides us with a way of thinking about how to answer this question. We should compare these two governments in terms of the extent to which they frustrate the plans of those who are subject to them. The government that produces the greater amount of frustration is the one that is worse from the standpoint of political freedom. By referring to this standard, we can gauge, even if only roughly, the significance of different categories of state action, such as:

1. that which subjects citizens to both interference and domination
2. that which subjects citizens to domination, but not interference
3. that which subjects citizens to interference, but not domination

In principle, an instance of state action that falls under any one of these categories can be worse (in terms of reducing political freedom) than an instance that falls under any of the other two. But, in practice, state actions that fall under the first category are likely to be the greatest threats to political freedom. The reason for this is that when state action dominates as well as interferes, it is much harder for those who are subject to this action to plan around it. This is why many writers in the liberal tradition have stressed the importance of the rule of law to a free society.[38] If we can know in advance the laws and rules that will constrain us, then we can take into account this knowledge when we formulate our plans and deliberate about how best to pursue them. But if we are subject to a state that arbitrarily and unpredictably interferes with us, then its actions are likely to be far more disruptive to our plans.

I doubt that much of anything useful can be said in the abstract about state action that falls under categories (2) and (3). We need to look at the concrete consequences of such types of action to determine their impact on political freedom. But an example might shed some light on the matter. Consider compulsory military service. Suppose that State A announces that it plans to institute a mandatory five-year service requirement for approximately one-fourth of all male citizens between the ages of eighteen and forty-five, but the state does not specify how it will select them or when the requirement will take effect. This announcement would, in all likelihood, substantially disrupt the plans of many citizens, and it would do so even if the state eventually drops the idea. Here domination

---

38 See John Locke, *Two Treatises of Government*, ed. Peter Laslett (Cambridge: Cambridge University Press, 1988); F. A. Hayek, *The Constitution of Liberty* (Chicago: University of Chicago Press, 1960); and John Rawls, *A Theory of Justice* (Cambridge, MA: Harvard University Press, 1971), 206–13.

would occur in the absence of interference. Now, contrast State A with State B, which enacts the same five-year service requirement but does so according to fair and publicly known rules. On the assumption that there is a genuine public need for military service, this state action plausibly could be described as interference without domination. Since the requirement would be administered according to known rules, it would not substantially disrupt the lives of those who are not selected to serve; those who are selected to serve will at least know when their service will begin and end, and they can take some steps to plan around it.

Nevertheless, even when State B's interference is predictable, nonarbitrary, and, thus, does not constitute domination, it still compromises freedom. The men who are selected to serve in State B will have to spend five years in the military. For many of them, the disruption that this will cause to their plans will be substantial. It will likely be much more substantial than the disruption that is caused to one's plans when one is merely vulnerable to being conscripted into military service at some unspecified time. So, in comparing State B's action with the noninterfering domination by State A, which merely announces an arbitrary plan to begin conscription, we would need to weigh the greater degree of frustration that State B would cause a smaller number of people against the lesser degree of frustration that State A would cause a larger number of people. In short, when assessing political freedom, we must consider both the intensity of the frustration that is caused by a state action and the number of people who are adversely affected.

Of course, a good deal more work needs to be done in order to make this kind of comparison even tolerably precise. I have said nothing, for example, about how we should measure the intensity of frustration that a given state action causes to a given person's plans. But my ambition, here, is not to work out a metric for measuring political freedom.[39] I have simply aimed to give some idea of how freedom as the nonobstruction of planning would approach the task of comparing and aggregating instances of interference and domination. My claim is not that this task will be easy or straightforward, but only that this ideal of political freedom at least provides us with a standard for doing it. In this respect, the ideal of political freedom as nonobstruction of planning fares better than both freedom as noninterference and freedom as nondomination in responding to the problem of pluralism.

Moreover, as we have seen, in responding to this problem, freedom as the nonobstruction of planning does not blur the distinction between political freedom and its value. According to this ideal, some citizens may be free, but not in a position to enjoy their freedom. Others may be free to pursue their plans, but their plans may be worthless or ill advised. Indeed, for some citizens, it will be true that they would be better off if they had much less political freedom. This is as it should be. The freedom-supportive state is not

---

39 Perhaps no such metric is possible. The best we may be able to do is to make reasonable rough-and-ready judgments about what state actions (or what kinds of governments) cause more obstruction to planning than others.

necessarily the best state. Political freedom is one value among others. And in this essay I have said nothing about its importance as compared to other values with which it may come into conflict.

VII. REFINING THE IDEAL

In presenting the case for freedom as the nonobstruction of planning over its rivals, I have emphasized a number of key points. The ideal does well in assessing which is worse from the standpoint of political freedom, arbitrary liberal government or nonarbitrary illiberal government, as described in Section V. The ideal responds well to the problem of pluralism, and it preserves the integrity of political freedom by not conflating it with the value or the enjoyment that freedom might bring. But even if these points are sound, the ideal still might be unacceptable. It may succumb to the problem of unacceptable implications.

I cannot respond here to every possible objection that might be pressed against the ideal of freedom as the nonobstruction of planning. Instead, in this section, I shall consider two important problems that threaten its plausibility. The first problem concerns the dependence of plans on the institutional environments in which they are formed. The second problem concerns the *Brave New World* scenario that I mentioned at the beginning of this essay. Unfortunately, even with respect to these two problems, I shall not be able to respond to them in a fully satisfactory way. My more modest objective will be to suggest how these problems should be addressed. This, in turn, will lead to further refinement of the ideal of political freedom as the nonobstruction of planning.

The first problem I shall address calls attention to the fact that the plans of persons are dependent on the institutional contexts in which they live. This raises some difficult issues that we have not confronted. To view freedom as the nonobstruction of planning is to hold that a person's political freedom is reduced whenever his plans are obstructed by another agent, whatever those plans may be. But this leads to some counterintuitive implications. For some agents, while acting fully within their rights, obstruct the plans of other agents; other agents have plans that involve the deliberate violation of the rights of other persons. Do these possibilities not suggest that talk about the obstruction of plans must presuppose, at a fundamental level, a shared understanding of legitimate rights and entitlements? If so, it is not clear what the relationship is between this background understanding and political freedom.

To bring out the problem here, consider a simple example. If I own a tract of land and I erect a fence to keep you from walking across it, which you had planned to do, then I thereby obstruct your plans. If, however, I am prevented from erecting the fence, then my plans are obstructed. Whose plans should a freedom-supportive state favor? It might be said that, in answering this question, we should just abstract from ownership issues and compare the intensity of the obstruction of plans that occurs (or would occur) in this kind of case. But doing this would miss an important point. My plans are legitimate, whereas yours are not. Your plans, after all, involve violating my rights.[40]

To take account of this example, it is tempting to say that political freedom involves the nonobstruction of *legitimate* plans. But if we say this, then we need a background account of rights and entitlements in order to make sense of what counts as a legitimate plan. This is something that I have not provided. Moreover, it is hard to see how I could provide it simply by reflecting on the idea of nonobstruction of planning. The worry, then, is that freedom as the nonobstruction of planning, as I have so far described the ideal, is seriously incomplete as an account of political freedom.

In response to this worry one might note that the same problem confronts both of the rival ideals that we have considered. Proponents of freedom as noninterference and freedom as nondomination must explain the connection, if any, that exists between the freedom-reducing factors that they recognize and the rights and entitlements of citizens. So the problem that we are now considering is not a special one for freedom as the non-obstruction of planning. Still, it is a problem. It presents us with a dilemma. Either we embrace a moralized account of freedom as the nonobstruction of (legitimate) planning, in which case judgments of political freedom are parasitic on an undefended background account of rights and entitlements, or we say that judgments of political freedom are insensitive to such rights and entitlements, in which case we must embrace the counterin-tuitive implications that I mentioned above.

Fortunately, the dilemma is not as formidable as it appears. Even if freedom as the nonobstruction of planning does not give us a full account of political freedom because it depends on, but does not provide, a back-ground account of rights and entitlements, it does not follow that the ideal is empty or unimportant. An adequate justification of rights and entitlements will need to draw on a wide range of considerations. Some of these considerations will refer to values other than political freedom. This is why freedom as the nonobstruction of planning cannot generate, all by itself, a complete account of justi-fied rights and entitlements. However, on the assumption that the state should promote freedom, the justification of the rights and entitlements of citizens should be sensitive to considerations that bear on political freedom. For example, some assignments of rights and entitlements may fare very poorly in contributing to an environment that enables people to form plans and carry them out. Other assignments may fare much better in this regard. If so, freedom as the nonobstruction of planning would provide reasons for favoring the latter over the former.

Once again, an example may help to make this point clearer. In order to be successful, planning agents need to be able to coordinate their activities efficiently. Some institu-tional structures, such as competitive markets with well-defined property rights, foster

---

40 I am assuming here that I have justly acquired the land and have (legitimate) property rights in it.

coordination and efficiency much better than do other institutional structures, such as command economies or systems without well-defined private property rights. For this reason, freedom as the nonobstruction of planning should favor the former institutional structures over the latter.[41] There are, of course, numerous ways of specifying property rights in market societies. Reference to this ideal of political freedom may provide some guidance as to how those rights should be specified, but other considerations will bear on the matter as well. Indeed, there will likely be a plurality of different ways of reasonably specifying property rights, ways that are compatible with the goal of achieving an economic environment in which agents can efficiently coordinate their activities.[42] If so, then freedom as the nonobstruction of planning will not tell us which specification(s) we should adopt. But the ideal will tell us that a freedom-supportive state would uphold one of these reasonable specifications. Judgments of interference and domination, therefore, can be understood against the background of the existing system of property rights, so long as it falls within the range of the reasonable specifications.[43]

The suggestion, then, is that we can avoid being caught between the two horns of the dilemma. To avoid counterintuitive implications, judgments of interference and domination must be sensitive to existing assignments of rights and entitlements. Indeed, persons form their plans against the background of a shared understanding of these rights and entitlements. So, in a sense, we first need this shared understanding before we can talk sensibly about the freedom to pursue plans. But, at the same time, the main idea behind the ideal—that people should live in an environment in which they can best form and pursue plans—favors some assignments of rights and entitlements over others, even if this

---

41 It is true that some institutional structures that are not plausibly freedom-supportive nonetheless might do well in terms of the nonobstruction of plans. Feudal societies provided stable and predictable environments for those who lived in them, but they did not provide their members with a wide range of options. According to the ideal of political freedom that I am proposing, a freedom-supportive state is one that sustains a planning-friendly environment while providing its members with a wide range of opportunities.

42 In his groundbreaking paper "The Problem of Social Cost," *Journal of Law and Economics* 3 (1960): 1–44, Ronald Coase argues that so long as transaction costs are negligible and property rights are well-defined, economic agents will bargain their way to an efficient outcome, irrespective of the initial assignment of property rights. Assuming this theorem to be correct, it would have some bearing on the claims advanced here. Coase's argument suggests that in specifying property rights one important consideration is to do so in a manner that will minimize transaction costs between different agents. This, in turn, will enable them to coordinate their activities and pursue their plans more efficiently.

43 But, it may be asked, what if I live in a political society that does not have a system of property rights that is reasonable in this sense? Then freedom as the nonobstruction of planning will direct the state to reform its system of property law so that it becomes reasonable. There are numerous complications raised by this, however, that I shall pass over here.

idea does not specify a uniquely correct assignment. This means that judgments of political freedom are not simply parasitic on a background institutional structure.

Much more could be said about the complex relationship between institutions, rights, and freedom-reducing factors, but these brief remarks should, at least, allay the worry that freedom as the nonobstruction of planning is either deeply implausible or an empty ideal.

Let me turn, next, to the second problem that threatens the plausibility of this ideal. An ideal of political freedom that ties judgments of political freedom to the plans of those who are subject to the state's authority must address the following question. Can a person have his freedom reduced even when his plans have not been obstructed in any way? Suppose, for example, that my government prohibits foxhunting and that the option to go foxhunting is not one that I need to pursue for any of my present plans. Then does not my government restrict my freedom even though it does not obstruct my plans?[44] It is tempting to respond that while the option to go foxhunting is not relevant to my present plans, it may, for all I know, be relevant to my future plans. As a planning agent, I have a freedom-based interest not only in pursuing my present plans, but also in living in an environment that does not restrict my options in the future. So, when my government prohibits foxhunting, it limits my freedom by closing off a possible future option.

There is surely something credible to this response at first. After all, people do take up new plans, and sometimes the plans that they take up are ones that they never would have guessed they would take up. Nonetheless, the response rings hollow. With respect to at least *some* options (call them non-serviceable options), I can know with great confidence that I will not need them for any of my current or future plans. I can also know with great confidence that even if I had access to such options, I would not acquire any need for them. Yet, when I am prohibited from pursuing these options, is not my freedom still limited?

This question poses a version of the *Brave New World* problem. In *Brave New World*, the plans of the subjects of the state have been adjusted so that they do not conflict with the restrictions that are imposed on them. But it would be crazy to characterize this state as freedom-supportive. Of course, in *Brave New World* the state has manipulated its subjects. This manipulation is a form of freedom-reducing interference. But we can easily vary the example. Suppose that the subjects in this world have voluntarily adjusted their plans so that they do not conflict with the restrictions that are imposed on them.[45] Here it seems that freedom as the nonobstruction of planning will not be able to account for the subjects' lack of political freedom.

---

44   Alternatively, if my plans include the option to go foxhunting, and my government prohibits this option, do I become freer simply by abandoning the plan that includes this option? This is the classic problem of the contented slave.

45   See Elster's discussion of character planning in Jon Elster, *Sour Grapes: Studies in the Subversion of Rationality* (Cambridge: Cambridge University Press, 1983), 117–19.

Any account of political freedom that relates options to the subjective mental states of persons will run into this kind of problem.[46] To overcome it, we need to introduce an objective condition. Given the characterization of personal autonomy in Section II above, such a condition is readily available: *For a person to be politically free, he must have access to an environment that provides him with a wide range of valuable options.*[47] Since this condition does not depend on the subjective mental states of persons, it will not be satisfied in *Brave New World* scenarios. Thus, by calling attention to this objective condition, we can avoid the unacceptable implication that persons in such worlds could be politically free. But now an obvious objection comes into view. If we are going to insist on the objective condition, then all of the emphasis on the subjective plans of persons becomes strangely otiose, does it not? In seeking to overcome the problem of *Brave New World*, has freedom as the nonobstruction of planning effaced itself?

Fortunately, the answer is "no." The satisfaction of the objective condition is plainly insufficient for a freedom-supportive environment. The reason for this is that the importance of a given option for a person depends on the role that it plays (or would play) in his current (or future) plans. A state that provides its subjects with a wide range of valuable options, but systematically thwarts their plans either through interference or through domination would not be a freedom-supportive state. Thus, while satisfaction of the objective condition is important, it fails to explain the ways in which the freedom of persons can be curtailed even when they remain free to pursue a wide range of alternative plans.

Return now to the foxhunting example. Assume that the following is true for a given person: (a) the option to go foxhunting is not relevant to any of his current plans; (b) the option to go foxhunting would not be relevant to any of his future plans even if it were available to him; (c) the fact that this option is not relevant to his current plans and would not be relevant to his future plans is not the result of being manipulated by another

---

46 See the discussion in Richard Arneson, "Freedom and Desire," *Canadian Journal of Philosophy* 15, no. 3 (1985): 425–48.

47 This condition raises a number of difficult questions: How should options be individuated? What counts as a sufficiently wide range of options? What constitutes "access" to an option? And what functions does the state have in ensuring that this condition is met? I shall not attempt to provide answers to these questions here, but a few remarks are necessary to prevent misunderstanding. For the most part, valuable options can be provided by civil society. State action is not needed to create them. However, without state action, some citizens may find themselves in a situation in which they lack the resources needed to have access to these options. Does this show that the freedom-supportive state must also be (at least to some extent) a welfare state? Perhaps, but perhaps not. It is possible that civil society, through charitable and intermediate associations, could ensure that all citizens have adequate access to the options that they need in order to be politically free. But whether such welfare provision would be sufficient and whether it would increase or diminish interference and domination relative to state welfare provision are matters that cannot be pursued here.

person; and (d) he lives in an environment that provides him with a wide range of valuable options. Given these demanding conditions, freedom as the nonobstruction of planning yields the result that when the state prohibits this person from pursuing the option of foxhunting, it does not reduce his freedom. This is, I think, the right judgment to reach in this kind of example. The best case for thinking that the restriction of nonserviceable options does reduce the freedom of persons rests on the worry that if we do not affirm this view, then we will not be able to account for *Brave New World* scenarios. But conditions (c) and (d) rule out such scenarios.

Moreover, at this point, it is worth reminding ourselves that freedom as the nonobstruction of planning is an ideal of political freedom. It does not purport to offer a full account of the free person or the autonomous life. Its focus is on what the state should do if it wishes to promote freedom. Seen from this perspective, if the state prohibits an option that is not relevant to my plans, there is every reason to think that it will be relevant to the plans of others.[48] This is why, first and foremost, the prohibition would reduce freedom. Now, it might be objected that the state *could* prohibit me from pursuing the option without prohibiting others from doing so, and in this way diminish my freedom without denying the option to anyone who needs it to pursue his plans. But, if this were to happen, freedom as the nonobstruction of planning can still explain why this state action would be freedom-reducing. A state that aimed to reduce my options, but not the options of my fellow citizens, would be an arbitrary state. By singling me out, and by subjecting me to arbitrary interference, it would be dominating me. This would remain true even if its dominating interference foreclosed an option for which I had no use, given my current and future plans. This is true because, as we have seen, merely being subject to domination reduces freedom. In this case, it would be reasonable for me to believe that if my government singles me out with respect to this option, then it could do so in the future for other options that I do or would care about. And this reasonable worry itself would obstruct my ability to plan my life.[49]

Bringing together the points developed in this section, I can now state more completely the demands that freedom as the nonobstruction of planning imposes on a state. According to this ideal, the freedom-supportive state must (1) sustain a legal and economic structure that allows its subjects to coordinate their activities and plans efficiently; (2) ensure that all of its subjects have access to a wide range of valuable options; and (3) minimize the

---

48 It is logically possible, even if it is something that would scarcely ever happen, that a state might prohibit an option—such as the option to eat glass—that none of its citizens would ever have any need for in pursuing their plans. On the account of political freedom that I am defending, it would not be possible to account for why this would be a reduction in freedom—if it is indeed a reduction in freedom! I leave it to the reader to consider whether this is a troubling objection to this ideal.

49 In this case I am like the slave who has a liberal master. I am free to pursue my plans, but I stand under the shadow of a dominating presence that may intervene at any time to obstruct them.

interference and domination that frustrate the plans of those who are subject to its authority. The first and second of these demands are, in a sense, prior to the third; in the freedom-supportive state, persons will form and pursue their plans against the background of a shared understanding of their institutional rights, entitlements, and available options.

VIII. CONCLUSION

It is time to take stock. I began this essay by stressing the distinction between political freedom and the freedom that really matters. I asserted, but did not defend, the claim that the freedom that really matters is best understood in terms of personal autonomy. Assuming that this claim is correct, it is implausible to think that a state can make its subjects free. At best, it can assist them in becoming free or provide facilitative conditions for their freedom. An ideal of political freedom tells us what the state should do in this respect.

I have tried to show that freedom as the nonobstruction of planning is the best ideal of political freedom on offer. It does a better job of responding to the problem of integrity, the problem of pluralism, and the problem of unacceptable implications than do its main rivals, and it explains in a satisfying way why both interference and domination reduce freedom. It also explains why certain institutional structures, such as the rule of law and the market economy, are (plausibly) supportive of political freedom.

Notwithstanding its attractions, political freedom, as I have stressed throughout this essay, is but one ideal. It can conflict with other values. For this reason, we are not entitled to conclude that a state that best promotes freedom is the best state, all things considered. The freedom-supportive state, according to the ideal of political freedom that I have defended, is neither egalitarian nor perfectionist.[50] It need not ensure that all subjects have an equal set of opportunities, nor does it need to take steps to help people form and pursue valuable or worthwhile plans. This naturally raises the question of whether, and to what extent, political freedom should be compromised for the sake of these other values. But this is a question to be taken up on another occasion.

Philosophy, University of Arizona

---

50   This requires an important qualification. To the extent that freedom as the nonobstruction of planning rests on the ideal of personal autonomy, and to the extent that this ideal itself is a perfectionist ideal, then the freedom-supportive state, as I have characterized it, is perfectionist. The point in the text is that the freedom-supportive state need not favor some plans over others because of their intrinsic value or their contribution to human flourishing.

LaVergne, TN USA
13 August 2010
192942LV00002B/2/P